# ethics

TEACHER EDITION

## Ethics Teacher Edition

**Writers**
Kevin M. Collins, MDiv
Paul Hornor, MDiv
Bruce Ostrom, PhD
Tom Parr, ThM

**Writer Consultant**
L. Michelle Rosier

**Biblical Worldview**
Brian C. Collins, PhD
Bryan Smith, PhD

**Academic Integrity**
Jeff Heath, EdD

**Instructional Design**
Rachel Santopietro, EdD
Michael Winningham, MA

**Editor**
Kristian Römer, PhD (cand.)

**Editorial Assistant**
Pam Evans

**Cover and Lead Designer**
Emily Rush

**Designer**
Alayna Rowan

**Production Designer**
Sherry McCollough

**DesignOps Coordinator**
Kaitlyn Quevedo

**Permissions**
Maria Andersen
Ruth Bartholomew
Sharon Belknap
Sylvia Gass
Hannah Labadorf
Jennifer Walton

**Project Coordinators**
Allison Brooks
Heather Chisholm

**Postproduction Liaison**
Peggy Hargis

Teacher Edition photo credits: **cover** Pyrosky/E+ via Getty Images; **viii**bg, **xvii**bg Ton Photographer 4289/Shutterstock .com; **xix**tl Alberto Gagliardi/iStock/Getty Images Plus via Getty Images

Student Edition photo credits appear at the end of this book.

Teacher Edition text acknowledgments appear on-page with text selections.

Student Edition text acknowledgments appear within the notes at the end of this book.

The text for this book is set in Abril by TypeTogether, Adobe Hebrew, Adobe Minion Pro, Adobe Myriad Pro, Adobe Text Pro, Arial, Calibri by Monotype, Chelsea Market Pro by Crystal Kluge, DIN 2014 by Vasily Biryukov, Felt Tip Woman by Mark Simonson, Free 3 of 9 by Matthew Welch, Freight by Joshua Darden, Freight Sans by Joshua Darden, Futura PT by Paratype, Helvetica, Helvetica Neue, Noto Sans by Google, Sketchnote Text by Mike Rohde, Skippy Sharp by Chank Diesel, Times New Roman PSMT, Times New Romans PS, Times-Roman, Trade Gothic Next by Monotype, and Wingdings.



ISBN 978-1-64626-390-5

15 14 13 12 11 10 9 8 7 6 5 4 3 2 1

# contents

# biblical worldview shaping in *ETHICS*

Scan this code for a fuller discussion of these themes.

Ethics is the study of how humans, as creations of God who bear His image, should think, feel, and act in all areas of life. It involves reflection on the kind of character a person must have to act morally. It trains people how to reason morally about their actions. Ethics is the endpoint of a biblical worldview. It is the part of worldview that looks at how individuals and groups live out their worldview.

In this course, five worldview themes will help students relate ethics to the worldview concepts that they have already learned in previous courses: authority, creational order, man's chief end, virtue, and wisdom. Early in the course, students will primarily explain these themes. As the themes are repeated, students will evaluate ideas within them, formulate a biblical understanding of them, and apply what they have learned about these themes to real-life situations. High levels of internalization are expected whenever the students are required to apply their learning.

| | 1 | 2 | 3 | 4 | 5 | 6 | 7 | 8 | 9 | 10 | 11 | 12 | 13 |
|---|---|---|---|---|---|---|---|---|---|---|---|---|---|
| **AUTHORITY** | E | Ev | E | | E | | | E | E | | | | |
| **CREATIONAL ORDER** | E, F | Ev | | | | | | E | E, F | E(4) | E(3) | E(3) | E(4) |
| **MAN'S CHIEF END** | | Ev | E(3) | E | E, Ev | E | | E | Ev(2) | Ev(2) | Ev(2) | Ev | Ev(2) |
| **VIRTUE** | E | Ev(2) | | E, Ev, A | F(2), A | | | E | F(3) | Ev, F(2) | F(4) | F(3) | F(4) |
| **WISDOM** | | | E(3) | | | Ev, F, A | | E | A | A(3) | | Ev, A(2) | A(2) |

## KEY

**E — Explain** biblical teaching

**Ev — Evaluate** controversial concepts

**F — Formulate** a biblical understanding of a controversial concept

**A — Apply** a biblical understanding to life

Numbers in parentheses indicate how many times a level appears in a chapter (if more than once).

## AUTHORITY

Ethical decisions need to be rooted in a proper authority. Because there is only one God who made the world and everything in it, God is the ultimate ethical authority. Fallen humans set their own reason, intuition, or feelings as authorities in place of God's Word. Any truly ethical life will have to begin with the acknowledgement of God's authority in Scripture to guide human character, desires, and behaviors.

## CREATIONAL ORDER

When God created the world, He made not only the physical stuff of the universe, but also the moral structures by which it works. Though every ethical system is dependent on the creation order, every fallen system twists its understanding of the creational order in some way. As Christians evaluate ethical issues, they need to demonstrate not only what a right course of action is but also why that course of action makes better sense of the world that God has made than the fallen alternatives do.

## MAN'S CHIEF END

The Bible speaks of man's chief end in a number of ways: to be conformed to the image of God, to rule over creation under God's greater rule, to delight in God's law, to fear God, to be blessed, to seek first God's kingdom, to be mature in Christ, and more. These purposes are often summed up as "to glorify God, and to enjoy him forever" (*Westminster Confession of Faith* [Philadelphia: William S. Young, 1851], 387). Fallen man centers his chief end on man: either on doing good to others or on the happiness of self. Christians should be motivated to act ethically because they desire to glorify God by being conformed to His image, in obedience to His law and for the advancement of His kingdom—this is the life of true blessedness.

## VIRTUE

Virtue is moral excellence. God's goal is not only for Christians to do the right things; God's goal is for them to *be* the right kind of persons. In many ethical systems the means by which virtues are developed are moralistic. In reaction to moralism, many have emphasized authenticity rather than virtue. Christians develop virtue in dependence on the Holy Spirit so that they can become authentically virtuous.

## WISDOM

Wisdom is derived from observing the creational order through the lens of Scripture and being able to state what is learned in a way that guides all life. The fool is the person who lives against the grain of the created order and who seeks to divert the consequences of such a life rather than correct his or her way of life. This foolishness can be expressed with sophistication and developed into ethical systems. By contrast, Christians should grow in wisdom by learning how to apply the Bible to situations it does not directly address.

# building academic rigor with *ETHICS*

## 1 Desired Learning Outcomes

*What do I want students to learn?*

- Ethical virtues and wisdom in analyzing and applying creational norms, Wisdom Literature, and the biblical triad of faith, hope, and love to ethical decision-making
- Biblical and systematic theology skills in collecting and accurately summarizing biblical data and evaluating the ethical claims of others
- Skills in formulating biblical solutions to real-world ethical choices and applying a biblical worldview to their own ethical choices
- 21st-century skills—collaboration, creativity, critical thinking, problem solving, digital literacy
- Biblical worldview development in the topics of authority, creational order, man's chief end, virtue, and wisdom

## 2 Teaching and Learning Supports

*How will I help students learn?*

- Activate prior knowledge of Wisdom Literature and other biblical passages as they relate to specific ethical choices.
- Highlight essential questions and ethical and theological vocabulary.
- Use graphic organizers and educational technology to develop biblical and systematic theology skills.
- Use case studies to provide students with opportunities to evaluate various ethical claims.
- Provide learning experiences that allow students to utilize a biblical worldview in real-life ethical contexts.
- Guide visual analysis of infographics, images, charts, and graphs.
- Conduct class discussions and debates regarding ethical questions and choices.
- Guide students as they analyze articles, write biblical ethics statements, and formulate responses to ethical scenarios.
- Use Scripture memory, Thinking It Through questions, and prayer journals to help students develop their ethical decision-making skills.

## 3 Evidence of Understanding

*How do I evaluate student learning?*

- Assess the development of wisdom during instruction with preassessments, summative assessments, and chapter reviews.
- Monitor student development in biblical and systematic theology skills with graphic organizers and collaborative discussions.
- Make observations of class discussions involving visual analysis and ethical case studies.
- Assess development in ethical skills with student activities and prayer journals.
- Evaluate the products of collaborative research, visual analysis, and cross-curricular studies.
- Provide opportunities for students to research ethical topics and present results through Turn and Talks as well as Think-Pair-Share activities.
- Assess student analysis of ethical content and Scripture passages with writing prompts and student activities.
- Evaluate solutions to real-world ethical problems with formative assessments, writing prompts, or discussions.

building academic rigor with *ETHICS*

# a panorama of academic rigor

*Academic rigor is the educational experience that engages students in content appropriate to their academic level and helps them learn to analyze, evaluate, and ultimately create.*

## THE LEARNING ENVIRONMENT

Learning happens in a context. Physical and social environments create this context. For students to be stimulated and engaged and to perform at high levels, they need an environment that connects with and shapes their interests and values. Students need a flexible environment that adapts to remedy their deficits and capitalize on their proficiencies. They need an interactive environment that intrinsically motivates them by giving them structure, freedom, and choices in learning. They need a safe environment that invites questioning, risk-taking, and honest discussion. Most importantly, students need positive relationships with mentors and peers and one-on-one time with caring, responsible instructors and parents. This kind of environment does not happen by accident; an educational climate like this must be crafted.

## THE TEACHER'S ROLE

The teacher is the person who crafts this learning environment. The teacher creates a learning community with high educational expectations, ignites interest and passion to help students persevere in challenging educational tasks, and inspires them by providing models of learning. The teacher instructs growing learners, supporting, critiquing, and praising their efforts along the way. While laying a foundation for lifelong learning, the teacher helps students transfer their academic knowledge, understanding, and skills to life with the purpose of shaping students' worldview.

## THE LEARNING EXPERIENCE

The textbook opens doors to the world of the learning experience. It captures student interest and significantly contributes to the educational environment. Educational and technological resources enable the teacher to develop knowledge, understanding, and skills in a scaffolded sequence to build a foundation that students can transfer to life. Teachers use educational tools to craft relevant, authentic learning experiences that develop creativity and problem-solving skills in a variety of contexts. These kinds of learning experiences allow students to take responsibility for their learning in the present and discover the joy of serving God with their vocational knowledge and skills in the future.

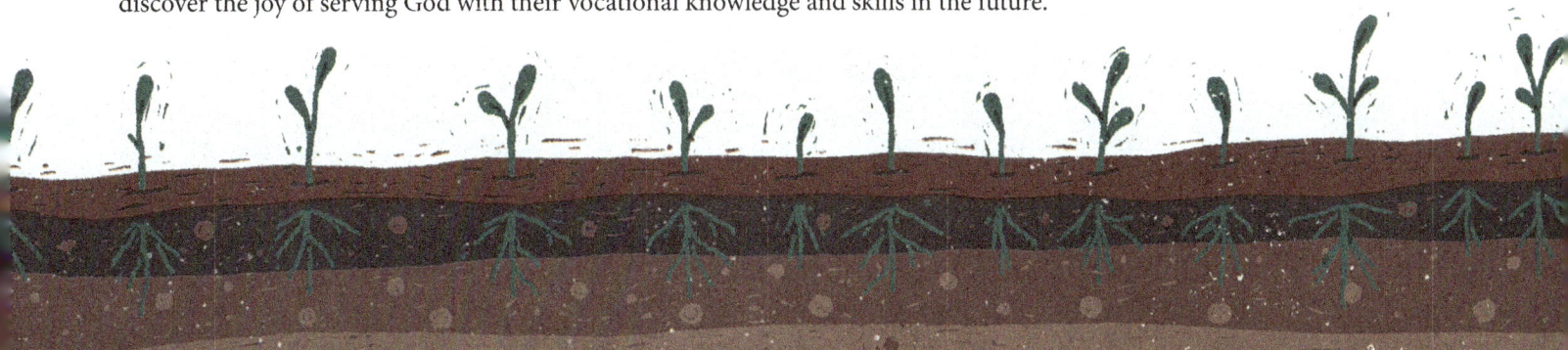

# technology solutions

## Why Educational Technology?

BJU Press has always maintained that the teacher is the key for learning in the classroom. The teacher knows best what the students require so they can accomplish educational objectives. The teacher guides and directs learning, using various methods to accomplish his or her purposes.

Today, teachers are expected to use technology to implement and supplement their methods. Of course, educational technology has always been around—it includes the alphabet, which allows us to visualize sounds and words, various devices used to write, and surfaces to write on. But when we think of technology in the twenty-first century, we picture digital devices, projections, and online interactivity. BJU Press's offerings are growing with the demand for educational technology in Christian schools. The purpose is not to have a shiny new gadget or method. The purpose is to equip today's teachers to fulfill the goal of Christian education: "to develop redeemed man in the image of God" (BJU Press, Handbook of Christian Education [2017], 33).

## What Does BJU Press Offer?

### *BJU Press Trove*

BJU Press Trove is the premier resource for teachers and students using BJU Press materials in schools. As a learning experience platform, it is the main digital companion to our books. In Trove, teachers and students alike can access and share resources, interact with assessments, and communicate seamlessly.

A powerful catalog of digital resources and robust lesson planning features support teachers' efforts to enhance their teaching strategies for greater depth and free up valuable time. With Trove, eTextbooks and eWorkbooks can be accessed anywhere and on any device. Students can read, take notes, and even complete assignments all within Trove.

The assessment builder gives teachers the power to customize assessments and take advantage of autogradability options—saving grading time and giving students immediate feedback on their performance. Assessments can also be printed out for conventional classroom use.

### Available Teacher Resources Include

- editable PowerPoint presentations
- lesson plan overviews
- various teaching aids, such as videos, maps, artwork, links, and charts
- test banks (select grades and subjects)
- eTexts (teacher and student editions)
- curriculum maps of BJU Press materials
- professional development (opportunities to earn CEUs)

BJU Press Trove provides practical resources to support Christian school teachers as they plan and teach.

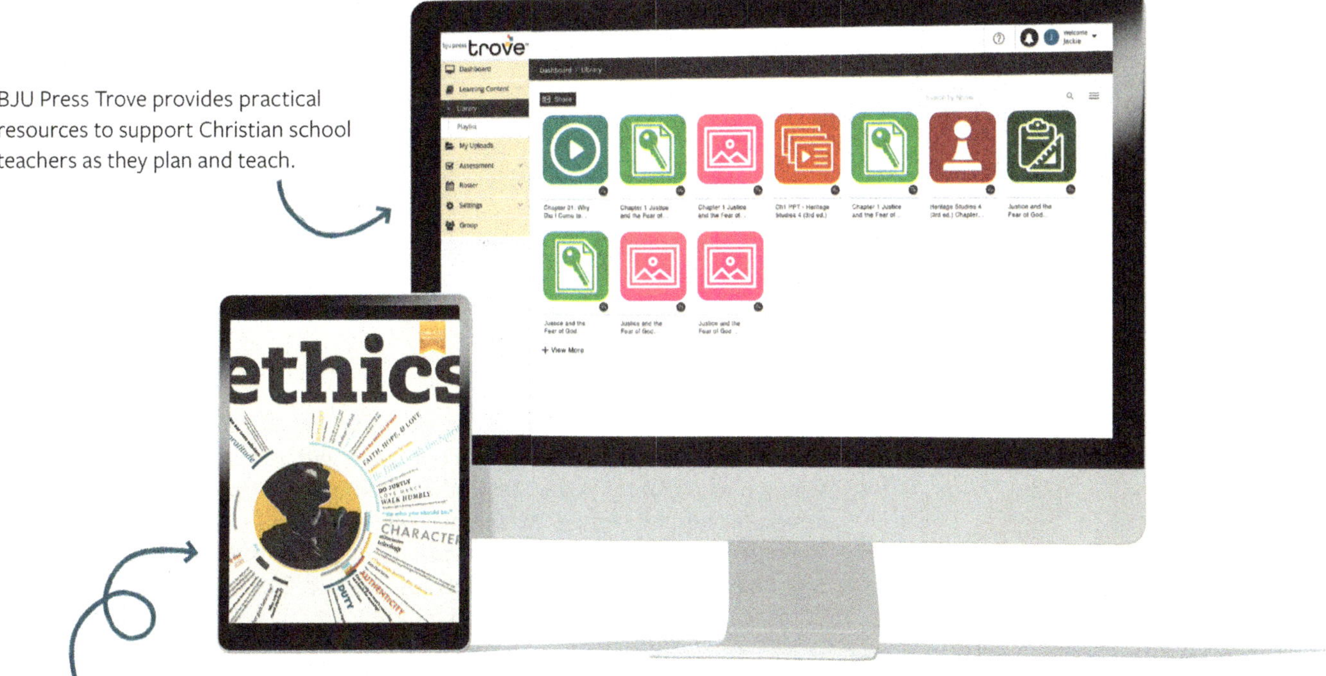


eTexts allow convenient access at home and school for both teachers and students.

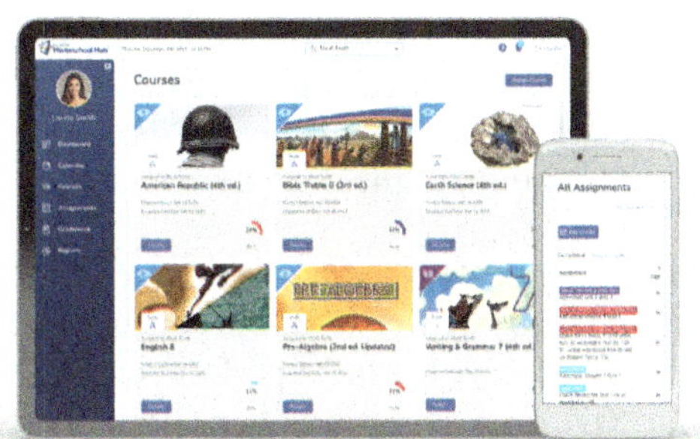

### *Homeschool Hub*

Homeschool Hub is the site where homeschool parents and facilitators access our digital resources, including links and select digital instructional aids that support the lessons. Homeschool Hub also provides a digital scheduler and gradebook.

### *AfterSchoolHelp*

AfterSchoolHelp allows your students to freely access tutorials and extra practice for select BJU Press math and English courses. The materials on AfterSchoolHelp align with the chapters of BJU Press textbooks. It also is the home of audio files for Spanish 1 and Spanish 2.

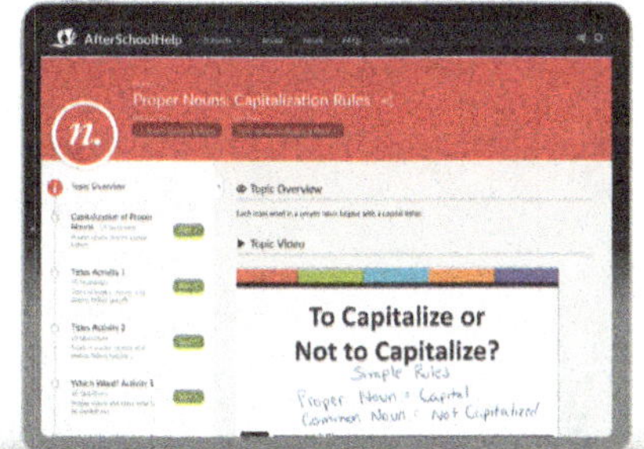


## How to Access Technology Offered by BJU Press

**BJUPressTrove.com** may be accessed by Christian schools that purchase annual access.
**HomeschoolHub.com** offers free access to homeschoolers using BJU Press materials.
**AfterSchoolHelp.com** offers free access to anyone who wants to use its resources.

# using your teacher edition

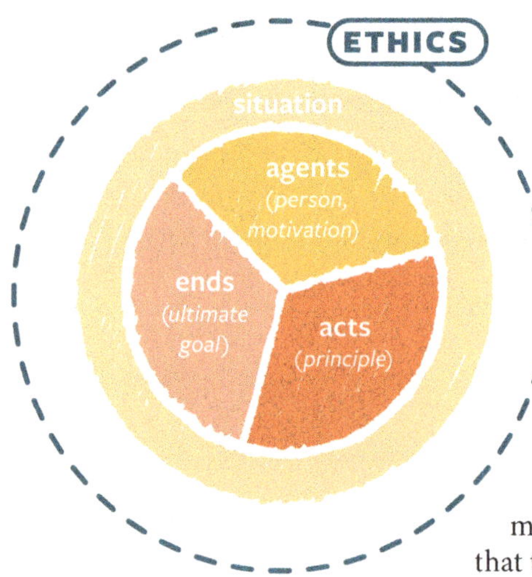


This course on Christian ethics is concerned with developing a certain kind of person who can think and act in the world in ways consistent with God's design for human beings. We follow a biblical method for handling ethics provided by Ken Magnuson in *Invitation to Christian Ethics: Moral Reasoning and Contemporary Issues* (Kregel Academic, 2020), which consists of three components: *acts, ends,* and *agents*.

## ACTS: WHAT'S THE STANDARD?

The component of *acts* most closely resembles the deontological approach, which focuses on rules that guide actions. Biblical truth (reflecting the created order) provides the authoritative, universal moral absolutes that humans need to govern themselves in this world. This course emphasizes four ways that the Bible provides ethical guidance: (1) direct commands, (2) general principles, (3) implications, and (4) descriptions and demonstrations of God's character.

Scripture reveals God's character as the ultimate standard of what is good and right. All human behavior is judged to be ethical or unethical based on whether it reflects the character of God. This course will teach students how to draw a line from God's character, revealed in Scripture and creation, to the daily decisions they must make in the world.

Discerning *creational norms* is also an essential skill for living life according to God's standard. Creational norms reveal God's good and moral design for His creation. Even though we can't go back and observe life in its perfect condition before the Fall, we can still discern from Scripture the reality of creational norms as a showcase of what is good and ethical. No one can excuse sinful and unethical living because all humans have been made in God's image, and therefore are responsible to reflect God in all the ways that a human can.

In Chapters 1–3, foundational matters of ethics are addressed. Rooting ethics in a biblical view of reality is essential for developing the students' ability to reason as Christians about controversial issues. The worldview paradigm—Creation, Fall, Redemption—is explicitly explained as it relates to the field of ethics. The more familiar students are with this biblical worldview, the better equipped they will be to grapple with specific ethical dilemmas that arise later in the textbook.

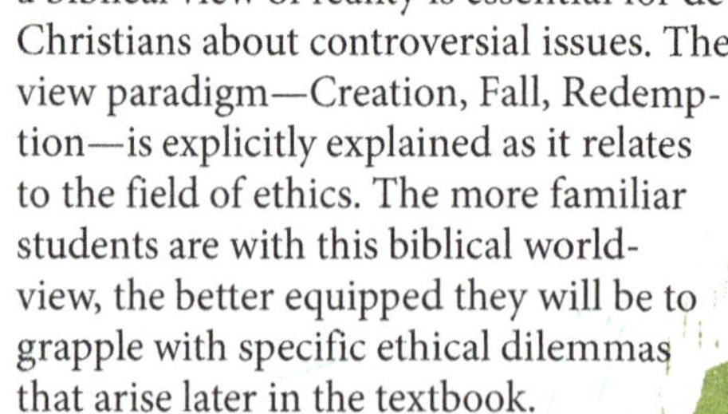

## ENDS: WHAT'S THE GOAL?

The component of *ends* most closely resembles the consequentialist, or teleological, approach, which focuses on the goals or results (the ends) of a given decision or action. Everyone makes choices with a particular goal in mind. Christians have a God-given goal: to glorify God by loving God and others. This course demonstrates the inseparable nature of the goal of ethics from the standard of ethics. God's revelation determines what loving Him and others looks like in the real world.

The goal of any ethical action must ultimately be to glorify God and enjoy Him through conformity to the image of Christ and through the advancement of His kingdom. This course is not a self-help manual on living a good life, nor does it provide a mechanical formula for moral improvement. Instead, God's redemptive work is emphasized throughout the textbook as the necessary condition for all ethical living.

Redemption enables believers to pursue God-glorifying decisions rather than self-centered ones. Christian ethics teaches students how to consider the consequences of their actions from a biblical perspective. To assist students in their pursuit of God-glorifying decisions, they will be prompted to ask the following questions: Will this decision conform me to Christ's image? Will it express my delight in God's law? Will it bless others by helping them to know and love God? Will it cause me to flourish as God intends? Will it advance God's kingdom in the world?

## AGENTS: WHAT'S THE MOTIVE?

The component of *agents* most closely corresponds to virtue ethics, which focuses on the person, or agent. To act ethically is not merely to do the right thing; it is to be the right kind of person doing the right thing for the right reasons. Virtuous character is foundational to carrying out God's commands to His glory. How could God's commands be rightly followed by a person whose inward character has not been transformed?

As Bryan Smith notes in the foreword:

> *God is interested in more than our decisions. It isn't just what we do that matters to Him; it's also who we are.... Of course, no textbook can make you a virtuous person. It takes the grace of God to do that. But a textbook can require you to reckon with God's grace by reading about it, meditating on it, and praying for it.*

Since Christians do not automatically become virtuous upon their conversion, they need to grow in virtue. Therefore, special attention is devoted in Chapters 4–7 to specific virtues for the purpose of developing Christlike character. Faith, hope, and love—the three central virtues—are foundational to all the rest. Additional virtues covered in the textbook are goodness, prudence, faithfulness, courage, self-control, humility, kindness, and gratitude—to name a few.

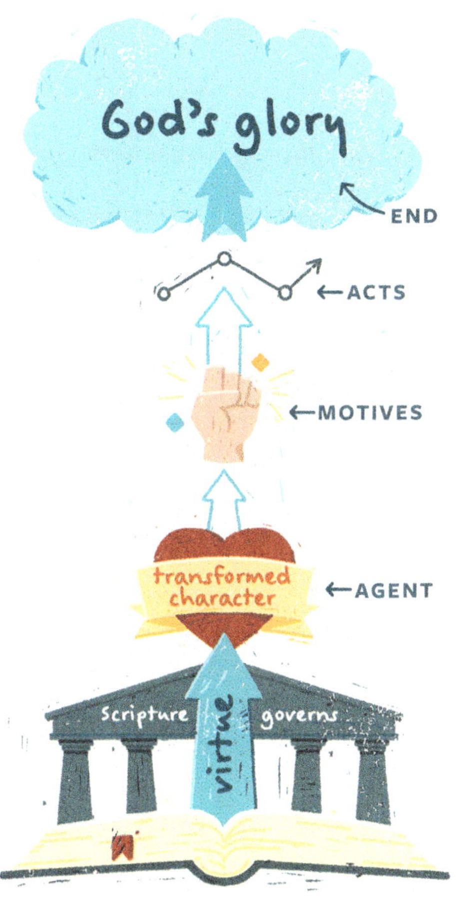

## CONTEXT: WHAT'S THE SITUATION?

The three main components—acts, ends, and agents—must all be applied to a specific ethical situation. Context is the additional element to making an ethical decision. What is the ethical issue that demands ethical decision-making?

In Chapters 9–13, each section will raise an ethical difficulty (an issue or scenario). Then each section will direct you to consider the Bible's teaching on how one ought to act. Each section will direct you to consider the end consequences to an individual or a society that does or does not conform to the biblical standard. And each section will direct you to consider the virtues and vices that motivate an agent's (a person's or society's) response. Because we live in a world that is full of sinful responses (both your own and others' responses that affect you), each section will conclude with how to biblically respond to troubling situations you may find yourself in.

All the components must work together. Magnuson summarizes the necessity and usefulness of all the components by saying the following:

> *The nature and character of God (corresponding to virtue ethics) is the source from which God's commands are given (corresponding to a form of deontology), and God's purposes or ends (corresponding to teleology) flow from his character and are indicated by his commands. Likewise, a person's character (virtue ethics) provides the foundation for keeping God's commands (deontology), which work together to fulfill the purposes for which human beings are created (teleology).*
>
> (TAKEN FROM PAGE 45 OF *INVITATION TO CHRISTIAN ETHICS: MORAL REASONING AND CONTEMPORARY ISSUES* © COPYRIGHT 2020 BY KEN MAGNUSON. PUBLISHED BY KREGEL PUBLICATIONS, GRAND RAPIDS, MI. USED BY PERMISSION OF THE PUBLISHER. ALL RIGHTS RESERVED.)

using your teacher edition

# product objectives

By the end of the course students should be able to do the following:

**Compare** and contrast various ethical systems.

**Apply** an approach to ethics that will enable them to grow in virtue and to relate biblical wisdom to a variety of ethical situations.

**Defend** biblical Christianity in a culture of competing truth claims and diverse lifestyles.

using your teacher edition

# resources

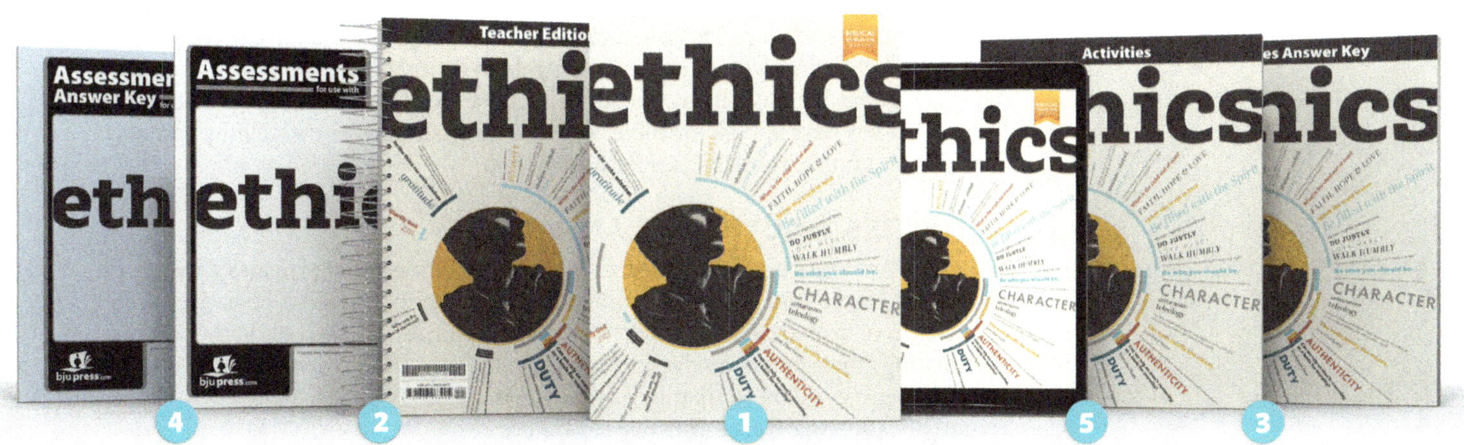


## ❶ STUDENT EDITION

*Ethics* Student Edition is an age-appropriate study of the branch of philosophy that studies how people should live. Each chapter and section in the Student Edition incorporate an essential question. These questions are designed to prompt students to think through the significance of that chapter's or section's topic. The questions engage students in making that topic meaningful and applicable to their lives.

Example of an essential question from Chapter 2:

Why is it so hard to make right decisions?

The Student Edition models for students how to apply Christian ethics to real-life situations. It is designed to be more than a summary of concepts related to ethics. Rather, it is designed to equip students to be faithful Christians regarding the ethical issues that surround them. Students will learn through careful analysis and evaluation of essential ethical principles how best to do this.

The main text of the Student Edition is supplemented with various features: ethical dilemmas, systematic theology, worldview considerations, and other related matters. The main text is also supported by a variety of artwork, photos, diagrams, and charts to aid visual learning, age-appropriateness, and readability.

The side margins provide explanations of key concepts and terms (starred words) to bolster student reading comprehension. Bolded words are Terms to Remember for which students may be assessed.

Thinking It Through questions supply reading checks or prompt in-class discussion. Chapter Reviews are structured according to Bloom's taxonomy to provide a brief review and application of the concepts before the chapter test.

## 2 TEACHER EDITION

*Ethics* Teacher Edition provides tools that will help you guide the students in understanding the material and developing critical-thinking skills. The sections contain a variety of teaching strategies, including use of technology, student collaboration, research, and visual analysis. The Teacher Edition also contains Explaining the Gospel, Instructional Aids, Glossary, Scripture Memory, Student Edition Scripture Index, and Student Edition Topical Index.

Though this course provides much material and many suggestions, it is simply a tool that should be tailored to your situation. For example, if you have several days a week for Bible class or if your students struggle to complete the exercises from the Activities, you may let students complete the exercises in class. On the other hand, if you have only a few days a week for Bible class or if your students are excelling, you may have them complete the exercises for homework.

## 3 ACTIVITIES & ACTIVITIES ANSWER KEY

*Ethics* Activities is a companion to the Student Edition that provides a variety of pages to reinforce student understanding and application of section objectives. The exercises have been designed to help students in a variety of ways: to do the work of formulating ethics for themselves, to apply an ethical model to specific situations, and to analyze and evaluate competing ethical views.

Activities Answer Key is available separately.

In addition to the exercises, Activities also includes prayer journals to teach students to pray specifically and scripturally based on each section's topic. Activities also includes each chapter's Scripture memory with a brief explanation of the significance of that passage.

## 4 ASSESSMENTS & ASSESSMENTS ANSWER KEY

*Ethics* Assessments includes printed assessments for evaluating student mastery of chapter and section objectives. Tests include various styles of questioning as well as application of Bible study skills. The assessments may be adapted to meet the students' individual needs.

Assessments Answer Key is available separately.

## 5 BJU PRESS TROVE

Digital instructional resources, such as videos, links, PowerPoint presentations, and Instructional Aids are available in BJU Press Trove. In addition, a bank of quiz and test questions for the instructor to use to generate individual tests is available in Trove.

# the teaching cycle

Scan this code for a fuller discussion of teaching strategies

## ENGAGE

Engage students by capturing their attention, activating prior knowledge, and motivating them to connect with new content.

- Preassessments
- Bell-ringer activities
- Essential questions
- Videos
- Visual analyses

## INSTRUCT

Instruct students by using direct, indirect, and interactive strategies to expand and extend their knowledge and skills.

- Direct instruction
- Discussions
- Quick Writes
- Bible studies
- Turn and Talks

## APPLY

Apply student learning by practicing knowledge and skills and connecting them to real life.

- Think-Pair-Share activities
- Discussions
- Scenarios
- Review activities
- Student Activities

## ASSESS

Assess student understanding by using a variety of tools to systematically evaluate knowledge, skills, attitudes, and beliefs in order to promote student learning.

- Tickets out the Door
- Formative assessments
- Summative assessments

## using your teacher edition

# teacher edition features

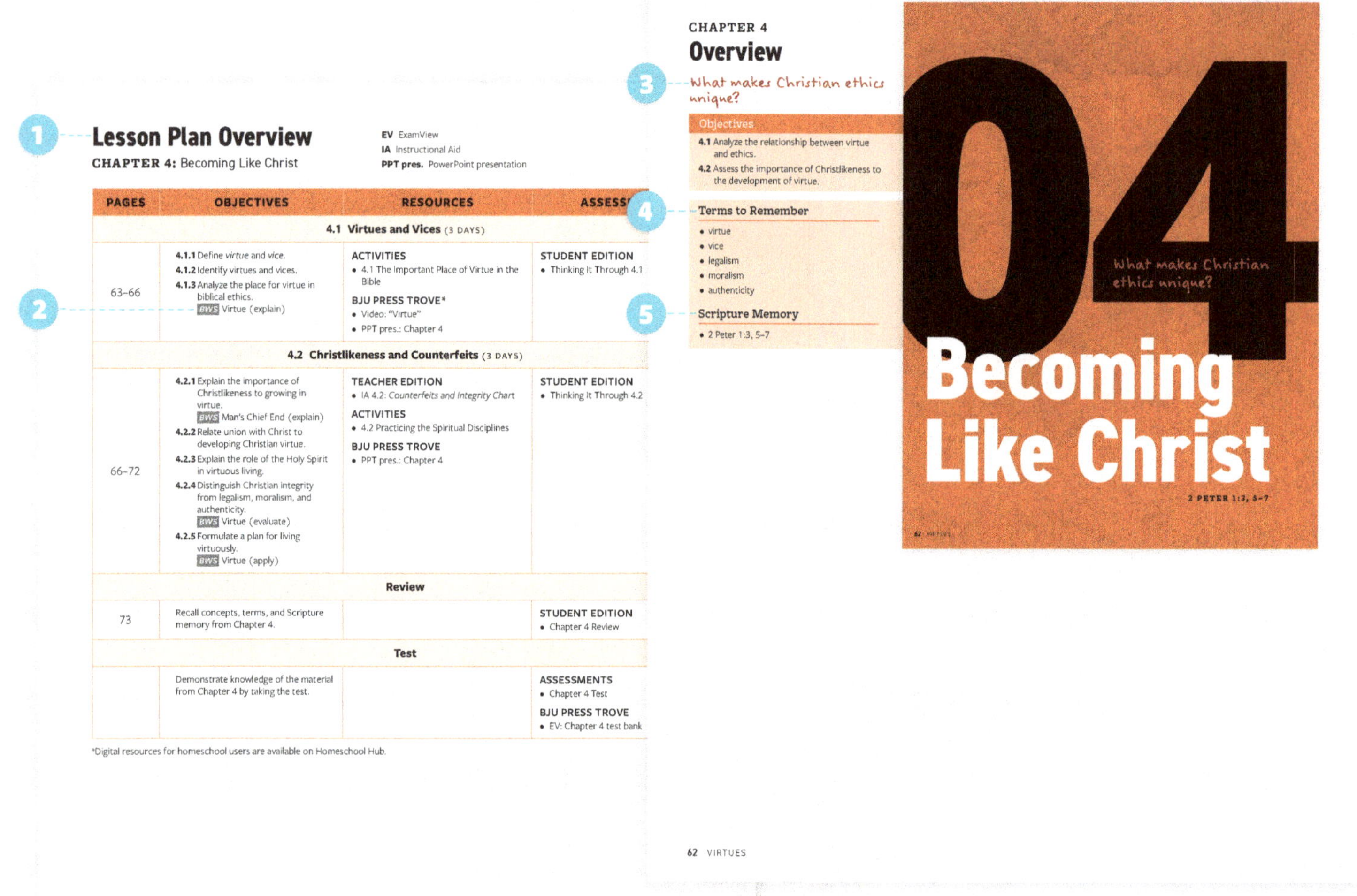

## Lesson Plan Overview

**CHAPTER 4:** Becoming Like Christ

**EV** ExamView
**IA** Instructional Aid
**PPT pres.** PowerPoint presentation

| PAGES | OBJECTIVES | RESOURCES | ASSESS... |
|---|---|---|---|
| | **4.1 Virtues and Vices** (3 DAYS) | | |
| 63–66 | **4.1.1** Define *virtue* and *vice*.<br>**4.1.2** Identify virtues and vices.<br>**4.1.3** Analyze the place for virtue in biblical ethics.<br>BWS Virtue (explain) | **ACTIVITIES**<br>• 4.1 The Important Place of Virtue in the Bible<br>**BJU PRESS TROVE***<br>• Video: "Virtue"<br>• PPT pres.: Chapter 4 | **STUDENT EDITION**<br>• Thinking It Through 4.1 |
| | **4.2 Christlikeness and Counterfeits** (3 DAYS) | | |
| 66–72 | **4.2.1** Explain the importance of Christlikeness to growing in virtue.<br>BWS Man's Chief End (explain)<br>**4.2.2** Relate union with Christ to developing Christian virtue.<br>**4.2.3** Explain the role of the Holy Spirit in virtuous living.<br>**4.2.4** Distinguish Christian integrity from legalism, moralism, and authenticity.<br>BWS Virtue (evaluate)<br>**4.2.5** Formulate a plan for living virtuously.<br>BWS Virtue (apply) | **TEACHER EDITION**<br>• IA 4.2: *Counterfeits and Integrity Chart*<br>**ACTIVITIES**<br>• 4.2 Practicing the Spiritual Disciplines<br>**BJU PRESS TROVE**<br>• PPT pres.: Chapter 4 | **STUDENT EDITION**<br>• Thinking It Through 4.2 |
| | **Review** | | |
| 73 | Recall concepts, terms, and Scripture memory from Chapter 4. | | **STUDENT EDITION**<br>• Chapter 4 Review |
| | **Test** | | |
| | Demonstrate knowledge of the material from Chapter 4 by taking the test. | | **ASSESSMENTS**<br>• Chapter 4 Test<br>**BJU PRESS TROVE**<br>• EV: Chapter 4 test bank |

*Digital resources for homeschool users are available on Homeschool Hub.

CHAPTER 4

## Overview

What makes Christian ethics unique?

**Objectives**

**4.1** Analyze the relationship between virtue and ethics.
**4.2** Assess the importance of Christlikeness to the development of virtue.

**Terms to Remember**

- virtue
- vice
- legalism
- moralism
- authenticity

**Scripture Memory**

- 2 Peter 1:3, 5–7

04
What makes Christian ethics unique?
Becoming Like Christ
2 PETER 1:3, 5–7

62 VIRTUES

CHAPTER 4 LESSON PLAN OVERVIEW L-62a

1. Lesson Plan Overviews appear at the beginning of each chapter. Each section is allotted a certain number of days of instruction. Review and test days are always allotted one day of instruction each.
2. Biblical Worldview Shaping themes are listed under the objectives they relate to.
3. Essential questions are probing worldview questions that the chapter or section aims to answer.
4. Terms to Remember are terms that are integral to the chapter's content.
5. Each chapter incorporates a Scripture passage relevant to the topic that the students are expected to memorize.

## 4.1 Virtues and Vices

### Engage

**VIRTUE**

Show the **video** "Virtue" to ... subject to students.

**TRANSFORMED TO BE VI...**

Guide a **visual analysis** of the ... page 63.

**What is the significance of each ... the diagram?** *The sun represents ... glory. The cross represents Christ ... work. The dove represents the Spi... work in the believer. The triangle ... the Trinitarian God. The dotted li... the work of all three persons affec... believer (from God as source thro... accomplishment by the Spirit's ap... The cross within the person shows ... transforming work within the beli... shadowed cross on the ground sho... internal transformation will be re... external ways as a witness.*

**What is the importance of the t... pictured in the diagram in relat... the topic of virtue in ethics?** *On... would be that a virtuous person n... all three persons of the Trinity as ... his or her virtue. Another exampl... that one's internal virtue is eviden... nally in transformed living (ethics...*

## 4.1 Virtues and Vices

*Why do virtues matter?*

**Objectives**

- **4.1.1** Define *virtue* and *vice*.
- **4.1.2** Identify virtues and vices.
- **4.1.3** Analyze the place for virtue in biblical ethics. BWS

**Biblical Worldview Shaping**

- **Virtue** (explain): God's goal is not merely to have people do the right thing but to become the right kind of person. (4.1.3)

**Printed Resource**

- Activity 4.1: The Important Place of Virtue in the Bible

**Digital Resource**

- Video: "Virtue"

**Suggested Reading**

- Berg, Jim. *Essential Virtues: Marks of the Christ-Centered Life.* Greenville, SC: JourneyForth, 2008.
- Davis, Andrew M. *An Infinite Journey: Growing Toward Christlikeness.* Greenville, SC: Ambassador International, 2014.
- Frame, John M. *The Doctrine of the Christian Life.* Phillipsburg, NJ: P&R Publishing, 2008. Pages 317–84.
- Grudem, Wayne. *Christian Ethics: An Introduction to Biblical Moral Reasoning.* Wheaton, IL: Crossway, 2018. Pages 107–14.
- Powlison, David. *How Does Sanctification Work?* Wheaton, IL: Crossway, 2017.



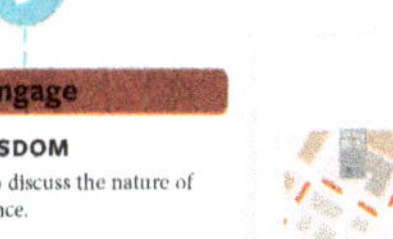

### Engage

**ARTIFICIAL WISDOM**

Ask a **question** to discuss the nature of wisdom and prudence.

**Can an artificial intelligence chatbot, like ChatGPT, be wise?** *Wisdom can't be obtained by finding the right information to answer a question or to find a solution. Wisdom is skill for life, and this involves knowing how to make ethical decisions and behave morally, which a chatbot is incapable of. Also, one cannot possess wisdom, or prudence, without having the fear of the Lord.*

**CORRECTING STUDENT MISCONCEPTIONS**

Use **direct instruction** to clarify that the opening illustration isn't saying that a supercomputer is or can be more prudent than a person. The illustration serves as an analogy for some aspects of prudence. Machines aren't people and therefore aren't able to be ethically responsible, or in this case, capable of the virtue of prudence. The designers and creators of computers are the responsible and moral parties.

### Instruct

**PRUDENCE INTERCONNECTING WITH THE OTHER VIRTUES**

Use **direct instruction** to teach that the virtue of prudence can never stand alone.

The prudent person must be motivated by love for God and others. His or her ends must be good, and the ultimate end must be the glory of God. And the means pursued must also be righteous. If a person uses his or her sharp mind to figure out how to get away with something sinful, or even if that person tries to achieve a good goal through sinful means, he or she is not exercising prudence but its counterfeit—either cunning or rashness.

Prudence is required when making a hard call. For example, Christians want to see lost friends come to Christ. However, it would be imprudent to continually pester a friend with the gospel—making it the first and dominant thing in every conversation, text, and phone call. It would also be imprudent to say nothing of Christ and the gospel to the friend. Neither course of action would advance the goal of seeing the friend come to Christ, and the latter would be unfaithful to the Great Commission. A prudent course of action would differ depending on the situation, but it would look to create opportunities for serious conversation about the gospel. It would communicate to the friend genuine concern for his or her eternal salvation. It would be patient but not complacent. There is no guarantee that a prudent course of action would result in the friend's conversion—that is up to God.

**SCENARIOS REQUIRING PRUDENCE**

Guide a **discussion** surrounding the following two scenarios requiring prudence.

**How would you practice prudence in the following scenario? You just graduated from high school and are looking forward to going to college. You have the opportunity to work for a friend from church, but you are set on going to college right away. Your dad, however, lost his job and has been without work for four months.** *You need to consider the fact that you don't qualify for many scholarships, your family doesn't have the money to pay for your first year of school and God has provided a good job for you. Prudence is required for you to determine whether to go to college right away or not.*

**How would prudence help your parents in the following scenario? Your family must relocate due to your dad's job. Your family is looking for a house, a church to join, and a good Christian school for you and your siblings in the new city you will be moving to.** *The parents need to decide on where to live, where to go to church, and which school (unless homeschool is considered) to put their children in. Juggling multiple priorities requires prudence.*



# Becoming Like Christ 04 Review

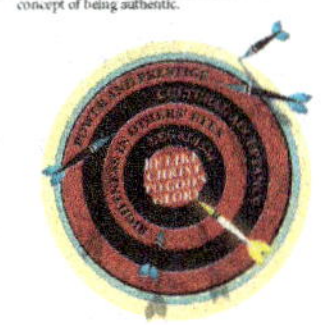

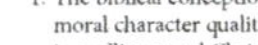

## Chapter 4 Review

**Terms to Remember**

- **virtue:** Rightly ordered love (Augustine, *City of God* 15.22), which manifests itself in a person's character and behavior.
- **vice:** A character trait or consistent behavior that is recognizably wicked or immoral; a deviation from God's upright standard. May be the exact opposite of a virtue or may be the twisting of a virtue into a counterfeit.
- **legalism:** Trying to earn justification with God through works, or trying to earn a higher standing with God by the performance of works or rituals.
- **moralism:** Trying to be a good, upstanding person through one's own good works; focused on social acceptability.
- **authenticity:** Being true to oneself, being transparent, and following one's heart—most often leading to transparent sinfulness.

**Understanding Ethics**

1. The biblical conception of achieving great moral character qualities must be rooted in godliness and Christlike righteousness rather than in self-achieved merit.
2. See the chart on page 65.
3. The study of ethics should relate to basic growth in Christlikeness or sanctification, which encompasses everyday life. It should not be limited to what we do; it should relate to who we are internally in our character, motivating what we do.
4. a wrong aim, source, and means of seeking to be virtuous
5. As heinous as his sinful hypocrisy was, he demonstrated a transformed life and received the promise of being the kingly tribe from which the Davidic Messiah would descend.

**Practicing Ethical Decision-Making**

6. The virtue of diligence can be twisted into workaholism to the neglect of other necessary or healthy responsibilities that God has also designed for us: relationships (friends, family), relaxation, commitment to church, and so on. Furthermore, the purpose for achieving a 4.0 could be of little value beyond self-focused pride.
7. The virtue of loyalty can be twisted into sinfully covering for others who are doing wrong. In fact, true loyalty must be prioritized to rightful God-given authorities, and true loyalty would seek to protect a sibling from harming himself or herself from the consequences of sinful living.
8. The virtue of courage can be falsely accused of being unloving, hateful, harsh, and prideful regardless of how carefully a pastor presents the Scripture's view and how it confronts sin and offers forgiveness to those who repent.

**Analyzing and Evaluating Ethical Claims**

9. Although it may be fair to say that a more realistic personality will be a more complex character, Christians should not exult in wicked personalities who end up doing the right thing. They should exult in personalities that are transformed to be the right kind of person.
10. It is true that Jesus confronted hypocrisy and injustice and helped the oppressed and that we too should pursue justice and do good to the oppressed, as these are defined by Scripture. However, to focus solely on these aspects of Jesus' life is to misunderstand His mission. Jesus came to save people from their sin by transforming them from the inside out. Only the gospel can truly change societies.



**6** Biblical Worldview Shaping themes are explicated under the section opener they relate to.

**7** Suggested Reading points the teacher to outside resources the teacher may read to supplement his or her teaching.

**8** Topic or skill headers indicate the subject of the following teaching.

**9** Teaching cycle headings (Engage, Instruct, Apply, and Assess) indicate the stage and progression of the learning cycle.

**10** Bold and italicized text indicates questions and answers for the students to gauge their understanding and to provide opportunity for their application.

**11** Glossary definitions of the Terms to Remember are provided for the teacher. Teacher Edition chapter review pages also provide the answers to the chapter review exercises in the Student Edition.

# foreword

When I was a senior in high school, what I wanted most was to be done with school. I didn't hate school. I liked learning, and I liked my friends. But I was ready to start enjoying the independence of adulthood. I got my wish. Before I knew it, I was walking across the stage to receive my diploma.

I found that adulthood did indeed come with a lot of independence. I had my own car, my own job, and my own bank account. I was able to choose the college I went to, and I chose my own major. But independence, I soon learned, was a two-edged sword. It allowed me to make my own decisions, but it also forced me to take responsibility for my actions. My decisions were my own now, not my parents'. If my car broke down, I paid for it. If I fell behind in my schoolwork, I had to reach out to my professor—he wasn't going to contact me.

Of course, I wasn't alone. Everyone I graduated with had to learn this lesson too. And some didn't learn it very well. Some of my friends managed to cram into the first three months after high school every bad decision a person could make in three months. That's when I learned another lesson: the decisions you make after high school are high-stakes decisions. When you make a bad choice at 10 years old, it doesn't follow you, not usually. When you make a bad choice at 18 or 22, it does. Bad decisions about relationships, substance use, marriage, conflict—these can destroy your life.

That's the reason we produced this course on ethics. Ethics is the study of right and wrong. It helps people make decisions that are morally good and shows them how to avoid the ones that are not. Our world is complex and messy. Doing the right thing is not always obvious. In fact, very often it's not. God has not left us to sort out such questions on our own. He has given us His Word and His Spirit. But we must learn how to make use of what He has given. That's what this course is meant to do for you—to show you how to make right decisions based on the wisdom of God in the Bible.

There are many books on ethics. But this one is different. It's focused on what the Bible teaches about ethics, and it gives a great deal of attention to being the right kind of person. God is interested in more than our decisions. It isn't just what we do that matters to Him; it's also who we are. That's why this course isn't just about issues—issues like abortion, euthanasia, racism, and cloning. It's also about virtues: love, righteousness, patience, and hope. The best way to learn how to make good decisions is to first learn to be a good person. Virtuous people tend to make virtuous decisions.

Of course, no textbook can make you a virtuous person. It takes the grace of God to do that. But a textbook can require you to reckon with God's grace by reading about it, meditating on it, and praying for it. It's my prayer that as you do these things this year, God will in His grace take hold of your life and do something wonderful in you and through you. Here's what I'm praying:

> That ye might be filled with the knowledge of [God's] will in all wisdom and spiritual understanding; that ye might walk worthy of the Lord unto all pleasing, being fruitful in every good work, and increasing in the knowledge of God; strengthened with all might, according to his glorious power, unto all patience and longsuffering with joyfulness. (Col. 1:9–11)

Bryan Smith, PhD
Assistant Director
Biblical Worldview Formation
BJU Press

# Lesson Plan Overview

**INTRODUCTION:** Introduction to Ethics
**CHAPTER 1:** Creational Foundations for Ethics

**EV** ExamView
**PPT pres.** PowerPoint presentation

| PAGES | OBJECTIVES | RESOURCES | ASSESSMENTS |
|---|---|---|---|
| **Introduction: What Is Ethics?** (3 DAYS) | | | |
| 2–4 | • Define *ethics*.<br>• Relate ethics to philosophy and biblical worldview. | **BJU PRESS TROVE***<br>• PPT pres.: Introduction | **STUDENT EDITION**<br>• Thinking It Through: What Is Ethics? |
| **Introduction: Why Study Ethics?** (2 DAYS) | | | |
| 5–9 | • Summarize the reasons to study ethics and the benefits of doing so.<br>• Explain the value of gaining spiritual wisdom in order to please God by making ethical choices.<br>• Formulate a plan to study ethics in a wise and godly manner. | **BJU PRESS TROVE**<br>• PPT pres.: Introduction | **STUDENT EDITION**<br>• Thinking It Through: Why Study Ethics? |
| **1.1 God's Character as a Foundation for Ethics** (3 DAYS) | | | |
| 13–16 | **1.1.1** Explain the basis for ethics.<br>*BWS* Authority (explain)<br>**1.1.2** Analyze the attributes of God that form the basis for ethics. | **ACTIVITIES**<br>• 1.1 God's Character Is the Starting Point<br>**BJU PRESS TROVE**<br>• Video: "Importance of Ethics"<br>• PPT pres.: Chapter 1 | **STUDENT EDITION**<br>• Thinking It Through 1.1 |
| **1.2 The Created Order as a Foundation for Ethics** (3 DAYS) | | | |
| 16–21 | **1.2.1** Define *creational norms*.<br>**1.2.2** Defend the existence of creational norms.<br>**1.2.3** Explain how creational norms are discovered.<br>*BWS* Creational Order (formulate)<br>**1.2.4** Explain the role of creational norms.<br>*BWS* Creational Order (explain) | **ACTIVITIES**<br>• 1.2 Creational Norms and Two Genders<br>**BJU PRESS TROVE**<br>• Link: He Made Them Male and Female<br>• PPT pres.: Chapter 1 | **STUDENT EDITION**<br>• Thinking It Through 1.2 |
| **1.3 The Image of God in Man as a Foundation for Ethics** (3 DAYS) | | | |
| 21–24 | **1.3.1** Define the *image of God in man*.<br>**1.3.2** Explain why the image of God in man is a fundamental creational norm for ethics.<br>**1.3.3** Explain why the image of God in man is key for human virtue.<br>*BWS* Virtue (explain) | **BJU PRESS TROVE**<br>• PPT pres.: Chapter 1 | **STUDENT EDITION**<br>• Thinking It Through 1.3 |

*Digital resources for homeschool users are available on Homeschool Hub.

| PAGES | OBJECTIVES | RESOURCES | ASSESSMENTS |
| --- | --- | --- | --- |
| **Review** | | | |
| 25 | Recall concepts, terms, and Scripture memory from Introduction and Chapter 1. | | **STUDENT EDITION**<br>• Introduction/Chapter 1 Review |
| **Test** | | | |
| | Demonstrate knowledge of the material from Introduction and Chapter 1 by taking the test. | | **ASSESSMENTS**<br>• Introduction/Chapter 1 Test<br>**BJU PRESS TROVE**<br>• EV: Introduction/Chapter 1 test bank |

INTRODUCTION

# Overview

*Why is studying ethics relevant to me?*

### Objective

- Explain the value of studying ethics.

### Terms to Remember

- ethics
- Christian ethics

## What Is Ethics?

*What is ethics all about?*

### Objectives

- Define *ethics*.
- Relate ethics to philosophy and biblical worldview.

### Suggested Reading

- Frame, John M. *The Doctrine of the Christian Life*. Phillipsburg, NJ: P&R Publishing, 2008. Pages 3–40.
- Grudem, Wayne. *Christian Ethics: An Introduction to Biblical Moral Reasoning*. Wheaton, IL: Crossway, 2018. Pages 23–40.
- Magnuson, Ken. *Invitation to Christian Ethics: Moral Reasoning and Contemporary Issues*. Grand Rapids, MI: Kregel Academic, 2020. Pages 14–22.

# Introduction to Ethics

*Why is studying ethics relevant to me?*

**morality:** often used synonymously with ethics, but can also refer more specifically to a society's conclusions regarding what is right and what is wrong

**creational norms:** the design of God's created order (the way things ought to be) translated into divine laws that govern the way human individuals and cultures ought to operate

## What Is Ethics?

Just do the right thing. Is that sufficient for you to be considered an ethical person? Or is ethics about something more than just making the right choices? How about one's motive, like seeking to please God? What about the standard that guides one's choices, like adhering to the Bible in obedience? Certainly, we have all done wrong things, made wrong choices, displeased God, and disobeyed the Bible's teaching. So we all have to come to grips with this topic—ethics. Is an ethical decision the same thing as a moral or right decision? Before this question can be answered, there needs to be a greater understanding of what ethics is and what the standard for ethics is. We'll get to those things in the foundations for ethics in Chapter 1. Ethics sounds like a good thing. But we'll need to start with some definitions to begin understanding everything that is involved in ethics.

### FOUNDATIONAL DEFINITIONS

**Ethics** is the branch of philosophy that studies how man ought to live. Ethics concerns itself with determining what is right and what is wrong. Ethics seeks to identify what is objectively good. Chapter 2 will provide a brief overview and critique of various secular ethical systems. As can be expected, there are right and wrong approaches to ethics.

The focus of this textbook's discussion of ethics will be Christian, not secular. Even though the term used is *ethics*, the emphasis is on ethics from a Christian viewpoint—one flowing from a biblical worldview. To truly know how to live in this world, we need a knowledge of God and His wisdom as revealed in His Word (Prov. 2:6; 9:10). Any morality* that people rely on to govern themselves is based on something. Only Christian ethics, based on understanding God and His ways through Scripture, is truly ethical.

You will learn in subsequent chapters that ethics has to do with acts (actions that conform to God's Word), agents (individuals who exemplify virtues and have certain motives), and ends (consequences).[1] In addition to these three elements, one must consider the circumstances of the ethical decision that must be made. More elaboration on this ethical model will be presented in Chapter 8.

**Christian ethics** seeks to determine how man ought to live in particular circumstances through studying God's Word, discerning God's creational norms,* and using moral reasoning. For the ethics to be truly Christian, a thorough consideration of the acts, agents, ends, and specific situation is necessary.

2

## Engage

### THE PLACE OF ETHICS IN PHILOSOPHY

Guide a **visual analysis** of the diagrams on page 2 in order to help orient students to the discipline of ethics and its place in the larger discipline of philosophy.

**What does the tree represent?** *the discipline of philosophy*
**What are the four branches on that tree?** *ethics, metaphysics, epistemology, and aesthetics (Students will learn more about these other branches later.)*
**Which branch does this book focus on?** *ethics*
**What ought the tree to be rooted in?** *the Bible*
**What might the sun, which is essential to growth, represent? What might the stained-glass outline allude to?** *God; pointing to God's glory in worship*
**What are three key elements in the work of ethics? What must those three elements be applied to?** *Acts (principle), agents (person, motivation), and ends (ultimate goal) must be applied to a situation (or context or circumstances). Another way to remember the key elements is to say it this way: principles must be applied by people to particular situations with the pinnacle in mind.*

## Instruct

### THE RELEVANCE OF STUDYING ETHICS

Ask the students this introduction's **essential question** to help them understand the relevance of studying ethics.

Making choices that align with Scripture is an essential part of Christian living. Learning about ethics will help you to do this in a manner that expresses your love for the Lord and for others. Since being a Christian does not automatically ensure we will make the right choice in every circumstance, we should be willing to invest some time and energy to grow in our ethical reasoning. Given the confusion of ethics in our culture, the urgency to study ethics could not be greater. As you develop the skills of ethics, you will be armed to navigate the confusion in a way that both guards your own heart and assists those needing clear ethical guidance for their own lives.

What is ethics all about?

### THREE KEY RELATIONSHIPS

Now that we have defined ethics, let's consider three key relationships that will help you understand how ethics fits with related areas of study.

First, consider how ethics relates to a biblical worldview. Developing a Christian ethic can only follow from the worldview framework found in God's Word: its presentation of reality in its Creation, Fall, Redemption storyline. The application of a Christian ethic follows from a careful consideration of the three ingredients of a biblical worldview: (1) the metanarrative,* (2) beliefs and values, and (3) personal and group behavior, which form culture. Your personal behavior and cultural engagement will be enhanced by your current study of ethics if you have already studied biblical doctrines and developed a biblical worldview. Unless you are grounded in the teachings of the Bible and you embrace a biblical worldview, you won't be able to consistently make ethical decisions. All ethical systems come from and reflect a worldview.

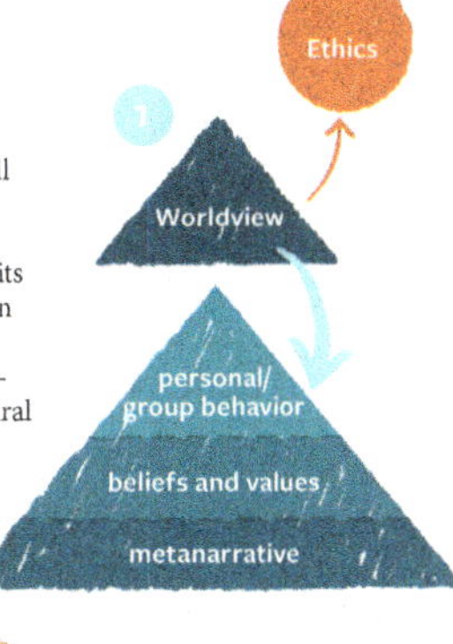


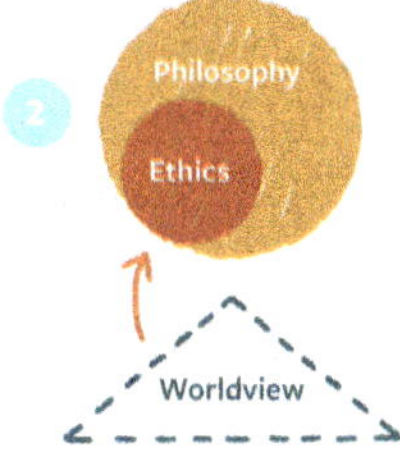


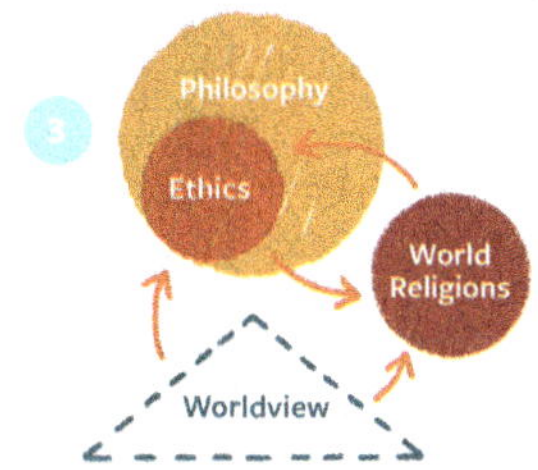


Second, consider how ethics relates to philosophy. *Philosophy* has been described as "the pursuit of a comprehensive understanding of all the world."[2] Philosophy uses reason to answer questions about the world and life. There are at least four main branches of philosophical study: metaphysics, epistemology, ethics, and aesthetics. You will learn more about these four branches in Chapter 2, but for now notice that ethics is one of philosophy's main concerns. Ancient Greek philosophers tried to figure out the meaning of life and how to live in the world without appealing to God or His Word. Even pagan philosophers realized that wisdom was needed to make good applications from reality to life. Christian philosophers have contributed to this discipline; so, as philosophy developed, it didn't remain totally godless. Each philosophical tradition has its own version of an ethical system.

Most secular philosophers maintain that wisdom can be obtained through reason and intellect alone, rejecting God's revelation. But man cannot be the final authority in his search for wisdom (Jer. 17:7–9; Mark 7:21–23). One of the problems with secular philosophy is its inability to explain truth, reality, and morality apart from God's revelation and thus its failure to consistently employ Christian ethics. Nevertheless, philosophy has had a major impact on ethics, using reason to arrive at some good answers to challenging scenarios. But a strict reliance on secular approaches to philosophy isn't an option for believers who want to develop a Christian ethic. Nonetheless, Christians shouldn't fear the helpful tools philosophy has harnessed (e.g., syllogisms, deductive and inductive reasoning, epistemological reflection, and math).

Third, ethics relates to world religions in that the teachings and practices of a religion influence the ethic that flows from those beliefs and traditions. Ethics is a component of religion as well as of philosophy. For example, Hindus in a high caste live "ethically" according to their religious worldview when they refuse to help Hindus who are part of lower castes. The high-caste Hindus' religion guides their beliefs and behavior. An ethic based on biblical Christianity, however, compels believers to be compassionate to others and to love all people indiscriminately (Luke 10:29–37). In this example, Scripture informs the religious practice which then forms the ethic of biblical Christians. The expression of one's ethics and the practice of one's religion are closely tied together.

**metanarrative:** an overarching storyline that attempts to explain all reality



## DEFINING ETHICS

Ask the students this section's **essential question** and use a **Quick Write** to help the students understand what ethics is about.

**What is ethics all about?**

**How would you distinguish Christian ethics from non-Christian ethics?**

**How would you distinguish ethics from morality?**

**How would you break down the key elements in an ethical system?**

*See page 2 and the top of page 3 for possible answers.*

## RELATING ETHICS TO BIBLICAL WORLDVIEW

Use a **Think-Pair-Share** to prompt students to analyze the relationships of categories.

**What do ethical systems reflect? Why is this significant?** *A worldview; ethical systems come out from and reflect worldview commitments. A worldview flows out of the teaching of God's Word and one's worldview and is more foundational than one's ethical system.*

**What are the three key ingredients of a worldview? Why is this significant?** *A metanarrative, beliefs and values, and personal and group behavior (which form culture); ethics reflects a metanarrative, beliefs and values, and the behavior of people or groups.*

## RELATING ETHICS TO PHILOSOPHY

Use a **Think-Pair-Share** to prompt students to analyze the relationships of categories.

**What are the four main branches of philosophical study?** *metaphysics (reality), epistemology (truth), ethics (morality), and aesthetics (beauty)*

**What does philosophy use to answer questions about the meaning of life and how to live in the world?** *human reason*

**One of the problems with secular philosophy is its inability to explain what three things apart from God's revelation?** *truth, reality, and morality*

**How does ethics relate to philosophy?** *Each philosophical tradition has its own version of an ethical system. The ethics flow from philosophical assumptions about the world.*

## RELATING ETHICS TO WORLD RELIGIONS

Use a **Think-Pair-Share** to prompt students to analyze the relationships of categories.

**How do world religions affect the ethics that develop downstream from religious beliefs and traditions?** *The teachings and practice of religions influence ethical behavior in that society.*

**What role does Scripture play in forming the ethic of biblical Christians?** *Scripture informs the religious practice which then forms the ethic of biblical Christians.*

**Of the three related areas of study (biblical worldview, philosophy, and world religions), which one is the most practical in how a person lives out the specifics of one's ethical system? Explain your answer.** *World religions; it is here that the "nuts and bolts" of one's worldview and philosophy find their expression.*

## FIVE BIBLICAL WORLDVIEW THEMES

Guide a **discussion** of the worldview themes and their relationship to ethics in order to reinforce the importance of biblical worldview integrated throughout the rest of the book and in all of one's ethical efforts.

**Which five biblical worldview themes impact your study of ethics?** *authority, creational order, man's chief end, virtue, and wisdom*

**How does each theme impact your study of ethics and your actual ethical living?** *See page 4 and compare student answers to the explanations found there.*

**How can these worldview emphases help you to apply ethics to your life?** *Recognize God as the ultimate authority in all things. Align your way of thinking with God's creational design of the world. Seek to glorify God now and look forward to enjoying Him forever. Develop virtuous character that reflects God's character. And grow in wisdom, so you can make ethical decisions and be a productive contributor to society and to God's kingdom.*

**What is an example of how at least one of the biblical worldview themes impacts your life ethically?** *One example relates to authority. If you seek to please God, then you won't accommodate a culture that rejects God's authority and thus justifies living immoral lifestyles.*

## RECURRING BIBLICAL WORLDVIEW THEMES

A biblical worldview is foundational to all your studies, not just to Bible class. In this course specifically, your attention will be drawn to various biblical worldview themes that impact your understanding of ethics. What follows is a brief summary of these themes.

### 1 Authority

There is only one God who made all things, and He is the ultimate authority. Fallen humans replace the true God and His revelation of Himself in His Word with other authorities such as reason, intuition, feelings, or religious texts. Truly ethical behavior can come only from submission to God and His Word.

### 2 Creational Order

God created not only the physical universe but also the moral norms by which people and societies function. Fallen humans twist God's moral order, and they make this twisted perspective seem normal. Christians should demonstrate why Christian ethics make better sense of the world God made than the alternatives.

### 3 Man's Chief End

God created mankind with many purposes that can be summed up in one "chief end," namely, "to glorify God, and to enjoy Him for ever."[3] Fallen humans replace this true goal for life with many false alternatives that leave the true God out. Christians demonstrate that right behavior is only found when one makes God the center of all motivations.

### 4 Virtue

God's goal is not merely for people to do the right thing but also to become the right kind of people. Fallen humans tend toward either external adherence to manmade rules or to displaying an "authentic" self, free from all constraints. The development of true virtue can only happen when the Holy Spirit regenerates a person and begins the work of sanctification.

### 5 Wisdom

Wisdom is the ability to discern creational norms, communicate them to others, and live by them. The fool lives against the grain of the creational order and develops sophisticated defenses for why he or she does so. The Christian grows in wisdom by learning how to apply the Bible and creational norms to situations the Bible does not explicitly address.

These worldview emphases constitute a helpful way to apply ethics to your life: Recognize God as the ultimate authority in all things. Align your way of thinking with God's creational design of the world. Seek to glorify God now and look forward to enjoying Him forever. Develop virtuous character that reflects God's character. And grow in wisdom, so you can make ethical decisions and be a productive contributor to society and to God's kingdom.

### Thinking It Through: What Is Ethics?

1. Define *ethics*.
2. Define *Christian ethics*.
3. How does ethics relate to biblical worldview, philosophy, and world religions?
4. Summarize the five biblical worldview themes that are woven into this textbook.

4

## Assess

Guide a **summative assessment** by directing students to answer the questions in Thinking It Through: What is Ethics?

### Thinking It Through: What Is Ethics?

1. Ethics is the branch of philosophy that studies how man ought to live. Ethics concerns itself with determining what is right and what is wrong. Ethics seeks to identify what is objectively good.
2. Christian ethics seeks to determine how man ought to live in particular circumstances through studying God's Word, discerning God's creational norms, and using moral reasoning.
3. Ethics relates to biblical worldview in that sound Christian ethics relies on a solid biblical worldview to guide it and provide a framework. A biblical worldview also helps Christians to make sense of the opposing worldviews.

   Ethics relates to philosophy in that philosophy is used to arrive at ethical conclusions. Philosophy has had a major impact on ethics, using reason to arrive at some good answers to challenging scenarios. Christians can use tools that philosophy provides in formulating and explaining Christian ethics.

   Ethics relates to world religions in that the teachings and practices of a religion influence the ethic that flows from those beliefs and traditions. A religious authority informs the religious practice which then forms the ethic of that religion.
4. Possible answers:
   - Authority: the ultimate authority of God as revealed in His Word
   - Creational Order: God's design and plan for creation
   - Man's Chief End: to glorify God and enjoy Him forever
   - Virtue: becoming the right person with the help of the Holy Spirit
   - Wisdom: rightly applying the Bible and creational norms to rightly relate to the world

## Why Study Ethics?

At the end of the day, everything you do is motivated by one thing or another. You do some things because you want to. You put on a jacket because you are cold. Or you wear a coat because your shirt underneath is dirty or wrinkled. And maybe you pull on a hoodie just because hoodies are comfy. But many things you just have to do, whether you like it or not. Helping pull weeds in the flower beds around your house and brushing your teeth before bed might fit this category. These things simply need to be done. Pulling the weeds may be motivated by the consequences of disobeying your parents' instructions. And brushing your teeth before bed is a habit, thanks to your parents and the dentist's drill.

### What are the personal benefits of studying ethics?

Do you need to be properly motivated to study ethics? Technically you don't need to be; perhaps you study it simply because you have to. But you will get so much more out of this course if you want to study it. The same can be said if you have a "meh" attitude toward your driving lessons. But if you don't pay attention and you don't put some effort into them, you might not pass your driving tests! You know you will personally benefit from being well-motivated for both driving lessons and this course. And the end results of both are very rewarding.

No one wants to be ill-prepared. Sure, there is skill in adapting, but no one wants to plan to be ill-prepared on purpose. Expanding your knowledge, growing spiritually, and improving your Christian testimony are all good reasons to study this material. But there are even more benefits of learning about ethics. Below is a brief elaboration on these good reasons for and benefits of studying this subject.

#### YOUR KNOWLEDGE

You should be motivated to study this textbook not only to be prepared for all the tests that will be coming your way but also to be prepared for life. Yes, life is full of ethical questions. Questions like whether doing a "greater good" justifies committing a "lesser sin." Or questions about who you should vote for in local or national elections. You will encounter an untold number of ethical situations that are difficult to untangle. You won't have straightforward answers for every ethical curiosity, but you will have a background in Christian ethics and a biblical framework at your disposal. Learning about faulty ethical approaches will also help you identify them and avoid them as you try to use a solid ethical model.

Knowing about ethics has another benefit. Studying ethics will familiarize you with commandments and principles from Scripture used to construct the Christian ethic, which contrasts with the secular ethics you will study. As you learn what God requires of His children, you will be challenged to align your life with what brings God glory (1 Cor. 10:31).

There is much knowledge to be learned in this course, but it is not knowledge merely for its own sake. Without insightful, accurate knowledge of ethical principles, ethical models, and ethical issues, your ability to make ethical decisions would be severely limited.

## Why Study Ethics?

### What are the personal benefits of studying ethics?

#### Objectives

- Summarize the reasons to study ethics and the benefits of doing so.
- Explain the value of gaining spiritual wisdom in order to please God by making ethical choices.
- Formulate a plan to study ethics in a wise and godly manner.

#### Suggested Reading

- See What Is Ethics?

### Engage

#### WHAT GETS YOU MOTIVATED?

Use a **bell ringer** activity to allow students to share what motivates them.

**What top three activities motivate your life the most? Persuade a classmate who may not be interested in that activity to get involved in at least one of those activities.** *Students may or may not be able to persuade a classmate to be motivated by the activities that motivate them.*

**What are some common reasons you're motivated to engage in an activity but someone else may not be?** *Usually, one person finds the activity fun, interesting, or beneficial in some way while the other person does not. Whatever the reason, if you're motivated about something, you must value it.*

#### BENEFITS OF STUDYING ETHICS

Ask the students this section's **essential question** to help them understand the personal benefits of studying ethics.

**What are the personal benefits of studying ethics?** *Expanding your knowledge, growing spiritually, and improving your Christian testimony are at least three benefits of studying ethics.*

### Instruct

#### THE BENEFIT OF STUDYING ETHICS: EXPANDED KNOWLEDGE

Use **direct instruction** to clarify the pitfalls and benefits of an expanded knowledge.

The Bible warns that knowledge puffs up (1 Cor. 8:1). You could be motivated by an expanded knowledge to benefit yourself in order to be highly esteemed by others. You could be motivated by an expanded knowledge to benefit yourself by outmaneuvering others, using your knowledge against them to get ahead for yourself. This is a pitfall.

On the other hand, you might be a person who wonders how someone could consider that expanded knowledge is of great benefit. You're not really all that motivated or interested in gaining a greater knowledge. This is another pitfall. God does not want us to operate in life out of ignorance (1 Pet. 1:14).

Knowledge, however, is vital to the Christian. You've probably heard the common saying that "knowledge is power." Although that saying can be abused (see the first pitfall described above), it contains a truth to be embraced. Having knowledge equips and enables us for our tasks in life. It helps us to avoid errors. It directs us to rightly pursue what is true, good, and beautiful. It is a key component for making ethical choices.

Christians must thoroughly know the principles in God's Word to guide their ethical living. Christians should know common, flawed ethical approaches promoted by the wisdom of the world to avoid falling prey to persuasive but destructive lies. You should be motivated to increase your knowledge for these reasons.

## THE BENEFIT OF STUDYING ETHICS: SPIRITUAL GROWTH

Provide a **journaling** opportunity for students to reflect on their own spiritual growth. Reinforce the biblical necessity of genuine Christians pursuing spiritual growth. Also, reinforce connecting spiritual growth to ethical living.

**Based on Colossians 1:10 and 2 Peter 1:5–10, what must Christians pursue?** *spiritual growth, growth in spiritual works and knowledge, and adding virtues to their faith*
**How does personal spiritual growth relate to ethics?** *Personal spiritual growth relates to ethical decision-making in everyday life. It is also involved in responding rightly to ethical issues in the culture, like abortion, civil disobedience, racial discrimination, stem cell research, and homosexuality.*

*The Spirit will produce fruit in Christians, demonstrated in how they live, which involves their ethical decision-making. Christians seek to grow in making the right choices as they yield to the Spirit's control. They rely on Him to help them grow more obedient to Christ.*
**Can you see spiritual growth in your own life? How does that spiritual growth affect your ethical decision-making? Can you see a difference in your life in the last year?** *Students should provide some concrete examples. Prompt students to share their thoughts if they wish.*
**How do you hope that this class will help you benefit in your own spiritual growth?** *Students should provide some concrete examples. Prompt students to share their thoughts if they wish.*

## THE BENEFIT OF STUDYING ETHICS: CHRISTIAN TESTIMONY

Guide a **discussion** about the benefit of studying ethics to bolster a solid Christian testimony in order to encourage students to focus on the value of such a pursuit.

**Why is it important to develop ethical character and behavior as a testimony to a watching world?** *Poor ethical character and behavior in the lives of professing Christians undermines a Christian witness. Stellar ethical character and behavior, though leading to persecution at times, will allow opportunities for greater witness to others. In addition, Christians may have a preserving influence on the society around them. Ethical living lifts high the name of Christ, pointing to His glory.*

### YOUR PERSONAL GROWTH

Another good reason to take this course seriously (and a benefit of doing so) is personal spiritual growth. Unit 2 is dedicated to growth in Christlikeness and specific virtues as the key to ethical Christian living. Every ethical decision is tied to Scripture and to the character of the person making the decision. Learning how to apply what you learn about ethics directly to your Christian living is both a goal and a blessing of this course. Thinking through issues like abortion, civil disobedience, racial discrimination, stem cell research, and homosexuality allows you to apply biblical truth and wisdom for spiritual growth in your life. This course is a tool to help believers be "fruitful in every good work" and increase "in the knowledge of God" (Col. 1:10). If you know the Lord, this course will also help you be more prepared to speak "the truth in love" (Eph. 4:15) with everyone you encounter.

### YOUR TESTIMONY

One more motivation to pay close attention to the content of this textbook is to develop a better Christian testimony before a watching world. Yes, the world loves to draw attention to the inconsistencies and sins of Christians. Believers are called to be "the salt of the earth" (Matt. 5:13). One effect of salt is preservation. When a society is left to its own devices, man's sinfulness sends that society on a downward trajectory (Gen. 6:5; Rom. 1:24–32). Believers who seek to live their lives according to a Christian ethical system showcase the value of what is right and shine light on the damage done by what is wrong. And Christians who are strong in their faith can remain faithful to the gospel message of Christ in the face of philosophical and religious opposition (Acts 5:40–42). This kind of testimony lifts high the name of Christ and draws attention to His unique and authoritative claims (John 14:6). Strong Christian testimonies—deeply rooted in Christian ethics—can continue to preserve a society even when most oppose God and His will.

Believers are also called to be "the light of the world" (Matt. 5:14). The "good works" (Matt. 5:16) this passage speaks of include behavior that is tied to a decidedly Christian ethic. Neither your own smarts nor your own feelings, no matter how much you trust them, qualify as an arbiter* in your ethical decision-making. Jesus is *the* Light of the World, and it is the message of His gospel that shines light into the darkened hearts of sinful people (John 8:12; 2 Cor. 4:4). Believers are commissioned to reflect Christ's light and make an impact on this dark world. Consider your own testimony and how you can improve it through studying ethics.

arbiter: a person who settles disputes

6

**How do you hope that this class will help you benefit in developing a better testimony for Christ?** *Students should provide some concrete examples.*

If you value spiritual growth, a solid Christian testimony, and a thorough knowledge of biblical principles to guide your understanding of right and wrong, then you should value the study of ethics. And if you value the study of ethics, then you should be motivated to actively engage in this course. Look to the Lord to give you this motivation and to help you maintain it as you seek to please Him.

### ETHICAL CHOICES, WISDOM, AND PLEASING GOD

We just looked at some reasons to study ethics and the benefits of doing so. In fact, every subject you study benefits you in some way. English—so you can communicate well. Math—so you can create things and understand much of God's orderly universe. History—so you aren't ignorant of the people and events that have led up to the present. Bible—in part, so you can learn how to live for God. Believers usually learn early after their conversion that they no longer live for themselves but for their Lord (1 Cor. 6:18–20). As we saw above, the more knowledge you have of God and His Word, the more opportunity you have to obey Him. And the purpose of knowledge is to gain wisdom for life, a life that is lived to glorify God (Prov. 1:1–7).

A key passage for the study of ethics is Colossians 1:9–12. The main goal for believers in this passage is found in verse 10: "walk worthy of the Lord." This one phrase is where the rubber meets the road for Christians. What someone thinks and believes directly affects their actions. But what someone thinks and believes is directly tied to what verse 9 says about believers being "filled with the knowledge of his will in all wisdom and spiritual understanding." Believers can't do the right thing (that is, make the ethical choice) without knowing how to arrive at that choice. Have you ever noticed that the Bible doesn't come out and give you answers to common yet high-impact life decisions—questions like where to go to college, what career to pursue, who to marry, how many children to have, what neighborhood to move into, or what church to join. Knowledge, wisdom, and spiritual understanding are not just about having information. Christians need the Holy Spirit to give them wisdom and understanding so that they can move from what they know generally about God's will from Scripture to making the best choice in a given situation. When Christians have spiritual wisdom and understanding, they will be able to truly "walk worthy of the Lord" (Col. 1:10).[4]

## Apply

### THE NEED FOR WISDOM

Guide a **discussion** about the need for wisdom in order to help the students understand its importance in living ethically.

Walk students through Colossians 1:9–12. Then return the focus to the first question.

**What do you need to walk worthy of the Lord, to be pleasing to Him (Col. 1:9–10)?** *the knowledge of His will along with wisdom and spiritual understanding*

**If your purpose should be to live a life that is pleasing to the Lord, walking worthy of Him, then what does that imply as the alternative possibility (Col. 1:9–10)?** *that you could walk in an unworthy manner that displeases Him*

Although believers have been justified by faith alone, they are still responsible to live obediently, just as a loving son or daughter seeks to please a loving parent. It is possible to grieve God by how you live (Eph. 4:30).

**What does a worthy walk that pleases God look like (Col. 1:10)?** *being fruitful in every good work and growing in the knowledge of God*

**How can you possibly live such a life (Col. 1:11)?** *only by the strengthening power of Christ that helps you patiently persevere with joy (delight in Him)*

**What can be your response to this work of God in your life (Col. 1:12)?** *thanksgiving that the Father included you in His inheritance as one of His saints, rescued from darkness to live in the light*

**Why do you need wisdom to walk worthy of the Lord?** *You must apply the knowledge of God's will specifically to your life. You have to make the connection between what the Bible says is God's moral will and the situation you are seeking to apply that to. That takes wisdom.*

**What are three examples of God's clear moral will discerned from Scripture and three examples of how that would be applied in ethical situations that might not be immediately clear, requiring wisdom?** *One example could be God's clear moral will to tell the truth. A situation of ethical difficulty might arise when telling the truth could hurt someone else that you believe you're supposed to be a loyal friend to (a competing virtue). You must rightly determine the priority of your obligations.*

## THE BEST APPROACH FOR STUDYING ETHICS

Guide a **group activity** to encourage students to collaborate on ideas for planning how to implement the key postures for approaching their ethical studies.

**How should you approach your study of ethics (manner, attitude, or posture)? Provide five keys and how you plan to implement each one on a routine basis throughout the course of this study.**

- *Prayer: One example is to treat the prayer at the beginning of the class hour as significant rather than routine; another example would be to set aside a time for prayer specifically for this class any time before studying.*
- *Humility: One example is to listen to the line of thinking all the way through before responding adversely or with irritation (whether that is something being explained in the textbook, by your teacher, or another student); submit yourself to the clear teachings of Scripture when you are out of line, even if the one calling your attention to that discrepancy didn't do it in the most humble or loving way.*
- *Reason: Make a commitment to use your brain to the full capacity that God has blessed you with. Make sure to submit your finite and fallen mind to the clear Word of God.*
- *Effort: Make a commitment to embrace the hard work of reasoning through difficult issues. Make a point to focus during class, when reading the textbook, and when studying. Don't begrudge researching difficult ethical issues. Recognize the value of hard work.*
- *Praise: Praise God for who He is and the opportunities and blessings He brings your way. When you're tempted to be discouraged because of all the ethical difficulties, make it a point to start thanking and praising God for the good and gracious things He provides, even in a fallen world.*

### THE RIGHT APPROACH TO STUDYING ETHICS

It is important to reiterate what is foundational to the study of ethics—the Bible. The right approach to these subjects is to keep the Bible's teaching on anything related to ethics front and center. We need Scripture to saturate our minds, hearts, and choices (Col. 3:16–17). Psalm 19:7–11 and the whole of Psalm 119 declare the necessity of Scripture for all of life, including when we are determining our ethics (see also 2 Pet. 1:3).

We have already covered *why* you should study ethics. Before embarking on the first chapter in our study of ethics, we want to look at *how* you should study ethics.

"Let the word of Christ dwell in you richly in all wisdom."
Colossians 3:16

*The basic reason that we should study ethics is to better know God's will for us.* WAYNE GRUDEM[1]

There's an old saying that when you're trying to do something correctly, you have to hold your mouth the right way. The saying is slightly humorous because it combines the reality of the effort required to do something right with the whimsical idea that the way you position your lips and tongue has a direct impact on accomplishing a task. This ironic saying is communicating in a light-hearted way that having the right posture helps get the job done. This is actually the case for many things in life. For example, posture is everything when it comes to your golf swing. The positioning of your shoulders, arms, hands, back, hips, and feet plays a huge role in a successful drive or putt. If you slouch or carelessly swing the club, the ball won't go where you want it to. The same principle applies to your study of ethics. The way you "carry yourself" as you approach your studies will have a lot to do with how successful you are.

#### Prayer[6]

If you are like many, prayer can be one of the last resources you use when you tackle your work. Maybe you rely on your brainpower and willpower entirely—or at least way before you consider praying about your work. Hopefully, you pray regularly for understanding and efficient learning as you study. If not, it isn't too late to start a new habit. And praying for wisdom as you learn to grapple with ethical choices will be essential! Believers have an advantage that unbelievers don't—the Spirit of God works in Christians and helps them understand matters that are spiritually discerned (1 Cor. 2:14–16). Starting now, get in the routine of praying before, during, and after your studies of ethics and ethical issues. And as you gain knowledge and grow from your studies, pray that God will establish the truth deep in your heart, so you can face college and the workplace convinced of the value of Christian ethics.

#### Humility

Humility is a Christian virtue that isn't highly sought after; by its very nature, it is not often publicly rewarded. Christians who are loving, kind, patient, or disciplined seem to be more readily acknowledged. But a humble person manifests meekness, confidence rooted in faith, and an absence of pride. You will gain a lot of knowledge this year. You will figure out things that many people much older than you don't know because they have never studied ethics. So here is a timely caution: stay humble, and don't let your new knowledge puff you up (1 Cor. 8:1). Humility can be one of your first requests as you pray for your efforts to learn and use this material.

8

### Reason

Human reason rightly has a bad reputation when it is held up as the ultimate standard for determining what's true. Reason that is not submitted to God and not viewed as deficient due to man's finiteness and fallenness is reason misused. But reason is a necessary tool for developing and communicating conclusions. Jesus and Paul used reason appropriately (Matt. 22:42–45; 1 Tim. 5:17–18). And that is because reason as a tool of thinking and communication isn't a boogeyman. You must be careful, though, that your "reasonable" extensions of what Scripture explicitly says don't go against other statements of Scripture. In ethics, this is key so you don't arrive at seemingly justified conclusions that in reality contradict clear biblical teaching. Use reason well, and use it submitted to the authority of God's revelation in His Word.

### Effort

Anything worth having requires effort. This saying applies to almost everything and most certainly to the subject at hand. You will need to be engaged and focused on the material as you work through each section and chapter. Of course, completing the assignments is part of the requirements for this course. But going beyond the classroom and homework, you will need to continue to work at coming to the best ethical decisions for countless situations. Consulting with others who are wise, mature Christians or who are knowledgeable on this subject will be key to your growth in these areas. Don't limit your study of what the Bible has to say on a given ethical topic to what this textbook presents. Search the Scriptures for answers and guidance in all subjects of study and areas of life (Acts 17:11; 2 Tim. 3:16–17).

### Praise

A final part of your approach to studying ethics should be praise and rejoicing. Just having a Bible class in school is a blessing and a privilege. God is the giver of all good things that we receive (James 1:17). To rejoice and praise God for His goodness, His care, and His love is a practice that should characterize every believer (Deut. 6:5; Ps. 146:2). Do you praise God for and rejoice over the material things you have? Do you thank God for your family and friends? One of the most helpful ways to begin this course is with praise to God for the opportunity to study ethics. To learn about ethics is to learn how to better please God with your motives, decisions, and actions.

As you embark on this journey, keep in mind that ethical issues constantly swirl around you. Be prepared to stop and think hard about what the Bible says about any given topic or situation—what your motives should be, what your goals should be, and what virtues you should emulate in choosing what you choose. It will be well worth it.

### Thinking It Through: Why Study Ethics?

1. Summarize the reasons to study ethics.
2. Summarize the benefits of studying ethics.
3. Explain the value of gaining spiritual wisdom in order to please God in making ethical choices.
4. How can you study ethics in a wise and godly manner?



## Assess

Guide a summative assessment by directing students to answer the questions in Thinking It Through: Why Study Ethics?

### Thinking It Through: Why Study Ethics?

1. You improve in knowledge, you grow personally, and your testimony is strengthened.
2. You will know better what God expects for your Christian living. You can discern between the right and wrong ethical systems.

   You grow personally as you learn how to better please God with your thoughts, motives, decisions, and actions.

   Your testimony improves in the sense that you align your ethical choices with what pleases God.
3. If the goal is to walk worthy of the Lord and please Him with your lifestyle, then gaining spiritual wisdom plays a crucial role in accomplishing that goal. Believers need God's wisdom to make good decisions. Left on their own, humans can't do the right thing. Ethical living that is pleasing to the Lord is possible only by getting wisdom from God to make those right choices.
4. Your disposition or attitude when approaching ethics plays a critical role in maximizing your learning and application of this material. A wise and godly manner in which to study this subject includes prayer, humility, reason, effort, and praise.

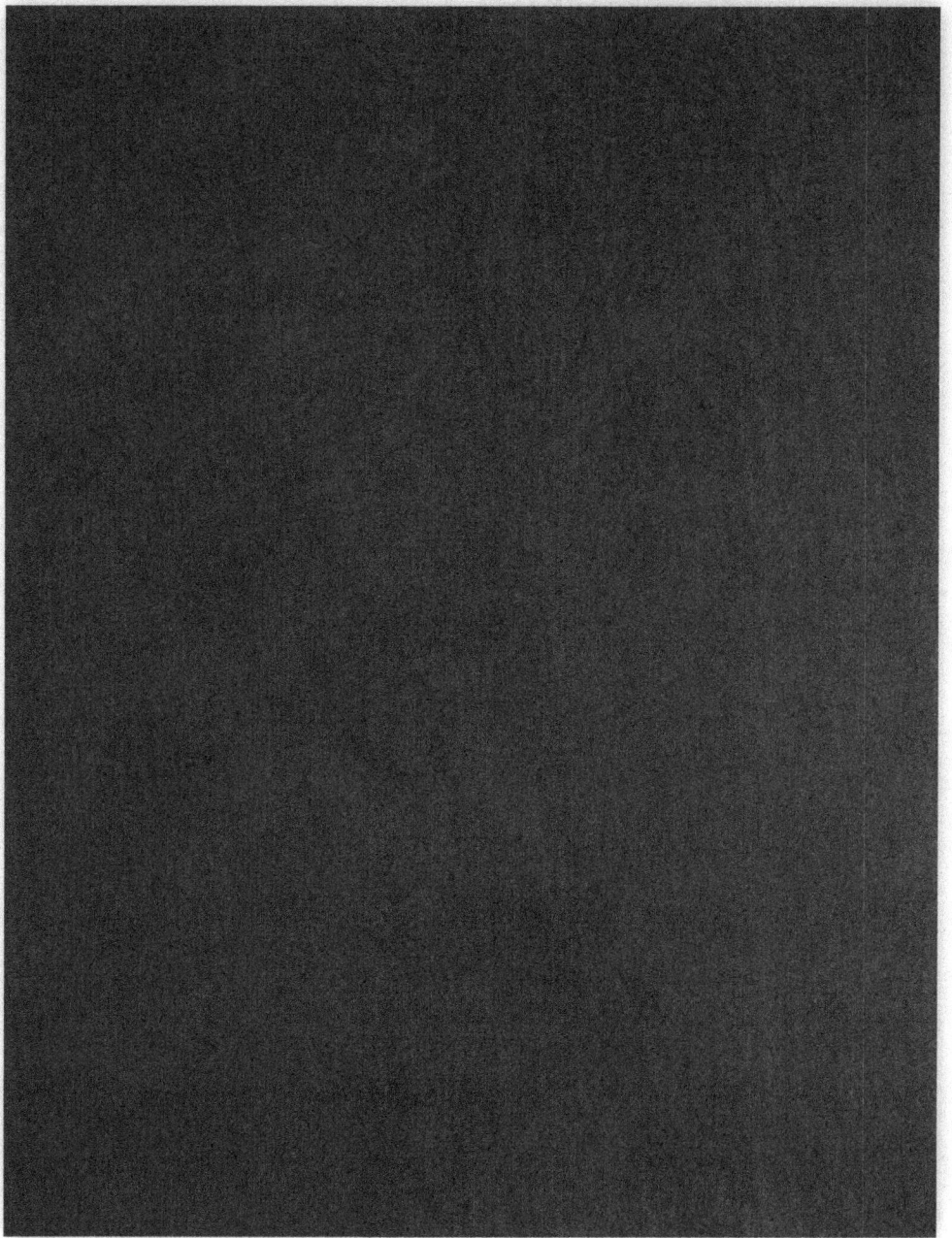

unit 1

# Foundations for Ethics

CHAPTER 1

# Overview

Who decides what's right and what's wrong?

**Objective**

**1.1** Analyze the basis for ethics.

### Terms to Remember

- creational norms
- image of God in man

### Scripture Memory

- Romans 1:18–20

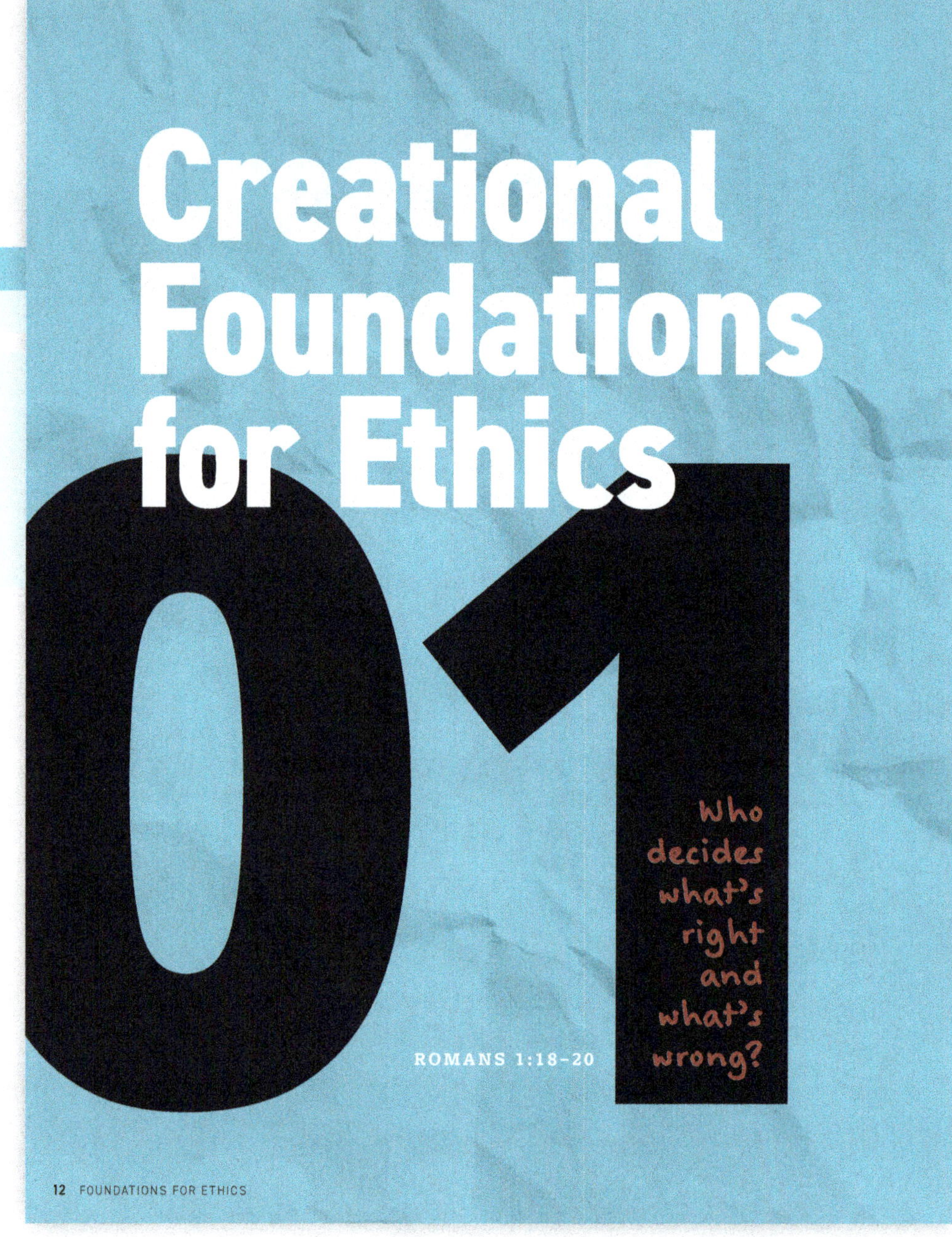

Creational Foundations for Ethics
01
Who decides what's right and what's wrong?
ROMANS 1:18-20
12 FOUNDATIONS FOR ETHICS

## 1.1 God's Character as a Foundation for Ethics

Soccer, which is called football by most of the global population, originated in England. A meeting in Cambridge in 1848 marks the official birth of soccer as an organized sport. The official rules for soccer have changed dramatically in its over one hundred seventy years of history. Take a look at this sample of rule changes or additions through the years:[7]

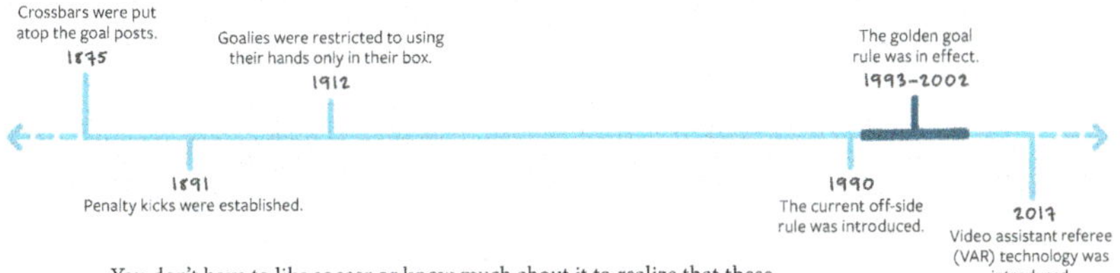
Crossbars were put atop the goal posts.
1875
Goalies were restricted to using their hands only in their box.
1912
The golden goal rule was in effect.
1993–2002
1891
Penalty kicks were established.
1990
The current off-side rule was introduced.
2017
Video assistant referee (VAR) technology was introduced.

You don't have to like soccer or know much about it to realize that these rule changes significantly modified the way the game is played. Why weren't the rules just established and never messed with again? Is there any guarantee that soccer as it is currently played will look the same fifty years from now?

The foundation for soccer has had an interesting progression. You will soon see that, unlike the foundation for soccer, the foundation for ethics does not fluctuate. When discussing something as important as ethics, to start by examining its foundations is not only logically important but also practically helpful. Any foundation you can think of, whether it be for a physical structure or an academic subject, can be damaged or undermined. And damaging or undermining a foundation affects everything above it. Let's begin examining the foundation for ethics.

## 1.1 God's Character as a Foundation for Ethics

*What is the basis for determining what's right and what's wrong?*

### Objectives

**1.1.1** Explain the basis for ethics. BWS

**1.1.2** Analyze the attributes of God that form the basis for ethics.

### Biblical Worldview Shaping

- **Authority** (explain): God's character is the basis for right and wrong. (1.1.1)

### Printed Resource

- Activity 1.1: God's Character Is the Starting Point

### Digital Resource

- Video: "Importance of Ethics"

### Suggested Reading

- Bridges, Jerry. *The Practice of Godliness.* Colorado Springs, CO: NavPress, 1983. Pages 49–66.
- Magnuson, Ken. *Invitation to Christian Ethics: Moral Reasoning and Contemporary Issues*. Grand Rapids, MI: Kregel Academic, 2020. Pages 70–74.

## Engage

### THE STRONGEST SUBSTANCE

Ask a **question** about the strongest substance on earth.

**What is the strongest naturally occurring substance known to man?** *diamonds (or lonsdaleite, an extremely rare substance)*

Because of their extremely high scratch resistance, diamonds can only be scratched by another diamond. Diamonds will not wear off easily. Transitioning to ethics, point out that a system of ethics will not wear off if it is built on God's character. Consequently, if a system of ethics is not built upon God's character, it will crumble and fail. Diamonds (or lonsdaleite) are among the strongest substances on earth. And God's character is the strongest foundation for ethics.

## Instruct

### THE IMPORTANCE OF ETHICS

Show the **video** "Importance of Ethics" to reiterate the significance of this course.

### SOURCES OF AUTHORITY

Guide a **Think-Pair-Share** for students to discuss the persons with the greatest authority in the world. Encourage the students to consider any sector in society, not just religious or political.

Guide a brief **discussion** asking and answering the following questions.

**Can you think of people in the past who have had great authority?** *Fidel Castro, Stalin, Mao Zedong, Napoleon, Alexander the Great*

Can you imagine these human authorities determining absolute morality for everyone else? When it comes to ethics, God's character is the standard for all that is good and bad, moral and immoral, right and wrong in the universe. God alone has absolute authority. Everyone and every institution are subject to His rule and authority. Even regarding ethical issues, God's character determines what is ethical or unethical for His creation.

**Why is God's character the source of absolute authority over all ethical and moral questions?** *God has always existed, and He is the Creator of all things (Gen. 1:1), which include ethics, morality, and determining what is right and wrong. God created all reality, so He holds the right to set up all the rules and laws of our existence as He sees fit based on His own character. But this God, who Himself is righteous, holy, and good, communicated His perfect character and attributes in His laws that govern His creation (Exod. 20:1–17). God is also the Sustainer of all things (Col. 1:15–17) and so His character governs the expectations He has for the humanity He created. God alone is the Judge and final Arbiter (Rev. 20:10–15). God's character serves as the standard against which all else is judged.*

### ATTRIBUTES OF GOD

Use a **misconception check** to gauge understanding of the reality that God defines the ethical nature of virtues. His attributes enable us to properly relate terms such as *love* and *goodness* to ethics.

**Do you agree with the popular saying, "Love is love"?** *This saying is absurdly false as it gives no definition of love. It leaves the door open for whomever to create his or her own definition. Love isn't abstract or unknowable. Love has a source, just like every other virtue.*

**Who gets to define what holiness, love, goodness, righteousness, and trustworthiness are and mean?** *The Creator and perfect Practitioner of love and the other attributes defines and exemplifies what they are and mean.*

Use **direct instruction** to further clarify the connection between God's character and ethics.

- God is holy (Isa. 6:3) and His holiness is the standard for our holiness (1 Pet. 1:14–16). Sin, evil, wickedness, vice, and anything bad is foreign to God's nature, and by that measure, sin and all its manifestations should not be part of a believer's life (1 Cor. 6:9–11).
- God determines what love is and judges every expression of love according to His perfect nature. Humans aren't able to define love based on their own feelings, emotions, or notions. God's love, as it translates into an ethical characteristic, is primarily seen in God's love for sinful humankind in the incarnation, life, death, and resurrection of Jesus Christ (John 3:16; Rom. 5:8). And Christ places love at the top of all virtues when it comes to relating properly to God and to others (Luke 10:27).
- The goodness of God is the standard for all forms of goodness among humanity (Pss. 86:5; 119:68). God's goodness does not contradict His justice. In meting out

What is the basis for determining what's right and what's wrong?

THE BASIS FOR ETHICS

Thankfully, the foundation for ethics is not based on something subjective, arbitrary, or susceptible to damage. God Himself, His character more precisely, is the basis for ethics. Why should God be a part of the conversation about ethics? And why must ethics be based on God's character? Follow along closely. God is self-existent and has always existed (Ps. 90:2; Isa. 40:28; John 8:58). God is Creator (Gen. 1:1; Heb. 11:3). God doesn't change; He is the same all the time (Mal. 3:6; James 1:17; Heb. 13:8). God is also infinite in power, knowledge, and wisdom. He is present everywhere all the time.

If you have studied *Bible Doctrines*, you probably realize we have described God's aseity,* eternality, immutability,* omnipotence, omniscience, and omnipresence. We have also affirmed that He is Creator of all things. God, therefore, is the sovereign ruler over all things everywhere at all times (Neh. 9:6; Isa. 37:16; Col. 1:16–17). There are no other contenders.

But God is not just powerful. He is also holy, just, and loving; He is good. Indeed, God's unchanging holiness, justice, love, and goodness define what those attributes mean. God's character is the standard by which such virtues are measured. There is no sure basis for ethics without God.

And God's character is not hidden. Scripture reveals God's nature and character, but creation itself also reveals to every person what God is like (Rom. 1:18–20, 32). And His character, as revealed in general and special revelation, gives us the standard for ethics. Who God is and how He acts determines what is right and what is wrong, and His character and work are known to some extent by all people.

As Creator and Sustainer of all things, God is also the supreme Judge of all (Gen. 18:25; John 5:22–27; 2 Cor. 5:10). The reality of an ultimate Judge who makes judgments informs us about the realities of right and wrong. Only God is capable of drawing up the boundaries for good and evil. Ken Magnuson summarizes this principle by saying,

> The ultimate source of morality is God, who created the universe with moral order—determined by his character, purposes, and will—and graciously reveals to human beings not only the reality of that order but also how to live according to that reality.[8]

So, God is the one who establishes the universal standards by which to make judgments. His holy character is the measure by which all else is measured (1 Pet. 1:15–16). God's character is the touchstone to achieve clarity on whether something is ethical.

What would happen to society if God's perfect and unchanging character weren't the basis for ethics? Chapter 2 will explain various faulty positions on ethics that people have come up with through the years. But imagine if the majority opinion of the masses determined what was ethically right. Or what if those in power—financially, politically, militarily, religiously—called the shots on what constituted right and wrong? The immorality, chaos, injustice, and subjectivity that could result from either of these options should be apparent. Grab a history book, or just read some news headlines, and you can see the horrible results of making anything but God the basis for ethics—results such as suffering, oppression, hatred, death, and celebration of sin and its consequences (Rom. 1:28–32).

asceity: self-existence

immutability: unchangeability

*"God is a Spirit, infinite, eternal, and unchangeable, in his being, wisdom, power, holiness, justice, goodness, and truth. . . . God's works of providence are, his most holy, wise, and powerful preserving and governing all his creatures, and all their actions."*

Westminster Shorter Catechism

14 FOUNDATIONS FOR ETHICS

**DEFENDING THE FAITH**

Is Too Much Authority a Bad Thing?

The fact that the God of the Bible is the one sovereign Lord over the entire universe, including ethics, frustrates many people. Granted, not all agree with the notion of God's universal lordship. But that is what the Bible teaches, and God's people should embrace the clear teaching of Scripture. A popular saying attributed to John Dalberg, Lord Acton, however, might come to mind when contemplating God's absolute authority over all things: "Power tends to corrupt and absolute power corrupts absolutely." Could this apply to God, even in the smallest way? Does the idea that "the guy with the biggest stick is the biggest bully" apply to God?

Continue reading this section to develop your answer more fully.

### ATTRIBUTES OF GOD

God's character is inseparable from His nature. We just looked at some attributes of God that describe His unique nature. Any ethical system that presumes to be based on any other grounds is faulty, deficient, and misleading. Let's consider more carefully some key attributes that lay the foundation for ethics.

#### *Holiness*

God is holy (Isa. 6:3). God is altogether perfect—in His self-existing triunity (transcendence) and in His interaction with all He created (immanence). God is pure and separate from any form of sin (Heb. 7:26). Holiness isn't only for God. God's people are called to live holy lives (Exod. 19:6; 1 Pet. 2:9). This God-imitating holiness is central to Christian virtue and ethics and comes to bear on challenging ethical situations we face.

#### *Love*

"God is love" (1 John 4:8). The love displayed and described by God is the love all ethical systems should imitate (1 John 4:9–11). Christ summarized what obedience to the law of God looks like in one word—love (Matt. 22:37–40). You would be hard-pressed to find a system of ethics that doesn't emphasize love—be it for nature, for others, or for oneself. But God has established what love is, what love does, and how people are supposed to love God and others.

#### *Goodness*

God is good (Mark 10:18). The God who is entirely good and delights in giving good gifts defines what goodness looks like (James 1:17). The ultimate display of God's goodness is sending Jesus to be sacrificed for undeserving sinners (Titus 3:4–5). The goodness of God is similar to His mercy. Mercy in lieu of justice can be ethical because of God's good and kind character (Rom. 11:22; James 2:13) and because Christ ultimately paid the price justice demands for those saved by mercy (Rom. 3:25–26).

#### *Righteousness*

Discussions of ethics always touch on the topic of right versus wrong, righteousness versus evil. God is righteous (Jer. 9:24). This attribute goes back to the idea mentioned above that God is Judge. And as Judge, God keeps His promises and judges righteously—always (Deut. 7:9; 32:4). The revelation of the God who declares and does the right thing in every instance gives biblical Christianity the only true starting point for ethics.

#### *Trustworthiness*

God is trustworthy (Isa. 12:2). This means that God is faithful and reliable. God's character is stable, permanent, and steadfast. Only God is unchanging. He will



justice on some, God is good; in pouring out mercy and grace on others, God is good (Rom. 9:14–15). God's goodness is part of His character, and how He relates to humanity doesn't change the reality of His goodness. That is the way it should be for people as well, especially for believers (Matt. 7:9–11).

- The righteousness of God very plainly corresponds to the realm of ethics. Abraham appealed to God's righteousness and just dealings when interceding for Lot and his family (Gen. 18:25). God's standard of righteousness and justice is the standard that governs all of humankind's interactions. Justice among humans must match the righteousness of God, reflecting His just actions and righteous nature.
- The trustworthiness of God is helpful to consider when discussing rooting ethics in God's character. Even though humans are creative in sinning and ethical scenarios can be very complicated, God's character is reliable, steadfast, unchanging, and entirely trustworthy. One can be secure in his or her ethical decisions that are submitted to the standard of God's character because God is wholly trustworthy (Isa. 26:3–4).

### GOD'S CHARACTER IS THE STARTING POINT

- Use **Activity 1.1** on page 1 to establish how the attributes of God as the basis for ethics impact Christian ethics.

## Apply

### WHO DECIDES WHAT'S RIGHT AND WHAT'S WRONG?

Ask students this chapter's **essential question** to help them understand that God decides what is right and wrong.

**A second question is this: Why are human authorities inadequate sources for determining right and wrong?** *Human authorities are finite, fallible, sinful, and subjective. Human authorities can do a good job governing and making decisions, but that only happens when their governance and decisions align with God's character and its outworking in the world.*

### WHAT IS THE BASIS FOR DETERMINING WHAT'S RIGHT AND WHAT'S WRONG?

Ask the students this section's **essential question** and guide a **discussion** of the answer and the reasoning behind the answer.

God's character determines what's right and what's wrong. And God's character is seen generally in creation and specifically in Scripture. God is over all, and His Word has absolute authority over humans, including their ethics.

## Assess

Use a **Ticket out the Door** to assess understanding of God's character as the foundation for ethics and His inherent authority to be that foundation.

**Why is a teenager obeying his or her parents by arriving home from a friend's birthday party on time ethically moral?** *God has placed parents as authorities over their children's lives. But parents are not only authorities in the lives of their children. Parents care for, protect, support, and strive to see their children succeed in life. And while God requires children to obey their parents, His own character of being a faithful Provider, wise Father, and powerful Protector also impacts a child's ethical obligation to obey his or her parents.*

Guide a **summative assessment** by directing students to answer the questions in Thinking It Through 1.1.

### Thinking It Through 1.1

1. God, His character more specifically, is the basis for ethics. There is no higher standard, no other authority that can determine what is ethical and what isn't. God's character is seen in how He exists as the triune God and how He interacts with His creation.
2. The reality of God and Him being God in all His ways qualifies Him to be the one to determine what is right and what is wrong. The triune God's perfect character dictates what is right, what is wrong, and the fact that those categories will forever be fixed.
3. God is the sovereign Ruler of all things everywhere at all times because of His aseity, eternality, immutability, omnipotence, omniscience, and omnipresence. God is also holy, loving, good, righteous, and trustworthy. Therefore, what He deems good is good, and what He declares evil is evil.
4. Holiness: God is perfect in His entire being, including being pure and separate from sin. All His dealings with people are also holy.

   Love: Because God is love, He defines what love looks like. Love for God and others is key to a Christian ethic because of God's amazing love.

   Goodness: God is good and delights in giving good gifts. His ultimate goodness was seen when He sent His Son to die on behalf of sinners.

   Righteousness: God always keeps His promises and always judges righteously. Because God is always right, He is the only true starting point for ethics.

   Trustworthiness: God is trustworthy, which means He is faithful, reliable, and unchanging. Even in the face of all the challenges we face in life, we can still trust all that God reveals to be true and sufficient because God is entirely trustworthy.

always be true to the righteous standard of His own character. The foundation for Christian ethics cannot be damaged because God can be trusted. Circumstances can change. We will face the consequences of bad decisions. But God is a rock (2 Sam. 22:31–33). Jesus called those who build their lives on His Word "wise" (Matt. 7:24–27). Only God can be trusted to order our decisions and behaviors (Prov. 3:5–7).

Since God is holy, loving, good, righteous, and trustworthy, anything in our lives that is contrary to these attributes is due to our fallenness. To live in a manner that doesn't reflect God's character is sinful (Exod. 34:6–9). This includes every unholy thought, every unloving motive, every bad consequence, and every unrighteous action.

God's character is the basis for ethics. There are two other related and complementary foundations for ethics that we will now turn to consider. Whereas this section presented *who God is* as the basis for ethics, the following sections will touch on aspects of *what God has done* to round out the foundations for ethics.

#### Thinking It Through 1.1

1. Explain the basis for ethics.
2. What is the basis for determining right and wrong?
3. Why is God the ultimate authority over all things, including ethics?
4. Summarize the attributes of God that form the basis for ethics.

## 1.2 The Created Order as a Foundation for Ethics

What do robins, butterflies, airplanes, and drones have in common? They all fly, obviously. Who made the robin and the butterfly? God did, of course (Gen. 1:20–21, 24–25). Who makes airplanes and drones? Well, people do, but they borrow from God's creation to make them. The flight of airplanes involves certain physical materials like metal, fiberglass, and fuel. But flight also involves properties such as lift, propulsion, drag, and aerodynamic design. A more challenging question is, Did God make flight, or did man invent it? Birds and insects have flown since the day they were created by God. So man hardly invented flight or came up with the required elements for it. The Wright brothers' predecessor George Cayley actually used birds in his research of how to form and use the wings of a glider or plane.[10] We can truly say that the pioneers of manned flight used the created order as a foundation for achieving sustained flight. Man tapped into certain laws of God's creation in order to create things that fly.

Flying a plane isn't the same as making ethical decisions—such as telling the truth on your income taxes or protecting the life of the unborn—is it? No, it's not. Scripture directly addresses these two ethical issues. Nevertheless, how God designed mankind also speaks to these scenarios. Christian ethics rightly starts with God's character as revealed in Scripture as a foundation for ethics. But Christian ethics also appeals to the created order and how it reflects the character of the one who created all things. And just as God created all the creatures that fly, He also established the physical principles of lift, propulsion, drag, and aerodynamic design required for flight. And just as God created a world in which governments necessarily exist and the unborn are persons who bear His image, He also established the ethical principles, like honesty and the protection of the vulnerable, required for people and societies to flourish. Such governing principles of God's creation are what we mean by creational norms. **Creational norms** are standards for how life in God's creation works, discerned by observing the design of the created order in light of Scripture's

16 FOUNDATIONS FOR ETHICS

## 1.2 The Created Order as a Foundation for Ethics

*What do creational norms have to do with ethics?*

### Objectives

**1.2.1** Define *creational norms.*

**1.2.2** Defend the existence of creational norms.

**1.2.3** Explain how creational norms are discovered. BWS

**1.2.4** Explain the role of creational norms. BWS

### Biblical Worldview Shaping

- **Creational Order** (formulate): Creational norms are discerned by observing the design of the created order through the lens of Scripture. (1.2.3)
- **Creational Order** (explain): Creational norms reveal God's good and moral design for His creation. Man is also responsible to pattern his life ethically after the creational norms. (1.2.4)

### Printed Resource

- Activity 1.2: Creational Norms and Two Genders

### Digital Resource

- Link: He Made Them Male and Female

teaching. Creational norms can be found in Scripture explicitly or can be discovered by viewing the world through the lens of Scripture.

### THE REALITY OF CREATIONAL NORMS

Scientists might speak of the laws of nature being constant and predictable. Scientists readily recognize that there are natural laws that govern our planet and the entire universe. Just think of the laws of thermodynamics. Scientists have observed certain behaviors and properties in nature that are predictable and consistent. For example, scientists have quantified and described the laws of thermodynamics. Or to reference something more familiar, a physical "law" of this world is that water boils at 212 degrees Fahrenheit at sea level. To mention the laws of nature is to identify certain constants or rules God built into His universe for it to function properly. Nature isn't some collection of random events! God made all things, and that includes how those things work underground, underwater, at sea level, on a high mountain, in the air, or in outer space.

Have you ever realized that attempting to violate natural laws has consequences? Have you ever tried to boil pasta at 175 degrees Fahrenheit? Of course not—unless you wanted to eat crunchy pasta. And if you ignore the law of gravity on a visit to the Grand Canyon or decide the laws of motion don't apply to you when crossing the street, you will soon find the consequences painful or fatal!

God's laws of creation, however, don't just include material things and their relationships. Other laws of creation—creational norms—come to bear on ethics because, in personal and interpersonal relationships, certain virtues and attitudes have been appointed by God for the well-being of individuals and societies.

Genesis 1 and 2 detail God's creation of the earth and the universe. Included in that creation account, though neither explicit nor detailed, are the natural laws that govern the physical world and the creational norms that govern the social world. Albert Wolters explains the breadth of God's design and purpose in everything He created by saying the following:

> All of human life, in all its vast array of cultural, societal, and personal relationships, is *normed* in this sense. The almighty Creator lays claim to it all; the universal Sovereign lays down his laws for it all; the absolute King requires his will to be discerned in it all.[11]

God employed His immeasurable wisdom and understanding in creating all things, including how all things relate to one another (Prov. 3:19–20). Before mankind fell and the plague of sin infected the world, God's creation perfectly aligned itself to God's design and purpose (Gen. 1:31). But in the Fall and the resulting Curse, sin brought confusion, corruption, and a twisting of God's holy and righteous standards among humans (Gen. 3:1–19).

Nevertheless, God's creational norms remain normative for His universe. God's laws that govern both the physical world and the social world are enduring. So before and after the Fall, the earth rotates on its axis and orbits the sun. And before and after the Fall, loving others is good, and unfounded and unjust hatred is evil. Loving others is the standard, the creational norm.

This enduring nature of creational norms can be seen in the fact that people have an innate sense of right and wrong. Various religions attempt to communicate this (faulty though their descriptions may be) in notions such as yin/yang, karma, and positive versus negative energy. God has made man in His image, and part of that design is that everyone has a sense of right and wrong within themselves as well as the sense that the world ought to operate a certain way (Rom. 2:15). You can observe how people have an instinct to pull someone out of harm's way with barely a moment's notice. You can observe how most people have an innate sense that compassion for the needy is praiseworthy. These are just two examples of how God has designed people to respond to and interact with one another.

## Suggested Reading

- Wolters, Albert M. *Creation Regained*. 2nd ed. Grand Rapids, MI: Eerdmans, 2005. Pages 16–27.

## Engage

### DISCERNING CREATIONAL NORMS FROM NATURE

Guide a **discussion** to help students understand how a small, seemingly insignificant creature can teach a huge lesson about ethical behavior.

**What small creature teaches a big lesson about ethical behavior?**

Ask each student that responds to explain their answer. If the ant is not mentioned after a few volunteers, ask a volunteer look up and read aloud Proverbs 6:6–11.

This proverb of the ant is a creational norm that directly translates to human behavior. Hard work that provides for one's needs doesn't only apply to the animal world. The apostle Paul brought over this creational norm seen in the ant, as well as other animals, to the human realm in his teaching in 2 Thessalonians 3:6–12, especially verse 10: "if any would not work, neither should he eat."

An ant is wiser than a lazy, slothful person. The creational norm is clear: diligent work provides for one's needs; failing to work leaves one in hardship. In this case, both nature and Scripture explicitly give us this teaching!

## Instruct

### DISCOVERING EXISTING CREATIONAL NORMS

Use **direct instruction** to defend the existence of creational norms and explain how they are discovered. Everything exists in a certain state (is), but that doesn't mean that everything *should* exist in that state (ought). Creational norms identify the *ought* of creation rather than merely describing what *is*.

Even though we can't go back and observe life in its perfect condition before the Fall, we can still discern from God's revelation in Scripture the reality of creational norms as a showcase of what is good and ethical. Albert Wolters states that we are to discern God's will in His creational norms (see page 17).

A word of caution is in order. We should not assume that every claim regarding a discovery of creational norms is actually a creational norm. Each claim needs to be tested by Scripture. Some creational norms are explicitly stated in Scripture (e.g., a marriage should be between one man and one woman for life). Other creational norms are not stated in Scripture but are deduced from careful observation of God's world. These statements need to be tested against Scripture.

For instance, one might say that a creational norm for a historian is to make careful and thorough use of primary source material, checking his sources against each other. Though the Bible doesn't say anything specific about this, it does say much about truth, and if someone argued instead that history is concerned with narratives, not facts, that statement would not align with Scripture.

Note that there may be a range of confidence about whether a given claim is creationally normative or not. We have absolute confidence about explicit statements of Scripture and less confidence about those things that we have deduced.

## QUALIFICATIONS FOR DISCERNING CREATIONAL NORMS

Use a **misconception check** for students to explain why the following statement is false.

**Unbelievers are equally capable of living ethically because they are hardwired to discern creational norms just like believers.**

Believers have more "tools" to learn how to live ethically. While it is true that all people have received the same general revelation and God's common grace is for all, the Holy Spirit assists believers in discerning creational norms through the fear of the Lord. Spirit-led fear of the Lord produces true wisdom that enables believers to live ethically before God and their neighbor.

Don't you want to build it the way it was designed?


### DISCOVERING CREATIONAL NORMS

How do you figure out how to do things you don't know how to do? YouTube! Prerecorded instruction is easier and quicker to get than finding someone and asking them for help. Before the advent of the internet, people used almanacs, manuals, and books in general to gain knowledge or learn a skill. Oral tradition has also been an important means of passing down insights and ways of doing things. Keep in mind the principle we are unpacking: creational norms are the built-in principles that reflect God's wise design of how all things should work. Wolters helps us again by saying it this way:

> Human civilization is *normed* throughout. Everywhere we discover limits and proprieties, standards and criteria: in every field of human affairs there are right and wrong ways of doing things. There is nothing in human life that does not belong to the created order.[12]

The question is, how should we, God's creatures, figure out how to align ourselves with the Creator's design of all things?

Let's consider how creational norms are related to farming. Farming must be learned to some degree. When God created the earth, He established how plants would grow, seed, and reproduce (Gen. 1:11–12). Man must discern and submit himself to the creational norms of agriculture in order to provide for himself, his family, and society as a whole. Who taught Adam how to tend to the Garden of Eden and subsequently to farm? God gave Adam and Eve certain tasks, so He, therefore, enabled them to accomplish those tasks (Gen. 1:26–28). After the Fall, Adam and Eve had to struggle with a cursed earth to get what they needed from it (Gen. 3:17–19). God's judgment even extended to how the creation worked. But they still were responsible to fulfill God's mandate and purposes. God's creational norms are still in operation, and we still need to find them out.

Scripture sheds light on how man learns to farm (Isa. 28:24–29). In sum, man is able to discover how to farm due to the creational norms God designed in man and nature. God teaches man how to farm! But God doesn't use specific Scripture passages to do this. A good farmer is a wise farmer because he taps into God's wisdom in how He designed certain plants and animals. This is a large part of God's common grace* that He gives to all. Common grace includes rain and sunshine as well as access to God's creational norms (Matt. 5:45; Acts 14:17).

But the teaching of the Bible can't be totally ignored either. Wisdom calls out to man for him to listen and reap the rewards of acquiring it (Prov. 1:20–23, 33; 3:13–18). Ignoring wisdom, which God offers to all and manifests in both Scripture and creation, is the result of sin and results in suffering (Prov. 1:22, 24–32). Read through Proverbs and notice how the miserable consequences of foolishness are due to violating both the laws of God's Word and the laws of God's creation (especially what we are calling creational norms).

#### *The Difference the Fear of the Lord Makes*

In the realm of ethics, not just in the physical world, man needs to discover creational norms; that is, man needs to discover God's *wisdom* built into the design of the world. Creational norms are discoverable. Various psalms affirm that the heavens and the heavenly bodies (19:1–4), man's body (94:9–10), and man's work (104:23–24) display God's knowledge and wisdom in establishing creational norms. As these physical things speak this way, they speak of their proper function.

Solomon's wisdom was displayed in how well he subdued creation and got the best out of every aspect of his kingdom (2 Chron. 9:3–6). Solomon's wisdom surely reached into the realm of ethics, as described in one of the most amazing accounts of Solomon's insight (1 Kings 3:16–28). In the example of Solomon, we see how God-given wisdom can enable a person to discover creational norms, put those norms to good use, and thereby achieve great things (1 Kings 3:5–13).

But there is no wisdom without the fear of the Lord (Prov. 9:10). If God isn't feared (reverenced) for who He is and for how He relates to man, then man will

**common grace:** God's grace to all humans, both believers and unbelievers, which includes God's restraint on man's sin and God's provision of general creation blessings

have a skewed perception of reality. God determines reality and governs all the laws He has set in place. So, if He is not part of a person's worldview, then that person's cultivation of the world will be limited and will lack the wisdom necessary to flourish. And even though unbelievers, who refuse to fear the Lord, can send man to the moon and take part in managing the global economy, their partial mastery of some creational norms doesn't lead to their spiritual and eternal well-being (Rom. 1:24–25, 32). The fear of the Lord precedes any measure of true wisdom and God-pleasing morality.

Read how Solomon used his God-given wisdom and recognition of creational norms in 1 Kings 3:16–28. What creational norms are displayed in this passage?

And the fear of the Lord is learned in Scripture. Notice the close relationship between the fear of the Lord and Scripture (Ps. 112:1; Eccles. 12:13). We've already established that God's character is the basis for ethics. To gain the wisdom we need to live ethically, we need more than creational norms. We need the Word to learn of God's character and to thereby know how to fear the Lord for who He is. Scripture is the lens that clarifies which path to take from the fear of the Lord to discerning and using creational norms.

### *The Difference the Spirit Makes*

Whereas all people are hardwired to be able to seek and find creational norms, it is believers who seek and find wisdom that comes from fearing God (Prov. 1:7; Job 28:28). Remember, wisdom is measured in part by how well you discern and align yourself to creational norms. Fleming James says it this way:

> Wisdom therefore was wrought into the constitution of the universe. It was independent of men, though in a real sense it existed specially for them. . . .
>
> In human life therefore wisdom meant conforming to the divine constitution of the world. One must find out what it is, then order himself accordingly. Of course this was but another way of saying that one must do the will of God.[13]

James helps us see the reality of creational norms and how we use wisdom to discover and apply them to our ethical living.

Believers should readily admit they lack wisdom in life in general and need God to give it to them (James 1:5)—not so much to figure out how to fly and farm, but to figure out how to live well with their neighbors and love other believers as they ought (Rom. 12:9–10; 1 Thess. 4:9). Having wisdom is connected with having the Spirit work in and guide your life (Acts 6:3, 10). Followers of Christ can claim God's promise that He will guide them as they walk by faith and seek to honor God with their ethical living (Prov. 3:5–6).



CREATIONAL FOUNDATIONS FOR ETHICS 19

## THE ROLE OF CREATIONAL NORMS

Use **one question and one comment** to develop summaries of the impact of creational norms on ethical behavior. Group the students and assign one of the creational norms from pages 20–21 to each group.

Instruct each group to create one summary comment of how their creational norm impacts ethical behavior. Instruct each group to also formulate one question regarding their creational norm that they will pose to the other groups to develop a collective answer.

See pages 20–21 for the summarized answers. Guide the discussion of the questions raised by each group.

# Apply

## RELATING CREATIONAL NORMS AND ETHICS

Ask this section's **essential question** to elicit an understanding that creational norms inform ethics.

**What do creational norms have to do with ethics?** *God's created order reflects His perfectly just and moral nature, which humans are responsible to observe. Since creational norms reflect God's character, they naturally contribute to our ability to discern ethical behavior.*

*In God's mercy, He has endowed humans with the necessary common grace to discover creational norms (Matt. 5:45; Acts 14:17) as well as the abilities to do that which is profitable for them and their neighbors (Isa. 28:24–29).*

## CREATIONAL NORMS AND TWO GENDERS

Use **Activity 1.2** on page 3 to apply creational norms to a very relevant topic. Use the **link** He Made Them Male and Female to access the article that the students will read for Activity 1.2.

### THE ROLE OF CREATIONAL NORMS

When you video call a friend who isn't in the same room as you, you aren't actually with that friend. Makes sense, right? You are using a device that has a camera, screen, and internet connection to imitate an in-person meeting. A video call lets you see and hear your friend, but the image on the screen isn't your friend. A face-to-face conversation would definitely be more direct and personal. But no one would say that you didn't interact and communicate with your friend on the video call. Using God's creation to discern God's will for a given situation is similar to a video call. Creation reflects and proclaims the character of the Designer. Much of what God desires for humans can be found in how He has set up our world. In our illustration above, the face-to-face conversation is akin to knowing God and His will through special revelation. It is definitely more direct and personal; it is a clearer and more explicit kind of communication of God's design for humanity. But the creational norms we find do reveal God's design and purpose for how all things should work, and they complement what is revealed in the Scriptures.

What do creational norms have to do with ethics?

| | SPECIAL REVELATION | GENERAL REVELATION |
|---|---|---|
| *Role* | helps accurately interpret creational norms | God's design reveals creational norms |
| *Type of Communication* | direct | indirect, implied |
| *Found in* | Scripture | creation |

Let's turn now to look at the role creational norms play. Consider the following creational norms.

- Creator-creature distinction
- Two genders, male and female
- Marriage, husband and wife
- Work-rest-work-rest rhythm
- Harmony and peace

Each of these norms directly impacts ethics. We read in God's Word and observe in God's creation what *ought* to be the ideal—the right and the good thing. On this side of the Fall, we experience how the *is* so often contradicts the *ought*. For example, according to God's character, the Bible's teaching, and what is generally observed in creation, the preservation of life and protecting the vulnerable is the *ought* in our world. (We find it natural for parents to protect and nurture their helpless young, for instance.) But in the natural world, some animals and even some plants eat or harm one another, and we find even some human parents who hurt or destroy their own children (what *is*, though it seems unnatural). Much of ethics tries to discover the *ought* when it comes to preserving life and protecting the vulnerable. This is because, unfortunately, the *is* contains so much hatred and mistreatment of people. This is true around the world and can be seen in many practices: murder, abortion, euthanasia, suicide, abuse, and torture. Repeatedly, the *is* as it plays out in society doesn't match the *ought* that creational norms teach in these situations. The *ought* reflects the divine creational norms. The *is* in the fallen world doesn't automatically match up with the *ought*.

Let's look at the items from the bulleted list above and see how the creational norms they teach serve as a foundation for our ethical considerations.

- Creator-creature distinction

  This governs how we relate to God and to one another. We aren't God; we are fallen, finite, and fallible creatures. God, therefore, should be feared. And we should show patience toward one another and love each other despite all our shortcomings.

- Two genders, male and female

  This norm is seen in nature as well as in the creation of Adam and Eve. There are men and there are women. Transgenderism and any other gender fluidity are counter to God's good design of mankind.

- Marriage, husband and wife

  God made Eve for Adam and Adam for Eve, and together they formed a family unit for life. Adultery, polygamy, polyamory, fornication, homosexuality, and bisexuality are all contrary to God's good design of marriage and sexuality.

- Work-rest-work-rest rhythm

  God created the world in six days and rested on the seventh. God ordained that humans work but also that they rest. Work is good. Rest is good. Workaholism and laziness are both contrary to God's good design for people in His world.

- Harmony and peace

  At the end of the creation account in Scripture, prior to the Fall, harmony and peace pervaded all creation. This included Adam and Eve's relationship with God and with one another. This also included the whole of the natural world—the planets, sun, moon, and stars as well as the oceans, rivers, and animals. Violence, vandalism, irresponsible pollution, and unjust wars are all contrary to God's good design of this world.

You will encounter people who reject the authority of Scripture, and their lives won't align with God's will. They base their ethical system on something other than God and His Word. But God has hardwired creational norms into every aspect of life. All people are without excuse when it comes to seeing the divine design in all things (Rom. 1:19–20; 2:1–2). Ethics is founded on the truths that creational norms reveal and which reflect God's character.

### Thinking It Through 1.2

1. Define *creational norms*.
2. Defend the existence of creational norms.
3. How are creational norms discovered?
4. How are creational norms related to ethics?
5. Give two examples of creational norms and explain how they relate to ethical issues.

## 1.3 The Image of God in Man as a Foundation for Ethics

Growing up, you most likely drew pictures, rode a bike, and climbed all over the playgrounds you would visit. Statistically, however, it is unlikely you are an artist or a competitive cyclist or a professional climber. It is easy to see the difference between dabbling in artistic expression, riding a bike around the neighborhood, and climbing playground equipment and their professional counterparts. Expressed more philosophically, there is a difference between *doing* an activity and *being* someone whose whole identity is wrapped up in that activity.



## Assess

Guide a **summative assessment** by directing students to answer the questions in Thinking It Through 1.2.

### Thinking It Through 1.2

1. Creational norms are standards for how life in God's creation works, discerned by observing the design of the created order in light of Scripture's teaching.
2. Creational norms exist in nature (gravity, temperature at which water boils, laws of thermodynamics, etc.) and in people (the conscience, sense of right and wrong, etc.). Manned flight is only possible because God created both the physical things as well as the principles or properties required for flight. Love and care are ingrained in all of us.
3. Wisdom is the primary way creational norms are discovered and utilized. God gives His common grace to all people, so everyone has access to many creational norms.
4. Aligning ourselves to creational norms helps us live a more ethical life. God's character as revealed in the Word is a believer's primary source for ethical living. But creational norms guide us in discovering what God's design and purpose are with all His creation, including how we interact with other people.
5. Answers will vary. See the five bullets on pages 20–21 for possible answers.

## 1.3 The Image of God in Man as a Foundation for Ethics

What does the image of God in man have to do with ethics?

### Objectives

**1.3.1** Define the *image of God in man*.

**1.3.2** Explain why the image of God in man is a fundamental creational norm for ethics.

**1.3.3** Explain why the image of God in man is key for human virtue. BWS

### Biblical Worldview Shaping

- **Virtue** (explain): Humans live ethically when they reflect the communicable attributes of God (i.e., virtues). (1.3.3)

### Suggested Reading

- See Section 1.1.

## Engage

### BEING VERSUS DOING

Use a **bell ringer** activity to invite students to share examples of someone or something behaving in a way contrary to their nature.

**You do what you are. "You are what you do" has it backward. What examples in life are slightly confusing because someone or something is behaving in a way contrary to their nature?** *For example, you might have a friend who surprised all his or her friends because of a stellar performance in a school play. This friend is very introverted and shy, but for the school play he or she transformed into an outgoing, expressive, and charismatic character. This friend was able to act contrary to his or her normal way of being for a play, but the limited "doing" didn't change this friend's "being."*

All humans are made in the image of God, and all believers are indwelt by the Holy Spirit. Believers have no excuse for *"doing"* contrary to their *"being,"* even though the reality of temptation and sin are always present this side of heaven.

This principle illustrates what it means to *be* human. You don't merely do human things, perform human activities, or act in human ways. You *are* a human, and everything you do is done as a human. The image of God in man is as fundamental to who you are as your humanity. Just as human beings are human from conception and forever more, every human being is also made in God's image (Gen. 1:26–27).

#### THE IMAGE OF GOD IN MAN

But what does it mean for man to be made in the image of God? This question has been the subject of much theological debate. Let's face it, it's an intriguing topic! Scholars and theologians throughout history have singled out various aspects of the image of God in man—man's body; man's relational abilities; man's mind, will, and emotions; and man's ability to work and create. Right away we can point out the deficiencies in elevating one aspect of man as *the* image of God in man. Man has a body, but he also has a soul. And God is spirit, so to hold that the image of God in man is merely related to man's physical body is unconvincing. Man is hardwired to be relational, but animals and angels also share certain aspects of this trait. Man thinks, decides, and feels, but so do angels and animals. Man (imperfectly) carries out God's original command to work, create, and maintain the natural environment where God placed him (known as the Creation Mandate [Gen. 1:28–30]). But this is one thing man *does* as a human; it isn't who he *is* as a person. In each case, singling out one manifestation of the image of God in man is too limiting.

The **image of God in man**, therefore, is the essence of being human, a status God bestows upon man whereby the whole person is made to be "like God in everything in which a creature can be like God."[14] God's image in man is comprehensive, encompassing all that man is, which directly relates to all that he does. As mentioned, man alone (both male and female) is specifically created in God's image (Gen. 5:1–2; 9:6). Not animals. Not angels. Adam and Eve were made in God's image, in His likeness, and were the king and queen (notice the lowercase) of the whole earth. God had endowed them with all their abilities, faculties, strengths, intelligence, and potential. Nevertheless, they were creatures with limited resources and capabilities. The Creator-creature distinction existed from the beginning, even before the Fall. Following the Creator-creature distinction, Herman Bavinck notes,

> God is the archetype, the exemplar, the original. We are only truly human to the extent that we display God, also in our daily lives. The human person, therefore, has to be viewed theologically, and also in ethics. Morality, too, finds its principle and standard in the relation in which a human being stands to God.[15]

So, man is made in God's image; he isn't God, nor can he become God. Even after the Fall, man retains the image of God, though the image is marred (Gen. 9:6). All the descendants of Adam and Eve are created in the image of God—there are no exceptions (Gen. 5:3).

"So God created man in his own image,
in the image of God created he him."
GENESIS 1:27
GOD
22 FOUNDATIONS FOR ETHICS


Being made in the image of God is a status that nobody can lose.

## Instruct

### THE IMAGE OF GOD IN MAN

Use **direct instruction** to help students recognize that the image of God in man is a creational norm.

Every human is made in God's image. The image of God in man is the essence of being human, a status God bestows upon humans. God's image in man is comprehensive, encompassing all that we are, which directly relates to all that we do.

So, what we do (ethical behavior) flows directly from who we are (made in God's image).

The image of God in man is also covenantal as well as creational. God is the Creator, and we cannot escape being in relationship with Him. Even when sinners refuse to acknowledge it, they're dependent on God's provisions for life and sustenance.

### ETHICS AND THE IMAGE OF GOD IN MAN

Use **direct instruction** to explain why the image of God in man is a fundamental creational norm for ethics.

Since every person is made in God's image, every person has the responsibility to live in such a way that reflects His design and purpose. The Fall in Genesis 3 corrupted human nature, but the design and purpose, as creational norms, remain. No one can excuse sinful and unethical living because all humans have been made in God's image to reflect God in all the ways that a human can.

Every ethical standard has a source, an absolute rule by which ethics is measured. God's character is that standard, and we learn about God through the Word and the creational order. But in addition to these external measurements, each person is made in God's image and given general revelation about the Creator, the absolute authority who should be obeyed and loved.

The ethical practice of Christian virtues is directly tied to humans being made in God's image. All people—every unborn baby and newborn infant, boy and girl, man and woman, and elderly man and woman—are deserving of ethical treatment by virtue of being made in God's image. Any harm to a person, physical or otherwise, is not only dehumanizing to that individual, but also a direct assault on the God in whose image he or she is made.

The Christian virtues that will be covered in Chapters 5–7 all flow and stem from God's character to give the foundation to ethics. And since humans are made in God's image, they must apply and demonstrate those virtues as they interact with others. These virtues include love, righteousness, goodness, diligence, faithfulness, patience, gentleness, kindness, compassion, joy, peace, and honesty. God possesses and displays each of these virtues perfectly. Individual human relationships and societies in general can only thrive and experience ethical interactions if these virtues are developed and practiced as foundations for their relationships. They undergird ethical human relationships so that the nature of God Himself is the foundation for our ethical behavior with one another as image bearers of that perfect and holy God.

## Apply

### THE RIGHT BEHAVIOR FOR THE RIGHT CONTEXT

Use an **analogy prompt** to discuss the following analogy.

**When it comes to ethical behavior, some people are like chameleons when they are around various types of people because . . .**
*. . . some people instinctively know how to behave when they are with a certain category of people: the elderly, foreign dignitaries, babies, parents, friends, siblings, and so forth.*

In other words, people act differently when the context of whom they are with changes. You wouldn't treat your grandmother the same way you treat a baby, a foreign dignitary, or your best friend.

### THE IMAGE OF GOD IN MAN AS A KEY CREATIONAL NORM

A master key is a key that can open multiple locks. The doctrine of the image of God in man is like a master key that can unlock both creational norms and ethics. On the one hand, the image of God in man is the creational norm foundational to all other creational norms. And on the other hand, the image of God in man is also important to ethics itself. Indeed, the image of God in man is the foundational creational norm for ethics. The natural next question is, How so?

What does the image of God in man have to do with ethics?

All people are "people-persons" to some extent. In other words, God not only created man with relational abilities but relational affinities (Gen. 2:18). Even introverts and loners need people. And the reality is, God designed the world for humans; so we interact with people. Even if you took a submarine to the bottom of the ocean or a rocket to outer space, chances are you would go with a few other people, and you would be dependent on a whole team of people! Our ethics, our moral decision-making and living, impacts people directly and constantly. Sure, you can live alone on the side of a mountain or on a deserted island, but your thoughts and actions are still ethical—you are a person created in the image of God.

The image of God in man is important and valuable—and not just because that is how God made man, but because God is to be praised and glorified for all His works (Ps. 145:3–4). The image of God in man is what gives man dignity, a dignity that sets him apart from the angels, animals, plants, and rocks. This is why murdering a person is such a high offense; God Himself is being affronted (Gen. 9:5–6). The person who was murdered was made in the very image and likeness of God. God places high value on how we treat people (Lev. 19:18; Mark 12:31). The ethical treatment of people made in God's image even includes how we talk about or to them (James 3:9). We practice Christian ethics with one another because man's dignity and value come from being made in the image of God.

Remember, you should locate your authority and ethical standards in the Scriptures and in the creational norms imbedded in creation. The image of God in man is to be the *north* on your compass of creational norms. The other creational norms make sense in light of the fact that man is created in the image of God. Unbelievers are also image-bearers and so are able to recognize man's unique status and value in God's created order. Whether or not they are willing to admit it, the golden rule in Scripture makes sense to them (Matt. 7:12). They actually can appreciate and respect that standard. That doesn't mean unbelievers will practice the golden rule out of fear of the Lord and love for God and their neighbor.

Consider any number of ethical situations if people didn't know that man has great dignity and value. (In man's sinful state, he often chooses to ignore or bury this truth [Rom. 1:25, 32]. But the truth is that man has great dignity and value because he is made in God's image.) Otherwise there would be no difference between a human, a bumblebee, and a frog. Any form of mistreatment, abuse, or murder of humans could be allowed under this paradigm. It is precisely because man is made in God's image that we must live ethically with each other.

Remember also that God's character is the basis for ethics. Even fallen man mirrors some of that character because only he is created in the image of God. So the ethics God lays out for man and has revealed to man is wrapped up in the image of God in man. The image of God in man directs all the creational norms as they relate to ethics.

### THE IMAGE OF GOD IN MAN AS KEY FOR HUMAN VIRTUE

Finally, consider that the image of God in man is key for human virtue. When considering ethical decisions, virtue is always part of the discussion. Augustine* briefly defined virtue as "rightly ordered love."[16] Virtue is morally commendable

**Augustine:** early church father of the fourth and fifth centuries



The lesson in this analogy is that believers are to treat all people according to a biblical ethic using Christian virtue because, regardless of their age or position in life, all people are made in the image of God.

## RELATING THE IMAGE OF GOD IN MAN TO ETHICS

Ask this section's **essential question** to evaluate student understanding of the image of God and ethics.

**What does the image of God in man have to do with ethics?** *The virtue by which we should live is seen in God's character. And God created humans in His image. Therefore, humans have a responsibility to treat others ethically to conform to the creational norm of personhood—being made in God's image.*

## THE KEY FOR HUMAN VIRTUE

Use **direct instruction** to explain Objective 1.3.3 with its corresponding focus on biblical worldview.

The image of God in man is key for human virtue. It is only because of each human's personhood, being made in the image of God, that virtue can be practiced. Only humans can live virtuously because only humans are made in God's image. This essence and status of man's personhood is a key component in ethical and virtuous behavior.

## Assess

### MUDDIEST OR CLEAREST POINT

Encourage students to provide **feedback** on which points seem the hardest to understand and which points they have a clear understanding of.

Guide a **summative assessment** by directing students to answer the questions in Thinking It Through 1.3.

### Thinking It Through 1.3

1. The image of God in man is a status God bestows upon humans. This means that the whole human is like God in every possible way that a creature can be like the Creator. It is comprehensive, encompassing all that we are, which directly relates to all that we do.
2. The image of God in man is the most important creational norm regarding ethics. Since humans are created in God's image, they have dignity, value, and worth. So, as we seek to treat one another ethically, the fact that we are created in God's image rises to the top as the foremost reason why we should seek to treat one another ethically.
3. Virtue is rightly ordered love. Virtue is made up of morally commendable motives for behavior.
4. The only way humans can imitate God's character in virtuous living, which is ethical living, is to somehow be endowed with the ability to be like God. God formed man in His image and likeness, which means humans can and should obey all their Creator's commands and fulfill their God-given purposes for living as God's image-bearers. In God's attributes one finds the virtues that he or she can and should endeavor to embrace.
5. The image of God in man has everything to do with ethics. Humans are distinct from angels, animals, and the rest of creation. Since we are made in God's image, we have the responsibility to be like God in all our ways. God made humans with this capability, and so all our relationships have a direct ethical implication. We are held to God's ethical standards because we are made in God's image.

motives for behavior. Virtue has less to do with *what* you do than it does with *why* you do what you do. Ultimately, we do what we love. Behaviors are directed by some form of virtue or lack thereof. Virtues and vices account for why you are acting the way you are acting—they explain who you are being, essentially. In a few chapters, it will become more apparent that virtue is an integral part of Christian ethics.

Man, made in the image of God, behaves either virtuously (according to God's character) or unvirtuously (utterly unlike God's character). A quick glance at two passages that list various Christian virtues (Gal. 5:22–23; Col. 3:12–15) shows how many correspond to the character of God. We can readily see the relationship between virtue and the image of God in man.

In Section 1.1 of this chapter, we discussed various attributes of God that form the basis of ethics. Fallen and sinful man can live according to God's holiness, love, goodness, righteousness, and trustworthiness only because he is created in God's image. Believers seek to be transformed into Christ's image (Rom. 8:29–30; 2 Cor. 3:18). People live ethically when they are conformed to God's attributes, to the virtues that are patterned after God's character. Unbelievers are also made in God's image. Anytime they display a form of virtue, any behavior that even slightly conforms to God's character, it is due to their nature as image-bearers and to common grace at work in their lives.

You might say your unsaved family members, neighbors, and friends are good people because they are kind, hard-working, compassionate, and self-disciplined. They might show a little mercy here and have a little hope there. But no one is good like God is good—*good* as in free from sin and *good* as in being incredibly generous because of His graciousness—including Christians (Mark 10:18; Rom. 3:10–12; 1 John 1:8). Nevertheless, every single person at times imitates aspects of virtue, because every human is created in the image of God. But only believers in Christ are indwelt by the Holy Spirit and are, therefore, able to conform their lives to the character of God and truly practice the virtues (Phil. 2:1–5).

#### THE CREATIONAL FOUNDATIONS FOR ETHICS

We have looked at three foundations for ethics—God's character, the created order, and the image of God in man. God Himself and His creation give us the foundation on which to build ethical conclusions. God's character is revealed in His Word and in creation. The created order displays God's good design for human life and flourishing. And the image of God in man provides the central creational norm for even aspiring to live ethically. In the next two chapters, you will learn about the Fall's effects on ethics and the role of redemption in ethics. The creational foundations are incredibly important as you start down the path of learning about ethics. But they are just that—the start.

#### Thinking It Through 1.3

1. Define the *image of God in man*.
2. Explain why the image of God in man is a fundamental creational norm for ethics.
3. Define *virtue*.
4. Explain why the image of God in man is key for human virtue.
5. What does the image of God in man have to do with ethics?

Introduction/ 01

# Review

CREATIONAL FOUNDATIONS FOR ETHICS

### Terms to Remember

- ethics
- Christian ethics
- creational norms
- image of God in man

### Scripture Memory

Romans 1:18–20

### Understanding Ethics

1. What is the value of studying ethics?
2. What is the basis for ethics?
3. What is the relationship of God to ethics?
4. What is the relationship of man to ethics?

### Practicing Ethical Decision-Making

5. What explanation would you give an atheist to explain why you both agree that murder is wrong?
6. Suppose you are on a town council and your vote will decide whether to use your town's limited funding on infrastructure improvements or renovating an old shopping mall. Which project would you choose? Explain why you made that choice from a biblical perspective.

### Analyzing and Evaluating Ethical Claims

7. What would you say to someone who defines ethical behavior as that which the majority of a society determines works best for the success of individuals in that society? Explain.
8. Defend the continuing role of creational norms as a foundation for ethics even after man's fall into sin.
9. Why does the image of God in man affect all our ethical decisions?

### Creating My Own Position Statements on Ethics

10. Suppose a friend says to you that there are no benefits to studying ethics. List the reasons why studying ethics is so beneficial.
11. Why should we approach ethics from a Christian perspective? Defend the understanding and implementation of ethics from a Christian, biblical worldview.

# Introduction/ Chapter 1 Review

## Terms to Remember

- **ethics:** The branch of philosophy that studies how man ought to live.
- **Christian ethics:** The branch of theology that studies how man ought to live in light of scriptural teaching, creational norms, and moral reasoning.
- **creational norms:** Standards for how life in God's creation works, discerned by observing the design of the created order in light of Scripture's teaching.
- **image of God in man:** The essence of being human; a bestowed status whereby the whole person is made to be "like God in everything in which a creature can be like God." (Taken from page 34 of *The Defense of the Faith*, 4th ed., by Cornelius Van Til, ed. K. Scott Oliphint. Copyright 2008, P&R Publishing, Phillipsburg, NJ.)

## Understanding Ethics

1. Studying ethics helps you improve in your knowledge of God, which informs how you live ethically. Also, you have the opportunity to grow personally in your Christlikeness and in your ability to love your neighbor better. And finally, studying ethics helps you improve your testimony. You will be more prepared to be salt and light in the world.
2. The basis for ethics is God's character. Who God is and how He acts determine what is right and what is wrong. His character can be discerned in special revelation and in the creational norms found in general revelation and the image of God in man.
3. God's relationship to ethics is the most critical aspect of ethics. There is no foundation of authority or absoluteness outside God and the aspects of His character that He shares with humans.
4. Ethics is of necessity practiced by humans as they relate to others. Humans are central to the outworking of ethics because they alone are made in God's image. Humans are to rightly steward the rest of God's creation, but how someone treats another person reveals much of what he or she thinks about God.

## Practicing Ethical Decision-Making

5. I would tell him that both he and I have an innate sense of right and wrong that was given to us by the God he doesn't believe in. I would explain the nature of creational norms and explain that things such as murder naturally feel wrong because they go against an innate sense of human worth and dignity that all humans have. Preserving and caring for life is how God designed the world.
6. Infrastructure improvements. (The shopping mall renovation can be a legitimate answer if the student argues a strong case, where a renovated mall brings more jobs and customers to the town.) Development of this answer will vary, but students should argue from the character of God as reflected in Scripture, creational norms, and the image of God in man. The image of God in man affects our ethical decisions more than any other creational norm. Steady and affordable power, clean and available water, and a good education (as examples of infrastructure issues) are all things that improve the lives of people who are made in God's image. The shopping mall needs to be updated, but the direct impact of that mall on the lives and well-being of the people in the town is most likely less than the good of investing in the infrastructure.

## Analyzing and Evaluating Ethical Claims

7. If humans or society were the final say on all things related to ethics, we would be in deep trouble. Humans are fallen, finite, and subjective. They are

proud and selfish too. If a man-made philosophy or false god were set up as a foundation to ethics, then falsehood and inconsistency would abound in that flawed system. Only God is reliable, trustworthy, true, and just.

8. The creational norms God embedded into creation remained there even after the Fall. Creation is good but it is broken, marred by the Fall and sin. One of God's creational norms is the image of God in man. That also was retained after the Fall, and humans are able to know certain things about God and the good creation He made. So we can and should appeal to creational norms to defend aspects of Christian ethics.
9. The image of God in man is foundational to all human interactions because each human is made in the image of God. But many of the world's ways of doing things are in large part due to their *not* acknowledging that man is created in God's image, leading to horrible consequences (e.g., abortion, euthanasia, suicide, transgenderism). To mistreat the pinnacle of God's creation is to disrespect God Himself.

## Creating My Own Position Statements on Ethics

10. Knowledge: Your knowledge of God's expectations for your Christian living improves. Applying that knowledge enables you to discern between the right and wrong ethical systems.

    Personal Growth: You grow personally as you learn how to better please God with your thoughts, motives, decisions, and actions.

    Testimony: Your testimony improves as you align your ethical choices with what pleases God.

11. Ethics are naturally Christian in that God's character is the basis for ethics. There are other ethical systems that don't share this assertion, but their systems are inconsistent, human-centered, and therefore flawed. Another reason ethics is Christian is that it is Christians who can truly and more fully live ethical lives that please God. Having a biblical worldview allows the Christian to succeed at engaging in all of life ethically and in a way that is consistent with the teaching of Scripture.

# Lesson Plan Overview

**CHAPTER 2:** The Fall's Effects on Ethics

**EV** ExamView
**PPT pres.** PowerPoint presentation

<table>
<tr><th>PAGES</th><th>OBJECTIVES</th><th>RESOURCES</th><th>ASSESSMENTS</th></tr>
<tr><td colspan="4">2.1 The Root Cause of All Ethical Difficulties (4 DAYS)</td></tr>
<tr><td>27–32</td><td>2.1.1 Explain how the Fall disrupts the functioning of the creational norms in the world.<br>BWS Creational Order (evaluate)<br>2.1.2 Describe the effects of the Fall on human nature.<br>BWS Virtue (evaluate)<br>2.1.3 Relate the effects of the Fall to the difficulty of making ethical choices.</td><td>ACTIVITIES<br>• 2.1 The Difficulty of Making Ethical Choices in a Fallen World<br>BJU PRESS TROVE*<br>• PPT pres.: Chapter 2<br>MATERIALS<br>• magnets and metallic objects</td><td>STUDENT EDITION<br>• Thinking It Through 2.1</td></tr>
<tr><td colspan="4">2.2 Faulty Approaches to Ethics (4 DAYS)</td></tr>
<tr><td>32–38</td><td>2.2.1 Explain the deontological approach.<br>2.2.2 Explain the consequentialist approach.<br>2.2.3 Explain the virtue ethics approach.<br>2.2.4 Explain the existentialist approach.</td><td>ACTIVITIES<br>• 2.2 Identifying the Ethical Approaches<br>BJU PRESS TROVE<br>• Video: "Major Ethical Systems"<br>• PPT pres.: Chapter 2</td><td>STUDENT EDITION<br>• Thinking It Through 2.2</td></tr>
<tr><td colspan="4">2.3 Evaluating the Faulty Approaches to Ethics (4 DAYS)</td></tr>
<tr><td>38–43</td><td>2.3.1 Evaluate the deontological approach.<br>BWS Authority (evaluate)<br>2.3.2 Evaluate the consequentialist approach.<br>BWS Man's Chief End (evaluate)<br>2.3.3 Evaluate the virtue ethics approach.<br>BWS Virtue (evaluate)<br>2.3.4 Evaluate the existentialist approach.</td><td>ACTIVITIES<br>• 2.3 Critiquing the Ethical Approaches<br>BJU PRESS TROVE<br>• PPT pres.: Chapter 2</td><td>STUDENT EDITION<br>• Thinking It Through 2.3</td></tr>
<tr><td colspan="4">Review</td></tr>
<tr><td>44</td><td>Recall concepts, terms, and Scripture memory from Chapter 2.</td><td></td><td>STUDENT EDITION<br>• Chapter 2 Review</td></tr>
<tr><td colspan="4">Test</td></tr>
<tr><td></td><td>Demonstrate knowledge of the material from Chapter 2 by taking the test.</td><td></td><td>ASSESSMENTS<br>• Chapter 2 Test<br>BJU PRESS TROVE<br>• EV: Chapter 2 test bank</td></tr>
</table>

*Digital resources for homeschool users are available on Homeschool Hub.

CHAPTER 2

# Overview

How can I identify problematic approaches to ethics?

## Objectives

**2.1** Identify the cause of the difficulties in living ethically.

**2.2** Describe faulty approaches to practicing ethics.

**2.3** Evaluate faulty approaches to practicing ethics.

### Terms to Remember

- naturalistic fallacy
- deontological ethics
- categorical imperative
- consequentialist ethics
- utilitarianism
- situation ethics
- ethical egoism
- virtue ethics
- existentialist ethics
- internal consistency
- external coherence

### Scripture Memory

- Romans 3:10–12

The Fall's Effects on Ethics

ROMANS 3:10–12

02

How can I identify problematic approaches to ethics?

26 FOUNDATIONS FOR ETHICS

## 2.1 The Root Cause of All Ethical Difficulties

Have you ever played with magnets, seeing how far away one magnet could be from another before—SNAP!—they were inescapably drawn together? When you were a child, it was rather fun to play with magnets.

You might be amazed to know the strength of a magnet used for industrial purposes. For instance, a Neodymium Iron Boron (NIB) magnet is the strongest class of magnets on earth. They are extremely powerful because of their energy density. An NIB magnet is so strong that, if attracted to something, it could fly across the room, and its high speed and momentum could shatter your bones if you put your hand in its path.[1]

Have you ever known the right thing to do, and yet felt yourself strongly pulled in the opposite direction? You may have even had a clear idea of the negative consequences of doing the wrong thing. You may have had a definite understanding of why choosing right would be the best thing for you and others. And yet, within, you still found yourself yearning to fulfill desires that you knew were wrong and destructive. In the end, you gave in and satisfied your desires.

Apart from the grace of God, our fleshly desires draw us with a force greater than that of an NIB magnet to give into temptations. Whether it comes out in the media we consume or the pictures we view online or the things we find spewing out of our mouths in response to our classmates, siblings, or parents, we feel in us this strong pull to do the opposite of what we know to be right (Rom. 7:7–25).

Are we excused for our responses, then, because something within seemed to inescapably pull us to feel, desire, think, do, or say something? No, but this answer can only be properly understood from a biblical understanding of the Creation, Fall, Redemption storyline. More specifically, a sound understanding of the difficulty of making ethical choices comes from a sound understanding of the biblical doctrines of man, sin, and salvation—all grounded in the reality of that biblical storyline. In other words, we must be grounded in the biblical presentation of truth and reality before we can understand why ethical living is so difficult. The truth and reality of the Fall's effects explain why it is so hard to make ethical decisions and why so many people have embraced fallible ethical systems.



## 2.1 The Root Cause of All Ethical Difficulties

*Why is it so hard to make right decisions?*

### Objectives

**2.1.1** Explain how the Fall disrupts the functioning of the creational norms in the world. BWS

**2.1.2** Describe the effects of the Fall on human nature. BWS

**2.1.3** Relate the effects of the Fall to the difficulty of making ethical choices.

### Biblical Worldview Shaping

- **Creational Order** (evaluate): The Fall has bent the creational order so that simply looking at what *is* in creation is no longer an accurate guide for what *ought* to be. (2.1.1)
- **Virtue** (evaluate): Humans no longer love what is right and often use their intellect to justify wrong choices. They often lack the will to do what they know to be right. (2.1.2)

### Printed Resource

- Activity 2.1: The Difficulty of Making Ethical Choices in a Fallen World

### Materials

- magnets and metallic objects

### Suggested Reading

- Frame, John M. *The Doctrine of the Christian Life*. Phillipsburg, NJ: P&R Publishing, 2008. Pages 41–130.
- Grudem, Wayne. *Christian Ethics: An Introduction to Biblical Moral Reasoning*. Wheaton, IL: Crossway, 2018. Pages 40–43.
- Magnuson, Ken. *Invitation to Christian Ethics: Moral Reasoning and Contemporary Issues*. Grand Rapids, MI: Kregel Academic, 2020. Pages 24–63.

### Engage

#### THE STRENGTH OF DESIRES

Conduct an **object lesson** using magnets and metallic objects to illustrate the strength of desires. The farther away the metallic object is, the less the force of attraction, or if exchanged for a wooden object, the force of attraction is gone. Christians may resist temptation by staying away from it and by having Christ change their natures. Although there's always the pull of the sin nature until glorification, that pull can wane in strength.

### Instruct

#### DESIRES, SIN, AND PERSONAL RESPONSIBILITY

Use a **misconception check** to reinforce the biblical position on personal responsibility for desires.

Select the correct answer.

- Strong desires are a part of who I am; I'm not ethically responsible for them. I was born that way.
- Strong desires are nothing more than temptations I live with. I can't do anything about them.
- Strong desires can be rooted in original sin that I must put to death. I'm ethically responsible.

The third choice is best (Gen. 6:5; Exod. 20:17; Jer. 17:9; Rom. 6:16; James 1:13–15; 1 John 2:15–17).

## THE FALL'S EFFECTS ON THE CREATED ORDER

Scripture highlights the Fall's effects on the created order in two key passages: Genesis 3:16–19 and Romans 8:18–23. Both passages remind us that the world we live in is not the way creation was designed to be. We live in a world full of physical problems, causing all kinds of ethical difficulties. Solutions to those problems are elusive—some proposed solutions are wrong while others are difficult to accept. For example, why do the fields of bioethics and medical ethics exist? The Fall's effects on our physical world have led to the need for such fields of study.

### *Genesis 3:16–19*

Let's consider the significance of Genesis 3:16–19 in the larger context of the creation narrative. Genesis 1:31 affirms that God made our world *very* good. As defined by God's own goodness, this means that everything in the created world was free from the slightest taint of badness. No aspect of the world was in decline or disrepair. All the natural laws* that governed the physical universe were fully functioning according to God's perfect design. Not only that, but all the processes for *our* functioning within this world were built into the created order, conformed to the perfect wisdom of God (Prov. 3:19; 8:22–31). In other words, God built norms into His creation for living wisely based on how He designed us to function in it.

These original realities—natural laws and creational norms in a perfectly good world—are immensely valuable for ethics; they give us the standard for how things *ought* to be (pointing to the basis for our ethic). God designed the world to work in a moral way that conforms to His character. Both the structures for the physical world and the structures for society in that world find an absolute and ultimate basis in God's character, which is reflected in His design.

But Genesis 3 reveals a major problem that intrudes into this perfect world. Sin entered the world when Adam and Eve chose to disobey God in the garden. And that sin had far-reaching effects on the rest of humanity and on the rest of the world. Its effects extend as "far as the curse is found," which is to say, throughout creation. That Curse is summarized in Genesis 3:16–19. The effects of the Fall ruin the human ability to function according to creational norms, according to God's law, according to God's wisdom, and according to God's righteous character. Humans still image their Creator, but they do so in a distorted, marred, and twisted way.

In Genesis 1:28, God gave humans the task of the Creation Mandate: to fill and subdue the earth. In Genesis 3:16–19, God frustrated that task by making childbirth painful, marriage difficult, and work laborious. This was God's just judgment for humans choosing to live life apart from Him. He gave them a taste of what life is like apart from Him fully upholding the world. Therefore, the world as it operates now cannot be the most accurate guide for our ethic. It is broken.

**natural laws:** moral norms rooted in God's character, which God established in the creation

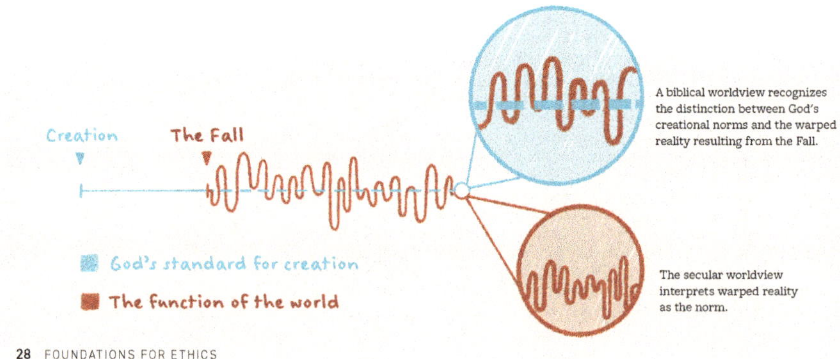

Creation
The Fall
God's standard for creation
The function of the world
A biblical worldview recognizes the distinction between God's creational norms and the warped reality resulting from the Fall.
The secular worldview interprets warped reality as the norm.


28 FOUNDATIONS FOR ETHICS

## CREATIONAL NORMS DISRUPTED BY THE FALL

Use **direct instruction** to define creational norms and to describe how they're disrupted by the Fall.

Creational norms refer to God's wise design built into the world for the successful functioning of people within this world. Natural laws refer to the physical ordering and design for this world's functioning (e.g., gravity), while creational norms focus on how humans ought to operate in this world (e.g., male headship in 1 Tim. 2:11–15).

Both the Curse on the physical world and the sinful nature of people in the world disrupt the functioning of the world and the functioning of people in the world in alignment with these natural laws and creational norms. The world has been marred by the effects of the Fall, and people transgress God's good ways. These realities raise ethical challenges in our world.

## THE BASIS FOR ETHICS IN A FALLEN WORLD (GENESIS 3:16–19)

Conduct a **Think-Pair-Share** to prompt collaboration on identifying and avoiding a common fallacy.

Because the world is fallen, a person must distinguish between the created order (both natural law and creational norms) and the fallen effects on that created order in order to correctly discern an ethical basis for their choices. A common fallacy occurs when people assume that the way the world is characterizes how the world should be, ignoring the effects of the Fall.

Choose one of the following spheres or issues. Give an example of a creational norm, an aspect of the Fall that complicates discerning the norm, and then demonstrate that it is possible to reason from the norm to the ethical obligation:

- Family
- State (government)
- Gender
- Abortion (and the laws and penalties currently in place)
- Business practices
- Scientific research practices
- Other topics of your choice

Possible answer: God made male and female (Gen. 1:27), and this creational norm is evident in the different characteristics that distinguish males and females from one another and in the fact that virtually all cultures around the world and throughout history have recognized this distinction. Some people are born with disorders of sexual development which may make normal male and female characteristics ambiguous. Christians recognize that one of the consequences of living in a fallen, cursed world are genetic and hormonal problems. Disorders of sexual development do not disprove the gender binary; they prove it, as the exception proves the rule.

## RIGHTLY APPEALING TO THE NATURAL WORLD FOR AN ETHICAL BASIS

Guide a **discussion** to help students understand a legitimate use of appeals to the natural law for ethics. Creational norms and natural laws have not disappeared after the Fall. The Bible tells us about God's original design so that we can spot how the world was originally intended to be. Christians may appeal to this order in creation. The unbeliever's conscience also testifies to it, even if he or she does not begin with the starting point of God's special revelation.

**How do the truths from Matthew 7:9–12 apply to unbelievers in their treatment of their own children and in their treatment of others?** *This passage makes an observation that fallen people generally care for their children because they have a natural tendency built into them (despite their original sin) to take good care of their own offspring. Generally, even unsaved people recognize the goodness of the "golden rule": do to others what you would have them do to you (e.g., showing mothers ultrasounds so that they can see the life in their womb; demonstrating the profit of treating customers well and with honesty in business dealings).*

Those who fail to take into account the brokenness of this world can fall into an error called the **naturalistic fallacy**. This fallacy assumes that what is natural is good. In other words, it assumes that if a behavior is found in nature, it must be morally acceptable. In a secular evolutionary worldview, there can be no transcendent* basis for morality, no authority greater than the consensus of human authorities. Without a transcendent, external authority revealing what is right and wrong, secularists can appeal only to nature. Christians, on the other hand, rely on what God's revelation has prescribed. God's revelation interprets the world, helping Christians to discern what is creational and what is fallen. Because Scripture tells Christians how the world ought to be, Christians may appeal to natural law, a subset of creational norms. However, they must discern such creational norms or natural law in light of special revelation.

The naturalistic fallacy is on full display in some recent claims that homosexual behavior is justified because we observe that behavior in the animal kingdom. You have to wonder how many other animal behaviors these people would appeal to as the basis for their morality. Certainly they wouldn't recommend eating one's mate, killing a competitor, or stealing another's offspring—all commonly observed behaviors in a cursed natural world. The naturalistic fallacy leads to people living like animals. But in the biblical worldview, people are not animals, nor should they behave as such (Gen. 1:26–27).[2]

Indeed, Christians should appeal to the natural world in their ethical reasoning. But they must also take into account that the world is not the way it should be. The Christian ethic stands firmly in the created order's design. But Christians must distinguish between the created order and the Fall's effects on that created order. God's special revelation helps Christians discern these things so that natural law can be more accurately understood. Yet, by God's common grace, even unbelievers may glean some moral grounding by their observations of God's design in this fallen world (Prov. 8:4). They may be inconsistent in their understanding and application of the morality ingrained into the design of this world, but even those without the benefit of God's special revelation have the witness of their own consciences (Rom. 2:14–15). Natural law may be a starting point for a Christian's appeal to an unbeliever. But the Christian must ultimately appeal to the special revelation of God's Word to properly interpret that natural law.

You wouldn't pull a broken lamp out of a package and assume that's the way it was designed to be. God did not create imperfection; sin has marred His perfect design.

#### *Romans 8:18–23*

One final word on the Fall's effects on the created order. Romans 8:18–23 reveals the reason for humankind's desperate efforts to alleviate the ethical difficulties of living in a fallen world. We (and the created order) groan under God's judgment, the Curse, which affects all creation (Rom. 8:20–22). We long for redemption, for restoration. The problems that come from living in a fallen world bring us great discomfort (and worse). Since God's Creation Mandate has tasked us with the stewardship of creation, it is good and right to work against the effects of the Fall by seeking to solve or to better cope with these effects. Ultimately, only Christ's final redemption will rescue us. And these effects of the Fall (including the Curse) point people to the need for a Savior. Yet, God would have us show love and compassion by ameliorating* the effects of the Fall in the lives of our families and neighbors.

Still, *what* should be identified as an effect of the Fall and *how* those effects should be addressed is subject to ethical debate. Should humans be

**transcendent:** pertaining to the things of God beyond the earthly human experience

**ameliorating:** making better



**How and why should these appeals be followed up with an appeal to the gospel?** *Only special revelation properly interprets the natural law, and only the gospel can empower internal change in character and real conformation to that law. Certainly, a culture that externally conforms to the biblical ethic will be a nicer place to live in. But that culture can be full of Pharisees headed to Hell, unless they repent. In fact, this is the point of Matthew 7 in context: one's righteousness must exceed the righteousness of the Pharisees, whose external conformity can't possibly match up to God's perfect demands.*

## THE NEED TO SOLVE ETHICAL PROBLEMS IN A FALLEN WORLD (ROMANS 8:18–23)

Use a **Quick Write** to preassess student understanding of ethical problems in the modern world.

Because the world is fallen, people need to solve ethical problems that arise due to the brokenness of the world they live in.

**Should humans be attempting to do gene therapy to fix genetic diseases like Down syndrome and muscular dystrophy so that one day these diseases will no longer exist in our world?** *Theoretically, there's nothing wrong with trying to prevent a disease or to fix the brokenness of a disease any more than there would be for fixing a broken bone. It would be wrong to seek to rid the world of people suffering from those diseases, but it's not wrong to seek to overcome the diseases. The difficulty at this point with gene therapy isn't with whether it would be a good thing to achieve the end goal of healing people. The difficulty is whether we have the ability to do so without long-term negative side effects as we try to figure out how to accomplish this. People must weigh the risks of experimentation that could cause permanent damage, especially on possible offspring if the gene therapy is being done on a germline.*

**Should humans be doing gene therapy to produce babies with blue eyes rather than brown eyes?** *No, creating what has been termed "designer babies" is different from fixing a disease that is the result of brokenness from the Fall. Humans should be satisfied with the diversity of God's good creational design and leave those attributes to His sovereignty.*

You're probably not involved in making difficult scientific decisions at this point in your life. However, with some simple life choices, you can make a practical difference to help people who are suffering from the effects of the Fall.

**What are some decisions that you can make to help people who are suffering from the effects of a broken world?** *Possible answer: Refusing to park in a handicap spot when it would be convenient to do so (even if for a seemingly short time) not only is an example of obeying the law, but it also shows that you love and respect your neighbor, whose functioning in this world has been made difficult by physical suffering.*

## STRUCTURE AND DIRECTION

Use a **Turn and Talk** to invite students to collaborate on the concepts of structure and direction and their applications.

**What is structure and direction?** *Structure refers to creational norms (the way God designed the world to function), and direction refers to the use of the created thing toward or away from its God-given creational norm or design.*
**Why are these labels helpful and important?** *When doing ethics, we don't want to confuse fallen direction with creational structure.*
**What are some examples of structure, along with corresponding examples of direction both toward and away from that structure?** *Possible answer: Music in general (with all the "raw materials" available) would be a part of God's creational structure; specific musical styles of communication (genres) would be the direction (the use of those raw materials to communicate a certain way) either toward or away from a structure of fitting communication.*

## THE FALL'S EFFECTS ON HUMAN NATURE

Guide a **group activity** to allow students to create an overview of the Fall's effects on the mind, will, and emotions. Possible formats include a chart, graphic organizer, or diagram. Students should design something that visually communicates the holistic effects of the Fall, and they should provide biblical support for the Fall's effects on each element.

attempting to do gene therapy? Should they be doing gene therapy to fix genetic diseases like Down syndrome and muscular dystrophy so that one day these diseases no longer exist in our world? Should they be doing gene therapy to produce babies with blue eyes rather than brown eyes? These and many other issues will be addressed in Unit 3.

**Structure and Direction**

One helpful paradigm for understanding the Fall's effects on the creational order is called structure and direction. Structure refers to the creational norms, the way God wisely designed the world to function. Direction refers to the use of a created thing either toward or away from its God-given creational norm or design.[3] When doing ethics, we don't want to confuse fallen direction with creational structure.

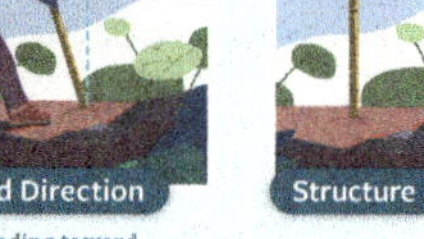

Bending toward fallen human nature

God's created order

Bending back toward the intended order

### THE FALL'S EFFECTS ON HUMAN NATURE

The Fall's effects on human nature are all-encompassing and inescapable. Every part of every human has been affected by the Fall. The Fall's effects are as pervasive as the air we breathe. "Who can say, I have made my heart clean, I am pure from my sin?" (Prov. 20:9). "If we say that we have no sin, we deceive ourselves, and the truth is not in us. . . . If we say that we have not sinned, we make him a liar, and his word is not in us" (1 John 1:8, 10). Not even the most righteous person on earth is free from sinning (Eccles. 7:20). It is a given that all people succumb to sin (1 Kings 8:46). The law of God was designed to shut the mouths of those who think they could claim to be without sin (Rom. 3:19–20; 7:7; Gal. 3:22). In fact, "all we like sheep have gone astray; we have turned every one to his own way; and the Lord hath laid on him the iniquity of us all" (Isa. 53:6). Even our best works don't come close to an acceptable standard (Isa. 64:6). The reality of our sin nature within us evidences itself in our actions (Rom. 3:10–18). And all of this is due to our standing "in Adam" (Rom. 5:12; see also Ps. 51:5), which imputes guilt and transmits corruption.

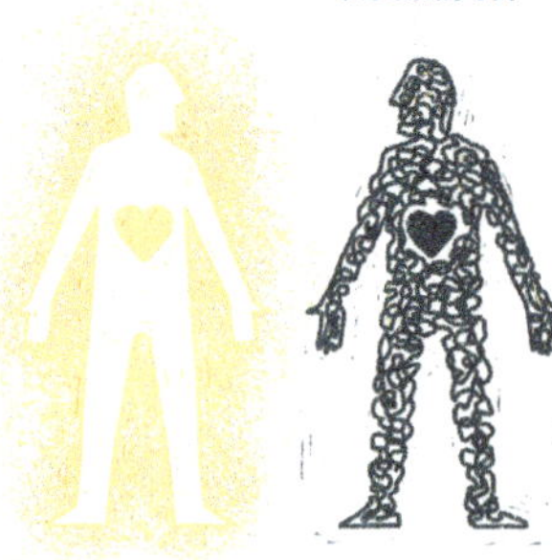


#### *The Fall's Effects on the Mind*

Has the mind of every person been affected by the Fall? Yes! Apart from the glorious gospel, regeneration and illumination by the Holy Spirit, and spiritual union with Christ, all people have their minds blinded by "the god of this world" (2 Cor. 4:4; see also 1 Cor. 2:14; Eph. 1:17). In rebellion, they suppress the truth (Rom. 1:18–25; see also John 8:45). Before salvation, people are characterized by ignorance and a darkened mind because of their desire to justify their sin (Eph. 4:17–19; Titus 1:15). For example, some of the most "enlightened" cultures have tried to intellectually justify mistreating fellow human beings.

#### *The Fall's Effects on the Will*

Has the will of every person been affected by the Fall? Yes! Everything a person chooses to do comes from the heart (Prov. 4:23; Matt. 15:17–20). And before God makes us alive to Himself, the condition of the heart is completely dead, unresponsive to God and His righteousness (Eph. 2:1–3). Apart from God's saving grace, all people are slaves to sin (John 8:34; Rom. 3:10–18; 6:16; 8:5–8).

For example, many people with addictions know what they ought to do, but they do not have the willpower within themselves to say no.

*The Fall's Effects on the Emotions*

Have the emotions of every person been affected by the Fall? Yes! We delight in sin (Prov. 2:14; Rom. 1:32). We become unrighteous in our anger (Prov. 14:29; James 1:19). We love and lust after the things of the flesh—even Christians must put these desires to death (Col. 3:5–10; 1 John 2:15–17). For example, even David, "a man after [God's] own heart" (1 Sam. 13:14), was drawn into impurity by desires he felt compelled to satisfy.

The mind, will, and emotions all work together simultaneously according to the affections that drive them. Our affections are the inclinations (formed by our values) that drive all we are and do because they are like the control center of our hearts. Either they are submitted to Christ's lordship or they are idolatrous. Before salvation, humans are idolatrous to the core (Jer. 17:9; Rom. 1:25). The fear of God is a holy affection, but instead of fearing God, unbelievers scorn His commandments and instruction so they can continue in their sin (Prov. 1:7).



*Common Grace: The Spirit's Restraint on the Fall's Effects*

If every part of every person has been affected by the Fall, then does this mean that every person is as bad as he or she could be? No! But no person can credit themselves for doing better than the worst he or she *could* do (1 Cor. 10:12–13; 2 Tim. 3:13). Not all people manifest badness in the same way or to the same extent. But that's due to God's gracious restraint through a variety of means: conscience, fear of consequences, the undeniable design of this world and how it works, the influence of God's people for the good of society, and the direct restraint of the Holy Spirit (Ezra 5:3–5; 6:6–12; Esther 2:21–23; 4:14; 8:7–14; Dan. 3:28–29; Matt. 7:9–11).

### THE FALL'S EFFECTS AND THE DIFFICULTY OF MAKING ETHICAL CHOICES

When you think of making difficult ethical choices, you may be thinking of things like capital punishment, stem cell research, and immigration laws. These things may seem distant and irrelevant to your personal life. But ethical decision-making has as much to do with our daily lives as it has to do with the major debatable issues of the day.

"Should I break a school rule because I think that it doesn't make sense? I could give an intellectual explanation for why it's an unnecessary rule. My friends all agree with me."

"Should I deliberately choose to cheat on a test even though I know it's wrong? I need to get a decent grade to go on the school's mission trip. I'm sure I can do some great spiritual good that will make up for cheating on an insignificant test."

"Should I date the guy or girl my parents disapprove of? I just can't help but like him or her. My parents' reasons for disapproving are so unconvincing."

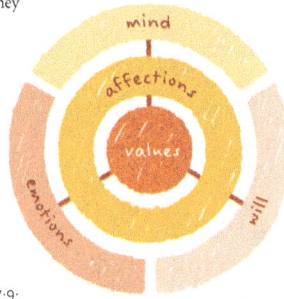

Why is it so hard to make right decisions?

Do you see how the Fall affects our minds (intellectual justifications), wills (the end justifies the means we choose), and emotions (forbidden desires)? We have to make ethical choices all the time. The effects of the Fall on the created order and on human nature make it difficult to make ethical choices. The issues in this world, in every aspect of life, can be complex. And the people trying to solve problems are plagued by rebellion (fallenness) or by limited understanding (finiteness). Even saved people are still affected by the Fall—they are not yet perfected and glorified. Saved people are still finite—they don't have all the facts (with absolute certainty) as they seek to make the right decisions.

The effects of the Fall on individuals have ramifications for the cultures and subcultures of groups of individuals who interact together—in families, churches, friend



## COMMON GRACE

Use a **misconception check** to assess student understanding of how or whether fallen unsaved people can do good.

Choose the best answer.

- Unsaved people affected by the Fall in the minds, wills, and emotions can do only bad.
- Since unsaved people do good things, they haven't really been fully affected by the Fall in their minds, wills, and emotions.
- Unsaved people get some credit for having some intrinsic goodness within themselves, which explains why they can do right.
- Unsaved people sometimes do right because of God's common grace that restrains their sin. God gets the credit for any good they do.

The last answer is the best one.

## Apply

## THE DIFFICULTY OF MAKING ETHICAL CHOICES IN A FALLEN WORLD

Use **Activity 2.1** on pages 5–6 to apply the information in the section.

## Assess

Use a **Ticket out the Door** to prompt students to reckon with the effects of the Fall and its ramifications on whole cultures or subcultures, as well as the difficulties of responding rightly to the sinful world around them.

**What could be one example of fallenness that makes ethical decision-making difficult in light of the pressures of your surrounding culture?** *Possible answer: peer pressure to get drunk or to have sex outside of marriage*

Guide a **summative assessment** by directing students to answer the questions in Thinking It Through 2.1.

## Thinking It Through 2.1

**1a.** Genesis 3:16–19; Romans 8:18–23

**1b.** Genesis 3:16–19 reveals that the effects of the Fall ruin the human ability to function according to creational norms because of the brokenness of the world caused by human sin. As a result, the world as it operates now is not the best guide for what ought to be, apart from the lens of special revelation showing us what is creational and what is fallen.

**1c.** Romans 8:18–23 reveals that the whole world groans as a result of the Curse, and so humans must work against these effects as they seek to fulfill the Creation Mandate. This raises ethical questions as to what should be pushed back against and how.

**2a.** The naturalistic fallacy assumes that what is natural is good. In other words, it assumes that if a behavior is found in nature, it must be morally acceptable.

**2b.** Many people rely solely on what science describes as the way the world is functioning to determine the ethic of how they ought to behave. This is a flawed basis for ethics.

**3.** Yes, Christians may appeal to the natural world and natural laws. But it can only be done as a starting point, since the natural world and its laws must be interpreted by the special revelation of God. God's Word reveals what is creational and what is fallen. The Christian must direct the unbeliever to the ultimate interpretation of the natural world found in God's Word. The natural world apart from God's Word is not a sufficient source from which one can rightly form ethical positions.

**4.** The Fall has had effects on the mind (John 8:45; Rom. 1:18–25), will (Prov. 4:23; Matt. 15:17–20; John 8:34), and emotions (Prov. 2:14; Rom. 1:32; Col. 3:5–10), all driven by the affections (Jer. 17:9; Rom. 1:25).

**5.** Making right decisions can be hard because of our fallenness (affecting our mind, will, emotions, and affections) and finiteness (limited understanding). The problems that humans try to solve in a broken world can be complex. Humans often ignore, manipulate, violate, or poorly understand and apply their own belief and value systems.

groups, societies, governments, educational institutions, businesses, art guilds, and the list could go on. These groups are affected by the fallen understandings, choices, and feelings of people who work together. All this fallenness and finiteness make it a struggle to properly answer important questions: How should they behave? How should they solve problems?

Ethical decision-making relates to both our responses to issues or problems in this world and the desires of our hearts. Our belief and value system should direct our responses. But too often we ignore or manipulate our belief and value system to justify wrong responses. We can be ignorant of what our own professed belief and value system would demand (we're finite). But we can also violate our own professed belief and value system (we're fallen). If we're Christians, we should desire to better match what we say we believe and value with the reality of our ethical choices and our daily lives.

Even if we ourselves are determined to live right, we have to respond to a sinful world around us that often won't cooperate with our desires to live ethically. We live in a sinful world that is bent on fulfilling its own idolatrous rebellion—people doing things their own way, prioritizing the wrong things, and not wanting to admit that their separation from God is the cause of many of the world's problems. This world system has developed a number of faulty approaches to practicing ethics. Believers need to understand what these approaches are and why they are faulty so that they don't end up conforming themselves to unbiblical ethical systems.

### Thinking It Through 2.1

1. a. Identify two key passages about the Fall's effects on creation.
   b. According to one of the key passages, how does the Fall affect our ability to fulfill our responsibilities?
   c. According to the other key passage, how do the Fall's effects on the created order impact ethics?
2. a. Define the naturalistic fallacy.
   b. Explain how the naturalistic fallacy relates to ethics.
3. Should Christians appeal to the natural world or to natural laws to forward their ethical positions? Explain your answer.
4. Identify the areas in which the Fall has had an effect on human nature. Provide at least one supporting Scripture reference for each of the areas.
5. Why is it so hard to make right decisions?

### 2.2 Faulty Approaches to Ethics

What do you think of the soldier who throws himself on a grenade to save the lives of others? He lives by a duty to a principle greater than himself and his own happiness. But what would you think of a soldier who continued to fight decades after he was informed that an official surrender had been declared? Should his commitment to his own ideals and his own perception of duty make no concession to other factors whatsoever? What about you? Should you make choices based on self-sacrificial duty to absolute principles, even if that means negative consequences to yourself or to society as a whole?

What do you think of a politician who takes bribes? He lives by doing whatever he can get away with while most benefiting himself. But what if the bribes resulted in saving thousands from being executed by an authoritarian dictator? The politician might justify benefiting from the bribes because of the risk he was taking and because he was benefiting many others in the end. What about you? Should you make choices based on what brings you the most happiness? Should you make choices



## 2.2 Faulty Approaches to Ethics

*What are some wrong ways to practice ethics?*

### Objectives

**2.2.1** Explain the deontological approach.

**2.2.2** Explain the consequentialist approach.

**2.2.3** Explain the virtue ethics approach.

**2.2.4** Explain the existentialist ethics approach.

### Printed Resource

- Activity 2.2: Identifying the Ethical Approaches

### Digital Resource

- Video: "Major Ethical Systems"

### Suggested Reading

- See Section 2.1.

based on what brings the most happiness to society as a whole—regardless of the means used to achieve that end?

What do you think of a professional athlete who skips practice and hogs the ball because she is by far the best player? She says, "I can't help being that way—that's just who I am." But what do you think of an Olympic athlete who helps up a fallen runner—even though it means losing the race? She explains the action to reporters this way: "That's just who I am and how I was raised." What about you? Should you make choices based on being true to yourself?

Do you generally live by strictly adhering to unbendable rules? Do you generally live by trying to achieve the best results—relative to your own desires, situations, or cultural expectations? Or do you generally live by attempting to be your most authentic self—whether that's who you are naturally or who you ideally want to be?

Of course, people are complex and will act according to a combination of approaches. Still, formal secular philosophers tend to operate according to one of four overall approaches. These four approaches to ethics can be labeled deontological ethics, consequentialist ethics, virtue ethics, and existentialist ethics.

### How Does Ethics Relate to Philosophy?

If you take an Introduction to Philosophy class in college, you will probably learn that philosophy entails four branches:

1. **metaphysics** (including ontology and cosmology)**:** the study of nature and reality itself (including the essence of existence as well as the nature and origin of the universe)
2. **epistemology:** the study of knowledge—how we know what is true and how we know what we know
3. **ethics:** the study of what *ought* to direct behavior, attitudes, and character (what makes something right or wrong)
4. **aesthetics:** the study of beauty

Since ethics is one major branch of study within the larger discipline of philosophy, it is something that most philosophers have wrestled with through the centuries. The four major ethical systems outlined in this chapter can be matched with proponents* who were major philosophical thinkers. These philosophers represent the human quest to discover a solid basis for knowing how to live life well or rightly. Due to the image of God in man and the human conscience, many have been concerned about ensuring moral living. God built this need into us. But this quest has been misdirected by human sinfulness. The biggest failure of most philosophers is that they don't rely on special revelation. Instead, they locate a basis for ethics in their reason, personal intuitions, or observations of the world. Therefore, they can never find a sure standard. Apart from God and His revelation, philosophers stumble in the dark, run into dead ends, and fall off cliffs in a fruitless quest for truth and righteousness. The problem isn't with the quest for better decision-making. And philosophers sometimes do stumble upon some truth. But half-truths lead to faulty systems and conclusions too.

The seeming futility of trying to find a sure standard has led to some giving up and not caring about ethics. But this too is an effect of the Fall. Christians should certainly care about how to live. They should be concerned about the destructive behavior in their own lives as well as in society. They should lead the way in knowing and practicing right behavior. Will you be such a leader? This textbook equips and enables you to be that much-needed leader in your areas of influence.

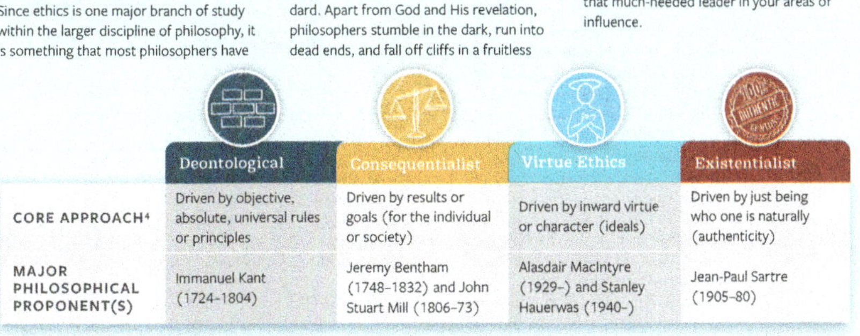

| | Deontological | Consequentialist | Virtue Ethics | Existentialist |
|---|---|---|---|---|
| CORE APPROACH[4] | Driven by objective, absolute, universal rules or principles | Driven by results or goals (for the individual or society) | Driven by inward virtue or character (ideals) | Driven by just being who one is naturally (authenticity) |
| MAJOR PHILOSOPHICAL PROPONENT(S) | Immanuel Kant (1724–1804) | Jeremy Bentham (1748–1832) and John Stuart Mill (1806–73) | Alasdair MacIntyre (1929–) and Stanley Hauerwas (1940–) | Jean-Paul Sartre (1905–80) |

**proponent:** a person who advocates for something

THE FALL'S EFFECTS ON ETHICS 33

## Engage

### MAJOR ETHICAL SYSTEMS

Show the **video** "Major Ethical Systems" to generate student interest on major ethical systems.

### FOUR APPROACHES FOR HOW TO LIVE

Use a **Four Corners** activity to preassess student tendencies toward one of the four approaches.

Choose the corner of the room that best represents your tendencies:

- Corner 1: You generally live by strictly adhering to unbendable rules.
- Corner 2: You generally live by trying to achieve the best results—relative to your own desires, situations, or cultural expectations.
- Corner 3: You generally live by attempting to be your most authentic self—who you are naturally.
- Corner 4: You generally live by attempting to be your most ideal self—who you ideally want to be.

**Why do you think you have this tendency?** *Students may refer to their personalities, experiences, reactions against observations they've made about other positions, family upbringing, cultural influences, biblical training, and so on.*

**What are some potential flaws with your tendency?** *Possible answers:*

- *Corner 1: legalistically abiding by the letter of the law, ignoring the spirit of the law, and thus failing to care for people's needs; for example, insisting on stopping at a stop sign even though it is a high crime area where carjackings occur*
- *Corner 2: justifying doing wrong in order to accomplish what you want; for example, cutting some corners in a sports practice drill so that your group will be rewarded*
- *Corner 3: In an attempt to avoid hypocrisy, someone may end up being transparently sinful without recognizing that as problematic; for example, justifying cutting others down with sarcasm because that's just who I am, and others need to take a joke.*
- *Corner 4: In an attempt to attain moral high ground, a person may become burdened by perfectionistic self-effort toward reform; for example, an ideal of getting up at 5:30 every morning to pray for an hour to seem more spiritual than anyone else in your class.*

## Instruct

### THE RELATIONSHIP OF ETHICS TO PHILOSOPHY

Guide a **discussion** to orient students to place ethics within the larger discipline of philosophy and to answer this section's essential question.

**What are the four branches of philosophy?** *See the numbered terms on page 33.*

**What is the ultimate reason that philosophers fail to arrive at a consistent ethical standard for living?** *They are trying to find a standard apart from the special revelation of God's Word.*

**How would you explain the four major approaches to ethics by philosophers? What are the representatives of each approach?** *See the chart on page 33.*

## THE DEONTOLOGICAL APPROACH

Use an **RSQC2** after-reading activity to challenge students to process and communicate what the deontological approach is all about.

**Recall and list the most important ideas that make up the deontological approach.** *Answers should include the following major concepts and influences: the categorical imperative or universal norms; objective, absolute, and universal rules; focus on duty and self-sacrifice; a good will of pure disinterested motives and refusing to use people as a means to an end; loyalty to a principle, regardless of end results; Immanuel Kant (the order of importance in this list may vary).*

**Summarize each important idea in one sentence.** *Possible answers:*

- *The categorical imperative is something that all people must do if they are acting according to a principle that they believe would guide all people, no matter the circumstances.*
- *Objective refers to rules that must be discovered as true, regardless of what one thinks.*
- *Absolute refers to something that is binding with few, if any, exceptions.*
- *Emphasis on duty and self-sacrifice; one is guided by a commitment to a higher principle rather than self-benefit or results.*

**What key question would you want answered about this approach?** *Students may wonder whether there are any other categorical imperatives, who gets to determine them, or what governs whether good will, loyalty, and duty are rightly defined and rightly directed.*

**How would you connect the ideas in this approach to the chapter and to this section's essential question?** *Students should recognize that this approach is flawed when it is detached from the revealed universal principles of God's Word. They may also note that this approach does not rely on God's grace for ethical transformation.*

**Do you have any comments about your initial thoughts about this approach to ethics?** *Students may share a variety of positive, negative, or tentative impressions about this approach.*

### What are some wrong ways to practice ethics?

#### THE DEONTOLOGICAL APPROACH

In general, **deontological ethics*** is governed by objective, absolute, universal rules or principles. *Objective* means that these rules are true regardless of what a person thinks of them or whether he or she understands them. They must be discovered. *Absolute* means that these rules are binding (with few if any exceptions). They are founded on definite, unchanging principles regardless of the circumstances. *Universal* means that these rules apply to everyone, everywhere, and at all times. They are to be enforced without partiality.

Immanuel Kant

Immanuel Kant is one of the most famous and influential philosophers to this day who promoted this approach to ethics. Someone who is driven by a Kantian deontological ethic is driven by duty above all else. This duty may even require self-sacrifice. It entails not only doing the right thing but being motivated to do it with the purest of motives. The purest of motives requires disinterest in benefiting oneself by the outcome of one's actions. One's own desires may need to be set aside. Positive or negative outcomes don't determine the goodness or badness of an act. Abiding by the principle is what matters. The ends (the ultimate goals or outcomes) do not justify the means (the method used to achieve the outcomes).

None of this means that specific, different situations don't matter. People may act in a variety of ways in different situations, but the underlying principle must not be violated. In other words, a single principle (like keeping one's promises) can have multiple, varying applications so long as the principle is not violated in any situation.

One of the major questions for this approach is how to discover these rules or principles. The secular philosopher rejects God and His Word as a source for absolute rules of morality. So, without special revelation, philosophers are left with their observations of the natural world. They seek to discover, by reason and observation alone, natural law principles for how this world operates and how everyone in this world must operate in all times and all places. They ask, "Do we want _____ to be a universal norm (regardless of potential outcomes at certain times)?" For example, do we want permissibility of lying to be a universal norm (even if in some circumstances it might benefit me)? What would it do to society as a whole if all kinds of people could come up with all kinds of justifications for lying? The world would spin out of control! (So, consequences are not completely left out of consideration, but the principle is what *determines* morality regardless of the consequences.)

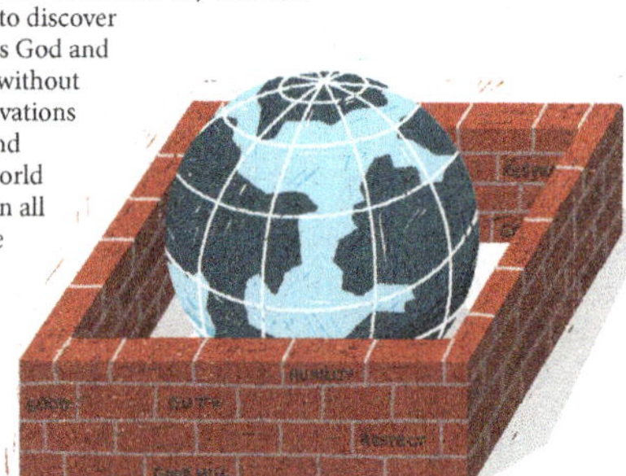

Immanuel Kant is famous for stating the following as the fundamental basis for the ethic that he promoted: "Act only according to that maxim by which you can at the same time will that it should become a universal law."[5] Kant sought to discover whether there was anything good at all times, regardless of circumstances. He concluded that a good will was the answer, for it was never criticized in any circumstance.[6] But how should one define and describe a good will? He defined a good will as one that does its duty for the sake of duty itself. In other words, you don't make ethical decisions as a means to benefit yourself. Your ultimate commitment is to abide by principles of duty.[7]

**deontological ethics:** ethical model which says that ethical choices are governed by objective, absolute, universal rules or principles and a selfless commitment to duty

But how do we know what our duties are? Kant's answer has become known as the categorical imperative. A **categorical imperative** is something that all people must do if they are acting according to a maxim (or principle) that they believe would guide all people to do the right thing. This maxim is true no matter the circum-

34 FOUNDATIONS FOR ETHICS

stances. In other words, the duty to the principles is not a *hypothetical* imperative (if this, then you must do this). How does one find out a categorical imperative? By asking, "What if everybody did it?"[8] More specifically, Kant used three ideas to identify a categorical imperative:

1. Act according to ethical principles that you can will to be universally followed.
2. Act according to principles that you could will to be universal laws of nature.
3. Act so as to treat human beings always as ends, never as mere means.[9]

Today, this kind of ethic is used by many different religious and secular people. They tend to be moralists (or legalists) who rely on their own goodness and good works. They ground their morality in their own reason and in observation of the natural world. Some may appeal to the Bible, but typically not as the inerrant, sufficient, and absolute special revelation of God. Other sources of absolutes must be appealed to over and above the Bible: church dogma, other religious books, false prophets, or other scientific and philosophical reasoning.

### THE CONSEQUENTIALIST APPROACH

**Consequentialist ethics*** is a teleological approach (from the Greek word *telos*, meaning "end"). In general, this approach allows for judgments and choices based on goals or results ultimately determined to be good by the desires of either the individual or society. Self-determination (or social determination)—and not discoverable rules—dictate how one should live. Every situation calls for a new evaluation of what the individual (or society) would most like to achieve in the end (sometimes regardless of the means used to get there). The best choices will bring the most happiness to the individual or to society as a whole; this defines what is good.

People who are driven by a consequentialist ethic are driven by results. They must do whatever they foresee will bring about the greatest happiness or the highest good. In this approach, the acts themselves are never in and of themselves good or evil, right or wrong. They are determined by their outcomes or consequences. Sometimes the outcomes can be viewed as one's fate. If good things happen to you, then you know that the universe is happy with you and you made the right choice. If bad things happen to you, then you know that the universe is angry with you and you made the wrong choice.

This approach rejects the inflexible rules of absolute, universal moral norms (the deontological approach). It rejects the idea of intrinsic good and evil. But most consequentialists also reject the complete subjectivity of existentialism—that a person can live out his or her own behavior regardless of the outcomes that affect others. However, some consequentialists end up going that route in the end.

Of all the approaches, this one has the most variations in how it is actually understood and practiced. For example, everyone in this category believes that humans ultimately seek happiness or pleasure (the highest good and the end goal). But from ancient times, groups differed on what this meant and how it was achieved. The Cyrenaic school of hedonists believed that the most intense, immediate pleasures were the best. In contrast, the Epicurean hedonists believed they needed to look for what would produce the most pleasure *and* the least amount of pain in the long run. They sought calmness without disturbance. Still another version comes from Aristotle, who defined the highest good as simple well-being—what everyone wants.

The most common version of the consequentialist approach is **utilitarianism**. Jeremy Bentham and John Stuart Mill are two famous and influential philosophers who promoted it. This view teaches that the utility, or usefulness, of an action in bringing about an intended, helpful end determines what is right or best. The idea that the end justifies the means or the rule of thumb that we should do the greatest good for the greatest number of people is a classic way of expressing utilitarianism.

**consequentialist ethics:** ethical model which says that ethical choices are governed by the results or ends they will achieve. The proper end is that which achieves the greatest amount of good. The good is often happiness, as defined by the individual or by society



## THE CONSEQUENTIALIST APPROACH

Instruct students to create a **concept map** in order to compare and contrast consequentialism and its subcategories (utilitarianism, situation ethics, and ethical egoism). This could be expanded to contrast consequentialism with the other ethical approaches as well.

Answers should sufficiently summarize and explain the material on pages 35–36.

## LIVING AS A CONSEQUENTIALIST

Use a **Think-Pair-Share** to assess whether students understand the nuances of the differing consequentialist approaches.

**How do you think each of the different kinds of consequentialists would operate and explain their actions in the following scenario? You're a small business owner who is trying to get off the ground and grow your business into a success. But you've found it a lot more difficult than you could have imagined. Your end goal is to be a success.** *Possible answers:*

- *Utilitarianism: High-level employees are given good benefits, but low-level, easily replaceable employees are given minimal benefits as a cost-savings measure.*
- *Situation Ethics: Lower prices are offered to customers through doing cash deals under the table where taxable income is not reported to the government.*
- *Ethical Egoism: Decent customer service is provided, and deals are made with suppliers to leverage market power so that prices can be lowered to put a rival out of business. Once a near monopoly is gained, prices are significantly raised.*

**Which consequentialist label would you give to the following scenario? You're an avid fisher who gets into competitive fishing. Your end goal is to win for both the prestige and prize money.** *Ethical Egoism*

## REFLECTING ON THE CONSEQUENTIALIST APPROACHES

Lead a **discussion** about the essentials of the consequentialist approach in order to reinforce what is foundational to it.

**What are three essential characteristics of a consequentialist ethic?** *a focus on goals or results; driven by foreseeing what will achieve the greatest good or happiness for the individual or society; good and evil (right and wrong) not intrinsic but determined by consequences*

**What are two distinctives of consequentialism that contrast it with the deontological approach?** *What is right and good is self-determined or socially determined rather than determined by discoverable rules; it rejects the inflexibility of absolute, universal rules that determine intrinsic good or rightness.*
**What is one comment you would like to make about your initial thoughts about this approach to ethics?** *Students may share a variety of positive, negative, or tentative impressions about this approach.*

## THE VIRTUE ETHICS APPROACH

Use a **Likert scale** to discuss and assess student understanding of virtue ethics.

**Do you strongly agree, somewhat agree, somewhat disagree, or strongly disagree with the following statement? "Focusing on who I should be as a person of virtue is all that's necessary for determining what is ethical and how to live ethically."** *It's likely that students will tend to somewhat agree or strongly agree with the statement. Virtue ethics is an important part of biblical ethics, but as a stand-alone ethical theory it is flawed.*
**What distinguishes virtue ethics from the deontological and consequentialist approaches?** *Rather than considering principles (deontological) or outcomes (consequentialist), this approach relies on instilling virtuous character in people so that they'll just do the right thing in a situation.*
**What does virtue ethics minimize focus on and maximize focus on?** *It minimizes focus on the issues (doing what I should do) and maximizes the focus on the person (being who I should be).*
**How do people know what it is to be virtuous and how do they become virtuous?** *In non-Christian forms, they know what it means by contemplating it or learning it in a community. They become virtuous by self-effort and self-reform.*
**What role and what importance does the community often play in virtue ethics?** *In forms of virtue ethics where the Bible or some other standard of virtue ethics is not recognized, the community is often key for defining and applying what virtue ought to look like, for teaching people to build this character and pursue virtue, and for cultivating it into people.*

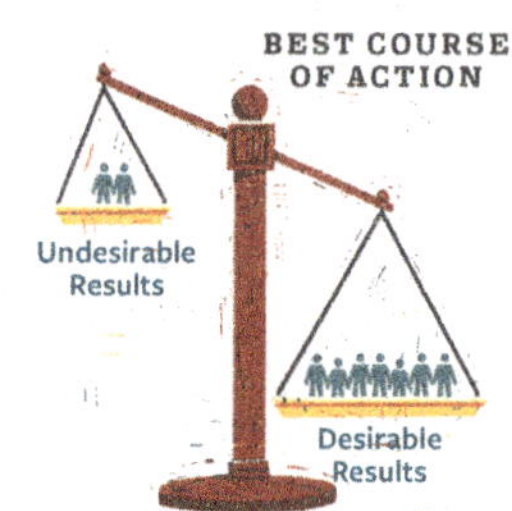


Bentham and Mill emphasized doing the most possible good for society as a whole. Bentham believed that achieving the best for all would benefit the individual self the most too. Mill believed that achieving the best for all was just a necessary part of being a social being. Regardless of the motives for doing the best for all, they both represent the utilitarian version of consequentialist ethics.

To clarify, not everyone who is a consequentialist ignores the means to the end (how the result is achieved). Ken Magnuson clarifies that "it might be more accurate to say that acts that produce a balance of desirable over undesirable results are right, while acts that produce a balance of undesirable over desirable results are wrong."[10] Some consideration is given to whether it is worth doing such and such to achieve a given end. How valuable is that end compared to the cost it takes to get there? But this is simply a pragmatic consideration.

Another version of the consequentialist ethic is known as **situation ethics**, a form of ethical relativism. Joseph Fletcher is the most famous proponent of this approach. Fletcher argued that the only governing principle for determining what is ethical is that of love. And this principle isn't defined absolutely. A person must figure out what love would look like in every new situation, and people's conclusions may legitimately differ. What's right for me is right for me, and what's right for you is right for you. No authority governs anyone.

Yet another version of the consequentialist ethic is known as **ethical egoism**. This version can be defined as pure, individual self-interest. This often comes with a bare admission that a person couldn't care less about others. The only thing that matters is the self-fulfillment of what the individual most desires for happiness. This philosophy has been happily embraced by totalitarian dictators like Mao Zedong. This kind of ethic has been, and continues to be, used by many different religious and secular people. Summarizing ethical thought, "especially from the eighteenth century to the middle of the twentieth century," ethicist Ken Magnuson opines:

> Moral philosophy has been dominated by deontology and consequentialism, as the two main frameworks for ethics. It has seemed that either ethics is about doing the right thing, regardless of the consequences, or doing whatever it takes to make sure things turn out right. . . . While recognizing that a number of smaller trails have been made, two of the main paths have been the deontological commitment to principles and rules, and the consequentialist focus on result.[11]

Today those religious and secular people tend to be libertines (given to license and lawlessness) or pragmatists (not lawless, but with a subjective basis for the laws they want to impose to achieve their version of the greatest good). They ground their morality in self-interest or in a supposed omniscience of what will turn out to be good for everyone else. Some may appeal to the Bible's ethic of love, but that term is usually gutted of any meaning given in the concrete commands of God's Word. Subjective desires reshape the Bible to fit one's own desired goals.

### THE VIRTUE ETHICS APPROACH

The goal of **virtue ethics*** is to work a value system into people thoroughly—in other words, to build character. In general, this approach relies on ancient Greek and medieval Christian definitions of virtue. When faced with an ethical question, the moral intuition of the virtuous person takes over so that he or she will almost automatically know what to do because of who he or she is. Such a person can be guided by virtuous character rather than considering principles (the deontological approach) or outcomes (the consequentialist approach) at the crux of a decision.

The idea is that a person of good character, someone who is virtuous, will choose the best course of action when confronted with an issue. This approach presumes that people know what it is to be virtuous either by their own contemplation of virtue or from being taught to be virtuous within a particular community. Through one of these two means, a person's character can be formed as virtuous. This approach minimizes the focus on the issues (doing what I should do) and maximizes the focus on the person (being who I should be).

**virtue ethics:** an approach to ethics that focuses on discerning what virtues lead to a flourishing life and on developing those virtues so that they become habitual

People who are driven by the virtue ethics approach often focus on cultivating ideal character traits so that, when confronted with a situation, they will choose the best course of action. Figuring out the character traits to cultivate could depend on the individual or the community to which a person belongs. Magnuson puts it this way:

> Rather than speaking of our duty to a universal moral principle or of the responsibility to make sure things turn out right, we might say that moral obligation is derived from the nature of virtue (what virtue demands) or from community expectations (what a virtuous community demands).[12]

The more a virtuous person is in tune with himself or herself (or with the expectations of the community), the more that person will know what to do in any given situation. The key is to become who you ought to be (character) on the basis of either virtue itself or what the community demands, and then let your actions flow out of who you are.

Virtue ethics says that good character can be cultivated and internalized so that it becomes one's nature.

Aristotle emphasized ideal character as a basis for ethics (as well as consequentialist outcomes). But some of the most influential representatives of the virtue ethics approach (in terms of living up to ideal character within a community) would be the more recent philosophers Alasdair MacIntyre and Stanley Hauerwas. They emphasize what it means to live a good life in community: displaying virtuous character in the unfolding story of this world. As such, they are critical of what they perceive to be poor character traits that degrade a flourishing community.

Versions of this approach have grown in popularity today. Many who reject traditional and conservative morality attack the social norms of previous generations by critiquing them through the lens of a new morality under the guise of virtue. The tables have turned, and those who once promoted virtue are now told that they are the ones who are not virtuous. Good is called evil, and evil is called good.

### THE EXISTENTIALIST APPROACH

**Existentialist ethics*** grounds ethics in the individual person. The existentialist looks at habits and customs and cultures and deems them to be shams. Instead of conforming to others' expectations, the existentialist must choose the right way to exist in this world. And in doing so, the existentialist defines existence. Existentialists were concerned that many people mindlessly conformed to conventional morality without having personal integrity. The existentialist wanted people to feel the weight of the choices they made and for which they alone were responsible.

Jean-Paul Sartre is the best, or perhaps the worst, representative of an existentialist approach to ethics. He believed in absolute human freedom—individuals must create for themselves their own identities (or essences) by the choices they make and thus can be whatever they want to be. (There is no inherent human nature or natural law that a person must conform himself to.) His view seems very triumphalist in that humans can achieve who they want to become. But each individual also bears sole responsibility for failure. Therefore, there is no objective meaning to existence, only the meaning the individual creates. This view can lead to great despair. Sartre's view also teaches that no outside constraints should inhibit people from being who they wish to become. There are no moral restraints. In the end, this ethic mirrors ethical egoism. But the route to living for absolute self-interest is cerebral (introspection on being one's true self) rather than pragmatic (what works).

This cord is holding me back.

Do divers need safety lines?
"Let us break their bands asunder, and cast away their cords from us."
Psalm 2:3

Although pure existentialist philosophy is less popular than it used to be, our postmodern culture is overrun by those who live according to self-defined identity and who throw off all moral constraint. Radically subjective notions of truth, meaning, and goodness abound. The self-determined ethics of existentialism is very much alive.

**existentialist ethics:** ethical model which says that ethical choices are determined by the freely choosing individual; in the absence of absolute truth or meaning, the individual creates his or her own meaning and essence by the choices he or she makes and must take full responsibility for the outcome of these choices

## THE EXISTENTIALIST APPROACH

Use a **Quick Write** to prompt students to summarize and explain in their own words the key features of the existentialist approach.

**What is the basis, motivation, and general approach of existentialist ethics? Who is one of the major representatives of it? How is it different from ethical egoism?** *The basis is found in the individual person.*

*The motive that drives the existentialist is to be freed from the external constraints of conventional morality that often feed into hypocrisy and undermining one's true authentic self.*

*The existentialist approach rejects living in conformity to others' expectations (it rejects any kind of conformity to human nature or natural law) in favor of defining one's own existence by creating one's own identity in expression of one's true self. However, this triumphalism of self-determination also puts a burden on people to self-achieve, which can lead to self-destruction and despair because of failure.*

*Jean-Paul Sartre is one of the major proponents of this approach.*

## ANSWERING THE ESSENTIAL QUESTIONS

Use a **Think-Pair-Share** activity to prompt students to answer this section's and chapter's essential questions based on content in the textbook and based on their own preunderstanding of a biblical worldview.

**What are some wrong ways to practice ethics, and how can you identify these problematic approaches to ethics?** *The common denominator in each of these faulty approaches is that they tend to look for the origin and basis of morality in humans or in this world (what is). They leave the discovery of ethical norms to human reasoning or observations and have disconnected their ethic from Scripture. Thus, they end up idolizing bits and pieces from the fuller biblical ethic. In addition, the motives and methods can be flawed since people are not seeking to glorify God or obey Him by means of the empowerment of the Holy Spirit through sanctifying gospel grace.*

# Assess

## CHANGE OF MIND?

Allow for student **reflection** or redo the **Four Corners** activity to see if students have changed their minds about their tendencies now that they have a better understanding of each option.

Students should complete the following prompts:

"I became more aware of . . ."
"I changed my mind about . . . because . . ."
"I was surprised about . . ."
"I most related to . . ."

## IDENTIFYING THE ETHICAL APPROACHES

Use **Activity 2.2** on pages 7–8 to apply the information in the section.

Guide a **summative assessment** by directing students to answer the questions in Thinking It Through 2.2.

## Thinking It Through 2.2

**1.** Ethics is one major branch of study within the discipline of philosophy. Many philosophers wrestled with ethical questions and came up with ethical systems.

**2a.** the deontological, consequentialist, virtue ethics, and existentialist approaches

**2b.** The deontological approach is governed by objective, absolute, and universal rules, principles, or maxims.

The consequentialist approach allows for judgments or choices based on goals or results determined by the desires of individuals or society.

The virtue ethics approach relies on the inculcation of values from contemplating them or learning them in community so that one simply knows what to do because of who he or she is in character or virtue.

The existentialist approach relies on being authentic—true to oneself.

**2c.** People who follow Kant's deontological approach are driven by disinterested duty.

People who follow the consequentialist approach are driven by results—usually the greatest happiness or highest good.

People who follow the virtue ethics approach are driven by living up to ideals or community expectations.

People who follow the existentialist approach are driven by being true to themselves.

**3.** Immanuel Kant best represents the deontological approach. Jeremy Bentham and John Stuart Mill best represent a consequentialist approach. Alasdair MacIntyre and Stanley Hauerwas best represent a virtue ethics approach. Jean-Paul Sartre best represents an existentialist approach.

**4a.** All these approaches are consequentialist in that people are driven by results or goals in a situation.

**4b.** Utilitarianism teaches that the most useful action for a desired end is what is good. Do the greatest good for the greatest number of people. The end justifies the means.

Situation ethics teaches that every individual must determine what is the most loving act in any given situation.

Ethical egoism teaches pure, individual self-interest often without regard to others or society.

#### CONCLUSION

The common denominator in each of these faulty approaches is that they tend to look for the origin and basis of morality in humans or in this world (what is). They leave the discovery of ethical norms to man's own reasoning or observations. Even many of those who use a holy book tend to look elsewhere for ethical foundations. Many believe that the holy book or religion resulted from an evolutionary process, such that society developed and constructed the religion for pragmatic reasons (such as survival).

So far, we have only described the faulty approaches to ethics by summarizing what they teach. In the next section, we will critique them, exposing their central errors. In Chapter 8, we'll attempt to construct the best Christian methodology for ethical decision-making.

#### Thinking It Through 2.2

1. How does ethics relate to philosophy?
2. a. Identify the four major ethical systems outlined in this chapter.
   b. Explain the basis for each ethic.
   c. Explain what drives people in each ethic.
3. Identify at least one major proponent who best represents each of the major ethical systems.
4. a. Explain how utilitarianism, situation ethics (ethical relativism), and ethical egoism are all similar.
   b. Explain how utilitarianism, situation ethics (ethical relativism), and ethical egoism differ.
5. What is a categorical imperative in the view of Immanuel Kant?

### 2.3 Evaluating the Faulty Approaches to Ethics

Have you ever committed to something that sounded good when you first heard about it, only to find out in the end that you hadn't really understood what you were committing to? Certainly, some part of what you had heard sounded beneficial or attractive. But another part was hidden or obscure. Once that part was revealed or made clear, you realized your obvious mistake. Maybe an advertiser pulled you into a bad purchase by using a gimmick or a friend tricked you into some lousy work or a raw deal of a trade. Or maybe it was something far more serious. Our sinful thinking and desires can also take us further than we want to go, and the price we pay is far greater than advertised by our self-deceived hearts.

Each faulty ethical approach has something within it that sounds beneficial or attractive. One piece of it may be right. But overall, each system is misdirected. If you found yourself drawn toward one ethical approach or another outlined in the last section, then you need to step back and consider what's really being sold by each system.



**5.** It is something that all people must do if they are acting according to a maxim (or principle) that they are convinced would guide all people to do the right thing. This maxim is always true no matter what the circumstances are.

## 2.3 Evaluating the Faulty Approaches to Ethics

*Why are secular approaches to ethics wrong?*

### Objectives

**2.3.1** Evaluate the deontological approach. BWS

**2.3.2** Evaluate the consequentialist approach. BWS

**2.3.3** Evaluate the virtue ethics approach. BWS

**2.3.4** Evaluate the existentialist approach.

### Biblical Worldview Shaping

- **Authority** (evaluate): Non-Christian deontological ethics all place authority in something other than God and His Word. (2.3.1)
- **Man's Chief End** (evaluate): The only consequence that can be ethically determinative is the glory of God, and people need revelation from God to know what brings Him glory. (2.3.2)
- **Virtue** (evaluate): No person can be virtuous apart from the Holy Spirit. (2.3.3)

How do you step back and consider each system? Here are three rules of thumb to help you.

- Look for **internal consistency**—that is, does the ethical system contradict or undermine itself?
- Look for **external coherence**—that is, does the ethical system match up with how things work in real life (according to the wisdom of God's creational design)?
- Look to God's Word—that is, does the ethical system in any way contradict the explicit teachings or underlying principles and clear implications of God's Word?

The last rule of thumb presupposes that you are a Christian who trusts God's mind over your own. God's revelation is the ultimate and clearest lens for evaluating all things, for we are finite and fallen. However, the other two rules of thumb are helpful tools. Perhaps the unbeliever will not listen to the correct presuppositions found in God's Word for interpreting the evidence in this world. The other two rules of thumb can remove the unbeliever's confidence in faulty ethical systems, leaving him or her helpless and in need of something else (Prov. 26:4–5; 2 Cor. 10:5). Then you can present the biblical truth.

#### PROBLEMS WITH THE DEONTOLOGICAL APPROACH

Don't Christians commit themselves to a self-sacrificial duty to obey objective, absolute, universal moral principles or rules? Don't Christians believe that motives and means to an end are just as important as the outcome? Don't Christians believe it's wrong to live for pleasure or to use people to achieve selfish ends? Yes! These questions highlight some of the strengths of the deontological approach. But a one-dimensional deontological approach is also filled with weaknesses, making the approach problematic overall.

The deontological approach (if it is not grounded in Scripture) has no sure *basis* for determining objective, absolute, universal moral principles because it rejects (or supplements) the all-sufficient Word of God and replaces it with human reason. God is replaced and humans are given independent authority to determine which maxims *they* wish were universal laws. This approach is contrary to the Word of God. Our only source of *authority* for universal absolutes is Scripture itself.

Human logic is limited and fallible. Trying to find a universal absolute principle outside oneself without a transcendent, personal Being (and His revelation) becomes impossible. This is made more obvious by observing the futile efforts of those who have tried to operate according to the deontological approach without God and His Word. On the one hand, they struggle to come up with very many unarguable categorical imperatives (universal absolutes everyone must obey regardless of the time or situation) even among themselves. When a supposed categorical imperative is settled on (for example, Kant's idea of acting from a good will, which always does its duty without self-interest), the imperative is usually so generalized and non-specific that it is hardly useful, because people may apply it in contradictory ways in a specific situation. (Does a good will, which selflessly fulfills its duty, mean prioritizing my duty to my wife or to my children in this situation?) It is difficult to get this approach to cohere with or at least be useful in real life.

On the other hand, the deontological approach can devolve into making tons of specific rules into categorical imperatives. (Never go over the speed limit! In any situation?) So what might be a good rule in most specific situations becomes unbending

*Why are secular approaches to ethics wrong?*

THE FALL'S EFFECTS ON ETHICS 39

### Printed Resource

- Activity 2.3: Critiquing the Ethical Approaches

### Suggested Reading

- See Section 2.1.

## Engage

#### ALL THAT GLITTERS IS NOT GOLD: FLAWED ETHICAL SYSTEMS

Use a **bell ringer** activity to invite students to relate a common experience to the attractive but flawed ethical systems.

**Have you ever committed to something that sounded good when you first heard about it, only to find out in the end that you hadn't really understood what you were committing to?** *Invite several students to share their experiences.*

## Instruct

#### HOW TO EVALUATE ETHICAL SYSTEMS

Guide a **discussion** about the three rules of thumb for evaluating ethical systems in order to provide these as tools students can use throughout the year.

**What are the three rules of thumb provided in the textbook as tools for evaluating ethical systems?** *internal consistency, external coherence, and God's Word*

**What is the significance of each one?** *Internal consistency evaluates whether a system contradicts or undermines itself.*

*External coherence evaluates whether a system matches up with how things work in real life.*

*God's Word provides explicit and direct teachings, principles, or implications that will uphold or critique human systems of thought.*

**Which rule of thumb should be most important for Christians? How are the other rules of thumb valuable, nonetheless?** *God's Word is the Christian's ultimate authority. The creational norms (external coherence) follow from and are interpreted by God's Word, revealing God's character reflected in His design of how the world functions. Christians can be confident that the biblical worldview, though containing paradoxes, is internally consistent, while every false worldview is internally inconsistent.*

**What strategy can Christians use with unbelievers who do not respect God's Word?** *When unbelievers refuse to listen to the correct and clear presuppositions of God's Word, Christians should remove the unbelievers' comfortable confidence in their false systems by showing the lack of internal consistency and external coherence of their false systems. Then Christians can show unbelievers the truths of God's Word to support the correct system.*

#### POSITIVES AND NEGATIVES OF EACH APPROACH

Instruct students to create **T-Charts** of the positives and negatives of each approach. The T-Chart could be used as a concise study guide. See the Thinking It Through 2.3 answers for suggestions of what could be placed in the T-Charts.

## Apply

#### PROBLEMS WITH EACH APPROACH

Divide students into at least four groups for a **group activity** in order to discuss the problems of each of the four approaches and examples of those problems. See possible answers below.

- Deontological: When a rule is so generalized or absolutized, it doesn't help much in real life. For example, the popular maxim "Choose kindness" sounds wonderful, but what is it designed to disallow and who would be found guilty of violating it? You have to wonder if

Jesus Himself would be condemned for some of His harsh confrontations toward unrepentant, hardened sinners. You need something more specific from the Bible to guide you in how to actually live out this maxim correctly.
- Consequentialist: To gain greater security, voters support politicians and their measures that sacrifice freedom.
- Virtue Ethics: Loving one's neighbor is described and applied in various contradictory ways by people who have one agenda or another.
- Existentialist: The advice to "keep being you" and "keep loving who you are" regardless of the negative consequences of your immoral lifestyle might sound reassuring to an unbeliever. But this attitude only furthers self-destruction and the destruction of others.

## EVALUATING CONTEMPORARY EVENTS

Guide a **current events** activity to show the relevance and commonality of these four flawed ethical approaches. Students should locate an article or website that exemplifies one or more of the flawed approaches and then critique them.

## Assess

## MUDDIEST OR CLEAREST POINT

Allow students to **reflect** on which points seem the hardest to understand and which points were made clear in their minds.

## THE BEST AND WORST PROBLEMATIC APPROACHES

Use a **Ticket out the Door** to assess student postures toward the flawed approaches.

**Which approach do you think is most flawed? Why?** *The existentialist or ethical egoism form of consequentialism seems the most destructive and furthest from the biblical ethic followed by situation ethics. The first two options provide little restraint on the sinful anarchy of people. The last option is extremely subjective. Students could pick other options for other reasons: the tyranny of a flawed deontological system can also wreak havoc.*

**Which approach do you think is closest to Christian tendencies? Why?** *The deontological approach is often pinpointed as a Christian approach when it is modified and guided by God's revealed Word. However, it is still too narrow to fully capture the Christian ethic (see Chapter 8). Students could pick another option such as virtue ethics since the Bible emphasizes being the right kind of person inwardly. But students are probably guided by a biblically informed deontology when choosing this category.*

## CRITIQUING THE ETHICAL APPROACHES

Use **Activity 2.3** on pages 9–10 to apply the information in the section.

in any and all situations regardless of other factors. And this leaves people weighed down under heavy, restrictive burdens. The impersonal rule becomes senseless, and the people who legalistically follow the rule may reveal themselves to be uncaring (by following the letter of the law over the spirit and intended purpose of the law, at the expense of others). Again, it is difficult to get this approach to cohere with real life.

Other criticisms have been leveled against the deontological approach. While duty is a laudable motive, is it the only acceptable motive? Which duty do I follow when I have equal, competing duties? Who gets to determine my duties? Must I always be completely disinterested in receiving any benefit from what I do, or else I become an immoral person? Isn't there a difference between using someone only for self-interest and benefiting from someone (finding mutual benefit agreed upon by both parties)? Isn't it possible to pursue and achieve happiness (the end goal of the consequentialist approach) by fulfilling my duties? Is happiness at odds with fulfilling duty? Does God's Word teach me to shun happiness or to find happiness in the right source?

In sum, only divine revelation (without other competing authorities) can provide the basis for universal moral absolutes. Appeals to other sources of authority for absolute moral rules can lead to burdensome, legalistic human traditions (Matt. 15:1–20; 23:1–33). John Frame critiques this lack of internal consistency:

> Kant claims to avoid any appeal to consequences (the teleological approach) or inclination (the existential approach). But he tests the universality of maxims precisely by showing the consequences of their universal affirmation. And in the end he judges these consequences according to his inclinations: his desire to live in a world in which promises exist, but cruelty does not, and everyone treats everyone else as an end.[13]

Even with the benefit of receiving the Bible's own universal absolutes, Christians don't use these alone in ethical decision-making. Biblical absolutes ground and direct the Christian. But other complementary* considerations must factor in as well.

### PROBLEMS WITH THE CONSEQUENTIALIST APPROACH

Don't Christians calculate the cost and consider how their actions affect others? Aren't they driven by doing the most loving thing in any given situation? Aren't all people inescapably bound to aim at accomplishing some goal or purpose in all that they do? Isn't it natural (by God's design) that humans normally seek self-preservation and seek to find delight in what they do in life? Yes! One might even argue that it is best to attempt to do the greatest good for the greatest number of people due to human limitations. These questions highlight some of the strengths of teleological considerations. But a one-dimensional consequentialist approach (the consequences becoming the basis of the ethic and not just one consideration among several) is also filled with weaknesses, making the approach problematic overall.

The consequentialist approach makes results the absolute measure of what is right and wrong. Although the consequences should be considered as a factor, they should not ultimately determine what a person ought to do in a situation. Can finite human beings always accurately predict the outcome of actions—especially when there is a whole web of decisions involved and many people making those many decisions over many years with billions of factors at play across a whole society? Making choices based on an obvious-enough outcome can only take place in very simple, limited situations. So the approach might work out sometimes, but it's not usually a workable approach in much of real life since nobody can truly predict all the effects in the long run. It lacks external coherence.

Who gets to decide (and when) whose perspective is most accurately judging whether an outcome will bring about the greatest good for an individual or society in the long run? One generation may be confident that certain choices are right and good. So those choices are judged to be moral in that generation. But then the next generation observes that the outcomes of those choices actually produced all kinds of harm (or at least what the next generation defines as harm). The next generation

**complementary:** completing by adding benefit without contradicting or undermining

judges the previous generation as immoral (even if the previous generation never purposed to cause harm). There is no sure standard of right and wrong—only perspective (postmodernism embraces this as true rather than seeing it as a problem). A person can be a hero in one generation and demonized in the next. This approach is internally inconsistent; it undermines itself as a consistent guide for ethical choices.

Here's another problem: How would you like to be in a minority population that doesn't matter to a majority population that operates according to the greatest good for the greatest number of people? Wouldn't you cry foul when you yourself suffered? The idea that "might makes right" has led to many atrocities throughout history. More than that, the Bible supports the intrinsic worth and proper treatment of every individual because all people are made in God's image. It is possible to do the greatest good for the greatest number of people as long as nothing immoral is being done to individuals (administrative rules often work this way). But as soon as the minority are suffering due to immoral actions (which can only be determined outside a consequentialist approach, by the way), then the utilitarian approach becomes problematic to the Christian.

Other criticisms have been leveled against the consequentialist approach. While people may find it attractive to live for pure self-interest (ethical egoism), the pleasurable results are usually short-lived. Their immoral living will produce painful consequences in the end. But consequentialists have a very difficult time measuring the balance between pain and pleasure in order to determine what to do. There are too many factors, and the judgments are too subjective. Even if they were to agree on a course of action, the judgment would boil down to agreed-upon preferences. Consequentialism can never tell someone what is actually right or wrong in and of itself. Situation ethics suffers from all these problems as well. It sounds good that we should operate by the rule of love in all situations. But how is love defined, and what does it actually look like without any direction from God's moral law? "Love" turns out to be nothing more than a person's subjective preferences.

In sum, only God's glory can be our ultimate end. And only God's commands in God's Word can describe what it actually looks like to pursue that end. God's commands describe what it looks like to love God and others—the two Great Commandments that sum up what ought to motivate us and how we can glorify God in all of life (Matt. 22:37–40). We need the specific direction of God's Word to guide us in our judgments. Both the means we use and the ends we achieve are important to God.

## PROBLEMS WITH THE VIRTUE ETHICS APPROACH

Don't Christians need to focus on being the right kind of people so that what they do flows out of who they are? Shouldn't Christians cultivate virtues? Aren't some ethical difficulties easy to resolve once a person becomes virtuous and thus sees the situations with clarity? Yes! These questions highlight some of the strengths of the virtue ethics approach.

Another strength of the virtue ethics approach is that it shifts the focus from the most difficult ethical choices that few people ever face in life (or that people rarely face) to focus on the moral choices we all have to make every day. The study of ethics should not be reduced to hard-to-solve ethical difficulties. The study of ethics should



THE FALL'S EFFECTS ON ETHICS 41

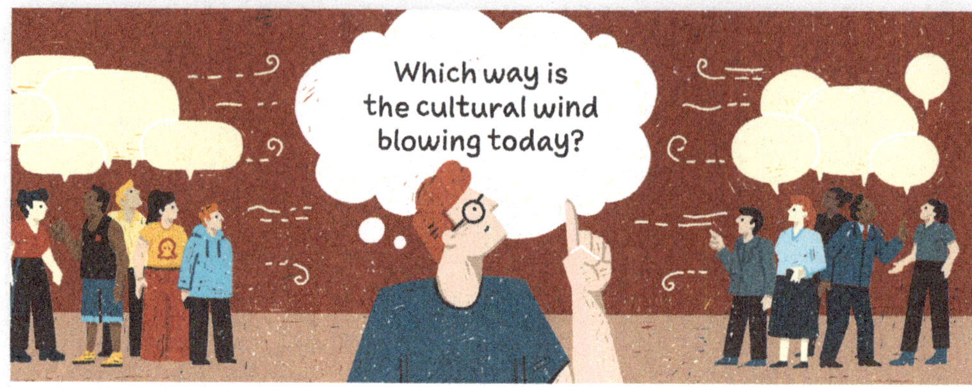


relate to basic growth in Christlikeness or sanctification (see Chapter 4). The hard cases should indeed be better resolved by the spiritually mature who have developed virtuous character (although even then the course of action isn't automatic—based simplistically on who I am). The Bible emphasizes that actions flow from the heart and that hypocrisy makes even right actions wrong.

But a one-dimensional virtue ethic has significant weaknesses as well. Virtue ethics tends to avoid evaluating specific acts and can neglect the reality of universal moral norms. Different groups of people will define what is virtuous differently. For instance, Aristotle thought the most virtuous man was "the one who thinks himself worthy of great things and really is worthy of them."[14] But Jesus said, "Blessed are the poor in spirit" (Matt. 5:3). Virtue ethics alone cannot decide what is truly a virtue and thus worth pursuing. If this decision is made on the basis of a community's values rather than upon universal moral norms, then virtue ethics becomes relative to that community.

In addition, even if everyone could agree on what a virtue is and what it looks like and how it should be applied, how does a person *become* inwardly virtuous? John Frame observes the problem that non-Christian virtue ethicists have with this question:

> Aristotle teaches that we need to have virtuous dispositions to perform virtuous acts; but we need to perform moral acts in order to form the habits that produce virtuous dispositions. Aristotle is aware of this circularity and counsels readers to begin the process by doing things that "resemble" virtuous acts. But how one gets from resemblance to actuality is a mystery.[15]

One of the possible strengths of virtue ethics can also be one of its greatest weaknesses. Many who make use of virtue ethics make use of storytelling with model characters in order to inspire students to build character in their own lives. They may even use the Bible for character-building. But this moralistic approach to the Bible can reduce the Bible to a book of fairy tales with moral lessons that are simply useful to instill character into people—much like Aesop's fables.

The Bible does recount historical narratives with biblical persons who can be held up as examples (both negative and positive) to learn from. But the Bible is much more than this; it is not merely an ethical guidebook. The Bible explains truth and reality according to the historical unfolding of one overarching redemptive plan that all the individual historical accounts plug into. The Bible is primarily about God and His redemptive plan. Many of the biblical stories are meant to point us to our own inability to produce virtuous character within ourselves. The source of character must be the transforming work of Christ (see Chapter 4). Many virtue ethicists (even those in a broadly "Christian" tradition) miss or minimize the gospel.



42 FOUNDATIONS FOR ETHICS

### PROBLEMS WITH THE EXISTENTIALIST ETHICS APPROACH

Don't Christians need to avoid mere external adherence to conventional morality? Don't Christians need to be who they really are, avoiding hypocrisy? Don't they need to examine their hearts to ensure that they have integrity, that their inner persons and their outward actions are not at odds with each other? Don't they need to take responsibility for their own choices? Yes! There are even some strengths in the existentialist approach. However, this approach tends to be worse than the others because it explicitly denies an objective moral order outside the individual. The existentialist approach can lead to the absolute anarchy of the individual who wants freedom to become whoever he or she wishes to become (in the name of authenticity). When many such people wish to become all that is antithetical to virtue, their society becomes less and less moral, and existentialism provides no mechanism or basis for restraining the disorder and immorality. Eventually that society will implode upon itself. God has not called us to be people of authenticity (in contrast to hypocrisy); God has called us to be people of integrity.

In sum, virtue (who I am on the inside) must be defined, described, and applied according to moral norms found in the Bible and in the design of God's creation. A person's ethical choices will reveal the fruit of true virtue versus hypocritical claims to virtue. Without any moral restraint from external absolutes or inward virtue, a society is doomed to self-destruction.

"You do you."

Less-structured rules of the road can lead to more chaotic driving. How does this image illustrate the ideology and outcome of the existential worldview?

### CONCLUSION

Chapter 8 will present a biblical approach, or methodology, for making ethical decisions. This approach brings together the need to act according to absolute principles (acts) by rightly motivated virtuous people (agents) to the glory of God (ends). In other words, elements seen in the deontological, consequentialist, and virtue ethics approaches must all be put together and rightly prioritized in a biblical approach to ethics.[16]

#### Thinking It Through 2.3

1. List and explain three rules of thumb for critiquing the ethical approaches.
2. Summarize at least two strengths of the deontological approach.
3. Summarize at least two weaknesses of the deontological approach.
4. Summarize at least two strengths of the consequentialist approach.
5. Summarize at least two weaknesses of the consequentialist approach.
6. Summarize at least two strengths of the virtue ethics approach.
7. Summarize at least two weaknesses of the virtue ethics approach.
8. Summarize at least one strength of the existentialist approach.
9. Summarize at least one weakness of the existentialist approach.



Guide a **summative assessment** by directing students to answer the questions in Thinking It Through 2.3.

#### Thinking It Through 2.3

1. See bullet points on page 39.
2. Strengths include relying on objective, absolute, and universal principles; driven by self-sacrificing duty; commitment to right motives and not just using people for an end; refusal to live according to selfish ends and mere self-pleasure.
3. Weaknesses include that it replaces a personal God with impersonal logic; its universal principles tend to be too generalized to be useful or applied without contradiction; rules are absolute, regardless of other factors; it assumes self-sacrificing duty is the only laudable goal; it cannot settle conflicting duties; it pits happiness against duty; it gives no place for self-interest or benefiting from others; it leads to making judgments due to consequences or preferences.
4. Strengths include counting the cost; considering how my actions affect others; seeking to be loving; seeking to be goal-oriented and purposeful; self-preservation; delighting in life; doing the greatest good for the greatest number.
5. Weaknesses include that it makes the results the ultimate determination for right and wrong rather than being just one factor to weigh; it can predict results only in very limited, simplistic situations and not in more complex, long-term situations; it has no sure perspective to judge the results as good and beneficial, or the opposite; individuals and minorities suffer under the atrocities of the mighty or the majority; it fails to give intrinsic worth to everyone; pleasures and preferences can be short-sighted and damaging; love is poorly defined.
6. Strengths include focusing on being the right person; focusing on cultivating virtues like prudence and wisdom; finding clarity in what to do as a result of being mature in virtue; emphasis on everyday living, rather than limited to hard cases; guarding against hypocrisy (just because someone does the right thing doesn't make that person moral).
7. Weaknesses include that people of high character still disagree on a course of action (their intuitions clash); general virtues are understood and applied differently based on personal values; norms are founded in subjective, changeable communities, rather than in transcendent, universal norms; virtues are cultivated through man-centered self-achievement; the Bible is reduced to a moralistic guidebook, rather than relied upon as the gospel that transforms from within through the work of Christ.
8. Its strength is that it guards against hypocrisy or that it takes responsibility for one's actions.
9. Its weakness is that it elevates sinful authenticity over virtue. Existentialists justify absolute personal freedom and anarchy, leading to the destruction of societies through immorality.

# Chapter 2 Review

## Terms to Remember

- **naturalistic fallacy:** This fallacy assumes that what is natural is good. In other words, it assumes that if a behavior is found in nature, it must be morally acceptable.
- **deontological ethics:** Ethical choices are governed by objective, absolute, universal rules or principles and a selfless commitment to duty.
- **categorical imperative:** A maxim (or principle) that a person is convinced would guide all people to do the right thing if it were a universal law. This maxim is always true regardless of circumstances and is an obligation for all people at all times, according to Kant's formulation.
- **consequentialist ethics:** Ethical choices are governed by the results or ends they will achieve. The proper end is that which achieves the greatest amount of good. The good is often happiness, as defined by the individual or by society.
- **utilitarianism:** The most common consequentialist approach to ethics. Believes that the utility (usefulness) of an action to bring about an intended helpful end determines what is right or best. The end justifies the means, and the proper end (or goal) is to do the greatest good for the greatest number of people, usually understood as that which brings the most happiness and the least pain.
- **situation ethics:** A consequentialist ethical approach. A form of ethical relativism that holds that a person should always act in the way that is most loving in each situation. Love is not tied to any moral absolutes, and what love requires may be different in different situations for different people.
- **ethical egoism:** A consequentialist approach in which pure, individual self-interest directed toward fulfillment of personal happiness is the governing goal.
- **virtue ethics:** An approach to ethics that focuses on discerning what virtues lead to a flourishing life and on developing those virtues so that they become habitual.
- **existentialist ethics:** Ethical choices are determined by the freely choosing individual. In the absence of absolute truth or meaning, the individual creates his own meaning and essence by the choices he makes and must take full responsibility for the outcome of these choices.

# 02 Review

THE FALL'S EFFECTS ON ETHICS

### Terms to Remember

- naturalistic fallacy
- deontological ethics
- categorical imperative
- consequentialist ethics
- utilitarianism
- situation ethics
- ethical egoism
- virtue ethics
- existentialist ethics
- internal consistency
- external coherence

### Scripture Memory

Romans 3:10–12

### Understanding Ethics

1. What is the value of living in a world with natural laws and creational norms?
2. Based on the Fall's effects on the created order and human nature, explain why it is so hard to make right decisions.
3. Summarize each of the four faulty approaches to ethics. Identify the major proponent(s) of each approach.
4. What do most philosophers who are driven by results identify as the ultimate goal of all people (or the highest good)? How would you differentiate Cyrenaic hedonists and Epicurean hedonists who followed this line of thinking?

### Practicing Ethical Decision-Making

5. Summarize how each of the four faulty ethical approaches would respond to the scenario below, and briefly explain the reasoning behind each.

   A store manager asks you to set aside some extra inventory without documenting it because he wants to give the product to charity without receiving any recognition for doing so.

6. Summarize how each of the four faulty ethical approaches would respond to the scenario below, and briefly explain the reasoning behind each.

   Your best friend asks you to help him or her cheat on a test.

### Analyzing and Evaluating Ethical Claims

7. How would you respond to someone who claims that the family unit can be defined however one wishes (two dads, two moms, marriage is unnecessary for a couple, and so on) because society is no longer bound by the traditional family setup? What fallacy has this person embraced?
8. How would you respond to a claim that a soldier cannot confiscate an enemy's weapons because stealing is wrong? What fallacy has this person embraced?
9. How would you respond to a claim that you can steal a computer because you have been disadvantaged in life and this tool will help you to graduate from college and do a lot of good for others in return one day? What fallacy has this person embraced?
10. How would you respond to a claim that all virtuous people will know by intuition (without needing to evaluate the complexities of the situation in the light of moral absolutes) whether the law should force the descendants of American slaveholders to compensate the descendants of American slaves for loss and disadvantage? What fallacy has this person embraced?

### Creating My Own Position Statements on Ethics

11. Summarize your own position on the effects of the Fall on the created order and on human nature.
12. Summarize your own position on the best approach to ethics.



- **internal consistency:** The test of whether an ethical system contradicts or undermines itself.
- **external coherence:** The test of whether an ethical system aligns with real life.

## Understanding Ethics

1. They give us the standard for how things ought to be (the basis for our ethics). God designed the world (the structures for the physical world and for society) to work in a moral way that conforms to His character.
2. It is hard to make ethical decisions because the Fall has affected the created order (so we have to differentiate what is creational and what is fallen) and our minds, wills, emotions, and affections (so it is hard to make correct judgments, be correctly motivated, and make right choices based on right desires).
3. The deontological system is best represented by Immanuel Kant. Its core approach is based on objective, absolute, and universal rules or principles for everyone.

   The consequential system is best represented by Jeremy Bentham and John Stuart Mill. Its core approach is based on results or goals (for the individual or society).

   The virtue ethics system is best represented by Alasdair MacIntyre or Stanley Hauerwas. Its core approach is based on cultivating inward virtue or character (ideals).

The existential system is best represented by Jean-Paul Sartre. Its core approach is based on just being who I am naturally (authenticity).

4. They identify happiness or pleasure as the highest good. Cyrenaic hedonists believed that the most intense, immediate pleasures were the best, while Epicurean hedonists believed they needed to look for what would produce the most pleasure and the least amount of pain in the long run.

## Practicing Ethical Decision-Making

5. Following the deontological approach, one might be perplexed about dutifully following the instructions of one's direct manager. In the end, one's duty to follow the rules of documenting all the inventory and one's duty to the owner should overrule.

   Following the utilitarian approach, one would be less likely to strictly follow the letter of the law on documenting all the inventory, especially if convinced that the reason is for a good cause.

   Following the virtue ethics or existentialist approach, one could stand for honesty if that is a virtue in one's ethical system. It may not be.

6. Following the deontological approach, one might be conflicted over duty to a friend, but most likely one would ultimately submit to the highest duty to the teacher and school and to the moral principle of honesty.

   Following situation ethics, a subset of the consequentialist approach, one would be more likely to justify loving one's friend if that friend had a good enough excuse for needing the answers.

   Following the virtue ethics approach, a person may know that society frowns upon dishonesty, so for that reason the person would refuse to participate.

   Following the existentialist approach, one would be most committed to freedom from authority to achieve one's own needs. This could lead to refusing to help to avoid any detrimental punishment, or it could lead to helping the friend because of some personal benefit.

## Analyzing and Evaluating Ethical Claims

7. The person and situation may call for a discerning and compassionate response (in how the truth is communicated).

   But fundamentally, this person has succumbed to the naturalistic fallacy: what is natural (in society) is (morally) good. Instead, biblical principles undergird the traditional family setup. God designed the world for one man and one woman to be joined in marriage and to reproduce so that (ideally) a mother and father raise children. Fallenness affects this ideal (through death, divorce, inability to reproduce).

8. Answers may vary. This is an example of making a general rule (a categorical imperative) into an absolute, regardless of the situation (a deontological approach). This is not a matter of the end justifies the means. It is, in fact, a situation in which it is possible to act ethically as one ought in fulfillment of one's rightful duty in a way that is only seemingly contrary to a particular categorical imperative.

9. Answers may vary. This is an example of the ends justifying the means rather than recognizing moral absolutes (a consequentialist approach). People can easily come up with some kind of a justification for achieving a laudable goal through sinful means.

10. Answers may vary. This is an example of assuming one's conclusion on what a virtue will look like in real life (a virtue ethics approach). Many people have virtuous ideals but fail to rightly apply the generalized virtue to situations. Just because someone seeks to cultivate virtuous ideals does not mean that that person will by intuition simply know what the right thing to do is apart from biblical principles and careful analysis of a situation. Many self-proclaimed virtuous people hotly disagree on the right response to the situation, even though they may agree on the virtues in the abstract.

## Creating My Own Position Statements on Ethics

11. Ideally, students will reflect a biblical view of the effects of the Fall as enunciated in Section 2.1.

12. Ideally, students will enunciate the need to be transformed persons (virtues) who are able to apply God's norms in creation and Scripture (rules) to specific situations, all for God's glory (results).

# Lesson Plan Overview

**CHAPTER 3:** The Role of Redemption in Ethics

**EV** ExamView
**PPT pres.** PowerPoint presentation

| PAGES | OBJECTIVES | RESOURCES | ASSESSMENTS |
|---|---|---|---|
| **3.1 Redemption and the Law** (3 DAYS) | | | |
| 46–50 | **3.1.1** Relate God's commandments to His character.<br>**3.1.2** Infer the ethical nature of the two Great Commandments.<br>**3.1.3** Relate the Ten Commandments to ethics.<br>**3.1.4** Analyze how the Mosaic law relates to Christians under the New Covenant.<br>*BWS* Authority (explain)<br>**3.1.5** Relate what Christ has done (indicatives) to our ability to obey the law of Christ (imperatives). | **ACTIVITIES**<br>• 3.1 Delighting in God's Law<br>**BJU PRESS TROVE***<br>• Link: Union with Christ in Pastoral Ministry<br>• PPT pres.: Chapter 3 | **STUDENT EDITION**<br>• Thinking It Through 3.1 |
| **3.2 Redemption and Wisdom** (3 DAYS) | | | |
| 50–54 | **3.2.1** Define *wisdom*.<br>**3.2.2** Relate gaining wisdom to the observation of God's creation.<br>*BWS* Wisdom (explain)<br>**3.2.3** Relate wisdom to God's law.<br>*BWS* Wisdom (explain)<br>**3.2.4** Relate wisdom to applying creational norms to the Christian life.<br>*BWS* Wisdom (explain) | **ACTIVITIES**<br>• 3.2 Growing in Wisdom<br>**BJU PRESS TROVE**<br>• Link: Four Ways to Live More Ethically<br>• PPT pres.: Chapter 3 | **STUDENT EDITION**<br>• Thinking It Through 3.2 |
| **3.3 Redemption and Man's Chief End** (3 DAYS) | | | |
| 54–58 | **3.3.1** Explain man's chief end.<br>**3.3.2** Relate man's chief end to the pursuit of Christlikeness.<br>*BWS* Man's Chief End (explain)<br>**3.3.3** Relate seeking the kingdom of God to man's chief end.<br>*BWS* Man's Chief End (explain)<br>**3.3.4** Relate blessedness to man's chief end.<br>*BWS* Man's Chief End (explain) | **ACTIVITIES**<br>• 3.3 Living for God's Glory<br>**BJU PRESS TROVE**<br>• PPT pres.: Chapter 3 | **STUDENT EDITION**<br>• Thinking It Through 3.3 |
| **Review** | | | |
| 59 | Recall concepts, terms, and Scripture memory from Chapter 3. | | **STUDENT EDITION**<br>• Chapter 3 Review |
| **Test** | | | |
| | Demonstrate knowledge of the material from Chapter 3 by taking the test. | | **ASSESSMENTS**<br>• Chapter 3 Test<br>**BJU PRESS TROVE**<br>• EV: Chapter 3 test bank |

*Digital resources for homeschool users are available on Homeschool Hub.

COLOSSIANS 3:1–3, 12

# The Role of Redemption in Ethics

*How can I live according to a Christian ethic?*

THE ROLE OF REDEMPTION IN ETHICS 45

CHAPTER 3

## Overview

*How can I live according to a Christian ethic?*

### Objectives

**3.1** Relate God's law to personal ethical choices.

**3.2** Analyze the role of wisdom in ethics.

**3.3** Relate biblical motivations to making ethical choices.

### Terms to Remember

- volunteerist perspective
- covenantal identity
- wisdom
- kingdom of God
- beatific vision

### Scripture Memory

- Colossians 3:1–3, 12

# 3.1 Redemption and the Law

## How can I delight in God's law?

### Objectives

**3.1.1** Relate God's commandments to His character.

**3.1.2** Infer the ethical nature of the two Great Commandments.

**3.1.3** Relate the Ten Commandments to ethics.

**3.1.4** Analyze how the Mosaic law relates to Christians under the New Covenant. *BWS*

**3.1.5** Relate what Christ has done (indicatives) to our ability to obey the law of Christ (imperatives).

### Biblical Worldview Shaping

- **Authority** (explain): Christians are under the new covenant, but they should learn from how God applied creational norms for Israel. (3.1.4)

### Printed Resource

- Activity 3.1: Delighting in God's Law

### Digital Resource

- Link: Union with Christ in Pastoral Ministry

### Suggested Reading

- Wolters, Albert M. *Creation Regained: Basics for a Reformational Worldview*. 2nd ed. Grand Rapids, MI: Eerdmans, 2005. Pages 13–20.

## 3.1 Redemption and the Law

Christian ethics addresses us as whole persons—our character, motivations, actions, and relationships. It aims to restore the image of God in man through the redemptive work of Jesus Christ. It neither minimizes outward conduct nor does it reduce morality to outward conduct. It transforms heart motivations. It recognizes the reciprocal relationship between character and actions (actions flow from character and also shape character). And it provides the universal moral norms necessary for determining right and wrong.

Without the universal moral norms of God's law, individuals and societies are bereft of an objective standard for assessing right and wrong. What is moral becomes a matter of personal preference or the consensus of a particular society. But these are ever-changing standards. The unchanging norms of Scripture provide us with the reliable compass we need to navigate the ethical currents of life.

Christians approach the task of ethics with an awareness of God's character revealed in creation, in His law (summarized in the Ten Commandments), and in the person and work of Jesus Christ. We follow the Bible's storyline so that our ethic is built according to the covenantal structure* of redemptive history. Then we draw on our new identity in Christ to apply ethics to our lives.

**covenantal structure:** the scaffolding for the biblical storyline formed by a series of covenants between God and certain individuals in redemptive history, beginning with the Adamic Covenant and concluding with the New Covenant

## Engage

### BY WHAT STANDARD?

Conduct a **Think-Pair-Share** in which the students answer the following question.

**What ethical standards in secular societies compete with God's law, and why are they unsustainable?**

Direct the students to share their answers with a partner.

## Instruct

### GOD'S CHARACTER AND GOD'S LAW

Guide a **preassessment** of student understanding of the relationship between God's character and God's law.

**Why do you think God's law, such as His law against adultery, was not an arbitrary decision on God's part?** *God's law reflects His holy character, and His law could never contradict His own character.*

**Why does the quality of life deteriorate for societies that reject God's law?** *Since humans were made to reflect God's holy character, they cause harm to themselves when they act contrary to the way God designed them to act.*

**Regarding the two Great Commandments, why should people not be allowed to decide on their own what it means to love God and to love their neighbor?** *People will be tempted to fill the love commands with their own fallen concepts of what love should look like.*

**If people really loved God and loved their neighbor, what would their conduct look like?** *It would look like conduct that is consistent with the Ten Commandments.*

**What two things regarding God's law does the plan of redemption accomplish for fallen people?** *The plan of redemption deals with the penalty of the law hanging over us because of our sin, and it gives us a new power to delight in the law.*

### GOD'S LAW: TWO ERRORS

Guide a **misconception check** about God's law by addressing two common errors.

**What do you think are some common errors people make with respect to God's law?** *The first error is to divorce God's law from God's character, and the second error is to divorce God's grace from one's obedience to*

## GOD'S CHARACTER AND GOD'S LAW

God's moral law is a reflection of His holy character. It is not an abstract code of ethics found in His personal library. Human judges are under the law by which they adjudicate* legal disputes. In this case the law exists outside the judge. But if God's law existed outside Himself, it would not be a reflection of His own character. It's important to understand that God does not declare, for example, murder and adultery wrong because that's what the moral universe imposes on Him.

God's Law
God's Moral Standard
God's Character

But if universal moral norms are not independent of God, does this mean that God's law is arbitrary? In other words, could God have made up an entirely different set of laws from the ones He has given to us? Instead of declaring murder and adultery wrong, could He have declared these things to be right? This faulty view is known as the **volunteerist perspective**. It maintains that God's law is whatever God wills it to be. We need to understand that even though this view seems to elevate the sovereignty of God, it makes ethical behavior arbitrary.

Contrary to volunteerism, biblical Christianity maintains that God only wills that which is consistent with His holy character. When God's law is divorced from His good character, ethics loses its grounding. Ethics is not arbitrary; it could not be other than it is because God's character could not be other than it is. Nor is there some moral standard external to God; right and wrong are established by God's character. His commands to not murder and to not commit adultery reflect who He is. He is the God of life, and therefore murder is always wrong. He is the God of faithfulness, and therefore adultery is always wrong.

### *The Two Great Commandments*

There are a lot of laws in the Mosaic code, so God in His wisdom boils them down into two Great Commandments: to love God supremely and to love others as oneself (Lev. 19:18; Deut. 6:5; Matt. 22:36–40). The ethical implications of the two Great Commandments are obvious. If we loved God perfectly, we would seek to please Him in our thoughts, motives, and actions. If we loved people perfectly, we would seek their good in every situation. Though no one does this perfectly, this is the standard to which we are called.

There is a great simplicity in being able to boil down all ethical choices to these two laws. And yet, the two Great Commandments are so broad that we might be tempted to fill the love commands with our own fallen concepts of what love should look like. The Ten Commandments define what it means to love God and others, and other laws in the Pentateuch explain them further and apply them to specific situations.

### How can I delight in God's law?

Christian love for God and for others is predicated on God's love for us. As the apostle John wrote, "Herein is love, not that we loved God, but that he loved us, and sent his Son to be the propitiation for our sins. . . . We love him, because he first loved us." (1 John 4:10, 19). Redemption does not come at the expense of God's law; it comes at the expense of God's own Son. The plan of redemption accomplishes two things: it deals with the penalty of the law hanging over us for our sin, and it gives us a new power to delight in the law. God is not only the standard of love; His love for us also enables our love for Him and for others.

### *The Ten Commandments*

We can relate the two Great Commandments to the Ten Commandments by asking two questions: What does love for God look like? Answer: having no other gods before Him, not making an image of Him and bowing before it, honoring His name, and honoring His day of worship (Exod. 20:3–11). What does love for people look like? Answer: put in positive form, the commandments teach us to honor our parents, respect human life, remain faithful in marriage, respect people's property, speak the truth, and rejoice in our neighbor's blessings (Exod. 20:12–17). But even the Ten Commandments are broad statements. God's people need further help knowing how to apply these commands to their lives. Many of the commands in the rest of the Pentateuch seek to do this.

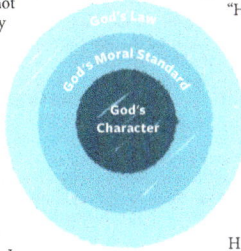

**adjudicate:** to come to a judicial decision; to act as judge



*God's law.*

Point out that, first, there is a misconception that God's law is above God. While a human judge is under the law, that is not the case with God. In other words, the law is not an independent, abstract code of ethics floating above God. Rather, God's law flows from who God is.

**Why does this distinction matter?** *If God's law existed outside Himself, then something greater than God would exist, which is an impossibility.*

Second, there is a misconception that people can keep God's law without depending on God's grace. Moralism is a real danger, even among professing Christians. The notion that fallen humanity can obey God's law apart from grace is a notion that nullifies Christ's redemptive work. To obey God's law from the heart, one must possess God's saving grace, experienced solely through a living faith in Jesus Christ. While it is true that unbelievers do good acts because of God's common grace (Matt. 7:11), their external morality falls short of that God-glorifying obedience found in believers (Matt. 5:19–20, 48).

## THE CHRISTIAN AND THE MOSAIC LAW

Use **direct instruction** to introduce the necessity of setting God's law in the flow of redemptive history (i.e., the importance of the covenantal structure of the Bible's storyline).

Explain that to understand how God's law works in Christian ethics, we need to read the Bible in its full context and on its own terms. The Bible's story is a story of redemption, and it is structured according to God's covenants, beginning with the Adamic Covenant and concluding with the New Covenant. These covenants are important because they highlight God's gracious character in giving and fulfilling His holy law. Unless God freely established a covenant with us, we could never be in a right relationship with Him. God always takes the initiative with us.

Point out that there are two things to keep in mind regarding the Mosaic Covenant. First, we must emphasize that Israel was under the Mosaic law as a covenant. Thus, obedience to the law was a condition if Israel was to experience God's promised blessing. Second, Israel's failure to meet the conditions of the covenant highlighted the need for a Mediator who could perfectly meet the conditions on behalf of sinners. By fulfilling the Mosaic law as humanity's representative, Christ was able to establish the New Covenant, and with it a new power to obey those aspects of the Mosaic law still in effect (e.g., creational norms such as marital faithfulness).

Mention that any approach to ethics that ignores this covenantal structure is doomed to failure. Yet how many religious people assume that brute law is sufficient to achieve an ethical society? "If people would only stop misbehaving and do the right thing, everything in society would be fine."

But without the gospel—the person and work of Christ—the law will only crush people. To establish an ethical society consistent with God's law, we must teach God's law in a way that situates it within its redemptive-historical context. The result of such teaching will help people see their need for the indwelling Holy Spirit, promised under the Old Covenant and fulfilled in the New Covenant by the redemptive work of Christ. It is by the Spirit that God's law is written on the hearts of God's people. Therefore, it is contrary to the work of the Spirit for a Christian to dismiss God's law. If we love God, we will delight in His law.

As the moral standard for human society, the Ten Commandments reflect the creational norms given to Adam, which in turn reflect God's character. After mankind fell into sin and God moved the plan of redemption forward by calling Israel to be His people, God gave Israel the law, which was a statement of creational norms and their applications. Even though some people read the Mosaic law as if it is arbitrary, it is not. The creational norms that it expounds are rooted in God's own character.

### THE CHRISTIAN AND THE MOSAIC LAW

The ethical nature of the Ten Commandments must not be abstracted from its redemptive-historical context. The Mosaic law was given shortly after God delivered Israel from Egyptian bondage (Exod. 20:1). The laws that God gave through Moses reflect that historical context. One author says, "The Mosaic law was the divinely accredited implementation of creational law for ancient Israel."[1] This means that God took creational norms and applied them to Israel's particular time and place. For instance, in Israel's time and place, the flat roofs of houses were places where people lived. The law required the Israelites to build a low wall around the rooftops so that people would not accidentally fall off the roof and die or injure themselves (Deut. 22:8). This was God's specific application of the fifth commandment, which concerns itself with the protection of human life.

#### *The New Covenant and the Law*

Despite Israel's privilege of receiving the law, its moral failure was evident from the start and therefore hinted at the need for a better covenant (Deut. 31:20, 27; Jer. 31:31–34). Israel's problem with disobedience was not unique to that nation. Violating God's creational norms, which are reflected in His moral law, is a universal problem. We are all guilty and therefore deserving of the death and curses threatened in the law. Humanity's long-awaited hope rested on God's promised Messiah.

By fulfilling the Old Covenant law, Christ ushered in the New Covenant and thereby changed the way His people relate to the law (Rom. 7:1–6; 8:3–4). Christians are not under the Mosiac law as a covenant; that was Israel's relationship to the law. Christ was born under the law-covenant in order to fulfill its demands and its penalties (Gal. 4:4). Because Christ fulfilled the law for us, we can enjoy through faith in Him the undeserved life and blessings promised in the law. God's people no longer receive His law from the thunder of Sinai, causing them to shrink back in fear; they now receive it from the hand of Christ on lovely Mount Zion, causing them to walk in loving obedience (Heb. 12:18–24; 1 Cor. 9:21).

But this does not mean the Mosaic law has no relevance for the Christian today. There is much the Christian can learn by observing how God made specific application of creational norms to Israel's particular time and place. As Wolters puts it,

> Insofar as the Mosaic law is addressed to a particular phase of the history of God's people it has lost its validity, but insofar as it points to the enduring normativity of God's creation order it retains its validity. . . .
>
> . . . In the Old Testament the explanations [God] gave included detailed instructions for the implementation of the blueprint; that was by way of apprenticeship. In Christ we are journeyman builders—still bound to the architect's explicit directions, but with considerable freedom of implementation as new situations arise.[2]

God's applications for Israel help Christians understand how to apply general laws like the Ten Commandments or the two Great Commandments to their own time and place.

Christians must ask when reading the Mosaic law, What part is universally normative because it is rooted in creation? What part is an application to Israel's time and place? And what can we learn from how God applied creational norms to Israel that should inform how we apply creational norms to our own situation? Thus, while Christians are not under the Mosaic law as their covenant, they are not released from all of God's laws either. Instead, Christ has fulfilled the law on our behalf to save us and then enable us to obey His law.

***The Holy Spirit and the Law***

Though Christians are not saved by keeping the law of God, they're not without the law of God (Rom. 3:20, 31). Christians refusing to obey God's law because they are under grace is incompatible with the New Covenant promise of the Spirit. The Old Testament prophets summed up God's promise this way: "I will put my spirit within you, and cause you to walk in my statutes" (Ezek. 36:27), and "I will put my law in their inward parts, and write it in their hearts" (Jer. 31:33).

*Though a believer be less under the power of the law than others... [h]e sees more of its spirituality and holiness.* JOHN OWEN[3]

God's promise to put His Spirit within His people corresponds with His promise to put His law within them. This law refers to the moral norms written in creation, then written on tablets of stone for Israel, and now written in the believer's heart. The difference now is that believers have the Spirit to empower them: "I will . . . cause you to walk in my statutes" (Ezek. 36:27). The Spirit is the wind in our sails of faith, enabling us to choose what is pleasing in His eyes. This is a blood-bought gift because Christ purchased our Spirit-enabled obedience by His death (2 Cor. 1:20). Therefore, the reality of the indwelling Spirit assures believers that they can keep His law as they yield to the Spirit.

## OBEDIENCE AND THE LAW OF CHRIST

Christian ethics does for our moral reasoning what other ethical systems cannot. It provides moral sanity in a morally insane world. At the same time, it offers hope for people who have fallen short of God's moral law and are looking for help.

***Indicatives and Imperatives***

Believers are often conscious of their weaknesses. The high ethical demands of God's moral law leave many feeling overwhelmed. Where can they find help to obey? The Spirit's work in them, as we noted, is one answer. Learning "the grammar of the gospel"[4] is another.

We learned in our English grammar studies the difference between the indicative mood and the imperative mood. The indicative mood refers to a factual statement, something that is true. The sentence "I am crucified with Christ" (Gal. 2:20) is in the indicative mood. The imperative mood refers to a command, something we must do. The sentence "Present your bodies a living sacrifice, holy, acceptable unto God" (Rom. 12:1) is in the imperative mood.

With respect to the gospel, the indicatives refer to what Christ has done, is doing, and will do for us, while the imperatives refer to what we must do as His redeemed people. The indicatives always precede and serve as the incentive for the imperatives. In other words, the love of Christ for us, expressed in our costly redemption, results in our love for Him, expressed in our joyful obedience. The fact that Christ has liberated His people to live righteously means that they really can live righteously (in dependence upon Him). Freedom to obey does not mean it's easy or that Christians can obey without a fight. It means that, for all the obstacles in their pathway, they can have ever-increasing victories in the fight for faith and obedience (1 Tim. 6:12; Rom. 8:37).



## UNION WITH CHRIST

Use the **link** Union with Christ in Pastoral Ministry to access the audio the students will listen to about the role of union with Christ in living out the Christian ethic.

## Apply

## OBEDIENCE AND THE LAW OF CHRIST

Guide a **discussion** to help students understand that the work of Christ is an essential ingredient to ethical living.

The two features to emphasize are (1) living out the Christian ethic depends on understanding the grammar of the gospel and (2) living out the Christian ethic depends on a growing understanding of the believer's identity in Christ.

First, *indicatives* (what Christ has done) precede and empower the *imperatives* (what Christians must do).

**How does knowing Christ and what He has done to secure our salvation impact the way we live as Christians?** *It changes how we think of obedience. Christ has freed believers from the heavy burden of perfectionism. Therefore, they are free to grow in obedience without fearing that God will cast them off when they fall short of perfect obedience. It encourages persistence in the face of difficulties. Nothing impedes obedience like despair over one's failure. And nothing cures such despair like the joy of being fully accepted in Jesus Christ. Failure in the Christian life can be very discouraging, especially for young believers who may become impatient with their progress of sanctification. Christians need not despair; God is pleased with their progress because they are His children, fully accepted in the Lord Jesus Christ. Therefore, the power for ethical living is found in the continual resting upon Christ and His finished work.*

Second, growing in our understanding of our identity in Christ is an immense help for ethical living.

**How can people who have sinned ever see themselves as anything but moral failures?** *Many people wrongly assume they can see themselves as moral winners only after they achieve some moral success. But this is not a Christ-centered approach to ethics. Christian ethics, instead, starts with the premise that sinners who trust in Christ are moral winners by virtue of their union with Christ. Christ won the moral battle for us, and His victory over sin has become the believer's victory.* **Why is it important for believers to pursue ethical living from a position of victory in Christ?** *Christians pursue ethical living from a position of victory, not from a position of personal defeat. Christian identity means that we are who God says we are, not what our feelings tell us, nor what other people say about us. Without this liberating gospel truth, ethical living is not possible.*

## DELIGHTING IN GOD'S LAW

Use **Activity 3.1** on pages 11–13 to apply the information in this section.

## Assess

Guide a **summative assessment** by directing students to answer the questions in Thinking It Through 3.1.

### Thinking It Through 3.1

1. God's moral law reflects His holy character. The law is not an abstract code of ethics floating above His head. At the same time, God did not arbitrarily decide what laws to hand down to humanity. For example, His commands to not murder and to not commit adultery reflect who He is. He is the God of life, and therefore murder is always wrong. He is the God of faithfulness, and therefore adultery is always wrong.
2. If we loved God perfectly, we would seek to please Him in our thoughts, motives, and actions. If we loved people perfectly, we would seek their good in every situation. Though no one does this perfectly, this is the standard to which we are called.
3. The Ten Commandments give concrete expression to the two Great Commandments. Loving God means having no other gods before Him, not making an image of Him and bowing before it, and honoring His name and His day of worship and rest (Exod. 20:3–11). Loving people means honoring our parents, respecting human life, remaining faithful in marriage, respecting people's property, speaking the truth, and rejoicing in our neighbor's blessings (Exod. 20:12–17).
4. Christians are not under the Mosaic Covenant, which Christ has fulfilled. But Christians should discern the universal creational norms that were being applied in the Mosaic law. And Christians should learn from how God applied those norms to Israel's time and place as they seek to apply those same norms to their own situations.
5. The grammar of the gospel refers to the indicatives (what Christ has done for us) and the imperatives (what we must do as His redeemed people). Indicatives always precede and serve as the incentive for the imperatives. The fact that Christ has liberated His people to live righteously means that they really can live righteously (in dependence upon Him).

#### *Christian Identity and Christian Ethics*

Ethical living is the outworking of a believer's new identity in Christ. It's not a self-help strategy for improving our moral character. Nor is it merely a matter of imitating Christ's life. Imitation is not possible without identification. In other words, we must be united to Christ by faith in order to become like Him.

Identification flows in two directions. First, Christ identified with sinners by taking on the likeness of sinful flesh and nailing it to the cross (Rom. 8:3). Second, those who trust in Christ are identified with Him in His life, death, and resurrection (Rom. 5:17; 6:4–5). This is a covenantal identity. Our old identity in Adam (sin and death) has been replaced with our new identity in Christ (righteousness and life).

Ethical systems that ignore the biblical teaching of **covenantal identity*** are doomed to failure. The current crisis in our world is a crisis of identity. People no longer know who they are. Burdened with the unbiblical notion that they can create their own identity, people are floundering to make sense of life and of their place in the world. Popular culture says, "Be true to yourself" (an expression of ethical egoism or existentialist ethics). Although this mantra is trumpeted as individual freedom, the despair of so many who follow it is evidence that it isn't freedom.

Freedom doesn't come from rejecting the fundamental nature of our humanity—namely, that we are the very image of God. It comes from being restored to this noble dignity, becoming what we were created to be as mirrors of God's holy character. The mystery of Christian ethics is that believers are gradually being restored in Christ to this original design as they trust and obey.

It takes biblical wisdom to resist the deceptive appeal of other ethical systems and believe that Christian ethics is the right way because it is God's way. Implementing the Christian ethic boils down to this simple principle: become what you are in Christ. In other words, know who you are, Christian. You are one who has been raised with Christ and seated with Him in heaven. Now, live in the light of this glorious fact (Col. 3:1–17)!

#### Thinking It Through 3.1

1. What is the proper way to think of God's law in relationship to His character?
2. What would our ethics look like if we obeyed the two Great Commandments?
3. How do the Ten Commandments relate to the ethic of loving God and loving people?
4. How does Christ's fulfillment of the Mosaic law change the way Christians relate to it?
5. How does the grammar of the gospel help Christians keep God's law?

### 3.2 Redemption and Wisdom

#### How does wisdom help me live ethically?

Christian ethics is more than just following a list of detailed rules. Especially in the New Testament, God wants Christians to understand the laws He has revealed and then reason the specific applications needed in their own situation. And already in the Old Testament Wisdom Literature, God was preparing His people for this task. Wisdom and law are closely connected because both are based on creational norms. Wisdom is the ability to discern those norms and live by them out of a heart of love for the Creator. It is also the ability "to summarize those principles in a succinct and memorable fashion."[5]

**covenantal identity:** who a person is—based not on individual characteristics but based on his or her relationship to a representative head whom God established, either Adam or Christ

Since these norms are rooted in creation, the wise person is a careful observer of creation to see how God designed it to work. However, to rightly understand what

50 FOUNDATIONS FOR ETHICS

## 3.2 Redemption and Wisdom

### How does wisdom help me live ethically?

#### Objectives

**3.2.1** Define *wisdom.*

**3.2.2** Relate gaining wisdom to the observation of God's creation. BWS

**3.2.3** Relate wisdom to God's law. BWS

**3.2.4** Relate wisdom to applying creational norms to the Christian life. BWS

#### Biblical Worldview Shaping

- **Wisdom** (explain): Wisdom is gained by observing through the corrective lenses of Scripture how God made His creation to function. (3.2.2)
- **Wisdom** (explain): Since both law and wisdom are applications of creational norms to everyday life, there is a close connection between law and wisdom. (3.2.3)
- **Wisdom** (explain): Growing in wisdom is a necessary part of the Christian life. (3.2.4)

#### Printed Resource

- Activity 3.2: Growing in Wisdom

#### Digital Resource

- Link: Four Ways to Live More Ethically

#### Suggested Reading

- Longman, Tremper, III. *How to Read Proverbs.* Downers Grove, IL: InterVarsity Press, 2002. Pages 14–19.

he or she is seeing, the wise person needs the corrective lenses of Scripture. Thus law and wisdom focus on the same thing. But, while in the Mosaic law God made the applications, the wise person needs to work those applications out using wisdom—still looking to the law for further guidance. Wisdom in applying creational norms is a fundamental task of the Christian life. It is something we do every day as well as when we are faced with hard ethical choices.

As we progress in this section, we'll consider how observing creational norms relates to gaining wisdom, how God's law relates to wisdom, and how creational norms apply to the Christian life.

### WISDOM AND DISCERNING CREATIONAL NORMS

Other ethical systems are like a Picasso painting; their secular attempts to reassemble the broken pieces of our lives are unsuccessful. If you've seen many Picasso paintings, you know that the artist often portrayed people as fractured and disjointed. Fallen people are not always as they appear. They strive to give the appearance of a life put together, but the pieces of their lives are in the wrong place. Picasso's fractured people appear foolish and bizarre, and in a way they are a parable of the foolish and sometimes bizarre results of man's efforts to repair himself apart from Christian redemption.[6]

*Weeping Woman* by Picasso

If we could obtain wisdom on our own, we wouldn't need the Lord Jesus Christ. Sadly, many people approach wisdom the way they approach salvation. Trusting in themselves, they exalt the wisdom of man above the wisdom of God. But those who trust in the person and work of Christ discover in Him the fountain of all wisdom (1 Cor. 1:30). It is through Him that Christians become wise.

To be wise is to be discerning, prudent, and virtuous (among other attributes). Discernment is the ability to determine the best course of action in a given situation. Prudence is the ability to be reasonable and cautious in addressing difficulties. And to be virtuous is to be righteous and just in dealing with others. We will not possess wisdom without possessing these qualities in some measure.[7]

Yet there is no quick and easy formula for acquiring wisdom. Wisdom is an art that Christians develop over time as they walk with God. We may define **wisdom** as the art of living well by observing creational norms through the lenses of Scripture, by listening to the counsel of the wise, and by being conscious that all life is lived before the face of God.

> *Wisdom is living out the whole of life with a constant awareness of accountability before a loving, gracious, and just Creator and Redeemer.* O. PALMER ROBERTSON[8]

#### *Wisdom and the Observation of God's Creation*

True wisdom begins with a humble reverence for God (Prov. 9:10). This includes the recognition that He is an infinitely wise Creator who has purposefully ordered His creation. When God fashioned the world in its physical and moral dimensions, wisdom was by His side (Prov. 8:30). Therefore, pursuing wisdom in our lives "offers us the key to interpreting our world: its beginnings, its purpose, its shape and its direction."[9] To correctly interpret the world, we must assume the right posture before God. We have to be teachable and willing to learn God's viewpoint.

When you purchase a new piece of technology, such as a smartphone, you recognize that the device is created to operate according to the design of its creator. An insightful operator learns the device's proper function and uses it as its creator intended. God's creation is similar in that He designed it to function one way and not another. Our job is to carefully observe what God has written into creation. When we do, we gain wisdom.



- Robertson, O. Palmer. *The Christ of Wisdom: A Redemptive-Historical Exploration of the Wisdom Books of the Old Testament*. Phillipsburg, NJ: P&R Publishing, 2017. Pages 5–16.

## Engage

### GROWING IN WISDOM

Use a **Turn and Talk** to allow students to answer the following questions.

**Why should we not think that a Christian automatically knows how to resolve complex ethical problems?** *Even Christians need to grow in wisdom so that they can know how to resolve such problems.*
**What does it mean for Christians to grow in wisdom?** *It means learning how to discern creational norms and how to live consistently with those norms out of love for God.*
**Since Christians can observe God's norms by looking at creation, why do they need the Scripture?** *Scripture is the corrective lens that helps Christians see creation as God made it to function.*
**What spiritual obstacle do you think prevents many young Christians from growing in wisdom?** *Elicit the following answer: pride in thinking they know it all.*

## Instruct

### WISDOM AND DISCERNING CREATIONAL NORMS

Guide a **visual analysis** of the Picasso painting on page 51 to illustrate the futility of non-Christian ethical systems in addressing human brokenness.

**How would you describe Picasso's depiction of the woman?** *fractured, disjointed*
**Would you surmise that Picasso's view of reality is hopeful or pessimistic?** *pessimistic*
**From a biblical standpoint, what is the real nature of man's fractured state?** *The image of God in man is fractured due to sin, and it stands in need of restoration.*
**In what way does Picasso's painting illustrate non-Christian ethical systems?** *Like people in a Picasso painting, humans remain fractured if they rely on non-Christian ethical systems.*
**Why do you think non-Christian ethical systems fail to restore broken people?** *They exalt human wisdom, which ignores the person and work of Christ, the fountain of all wisdom.*

## MONEY, SEX, AND POWER: WHO DECIDES?

Use **direct instruction** to discuss the necessity of being teachable and willing to learn God's viewpoint if one is to discover the creational norms regarding money, sex, and power.

Money, sex, and power are three areas of life that everyone cares about to some degree. However, people bring different ideas about how these things are supposed to function in everyday life. The question is, Who decides? Should the individual decide? society? God?

This question directly relates to the issue of creational norms. If there is no God who decides, then there are no creational norms for us to learn. Deciding what to do with money, sex, and power is left to the individual or to the society. But if there is a God who decides, then we would expect that ignoring His design would end in frustration and disappointment. And does this not aptly describe the condition of secular societies?

God has created the world with His intentions encoded into it. If we listen to Him, we can learn how money, sex, and power (along with a range of other issues) are supposed to function. This means that the starting point for wisdom is to read what the Creator has written into His creation (i.e., creational norms). Therefore, it is essential that people assume a posture of humility before their Creator if they are to see and understand how money, sex, and power can be utilized to the glory of God and to the flourishing of human society.

## WISDOM AND THE CORRECTIVE LENSES OF SCRIPTURE

Guide a **discussion** to present Scripture's role in developing wisdom for rightly perceiving creational norms.

We all live in the same created world. Yet people vehemently disagree on the most basic issues of morality. If people could arrive at a correct understanding of God's intention solely by observing creation, then we should expect human beings to be in complete agreement.

**So why aren't humans in agreement?** *Sin has distorted the way people see reality. But the problem is even worse than that. Sin deceives people into thinking they can correctly perceive reality independent of God. Therefore, human beings are in this befuddled condition of being wrong about many things while convincing themselves they're right. This explains how our society can confidently assert that homosexual behavior is right despite God's unambiguous intention for human sexuality, which He clearly demonstrates in His design of humans as male and female.*

**Why do we need Scripture in order to be wise?** *Scripture provides the corrective lenses for rightly seeing creational norms. The problem is not with the creational norms; they are visible and recognizable. The problem is with fallen humanity's stubborn refusal to see what is there. Scripture speaks with clarity and power. It gives sight to the blind, so that we can see things in creation as they really are.*

**How does Scripture help us see the world accurately?** *By looking at creation through Scripture, we learn how to distinguish creational norms from that which is fallen in creation. Not everything in fallen creation is what God originally intended (i.e., sin and its consequences). The concept of "structure and direction" is a vital tool for looking at culture and identifying what is creational about it and what is fallen about it. Wisdom is knowing how to apply Scripture in a way that pushes fallen creation back in the direction of God's original design.*

**How does God's law and the Wisdom Literature of the Bible help us regarding creational norms?** *They help us to see the consistency of God's intentions for society. That which God intends for humans in every culture throughout time is found in the harmony of God's Law, the Bible's Wisdom Literature, and creational norms. They all speak with one voice, because all three originate with God. Christians can, and should, bear witness to the society around them about God's good intentions for humanity.*

Let's consider the following examples: money, sex, and power. We choose these examples because people have strong ethical disagreements about them. So we start with a basic question: Who determines how these things should function? What is the good, right, and just way for people to utilize these things? Do human beings get to arbitrarily decide, or has God structured His creation such that money, sex, and power are to be handled according to His wise purposes? How you answer these questions indicates whether you have insight.

### *Wisdom and the Corrective Lenses of Scripture*

Wisdom is more than affirming that God has ordered creation; it's a matter of being attuned to that order and conforming our lives to it. God's intention has always been that people would do this in dependence upon Him. But we now live in an upside-down world, meaning people interpret reality according to their own imaginations. Everything is backward: the wisdom of God is made to appear foolish, and the foolishness of the world is made to appear wise (Rom. 1:22; James 3:14–16). Sin has impaired our ethical vision so that we don't perceive reality as it is.

Reading God's ethical intentions for society off the pages of creation requires the corrective lenses of Scripture. By looking at the world *through* Scripture, we see God's creational norms more clearly, but we also see how sin has distorted these things. For example, with a biblical lens we see the goodness of work and of building wealth, but we also see workaholism, laziness, and greed for the distortions they are. Similarly, we see God's purposeful distinction of men and women, but we also see gender confusion and the abuse or reversal of gender roles. Likewise, we see the goodness of humans exercising dominion over creation, but we also see animal abuse and poor stewardship of natural resources. The question is, How do we get back on track with creational norms?

The answer points us back to the important concepts of *structure* and *direction*. Recall that structure has to do with creational norms, the way God wisely designed the world to function. Direction has to do with what humans do with a created thing, bending it either toward or away from its creational

52 FOUNDATIONS FOR ETHICS

design.[10] In the Fall, humans pushed creation in the wrong direction, which is one of the reasons we need the corrective lenses of Scripture to guide our observations of creation. One mistake many people make is to identify bad direction with structure. For instance, people assume that if they have a desire for something, that desire must indicate something about the way God made them. But they don't stop to ask whether their desires are consistent with God's structure or are the result of pushing God's structure in a fallen direction. Pushing structure in a good direction requires wisdom, because it is often not easy to undo the way bad direction has twisted things and to move back toward creational structure.

#### *Wisdom and the Law of God*

God's law is an explicit revelation of God's wisdom. We can inductively gain some wisdom by observing God's world. But we can also deductively receive wisdom by listening to God directly telling us what we ought to understand when we observe God's world. The Wisdom Literature takes us a step beyond the law of Moses. In the New Testament, God's people have to make their own applications of God's law to their time and place. Wisdom Literature is an Old Testament preparation for that task.

As we carefully listen to the voice of wisdom, we will hear the same truth we hear in God's law. In other words, the moral substance of the Bible's Wisdom Literature echoes the moral substance of God's law. Both share the same purpose and goal: to realign God's people with creational norms so that they can flourish as individuals and as a community of believers.

A few examples from the Ten Commandments and the book of Proverbs will make this clear. First, God's law reaffirms man's subordinate position before his sovereign Creator (Exod. 20:2–3). Wisdom echoes the Creator/creature distinction. It instructs us to not be wise in our own eyes but to trust God and acknowledge Him in all our ways (Prov. 3:5–7). Second, God's law harkens back to the creational norm of marriage as the appointed realm for human sexuality (Gen. 2:18–25; Exod. 20:14). Wisdom raises her voice in agreement: sexual immorality is a fire that burns, but sexual faithfulness in marriage is a satisfying fountain (Prov. 5:15–19; 6:27–29). Third, God's law reiterates the work/rest rhythm of life that we see at the beginning of creation (Gen. 1:31–2:3; Exod. 20:8–11). Wisdom lends her voice to this commandment, reminding us that work brings profit, but we should discern when to cease from work and should not put our trust in wealth (Prov. 14:23; 24:4–5).

### WISDOM AND APPLYING CREATIONAL NORMS

Redemption does not rewrite creational norms; it reorients people to those norms. It restores the Christian's capacity for discernment, prudence, and virtue so that he or she can go with the grain of creation instead of against it. It redirects us to our gracious Redeemer who beckons, "If any of you lack wisdom, let him ask of God, that giveth to all men liberally, and upbraideth not; and it shall be given him" (James 1:5).

It pleases God when we trust Him for what we lack. He will not hold our foolishness against us when we exchange it for His wisdom. After all, one of the ways we gain wisdom is by learning from our poor choices and changing our conduct as a result.[11] Learning how to apply creational norms in the context of a fallen world is a necessary part of the Christian life. Although the Bible is sufficient for providing us with wisdom, it doesn't provide simple solutions to every problem we encounter. That's why we need the Holy Spirit to make us wise and to enable us to live wisely.

Consider the application of creational norms to making decisions about what to purchase with our money. Every decision we make with money is an ethical decision. Scripture has a lot to say about money, but it doesn't tell us whether we should purchase one brand of tennis shoes or another. But what if you discover that



## Apply

### WISDOM AND APPLYING CREATIONAL NORMS

Use **direct instruction** to relate wisdom to living ethically in a fallen world.

Remind the students that life in this world is not as it was before sin entered it, nor is it the way things will be when God's redemptive work reaches its conclusion. As much as we might wish, we do not get to make ethical choices in a sin-free environment. That day is coming for believers. Until then, Christians must face the complexity of sin when wrestling with ethical decisions.

### HOW TO LIVE WISELY IN A FALLEN WORLD

Guide a **Think-Pair-Share** to allow students to brainstorm ideas for living ethically in a fallen world.

- Recognize your need to grow in sanctification. This includes growing in discernment, prudence, and virtue.
- Be willing to learn from your mistakes. Acknowledge your lack of wisdom and ask God to supply you with wisdom.
- Remember your dependence on God's Spirit when searching the Scriptures for the wisdom you need. God promises to help you.
- When you notice a sinful practice in your circle of influence or in society at large, consider what creational norms and biblical principles might help. If possible, correct the sinful practice by speaking truth in love. If not, choose by God's grace not to go along with the practice. Be countercultural without being quarrelsome.
- Do not become impatient when your effort to move a situation toward creational norms faces a setback. Change takes time. Remember that the goal is to please the Lord in all you do. You can trust Him with the results of your efforts, for your labor in the Lord is never in vain.

### GROWING IN WISDOM

Use **Activity 3.2** on page 15 to apply the information in this section. Use the **link** Four Ways to Live More Ethically to access the article that the students will read for Activity 3.2.

## Assess

Guide a **summative assessment** by directing students to answer the questions in Thinking It Through 3.2.

### Thinking It Through 3.2

1. We may define wisdom as the art of living well by observing creational norms through the lens of Scripture, by listening to the counsel of the wise, and by being conscious that all life is lived before the face of God.
2. True wisdom begins with a humble reverence for God (Prov. 9:10). This includes the recognition that He is an infinitely wise Creator who has purposefully ordered His creation. When God fashioned the world in its physical and moral dimensions, wisdom was by His side (Prov. 8:30). To correctly interpret the world, we must assume the right posture before God. We must be teachable and willing to learn God's viewpoint.
3. Sin has impaired our ethical vision so that we don't perceive reality as it is. By looking at the world *through* Scripture, we see more clearly God's creational norms; but we also see how sin has distorted these things. In the Fall, humans pushed creational norms in a bad direction, which is one of the reasons we need the corrective lenses of Scripture to guide our observations of creation.
4. The Wisdom Literature takes us a step beyond the law. In the New Testament, God's people must make their own applications of God's law to their time and place. The moral substance of the Bible's Wisdom Literature echoes the moral substance of God's law. Both share the same purpose and goal: to align God's people with creational norms so that they can flourish as individuals and as a community of believers.
5. Because the Bible does not address every specific situation that we encounter in life, we will need to grow in wisdom as we seek to apply biblical principles and creational norms.

one company is using slave labor to manufacture their tennis shoes while another company has a volunteer workforce that is well compensated? Should these factors influence your purchasing decision?

How might you apply creational norms to this situation? You could point to the fact that slavery is a distortion of the Creation Mandate, a result of the Fall. You could point to the fact that we are responsible to steward our possessions in a way that leads to human flourishing. These are wisdom issues, and they directly relate to how you should respond to the above scenario.

Although the Fall has complicated our decisions in life, Christians can respond to these challenges by paying attention to God's creational norms. We will need Scripture to help us correctly interpret creational norms, and we will need wisdom to sort through the various issues that arise. Redemption means that Christians possess the resources to grow in wisdom and push further and further toward God's creational norms.

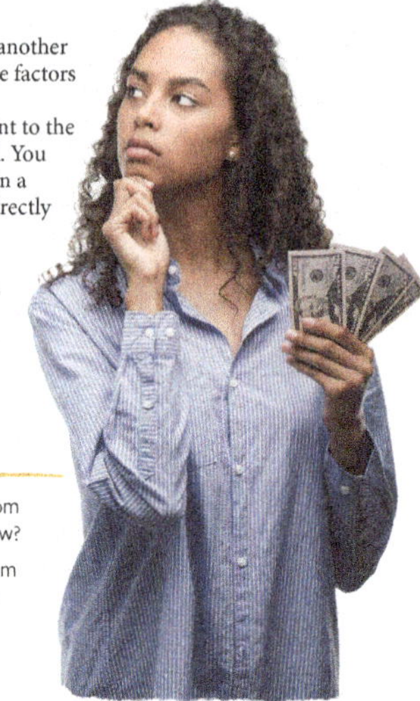

### Thinking It Through 3.2

1. How is wisdom defined?
2. How does a Christian's reverence for God impact his or her interpreting of creational norms and increasing in wisdom?
3. Why do people need the corrective lenses of Scripture to correctly discern creational norms?
4. How does the Bible's Wisdom Literature relate to God's law?
5. How does growing in wisdom enable Christians to realign with creational norms?

## 3.3 Redemption and Man's Chief End

A biblical ethic is not only about following the right rules. It is also about having the right goals and acting in such a way that those goals are furthered. Scripture gives Christians many goals, but these can all be boiled down to the one goal of glorifying God. God's glory is His excellence put on display, and when we glorify God, we honor and praise God for His excellence and seek to make His excellence visible to everybody.

One way to glorify God is by pursuing Christlikeness. God created humans originally as bearers of His image. This is a foundational truth, one which undergirds much of ethics. Sin has twisted that image of God in man. But Christ is the image of God, and the image of God in man is restored in us as we become more and more Christlike.

Similarly, God created man to rule over the earth under His greater rule. In and after the Fall, man has attempted to rule the world apart from God. The kingdom of God is the reign of man over the world under God's greater rule. This is ultimately fulfilled in the man Christ Jesus, but all those in Him are also to reign with Him and so fulfill God's plan for creation.

When humans pursue these goals, the result is blessedness—happiness in the richest sense of the word—human flourishing. Everybody is pursuing happiness, but when it is pursued apart from the glory of God, it is a shallow and fleeting happiness. The Christian who pursues God's way may suffer much now, but in the end he or she will flourish "like a tree planted by rivers of water" (Ps. 1:3). So in making ethical choices, the Christian should ask: Is this choice going to glorify God? Will it make me more Christlike? Will it advance God's kingdom? And will it make me a person who is happy in God?



## 3.3 Redemption and Man's Chief End

### Why do I do what I do?

### Objectives

**3.3.1** Explain man's chief end.

**3.3.2** Relate man's chief end to the pursuit of Christlikeness. BWS

**3.3.3** Relate seeking the kingdom of God to man's chief end. BWS

**3.3.4** Relate blessedness to man's chief end. BWS

### Biblical Worldview Shaping

- **Man's Chief End** (explain): Being transformed into Christ's image restores the image of God in man that was marred by the Fall. (3.3.2)
- **Man's Chief End** (explain): Seeking first the kingdom of God is seeking for all people to submit to God in every part of their lives. (3.3.3)
- **Man's Chief End** (explain): Being formed into Christ's image and seeking God's kingdom above all else are the best ways to glorify God and enjoy Him forever. (3.3.4)

### Printed Resource

- Activity 3.3: Living for God's Glory

### Suggested Reading

- Mathis, David. "We Will See His Face: What Is the Beatific Vision?" Desiring God (website), March 11, 2021.

### GOD'S GLORY AND MAN'S CHIEF END

The Bible provides a number of purposes for which God made man: to be conformed to God's image and to rule over creation under God's greater rule (Gen. 1:26–28); to delight in God's law (Ps. 1:1–3); to fear God (Prov. 1:7); to trust in God with all one's being and acknowledge Him in all one's ways (Prov. 3:5–6); to be blessed or to flourish (Ps. 1:1; Matt. 5:3–12); to walk worthy of God and do good works, which glorify the Father (Matt. 5:16; Col. 1:9–12); to seek first God's kingdom and righteousness and enter that kingdom (Matt. 5:20; 6:33); to be conformed to the Son's image for the Son's glory (Rom. 8:29); to be holy, blameless, pure, and righteous so that God receives glory (Eph. 1:3–4; Phil. 1:9–11); to be mature in Christ (Col. 1:28–29); to attain the Sabbath rest (Heb. 3–4). These various purposes are often summed up as "to glorify God, and to enjoy him forever."[12] According to Scripture, an action is considered morally good when it springs from a motive to glorify God (Matt. 5:16; 1 Cor. 10:31; 1 Pet. 4:11).

Why do I do what I do?

Knowing and enjoying God are essential to glorifying God. The tendency of the fallen human heart is to reduce morality to mere duty as though joy in God were irrelevant in the performing of our duty. But this is to rob God of His glory. A person who dutifully serves God without gladness of heart communicates that God is not worthy of service. Thus, God told the Israelites that He would hand them over to their enemies if they did not serve Him "with joyfulness, and with gladness of heart" (Deut. 28:47). That's how seriously God takes His glory and our happiness in Him.

Therefore, duty without delight is an insufficient motive for Christian ethics. It is by our delights that we show what is valuable to us, and it is by our greatest delight that we show what is most valuable to us. Since God is the most valuable being in the universe, it is only fitting that He be our greatest delight. To act morally includes acting from a genuine delight in God and His worth, which is the same as glorifying God. This is the teleology* of Christian ethics. In other words, God is not a means to some other good. He is our greatest good, and therefore He is the chief end for which we live, move, and have our being (Ps. 73:25; Acts 17:28).

*Thou madest us for Thyself, and our heart is restless, until it repose* in Thee.*

AUGUSTINE[13]

#### DEVELOPING ETHICAL SKILLS

**What If My Duty Doesn't Delight Me?**

Some may wonder whether an emphasis on delighting in God weakens duty. The argument is that doing the right thing is often difficult, and in order to fulfill our duty, we need a commitment to doing the right thing even when we don't feel like doing it. "Should people wait until they feel pleasure in God before doing their duty?" some would ask. The problem with this line of thinking is that it assumes that delighting in God is one thing and that doing our duty is another, whereas the Bible teaches that delighting in God is an important part of our duty (Ps. 37:4). It is surely true that we must do our duty even when duty calls for work that doesn't inherently delight us (or when fulfilling our obligations might cost us something). But there's a difference between delighting in God and delighting in specific tasks. In fact, that's the beauty of doing all we do for the glory of the God: even the most menial tasks become meaningful and worthy of our best efforts if we are doing them for our Creator, and living for our worthy Redeemer helps us do the right thing even when it's costly and doesn't make sense to a godless world.

**teleology:** referring to the end goal
**repose:** to lie or be at rest



## Instruct

### GOD'S GLORY AND MAN'S CHIEF END

Guide a **Bible study** about what it means to glorify God. Divide the students into four groups and direct them to look up the following Bible verses.

- Group 1: ruling over creation under God's greater rule (Gen. 1:26–28); delighting in God's law (Ps. 1:1–3); fearing God (Prov. 1:7)
- Group 2: acknowledging God in all our ways (Prov. 3:5–6); living a blessed life according to God's Word (Ps. 1:1; Matt. 5:3–12); walking worthy of God and doing good works (Matt. 5:16; Col. 1:9–12)
- Group 3: seeking God's kingdom and righteousness (Matt. 5:20; 6:33); being conformed to the image of Christ (Rom. 8:29); being holy, blameless, pure, and righteous (Eph. 1:3–4; Phil. 1:9–11)
- Group 4: being mature in Christ (Col. 1:28–29); attaining the Sabbath rest (Heb. 3–4); striving to do everything for God's glory (1 Cor. 10:31)

Encourage students to share how they can glorify God based on the verses read.

## Engage

### YOUR MOTIVATIONS MATTER

Ask the students this section's essential question to awaken them to the motivations that drive their choices in life. Use questions such as the following to encourage an honest response.

**Do you ever do the right thing for the wrong reasons?** *Since every sinner has done that, the answer should be "yes."*
**What would be some wrong reasons for serving in the church?** *Possible answers: to be seen by others, to feel superior to others, to attempt to gain salvation and forgiveness of sins*
**Why do heart motivations matter to God as much as the actions we perform?** *Our devotion to God exists at the most basic level in heart motivations. One may do many outwardly good things without devotion to God.*
**What should be our *ultimate* motivation in all that we do?** *the glory of God*
**What could be some additional acceptable motivations for our actions?** *doing good to others and seeking our own happiness in righteous ways*
**Are the pursuit of God's glory and the pursuit of our own happiness necessarily at odds with one another?** *not when the happiness we seek is found in knowing God and enjoying all things for God's glory*

## CHRISTLIKENESS AND THE KINGDOM OF GOD

Lead a **discussion** to help students understand the cost of ethical living as it relates to being like Christ.

Explain that people often think that doing the right thing will be rewarded and that doing the wrong thing will be punished. And in a society that operates according to God's Word, that is how things work.

**But what happens when a society is corrupt? What happens when those in authority reward evil and punish righteousness?**

When Jesus was arrested, Pilate gave the blood-thirsty crowd a choice. Pilate could release Jesus, the Prince of Peace and Author of Life, or he could release Barrabas, an unruly rebel and a murderer. The crowd chose Barrabas, and Pilate consented to their evil choice.

Point out that biblical history and church history are filled with periods in which the ruling authorities punished God's people for refusing to bow to the idols of the day. For example, Shadrach, Meshach, and Abednego refused to bow to Nebuchadnezzar's golden image, and they were thrown into a fiery furnace as a result; yet God rescued them (Dan. 3). Also, one thinks of persecutions of Christians during the reign of the Roman emperors.

To follow Christ and to choose righteousness over evil in our own day may come at a cost. It may be a financial cost, as when a business in the marriage industry is penalized for refusing to participate in a same-sex wedding.

Whatever the cost may be for living ethically, Christians should remember that they are called to be like Christ. Specifically, Christians should consider Christ's pattern of humiliation and exaltation. It can be difficult to suffer for doing what is right, but such was the life of our Master.

**If Christ suffered for doing what pleased God, should His servants expect any different?**

The good news is that God will one day reward His people by granting them a share in Christ's exaltation. The day is coming when righteousness will cover the earth and evil will finally be punished.

## ETHICS AND THE KINGDOM OF GOD

Instruct students to create a **T-Chart** to compare the values of the kingdom of God with the values of the world. Use the Beatitudes in Matthew 5:3–12 for this activity. On one side of the chart, instruct students to list the values of the kingdom of God. On the other side students should list the values of the world. Mention that the world's values will be the opposite of God's values. The following is an example of a completed chart.

| GOD'S VALUES | WORLD'S VALUES |
|---|---|
| **1.** poor in spirit, humility | **1.** boast in your accomplishments |
| **2.** mourning, godly sorrow | **2.** self-pity or indifference |
| **3.** meekness | **3.** ruthless ambition |
| **4.** hunger and thirst for righteousness | **4.** hunger and thirst for material gain |
| **5.** mercy, forgiveness | **5.** holding grudges, vengeance |
| **6.** pure in heart | **6.** lust for power, pleasure, and position |
| **7.** being a peacemaker without compromising truth | **7.** superficial peace at the expense of truth or causing strife to get ahead |
| **8.** suffering for Christ's sake | **8.** preferring temporary comfort over doing the right thing |

### CHRISTLIKENESS AND THE KINGDOM OF GOD

Christian ethics measures the good by considering what leads to the honor and glory of God. For our purposes, we'll consider two ways Christians are called to honor God. The first is by being conformed to the likeness of Christ, and the second is by pursuing Christ's kingdom instead of the values of the world. Honoring God is not limited to these two areas, but these are two important areas that relate to man's chief end.

#### *Christlikeness*

As God's image-bearers, we were created to prioritize the glory of God above everything. Since Christ is "the image of the invisible God" (Col. 1:15), He is well suited to restore human beings to their original purpose. Christians are gradually restored as God's image-bearers by regularly beholding God's glory in the face of His Son (2 Cor. 3:18; 4:5–6).

To be like Christ is to find satisfaction in doing the will of God (John 4:34). This points to a vital principle in Christian ethics. Walking the path of obedience will at times be costly to our personal comfort. The degree to which Christians are motivated by the glory of God is the degree to which they will gladly sacrifice personal comfort in doing the will of God.

Being satisfied in God doesn't mean that we avoid the path of pain; it means that we draw strength to endure adversity from our satisfaction in God. Even Jesus chose to endure crucifixion "for the joy that was set before him" (Heb. 12:2). He likewise motivated His disciples to endure temporary hardships with the promise of everlasting joy (Matt. 5:10–12).

Therefore, pursuing Christlikeness entails following Him in His humiliation* in the assurance of one day sharing in His exaltation* (Matt. 16:24; Rom. 8:17). When faced with the choice between personal comfort and faithfulness to God, we should choose faithfulness to God (Luke 9:58; Rev. 2:10). This response glorifies God because it reflects the way Christ responded throughout His earthly life.

#### *The Kingdom of God*

Part of the challenge of Christian ethics is learning how to live in the world without adopting the values of the world (John 17:14–17). An ethical person is one who correctly perceives the true value of things based on a biblical evaluation. He or she understands that not everything in the world that glitters is gold and that the things of God appear unattractive to the undiscerning. While the things of this world can be deceptively attractive, Christians can—by the grace of God—resist their allure because they've discovered in the kingdom of God the "pearl of great price" (Matt. 13:46).

**humiliation:** the appointed path of suffering that Christ endured as His people's representative head and the pattern of life to which Christians are called as His faithful followers

**exaltation:** the triumphant end to an obedient life of humiliation, which Christ experienced in His resurrection and enthronement and which He secured as the destiny for His believing people

56 FOUNDATIONS FOR ETHICS

The **kingdom of God** refers to the reign of the risen and enthroned Lord Jesus Christ. The kingdom of God includes Christ bringing the saints to fulfill the Creation Mandate as well so that they rule the creation as God intended. In 1 John 2:15, the phrase "things that are in the world" refers to the various forms of thinking and living that are in opposition to Christ's reign. These include "the lust of the flesh, and the lust of the eyes, and the pride of life" (1 John 2:16), all of which describe a life dominated by the senses and the pursuit of self-centered pleasure. Since glorifying God means making much of Him, what better way for us to make much of God than by pursuing His kingdom over the fleeting pleasures of this world?

Entrance into the kingdom through faith in Christ is the beginning of a lifelong pursuit of the kingdom of God (Matt. 6:33). Learning how to live as citizens of the kingdom does not happen all at once. The ethics of the kingdom are counterintuitive to our fallen nature. For instance, those who are blessed in the eyes of heaven are poor in spirit, they mourn their sin, and they hunger and thirst for righteousness (Matt. 5:3–4, 6). Known as the Beatitudes,* the sayings of Jesus in Matthew 5:3–12 exalt character traits that are the opposite of what the world esteems. And yet, what makes these character traits attractive in believers is that they draw attention to the worth of Christ and His redemptive work.

"But lay up for yourselves treasures in heaven, where neither moth nor rust doth corrupt, and where thieves do not break through nor steal: for where your treasure is, there will your heart be also."
Matthew 6:20–21

### BLESSEDNESS AND MAN'S CHIEF END

It's interesting to observe how Jesus motivated ethical living. He wasn't reticent to warn people of the dangers of an unethical life, yet His preference seemed to have been setting before believers the unfathomable blessings awaiting those who live for the kingdom of God rather than for the lusts of the world. "Blessed are the meek: for they shall inherit the earth," He said (Matt. 5:5). And "Blessed are the pure in heart: for they shall see God" (Matt. 5:8).

The word translated *blessed* can also be translated as *happy*, and it refers to God's favor upon His people, which is the source of all their happiness. The biblical perspective on happiness includes human flourishing in the physical world. As the above Beatitudes indicate, the chief privilege of the redeemed will be to behold God's glory in the new creation as they rule with Christ.

#### *Blessedness: Inheriting the Earth*

Christ has promised that His people will inherit the earth, which means they will rule forever with Him in the new creation. This future state of blessedness is the spiritual birthright of every believer (Gal. 3:29; 4:7), and it directly relates to man's chief end. God's original purpose was for His image-bearers to glorify Him by ruling the earth under His sovereign reign and provision (Gen. 1:26–28). Despite the disruptive impact of the Fall on man's rule, God's purpose will be fully restored when Christ returns to be glorified in His people (2 Thess. 1:10).

Meanwhile, our current situation is one in which Christians suffer many wrongs. When this happens, it doesn't feel like a state of blessedness; it feels more like being on the losing side of history. Instead of retaliating against those who wrong us, the Christian ethic challenges us to respond with meekness.

Meekness is the ethical virtue that Jesus commends in the third beatitude. It refers to the "moral quality of humility and gentleness, usually exhibited during suffering or difficulty and accompanied by faith in God."[14] Although it currently looks as though the earth goes to the ruthlessly ambitious, the surprising turnabout is that it eventually goes to the meek. Jesus guarantees it. Therefore, Christians can experience blessedness here and now as they await that coming day.

**Beatitudes:** the supreme blessings that Jesus pronounced upon His believing people in the Sermon on the Mount



## Apply

### BLESSEDNESS AND MAN'S CHIEF END

Have students create a **scenario** to relate the Christian's future world of blessedness with living ethically in the present world.

In the scenario, one student is finding it difficult to live a biblically ethical life, while the other student is there to provide the struggling student with answers. Students could work in groups to create the backstory and details and then brainstorm to come up with answers similar to the suggested content below.

Since doing the right thing is often difficult, Christians may wonder how they can persist in living an ethical life. The more familiar believers are with the future world awaiting them and the more confident they are that it is coming soon, the better equipped they will be to endure hardships in the pathway of obedience to God. Two realities of the future world are especially worthy of constant remembrance: (1) living in a morally and physically perfect world, reigning with Christ, and (2) seeing and enjoying the glory of God in the face of Christ.

Both realities are promised to all believers. Just as runners focus on the prize that awaits them at the finish line as a means of motivating them in the race, so Christians should focus on their glorious future as a means of motivating them in their ethical choices. The hardships of this life are temporary, but the joys of the life to come are eternal. One may ask whether it is even possible for a Christian to remain faithful unto death without keeping these realities in view all the time. It would seem unlikely. The temptations to compromise are too great and too many to be resisted by anything less than the hope of a blessed future with Christ. Therefore, it is essential to nurture our faith in God's promise about these realities if we are to persist in an ethical life that pleases the Lord. To do that we must treasure God above everything this world has to offer, and we must hold on to the promises of God: the promises of inheriting the earth and seeing God face-to-face.

### LIVING FOR GOD'S GLORY

Use **Activity 3.3** on pages 17–18 to apply the information in this section.

## Assess

Guide a **summative assessment** by directing students to answer the questions in Thinking It Through 3.3.

### Thinking It Through 3.3

1. According to Scripture, an action is considered morally good when it springs from a motive to glorify God (Matt. 5:16; 1 Pet. 4:11).
2. A person who dutifully serves God without gladness of heart communicates that God is not worthy of service. To act morally is to act from a genuine delight in God and His worth, which is the same as glorifying God. Moreover, the Bible teaches that delighting in God is our duty (Ps. 37:4).
3. Christians are gradually restored as God's image-bearers by regularly beholding the glory of God in the face of Christ (2 Cor. 3:18; 4:5–6).
4. Being satisfied in God doesn't mean that we avoid the path of pain; it means that we draw strength to endure adversity from our satisfaction in God. Even Jesus chose to endure crucifixion for the joy that was set before Him (Heb. 12:2). He likewise motivated His disciples to endure temporary hardships with the promise of everlasting joy (Matt. 5:10–12).
5. Part of the challenge of Christian ethics is learning how to live in the world without adopting the values of the world (John 17:14–17). While the things of this world can be deceptively attractive, Christians can—by the grace of God—resist their allure because they've discovered in the kingdom of God the "pearl of great price" (Matt. 13:45–46). Since glorifying God means making much of Him, what better way for us to make much of God than by pursuing His kingdom over the fleeting pleasures of this world.
6. They draw attention to the worth of Christ and His redemptive work.
7. The chief privilege of the redeemed will be to behold God's glory in the new creation as they rule with Christ.
8. The consummation of redemption is when believers see God face-to-face (Rev. 22:4). Instead of hiding from Him as Adam and Eve did after they sinned in the garden (Gen. 3:8), Christians will dwell in the holy presence of God and never feel the slightest inclination to hide from Him (Rev. 21:3). This is the blessed life for which we were made but then lost because of our sin. Christ has come and recovered all this for us.

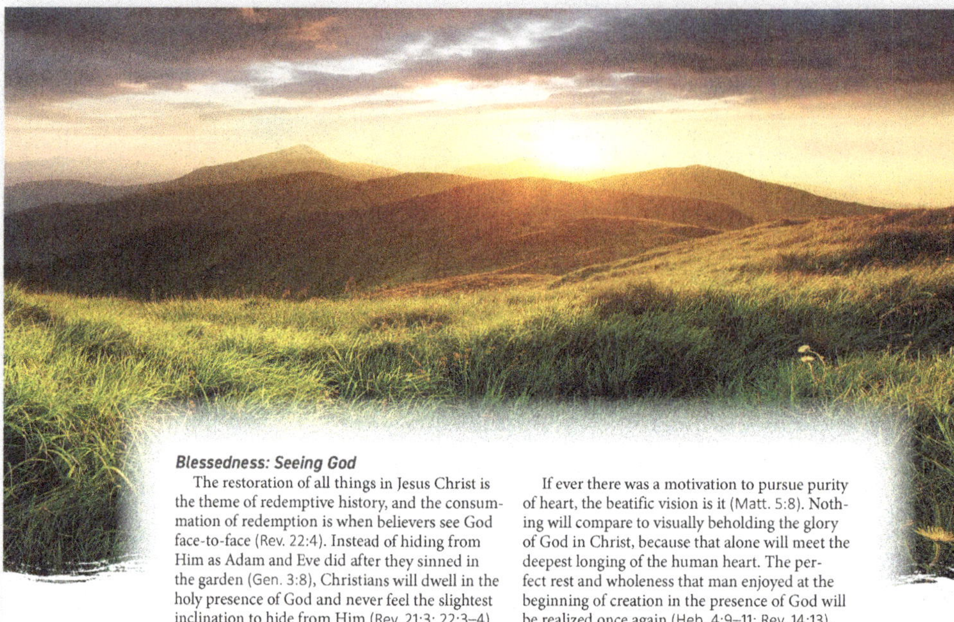

***Blessedness: Seeing God***

The restoration of all things in Jesus Christ is the theme of redemptive history, and the consummation of redemption is when believers see God face-to-face (Rev. 22:4). Instead of hiding from Him as Adam and Eve did after they sinned in the garden (Gen. 3:8), Christians will dwell in the holy presence of God and never feel the slightest inclination to hide from Him (Rev. 21:3; 22:3–4). This is all the more stunning when we recall that God told Moses that no man can see His face and live (Exod. 33:20).

**beatific vision:** "the sight that makes happy,"[16] specifically the direct sight of God Himself, which believers will experience in their glorified state

By faith Christians currently behold the glory of God in the face of Christ (2 Cor. 3:18). But one day faith will give way to sight. Then our eyes will look upon Him with the greatest satisfaction, and we will experience what Christians call the **beatific vision**.* We cannot imagine what this immediate sight of God will be like, but we do know that Jesus Christ is central to the beatific vision. There's no sight of God apart from Him (John 14:8–9; Col. 1:15).[15]

If ever there was a motivation to pursue purity of heart, the beatific vision is it (Matt. 5:8). Nothing will compare to visually beholding the glory of God in Christ, because that alone will meet the deepest longing of the human heart. The perfect rest and wholeness that man enjoyed at the beginning of creation in the presence of God will be realized once again (Heb. 4:9–11; Rev. 14:13). But this inheritance, according to Jesus, belongs to the pure in heart.

God is the believer's greatest inheritance for now and for eternity (Pss. 16:5; 73:26). Seeking to be Christlike, to advance God's kingdom, and to flourish (now and eternally)—all for the glory of God—these are essential parts of ethical decision-making. This is the blessed life for which we were made but then lost because of our sin. Christ has come and recovered all of this for us.

### Thinking It Through 3.3

1. According to Scripture, what motive is necessary in order for an action to be morally good?
2. Why is it impossible to dutifully serve God without also delighting in Him?
3. How does God's glory revealed in Christ help to restore Christians as God's image-bearers?
4. How does being motivated by the glory of God and the enjoyment of God enable Christians to be like Christ?
5. How does being motivated by the glory of God and the enjoyment of God enable Christians to pursue the kingdom of God over the things of the world?
6. How do the character traits commended in the Beatitudes glorify God when they are manifested in a believer's life?
7. Based on the Beatitudes regarding the meek and the pure in heart, what will be the chief privilege of the redeemed?
8. How does the redemption accomplished by Christ relate to the blessing of seeing God?

58 FOUNDATIONS FOR ETHICS

THE ROLE OF REDEMPTION IN ETHICS

# Review 03

### Terms to Remember

- volunteerist perspective
- covenantal identity
- wisdom
- kingdom of God
- beatific vision

### Scripture Memory

Colossians 3:1–3, 12

### Understanding Ethics

1. Summarize how God's character and God's law should inform our ethics.
2. Explain why redemption is necessary for ethical living.
3. Explain why humility before the Creator is necessary to wisely discern creational norms.
4. Summarize how the New Covenant promise of the Spirit and the grammar of the gospel help Christians to obey God's law.

### Practicing Ethical Decision-Making

5. Scripture has a lot to say about money, but it doesn't tell us whether we should purchase one brand of tennis shoes or another. How would you respond in the following situation?

   You're interested in purchasing a new pair of tennis shoes, but the ones you want are manufactured by a company that uses slave labor.

6. How might you utilize the biblical teaching regarding the Christian's new identity in Christ to address the following situation?

   Suppose a new Christian is tempted to lie to his parents. He used to lie to them regularly because he feared their rejection. He comes to you for advice on how he can be truthful with them.

### Analyzing and Evaluating Ethical Claims

7. How would you respond to the claim that God's law is too restrictive of human freedom and that the only reason God imposes His law is because He wants to withhold good things from people?
8. How would you respond to the claim that Christians are not obligated to keep God's law because they are under grace?
9. How would you respond to the claim that a desire to help people is the only motive necessary for a deed to be considered morally good?
10. How would you respond to the claim that a blessed life only relates to spiritual blessings and does not have anything to do with Christians ruling on the earth?

### Creating My Own Position Statements on Ethics

11. Summarize your own position on whether people need Scripture to accurately discern creational norms for ethical living.
12. Summarize your own position on the best way to motivate ethical living.

THE ROLE OF REDEMPTION IN ETHICS 59

# Chapter 3 Review

## Terms to Remember

- **volunteerist perspective:** The belief that God's law is simply whatever He wills it to be and that right and wrong could have been opposite what they are, merely at God's whim.
- **covenantal identity:** Who a person is—based not on individual characteristics but based on his or her relationship to a representative head whom God established, either Adam or Christ.
- **wisdom:** The art of living well by observing creational norms through the lenses of Scripture, by listening to the counsel of the wise, and by being conscious that all life is lived before the face of God.
- **kingdom of God:** The reign of the risen and enthroned Lord Jesus Christ; includes Christ bringing the saints to fulfill the Creation Mandate as well, so that they rule the creation as God intended.
- **beatific vision:** "The sight that makes happy," (David Mathis, "We Will See His Face") specifically the direct sight of God Himself, which believers will experience in their glorified state.

## Understanding Ethics

1. Our ethics depends on having an absolute standard of right and wrong. God has revealed the standard to humanity in His law, which reflects His holy character.
2. Redemption is necessary for ethical living because fallen humans cannot sincerely obey God's law apart from the person and work of Christ.
3. Fallen humans' prideful condition leads them to think they can decide for themselves right from wrong. Humility recognizes the Creator's right to determine these things, which is the starting point for wisely discerning creational norms.
4. Christians are not alone in their efforts to keep God's law; the Spirit who writes the law upon their hearts is present to help them obey. The grammar of the gospel helps Christians obey by grounding their obedience in the atoning work of Christ on their behalf.

## Practicing Ethical Decision-Making

5. Answers should be based on a biblical view of labor, not one's personal desire for the shoes.
6. Answers should emphasize that because the believer's new identity is in Christ, he or she doesn't need to fear other people anymore.

## Analyzing and Evaluating Ethical Claims

7. Answers should highlight God's good character as the source of His law. To suggest that God gave His law because He wants to withhold good things from people runs contrary to God's character.
8. Answers should stress that grace liberates Christians to obey God's law. To suggest that grace renders obedience to God's law irrelevant contradicts Scripture and the New Covenant promise of the Spirit who writes God's law upon believers' hearts.
9. Answers should point out that many people perform seemingly good deeds without an aim to glorify God. Because such deeds ultimately dishonor God, they cannot ultimately be considered morally good.
10. Answer should point to the biblical promises of physical blessings. Denying the physical blessings of the future eternal state is to reject the biblical promises.

## Creating My Own Position Statements on Ethics

11. Students should answer based on their honest response to the lesson.
12. Students should answer based on their honest response to the lesson.

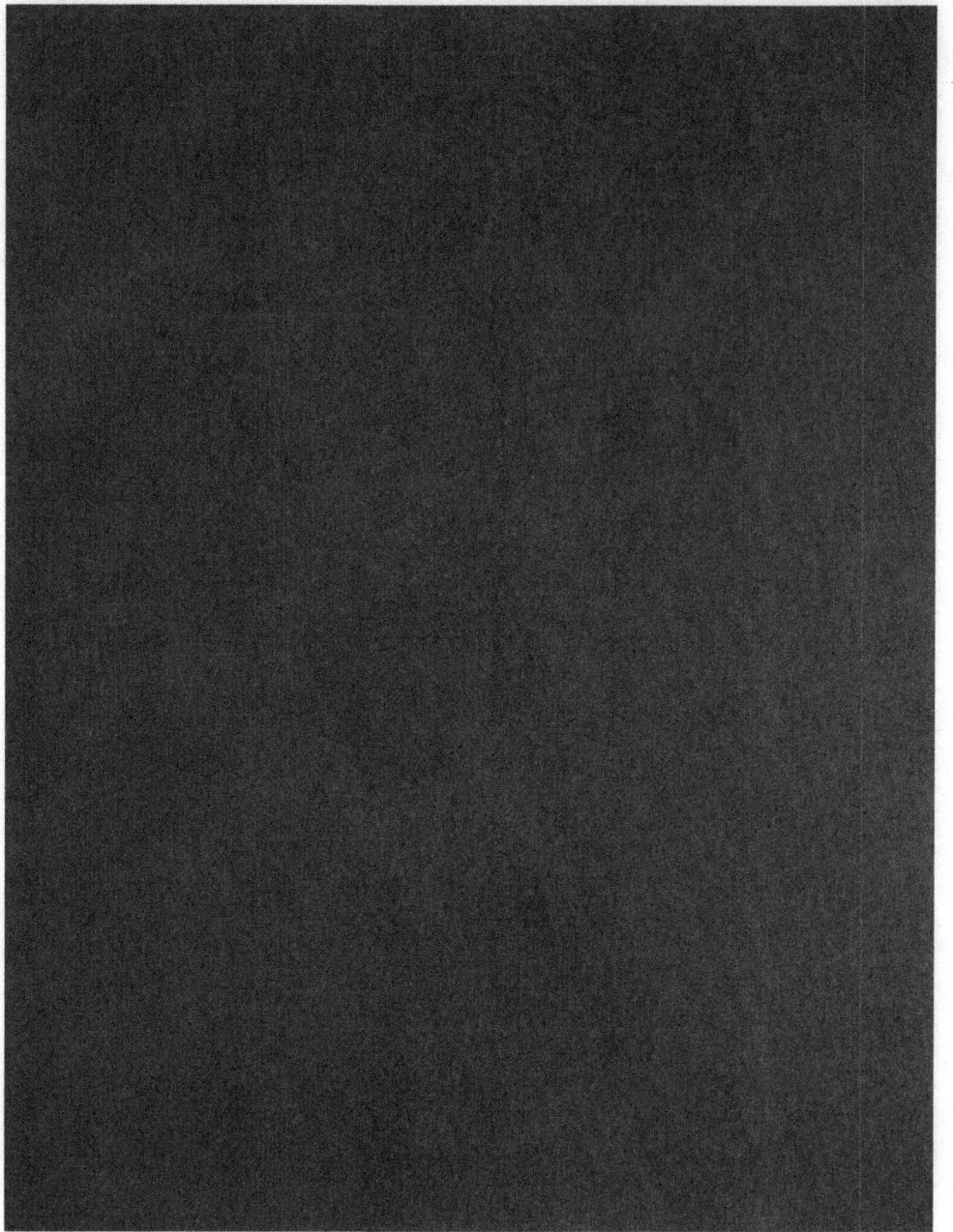

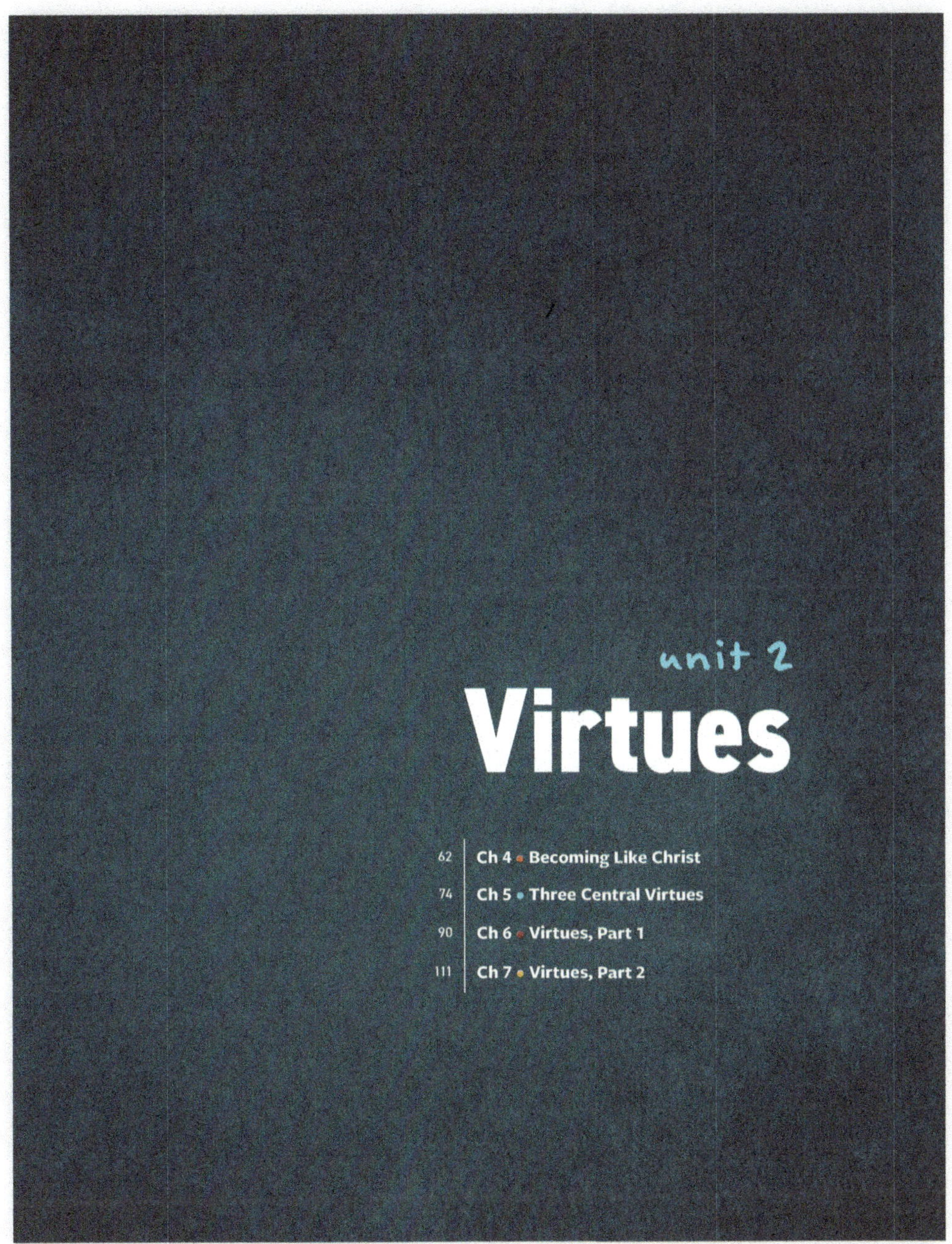

unit 2

# Virtues

# Lesson Plan Overview

**CHAPTER 4:** Becoming Like Christ

**EV** ExamView
**IA** Instructional Aid
**PPT pres.** PowerPoint presentation

| PAGES | OBJECTIVES | RESOURCES | ASSESSMENTS |
|---|---|---|---|
| **4.1 Virtues and Vices** (3 DAYS) | | | |
| 63–66 | **4.1.1** Define *virtue* and *vice*.<br>**4.1.2** Identify virtues and vices.<br>**4.1.3** Analyze the place for virtue in biblical ethics.<br>BWS Virtue (explain) | **ACTIVITIES**<br>• 4.1 The Important Place of Virtue in the Bible<br>**BJU PRESS TROVE***<br>• Video: "Virtue"<br>• PPT pres.: Chapter 4 | **STUDENT EDITION**<br>• Thinking It Through 4.1 |
| **4.2 Christlikeness and Counterfeits** (3 DAYS) | | | |
| 66–72 | **4.2.1** Explain the importance of Christlikeness to growing in virtue.<br>BWS Man's Chief End (explain)<br>**4.2.2** Relate union with Christ to developing Christian virtue.<br>**4.2.3** Explain the role of the Holy Spirit in virtuous living.<br>**4.2.4** Distinguish Christian integrity from legalism, moralism, and authenticity.<br>BWS Virtue (evaluate)<br>**4.2.5** Formulate a plan for living virtuously.<br>BWS Virtue (apply) | **TEACHER EDITION**<br>• IA 4.2: *Counterfeits and Integrity Chart*<br>**ACTIVITIES**<br>• 4.2 Practicing the Spiritual Disciplines<br>**BJU PRESS TROVE**<br>• PPT pres.: Chapter 4 | **STUDENT EDITION**<br>• Thinking It Through 4.2 |
| **Review** | | | |
| 73 | Recall concepts, terms, and Scripture memory from Chapter 4. | | **STUDENT EDITION**<br>• Chapter 4 Review |
| **Test** | | | |
| | Demonstrate knowledge of the material from Chapter 4 by taking the test. | | **ASSESSMENTS**<br>• Chapter 4 Test<br>**BJU PRESS TROVE**<br>• EV: Chapter 4 test bank |

*Digital resources for homeschool users are available on Homeschool Hub.

**CHAPTER 4**

# Overview

*What makes Christian ethics unique?*

## Objectives

**4.1** Analyze the relationship between virtue and ethics.

**4.2** Assess the importance of Christlikeness to the development of virtue.

### Terms to Remember

- virtue
- vice
- legalism
- moralism
- authenticity

### Scripture Memory

- 2 Peter 1:3, 5–7

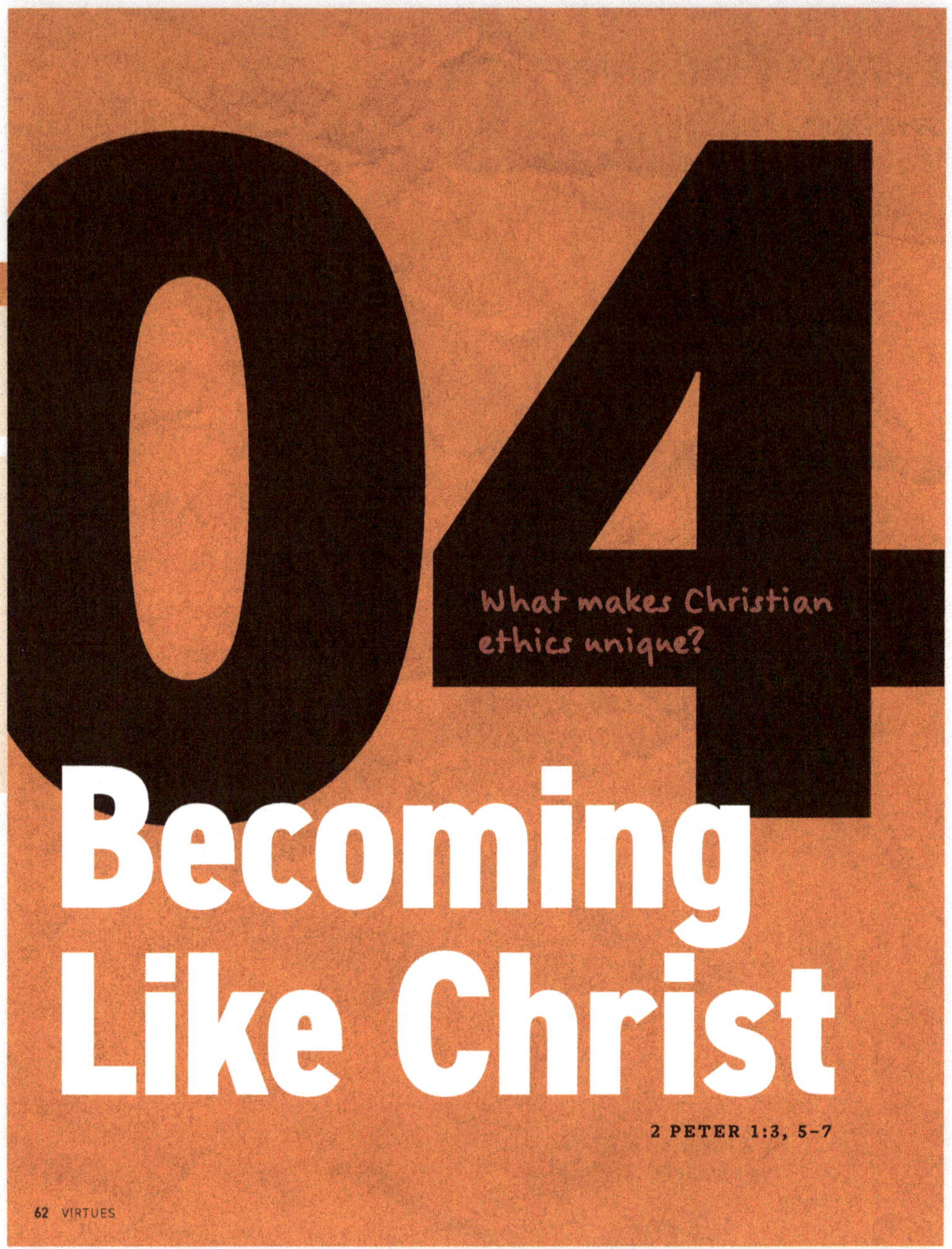

04
What makes Christian ethics unique?
Becoming Like Christ
2 PETER 1:3, 5-7
62 VIRTUES

## 4.1 Virtues and Vices

### DEFINING VIRTUE

Has anyone ever told you that patience is a virtue? Perhaps someone said it in jest because you were grumbling about having to wait longer than expected. But what does that saying even mean? What is a virtue?

The Greek word for virtue (*aretē*) can be found five times (in three passages) in the New Testament (Phil. 4:8; 1 Pet. 2:9; 2 Pet. 1:3, 5). But the *concept* is found throughout Scripture (see Gal. 5:19–23). The Bible calls us to be virtuous by emphasizing that a virtuous person is one of excellent moral character[1]—being righteous, godly, and Christlike. In fact, the two Great Commandments—to love God and to love others—are commands to be virtuous by reflecting God's character, the source of all virtue.

Originally, the word *virtue* related to a person excelling in any number of ways, including accomplishing a task such as a well-built (virtuous) boat. Eventually, one of the most common uses of the word had to do with mastering or achieving excellence in particular character qualities. In the ancient Greek culture, this moral excellence was usually understood as the result of a person's own effort to produce these qualities in himself or herself; thus, the person merited praise for being so excellent or virtuous. A person became renowned (obtained glory) for being virtuous (excelling in good character).[2]

In contrast, Christians look to God in order to become virtuous. God, through the gracious working of the Spirit (who unites us to Christ and lives in us), gets all the credit for anything good about who Christians *are* or what they *do* (Phil. 2:13; Gal. 2:20). Nevertheless, Christians are exhorted to diligently and actively make every effort to cultivate excellent (virtuous) character traits. God gets the credit for enabling our efforts (2 Pet. 1:5; see also Phil. 2:12). When the Holy Spirit was granted to us, transforming our nature, we were given all that we needed for godliness. In fact, our calling is to reflect "the praises" (*aretē*: excellencies) of our God to a watching world (1 Pet. 2:9; see also Matt. 5:16). All this is in the context of being distinct from a world driven by lust for vices (Phil. 4:8; 1 Pet. 2:11–12).

BECOMING LIKE CHRIST 63

## Engage

### VIRTUE

Show the **video** "Virtue" to introduce the subject to students.

### TRANSFORMED TO BE VIRTUOUS

Guide a **visual analysis** of the diagram on page 63.

**What is the significance of each part of the diagram?** *The sun represents God in His glory. The cross represents Christ and His work. The dove represents the Spirit and His work in the believer. The triangle represents the Trinitarian God. The dotted line shows the work of all three persons affecting a believer (from God as source through Christ's accomplishment by the Spirit's application). The cross within the person shows Christ's transforming work within the believer and the shadowed cross on the ground shows that that internal transformation will be reflected in external ways as a witness.*

**What is the importance of the truths pictured in the diagram in relation to the topic of virtue in ethics?** *One example would be that a virtuous person must credit all three persons of the Trinity as the source of his or her virtue. Another example would be that one's internal virtue is evidenced externally in transformed living (ethics).*

## 4.1 Virtues and Vices

Why do virtues matter?

### Objectives

**4.1.1** Define *virtue* and *vice*.

**4.1.2** Identify virtues and vices.

**4.1.3** Analyze the place for virtue in biblical ethics. *BWS*

### Biblical Worldview Shaping

- **Virtue** (explain): God's goal is not merely to have people do the right thing but to become the right kind of person. (4.1.3)

### Printed Resource

- Activity 4.1: The Important Place of Virtue in the Bible

### Digital Resource

- Video: "Virtue"

### Suggested Reading

- Berg, Jim. *Essential Virtues: Marks of the Christ-Centered Life*. Greenville, SC: JourneyForth, 2008.
- Davis, Andrew M. *An Infinite Journey: Growing Toward Christlikeness*. Greenville, SC: Ambassador International, 2014.
- Frame, John M. *The Doctrine of the Christian Life*. Phillipsburg, NJ: P&R Publishing, 2008. Pages 317–84.
- Grudem, Wayne. *Christian Ethics: An Introduction to Biblical Moral Reasoning*. Wheaton, IL: Crossway, 2018. Pages 107–14.
- Powlison, David. *How Does Sanctification Work?* Wheaton, IL: Crossway, 2017.

For the Christian, **virtue** can be defined as rightly ordered love.[3] Everything we do is motivated by love (properly directed or misdirected). What we love directs our commitments. If we are committed to the right things according to the right priorities, then we are virtuous. Since Christ is the source and enabler of our virtue, virtuous character entails reflecting Christ, motivated by a love for Him. And this sums up the ultimate goal of every Christian: to glorify God by being like Christ (Rom. 8:29; see also Matt. 22:37–40).

> *A virtue ethic that is Christian will focus on a description of the regenerate heart.*
> JOHN FRAME[4]

This ultimate goal should direct all Christian ethics. What we do must be directed by who we are. Becoming *who we ought to be* can only be accomplished by the internal transformation resulting from Christ in us. And "Christ in us" comes through the redemptive work of God when we accept the gospel. The gospel works itself out in ethical living (Eph. 2:10; 4:13, 20; Phil. 2:12–13; James 2:14–26) because true repentance (stemming from true transformation) bears fruit (Luke 3:8). Just as the fruit of a tree evidences what kind of tree it is, so also our actions evidence what kind of people we are (Prov. 20:11; Matt. 7:16–17; 12:35).

A true Christian will be motivated by a whole web of virtues, reflecting Christlikeness. It is not enough to do the right thing outwardly; God examines the heart motivations as well (Deut. 6:5–6; Matt. 22:37; 23:5). Apart from Christ, the unbeliever will lack the power to be consistently and genuinely virtuous. When the unbeliever is in some sense virtuous, all credit goes to the restraining work of the Holy Spirit (God's common grace) and the image of God remaining in that person.

### DEFINING VICE

The word **vice** generally refers to a character trait or behavior that is recognizably wicked or immoral. Someone who is characterized by a vice has been overcome by a particular destructive habit. When bad behavior characterizes a person, those actions evidence the internal heart of that person (just as virtue is a matter of the heart). Vice is a deviation from God's upright standard (Gal. 6:1). The Bible speaks of the crooked person (Prov. 3:32; 11:3, 6; 21:8). This is the person characterized by vice—the opposite of the upright person.

A vice could be the exact opposite of a virtue. But it could also be the twisting of a virtue into something that appears like a virtue at first but in the end is a counterfeit. Often, "the prince of the power of the air" (Eph. 2:2) takes the second, more deceptive, approach; this world's system touts a virtue (like love, justice, or compassion) but misdefines or misapplies it. Or someone accomplishes a moral end but does so for the wrong reason. If someone has selfish motives for doing the right thing, is that person virtuous (Prov. 15:8; Matt. 6:1–8)?

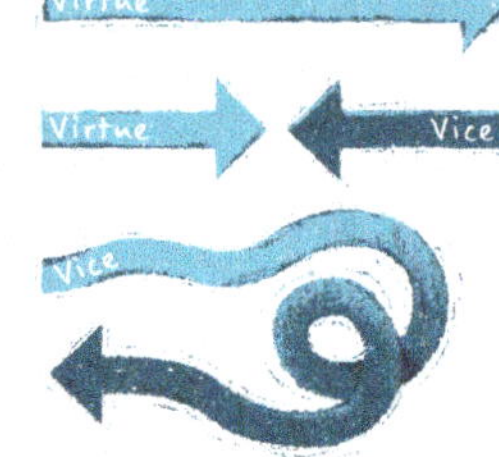


In Chapters 5–7, you will be studying various virtues and vices. You will have to carefully examine the meaning, motives, and ends associated with each virtue in order to rightly understand each and to avoid vices that are portrayed as virtues. Then in Chapters 9–13, you will be grappling with specific ethical issues. When you do, one key will be to evaluate the motives of people in various situations. Are they truly motivated by virtue? Or do they portray themselves as virtuous while succumbing to vice?

At this juncture you may be wondering to yourself why one character trait or action should be considered a virtue and another a vice. Why is "good" good and "bad" bad? Is it random? Do societies choose (and change the definitions in each new



## Instruct

### UNDERSTANDING VIRTUE

Guide a **discussion** about the term *virtue* in order to clarify what it is and how it comes about.

**What are three key passages in which the term *virtue* (*arete* sometimes translated as "excellence" or "praise") is used in the Bible? Allow the students time to look for and read through the passages and then answer.**

- *Philippians 4:8 is encouraging Christians to dwell on things that are virtuous or morally excellent in character. They should not be filling their lives with things that are characterized by vice.*
- *1 Peter 2:9 describes Christians as people who should be characterized by a public witness that reflects God's own morally excellent or virtuous character. God's people should be like Him.*
- *2 Peter 1:3, 5 declares that the believer's calling is to virtue or moral excellence. Thus, those growing in sanctification will build on their faith virtuous character as evidence of God's transforming work and calling.*

**Although the term *virtue* is used only a few times, what are some other biblical concepts that parallel this call to virtue? What are some example Scripture passages? (Students may do a word search of the terms with a Bible software program.)** *Whenever the Bible calls on Christians to be godly, it is calling on them to be virtuous because God and His righteousness are the source and standard of virtue. Examples might include Titus 2:12, Colossians 3:10, and James 1:20.*

**How was the term *virtue* used historically? How is it used in the Bible? Why is this an important distinction?** *The historical use had to do with achieving excellence in character by one's own efforts. In contrast, Christians look to God to become virtuous as they actively cultivate excellence. This distinction is important because God must receive the credit for the good we do (Phil. 2:13; Gal. 2:20).*

**In the context of Christian ethics, how should the term *virtue* be defined? Why is this important in relation to ethics?** *It should be defined as rightly ordered love (Augustine,* City of God *15.22, trans. Marcus Dods, with an introduction by Thomas Merton [New York: Modern Library, 1993], 511.). Virtue is reflecting Christ in all we do, motivated by a love for Him. The ultimate goal of glorifying God by being like Christ should direct all Christian ethics.*

**What is the only way for a person to become truly virtuous? How can you explain the seemingly virtuous actions of the unbeliever?** *By having Christ in us through the internal transforming work of the gospel; the image of God remains in the unbelievers, and common grace restrains their sins.*

### UNDERSTANDING VICE

Use a **Turn and Talk** to prompt students to collaborate on answers based on the textbook.

**What is a vice? What's the source of vice? In what two ways does vice contrast with virtue? Who decides whether something is a virtue or a vice, and could it be any other way? Why shouldn't you glory in vice?** *See pages 64–65 to evaluate student answers.*

### DEFINING VIRTUES

Guide a **discussion** about obtaining a knowledge of virtues so that students recognize the importance of all of God's Word and of the necessary internal transformation that comes from personally knowing God through Christ.

**Where do we look to obtain a knowledge of what the virtues are in contrast to the vices?** *God's Word, which reveals God's character*

**Is the Old Testament irrelevant to the New Testament Christian's ethical living? Why or why not?** *No, the Old Testament remains relevant because it reveals God's unchanging character even though He was dealing*

generation)? Is it all just perspective? Maybe you do believe that God decides. But could God have chosen the opposite to be good?

The Bible gives clear answers to all the above questions. Virtue and vice are determined by God's own unchanging righteous character. Good matches up with who God is and with His design for this world. His design was created for our well-being. So, to behave badly is to be destructive to ourselves, to hurt others, and to blaspheme God through our selfish and prideful idolatry (which is what all sin is at its root). There is no virtue in choosing to be a person of vice. You will only destroy yourself and others in your rebellion. And God, the righteous Judge, will be victorious in the end. You should tremble in fear to even consider glorying in vice (Prov. 1:22–33; Heb. 10:26–31; 12:29; see also 2 Cor. 5:11).

### IDENTIFYING VIRTUES AND VICES

How can we find out what the virtues are? Where do we look to obtain such knowledge? Identifying the virtues comes through knowing God and His Word. He has revealed Himself, His character, through His self-revelation. The Old Testament remains important for ethics as a revelation of the unchanging God and His dealings with a particular people in a particular place. The Old Testament provides a value system. The Gospels emphasize the need for inward transformation to internalize that value system into our character. And the Epistles provide doctrinal explanations and direct instruction on how to behave in the church age. But above all, God has revealed Himself (His character) through His Son, Jesus Christ. God has supplied all that we need to be virtuous in Christ Jesus (2 Pet. 1:3). The promise found in 2 Peter 1:10–11 is the climax to the exhortations to put on the virtues in 2 Peter 1:5–8.

In Chapters 5–7, you will survey some of the virtues identified in God's Word. You will also encounter many vices, which contrast with these virtues. This survey is not exhaustive. But these virtues and vices play a major role in ethical decision-making. Thus, when you grapple with the issues in Chapters 9–13, these virtues and vices will play a major role in your analysis of what should be done in a situation.

| VIRTUES | VICES |
|---|---|
| faith | unbelief |
| love | lust, hate |
| hope | despair |
| righteousness | ungodliness |
| goodness | corruption |
| prudence | rashness, cunning |
| diligence | sloth, laziness |
| faithfulness | disloyalty |
| courage | recklessness, cowardice |
| self-control | self-indulgence, addiction |
| temperance | addiction, asceticism |
| patience | strife |
| humility | pride |
| meekness | anger |
| gentleness | harshness |
| kindness | cruelty |
| compassion | indifference |
| gratitude | ingratitude |
| joy | despair |
| peace | worry |
| honesty | dishonesty, falsehood |

### UNDERSTANDING THE IMPORTANCE OF VIRTUE IN CHRISTIAN ETHICS

Why do virtues matter?

In Section 2.2 you learned about virtue ethics, and in Section 2.3 you learned about the problems with certain forms of the virtue-ethics approach. But the problems with that approach should not lead us to reject the important place for Christian virtue ethics. The problems that can arise in virtue ethics are removed when the virtues are properly defined, described, and applied by moral norms found in the Bible and in the design of God's creation. The problems are removed when the source of virtue is the transforming work of the gospel (Christ in us).



*with a particular people in a particular place with a different responsibility under the Old Covenant. The Old Testament still provides a value system rooted in God's character (2 Tim. 3:16–17).*

**What fact do the Gospels emphasize regarding the value system that the Old Testament illustrates?** *People need to be inwardly transformed in their character to live out that value system. The Gospels do not overturn that value system but emphasize the need to internalize it by the work of Christ.*

**What value do the Epistles provide for directing the Christian ethic?** *They provide doctrinal explanations (indicatives) that ground the instructions (imperatives) for how to live in the current church age.*

**What, or who, is the greatest exemplar of Christian virtue?** *Jesus Christ perfectly models virtue.*

**How is it possible for Christians to follow Christ's example?** *God has supplied all that we need to be virtuous in Christ Jesus (2 Pet. 1:3) so that believers' lives will be characterized by virtues (2 Pet. 1:5–8).*

## IDENTIFYING VIRTUES AND VICES

Use a **cooperative group activity** to prompt students to match each virtue and vice with an example.

Divide students into groups. Groups should write down an example that illustrates someone characterized by a virtue or a vice. Then they should switch papers and identify the vice or virtue that the other group was seeking to exemplify. Use the T-Chart on page 65 for a list of virtues and vices.

# Apply

## VIRTUE'S IMPORTANCE IN CHRISTIAN ETHICS

Guide a **discussion** on this section's essential question to apply the importance of virtue to all of life.

**Why do virtues matter? How does the focus on virtue affect one's approach to ethics?** *God's goal is not merely for people to do the right things. God's goal is for people to be the right kind of people. The focus on virtue forces attention on who people are and not just what they do.*

**Is doing the right thing, regardless of a person's character, sufficient for an action to be ethical?** *If a person does the right thing, then negative effects on other people and society are certainly lessened, and we can appreciate that. But doing the right thing does not make an action truly ethical if one's character is marked by a rejection of God.*

**How does the focus on virtue change the scope of ethics? What are some examples?** *The scope of virtue ethics includes basic growth in Christlikeness or sanctification in all the practical areas of life and not just hard-to-solve ethical difficulties. For example, it's not difficult to understand that cheating on a test is wrong. The difficulty is in doing the right thing due to cultivating the right character.*

**What happens when people cultivate virtue by means other than the transforming work of the gospel?** *a counterfeit of virtue that will be based on a works righteousness that falls short and leads to hypocrisy*

**What is an example of how a virtue could be misdefined or misapplied if that general concept is detached from the moral norms found in God's Word or creational norms found in God's world?** *Courage could be distorted into recklessness when a person puts his life or health at risk for something that is not worth it. A person could appeal to the virtue of loyalty as an excuse for not exposing the wrongdoing of a friend or employer. Someone might appeal to patience or kindness to justify avoiding a needed public confrontation with someone who is teaching error.*

## THE PLACE OF VIRTUE IN THE BIBLE

Use **Activity 4.1** on page 19 to apply the information in the section.

## Assess

### CAN EVIL PEOPLE DO GOOD THINGS?

Use a **Think-Pair-Share** to prompt students to grapple with what it means for evil people to do good things.

**If a very bad person can do good things and a very good person can do bad things, then does virtuous character matter? (You may choose to provide students hints to guide them: see Matthew 7:9–11; Psalm 51.)** *All people are born sinners and are thus bad. By God's grace, however, sinners still do many things that are good. If everyone was as bad as they could possibly be, life in God's world would simply cease to function (imagine if every parent tried to starve or poison their children)! When the best it can be said of a person like Hitler is that at least he was kind to dogs, that hardly undermines the claim that Hitler was evil. On the other hand, even those whom God chooses to be His own are born sinners, and in this life they still battle with sin. Their claim to be good rests not in themselves but in God. When they do wrong, they repent of their sin and seek God's forgiveness.*

Guide a **summative assessment** by directing students to answer the questions in Thinking It Through 4.1.

### Thinking It Through 4.1

1. rightly ordered love (Augustine, *City of God* 15.22)
2. a character trait or consistent behavior that is recognizably wicked or immoral; a deviation from God's upright standard; may be the exact opposite of a virtue or may be the twisting of a virtue into a counterfeit
3. See the chart on page 65.
4. The Old Testament continues to be a revelation of the unchanging character of God, providing a value system for what should be considered virtuous in ethics.
5. God's goal is not merely for people to do the right things. God's goal is for people to be the right kind of people.

GRAPPLING WITH ETHICAL ISSUES

**Can Evil People Do Good Things?**

Would it surprise you if you were told that Adolf Hitler had a great affection for his dogs? How could such a cold-hearted individual warm-heartedly and cheerfully love anything?

On the other hand, can good people do evil things? Would it surprise you if you were told that the man after God's own heart committed adultery—and murder to cover up that adultery? How could a person with such a passion to love God fall into such gross sin?

If a very bad person can do good things and a very good person can do bad things, then does virtuous character matter?

Ethicist Ken Magnuson highlights the importance of virtue in ethics by emphasizing that this approach to ethics

> deals better with the majority of ethical choices in part because such everyday situations are more common than quandaries, and require virtues that direct the will to do what we ought to do, rather than intellectual problem-solving skills that settle moral dilemmas. . . . As we learn what to do in everyday situations, we develop virtue and character, along with wisdom, that helps to prepare us even for moral quandaries.[5]

Therefore, the study of ethics should not be reduced to hard-to-solve ethical difficulties. The study of ethics should relate to basic growth in Christlikeness or sanctification. We will turn our attention to this in the next section. This focus is a much-needed corrective regarding a much-neglected piece of ethics. The study of ethics has most often focused on what people *do*, especially in difficult scenarios where the right choice is not obvious. But most of life relates to moral decision-making in everyday-living scenarios. These scenarios are the focus of the Wisdom Books (especially the book of Proverbs). The Bible makes a concerted effort to connect what we *do* to who we *are* inwardly (our character). The important place for virtue in Christian ethics is this: God's goal is not merely for people to do the right things. God's goal is for people to be the right kind of people.

Christians do need to focus on being the right kind of people so that what they do flows out of who they are. Christians do need to cultivate virtues. Some ethical difficulties are indeed very easy to resolve once a person becomes virtuous and thus sees the situation with clarity. However, virtue in a truly biblical ethic will contrast greatly with the notion and application of "virtue" in non-Christian (or pseudo*-Christian) ethics. That's why it is so important to place one's understanding and application of virtue in the context of the gospel, in the context of the redemptive storyline of Scripture.

> [A Christian virtue ethic] provides a window into the soul. JOHN FRAME[6]

#### Thinking It Through 4.1

1. Define *virtue*.
2. Define *vice*.
3. Identify one virtue and the counterpart vice(s).
4. Why is the Old Testament still valuable to the study of ethics?
5. Why does virtue matter in Christian ethics?

### 4.2 Christlikeness and Counterfeits

In the last section we asked, What is virtue? How should it be defined or understood? Why is it important to Christian ethics? In this section we ask, Why should a person want to be virtuous? Where can a person turn for power to be virtuous? How can a person take the necessary steps to become virtuous?

Have you ever been trying to accomplish something only to find yourself failing over and over again? You just couldn't figure out the key to success. Then perhaps someone came alongside and pointed out that you would never succeed until you changed one key ingredient. When that person revealed the key ingredient that was missing, everything clicked.

How important is Christ to growing in virtue? He is the key ingredient. Christ is at the center of it all—not as a magic potion or formula to gain power. A life that is

**pseudo:** false, counterfeit, pretended, spurious

66 VIRTUES

## 4.2 Christlikeness and Counterfeits

*How can I become a virtuous person?*

### Objectives

**4.2.1** Explain the importance of Christlikeness to growing in virtue. BWS

**4.2.2** Relate union with Christ to developing Christian virtue.

**4.2.3** Explain the role of the Holy Spirit in virtuous living.

**4.2.4** Distinguish Christian integrity from legalism, moralism, and authenticity. BWS

**4.2.5** Formulate a plan for living virtuously. BWS

### Biblical Worldview Shaping

- **Man's Chief End** (explain): God's goal for Christians is to restore the image of God by having Christ formed in them. (4.2.1)
- **Virtue** (evaluate): Moralism and authenticity are distortions of Christian integrity. (4.2.4)
- **Virtue** (apply): Becoming a virtuous person is at the heart of being a Christian and of Christian ethics. (4.2.5)

### Printed Resources

- Instructional Aid 4.2: *Counterfeits and Integrity Chart*
- Activity 4.2: Practicing the Spiritual Disciplines

truly wrapped up in Him, relying on Him, and guided by Him can be transformed little by little into more and more virtuousness—Christlikeness (2 Cor. 3:18).

You can be filled with hope and confidence that you can grow in virtue when Christ is at the center of your efforts (rather than trying to grow through self-effort). You can know that calls to virtuous living are on track when those exhortations are Christ-centered and gospel-driven. Our growth in virtue comes from focusing on Christ (aim), drawing from the wellspring that is in Christ (source), and depending on the gracious work of the Holy Spirit to grow us in Christ (means).

#### SEEKING TO BE VIRTUOUS: CHRISTLIKENESS (THE AIM)

How can I become a virtuous person?

Perhaps you've had the opportunity to learn about target shooting—whether at a camp, from a family member, or from a certified instructor. If so, one of the first and fundamental lessons you learned (after range safety) was how to take aim. Even a slight misadjustment, breathing at the wrong time, or the way you hold your equipment can ruin your aim. Taking aim requires careful concentration, avoiding all other distractions. But above all, you should make sure all that effort is aimed at the right target in the first place!

Why should a person want to be virtuous? Is that person aiming at the right target? Many people seek to be virtuous (or at least to be seen by others as virtuous). But far too many seek to do so for the wrong reasons. They're aiming to achieve something other than what they should. Does the motive or the goal matter as long as a person does the right thing?

The Bible has a lot to say about the inward heart motivations for why we do what we do (1 Sam. 16:7; Ps. 44:21; Prov. 4:23). Are people aiming at the right target when they go through the motions of empty religious ritual (Isa. 1:10–18)? What do they think they're accomplishing? The problem of aiming to look good on the outside comes to a head in the Gospels. Jesus repeatedly confronted the religious leaders' hypocrisy (Matt. 6:1–8, 16–18; 15:8–20; 23:3–7, 23–27). They weren't aiming to love God and others; they wanted power and prestige.

The Bible warns against being deceived by those who flatter with their seemingly virtuous words and actions but whose hearts are wicked (Prov. 23:6–8). Lots of people say they desire to be virtuous, but few people arrive at the right destination. Their goal, purposes, motives, desires, and focus are misdirected. They are seeking to be righteous in the eyes of others (leading to moralism). Or maybe they are seeking to be culturally accepted, conformed to the spirit of the age; in our age, that often means heeding the call to "just be who you are" (leading to lawless "authenticity"). Externally living up to ideals (being a moralist) and redefining vice as virtue (being an authentic lawless person) both aim at fulfilling a person's (or society's) idolatry, and thus the aim turns out to be self-serving.

In contrast, the Christian aims to be like Christ (Rom. 8:29; 2 Cor. 3:18) to the glory of God (1 Cor. 10:31). Christians live to please God (Eph. 4:1; Col. 1:10) and to love others (1 John 4:7–8). God's goal for Christians is to restore the image of God by renewing them in the image of Christ (Col. 3:10). Christians should be motivated to act ethically because their desire to glorify God conforms them to His image, encouraging them to obey His law and advance His kingdom. This is the life they believe will truly flourish (Ps. 1:1–6). Aiming for something other than Christlikeness will result in being off target for becoming a truly virtuous person. Becoming virtuous cannot truly happen apart from being conformed to the likeness of Christ.



## Suggested Reading

- See Section 4.1.
- Hughes, Barbara. *Disciplines of a Godly Woman*. Wheaton, IL: Crossway, 2001.
- Hughes, R. Kent, and W. Carey Hughes. *Disciplines of a Godly Young Man*. Wheaton, IL: Crossway, 2012.

## Engage

### THE KEY INGREDIENT FOR SUCCESS

Use a **bell ringer** activity to make a connection to an essential key ingredient for succeeding in an endeavor. Make the parallel to Christ's place in one's endeavor to become virtuous.

**Has there been a situation where you were finding it difficult to accomplish something until someone tipped you off to a key for success, which enabled you to accomplish it?** *Possible answers: Making three pointers in basketball more effectively; if you keep hitting where the rim is bolted to the backboard, then back up a step and you'll start hitting the shot.*

**How important is Christ to growing in virtue?** *He is the key ingredient. Being transformed into Christlikeness is one and the same as being virtuous. However, many people think that they can become virtuous through self-effort and self-reform apart from Christ's transforming them internally.*

## Instruct

### MOTIVES FOR BECOMING VIRTUOUS

Guide a **group activity** to prompt students to collaborate and to present answers to the questions in order to reinforce the importance of a right aim.

**What are some aims (goals, purposes, motives, desires) people seek to become virtuous? Exemplify or illustrate these differing aims. Why is having the correct aim necessary?** *Possible answers:*

- *Moralism: People are motivated to be seen as virtuous by others by externally living up to ideals for self-serving reasons. For example, this is exemplified in someone who actively participates in church activities with faithful dedication and speaks out in favor of pious living, all while participating in grievous unrepentant sin as a pattern for years until he or she gets caught. Then that person leaves the faith to persist in sin rather than repenting to be restored.*
- *Authenticity: People aim at just being who they naturally are, redefining vice as virtue as they aim to fulfill their own idolatrous desires. For example, this is exemplified in someone who claims that Christians can dismiss biblical commands regarding God-given roles because those commands are culturally outdated.*
- *Christlikeness: Christians aim to be like Christ to the glory of God because that is their chief end, to be restored into the image of God. They live to please God by loving Him and others in accordance with His commands. Therefore, they want to live ethically to glorify God, to be conformed to His image, and to advance His kingdom. This aim is absolutely necessary for becoming a truly virtuous person; it cannot happen apart from being conformed to the likeness of Christ. For example, this is exemplified in someone who self-sacrificingly and anonymously provides charitable support for a fellow church member because he or she wants to relieve that person's difficulty.*

## THE SOURCE THAT ENABLES ONE TO BE VIRTUOUS

Guide a **discussion** to reinforce the importance of the right source.

**Why is the source that enables one to be virtuous just as important as the right aim?** *A person must be connected to Christ to make the desire to be Christlike a reality.*
**What biblical truth plainly demonstrates the need for an inward source of virtue?** *People's inability to keep the Old Testament law demonstrated they needed to be changed from the inside to become virtuous, obedient people.*
**What does the Bible identify as the source? What provides that source?** *The source that enables virtuous living is Christ in us. The New Covenant provides that inward heart change through the Spirit who unites us to Christ at regeneration.*
**What other sources do people look to other than the gospel, or Christ?** *Possible answers: themselves, human tradition, moralistic approaches to the Bible, false religion, friends, the culture, psychology*

### ENABLED TO BE VIRTUOUS: CHRIST (THE SOURCE)

Have you ever heard the retort, "Consider the source"? Maybe you were repeating some claim or opinion that you had heard. Then your friend asked you, "Who told you that?" When you revealed where you had gotten your information, your friend responded, "Consider the source." Your friend was implying that you got bogus information from a poor source.

Where can people turn to enable themselves to be virtuous? The Old Testament law demonstrated that people needed to be changed from the inside out because they had no ability within themselves to keep the law, to be virtuous (Deut. 30:6; Acts 15:10; Gal. 3:21–22). The New Covenant provides for this needed inward heart change (Jer. 31:31–34). Only in a believer's new life in Jesus can this heart transformation occur (John 3:3). The source for virtue comes from Christ in us (Gal. 2:20). Lots of people claim to have discovered the secret to success or to spirituality, but few of them are drawing from the wellspring of living water offered by Christ (John 4:10–14). The basis of their morality is something other than Christ.

The Christian relies on his or her union with Christ (1 Cor. 12:13). At salvation, the believer is united to Christ and regenerated by the Holy Spirit, transforming his or her inward character (2 Cor. 5:17). Regeneration fundamentally changes the orientation of the believer, releasing the believer from slavery to sin (Rom. 6:1–23). Regeneration and the Spirit's indwelling provide the Holy Spirit's empowerment to overcome sin rather than remain enslaved to its pull. If you have been born again, the source of virtue, righteousness, and godliness is Christ living in you (Gal. 2:20). And if He lives in you, the evidence will work itself out in how you live (Phil. 2:12–13; Eph. 2:10).

A person cannot only have a desire to be like Christ (the aim); he or she must be connected to Christ (the source) to make that desire a reality. Developing Christlike virtue flows from union with Christ (John 15:1–14). There is no other way to properly develop virtue than to be connected to Christ by regeneration and saving faith.

> *In . . .* Pilgrim's Progress, *John Bunyan did a masterful job of portraying our ongoing reliance on Christ's ministry for the maintenance of the work of grace in our soul.*
> ANDREW DAVIS[7]

### BECOMING VIRTUOUS: THE SPIRIT'S WORK (THE MEANS)

Have you traveled around the country or even internationally? Getting from point A to point B could happen in any number of ways—different modes of transportation and different routes. It doesn't matter how you get to some places as long as you reach your destination. But some places require a specific route. Sherpas guide mountain climbers because they know the path to take.

Growing in virtue requires one definite means to get to that end. Sure, different people will be in different situations, have various trials, and have varying stories of how God has worked in their lives. But ultimately, all believers share in common the one and only means of growing in virtue through those various circumstances: the work of the Holy Spirit in their lives (Rom. 8:2–5, 13). In fact, living virtuously is one and the same as displaying the fruit that comes from the Spirit (Gal. 5:22–23).

How can a person take the necessary steps to become virtuous? There's no formulaic shortcut; there's no earning brownie points with God by going through ritualistic motions. Rather, Christians live out a loving relationship with God by carefully discerning what is pleasing to the Lord (Eph. 5:1–2, 10, 15). And Christians do this in the power and by the guidance of the Holy Spirit.

The work of the Holy Spirit is the instrument God uses in our lives to sanctify us. Even though we ourselves have an active role to play in yielding ourselves to be filled or controlled by the Spirit (Eph. 5:1, 18; see also Rom. 12:1–2; 2 Cor. 7:1; Phil. 2:12–13; 1 Thess. 4:3; Heb. 12:14), the Spirit plays the central role in empowering us so that Christ lives through us (Gal. 5:16–17, 25; see also Eph. 4:16–24). The Bible's descriptions of the Holy Spirit's role in sanctification are all-encompassing: the Holy Spirit leads the believer (Rom. 8:13–14, 26), imparts virtues (Gal. 5:22–23), bestows gifts (Rom. 12:6; 1 Cor. 12:4), prompts and guides to live by a new law—"the law of the Spirit of life in Christ Jesus" (Rom. 8:2; see also Rom. 8:4; Gal. 5:6; 6:2)—and renews the intellect and will (1 Cor. 2:10; 2 Cor. 5:17; 1 Thess. 5:23). Believers should be characterized by living and walking in the Spirit (Rom. 8:1, 4, 9–11; 1 Cor. 6:19; Gal. 4:6).

Christian growth (growing in virtue by the Spirit's work) takes place gradually and progressively through the habits of the spiritual disciplines: Bible reading, prayer, communion with the saints in the work of the church, and consistently battling against our still-present sin nature as well as the temptations all around us in the world. Indeed, the flesh, the Devil, and the world will always be with us until we are present with the Lord and glorified in heaven (Gal. 5:16–17; 1 Pet. 5:8; 1 John 2:15–17). And no Christian enters the kingdom of God by skipping suffering, which includes having to reckon with the unethical acts of others against them (Acts 14:22; 2 Thess. 1:4–5).

BECOMING LIKE CHRIST 69

## THE MEANS OF BECOMING VIRTUOUS

Use a **Quick Write** to reinforce the importance of the correct means.

**How can a person take the necessary steps to become virtuous? What is the person's role in this?** *We depend on the gracious work of the Holy Spirit to grow us in Christ so that we bear the Spirit's fruit. Although the Spirit is the means God uses to grow us, each person is responsible for actively yielding themselves to the work of the Spirit. This takes place as people give opportunities for the Spirit to work in them as they purposefully participate (not mechanically or ritualistically) in the spiritual disciplines: prayer, Bible study, local church involvement, and putting sin to death.*

## COUNTERFEITS OF VIRTUE

Use **Instructional Aid 4.2** in order to have students contrast the three counterfeits of virtue and the biblical solution, integrity.

### COUNTERFEITS OF VIRTUE: MORALISM AND AUTHENTICITY

The importance of the correct aim, source, and method is that they determine the true achievement of genuine virtue, keeping us on the path of growth in true holiness. This is well illustrated in John Bunyan's *Pilgrim's Progress*. The main character, Christian, soon finds out that Worldly Wiseman misdirected him to the Village of Morality. Evangelist has to redirect Christian to the Wicket Gate so that he will find true relief from his burden of sin at the foot of the cross. Later, Christian encounters Formalist and Hypocrisy, who are convinced they have a better path than the straight and narrow way up the Hill of Difficulty. Their "easier" routes lead to Danger and Destruction, where they wander lost in the woods and mountains. Only the straight and narrow path up the Hill of Difficulty can lead Christian to his eternal destiny with God.

People are always looking for an easy and happy way to both look good to others and enjoy their own idolatrous ends. Three of the most common ways to appear virtuous while remaining idolatrous are the pathways of legalism, moralism, and authenticity.

Christian climbing the Hill of Difficulty

#### *Legalism*

**Legalism** involves trying to earn a right standing with God (justification) through works. It can also refer to trying to earn a higher standing with God by the performance of works or rituals—as if going through external motions automatically brings about inward spirituality that would be acceptable to God. It minimizes or ignores horizontal relationships in the here and now to focus on vertical efforts to win God's favor. However, it tends toward pride and hypocrisy or guilt and hopelessness.

#### *Moralism*

**Moralism** involves trying to be a good, upstanding person through one's own good works. Although this is similar to legalism, it is more focused on social acceptability. The moralist is less concerned with right standing before God than with being approved as a good person by others. The focus is on the horizontal relationship with other people rather than the vertical relationship with God.

Moralism can sometimes be observed in a person who focuses on doing good works in the community: serving in soup kitchens, doing volunteer work in hospitals, raising awareness about human trafficking, funding projects in third-world countries for clean water, becoming a political activist to fight injustice—the list could go on. Moral-

ism can sometimes also be observed in a person who dutifully attends church, prays piously, and puts money in the offering plate. If you were to observe this person, he or she might appear to be a very upright person (particularly when compared with many others in this world who live openly vile lives). But could you spot a moralistic person as a counterfeit? Could you spot the wrong aim, source, and means in your own attempts to be a virtuous person?

It's not as though Bible-believing Christians shouldn't participate in these kinds of works. But what's missing from the moralist's efforts? What is it about what the moralist does that makes his or her works misdirected, prioritized incorrectly, and insufficient? Is the moralist truly aiming at Christlikeness, drawing from the resources found in Christ, and being guided and transformed by the Holy Spirit? When outwardly good works are disconnected from the gospel, done for the wrong reasons, empowered by the wrong source, and misguided to achieve some self-serving purpose, then this is all self-righteousness, not virtue. Ultimately, the moralist is a hypocrite, because whether he or she realizes it or will admit it, he or she behaves "morally" for self-serving or merely horizontal purposes. Don't be a moralist; don't be a hypocrite.

#### *Authenticity*

In reaction to hypocrisy, **authenticity** has become very popular. You're told to be yourself, to be true to yourself, to be real, to be transparent, to follow your heart, to fulfill all your dreams. But the rage for authenticity is a counterfeit contrast to hypocrisy. Yes, Jesus called on the Pharisees not to be hypocrites. But His solution was far from calling on them to be themselves. He called on people to deny themselves (Matt. 16:24). His solution was far from calling on the Pharisees to become authentically or transparently sinful. Rather, He called on them to come to Him for genuine, inward transformation (Matt. 5:17–20).

Our natural desires are sinful because we are sinful beings by nature: our minds, wills, and emotions are driven by the fallen desires of our affections. To let go of any inhibitions in order to "be true to ourselves" would be the surest way to embrace what's most vile. Having to say no to our sinful desires, having to discipline ourselves to be obedient, has nothing to do with hypocrisy (unless such efforts focus on the wrong aim, draw from the wrong source, and make use of the wrong means). Hypocrisy would be pretending our obedience to Christ were entirely our own or pretending to be obedient while secretly finding a way to be disobedient (Acts 5:1–11). Working hard toward godliness is not the same as hypocritical lying (1 Tim. 4:7).

Jesus calls on us to have integrity. The difference between *authenticity* and *integrity* couldn't be greater. Instead of "just being ourselves," Jesus calls us to become, by God's grace, who we ought to be.

integrity= being who God wants me to be

authenticity= being "my true self"

### CONCLUSION

Our culture redefines virtue as vice and vice as virtue. It also cancels or shames those who transgress its notions of virtue. In such times, nothing is needed more than our Creator's law and our Redeemer's gospel. Our Creator's law can restore moral sanity by showing us what actual virtue is. But that same law also exposes our own *lack* of true virtue. For such self-destructive rebels, the gospel provides the hope-giving forgiveness for the most unvirtuous, hypocritical people—truly good news. Wretches like you and me can be redeemed to live a life of integrity. Judah, the man who was ready to burn Tamar to death for prostitution when in fact he was the one who had gone to her for immoral relations (Gen. 38:24–26), later demonstrated profound virtue and a changed life when he was willing to sacrifice himself for Benjamin (Gen. 44:18–34). He, rather than his firstborn brother, was exalted by God and became the father of the kingly tribe from which the Davidic Messiah would come (Gen. 49:8–12).

Becoming a virtuous person is at the heart of Christian ethics. You can only realistically plan to live virtuously once you have been transformed by the power of the



## Apply

### A PLAN FOR LIVING VIRTUOUSLY

Use a **Ticket out the Door** as a prompt to help students plan to practice the spiritual disciplines.

If practicing the spiritual disciplines is key for Christians to become virtuous people, then Christians should be purposeful and diligent in practicing these disciplines. They will need to plan to prioritize practicing these disciplines.

Answer the following questions to help yourself plan and prioritize practicing the spiritual disciplines.

- What tools can you use?
- Where will you seek out a quiet time with the Lord?
- When will you set aside time for prayer and Bible study as well as accountability with a parent or mentor?
- How often and how long should you set aside quiet time versus the other optional activities you prioritize?
- Whom will you seek to mentor you?
- Why would you plan and prioritize practicing the spiritual disciplines?

Helpful resources to encourage the practice of the spiritual disciplines are in the Suggested Reading.

### UNIQUENESS OF CHRISTIAN ETHICS

Ask this chapter's **essential question.**

**What makes Christian ethics unique?**
*Contrary to other ethical systems, Christian ethics focuses on having a right relationship with God. The gospel transforms the person from within, which alone enables a person to become a virtuous person.*

### PRACTICING THE SPIRITUAL DISCIPLINES

Use **Activity 4.2** on page 21 to apply the information in the section.

## Assess

Guide a **summative assessment** by directing students to answer the questions in Thinking It Through 4.2.

### Thinking It Through 4.2

1. to be Christlike to the glory of God
2. through union with Christ (being connected to Him by the regenerating work of the Holy Spirit)
3. by relying on the guidance and sanctifying work of the Holy Spirit while practicing the spiritual disciplines

**4a.** legalism, moralism, and authenticity

**4b.** Legalism involves trying to earn a right standing with God (justification) through works. It can also refer to trying to earn a higher standing with God by the mere performance of works or rituals—as if going through external motions automatically brings about inward spirituality that would be acceptable to God. It minimizes or ignores horizontal relationships in the here and now to focus on vertical efforts to win God's favor.

Moralism involves trying to be a good, upstanding person through one's own good works with a focus on social acceptability (the horizontal dimension). But all these good works are misdirected and insufficient—not aimed at Christlikeness, drawing from the resources found in Christ, or guided by the sanctifying work of the Spirit.

Authenticity involves being your most natural (sinful) self by following your heart and fulfilling all your natural desires without any restraint or inhibitions.

**4c.** Legalism ends in pride and hypocrisy or guilt and hopelessness. Moralism ends in self-righteous hypocrisy. Authenticity ends in transparent sinfulness that embraces what is vile.

5. inward transformation that results in integrity
6. Once a person has been transformed by the gospel and connected to Christ, the Christian must begin practicing the spiritual disciplines to grow in virtue. The Christian must plan to set aside the time and resources to be actively engaged in these spiritual disciplines.

gospel and united to Christ. But your regeneration and conversion are the starting line, not the finish line. Planning to be a virtuous person begins by rightly understanding the virtues and how they relate to practical issues of life. By God's grace, the Holy Spirit will begin to sanctify you as you seek to grow through the spiritual disciplines and look to Him for wisdom in applying the Word of God to your circumstances. Plan to be in God's Word; to pray; to learn from your pastors, teachers, and other spiritual mentors in the church; and to engage in the fight against sin day in and day out.

As you study the virtues in the next three chapters and apply those virtues to ethical decision-making (in Unit 3 on ethical issues), remember the dangers of misdefining virtue, having inappropriate aims, relying on incorrect sources, and using wrong means for achieving virtue. These are common mistakes not only in non-Christian ethical systems but even among Christians, who are subject to missteps along the way as they seek to be virtuous.

### Thinking It Through 4.2

1. Why should a Christian seek to be virtuous? (What's the correct aim?)
2. How is a person enabled to be virtuous? (What's the correct source?)
3. How can a person take the necessary steps to become virtuous? (What's the correct means?)
4. a. Identify three counterfeits of true virtue.
   b. Describe each counterfeit and explain what makes each a counterfeit.
   c. What is the end result of each counterfeit?
5. What is Jesus' solution to hypocrisy?
6. How can you plan to become virtuous?

# Review

BECOMING LIKE CHRIST

### Terms to Remember

- virtue
- vice
- legalism
- moralism
- authenticity

### Scripture Memory

2 Peter 1:3, 5–7

### Understanding Ethics

1. Contrast the biblical concept of virtue to that of Greek culture.
2. Identify at least three virtues and the contrasting vices.
3. Why shouldn't the study of ethics be reduced to hard-to-solve ethical difficulties?
4. What three elements necessary for growing in true virtue can lead to virtue counterfeits when wrongly oriented?
5. How does the life of Judah illustrate the hope for forgiveness and true transformation offered in the gospel?

### Practicing Ethical Decision-Making

6. Analyze the scenario below to determine where virtue could be subtly twisted into a vice.

   A college student works diligently to achieve a 4.0. He or she focuses all attention on studies and will not allow any other activity to interrupt those studies.
7. Analyze the scenario below to determine where virtue could be subtly twisted into a vice.

   Even though you know your sibling is sneaking out of the house at night, you cover for him or her because you believe in staying loyal to your closest sibling.
8. Analyze the scenario below to determine how a virtue could be wrongly accused of being a vice.

   A pastor confronts sinful, unethical practices in the culture. He calls on people to repent to receive God's forgiveness.

### Analyzing and Evaluating Ethical Claims

9. How would you respond to the following claim? The greatest heroes in movies and literature are not the simplistically virtuous personalities. The greatest heroes are the complicated personalities who choose to do good despite having major flaws. This proves that inward character is far less important than some people make it out to be.
10. How would you respond to the following claim? Jesus was a great man who showed us how to be better people. We should follow his example by overturning unjust systems and doing good to the oppressed in society.

### Creating My Own Position Statements on Ethics

11. Write a position statement on the aim, source, and means that you would like to be your own in pursuing virtue. Personalize it and make it more specifically applicable to your own life situation.
12. Write a biblically based position statement on the concept of being authentic.

# Chapter 4 Review

## Terms to Remember

- **virtue:** Rightly ordered love (Augustine, *City of God* 15.22), which manifests itself in a person's character and behavior.
- **vice:** A character trait or consistent behavior that is recognizably wicked or immoral; a deviation from God's upright standard. May be the exact opposite of a virtue or may be the twisting of a virtue into a counterfeit.
- **legalism:** Trying to earn justification with God through works, or trying to earn a higher standing with God by the performance of works or rituals.
- **moralism:** Trying to be a good, upstanding person through one's own good works; focused on social acceptability.
- **authenticity:** Being true to oneself, being transparent, and following one's heart—most often leading to transparent sinfulness.

## Understanding Ethics

1. The biblical conception of achieving great moral character qualities must be rooted in godliness and Christlike righteousness rather than in self-achieved merit.
2. See the chart on page 65.
3. The study of ethics should relate to basic growth in Christlikeness or sanctification, which encompasses everyday life. It should not be limited to what we do; it should relate to who we are internally in our character, motivating what we do.
4. a wrong aim, source, and means of seeking to be virtuous
5. As heinous as his sinful hypocrisy was, he demonstrated a transformed life and received the promise of being the kingly tribe from which the Davidic Messiah would descend.

## Practicing Ethical Decision-Making

6. The virtue of diligence can be twisted into workaholism to the neglect of other necessary or healthy responsibilities that God has also designed for us: relationships (friends, family), relaxation, commitment to church, and so on. Furthermore, the purpose for achieving a 4.0 could be of little value beyond self-focused pride.
7. The virtue of loyalty can be twisted into sinfully covering for others who are doing wrong. In fact, true loyalty must be prioritized to rightful God-given authorities, and true loyalty would seek to protect a sibling from harming himself or herself from the consequences of sinful living.
8. The virtue of courage can be falsely accused of being unloving, hateful, harsh, and prideful regardless of how carefully a pastor presents the Scripture's view and how it confronts sin and offers forgiveness to those who repent.

## Analyzing and Evaluating Ethical Claims

9. Although it may be fair to say that a more realistic personality will be a more complex character, Christians should not exult in wicked personalities who end up doing the right thing. They should exult in personalities that are transformed to be the right kind of person.
10. It is true that Jesus confronted hypocrisy and injustice and helped the oppressed and that we too should pursue justice and do good to the oppressed, as these are defined by Scripture. However, to focus solely on these aspects of Jesus' life is to misunderstand His mission. Jesus came to save people from their sin by transforming them from the inside out. Only the gospel can truly change societies.

### Creating My Own Position Statements on Ethics

11. Christians should reflect aiming at Christlikeness, drawing from resources found in Christ, and relying on the Holy Spirit to grow in Christ. Students should describe what exactly this would look like in their lives.
12. Answers may draw on other resources than the textbook. Authenticity should be critiqued as an unbiblical concept, since the Bible never calls on us to be ourselves since we are naturally sinful. Rather, the Bible calls on us to be people of integrity, being conformed to Christ in us. We are to match our lives with who we truly are when our identity is in Christ. We are to be honest and transparent, but we are also called on to be obedient, fighting against our natural sinful tendencies. And we need not openly share all our sinful struggles publicly when those sins are most appropriately dealt with in private with God and with the other people who rightfully need to know (spiritual leaders, the party with whom we need to be reconciled).

# Lesson Plan Overview

**CHAPTER 5:** Three Central Virtues

**EV** ExamView
**PPT pres.** PowerPoint presentation

| PAGES | OBJECTIVES | RESOURCES | ASSESSMENTS |
|---|---|---|---|
| | **5.1 The Virtue of Faith** (3 DAYS) | | |
| 75–79 | **5.1.1** Define *faith*.<br>**5.1.2** Explain the object of faith.<br>BWS Authority (explain)<br>**5.1.3** Explain how walking by faith and not by sight motivates virtuous living.<br>BWS Man's Chief End (explain) | **ACTIVITIES**<br>• 5.1 Examining My Faith<br>**BJU PRESS TROVE***<br>• PPT pres.: Chapter 5 | **STUDENT EDITION**<br>• Thinking It Through 5.1 |
| | **5.2 The Virtue of Love** (3 DAYS) | | |
| 79–84 | **5.2.1** Compare and contrast various definitions of love.<br>**5.2.2** Defend the biblical definition of love.<br>**5.2.3** Explain how love for God motivates ethical choices.<br>BWS Virtue (formulate)<br>**5.2.4** Explain how a desire for others' true good motivates ethical choices.<br>BWS Virtue (formulate)<br>**5.2.5** Formulate a plan to grow in love.<br>BWS Virtue (apply) | **ACTIVITIES**<br>• 5.2 Evaluating Definitions of Love<br>**BJU PRESS TROVE**<br>• Link: 5 Definitions of Love<br>• PPT pres.: Chapter 5 | **STUDENT EDITION**<br>• Thinking It Through 5.2 |
| | **5.3 The Virtue of Hope** (3 DAYS) | | |
| 84–88 | **5.3.1** Define *hope*.<br>**5.3.2** Relate God's character and nature to the virtue of hope.<br>**5.3.3** Contrast hope in God with misplaced hopes.<br>**5.3.4** Contrast the virtue of hope with a utilitarian ethic.<br>BWS Man's Chief End (evaluate)<br>**5.3.5** Apply the virtue of hope to being a hopeful person. | **ACTIVITIES**<br>• 5.3 Becoming a More Hopeful Person<br>**BJU PRESS TROVE**<br>• PPT pres.: Chapter 5 | **STUDENT EDITION**<br>• Thinking It Through 5.3 |
| | **Review** | | |
| 89 | Recall concepts, terms, and Scripture memory from Chapter 5. | | **STUDENT EDITION**<br>• Chapter 5 Review |
| | **Test** | | |
| | Demonstrate knowledge of the material from Chapter 5 by taking the test. | | **ASSESSMENTS**<br>• Chapter 5 Test<br>**BJU PRESS TROVE**<br>• EV: Chapter 5 test bank |

*Digital resources for homeschool users are available on Homeschool Hub.

## CHAPTER 5
# Overview

Why are faith, love, and hope the central virtues?

### Objectives

**5.1** Relate the virtue of faith to living ethically.

**5.2** Relate the virtue of love to living ethically.

**5.3** Relate the virtue of hope to living ethically.

### Terms to Remember

- faith
- love
- hope
- utopian

### Scripture Memory

- 1 Corinthians 13:13

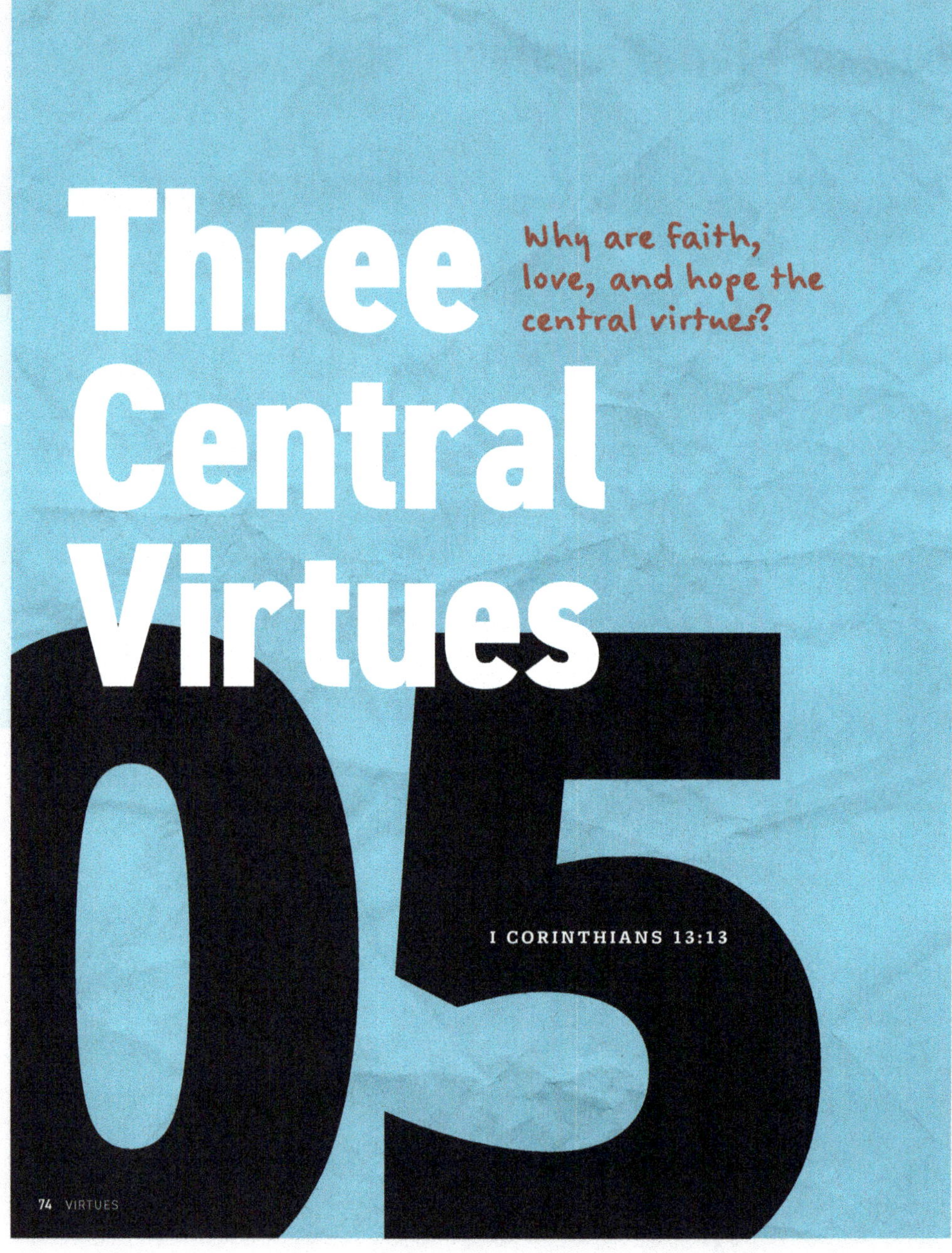

Developing Christlike virtues for the glory of God is an essential goal of Christian ethics. Each virtue is like a distinct thread in a multicolored garment that adorns believers with the enduring beauty of the gospel (1 Pet. 3:3–4). It's no accident that our culture's overemphasis on outward beauty coincides with a neglect of the New Testament virtues. When the true beauty of the inner person—with the virtues of faith, love, and hope—disappears from a culture, all that is left is a shallow fixation on outward appearance. Yet there is something exceedingly attractive about a genuinely faithful, loving, and hopeful Christian.

A survey of the New Testament reveals that faith, love, and hope are purposefully integrated, suggesting that this triad of virtues is foundational to all other biblical virtues. The earliest grouping of these three virtues appears in 1 Thessalonians, where the apostle Paul commended the believers for their work of *faith*, labor of *love*, and steadfastness of *hope* (1 Thess. 1:3).[1] A couple of observations about this passage are worth noting.

First, while all three virtues are distinct from one another, they're like a threefold cord that cannot be broken. Christian living in the present is bound by all three. It's inconceivable that a Christian could have faith without also possessing love and hope and vice versa. Second, an argument can be made that the New Testament's usual ordering of the virtues is significant. A Christian first comes to *faith*, then lives on the basis of *love* to God and neighbor, then perseveres through hardship and persecution by *hope* in what is to come.[2] This order will serve as the outline for our present study.

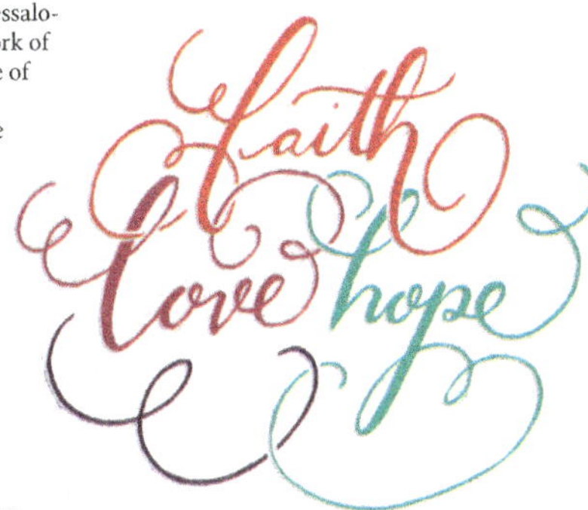


## 5.1 The Virtue of Faith

From a biblical standpoint, no act is truly ethical unless done from faith (Rom. 14:23; Heb. 11:6). Faith in God is a virtue because it is fitting for dependent creatures to trust their Creator. The word *fitting* refers to something that functions properly. For example, the eye is made for seeing, the ear for hearing, and the nose for smelling. Our senses were fitted to relate to the outside world. Likewise, our human constitution was originally fitted for faith in God. Before sin entered the world, it was natural for human beings to rely on God for their every need. God delights in providing for His believing children as their heavenly Father (Matt. 6:8; Luke 12:32). Faith magnifies God's roles as the Creator and Provider, and this is what makes faith virtuous. We can see this more clearly by contrasting faith with unbelief.



## 5.1 The Virtue of Faith

What role does faith play in living ethically?

### Objectives

**5.1.1** Define *faith*.

**5.1.2** Explain the object of faith. BWS

**5.1.3** Explain how walking by faith and not by sight motivates virtuous living. BWS

### Biblical Worldview Shaping

- **Authority** (explain): Faith must be grounded in the proper authority to be virtuous. (5.1.2)
- **Man's Chief End** (explain): Trust in the promises of God is a firm foundation for ethical behavior in the face of present temptations and trials. (5.1.3)

### Printed Resource

- Activity 5.1: Examining My Faith

## Engage

### FAITH, LOVE, AND HOPE: VIRTUES THAT SUPPORT ALL OTHERS

Use this chapter's **essential question** to explain why faith, love, and hope are the central virtues.

Write the following virtues for display.

- goodness
- courage
- self-control
- patience
- meekness
- kindness
- compassion
- gratitude
- honesty

Use the following questions to connect the three central virtues with the virtues listed for display.

**Which virtue can you most easily connect to either faith, love, or hope?** *Allow time for students to make their selection (e.g., gratitude requires faith in God's provision, compassion requires love for people who are hurting, and meekness requires hope in God's promised future).*

**Why are people without faith in God unable to *genuinely* exercise any of these virtues?** *Without a right relationship with God, it is impossible to genuinely exercise virtues because all virtues spring from Him.*

**How does love for God and love for people enable the *genuine* exercise of these virtues?** *Love is necessary to strengthen a person for the exercise of all the virtues.*

**Why is Christian hope necessary for the *genuine* exercise of these virtues?** *People need hope to be virtuous in trying circumstances.*

**Why do unbelievers who lack the virtues of faith, love, and hope appear at times to be virtuous?** *There are various reasons: God's common grace, the image of God in man, and self-righteousness.*

## Instruct

### THE NATURE OF FAITH

Guide a **preassessment** of student understanding on the nature of genuine faith.

**What are the three components of genuine faith?** *knowledge, assent, and confidence*
**Why is blind faith (i.e., faith without knowledge) not a virtue?** *For faith to be virtuous, it must know what to believe concerning God.*
**What does it mean to assent to the content of Scripture?** *to agree that the things written in Scripture are true*
**Why are knowledge and mental assent, by themselves, insufficient to constitute a living faith?** *A living faith must also have the element of confidence.*

Use **direct instruction** to present the difference between profession of faith and possession of faith.

Point out that not everyone who says he or she has faith truly has faith. James teaches this in his epistle (James 2:14). There are some people in the church whose faith goes no further than mental assent. They say they believe in Christ and in biblical truth, but their lives give no evidence of a living faith. They have what we might call a *dead* faith, or an *empty* faith. Though they profess faith, they do not possess faith.

Jesus spoke of false professors when He said, "Many will say to me in that day, Lord, Lord, have we not prophesied in thy name? and in thy name have cast out devils? and in thy name done many wonderful works? And then will I profess unto them, I never knew you: depart from me, ye that work iniquity" (Matt. 7:22–23). There are three observations from this passage.

1. These individuals profess Jesus as Lord.
2. Their profession consists of knowledge and assent. It is true that Jesus is Lord, and these individuals are assenting to this truth.
3. Jesus tells them that their faith is not real. Like Judas, these individuals cast out demons and do many wonderful works, but their hearts do not embrace Jesus with confidence—the third and crucial element of genuine saving faith.

To possess faith, a person must have all three elements of faith—knowledge, assent, and confidence. Genuine faith does not have to be perfect faith. It may be as small as a mustard seed (Luke 17:6). What matters is that faith embraces Christ as revealed in Scripture, and that its genuineness can be seen in our lives as we continually surrender to Christ's lordship. Virtues that are truly virtuous can grow only in this kind of faith-relationship with God.

Unbelief in God, His Word, and His promises is a vice because of what it says about God. It says that God is untrustworthy, which is a lie against His holy character. It says that God's Word is unclear and unreliable, which is an insult to His gracious self-revelation. And it says that God's promises are uncertain, which is a slight against His perfect faithfulness. We could multiply the examples, but the important thing to note is how faith and unbelief find their meaning, not in abstraction from God, but in direct relation to God and His revelation.

#### THE NATURE OF FAITH

One Protestant reformer said, "We shall possess a right definition of **faith** if we call it a firm and certain knowledge of God's benevolence toward us, founded upon the truth of the freely given promise in Christ, both revealed to our minds and sealed upon our hearts through the Holy Spirit."[3] As this definition indicates, biblical faith consists of three inseparable components—knowledge, assent, and confidence. Faith knows something of the content of God's Word (knowledge), agrees that these things are true (assent), and exercises personal reliance on God for the fulfillment of all His promises (confidence).

##### *Faith Includes Knowledge*

How can one believe without first knowing what he or she is supposed to believe (Rom. 10:14)? Biblical knowledge is necessary if faith is to be rooted in reality. Those who set faith in opposition to knowledge are equating faith with fantasy, a kind of unfounded wish. But there's no virtue in wishful thinking. Instead, God is honored when we trust Him because we know, based on Scripture, "that he is, and that he is a rewarder of them that diligently seek him" (Heb. 11:6).

##### *Faith Includes Assent*

The difference between knowledge and assent is one of agreement. Many unbelievers know the content of Scripture; they simply don't believe it to be true. They know, for example, that the Bible teaches that Christ was crucified and raised from the dead, but they don't agree that Scripture gives an accurate historical account of these things. Faith, on the other hand, accepts the self-authenticating* evidence of Scripture (Heb. 11:1). Faith rightly perceives the divine authorship of Scripture and therefore assents to the truth of what it teaches.

##### *Faith Includes Confidence*

Knowledge and assent by themselves, however, are insufficient to constitute a living faith. Even the demons know and assent to the truth of Scripture (James 2:19). They understand the truth about God and His mighty acts in history. After all, they knew that Jesus was the Holy One of God who came to destroy them (Matt. 8:29; Luke 4:34).

Therefore, in order for faith to be genuine, it must include the element of confidence—a heartfelt commitment by which we rest in Christ as a result of the Holy Spirit opening our eyes to see the truth and to sense the glory of it so that our minds are held captive by it. Confidence is faith's capstone to knowledge and assent because it heartily approves of what it knows to be true about God, His Word, and His promises.

*If you have faith, you have infinitely more than he who has all the world.*
CHARLES SPURGEON[4]

**self-authenticating:** demonstrating its own truthfulness

### THE OBJECT OF FAITH

Where we place our trust is of great ethical significance. As the psalmist wrote, "Some trust in chariots, and some in horses: but we will remember the name of the Lord our God" (Ps. 20:7). Chariots and horses were tangible symbols of technological and military strength in the ancient world, and Israel was frequently tempted to trust in these things for its protection. As Isaiah wrote, "Woe to them that . . . trust in chariots, because they are many; and in horsemen, because they are very strong; but they look not unto the Holy One of Israel, neither seek the Lord!" (Isa. 31:1). Whether the technology is ancient or modern, the choice remains the same for every generation: Will we trust in our own ingenuity and strength, or will we trust in the Lord?

What role does faith play in living ethically?

#### *Trusting God and His Word*

Biblical faith has God as its object; it rests on Christ and no other (Rom. 5:1–2; 1 Cor. 2:5). Faith is nothing if it is not directed toward the right person. In the absence of God, secular society has normalized the notion of self-confidence. To have confidence means to firmly trust, or to fully rely upon. Therefore, we should question the wisdom of frail and dependent creatures investing confidence in themselves. This is like telling people to be their own shelter in the midst of a storm. While people may legitimately have a limited confidence in their abilities or in the abilities of others, absolute faith is only valid if the object of faith is self-sufficient and great enough to bear the weight of the world. And since God alone fits this description, He alone is worthy of our complete and unreserved confidence.

To clarify, we cannot separate faith in God from faith in His Word (Rom. 10:17). Building our faith upon the proper authority of Scripture is necessary for faith to be virtuous because it is in the Bible that we learn the things to believe—things that are true and trustworthy and things that feed and fuel our faith (Rom. 1:16–17). Remove the Bible from the Christian faith, and the Christian faith ceases to exist—and with it the virtue of faith itself. Trusting the Bible means receiving it with all the authority that comes from God Himself and then living in its truth and power.



## THE OBJECT OF FAITH

Guide students in a **role-play** in which they interact with people who place their trust in the wrong thing. Direct students to respond to the following simulations.

**Someone says, "I don't need anyone to help me. I can look out for myself. There's no situation I cannot handle."** *This person fails to recognize his own limitations. All human beings are fragile creatures who need God's help all the time. Every person lives, moves, and has his or her being in God (Acts 17:28). People who think they don't need God's help are deceiving themselves. Those who trust themselves will eventually discover a situation they cannot handle.*

**Someone says, "I believe that money is the solution to my problems. The more that I have, the happier I am. People may call me shallow and materialistic, but I've yet to see a poor person that is happy."** *While money is a tool that can solve some problems, such as paying for a plumber to fix a broken sink, humanity's greatest problems cannot be solved with money. Our need for forgiveness of sin, reconciliation with God, and loving relationships cannot be bought. Furthermore, many poor Christians have experienced greater happiness in God than the wealthiest unbelievers have experienced in money.*

**Someone says, "I trust in God, but I don't believe everything that the Bible teaches. Besides, I can hear God speaking to me more powerfully outside the Bible."** *God has revealed Himself in the Bible. We cannot separate faith in God from faith in His Word. It is in the Bible that we learn who God is. A person who does not believe what God has revealed in Scripture does not trust God. God always speaks through His Word and never apart from His Word.*

## VIRTUOUS FAITH

Guide a **discussion** to help students understand that faith must be grounded in the proper authority to be virtuous.

**If a person has sincere beliefs, why does it matter *what* the person believes?** *What a person believes matters because truth matters. Sincerity is important when believing the truth, but sincerely believing what is false is not a virtue.*

**What makes faith virtuous?** *Faith is virtuous when the object of faith is God as revealed in His Word.*

## TRUSTING GOD'S PROMISES

Guide a **Bible study** to direct students to place their trust in God's promises. Instruct students to look up the following passages in Isaiah and identify the specific promise of God in each passage.

- Isaiah 26:3 (perfect peace)
- Isaiah 40:31 (renewed strength)
- Isaiah 41:10 (strength and help)
- Isaiah 43:2 (protection in trials)
- Isaiah 54:10 (unfailing kindness)
- Isaiah 54:17 (vindication of the righteous)

## EXAMINING MY FAITH

Use **Activity 5.1** on pages 23–24 to apply the information in the section.

## Apply

### FAITH AND ETHICS

Ask students this section's **essential question** to discuss faith's role in ethical living.

### THE POWER OF WALKING BY FAITH

Guide a **discussion** on Hebrews 11 to strengthen students' faith in God. Explain that the biblical characters of Hebrews 11 are presented as examples of genuine faith for believers to follow.

**What did Abel do by faith?** *He offered to God a better sacrifice than Cain.*
**How was Enoch rewarded for his walk of faith?** *He was taken to heaven without dying.*
**What is impossible to do without faith?** *to please God*
**How did Noah respond in faith to God's warning of coming judgment?** *Noah prepared an ark to save his house.*
**What did Abraham do by faith when God first called him?** *Abraham left his home country, not knowing where he was going.*
**What future promise encouraged Abraham as he sojourned in the Promised Land?** *a city built by God*
**What was Sarah able to do by faith when she was in her old age?** *She was able to conceive and deliver a child.*
**When God called Abraham to sacrifice Isaac, what did Abraham believe that God could do?** *raise Isaac from the dead*
**Why did Abraham believe God would deliver Isaac from death?** *because Isaac was God's promised seed through whom He would provide the Messiah*
**How did Moses' parents show faith when they hid baby Moses for three months?** *They did not fear the king of Egypt and his order for Hebrew male babies to be killed upon birth.*
**How did Moses' decision to suffer with God's people demonstrate his faith?** *He esteemed the reproach of Christ of greater value than the riches of Egypt.*
**How was Moses able to endure the king of Egypt's anger without fear?** *Moses looked with the eyes of faith to the invisible God.*
**What did God do for Moses and Israel at the Red Sea?** *God caused His people to cross on dry ground, and He drowned the Egyptian army.*
**How did the Israelites show their faith in God when they came to the walls of Jericho?** *They walked around the walls seven times as God had instructed, and the walls fell.*

#### Taking Hold of God's Promises

As faith leans in to what the Bible says, it is listening to the very voice of God. One way God speaks to us in Scripture is through His promises. A divine promise is an assurance from God that He will act to accomplish His good purposes for those who are in Christ. The promises of God range from supplying our daily needs to completing our salvation when Christ returns (Matt. 6:8, 33; Phil. 1:6). Whether the need is for help in times of distress, strength to act virtuously, or grace to persevere in the Christian life, God supplies the believer's every need. The guarantee that He will do this is found in the "exceeding great and precious promises" of Scripture (2 Pet. 1:4).

But faith must take hold of these promises. It does a person no good to leave the promises dangling in the air. When a particular need arises, faith goes into action by embracing one of God's promises. Trusting in the promises of God is a firm foundation for ethical behavior in the face of present temptations and trials. For example, you may be tempted to retaliate in anger when treated unjustly. Resisting this temptation is possible as you trust God to avenge all wrongs (Rom. 12:19). God has promised to do this. If you trust Him, your ethical response to a personal injustice will not involve taking vengeance into your hands.

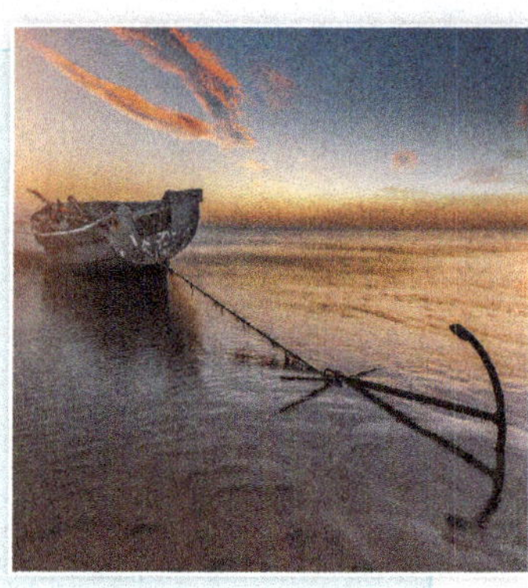

#### THE POWER OF WALKING BY FAITH

In the book of Hebrews, there's an entire catalog of believers who are commended for their faith (Heb. 11). What stands out about them is that their faith in God was not static but active and powerful; it made a practical difference in their lives under very difficult and trying circumstances. They looked beyond their immediate circumstances to God's greater kingdom purposes, trusting that God was with them by working providentially behind the scenes (see Heb. 10:32–39). In other words, they walked by faith in the unseen rather than fixing their eyes on what is seen (2 Cor. 4:18; 5:7).

Christian ethics depends on a clear teleological focus. As a reminder, *teleological* refers to the end goal behind our choices. But we cannot see the end goal except with the eyes of faith. Therefore, it is vital that we cultivate our faith so that we can make ethical choices consistent with a biblical teleology.

##### *Forward-Looking Faith*

Faith possesses power largely in its ability to look forward to the unseen future, a future defined by the trajectory of redemptive history, which culminates in the triumphant return of Christ. Whenever Christians face trouble and distress, or even comfort and pleasure, it is tempting to see the present, visible world as all of reality. But faith understands there's an unseen reality with which we must reckon. Faith knows of the coming judgment and the coming rewards, and it lives life in light of those realities.

When God called Abraham to leave his home country for a land that God had promised, Abraham obeyed in faith even though he didn't know where he was going (Heb. 11:8–9). When Abraham's wife, Sarah, was beyond the age to conceive a child, she trusted God to fulfill His promise for a child (Heb. 11:11). They and their descendants lived as exiles in the world, looking forward to that better country God had prepared for them (Heb. 11:13–16). Their forward-looking faith enabled them to act in their present circumstances based on what God would do for them in the future.

This highlights an important lesson about the relationship between faith and ethics. The degree to which a believer is confident God will act exactly as He has promised is the degree to which a believer will base his or her decisions on the promises of God rather than on his or her limited perception.



**How did Rahab show her faith in God?** *She hid the Israelite spies, and she didn't die with those who refused to believe.*
**What wonderful things are mentioned in Hebrews 11:33–34 that believers experienced by faith?** *conquered kingdoms, administered righteousness, obtained promises, shut the mouths of lions, extinguished the power of fire, escaped the sword, were made strong in weakness, became mighty in combat, forced foreign armies to flee*
**What painful trials mentioned in Hebrews 11:36–37 did believers endure by faith?** *They were stoned, sawn in two, tempted, killed with the sword, and they wandered around in sheepskins and goatskins, destitute, oppressed, and mistreated.*

## Assess

Guide a **summative assessment** by directing students to answer the questions in Thinking It Through 5.1.

### Thinking It Through 5.1

1. "Now we shall possess a right definition of faith if we call it a firm and certain knowledge of God's benevolence toward us, founded upon the truth of the freely given promise in Christ, both revealed to our minds and sealed upon our hearts through the Holy Spirit" (John Calvin, *Institutes of the Christian Religion* 3.2.7, vol. 1, ed. John T. McNeill, trans. Ford Lewis Battles, The Library of Christian

Acting ethically when pushed to one's limit requires a forward-looking faith. You may find yourself confronted with a situation that is extremely difficult to handle. Faith is often tested not merely by the severity of a trial but also by its duration. Part of you may look for an easy way out, even one that is sinful. But as you look forward to the day when God will deliver you from adversity, you will gain strength to persist in righteousness instead.

#### *Dependent Faith*

The most powerful dynamic of faith is the settled conviction that God loves His believing children in Jesus Christ (Rom. 5:8; 8:35; Eph. 1:3–5). As Christians grow in the certainty of the Father's love and care for them, they grow in their dependence upon Him. They readily admit to being little children before an all-powerful and all-wise Father, and they make regular appeals to Him for His enabling grace so as to respond in every situation with faithfulness to Him (Matt. 21:22; Heb. 4:16).

A dependent faith also means being convinced that God's ways are better than our own and that to be "rich toward God" (Luke 12:21) is better than to be rich in this world (Isa. 55:8–9; Prov. 15:16; Matt. 6:19–21). This was precisely the faith-ethic at work in Moses' decision to leave Pharaoh's palace, for he would "rather . . . suffer affliction with the people of God, than . . . enjoy the pleasures of sin for a season" (Heb. 11:25). Faith enabled Moses to make a difficult but rewarding choice. He looked beyond the passing treasures of Egypt to the greater wealth of Christ (Heb. 11:26).

To an unbelieving world, Moses' decision looks foolish. But to the eyes of faith, his decision makes perfect sense. God's love and care for Moses surpassed anything that Egypt could offer, and this belief influenced his ethical choices in practical ways. In a similar way, the biblical virtue of faith can influence our ethical choices as we rest assured of God's unfailing love in Christ.

### Thinking It Through 5.1

1. How is faith defined?
2. What are the three essential elements of faith, and what is the significance of each?
3. What does it mean for God to be the object of faith, and why is faith in His Word essential to that?
4. How do God's promises relate to faith and ethical behavior?
5. How does walking by faith and not by sight motivate virtuous living?
6. Why is a phrase such as "Believe in yourself" or "Have faith in yourself" bad advice?

## 5.2 The Virtue of Love

Love has a unique role among the central virtues. Whereas faith and hope are temporary (for these virtues will cease when the future glory becomes reality), the virtue of love never ends; it continues throughout eternity. This explains why Scripture speaks of love as the greatest virtue (1 Cor. 13:13).

In thinking carefully about the virtue of love, we need to understand that in a fallen world there's no virtue in the word *love* itself. Whether or not our love is a virtue depends on the object of our love. There's no virtue in loving what is evil. One of the most appalling features of fallen human nature is misdirected love, and that's all the more reason for us to rely on God's Word to get our bearings on what true love is. Our capacity for self-deception on this issue is far too great to rely on our feelings and the sentimental lyrics of popular love songs.

The virtue we're seeking to cultivate is not as obvious as people assume. What is love? Is it an emotion? An action? A commitment? All the above? Where does true



Classics, vol. 20 [Philadelphia: Westminster Press, 1960], 551).

2. Biblical knowledge: necessary if faith is to be rooted in reality

   Assent: rightly perceives the divine authorship of Scripture and therefore assents to the truth of what it teaches

   Confidence: a heartfelt commitment to rely on God for the fulfillment of all His promises.

3. Faith is only valid if the object of faith is self-sufficient and great enough to bear the weight of the world. And since God alone fits this description, He alone is worthy of our complete and unreserved confidence. We cannot separate faith in God from faith in His Word (Rom. 10:17). For faith to be virtuous, it must be built upon the authority of Scripture, because from the Bible we learn to believe the things that are true and trustworthy and that fuel our faith.

4. Faith must take hold of God's promises. It does a person no good to leave the promises dangling in the air. When a particular need arises, faith goes into action by embracing one of God's promises. Trusting in the promises of God is a firm foundation for ethical behavior in the face of present temptations and trials.

5. Whenever Christians face distress, or even comfort, it is tempting to see the visible world as all there is. But faith understands there is an unseen reality. Faith knows of the coming judgment and rewards, and it lives life in light of that. The degree to which a believer is confident that God will act exactly as He has promised is the degree to which a believer will base his or her decisions in life on the promises of God rather than on limited human perception.

6. We are frail and dependent creatures. God alone should be the object of our faith. He can do for us what we cannot do for ourselves.

## 5.2 The Virtue of Love

How do the things I love influence my choices?

### Objectives

**5.2.1** Compare and contrast various definitions of love.

**5.2.2** Defend the biblical definition of love.

**5.2.3** Explain how love for God motivates ethical choices. BWS

**5.2.4** Explain how a desire for others' true good motivates ethical choices. BWS

**5.2.5** Formulate a plan to grow in love. BWS

### Biblical Worldview Shaping

- **Virtue** (formulate): People who do not love God and others will not be able to make wise ethical choices because God's law is summed up as loving God and others. (5.2.3; 5.2.4)
- **Virtue** (apply): The student makes his own plans for becoming a more loving person. (5.2.5)

### Printed Resource

- Activity 5.2: Evaluating Definitions of Love

### Digital Resource

- Link: 5 Definitions of Love

### Engage

#### WE CHOOSE WHAT WE LOVE MOST

Use **direct instruction** to answer this section's essential question about how our choices arise from what we love most.

To love something is to prefer it over other things. Every choice people make in life is based on their preference for one thing over another. If they love something immoral, their choices will tend toward the immoral. Conversely, if they love God, their choices will tend toward the moral.

Sometimes a person has competing interests within his or her heart. One's ultimate preference will always prevail. For instance, a person who drives an older vehicle might like a newer car, but if the preference for saving money and avoiding debt is greater than the desire for a new car, then he or she will choose to keep the older car.

Christians wrestle with ethical decisions in a similar way. Imagine a Christian wrestling with the ethical choice of tithing on one's income. Although briefly contemplating using the tithe to purchase something, he or she chooses to tithe instead. The overriding factor in the decision was love for God. It is love for God that strengthens believers to make the right choices.

## Instruct

### CONTRASTING VIEWS OF LOVE

Guide a **discussion** about the way the word *love* is abused in secular society.

**How do you think secular society abuses the word *love*?** *by calling evil behavior loving and righteous behavior unloving*

**What sinful relationships does secular society justify in the name of love?** *same-sex relationships, adulterous relationships, and cohabitation*

**Why shouldn't people be allowed to let their feelings determine the meaning of love?** *God's Word defines the meaning of love, not human feelings.*

**Why do you think secular people view a biblical sexual ethic as unloving?** *They think it represses legitimate desires and denies them something good.*

**In seeking to correct people who equate love with individual feelings, how might you turn their argument against them?** *Show them the fallacy of their logic by equating love with behavior that they would oppose. Challenge them on the consistency of their position. Though they may oppose the behavior, if the person engaging in it calls it loving, how can they reasonably object to it? If they claim to object to the behavior because they think it is morally wrong, point out that they are being inconsistent with their own definition of love.*

### CONTRASTING LOVE SOME MORE

Use a **Turn and Talk** to prompt collaboration on answers based on the textbook.

**What two loves stand in contrast to the spiritual love of biblical Christianity?**

**What is wrong with making self-love the greatest love of all?**

love originate? What is the standard of love? What does it mean to love God and to love one's neighbor? Are we to love every person in the world equally? Is there a sense in which love and hate can be compatible under certain circumstances? These and many more questions indicate that love is not as simple as people suppose.

#### CONTRASTING VIEWS OF LOVE

There's a direct connection between the things we love and our ethical choices. If our love is misdirected, then our choices will be also. Erroneous conceptions of love can easily cloud our judgment and lead us to make choices that we mistakenly believe are moral, when in reality they are immoral. Love is commonly misdirected as self-love and as sentimental love. These are in contrast to the spiritual love of biblical Christianity.

##### *Self-Love*

Although there's a biblically proper way to think of self-love, the dominant view today involves a self-love that is inward-focused and self-absorbed. The song "Greatest Love of All" (most famously sung by Whitney Houston) is an example of self-love gone horribly wrong:

I found the greatest love of all inside of me.
The greatest love of all is easy to achieve.
Learning to love yourself is the greatest
love of all.[5]

There are several problems with this line of thinking. First, the idea that people should learn to love themselves assumes that they don't already, when in fact all people fervently love themselves. Second, love is not discovered by a person looking inward. It's a sad irony of our time that the more people turn within to find love the more lonely and unloved they feel. Third, this kind of love is not proper self-love but self-absorbed love. Self-absorbed love is a vice because it never goes any higher than one's private self-interest, never makes any sacrifices for the good of others, and paradoxically never considers its own best interest in an eternal sense. But the most problematic aspect of this thinking is that it elevates self-love above God's love, which is the greatest love of all.

##### *Sentimental Love*

Feelings of love are not a reliable measure of whether the love being expressed is appropriate, and yet a great many people make choices based on a certain kind of sentimental love. This is most obvious in the way our culture approaches romantic relationships, but it can manifest itself in any relationship.

The problem with sentimental love is not the fact that emotions are involved; biblical love includes godly emotions. The problem is in making private emotions rather than God's law the standard for what love looks like. Situation ethics, for example, teaches people to do the loving thing while rejecting biblical norms, as if people could somehow intuit on their own what the loving thing is. Unfortunately, many people violate God's law in their relationships, especially romantic relationships, under the guise of love. Despite the trail of misery and broken relationships in our culture, people continue to rely on their fleeting sinful passions, convinced that a relationship must be right if their hearts tell them it is right.

80 VIRTUES

**What is the problem with sentimental love?**

**What makes Christian love spiritual?**

*See pages 80–81 to evaluate student answers.*

### EVALUATING DEFINITIONS OF LOVE

Use **Activity 5.2** on page 25 to apply the information in the section. Use the **link** 5 Definitions of Love to access the video the students will watch for the activity.

### *Spiritual Love*

We can think of Christian love as spiritual love, which is to be distinguished from natural love. There is a natural affection that family members and friends have for one another, and this kind of love exists among non-Christians as well as Christians. It is called natural love because it springs from natural causes, such as when we love a friend because of his or her kindness toward us. Spiritual affection, however, does not arise from natural causes; it is the fruit of the Holy Spirit (Gal. 5:22). It is spiritual because it is a love that flows from God and thereby enables us to love as He loves (1 John 4:10, 19). To be clear, natural love and spiritual love are not in opposition. Christians should have both. Unbelievers may or may not have natural love, but apart from God's grace they will certainly lack spiritual love.

Spiritual love amplifies natural love.

But there's another sense in which Christian love is spiritual. As Augustine wrote, "I define '**love**' as any movement of the soul to enjoy God for God's own sake, and to enjoy one's self and one's neighbor for God's sake."[6] This alone makes love a true virtue for two reasons: it prioritizes love for God above all else, and it gains its strength to love others from loving God.

Spiritual love for God sets self-love in its proper context, such as when a believer approaches God for the pleasure of His presence and fellowship. And with respect to loving people, those who are most loving are those believers who seek their "*own* happiness in doing good to others."[7] Far from being a non-emotional, disinterested act, true biblical love regards the beloved with such delight that it is even willing to suffer for the good of the beloved. When we love like this, we can say that our love is Godlike (1 John 3:16).

> *Christian love will never be found except in a heart prepared by the Holy Spirit.*
>
> J. C. RYLE[7]

## THE CASE FOR CHRISTIAN LOVE

Christian love begins with God because "God is love" (1 John 4:16). Apart from Him, there would be no such thing as love. The greatest demonstration of God's love is the gift of His Son for the salvation of sinners (Rom. 5:8; 1 John 4:10). Loving as God loves is one of the evidences that a person has been born into God's family (1 John 4:7). "We love him, because he first loved us" (1 John 4:19). Similarly, we could say that we love others because God first loved us (1 John 4:11).

The two Great Commandments—love God and love others—speak to the moral obligation upon us to love (Matt. 22:37–39; Mark 12:29–31). The heart, mind, and body are under this obligation, and therefore we cannot limit love to one aspect of our humanity, as if love were only emotional or rational or volitional. As we'll see, Scripture takes a comprehensive view of love.

### *A Disposition of the Heart*

In overreacting to the sentimental love of the world, some Christians have discounted the emotions as an essential part of love. In addition, they reason that a moral obligation cannot extend to the emotions because people cannot control how they feel. "All that matters is doing the right thing," they say. A mother may not feel like sacrificing for the good of her children, but because it's the right thing to do, she makes sacrifices anyway. But is it really the case that the mother's emotional bond with her children plays no role in her sacrifice? She may not feel good about the sacrifice *per se*, but she could feel an affection for her children that would certainly motivate her sacrifice.

If we reduced love merely to a sacrificial action, as some would have it, we would actually contradict Scripture: "Though I bestow all my goods to feed the poor, and though I give my body to be burned, and have not [love], it profiteth me nothing" (1 Cor. 13:3). The logic of this passage is unavoidable; not all sacrificial actions flow from love. The apostle Paul was not making a case for non-sacrificial love; he was making a case for having the right disposition toward the objects of our love. As he wrote to the Thessalonian believers, "So being affectionately desirous of you, we were willing to have imparted unto you . . . our own souls, because ye were dear unto us" (1 Thess. 2:8). This is the disposition of a loving heart.

THREE CENTRAL VIRTUES 81

## THE CASE FOR CHRISTIAN LOVE

Guide students in a **debate** on whether love contains an emotional element to preassess current knowledge.

Assign one group of students to argue that emotions are not a necessary element to love. Assign the other group of students to argue that emotions are a necessary element to love. Divide students into the two groups randomly or according to which side they choose. Appoint a leader for each group. Then direct students to collaborate in their group for five minutes by having them (1) consider why their position is correct, (2) articulate why the other position is incorrect, and (3) provide a concrete example to defend their own position. Invite students to present their best arguments. Compare student responses with the information on page 81.

## Apply

## GOD'S LOVE EMPOWERS OUR OWN

Guide a **discussion** to explain that loving people depends on one's experience of God's love.

Non-Christians do not think of themselves as unloving. They have people in their lives for whom they have genuine affection and concern. They can point to many selfless deeds performed in the service of their family and friends to prove that they are loving people.

Although these unbelievers have not experienced the love of God in Christ, they do seem to care for other people.

**Given this reality, how can Christians maintain that loving people depends on their personal experience of God's love?**

- *Biblical love is more than a general concern for family and friends. It has a specific concern for the good of others as God defines the good. The greatest good anyone can do for another person is to show them the love of God by word and by deed. But unless a person has experienced God's love in Christ, he or she is unable to do this.*
- *Biblical love calls us to love our enemies. This is impossible to do unless we have come to the realization that God loved us when we were His enemies. This experience of God's love in salvation frees believers to love their enemies.*
- *Biblical love requires a level of sacrifice that is impossible unless the love of God has assured one of his or her eternal destiny with God. Many Christians have laid down their lives for the good of others because God's love set them free from the fear of death and the need to preserve their lives in this world.*

### *A Mindful Consideration*

Doing good to others presupposes that we know what constitutes the good, and therefore love will be well-informed as to how Scripture defines the good. According to the prophet Micah, God has shown us "what is good," which is "to do justly, and to love mercy, and to walk humbly with [our] God" (Micah 6:8). Therefore, one aspect of love is a mindful consideration of how best to relate to people in diverse situations. This is not as easy as people think. Doing justice and showing mercy take more than good intentions; they also take biblical wisdom and discernment.

For example, how we love victims of injustice will look different from how we love the perpetrators of injustice. Biblical love "rejoiceth not in iniquity, but rejoiceth in the truth" (1 Cor. 13:6). Therefore, it is loving to validate the experience of genuine victims and then to protect them from further abuse. And it is loving to hold perpetrators accountable for their actions and then to call them to repentance. What is good for one is not appropriate for the other. And biblical love understands how to make these important distinctions.

### *A Joyful Action*

Saying "I love you" to the people we love is perfectly normal. However, we understand that sometimes our actions do not match our words. The apostle John wrote, "Let us not love in word, neither in tongue; but in deed and in truth" (1 John 3:18). While John was not prohibiting readers from telling people of their love, he was stressing that actions speak louder than words and that we do well to express genuine love by deeds that meet real needs.

James made the same observation: "If a brother or sister be naked, and destitute of daily food, and one of you say unto them, Depart in peace, be ye warmed and filled," all the while refusing to help them, such words are of no value (James 2:15–16). When the apostle Paul sought to inspire the Corinthian church in their love, he held up the Macedonian believers as an example for them. When the Macedonians gave, "the abundance of their joy and their deep poverty" overflowed in a wealth of generosity (2 Cor. 8:2). Even if we are poor, we should be joyfully eager to support those in need because that's what real love does.

## RIGHTLY ORDERED LOVES

Cheerfully giving to those in need when you're in poverty is not natural. It's a strange ethical choice—that is, until we understand the idea of *rightly ordered loves* (remember the definition of virtue from previous chapters). A man who loves money more than God and more than people has wrongly ordered loves. But so does the

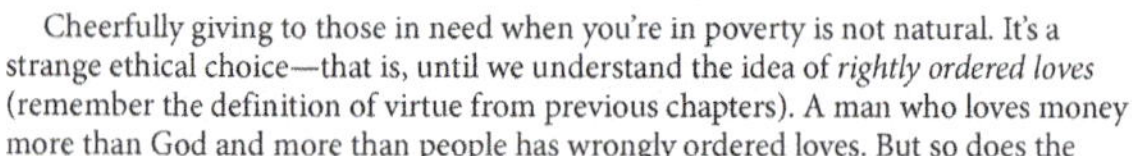

man who loves people more than he loves God; his loves are also out of order. Therefore, rightly ordered loves are necessary if we are to make right ethical choices.

How do the things I love influence my choices?

***Loving God above All***

The reason the Macedonian believers sacrificed financially for the support of other Christians was because the grace of God was powerfully at work in them (2 Cor. 8:1). Grace empowers believers to love God above all—above their possessions, their lives in this world, and their closest family members. The fact that Jesus calls the command to love God "the first and great commandment" (Matt. 22:38) is a strong argument for prioritizing love for God. Then there is the direct statement from Jesus that we are to prioritize love for Him above "father or mother . . . and . . . son or daughter" (Matt. 10:37).

And yet, when we prioritize love for God, the result is not less love for people but more love for them. Scripture teaches this explicitly. "By this we know that we love the children of God, when we love God, and keep his commandments" (1 John 5:2). It's impossible to truly love people with a biblical ethic without loving God above people.

natural love

LOVING GOD SUPREMELY

natural love expanded

Rightly ordered spiritual love increases our potential for loving others like a double concave lens refracts light and spreads it over a larger area.

The reasons for this are many, but here are a few to consider. First, by loving God above all, we do the greatest good for people, which is to set before them the worth and beauty of God for their enjoyment. The psalmist concurs, proclaiming, "My soul shall make her boast in the LORD: the humble shall hear thereof, and be glad" (Ps. 34:2). Second, by loving God above all, we are more scrupulous in keeping His commandments, including the commandments to love our neighbors and our enemies in all the ways God requires. Loving people can be hard, but loving God means having Him with us in the hard places. Third, by loving God above all, we relinquish all we have to His disposal. None are more generous to others than those who are convinced that God is their provider and their great reward. Fourth, by loving God above all, we lean more heavily on the Spirit's leading through the Scriptures and thereby possess the wisdom and grace necessary to do what is best for others. In each of these ways, our love for God releases an aroma of Christ which results in the good of others as they observe and experience His loving character reflected in us.

***Loving People Rightly***

Having considered how our love for God motivates ethical choices, we now turn our attention to how our love for people motivates our ethical choices. Our focus here is on what it means to love our neighbor as ourselves (Matt. 22:39). Whom we love and how we love are the two main issues before us.

There's a sense in which our love should be broad enough to include every human being, while at the same time we recognize the practical limits of our resources. We are to have a general goodwill toward humanity, desiring what is best for all people in all places. This sets us up to show love to the people within our sphere of influence regardless of who they are. Love shows no partiality based on ethnicity or socioeconomic status (Acts 10:34–43; James 2:1–13). At the same time, Scripture recognizes that our affections for family and friends will be stronger than they are for other people and that our duty to them takes priority (1 Tim. 5:8; Exod. 20:12; Eph. 6:1–4). This is not an absolute rule because there are occasions when our Christian ties take priority over our family ties (Luke 8:21; Gal. 6:10). The main point is that God has placed within our lives specific people for us to serve in real time and in real situations, albeit in various ways and to differing degrees depending on the circumstances.



## LOVE FOR GOD AND LOVE FOR PEOPLE

Use a **journaling** activity to prompt students to consider practical ways that their love for God can lead them to love people. Direct students to journal their answers as a prayer to God. Point to the following examples to assist students.

- Loving God can lead me to pray for peoples unreached with the gospel.
- Loving God can lead me to volunteer at my local food bank.
- Loving God can lead me to honor my parents by speaking respectfully to them.
- Loving God can lead me to sing in the church choir to assist the congregation's worship of God.
- Loving God can lead me to forgive a friend who apologized for some hurtful words spoken.
- Loving God can lead me to contemplate biblical solutions to ethical problems in the hopes of pushing my culture back toward creational norms.

The one constant in our love for people is that we have their best interests in mind, loving them as we love ourselves. We should treat others the way we want to be treated (Matt. 7:12). This includes actively performing deeds that will benefit them and refraining from deeds that would harm them.

With regard to harm, love for neighbor includes hating that which harms them. We must guard against the false dichotomy the world establishes between real love and an appropriate hate. The more we love people the more we will hate anything that ultimately threatens them, including the life-destroying decisions they may make. While people may struggle with the idea of a good hatred, everyone instinctively recognizes that indifference toward evil in the world is unloving. One of the most urgent ethical issues of our day is the protection of vulnerable people, which can be costly to those who stand up for them. But that's what biblical love does. It lays down its life for the good of others (John 15:13).

There are many practical ways to love others. We should not underestimate the power of rejoicing with those who rejoice (Rom. 12:15). For example, suppose a friend receives a new car from his parents, and he shares the good news with you. What is the loving response? Do you inwardly begrudge his new car because you're driving an old car or no car at all? Or do you put aside envy and share in your friend's blessing (1 Cor. 13:4)? The latter response is an ethical expression of Christian love because it flows from a genuine delight in your friend.

Christian love also recognizes and seeks to meet the greatest need that people have, which is spiritual and eternal in nature. As important as it is to feed a hungry person, it is infinitely more important to feed a spiritually hungry person with the Bread who supplies eternal life (John 6:35). We can and should do both. The church, however, has regularly faced challenges regarding its primary mission. As the reality of eternity recedes into the background of society and many temporal needs press upon us with immediate urgency, the church must remember that the gospel of Jesus Christ is what our neighbors need most urgently. The moment we lose sight of this is the moment we lose the Christian virtue of love.

### Thinking It Through 5.2

1. How does an unbiblical self-love differ from Christian love?
2. What is the biblical defense for understanding love as a disposition of the heart?
3. What is the biblical defense for understanding love as a joyful action?
4. How does prioritizing love for God motivate ethical choices?
5. How does love for others manifest itself in our ethical choices?

## 5.3 The Virtue of Hope

How can I be joyful when life is so difficult?

It's encouraging to know that God is actively at work on behalf of those who trust Him. Although God hasn't promised His people an easy life, He has promised that "all things work together for good to them that love God, to them who are the called according to his purpose" (Rom. 8:28). The "all things" includes even the bad things we experience. Everything from daily frustrations to the deepest hurts of life are woven into the fabric of God's redemptive purpose. Knowing this sustains the joy of many Christians in their darkest valleys.

The biblical view is realistic about the sorrows that accompany life. At the same time, it points forward to a day when God will wipe away every tear and restore this broken world (Rev. 21:4). For this reason Christians are able to grieve, not "as others which have no hope" (1 Thess. 4:13), but as those who eagerly anticipate the coming of the Lord (1 Thess. 4:14–18).

The virtue of Christian hope, therefore, reaches back to the past where God has acted redemptively in human history, ensuring that the ravages of sin and death are



## Assess

Guide a **summative assessment** by directing students to answer the questions in Thinking It Through 5.2.

### Thinking It Through 5.2

1. Unbiblical self-love is self-absorbed. Self-absorbed love is a vice because it never goes any higher than one's private self-interest, never makes any sacrifices for the good of others, and paradoxically never considers its own best interest in an eternal sense. Biblical love is spiritual—it is the fruit of the Holy Spirit (Gal. 5:22). It flows from God, and thereby enables us to love as He loves (1 John 4:10, 19). As Augustine wrote, "I define 'love' as any movement of the soul to enjoy God for God's own sake, and to enjoy one's self and one's neighbor for God's sake" (*On Christian Teaching* 3.10.16, in William Harmless, ed., *In His Own Words* [Washington, DC: CUA Press, 2010], 170).
2. If we reduced love merely to a sacrificial action, we would contradict Scripture—"though I give my body to be burned, and have not [love], it profiteth me nothing" (1 Cor. 13:3). The logic of this passage is unavoidable; not all sacrificial actions flow from love. The apostle Paul was not making a case for non-sacrificial love; he was making a case for having the right disposition toward the object of our love. As he wrote to the Thessalonian believers, "So being affectionately desirous of you, we were willing to have imparted unto you . . . our own souls, because ye were dear unto us" (1 Thess. 2:8).
3. The apostle John wrote, "Let us not love in word, neither in tongue; but in deed and in truth" (1 John 3:18). While John was not prohibiting readers from telling people of their love, he was stressing that actions speak louder than words, and we do well to express genuine love by deeds that meet real needs. James made the same observation: "If a brother or sister be naked, and destitute of daily food, and one of you say unto them, Depart in peace, be ye warmed and filled," all the while refusing to help them, such words are of no value (James 2:15–16).
4. When we prioritize love for God, the result is not less love for people, but more love for them. Scripture teaches this explicitly: "By this we know that we love the children of God, when we love God, and keep his commandments" (1 John 5:2). It's impossible to truly love people with a biblical ethic without loving God above people.
5. One of the most urgent ethical issues of our day is the protection of vulnerable people, which can be costly to those who stand up for them. But that's what biblical love does. It lays down its life for the good of others (John 15:13). In terms of our day-to-day treatment of others, there are many helpful ways we can love them. We should not underestimate the power of rejoicing with those who rejoice and weeping with those who weep (Rom. 12:15). These responses are ethical expressions of Christ's love in us when demonstrated from a genuine regard for those made in God's image. Biblical love also recognizes and seeks to meet the greatest need that people have, which is spiritual and eternal in nature. As important as it is to feed a hungry person, it is infinitely more important to feed a spiritually hungry person with the bread of eternal life (John 6:35).

## 5.3 The Virtue of Hope

How can I be joyful when life is so difficult?

### Objectives

**5.3.1** Define *hope*.

**5.3.2** Relate God's character and nature to the virtue of hope.

"swallowed up in [the] victory" of Christ (1 Cor. 15:54). It also reaches forward to the wrapping up of redemptive history when all of God's promises meet their final eschatological goal. Where true Christian hope exists, we find a tenacity among believers to move forward in God's ways even as they patiently wait for the completion of God's work.[9]

### THE SOURCE OF CHRISTIAN HOPE

Hope in the Lord rather than in our circumstances is what fuels our joy, and it is joy in the Lord that enables us to abound in hope. The reciprocal relationship between hope and joy is made explicit in Scripture: "Now the God of *hope* fill you with all *joy* and peace in believing, that ye may abound in *hope*, through the power of the Holy Ghost" (Rom. 15:13, emphasis added).

The fact that God is identified as "the God of hope" is a clear indication that He is the source of our hope. The verse above amplifies this point with the additional comment that God's Spirit empowers our hope. The Spirit is the guarantee of our promised inheritance until we acquire possession of it (Eph. 1:14).

Faith is also indispensable for keeping hope alive. Scripture indicates that it is "in believing" that we can "abound in hope" (Rom. 15:13). Only believers can have the true virtue of hope because God's promises of redemption are only given to believers (1 Pet. 1:3; Gal. 5:5).[10]

#### *Hope Defined*

Christian **hope** may be defined as "the expectation of the things that faith has believed to be truly promised by God."[11] Oliver O'Donovan describes hope this way: "When we hope, we begin from the problematic character of the present, from its ambiguity and unsatisfying incompleteness, and turn gratefully to the future judgment of God which perfects the imperfections of the present and promises completion."[12] The validity of hope is not based on what a person wishes *might* happen but on the certainty of what God promises *will* happen.

The impact of hopelessness on people's ethical choices can be seen all around us. How many people turn to substance abuse to escape feelings of hopelessness? How many people resort to crime and justify it because they see no other hope to improve their lives? How many marriages end in divorce because of hopelessness? How many people end their own lives in suicide because of hopelessness? And how many people despair from a guilty conscience for lack of hope in the Redeemer? These ethical failures are undeniably connected to the absence of the virtue of hope.

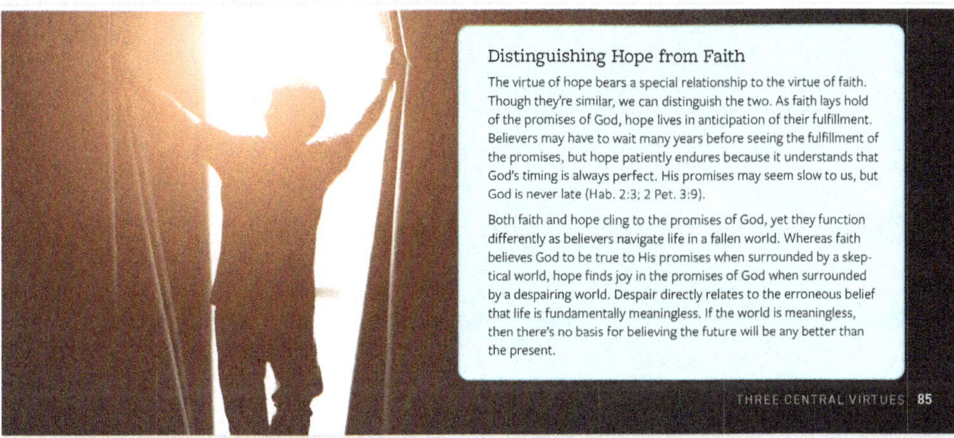

Distinguishing Hope from Faith

The virtue of hope bears a special relationship to the virtue of faith. Though they're similar, we can distinguish the two. As faith lays hold of the promises of God, hope lives in anticipation of their fulfillment. Believers may have to wait many years before seeing the fulfillment of the promises, but hope patiently endures because it understands that God's timing is always perfect. His promises may seem slow to us, but God is never late (Hab. 2:3; 2 Pet. 3:9).

Both faith and hope cling to the promises of God, yet they function differently as believers navigate life in a fallen world. Whereas faith believes God to be true to His promises when surrounded by a skeptical world, hope finds joy in the promises of God when surrounded by a despairing world. Despair directly relates to the erroneous belief that life is fundamentally meaningless. If the world is meaningless, then there's no basis for believing the future will be any better than the present.

THREE CENTRAL VIRTUES 85

**5.3.3** Contrast hope in God with misplaced hopes.

**5.3.4** Contrast the virtue of hope with a utilitarian ethic. BWS

**5.3.5** Apply the virtue of hope to being a hopeful person.

### Biblical Worldview Shaping

- **Man's Chief End** (evaluate): Without the Christian virtue of hope, people are tempted to use sinful means to achieve desired ends. (5.3.4)

### Printed Resource

- Activity 5.3: Becoming a More Hopeful Person

## Engage

### FACING TRYING CIRCUMSTANCES

Guide a **discussion** to engage students with this section's essential question.

**What are some common negative responses people have when facing trials?** *Possible answers: frustration, disappointment, anger, doubting God's goodness*

**Why do you think people have a difficult time being joyful when life is difficult?** *Possible answers: People base their happiness on circumstances rather than on God; people experience severe trials that seem to be pointless; people either lack the hope that their life will get better, or their hope has been greatly diminished, as may happen with believers from time to time.*

**How can I be joyful when life is so difficult?** *While it is natural for hardships to bring sorrow, believers can always take joy in their relationship with God.*

Ask volunteers to tell how their hope in the Lord has brought them joy in trials. Elicit examples such as the following:

- Being hopeful that God is working life's difficulties for my eternal good enables me to have joy in my trials.
- Being hopeful about God's promise of heaven, where there is no sin and suffering, brings joy to me in my present hardships.
- Being hopeful that my suffering as a believer is not meaningless but shares in the sufferings of Christ brings me joy.

### BECOMING A MORE HOPEFUL PERSON

Use **Activity 5.3** on page 27 to prepare the students for the section.

## Instruct

### THE SOURCE OF CHRISTIAN HOPE

Guide a **discussion** of Romans 15:13 to help students recognize the origin and nature of Christian hope.

**Why does the apostle Paul call God the "God of hope"?** *because God is the source of hope*

**What does the God of hope do for those who believe?** *He fills them "with all joy and peace in believing."*

**What is the result of a believer being filled with joy and peace?** *Believers "abound in hope."*

**How do we know that the Holy Spirit is the source of the believer's hope?** *Romans 15:13 says that believers "abound in hope, through the power of the Holy Ghost."*

### HOPE VERSUS FAITH

Use a **Turn and Talk** to help students distinguish hope from faith. Direct attention to the textbox on page 85 and encourage the students to use the following questions to guide their interaction with fellow students.

**How do faith and hope differ regarding God's promises?** *Faith takes hold of God's promises as being true. Hope waits patiently for the fulfillment of God's promises.*

**How do faith and hope function as believers navigate life in a fallen world?** *Faith counters the skepticism of the fallen world* *with the truth of God's promises. Hope counters the despair of the fallen world with the assurance of a better world to come.*

### BUILDING HOPE ON GOD'S UNCHANGING CHARACTER

Use **direct instruction** to explain that Christian hope is founded on the unchanging character and promises of God.

Christian hope is not wishful thinking. People often use the word *hope* as a synonym for something they wish would happen but cannot be certain will happen. For example, we might say that we hope a particular political candidate wins an upcoming election. Since we don't know for sure if the candidate will win, our hope in this context is tenuous.

Christian hope, however, is sturdy and certain because it rests on the unchanging character of God and His promises. Because God and His promises are unchanging, believers can be confident that the blessed life that God has promised will one day become a reality. Therefore, growing in the knowledge of God's character and promises is essential for growing in hope.

## Apply

### WHAT HAPPENS WHEN PEOPLE LACK HOPE?

Guide a **discussion** to help students recognize that using sinful means to accomplish a desired end is contrary to hope in God.

**How is it contrary to hope in God for someone to steal some food to feed his or her hungry family?** *The person is assuming that God is unable to provide and that having food is more important than trusting God.*
**How was it contrary to hope in God for Sarah and Abraham to enlist Hagar to bear them a son?** *They assumed that God's delay in providing the promised child meant that He needed their help.*
**How is it contrary to hope in God for a student to cheat in college out of fear of losing his or her scholarship?** *The student is assuming that taking shortcuts with studies is more beneficial than investing time in the studies and trusting God with the results.*

*Hope Well-Founded*

Unless God is capable of making good on His promises, there's no basis for hope. His character and nature must be what Scripture says they are in order for our expectations to be well-grounded. Every divine attribute serves as a certain anchor for hope. For example, God's truthfulness assures us that His promises are not empty, His infinite power guarantees that His promises will not fail, and His unchanging character undergirds the unchanging nature of His promises (Num. 23:19; Titus 1:2; Job 42:2; Mal. 3:6).

As if all this were not enough (when in fact God's character *is* enough), God goes the extra mile just to put our minds at ease. He confirms His promise with an oath (Heb. 6:17–18). God's character and God's oath give believers a double assurance that His promises are irrevocable.

The storms of life may rage against the believer, but the anchor of hope will keep the ship of faith from capsizing. How certain is this hope? It is as certain as the resurrection and ascension of Christ, the one who has entered within the heavenly temple as our "great high priest" (Heb. 4:14; see also 6:19–20). The believer can no more fall short of the promised inheritance than Christ can fail in His priestly work or cease to reign as our risen Lord.

*To hope is to exist in trust that God's constancy is such that the present is on the way to perfection.*

JOHN WEBSTER

THE SUBSTITUTES FOR CHRISTIAN HOPE

Christ is the only hope for a hopeless world (Col. 1:27). Those who reject the hope that God offers in the gospel must find substitutes to combat hopelessness. Money and family are common substitutes. Human progress is another one.

*The Myth of Progress*

The temptation for the modern world is to place its hope in science, technology, and political structures. Because these things have ameliorated* disease, poverty, and conflict, the assumption is that they will lead humans into a perfect world of peace and prosperity. While science, technology, and good political structures are not the enemy (they are all part of the Creation Mandate), people fail to appreciate their limits. Despite great advancements that have improved the quality of life, hopelessness remains a problem. Some of the most anxious and unsettled people in the world today are those who have benefited the most from mankind's achievements.

But there's an even bigger problem. Hope in human progress undermines the Christian ethic because it promotes a **utopian*** future in direct competition with God's eschatological hope. It is a fantasy to think that humans can usher in a perfect world. A little historical awareness, as well as a biblical doctrine of man, should put this myth to rest. Just think of the utopian leaders of the past who have employed unethical means in their attempts to usher in a "perfect" world—for example, Vladimir Lenin or Mao Zedong. The things sinners do to achieve their supposedly noble goals for a better future often violate God's good law and have resulted in some of the worst atrocities in history.

**ameliorated:** made better

**utopian:** relating to an ideal society of perfect peace, justice, and prosperity; often intended as a description of an unrealistic hope

86 VIRTUES

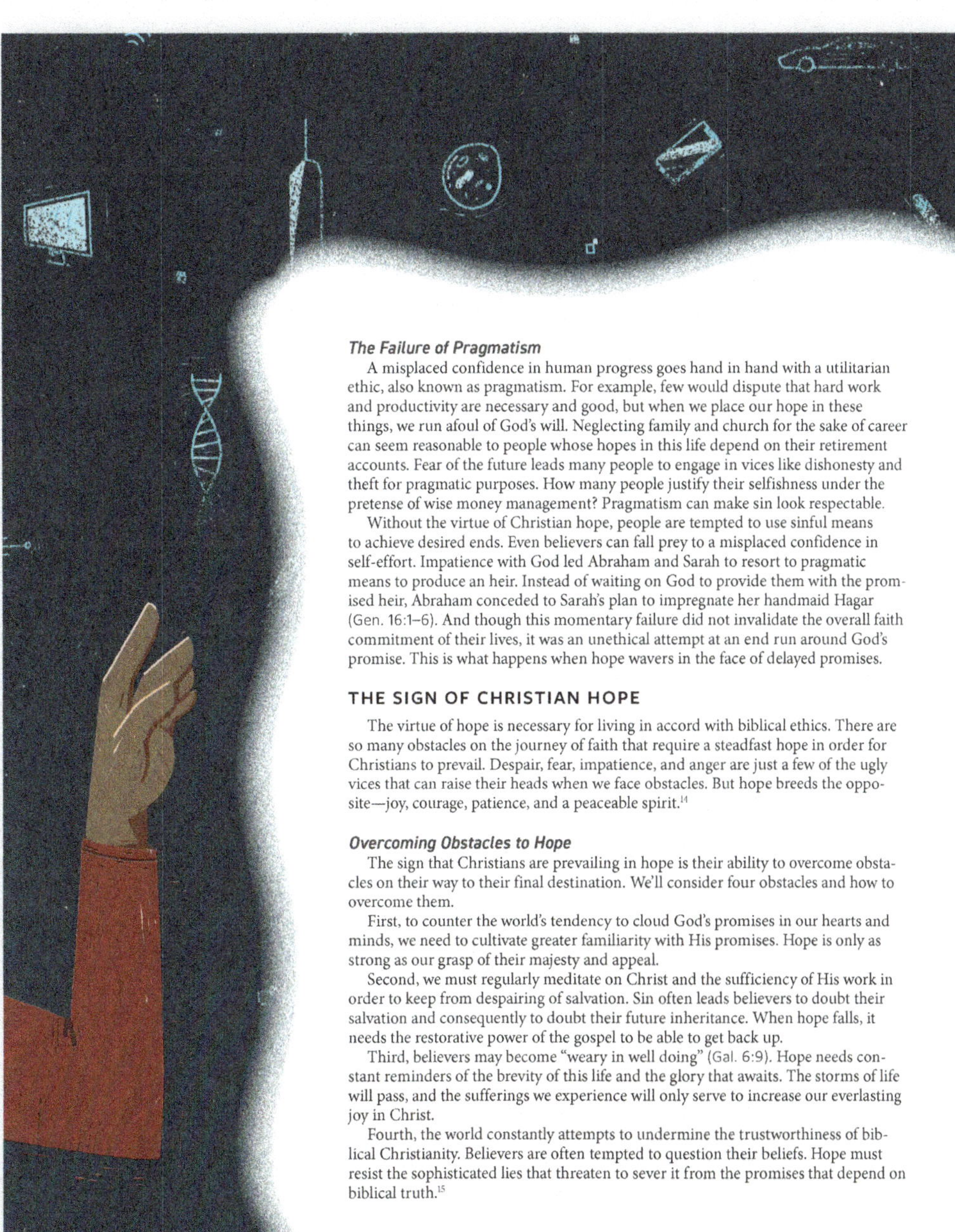

### *The Failure of Pragmatism*

A misplaced confidence in human progress goes hand in hand with a utilitarian ethic, also known as pragmatism. For example, few would dispute that hard work and productivity are necessary and good, but when we place our hope in these things, we run afoul of God's will. Neglecting family and church for the sake of career can seem reasonable to people whose hopes in this life depend on their retirement accounts. Fear of the future leads many people to engage in vices like dishonesty and theft for pragmatic purposes. How many people justify their selfishness under the pretense of wise money management? Pragmatism can make sin look respectable.

Without the virtue of Christian hope, people are tempted to use sinful means to achieve desired ends. Even believers can fall prey to a misplaced confidence in self-effort. Impatience with God led Abraham and Sarah to resort to pragmatic means to produce an heir. Instead of waiting on God to provide them with the promised heir, Abraham conceded to Sarah's plan to impregnate her handmaid Hagar (Gen. 16:1–6). And though this momentary failure did not invalidate the overall faith commitment of their lives, it was an unethical attempt at an end run around God's promise. This is what happens when hope wavers in the face of delayed promises.

## THE SIGN OF CHRISTIAN HOPE

The virtue of hope is necessary for living in accord with biblical ethics. There are so many obstacles on the journey of faith that require a steadfast hope in order for Christians to prevail. Despair, fear, impatience, and anger are just a few of the ugly vices that can raise their heads when we face obstacles. But hope breeds the opposite—joy, courage, patience, and a peaceable spirit.[14]

### *Overcoming Obstacles to Hope*

The sign that Christians are prevailing in hope is their ability to overcome obstacles on their way to their final destination. We'll consider four obstacles and how to overcome them.

First, to counter the world's tendency to cloud God's promises in our hearts and minds, we need to cultivate greater familiarity with His promises. Hope is only as strong as our grasp of their majesty and appeal.

Second, we must regularly meditate on Christ and the sufficiency of His work in order to keep from despairing of salvation. Sin often leads believers to doubt their salvation and consequently to doubt their future inheritance. When hope falls, it needs the restorative power of the gospel to be able to get back up.

Third, believers may become "weary in well doing" (Gal. 6:9). Hope needs constant reminders of the brevity of this life and the glory that awaits. The storms of life will pass, and the sufferings we experience will only serve to increase our everlasting joy in Christ.

Fourth, the world constantly attempts to undermine the trustworthiness of biblical Christianity. Believers are often tempted to question their beliefs. Hope must resist the sophisticated lies that threaten to sever it from the promises that depend on biblical truth.[15]



## OVERCOMING OBSTACLES: THE SIGN OF CHRISTIAN HOPE

Guide a **discussion** to prompt students to evaluate whether hope is alive and active in their lives.

**How can you know whether Christian hope is alive and active in your life?** *by taking note of whether you are overcoming obstacles to hope*

**What could you do to counter the world's tendency to cloud God's promises in your heart and mind?** *Students should identify specific promises of God with which they are cultivating greater familiarity.*

**What could you do to keep from despairing in your fight against your sin?** *Students should indicate whether they are regularly meditating on Christ and the sufficiency of His work.*

**What could you do to overcome any weariness from doing what is right in difficult situations?** *Students should indicate whether they are regularly contemplating the brevity of life and the glories that await believers.*

**What could you do to resist the world's temptation to question the trustworthiness of biblical Christianity?** *Students should identify ways they strengthen their confidence in Scripture.*

THREE CENTRAL VIRTUES 87

## Assess

Guide a **summative assessment** by directing students to answer the questions in Thinking It Through 5.3.

### Thinking It Through 5.3

1. Christian hope may be defined as "the expectation of the things that faith has believed to be truly promised by God" (James T. Dennison, Jr., comp., "Calvin's Catechism [1537]," in vol. 1, *Reformed Confessions of the 16th and 17th Centuries in English Translation* [Grand Rapids, MI: Reformation Heritage Books, 2008], 378). Both faith and hope cling to the promises of God, yet they function differently as believers navigate life in a fallen world. Whereas faith believes God to be true to His promises when surrounded by a skeptical world, hope finds joy in the promises of God when surrounded by a despairing world.
2. Unless God is capable of making good on His promises, there's no basis for hope. His character and nature must be what Scripture teaches in order for our expectations to be well-grounded. Every divine attribute serves as a certain anchor for hope. For example, God's truthfulness assures us that His promises are not empty, His infinite power guarantees that His promises will not fail, and His unchanging character undergirds the unchanging nature of His promises. As if this were not enough (though God's character is enough), He goes the extra mile just to put our minds at ease. He confirms His promise with an oath (Heb. 6:17). God's character and God's oath give believers a double assurance that His promises are irrevocable.
3. Those who reject the hope that God offers in the gospel must find substitutes to combat hopelessness. The temptation for the modern world is to place its hope in science, technology, and political structures. Because these things have ameliorated disease, poverty, and conflict, the assumption is that they will lead humans into a perfect world of peace and prosperity. Despite great advancements that have improved the quality of life, hopelessness remains a problem. But there's an even bigger problem. Hope in human progress undermines the Christian ethic because it promotes a utopian future in direct competition with God's eschatological hope. It is a myth to think that humans can usher in a perfect world.
4. A misplaced confidence in human progress goes hand-in-hand with pragmatism. For example, few would dispute that hard work and productivity are necessary and good, but when we place our hope in these things, we run afoul of God's will. Neglecting one's family and church for the sake of a career can seem reasonable to people whose hopes in this life depend on their retirement accounts. Fear of the future leads many people to engage in vices for pragmatic purposes. Without the virtue of Christian hope, people are tempted to use sinful means to achieve desired ends. Even believers can fall prey to a misplaced confidence in self-effort. Impatience with God led Abraham and Sarah to resort to pragmatic means to produce an heir. Instead of waiting on God to provide them with the promised heir, Abraham conceded to Sarah's plan to impregnate her handmaid Hagar (Gen. 16:1–6). This is what happens when hope wavers in the face of delayed promises.
5. See "Overcoming Obstacles to Hope" on page 87 for the correct answers.

***Finishing Well through Hope***

Believers are not called to "fix" the world; they're called to be faithful to the Lord who rules the world with sovereign might. We cannot fall for the world's imagined perfectibility of life in this fallen creation. The world cannot and will not achieve perfect peace and justice. Christ alone is qualified to realize these things for His people, and He will not do so until He returns. Therefore, hope fixes its eyes on Christ rather than on the hollow promises of political leaders.

This doesn't mean Christians can be inactive or disengaged from the culture. Christian hope is neither passive nor silent in the world; rather, it bears witness to the reign of Christ through a life of love and service. It motivates Christians to do the right thing for the right reasons, especially in difficult circumstances.[16]

One of the most powerful witnesses to the world is when Christians redeem the time by living in this present evil age as citizens of the age to come (Eph. 5:16).[17] Everything that a Christian does in the world will look different from the way the world does things. How Christians go about raising their families, pursuing a career, managing resources, and facing trials should all strike a distinctive note of hope.

Far from engendering complacency in believers, the virtue of hope empowers the most rigorous ethical behavior possible. Avoiding hardships and aspiring to an easy life here and now is not our hope. Our hope reaches for something greater and better. It reaches for God's best, rests in God's promises, and runs toward God's reward. It has one goal in mind—to finish well, hearing the Lord say, "Well done, thou good and faithful servant" (Matt. 25:21).[18]

#### Thinking It Through 5.3

1. How does the virtue of hope relate to the virtue of faith?
2. How do God's character and nature relate to the virtue of hope?
3. What is wrong with placing our hope in human progress?
4. What can happen when a person lacks biblical hope?
5. What four obstacles do we need to overcome to prevail in hope?

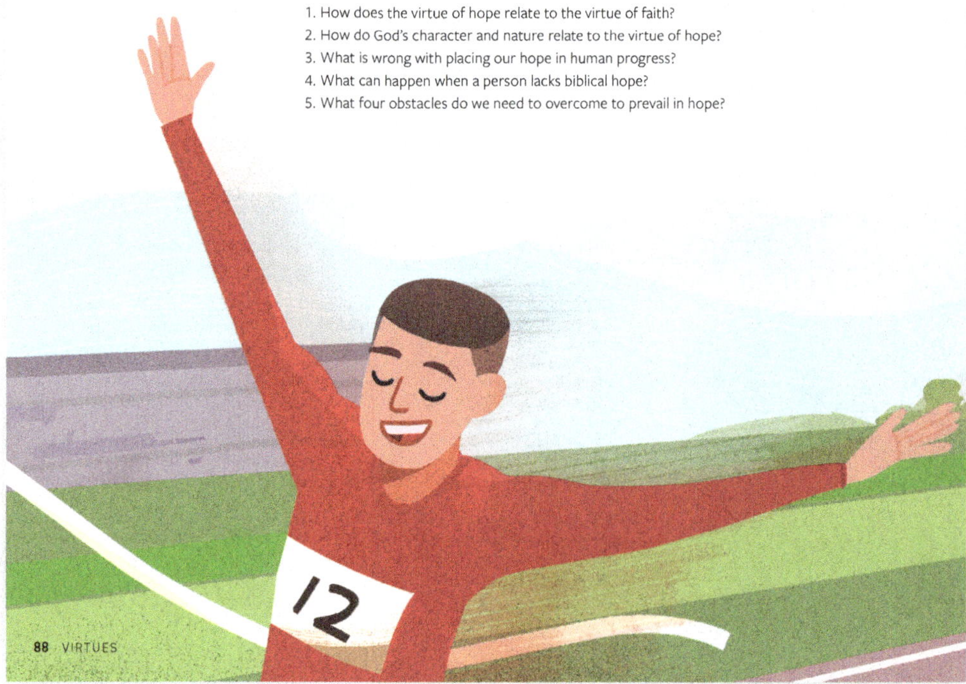

# Review 05

THREE CENTRAL VIRTUES

### Terms to Remember

- faith
- love
- hope
- utopian

### Scripture Memory

1 Corinthians 13:13

### Understanding Ethics

1. Explain the reason love is the greatest virtue.
2. Summarize the three essential elements of faith.
3. Explain the difference between biblical love and an unbiblical self-love.
4. How are faith and hope related?

### Practicing Ethical Decision-Making

5. The virtue of faith enables Christians to make difficult ethical choices. How would you respond in the following situation?

   You're struggling with some financial needs and learn of an opportunity to earn some money, but it involves engaging in sinful activity.

6. How would you apply the virtue of hope in overcoming the following obstacle?

   Suppose you are experiencing a long-term disability, and you're tempted to despair because it seems the suffering will never end.

### Analyzing and Evaluating Ethical Claims

7. How would you respond to the claim that the highest love is loving yourself?
8. How would you respond to the claim that mental assent alone is real faith?
9. How would you respond to the claim that biblical love is only an action and does not involve the emotions?
10. How would you respond to the claim that human progress is a sufficient hope for the world?

### Creating My Own Position Statements on Ethics

11. Summarize your own position on whether the virtue of love is ever compatible with hate.
12. Summarize your own position on the best way to address feelings of hopelessness.

# Chapter 5 Review

## Terms to Remember

- **faith:** "A firm and certain knowledge of God's benevolence toward us, founded upon the truth of the freely given promise in Christ, both revealed to our minds and sealed upon our hearts through the Holy Spirit" (John Calvin, *Institutes* 3.2.7).
- **love:** "Any movement of the soul to enjoy God for God's own sake, and to enjoy one's self and one's neighbor for God's sake" (Augustine, *On Christian Teaching* 3.10.16).
- **hope:** "The expectation of the things that faith has believed to be truly promised by God" (Dennison, Jr., "Calvin's Catechism," 378).
- **utopian:** Relating to an ideal society of perfect peace, justice, and prosperity; often intended as a description of an unrealistic hope.

## Understanding Ethics

1. Whereas faith and hope cease when the future glory becomes reality, love continues for all eternity.
2. Knowledge, assent, and confidence are the three elements of faith. Knowledge relates to the things that are believed. Assent is the recognition that the content of Scripture is true. Confidence is the heartfelt embrace of the truthful content of Scripture.
3. Biblical love is rooted in God's love and expressed toward people in ways that imitate God's love for people. This includes doing things that serve people's everlasting joy in God, even at great expense to oneself. Self-love, however, elevates personal and immediate gratification, even sacrificing the good of others for personal gain.
4. Faith takes hold of God's promises as true, and hope waits patiently for God to fulfill His promises.

## Practicing Ethical Decision-Making

5. Students should consider how trust in God for one's financial needs would enable them to resist the temptation to engage in sinful activity for the sake of monetary gain.
6. Students should consider how disabled believers might find strength to overcome despair by looking to God's promise of the future resurrection.

## Analyzing and Evaluating Ethical Claims

7. God's love is the highest love there is. To make self-love the highest love is to elevate self-love above God's love.
8. The demons possess mental assent, but they do not have faith. In addition, Jesus spoke of people who give lip service to His lordship, but they do not have faith in Him.
9. Scripture teaches that it is possible to perform actions that appear loving but are not. An action is not loving if it does not include the emotional element.
10. Human progress cannot usher in a perfect world. All such attempts in history have led to disaster. There is no basis in Scripture or history to conclude that human progress is a sufficient hope for the world.

## Creating My Own Position Statements on Ethics

11. Students should provide honest answers while also dealing with the arguments in the textbook that maintain the compatibility of the virtue of love with a biblical form of hate.
12. Students should provide their own position while also interacting with the strategies in the textbook for addressing hopelessness.

# Lesson Plan Overview

**CHAPTER 6:** Virtues, Part 1

**EV** ExamView
**IA** Instructional Aid
**PPT pres.** PowerPoint presentation

| PAGES | OBJECTIVES | RESOURCES | ASSESSMENTS |
|---|---|---|---|
| **6.1 Righteousness and Goodness** (3 DAYS) | | | |
| 91–95 | **6.1.1** Define *righteousness* and *goodness*.<br>**6.1.2** Compare and contrast Christian and non-Christian conceptions of righteousness and goodness.<br>**6.1.3** Contrast the virtues of righteousness and goodness with the vices of ungodliness and corruption.<br>**6.1.4** Develop a plan for growing in righteousness and goodness. | **TEACHER EDITION**<br>• IA 6.1: *Virtue and Vice Chart*<br>**ACTIVITIES**<br>• 6.1 The Essence of Virtue<br>**BJU PRESS TROVE***<br>• PPT pres.: Chapter 6 | **STUDENT EDITION**<br>• Thinking It Through 6.1 |
| **6.2 Prudence** (3 DAYS) | | | |
| 95–100 | **6.2.1** Define *prudence*.<br>**6.2.2** Compare and contrast Christian and non-Christian conceptions of prudence.<br>**6.2.3** Contrast the virtue of prudence with the vices of rashness and cunning.<br>BWS Wisdom (evaluate)<br>**6.2.4** Give examples of how prudence relates to ethical decision-making and ethical living.<br>BWS Wisdom (formulate)<br>**6.2.5** Develop a plan for growing in prudence.<br>BWS Wisdom (apply) | **TEACHER EDITION**<br>• IA 6.2: *Virtues and Vices in the Bible*<br>**ACTIVITIES**<br>• 6.2 Prudent Prudence<br>**BJU PRESS TROVE**<br>• PPT pres.: Chapter 6 | **STUDENT EDITION**<br>• Thinking It Through 6.2 |
| **6.3 Diligence, Faithfulness, and Courage** (3 DAYS) | | | |
| 101–6 | **6.3.1** Define *diligence*, *faithfulness*, and *courage*.<br>**6.3.2** Identify ways in which diligence, faithfulness, and courage can be misapplied to wrong goals.<br>BWS Man's Chief End (explain)<br>**6.3.3** Contrast the virtues of diligence, faithfulness, and courage with the vices of sloth, workaholism, disloyalty, recklessness, and cowardice.<br>**6.3.4** Give examples of how diligence, faithfulness, and courage relate to ethical decision-making and ethical living.<br>**6.3.5** Develop a plan for growing in diligence, faithfulness, and courage. | **ACTIVITIES**<br>• 6.3 The Place for Diligence, Faithfulness, and Courage<br>**BJU PRESS TROVE**<br>• PPT pres.: Chapter 6 | **STUDENT EDITION**<br>• Thinking It Through 6.3 |

*Digital resources for homeschool users are available on Homeschool Hub.

| PAGES | OBJECTIVES | RESOURCES | ASSESSMENTS |
|---|---|---|---|
| **6.4 Self-Control, Temperance, and Patience** (3 DAYS) | | | |
| 106–9 | **6.4.1** Define *self-control*, *temperance*, and *patience*.<br>**6.4.2** Compare and contrast Christian and non-Christian motives for self-control, temperance, and patience.<br>**6.4.3** Contrast the virtues of self-control, temperance, and patience with the vices of self-indulgence, addiction, asceticism, and strife.<br>**6.4.4** Give examples of how self-control, temperance, and patience relate to ethical decision-making and ethical living.<br>**6.4.5** Develop a plan for growing in self-control, temperance, and patience. | **ACTIVITIES**<br>• 6.4 A Dynamic Duo: Self-Control and Temperance<br>**BJU PRESS TROVE**<br>• PPT pres.: Chapter 6 | **STUDENT EDITION**<br>• Thinking It Through 6.4 |
| **Review** | | | |
| 110 | Recall concepts, terms, and Scripture memory from Chapter 6. | | **STUDENT EDITION**<br>• Chapter 6 Review |
| **Test** | | | |
| | Demonstrate knowledge of the material from Chapter 6 by taking the test. | | **ASSESSMENTS**<br>• Chapter 6 Test<br>**BJU PRESS TROVE**<br>• EV: Chapter 6 test bank |

CHAPTER 6

# Overview

With so many obstacles how do I navigate the right path?

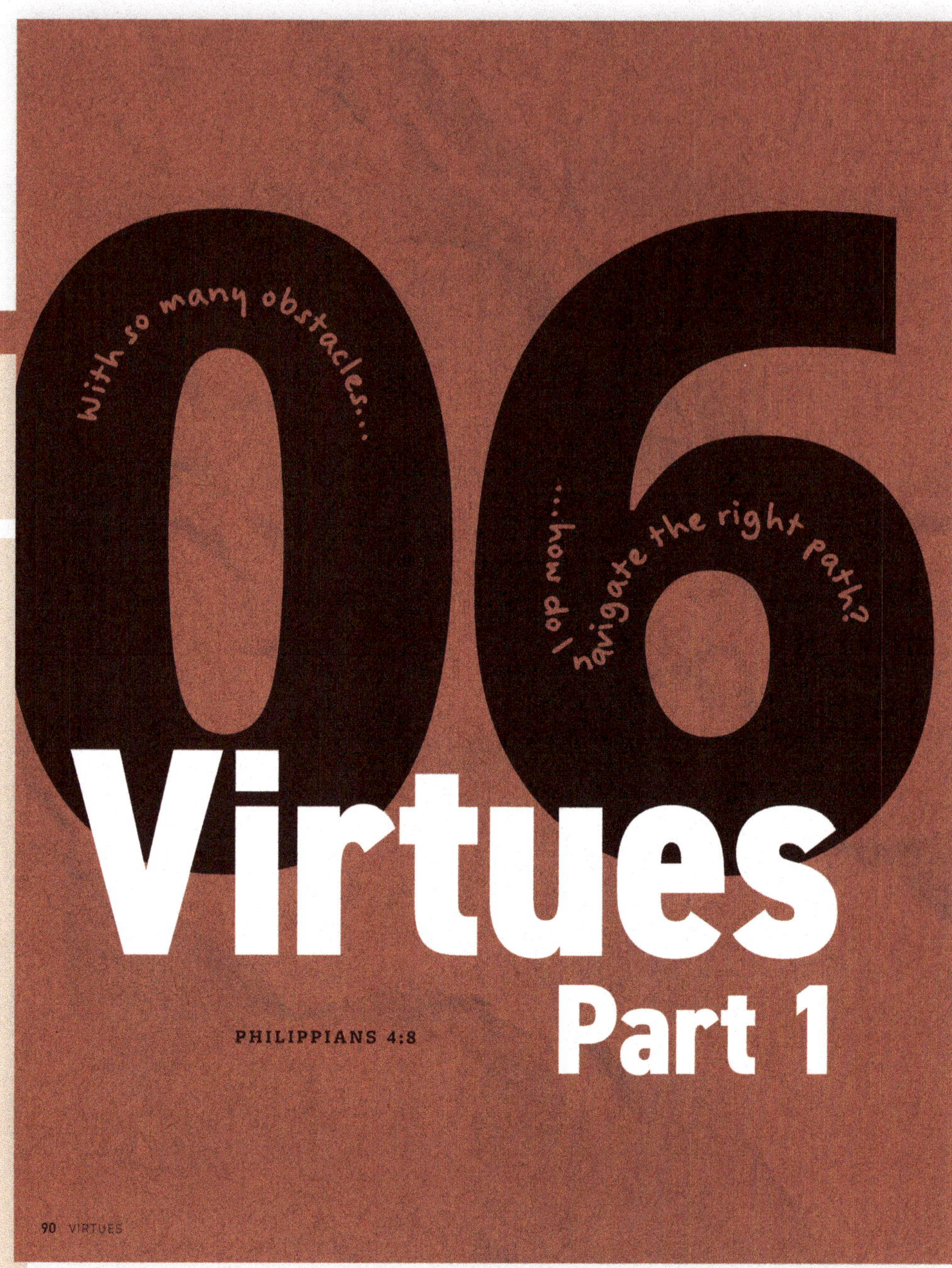

With so many obstacles...
how do I... navigate the right path?
06
Virtues
Part 1
PHILIPPIANS 4:8
90 VIRTUES

## Objectives

**6.1** Analyze Christian and non-Christian conceptions of each virtue.

**6.2** Evaluate Christian and non-Christian applications of each virtue.

**6.3** Formulate plans for growth in each virtue.

## Terms to Remember

- righteousness
- goodness
- ungodliness
- corruption
- prudence
- cunning
- rashness
- diligence
- faithfulness
- courage
- sloth
- workaholism
- disloyalty
- recklessness
- cowardice
- self-control
- temperance
- patience
- self-indulgence
- addiction
- asceticism
- strife

## Scripture Memory

- Philippians 4:8

## 6.1 Righteousness and Goodness

Have you ever felt crushed under the weight of your homework? Have you ever been on the brink of despair from trying to figure out how to do that big project? You might have approached your teacher with your frustration only to hear that you have all you need to do the assignments. You just need to sit down and do the work! That doesn't quite remove the feeling of being overwhelmed though, does it?

You should be aware by now that living a life marked by virtue is indeed a challenging task. Identifying virtues will be a helpful step toward living virtuously for God's glory. These three chapters on virtues should make you aware of most virtues, but they should also do much more than that. Our sin nature rebels against God's expectations (Rom. 7:20, 23). Our flesh lusts after complacency or any vice that seems more rewarding than letting virtue motivate our actions. Developing virtue in your heart so that it flows out into your thoughts and actions takes a lot of effort. Thankfully, like the illustration about the homework assignments above, believers have everything they need to develop virtue and live virtuously (2 Pet. 1:3–9). They aren't left to themselves to produce virtue in their lives.

You have learned what is the basis for ethical living and virtuous character—the character of God Himself (Exod. 34:6–7). You have also learned that believers can live ethically and virtuously by means of the Spirit's regenerative work and transformative power (Rom. 12:2; Titus 3:5). The next two virtues we will cover, like all virtues, seem so foreign to man in his natural state. By God's grace, believers are able to exemplify and practice righteousness and goodness. In fact, God commands and expects His children to live according to these two virtues (1 Pet. 1:15–16).

### DEFINING RIGHTEOUSNESS AND GOODNESS

Righteousness corresponds to the concepts of *rightness* and *right*, the opposites of wickedness and wrong. That much is easily observable from the root of the term and from looking at its antonyms.[1] Defining righteousness can't be done by simply saying that *x* is right and *y* is wrong. If something is to be determined to be right, then there has to be a standard by which to judge its rightness or wrongness. So the virtue of **righteousness** is the conformity of an individual's life to God's standards of moral perfection. If we kept our definition more general, we could say that righteousness is



## Engage

### A STARTING POINT FOR RIGHT AND WRONG

Guide a **Socratic seminar** where students in groups of two or three ask each other and respond to the questions below and any follow-up questions.

**What makes right right? What makes wrong wrong? If there are such things as moral absolutes in the universe, what are they? What makes an absolute standard an absolute standard?** *Answers should point to God, His character, and His purposes as found in the Word. This is the "ought" discussed in Chapter 1.*

Righteousness and goodness, along with the rest of the virtues, are truly virtuous when the starting point is God—His character and His divine purposes as found in Scripture.

## 6.1 Righteousness and Goodness

Why isn't it sufficient for me to identify what is right and what is good based solely on situations starting and ending well?

### Objectives

**6.1.1** Define *righteousness* and *goodness*.

**6.1.2** Compare and contrast Christian and non-Christian conceptions of righteousness and goodness.

**6.1.3** Contrast the virtues of righteousness and goodness with the vices of ungodliness and corruption.

**6.1.4** Develop a plan for growing in righteousness and goodness.

### Printed Resources

- Instructional Aid 6.1: *Virtue and Vice Chart*
- Activity 6.1: The Essence of Virtue

### Suggested Reading

- Berg, Jim. *Essential Virtues: Marks of the Christ-Centered Life*. Greenville, SC: JourneyForth, 2008. Pages 84–112.
- Bridges, Jerry. *The Practice of Godliness*. Colorado Springs, CO: NavPress, 2008. Pages 49–66, 193–204.
- ———. *Respectable Sins*. Colorado Springs, CO: NavPress, 2007. Pages 47–56, 105–16.

## Instruct

### VIRTUES AND VICES

Use **Instructional Aid 6.1** to orient students to the list of virtues and their corresponding vices they are learning about in Chapters 5–7.

### TWO CRITICAL KINDS OF RIGHTEOUSNESS

Use **Decisions, Decisions** to reinforce the difference between the two ways that righteousness applies to believers: salvific and ethical.

Instruct students to move to the side of the room that represents either Salvific Righteousness or Ethical Righteousness.

- The righteousness of Christ imputed to sinners (Salvific)
- The righteousness believers pursue (Ethical)
- The righteousness obtained by conforming one's life to God's perfect standards (Ethical)
- The righteousness that justifies sinful man before a holy God (Salvific)
- The righteousness provided for the believer by God (both)

any conformity to any standard. But not all standards are inherently upright, and not all that conforms to those standards is morally acceptable. For example, an exclusionary high school or college club might require prospective members to antagonize someone or deface school property for admittance. A foolish student might humiliate and hurt someone or commit vandalism, therefore meeting the standard to be admitted to the club. But in this case, since the standard itself would be unethical, the immoral conformity to it could not be deemed righteous. By His character, God Himself determines the standard for righteousness (Ps. 71:19; Isa. 5:16).

#### What Kind of Righteousness?

When you hear the word ***righteousness***, what do you think of? Some may think of the righteousness of Christ imputed to sinners who come to Him in repentance and faith. Many passages describe the kind of righteousness that justifies sinful man before a holy and righteous God (Rom. 1:17; 4:3; 2 Cor. 5:21). We might call this ***salvific*** righteousness, because apart from the righteousness of Christ, no one could be saved from the penalty of sin. This is God's righteousness.

But then there is the kind of righteousness that believers pursue as they seek to conform their lives to God's perfect standards. We might call this ***ethical*** righteousness. Romans 5:1–5 shows the strong connection between these two aspects of righteousness. Verse 1 says that sinners are "justified by faith"; the peace they now have with God is because of Christ's atonement for their sin and their receiving of His imputed righteousness. But notice the mention in verses 3–5 of various virtues that are produced in the lives of justified believers—faith, joy, hope, patience, and love. Paul also instructed Titus that righteousness should characterize the lives of believers (Titus 2:12). This is believers' ethical righteousness. But even this ability to practice righteousness is given to a believer by God; no believer can produce in himself or herself any amount of righteousness (Phil. 2:13).

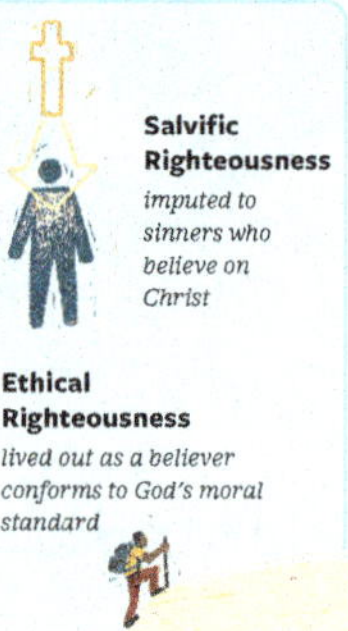

Salvific Righteousness
imputed to sinners who believe on Christ
Ethical Righteousness
lived out as a believer conforms to God's moral standard


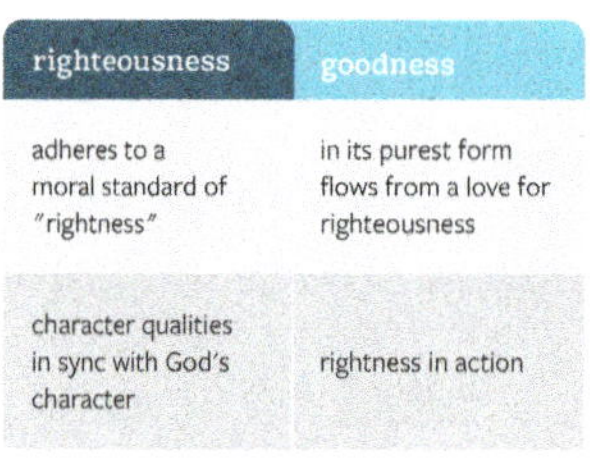

| righteousness | goodness |
|---|---|
| adheres to a moral standard of "rightness" | in its purest form flows from a love for righteousness |
| character qualities in sync with God's character | rightness in action |

Identifying something as righteous or unrighteous communicates whether an individual's actions conform to God's perfect standards. Goodness, on the other hand, flows from a heart that loves righteousness, resulting in generous and kind actions toward others. **Goodness** is generously seeking others' happiness and well-being, as determined by God's righteous standards. Goodness is truly virtuous when both generous motives and generous actions are directed by righteousness (see example in James 3:9–12). For example, unsaved people might have a good motive to protect young people who are driving home drunk or high from clubs, so their solution might be to create more clubs closer to residential areas of town. However, when believers critique this solution against righteousness, they should recognize that the solution falls short of actual goodness, since God condemns what goes on during clubbing as immoral, sinful behavior (Rom. 13:13; 1 Pet. 4:3). Goodness is present only when others benefit from a righteous motive, through moral means, and with upright consequences.

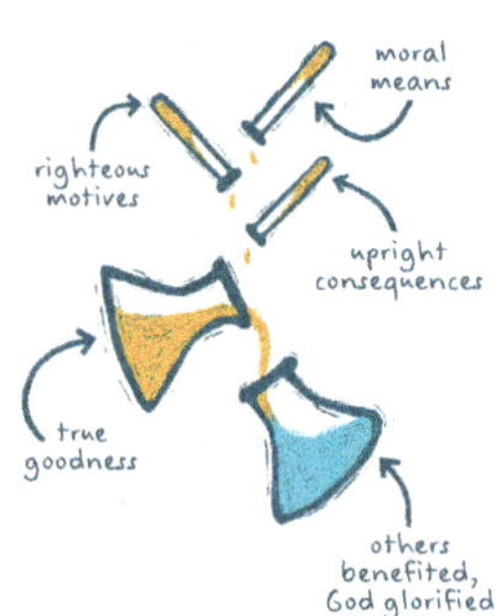


#### CONCEPTIONS OF RIGHTEOUSNESS AND GOODNESS

You have probably realized that righteousness and goodness are quite similar. Even though there is some overlap in how the Bible refers to these two virtues (Prov. 2:20; 14:19; Eccles. 9:2; Rom. 5:7), the two terms aren't identical in their meanings and uses. Their distinct-yet-close relationship is seen in passages that describe the righteous as doing good (1 Sam. 24:17; Eccles. 7:20) and in passages that use both words to describe one person or thing (Luke 23:50; Rom. 7:12). So a righteous individual does good things, and good character describes a righteous individual. We can even say that justice, the application of the righteous standard, is good even if the result is painful or sad (Deut. 19:13, 21). When God's standards of morality are upheld, the applications of those standards are good. Righteous justice is good because it meets God's standards and is met with God's approval (Ps. 11:5–7).

Why isn't it sufficient for me to identify what is right and what is good based solely on situations starting and ending well?

Since non-Christians don't appeal to God's standards, how do they determine what is righteous and what is therefore good to do? For many people, whatever they feel is right and good works for them. For many others, whatever the consensus of their society says is right and good sets the standard. Whatever worldview people have manifests itself when they appeal to whatever standard they use (some are conscious of their standard, while others are not). A person can live life according to any number of contradictory standards. Sometimes unbelievers borrow from the Christian worldview that has influenced a society in the past. By God's common grace, unbelievers can demonstrate some measure of apparent righteousness and show apparent goodness to others. Unbelievers, who are made in God's image, can be honest in business transactions, seek to alleviate poverty in their cities, and show love to their children (Matt. 7:11). Nevertheless, a broken foundation is still broken even if the roof doesn't cave in immediately.

An unbeliever might feel righteous ("justified") by arguing that he or she is in the right on the basis of the standard he or she appeals to. Unbelievers might feel they have done something good for someone when they make a philanthropic* gesture. They feel justified when they live in conformity to their self-established standards. But if the standards aren't God's standards, according to His character and how He designed the world, then no true righteousness or goodness is expressed.

True virtue comes out of a right relationship with God, aligns with God's standards, involves a right motive, fits the occasion, and seeks a right outcome.

### TWISTING RIGHTEOUSNESS AND GOODNESS

Society has a knack for bending God's structure (the design of His good, created order) in a sinful direction. The language society uses might seem innocent to some. But the ungodly world system we live in has mastered using virtuous-sounding words and redefining or reapplying them in ungodly and corrupt ways. A woman's "choice" becomes synonymous with killing her unborn baby, and "freedom" or "love" might mean living opposed to God's creation of men as men and women as women. These are clear examples of calling "evil good, and good evil" (Isa. 5:20). In the next unit, we will spend five chapters discussing a great variety of issues that require ethical decisions. Included in those chapters are the examples above, plus many more.

Sinners ignore God's design, rejecting that which reflects God's righteousness and goodness (Rom. 1:18, 25, 29, 32). The virtues that all Christians should strive by God's grace to develop can get twisted by a sinful society, which demonizes Christians for working toward true virtue. Vices are approved and virtues are repressed. Righteousness gets traded for ungodliness, and goodness gets traded for corruption.

The vice of **ungodliness** is anything that is contrary to God's nature or opposed to God's ways. The default mode of society, of all unregenerate people, can be summarized by this term. Those who are enslaved to sin and to its master wholly oppose God and His righteous standards (Eph. 2:1–3). Why is society approving of same-sex marriages? To violate God's righteous standards for marriage is to embody unrighteousness, which is ungodliness (Rom. 1:26–27, 29). What corresponds to righteousness is one man and one woman who are faithful to one another and submitted to God's design and purpose for marriage (Gen. 2:22, 24; Eph. 5:22–33).

The vice of **corruption** describes any harm done to God's good design and moral will for His creation. Similar to ungodliness, this term encompasses all the tragic

**philanthropic:** loving one's fellow men; benevolent; humane



## TWISTED RIGHTEOUSNESS AND GOODNESS

Use **Directed Paraphrasing** for students to summarize how the vices of ungodliness and corruption twist the virtues of righteousness and goodness, respectively.

**Ungodliness:** *anything that is contrary to God's nature or opposed to God's ways; the default mode of society and all unregenerate people*

God's standard (structure) of righteousness is bent in a sinful way, producing ungodliness.

**Corruption:** *any harm done to God's good design and moral will for His creation; encompasses the tragic consequences of the Fall and the Curse*

God's standard (structure) of goodness is bent in a sinful way, producing corruption.

### HOW TO GROW IN RIGHTEOUSNESS AND GOODNESS

Use a **journal entry** where students answer the questions found in the running text on page 95 to develop a plan for growing in righteousness and goodness.

**What do you need to do to recognize ungodly thought patterns or behaviors in your life?** *Objectively analyze your thoughts, desires, and actions, searching for any sinful patterns (Eph. 5:15–17). Get a trusted friend who can offer his or her perspective on your speech, attitudes, and actions. Ask your parents to be honest with you as well.*

**What routines could you set up to remind yourself of God's righteousness and His perfect standards?** *If you don't have a consistent time set up to read and meditate on God's Word, start one now (Ps. 1:1–6). Learning about God in the Bible allows you to recognize His work in your life and identify those aspects of your life that contradict His character.*

**How can you depend more on the Spirit's empowerment to live by God's standards of righteousness and goodness?** *Along with time in the Word mentioned above, prayer is how believers communicate with God and seek to line up their lives with the Spirit's leading (Matt. 6:9–13; Col. 4:2). Humble surrender is also necessary to submit to God's ways, truths, and commands.*

**What do you need to do to assess your motives, thoughts, and actions to know whether they have been corrupted by selfish or worldly influences?** *Pray and learn truths about God from the Word (Ps. 139:23–24).*

**How might you keep God's goodness fresh in your mind and heart so you can practice generous, no-strings-attached goodness to others?** *Recall all the blessings of your own salvation in Christ (1 John 4:10–11). Meditating on the gospel and its implications for your own life motivates you to love others in a way that allows the gospel to shine through that love. Christian love does good to others and reflects God's goodness (Gal. 5:14).*

consequences of the Fall and the Curse. Corruption twists goodness into a counterfeit. Being kind and helpful to classmates because you want them to vote for you for student council corrupts the virtue of goodness. Goodness is corrupted when there is an ulterior motive. Even something like a "white lie" is unrighteous. Pretending you didn't hear your parents call you corrupts the goodness you should do by acknowledging them. Your inaction shows you're seeking your own convenience over your parents' happiness and well-being, and your deception undermines the well-being of your relationship with them.

Examples of ungodliness and corruption abound. Excessive punishment for a simple infraction or crime is corrupt and ungodly. Even though punishment was applied, it wasn't done in a righteous manner. Therefore, it can't be classified as good. God has revealed His standard for righteous punishments for real offenses: true justice involves punishment that fits the crime committed (Exod. 21:23–25). When wrong is done and it is overlooked or covered up by those responsible for justice, the vices of ungodliness and corruption may also be at play. Punishment is in order when just and good laws are broken. But righteous punishment gets twisted into ungodliness when wrongdoing is either punished too severely or not severely enough. Authority figures who justly enforce righteous standards and laws do good, even to the offender, when they punish the offender appropriately. But failing to do one's duty of enforcing the law is a corruption of one's role.

What do the virtues of righteousness and goodness look like? In many ways they look like the opposite of ungodliness and corruption. Ungodliness and corruption are bent away from God's good creational structure. When believers' lives embody righteousness and goodness, they begin to untwist the mess ungodliness and corruption make.

#### GROWING IN RIGHTEOUSNESS AND GOODNESS

If you play an instrument or sing, what do you do when your instructor tells you that you need to improve in a specific area? Practice! If you don't practice playing your instrument or singing, you won't improve your skills. You need to know what to do, for sure, but then you really just need to apply what you have learned. Knowledge is important; that much should be obvious. But lots of focused practice is what you need in order to improve. Do you recognize your need to grow in the virtues of righteousness and goodness? Do you have a plan to grow?

Believers don't lack opportunities to practice growing in virtue. Each day contains temptations, challenges, and needs that can be met—all opportunities to practice a virtue rather than a vice by turning to God for help so that Christ lives through you (Gal. 2:20). But you can still neglect practicing virtues, as you might neglect picking up your instrument to practice. You might try to avoid or ignore temptations and difficult situations. But you can't avoid them all. And avoiding uncomfortable situations can reveal cowardice, a vice, rather than potentially displaying courage, a virtue. And just as you need knowledge and skill to perform well musically, you

## Apply

### THE NEED FOR VIRTUE

Ask this section's **essential question** to help students contrast the "end-justifies-the-means" mentality with biblical virtue. If we do not pursue virtues, even our best analysis of a situation will be flawed. We need virtue to realize that we lack virtue.

**Why isn't it sufficient for me to identify what is right and what is good based solely on situations starting and ending well?** *Righteousness and goodness are more trustworthy than an "end-justifies-the-means" mentality. We need a standard that won't change with the times, constantly adapting to cultural whims. Righteousness and goodness are determined by God, and we can recognize them as such when we are in a right relationship with God. A situation is right and good when it aligns with God's standards, involves a right motive, fits the occasion, and seeks a right outcome.*

### THE ESSENCE OF VIRTUE

Use **Activity 6.1** on page 29 to apply the information in the section.

## Assess

### RIGHTEOUS GOODNESS AND GOOD RIGHTEOUSNESS

Use a **Ticket out the Door** about the overlap between righteousness and goodness. The activity can be written or done verbally in pairs.

**What is the relationship between righteousness and goodness?** *Righteousness primarily refers to conforming to the correct standard, and goodness is about how conforming to that correct standard plays out in real life. Righteous individuals do good things, and good character describes a righteous individual. We can even say that justice, the application of the righteous standard, is good even if the result is painful or sad.*

need wisdom in order to live according to righteousness and goodness (Prov. 2:6–9). Virtuous living doesn't just happen. And it doesn't come about in your life without God giving you His wisdom.

Goodness is listed as a fruit of the Spirit (Gal. 5:22). Righteousness can be found in other lists of virtues (Rom. 14:17; Eph. 5:9). On the one hand, God enables believers to grow in these virtues. This growth includes gradually living more in conformity to God's perfect standards and gradually becoming more generous and benevolent in how they treat others. This enablement comes from the nature of salvation and how God works to bring about growth and change in His children (Rom. 8:29–30; Phil. 2:13). On the other hand, believers need to actively do their part in pursuing virtue and avoiding vice (Phil. 2:12).

What do you need to do to take notice of ungodly thought patterns or behaviors in your life (Eph. 5:15–17)? What routines could you set up to remind yourself of God's righteousness and His perfect standards (Ps. 1:1–6)? How can you increase your dependence on the Spirit's empowerment to live by those standards (Rom. 8:12–15; Gal. 5:16, 25)? And what do you need to do to assess your motives, thoughts, and actions to see whether they have been corrupted by selfish or worldly influences (Ps. 139:23–24)? And finally, how might you keep God's goodness fresh in your mind and heart, so you can practice generous, no-strings-attached goodness to others (Gal. 5:14; 1 John 4:10–11)? You need to plan to run away from sin and its tempting trappings and to run after righteousness and the virtues that enable you to imitate God's goodness (1 Tim. 6:11; 2 Tim. 2:22).

Remember, the goodness that should characterize your life flows from your joyful conformity to God's righteous standards (Ps. 119:97). God is powerful enough and gracious enough to grow these two virtues in your life. Trust that God will do so, and enjoy your participation in the Spirit's work in you.

### Thinking It Through 6.1

1. Define *righteousness*.
2. Define *goodness*.
3. Compare and contrast Christian and non-Christian conceptions of righteousness and goodness.
4. Contrast the virtues of righteousness and goodness with the vices of ungodliness and corruption.
5. What steps can you take to grow in righteousness and goodness?

## 6.2 Prudence

There was a time when computers filled entire rooms and had very limited capabilities. As computers gradually got smaller, supercomputers were developed and gained greater and greater capabilities. The smartphones most people carry today are just that: sophisticated supercomputers. Back in 1996, an IBM supercomputer called Deep Blue played chess against the world's number one chess master at that time, Garry Kasparov. The match ended with a victory for the human, but only after the machine had managed to win one of the six games. The tables were turned, though, in the following year's rematch. The final decisive game was won by Deep Blue—and in only nineteen moves. A machine had outplayed, outsmarted, and bested the greatest chess mind in the world. Processing chips had beaten a brain. Artificial intelligence had defeated genuine intelligence.[2]



Guide a **summative assessment** by directing students to answer the questions in Thinking It Through 6.1.

### Thinking It Through 6.1

1. the conformity of an individual's life to God's standards of moral perfection
2. generously seeking others' happiness and well-being as determined by God's righteous standards
3. A Christian conception of righteousness and goodness is rooted in what God has revealed to us in His Word. Righteousness is when believers live in conformity to God's standards of moral excellence through the power of the Holy Spirit. When a righteous motive informs righteous actions, then the result is goodness toward others. Non-Christians, however, conceive of righteousness as doing whatever they perceive to be right and just. Their basis is flawed, and often their motives are as well. The same can be said for a non-Christian conception of goodness: an action or result is deemed good when it conforms to one's own self-established standards. This is selfish and short-sighted because it ignores God's absolute standard.
4. Ungodliness stands in opposition to righteousness. Following the way of the world, fulfilling one's own desires and lusts, and removing God from one's life lead to an ungodly, unrighteous lifestyle. God's standards are ignored and therefore violated. Corruption stands in opposition to goodness. Rather than being kind, merciful, benevolent, and generous to others for their benefit, corruption spoils any good intentions, actions, and results for the benefit of self. When one neglects the well-being of others, then that is a corruption of the goodness that God expects people to have toward one another.
5. Learn about the righteousness believers have in Christ and what God's standards and expectations are for how His children should live. Pursue a love for God and others while fleeing sin and temptation. Realize that as you grow in certain virtues, other people will also grow alongside your efforts toward righteousness and goodness.

## 6.2 Prudence

How can prudence help me with my social media usage?

### Objectives

**6.2.1** Define *prudence*.

**6.2.2** Compare and contrast Christian and non-Christian conceptions of prudence.

**6.2.3** Contrast the virtue of prudence with the vices of rashness and cunning. *BWS*

**6.2.4** Give examples of how prudence relates to ethical decision-making and ethical living. *BWS*

**6.2.5** Develop a plan for growing in prudence. *BWS*

### Biblical Worldview Shaping

- **Wisdom** (evaluate): A wise person chooses the best means to reach the right goals. He avoids pursuing the right goals in counterproductive ways or using his reason and skills to pursue the wrong goals. (6.2.3)
- **Wisdom** (formulate): Prudence is necessary for developing other virtues since it enables a person to discern when a virtue is being deformed into a vice. (6.2.4)
- **Wisdom** (apply): Without prudence no person will be able to act ethically in all of life. (6.2.5)

### Printed Resources

- Instructional Aid 6.2: *Virtues and Vices in the Bible*
- Activity 6.2: Prudent Prudence

### Suggested Reading

- Timpe, Kevin, and Craig A. Boyd. *Virtues and Their Vices*. Oxford: Oxford UP, 2014. Pages 37–58.

**PRUDENCE DEFINED**

The virtue of prudence has much in common with the game of chess, at least the way someone like Garry Kasparov plays. Prudence is related to knowledge and wisdom. But prudence isn't simply having a lot of knowledge, nor is it only knowing the right thing to do. It is also knowing the best way to carry out the right thing. **Prudence** is the ability to choose the best course of action, having considered all the constraints of the situation, to obtain the most righteous and beneficial outcome. There are aspects of past knowledge, present discernment, and future considerations involved in the virtue of prudence. In our illustration above, the human or the computer could be described as more "prudent" than the other when winning a match. Having knowledge of the game of chess, an accurate analysis of the opponent and each move's implications, and foresight to plan out many moves in advance is essentially a version of chess prudence! But machines can't be virtuous; only people can. And the virtue of prudence can't be limited to running data through a predetermined algorithm. Prudence, like wisdom, involves the whole person—head and heart.

**PRUDENCE TODAY**

What concerns us, however, is the ethical nature of prudence as a virtue. Prudence must be present any time an ethical difficulty arises. We know loving God and loving others are explicit commands of Scripture that apply to all believers at all times (Matt. 22:36–40). *How* to love your neighbor who is an angry, cursing drunk most evenings and weekends requires prudence, among other virtues. You want to protect your family, but you don't want to appear unfriendly. You want to address your concerns about his effect on the neighborhood, but you want to keep the channels open for future, gospel-intentional communication. Both short-term and long-term implications of your decisions must be considered. When working through a difficult situation that requires multiple virtues, you will usually know what the various good options are. But you will need to assess the effects of doing the right thing on the various parties involved in that scenario. And to do all this, you need prudence.

What is the difference between what Christians and non-Christians understand prudence to be? In a moment we will look at multiple passages that teach how believers relate to prudence. But how is prudence viewed from the world's perspective? Some unbelievers may view prudence as overly cautious, such that those who practice it are prudes* or cowards—as if boldly and thoughtlessly doing whatever they want, no matter the consequences, is best for everyone. Prudence to unbelievers could be seen as excessive, unnecessary, and even legalistic—as if considering the situation, assessing how much they know about everything related to the situation, analyzing their motives, and calculating the effects on all involved would usually be unhelpful. But unbelievers don't shun prudence altogether. For those outside Christ who seek their own interests and promote their personal agendas, prudence can come in handy when it serves their best interests. For example, most people want an efficiently run government that makes buying and selling and moving about the nation easy. Christ Himself pointed out how prudent unbelievers can be when it comes to a construction project or military matters (Luke 14:28–32). This type of prudence generally serves their own best interests and isn't necessarily ethically motivated. Remember, God's common grace on all people enables them to imitate virtuous living, though that imitation is hollow.

As for the Christian's understanding, prudence is a biblical Christian virtue and therefore necessary for believers to practice. Prudence is a foundational virtue seen especially in the Wisdom Literature in the Old Testament (particularly Proverbs and Ecclesiastes). The Word of God informs a believer's motivations and conditions his

**prude:** someone who is excessively proper or modest in the way he or she speaks, dresses, and conducts himself or herself in general



## Engage

### ARTIFICIAL WISDOM

Ask a **question** to discuss the nature of wisdom and prudence.

**Can an artificial intelligence chatbot, like ChatGPT, be wise?** *Wisdom can't be obtained by finding the right information to answer a question or to find a solution. Wisdom is skill for life, and this involves knowing how to make ethical decisions and behave morally, which a chatbot is incapable of. Also, one cannot possess wisdom, or prudence, without having the fear of the Lord.*

### CORRECTING STUDENT MISCONCEPTIONS

Use **direct instruction** to clarify that the opening illustration isn't saying that a supercomputer is or can be more prudent than a person. The illustration serves as an analogy for some aspects of prudence. Machines aren't people and therefore aren't able to be ethically responsible, or in this case, capable of the virtue of prudence. The designers and creators of computers are the responsible and moral parties.

## Instruct

### PRUDENCE INTERCONNECTING WITH THE OTHER VIRTUES

Use **direct instruction** to teach that the virtue of prudence can never stand alone.

The prudent person must be motivated by love for God and others. His or her ends must be good, and the ultimate end must be the glory of God. And the means pursued must also be righteous. If a person uses his or her sharp mind to figure out how to get away with something sinful, or even if that person tries to achieve a good goal through sinful means, he or she is not exercising prudence but its counterfeit—either cunning or rashness.

Prudence is required when making a hard call. For example, Christians want to see lost friends come to Christ. However, it would be imprudent to continually pester a friend with the gospel—making it the first and dominant thing in every conversation, text, and phone call. It would also be imprudent to say nothing of Christ and the gospel to the friend. Neither course of action would advance the goal of seeing the friend come to Christ, and the latter would be unfaithful to the Great Commission. A prudent course of action would differ depending on the situation, but it would look to create opportunities for serious conversation about the gospel. It would communicate to the friend genuine concern for his or her eternal salvation. It would be patient but not complacent. There is no guarantee that a prudent course of action would result in the friend's conversion—that is up to God.

### SCENARIOS REQUIRING PRUDENCE

Guide a **discussion** surrounding the following two scenarios requiring prudence.

**How would you practice prudence in the following scenario? You just graduated from high school and are looking forward to going to college. You have the opportunity to work for a friend from church, but you are set on going to college right away. Your dad, however, lost his job and has been without work for four months.** *You need to consider the fact that you don't qualify for many scholarships, your family doesn't have the money to pay for your first year of school and God has provided a good job for you. Prudence is required for you to determine whether to go to college right away or not.*

**How would prudence help your parents in the following scenario? Your family must relocate due to your dad's job. Your family is looking for a house, a church to join, and a good Christian school for you and your siblings in the new city you will be moving to.** *The parents need to decide on where to live, where to go to church, and which school (unless homeschool is considered) to put their children in. Juggling multiple priorities requires prudence.*

or her choices (Ps. 119:97–104). To have ready access to a knowledge of what is pleasing to God, believers need to know what He has communicated in His Word. A prudent person can take this knowledge and determine the best way to apply it to specific situations. As you might expect, Proverbs in various places describes the value of wisdom and the benefits that applying wisdom (prudence) provides (4:7; 9:10; 13:10; 15:22).

A Christian demonstrates prudence by internalizing the wisdom in Scripture and applying it, living it out. Prudence is most needed when there are several goals that are biblical or several paths to reach a biblical goal but only one choice can be made. So, for example, it might be prudent to take a gap year after high school if you need to make some money prior to enrolling in a four-year degree program. But if you were able to secure a scholarship, it might not be prudent to wait a year. Many other ethical issues come up in either scenario though: Is your job conducive to moral living? What ethical issues, if any, come up frequently at your job? Is the college where you got a scholarship going to help you grow as a Christian? How wise is it to go into debt for college, and how much debt could you manage? A prudent person not only raises the questions necessary to make a wise decision; a prudent person is skilled in choosing the best goal from several legitimate alternatives and choosing the best means for reaching a given goal.

Another point that aids the Christian's understanding of prudence is that only believers can truly practice prudence. All the goals unbelievers have are in some way distorted or misplaced because they are not in service to the great goal of glorifying God and enjoying Him forever. So even good goals, like securing a quality education for their children, will be distorted. Instead of wanting their children to be well-educated so that they can serve God more effectively, they may be more concerned about their children's wealth or social status. These non-Christians may be very effective at reaching their goals, but it isn't really prudence if they're pursuing the wrong goals.

Christians might see the non-Christian pragmatic idea of what prudence is and then decide to shun prudence. Or they might think that since their goals are good and right, there is no need to worry about whether the *way* those goals are pursued is wise. However, the Bible teaches that even the Messiah needed the Spirit of the Lord to give Him wisdom and counsel (Isa. 11:2). The Spirit of God is also at work in believers, guiding them into truth and helping them see what good and right choices are (1 Cor. 2:12–13). Believers need to receive God's wisdom (James 3:17). Faithful believers are compared to "a faithful and wise servant" who carries out his master's charge (Matt. 24:45–46) and to the wise virgins who brought extra oil for their lamps (Matt. 25:1–13). Jesus illustrated the necessity of prudence by comparing His twelve disciples to "sheep in the midst of wolves" and urging them to "be . . . wise as serpents, and harmless as doves" (Matt. 10:16). A sheep among wolves must not only be careful, but also smart and wise to navigate life and not be harmed. Turning the appropriate knowledge into applied wisdom requires prudence. Snakes can be dangerous to other creatures, but they are also wise. Doves are weak, but they are also harmless to other creatures. Prudence determines how to apply both the wisdom of snakes and the harmlessness of doves to a given situation. And for believers to be like sheep, snakes, and doves (in appropriate ways) requires submission to the Lord and obedience to His Word, combined with a solid understanding of how the world works.

*In modern ethics, prudence is often reduced to utility or self-interest. The modern view of prudence is derived from a misunderstanding of prudence as pragmatic self-interest.*

CLARKE FORSYTHE

VIRTUES, PART 1 97

## ANTONYMS FOR PRUDENCE

Have students **list** synonyms for the words *cunning* and *rashness*.
*Possible answers:*

- *Cunning: shrewd, devious, slick, crafty, insidious, tricky, wily, deceitful*
- *Rashness: recklessness, anger, carelessness, violence, ignorance, shortsightedness*

Use **direct instruction** to explain that cunning and rashness are vices that contrast with prudence.

Sometimes shrewdness is presented as prudence. In reality, it is a vice masquerading as a virtue.

Rashness is the vice that is the opposite of prudence. To be rash is to act with full confidence of one's own impulses without seeking advice or taking the time to think through the consequences of actions.

## VIRTUE AND VICE LISTS IN THE BIBLE

Use **Instructional Aid 6.2** to familiarize students with where the Bible provides lists of the various virtues and vices.

## IDENTIFYING CUNNING AND RASHNESS

Use a **Turn and Talk** to evaluate why the scenarios below are examples of cunning and rashness, respectively.

- A politician knows that a certain bill, while not perfect, would advance both the national interest and the goals of his party and constituents. But he attacks the bill and those in the party who support it because they didn't support another bill that had no chance of passing. The politician does this to portray himself as a fighter to his voters, which puts him in a better position to run for higher office. The result is that the policy goals that he professed to support were not advanced, but instead his voters became more cynical toward the other party members.
- You get frustrated with slow traffic and immediately begin to drive recklessly.

## PRUDENCE REQUIRED

Guide a **discussion** that allows students to analyze and develop the two scenarios on pages 99–100.

**In the first scenario, what made the first approach imprudent?** *The first approach was too rash. You expressed your legitimate concern and said the right things, but you needed to have done it in a more loving way.*
**Is straight talking and strong, even loud, language ever prudent?** *Yes, the more serious the situation, the more prudent it is to use strong language. For example, if someone were about to be harmed, it would be prudent for you to shout, even make physical contact. And so, depending on the relationship and the direness of the situation, it can be entirely prudent for you to speak firmly and directly.*
**What made the alternative approach the prudent choice?** *You communicated truth in love without the berating and name-calling that the first approach had. Confrontation still took place, but love and care were communicated to the friend. Given the circumstances, it was the prudent choice.*

Direct attention to the Grappling with Ethical Issues box on page 100.

**In the second scenario, is it ever virtuous to fight?** *The second scenario is more complicated since it involves a potentially traumatizing and violent situation. This means that prudence plays an even more strategic role. Some might say that loving our neighbor (Matt. 22:39) wouldn't justify any type of fighting. Treating others as we want to be treated (Matt. 7:12) doesn't seem to justify a physical altercation either. But those norms must be applied to a situation (what about love for your friends?), and a broad knowledge of Scripture gives plenty of clues that violence isn't always wrong, even if it is usually to be avoided. Indeed, God Himself is described as "a man of war" (Exod. 15:3), and Christ mentioned the value of a sword in a perilous moment (Luke 22:36).*

### PRUDENCE FORGOTTEN

You've heard it said, "The end justifies the means." This sentiment is totally contrary to prudence. The virtue of prudence is evidenced through a combination of (1) the proper knowledge about an issue, (2) the specifics of the situation, and (3) the appropriate foresight—so that the best means available are used to reach the right goals. But does the final outcome really justify whatever has to be done to obtain it? This unethical mentality is widely accepted in our culture. But that thinking is pragmatic, which means that whatever needs to happen to obtain the desired end result is valid. In such thinking, prudence has been ignored. It has been deleted from the equation. Prudence isn't only choosing the most preferable end and getting there by causing the least amount of damage possible. Nor is prudence charting a path that is entirely ethical but landing on an unethical outcome.

1. knowledge of the issue
2. consideration of the situation
3. appropriate foresight

The vice of cunning fills the void that prudence leaves when it is ignored. **Cunning** involves shrewdness as well as deception. Like prudence, cunning employs a thorough analysis of the situation, but it does so to obtain something through immoral means or to an unethical end. Growing up you might have learned some of Aesop's fables. Do you remember the one about the fox and the crow? This fable portrays the fox as cunning and the crow as vain. But more importantly, this fable helps us learn about the difference between prudence and cunning. The fox employed a devious means to get a snack. It used a pragmatic approach in which cunning was a main ingredient. The fox was hungry, and the crow had cheese. The fox didn't want to go hungry, so he decided to take what wasn't his to take. But in order to do so, he needed smarts—the fox stooped to vice rather than rising to virtue. The fox utilized cunning means by flattering the crow to get it to open its beak and drop the cheese.[4] Cunning only served the fox's interest. This isn't virtuous prudence. This is the vice of cunning.

Do you ever notice your selfish motives for doing something nice for someone? Have you ever felt justified for pursuing a good cause but at the same time felt uncomfortable knowing that the way you were achieving it was wrong? The way of prudence offers a clean conscience as well as God's approval.

The vice of rashness also ignores prudence. But rashness is the opposite of cunning. While cunning uses deceptive yet calculated means to obtain a desired goal, **rashness** acts in the moment with no regard for whether one's actions are the best way, or even a good way, to reach a desired end. Rashness is impulsive and reckless. Rashness usually causes harm in the end because it doesn't take the end into consideration. Rashness works against the fruit of the Spirit and the rest of the virtues. And you can find terms related to rashness in a few of Scripture's lists of vices, often translated by words like *foolish* or *reckless* (Rom. 1:31; 2 Tim. 3:4; Titus 3:3). Sometimes people confuse rashness with boldness for the truth and for what is right. But rashness jumps in prematurely and adds to a problem rather than waiting to hear the whole story and then helping with a solution (Prov. 18:13).

Do you wait to hear both sides of a story? Do you ever stop to consider the short-term effects of your words and the long-term effects of your actions? Prudence demands that you do.

## PRUDENCE IN ACTION

Can we rightly say that prudence is necessary for all ethical decision-making? What does prudence look like in action?

Think of prudence like a quality control worker at a factory. You might have seen a video of one of these workers carefully watching a steady stream of product go by on a conveyor belt. This worker must remove defective items, ensure a constant flow of the product, and stop the belt immediately if something goes wrong. In this analogy, the conveyor belt is a complex ethical situation as it develops. The products going by are various virtues that rise to address the situation. Prudence knows what the virtues are and can identify them. When a vice (a virtue made defective) comes down the conveyor belt, prudence can identify it and remove it.

*Prudence is at the heart of moral character, for it shapes and directs the whole of our moral lives, and is indispensible to our becoming morally excellent persons.*

W. JAY WOOD[5]

### *Two Examples*

Prudence helps shape our daily habits and helps us make judgment calls. Our habits reveal much about who we are, and they require much effort to develop or change. We need prudence to establish and develop truly virtuous habits. Also, when we decide to do something we usually don't do (or decide not to do something we usually do), prudence comes into the picture if the actions in question are ethically significant. When we aren't choosing between clear vice and clear virtue, prudence helps us discern when exceptions to our normal habits of godly living are necessary and good.

For example, consider this first scenario: You have a friend who is starting to hang out with the wrong crowd. You want to be courageous and confront him about the path he is on because you are truly concerned for him. So, the next time you see him with those friends, you confront him in front of them, tell him he's being an idiot, and let him know those friends will ruin his life because if he continues to hang out with them, he'll most likely start doing drugs and committing small crimes with them. You tell him that, if he were smart, he'd walk away from them right now and cut off further friendship with them. Now, everything you said might have been true, but how you said it, when you said it, and even the words used to say it would have been imprudent.

*Prudence is essential for moral virtue because it provides the ineliminable* sound judgment required to practice any of the virtues in our particular moral circumstances.*

W. JAY WOOD[6]

Consider this alternative approach: You invite him over to your house so the two of you can have a private conversation. You tell him that you're really concerned about his new friends. You point out that, if he continues to spend time with them, he'll come under pressure to do drugs or to commit petty crimes. You let him know that they're likely to be friends only in the short term—but that the impact on his life would likely be long-term. Which approach is more likely to accomplish the goal you are seeking?

Here is a second scenario: You have (prudently) established the habit of not fighting and avoiding situations where you might be drawn into a fight. But one day while you're walking home from school, some guys show up out of nowhere and start harassing you and your friends. You do your best to ignore them, but they get in your face and start pushing you. They do the same to your friends. You ask them multiple times to leave you alone, but they don't. One of your friends is able to run away, and you yell after him to call the cops. At that point, you realize that these thugs are out to give you and your friends a serious beating. So, the prudent thing to do at that moment is to minimize the harm done to you and to your friends by resorting to self-defense; despite your usual habit, you end up in a fight. You aren't sure why these guys are acting so violently toward you and your friends. But you know they have it out for you. You can either get seriously beat up and watch them do the same to your friends, or you can try to forcibly make them stop as you yell for help and try to get to safety.

**ineliminable:** indispensable



*Prudence considers the scriptural commands and principles together with the current situation to devise the best way to obtain the best and most righteous result. The end in mind is to protect oneself and others who are innocently in harm's way; a good case can also be made that the most loving thing that can be done for bullies is to prevent them from using violence and intimidation. The police have been called because one of their purposes is to protect the innocent. But until they arrive, you have to make a decision regarding the best way for you and your friends to not suffer harm. Law enforcement officers might use batons, tear gas, tasers, or firearms to defuse the situation you are in. But they aren't there and might not arrive in time. You don't have any weapons, but you can fight back as best as you can and at least make the attackers focus on you, so they leave the rest of your group alone. Being willing to take a beating when that saves others from getting beat up can be a prudent and virtuous decision! Prudence rallies the virtues of courage and love and applies them wisely in this difficult situation.*

## Apply

### QUESTIONS OF PRUDENCE

Guide a **discussion** to answer this chapter's and section's essential questions.

**With so many obstacles (temptations, sin, a fallen world, and the consequences of sin), how do I navigate the right path?** *It is helpful to begin by asking, "What are the obstacles barring the way to the right path?" One challenge is wanting to make the right choices to get to the right path and stay there. If the obstacles are vices, they should be easy enough to spot. But sin is tricky, and it has a way of interfering in one's judgment.*

*Prudence and knowledge of Scripture are necessary when multiple virtues are needed at the same time to attain ethical motives, righteous actions, and good results. A hard decision taken in good faith while appealing to prudence and other necessary virtues can be the best option for believers. The right path always offers future opportunities to correct or to hone one's decisions.*

**How can prudence help me with my social media usage?** *Prudence provides insight into analyzing how to use your time and recognizing what tasks are helpful or harmful, moral or immoral, necessary or unnecessary, wise or unwise. Prudence cuts through the influential trends of social media, the amount of time spent on there, and what content is consumed or produced.*

Use a **Think-Pair-Share** to allow students to answer and discuss the questions below. This exercise expands on this section's essential question above as it pertains to dealing directly with another person on social media.

**Should I respond or keep scrolling?**

**Can I address the person on social media in person or through private correspondence?**

**Am I the appropriate person to address this other person? What is my relationship to them?**

**Should I consult an adult before I respond?**

**Can I address the person without attacking them but rather focus on the rightness or wrongness of the issue at hand?**

**Am I appropriately using the Bible when addressing another person?**

**Does this interaction require grace and mercy or direct confrontation?**

*Prudence helps sort through the whether, why, when, what, and how to say something on social media. It is a known fact that social media isn't the best place for many types of arguments or discussions. And it is questionable if many of these interactions should take place to begin with.*

Answering these and similar questions helps create healthy habits that reflect the virtue of prudence, among other virtues.

### PRUDENCE AT SCHOOL

Ask a **question** to encourage students to apply the virtue of prudence in a practical way.

**Would it be prudent to sign up for one more extracurricular activity at school when you already have a packed schedule?** *That depends. You must consider multiple factors in your decision: How are your grades doing? How would the new activity affect your work hours and study times? How helpful would that new activity be for the present and future? Are you managing your time well in getting physical rest, spiritual refreshment, and sufficient downtime?*

*Prudence in this case looks at the priorities of grades, work, rest, spiritual formation, and social activities, among other things. Prudence is required to analyze the current situation and project how one more activity could affect you in the long run. Even if there are immediate challenges, the long-term benefits might outweigh them.*

### PRUDENT PRUDENCE

Use **Activity 6.2** on page 31 to apply the information in the section.

## Assess

Guide a **summative assessment** by directing students to answer the questions in Thinking It Through 6.2.

### Thinking It Through 6.2

1. the ability to choose the best course of action, having considered all the constraints of the situation, to obtain the most righteous and beneficial outcome
2. Non-Christians practice a kind of prudence when they work hard to make good decisions and look ahead to potential problems. But all true virtue and wisdom are rooted in the fear of the Lord. In addition, prudence must be guided by the proper ultimate goal (glorifying God) and a proper understanding of God's moral law.
3. Rashness is the opposite of the cautious aspect of prudence. Cunning is the opposite of the selfless and compassionate aspect of prudence. Rashness endangers the ends, and cunning twists the means.
4. Prudence plays a role in all ethical decision-making. When a decision must be made to do the right thing, avoid the wrong thing, and see a good outcome, prudence helps guide that process. And there is no ethical living when vice-laden means are used for good outcomes or when virtuous means cause avoidable, bad outcomes.
5. Answers should generally include seeking the Lord to obtain wisdom and understanding in the Word through the Holy Spirit as you follow these steps:
   - Pause to think through all aspects of the challenging ethical situation.
   - Mentally tick off the virtues that are lacking from the situation or are necessary to help solve it.
   - Identify the vices involved in the situation or that might come up.
   - Don't lose sight of the overall goal, and seek the best outcome given the circumstances.

**GRAPPLING WITH ETHICAL ISSUES**

**Is It Ever Virtuous to Fight?**

How would you explain the use of prudence in the second scenario? Work through your response and then check with your teacher for the answer.

In the first scenario, the initial tension is between being courageous by telling a hard truth versus being cowardly by avoiding an uncomfortable conversation that could threaten your relationship (Eph. 4:15). Courage isn't the same as rashness, though, and the need for courage doesn't cancel the need for humility. And prudence should tell you that a gentle, yet direct, private conversation is more likely to achieve a good result than an in-your-face public confrontation. Prudence takes all this into consideration and values the virtue of courage enough to align with it and make an ethical decision (Heb. 3:13)—but acts courageously in the wisest way possible. Paul exhorts believers to be careful as they live for God amid the surrounding culture, which affects and influences them (Eph. 5:15–17). The current world system and those who are part of it go against God and His people. Prudence plays a major role in cutting through the bad motives that we or others might have and in determining the best means to arrive at a good end.

How can prudence help me with my social media usage?

#### PRUDENCE IN DEVELOPMENT

As you pursue prudence, you will develop more virtues than just prudence. Practicing prudence will also help you identify and avoid certain vices. What steps can you take to develop prudence? Be aware that caution by itself isn't prudence. But prudence often requires you to pause to consider all aspects of the ethical difficulty you have encountered. (Sometimes prudence entails thinking through possible ethical difficulties *before* encountering a crisis—as you can imagine, it would be helpful for our second scenario above!) What follows are various steps you can take toward developing prudence when you encounter your next ethical difficulty. Pray and ask God to give you the wisdom and understanding that He provides for you through Christ and by the Spirit. Only with the Lord's help will these steps help you grow in your exercise of prudence (Ps. 119:73; Eph. 1:16–17; James 1:5).

- Pause to think through all aspects of the challenging ethical situation (thus also practicing patience and humility).
- Mentally check off the virtues that are lacking in the situation or are necessary to help solve it (always remember faith, love, and hope).
- Identify the vices involved in the situation or those that might come up (always watch out for pride and selfishness).
- Don't lose sight of the overall goal, and seek the best outcome given the circumstances (and remember, prudence avoids cunning and rashness).

#### Thinking It Through 6.2

1. Define *prudence*.
2. How do Christian and non-Christian conceptions of prudence differ?
3. Contrast the virtue of prudence with the vices of rashness and cunning.
4. How does prudence relate to ethical decision-making and ethical living? Give examples other than those given above.
5. What can you do to grow in prudence?

100 VIRTUES

## 6.3 Diligence, Faithfulness, and Courage

Knights in the Middle Ages were known for their code of chivalry. Think of the stories of King Arthur and the Knights of the Round Table. Not that the men who fought the king's wars were virtuous or moral men, because most weren't. But the code of chivalry was meant to keep them in check and was intended to make them model subjects of the king and model members of the Roman Catholic Church. For example, knights were to defend the weak and vulnerable, respect women, support the Church, and be valiant in battle. Knights were also supposed to exhibit various virtues.

The three virtues presented in this section were included in the medieval knight's code of chivalry. Knights were to be diligent in serving the king, faithful to the Church and to the code, and courageous in battle.[7] As you have recently learned, lofty goals that are reached by unethical means don't qualify as virtuous and neither do ethical means that end with an immoral outcome. Hard work, loyal commitment, and bravery are important character traits, but they aren't virtuous in and of themselves. God's character is the basis and God's glory is the goal of all the virtues, including these three. Diligence, faithfulness, and courage, like all virtues, can fully be practiced only by believers. Only believers seek to glorify God by conforming to His character. So, what exactly are these three virtues?

### DEFINING DILIGENCE, FAITHFULNESS, AND COURAGE

**Diligence** can be defined as "*the exertion of the spiritual and physical powers of a believer whereby he willingly, joyously, and earnestly executes that task which God assigns him, doing so because it is the will of God.*"[8] Diligence is more than hard work. Diligence is dedication to do the will of God. And diligence approaches tasks and does them "heartily, as to the Lord" (Col. 3:23; see also Eccles. 9:10). This means that other virtues (honesty, prudence, kindness, etc.) are factored in so that diligence doesn't become consumed with only the work, the timeliness of completing the work, or the amount of effort put into the work. Paul exemplified diligence through his work ethic when he was in Thessalonica (2 Thess. 3:7–9). Paul and his companions worked hard in order not to be a burden to the church but also to set an example of what Christian diligence looks like. The virtue of diligence involves working hard for a good reason with a useful goal in mind.

**Faithfulness** is steadfast loyalty to that which is morally acceptable and good, despite difficulty and conflict. This virtue is related to faith (as seen in the root of the word) in that we are faithful toward those things that we believe in, that we think are trustworthy. Paul's life is an example of what faithfulness looks like for a believer (Phil. 3:12–21). Faithfulness isn't limited to maintaining faith in God, but it serves as a strong foundation for this virtue.

**Courage** is spiritual strength to unashamedly do the right thing at the right time even at risk of one's own harm.[9] The ideas of bravery and valor rightfully come to mind when we think of courage. And courage as a virtue, practiced by believers, takes bravery and valor to the spiritual realm of everyday living. Paul teaches about the armor of God, and courage is important for making use of this armor—even though we don't find the term in this passage (Eph. 6:10–20). Here we have a parallel with our knight illustration from above. Paul's encouragement to "be strong in the Lord" (6:10), the references to standing against all that comes against Christians

*Christlike wholeness requires the courage to do the right thing no matter what.*

JIM BERG[10]



## 6.3 Diligence, Faithfulness, and Courage

How should I respond when a friend asks to copy my homework?

### Objectives

**6.3.1** Define *diligence, faithfulness,* and *courage*.

**6.3.2** Identify ways in which diligence, faithfulness, and courage can be misapplied to wrong goals. BWS

**6.3.3** Contrast the virtues of diligence, faithfulness, and courage with the vices of sloth, workaholism, disloyalty, recklessness, and cowardice.

**6.3.4** Give examples of how diligence, faithfulness, and courage relate to ethical decision-making and ethical living.

**6.3.5** Develop a plan for growing in diligence, faithfulness, and courage.

### Biblical Worldview Shaping

- **Man's Chief End** (explain): Right goals are necessary for the virtues of diligence, faithfulness, and courage to be truly virtuous. (6.3.2)

### Printed Resource

- Activity 6.3: The Place for Diligence, Faithfulness, and Courage

### Suggested Reading

- Berg, Jim. *Essential Virtues: Marks of the Christ-Centered Life*. Greenville, SC: JourneyForth, 2008. Pages 161–73.
- Bridges, Jerry. *The Practice of Godliness*. Colorado Springs, CO: NavPress, 2008. Pages 147–56.
- Timpe, Kevin, and Craig A. Boyd. *Virtues and Their Vices*. Oxford: Oxford UP, 2014. Pages 177–98.

### Engage

#### CONNECTING THE VIRTUES OF DILIGENCE, FAITHFULNESS, AND COURAGE

Use a **bell ringer** activity to help the students connect and better understand the definitions of diligence, faithfulness, and courage.

**What are a few synonyms for the adjective *relentless*?** *continuous, never-ending, incessant, nonstop, persistent, tenacious*
**Who or what would you describe as relentless?** *Possible answers: a small child, a cough, a passionate person*
**How is diligence relentless?** *It doesn't give up. It works hard until it achieves its goal or that goal becomes unattainable.*
**How is faithfulness relentless?** *The relentless individual is faithful to the principles or convictions which energize said relentlessness.*
**How is courage relentless?** *Such persistence often requires courage to continue despite the temptation to stop or the criticism that comes with being so relentless.*

Relentlessness itself is no virtue. But to be relentless for the right reasons and in the right way can be a sign of diligence, faithfulness, or courage.

### Instruct

#### RELATIONSHIP TO OTHER VIRTUES

Use **direct instruction** to explain how diligence, faithfulness, and courage are practiced alongside and in combination with the rest of the virtues. They aren't practiced in isolation from the other virtues.

Virtues are not in competition with one another. Self-control and temperance don't cancel out diligence. Patience doesn't cancel out faithfulness. And neither does meekness, gentleness, or love cancel out courage.

Just as logs come together to build a sturdy cabin, the virtues are utilized with care and purpose to reflect Christlikeness and to embody the love of God and love for others.

## COMMON EXPRESSIONS OF DILIGENCE, FAITHFULNESS, AND COURAGE

Use a **journaling** activity to help students record common expressions of the virtues of diligence, faithfulness, and courage.

Diligence gets something done, faithfulness maintains a commitment to something, and courage does what is right for the right reasons no matter the cost.

**What are some examples of these virtues at work?** *Possible answers:*

- *Diligence: Consistent hard work at school or at a job even though it gets tough and the result isn't what one expected (e.g., low grades, low pay, a difficult environment to study or work in). Diligence is the stamina and endurance to finish the job one is responsible for.*
- *Faithfulness: A commitment to a sports team that you play on even though your team is in last place and many teammates have quit or play half-heartedly. Faithfulness is honoring your commitment by trying as hard as you can, regardless of the outcome.*
- *Courage: An unsaved family member or friend puts you on the spot about an LGBTQ+ issue he or she is excited about. Courage compels you to respond lovingly and respectfully without compromising on the truth of what God's Word teaches on the topic. Becoming estranged from that person who is close to you is a risk that is weighed, but courage says to let the fallout be what it may.*

(6:11, 13–14), and Paul's desire for personal boldness (6:19–20) all point to the virtue of courage.

### RELATIONSHIP BETWEEN DILIGENCE, FAITHFULNESS, AND COURAGE

So how are these three virtues related? Diligence gets something done. Faithfulness maintains a commitment to something. Courage does what's right for the right reasons no matter the cost.

Here is a scenario where all three virtues are required and seamlessly work together: a friend of yours, we'll call her Sandy, goes to a public high school. Sandy has a reputation, a good one, for being a thoughtful and strong Christian. Her teachers, though, are either atheistic or irreligious. As the school year goes on, the pushback from some teachers and classmates over how she practices her Christian faith increases. How should Sandy respond?

First, she needs to diligently study the Word (and maybe some other resources) in order to learn how to defend her faith and have the best possible answers for her detractors while maintaining a bold yet gracious attitude toward them. She can't learn everything in a matter of weeks or months, but she must display *diligence* in learning how to engage in apologetics with those at school (2 Tim. 2:14–15).

Second, Sandy must remain faithful to the Lord amidst the growing pressure against her for her Christian faith. Some unbelievers can be very antagonistic to Christians and even try to get a believer to leave the faith or slip up in their faith. Sandy must demonstrate *faithfulness* in her commitment to Jesus Christ as her Lord and her source of truth and confidence (Rom. 1:16).

And third, Sandy needs to be unashamedly courageous in her defense of the truth of the Bible and of the authority of Christ (Matt. 28:18; Eph. 3:12–13). She might be alone in her efforts or at least feel alone. She might not feel persuasive. But as Sandy trusts the Lord with the outcome, she shows *courage* by speaking up for her faith and not forsaking her beliefs despite harassment from those around her.

In short, Sandy's faithfulness to Christ and His Word leads to diligence in preparation and courage in proclamation as she faces those who oppose the gospel. And it's worth noting that Sandy's diligence (in preparation and in her general way of living) can contribute to courage (confidence in what she has to say and in her testimony) when the moment comes to speak (see 1 Pet. 3:14–16).

### MISAPPLICATIONS OF DILIGENCE, FAITHFULNESS, AND COURAGE

What distinguishes an advanced musician from a beginner? Many things undoubtedly, but would you say that both musicians have different knowledge about what to play on their instrument? Not necessarily. An advanced musician might play all the same notes and chords that a beginner has recently learned. But if both the beginner and the advanced musician played the same piece of music, the latter's rendition would be unquestionably better. Why? Because an advanced musician has learned by experience and practice what it means to play skillfully and artfully, beyond simply hitting the right notes.

What distinguishes a mature believer from an immature believer? Often, the difference between the two also comes down to being able to live skillfully and artfully, and this ability too is developed by experience and practice. Both believers are trying to apply the same virtues, but the mature believer has thoroughly internalized the virtues more and developed moral skill in applying them to specific circumstances in a balanced and grace-infused way. When it comes to applying diligence, faithfulness, and courage, such developed moral skill will help you apply each virtue in a careful fashion, with the right goals in mind. Practicing diligence, demonstrating faithfulness, and showing courage fall short of virtue if your goals and means aren't wise and ethical.



## VICES ARE THREATS, NOT ULTIMATUMS

Guide a **discussion** of the vices of sloth, laziness, disloyalty, recklessness, and cowardice.

Christians are called to diligence in the face of rampant sloth and workaholism. Christians are called to faithfulness despite the social acceptability of disloyalty. And Christians are called to courage, forsaking any shred of recklessness or cowardice.

Vices pose as threats to believers. But they are not ultimatums that believers must give in to, even in the thick of ethical difficulties.

**Why is sloth often not identified for what it really is?** *Those guilty of the vice of sloth are often clever in how they present excuses for their lack of diligence. Here are a few examples: "Not everyone is a go-getter." "Everyone works at a different pace." "It's not good to stress out." A desire to be slothful as well as the use of these excuses is unethical. We must keep in mind that diligence can be expressed regardless of one's personality or the pace at which one works.*

**Why does workaholism get a pass in some Christian circles?** *In general, Christian circles extol productivity and shun sloth. A danger, however, is that workaholism abuses a good principle (a diligent work ethic) and turns it into a vice and an idol. Another danger is that workaholism in one area is typically a sign of sloth in other neglected areas.*

**How does failing to commit or changing the terms of the commitment reflect disloyalty, not faithfulness?** *Faithfulness is deciding to commit to something good and staying committed to it. Even a partial commitment or one that changes over time displays the vice of disloyalty rather than the virtue of faithfulness. Disloyalty breaks the bonds of trust and loyalty between two or more people. And the disloyal party loses integrity.*

**How does the world twist being "true to oneself" even if that means reckless and irresponsible behavior?** *Many people blame their short temper on their genes or attribute their reckless behavior to their rough upbringing. It is common to shift blame and not take responsibility for bad and destructive behavior. But courage pursues the good of others by avoiding recklessness. And confessing your faults is one way you can demonstrate courage.*

**How does the world elevate looking out for oneself to the point where cowardice is approved of?** *If the mindset is that self-preservation is the highest good, then there is room*

***Misapplied Diligence***

God requires that we be diligent about important issues that affect our lives and relationships—including our relationship with God (Prov. 4:23; Phil. 2:12–13). That means that being diligent at just any task doesn't count for anything unless the goal is godly. For example, you might set for yourself the goal of being as healthy as you can possibly be. To achieve this sort of health and physical fitness will require great diligence. Your diligence might be exemplary in eating healthy foods, staying away from sodas, snacking only on fruits or vegetables, working out consistently, getting plenty of sleep each night, and having annual physicals that include bloodwork. This level of diligence, though it could be commendable, could also be misapplied, since seeking to achieve peak health and fitness can turn into an idolatrous pursuit. God expects us to be healthy so we can be good stewards of the bodies He has given us and so we can be able to fulfill His will for us (inferred from Gen. 1:26, 28, 31 and 1 Tim. 4:8). But God also expects us to diligently do many other things throughout our lifetimes, and these good responsibilities may conflict with such a rigorous health and fitness schedule. If we adjust the goal to rightly accommodate our physical limitations, realistic life stages, ministry opportunities, work responsibilities, spiritual growth, and family demands, then the virtue of diligence can truly be ethical in a measured pursuit of health and wellness. In other words, the fundamental virtue of *prudence* should help us order our responsibilities rightly. Truly living for God's glory involves diligently balancing our time and effort in all our areas of responsibility—not being excessively "diligent" in one area to the neglect of others.

***Misapplied Faithfulness***

If you get a job at a store or restaurant one day, or already have one, then you should be faithful to your agreement to work there. Your goals are to bring glory to God through your work and to provide for yourself financially. You need to work! Let's say that when you get your job, you and your boss agree that you will work Mondays through Saturdays. But after a few months, your boss schedules you to work on Sunday mornings. What do you do? You want to be faithful to your commitment to work for your employer. You also want to keep your job so you can provide for your needs. These are legitimate goals. Notice how the circumstances of your employment changed, though. Upon accepting the job, you weren't required to work Sunday mornings; now you are. A narrow "faithfulness" to your job for its own sake would cause you to be unfaithful to God's commands and expectations regarding church involvement (Heb. 10:25). The goal of being a faithful follower of Jesus, which includes consistent church involvement, needs to be addressed at this crossroads. This is an example of conflicting goals, both good. Blind faithfulness to one goal that causes unfaithfulness to a greater goal isn't ethical. Again, prudence should help you in ordering your priorities and understanding what faithfulness across the whole of your life's responsibilities would look like.

***Misapplied Courage***

Consider someone pursuing the goal of consistently confronting all the sin they perceive in their friends and fellow church members. To do this takes courage, lots of it. The goal seems commendable, and the path to achieve it does re-



*for cowardice to be viewed positively and not negatively. Those who make decisions to take care of themselves rather than conform to biblical standards of living are actually engaging in cowardice, even though the world may view them as brave. One example is a married person divorcing a spouse because he or she feels unhappy or unfulfilled. The world elevates cowardice and calls it courage.*

*Courage is a Christian duty but also a constant possibility for one who places himself in the almighty hands of God. It shows itself in patient endurance, moral steadfastness and spiritual fidelity.*
H. D. MCDONALD[11]

quire courage. But the goal can be easily misapplied because, first, we are fallible at detecting actual sin in the lives of those we would plan to courageously confront. In observing a friend strictly externally or with little context, there is a chance you are making a judgment based on your own preferences rather than on biblical teaching. Second, the Bible suggests that there may be times when it is appropriate to overlook an offense (Prov. 19:11; Acts 17:30; Rom. 3:25; 1 Pet. 4:8). Third, Christ was clear that it is far easier to see small faults in others than to see large faults in ourselves and that we should address our own sins first (Matt. 7:2–5). The goal of seeing believers repent of sin and pursue godliness is a great goal. Courage is truly ethical when a better goal is set up and followed—a goal for which prudence has balanced love, humility, mercy, concern for holiness, and wise understanding of various particular circumstances. Nonetheless, the goal of confronting clear and grave sin does require courage, and believers should actively seek to do so ethically (Gal. 6:1).

### Righteous Motives and Goals, but Bad Outcomes

God is glorified when your motives are in the right place and the goal you are reaching for is righteous. But you can't control all the circumstances that affect the outcome. You are responsible for your motives. You are responsible for how you go about living out the appropriate virtues and how you set the goal. God alone knows how all things will turn out and declares "the end from the beginning" (Isa. 46:10). He knows each of our motives and why we set the goals we set (1 Cor. 4:5). Using the example of diligence from above, let's say someone is diligent and careful to eat well and exercise frequently. This person is also as diligent as can be in all other responsibilities. The goal is right this time. But at age thirty-eight, this person finds out he or she has an aggressive form of cancer. Is this the individual's fault? Is this someone who was not diligent enough with their diet after all? Did God not see his or her just motives and righteous goal?

### TWISTING DILIGENCE, FAITHFULNESS, AND COURAGE

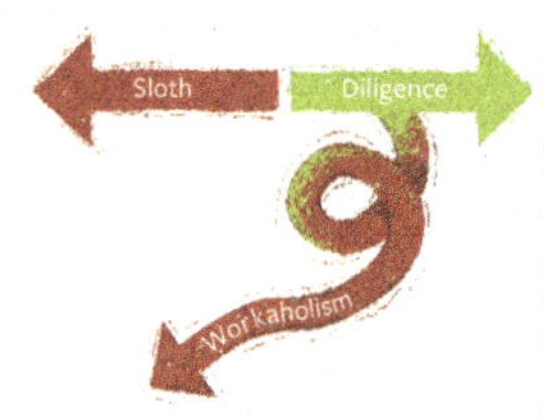


The easiest way to twist diligence is to pit the vice of sloth or laziness against a vice in the opposite ditch—workaholism. **Sloth** is laziness, a lack of motivation to do necessary and productive work—the opposite of diligence. One who is slothful is also foolish and ends up hurting him- or herself and others. In the book of Proverbs, the vice of sloth is exposed as destructive (Prov. 6:9–11; 13:4; 18:9; 19:15; 20:4; 21:25; 26:13–16). **Workaholism**, on the other hand, twists diligence, leaving no room for and giving attention to the other good and necessary parts of life that aren't work. It involves making an idol out of work and usually results in overworking one responsibility to the detriment of others. To be diligent at work is a good thing; it isn't workaholism, which twists the virtuousness of diligence.

You have probably faced the temptation to procrastinate getting your schoolwork done. Be careful! Habitual, prolonged procrastination is essentially the vice of sloth. The virtue of diligence would see you work ahead where possible and see you guard your time so as to get your schoolwork done when it's due. On the other hand, you may have been tempted to study all the time, neglecting time with the Lord or with family. That, too, is problematic. Be diligent in what God has called you to do right now. Don't be lazy and don't be a workaholic.

Faithfulness can also be twisted and brought down from its lofty position as a virtue to a lowly and distasteful vice—the vice of disloyalty. **Disloyalty**, the opposite

104 VIRTUES

## Apply

### RIGHTEOUS MOTIVES AND GOALS, BUT BAD OUTCOMES

Use a **Turn and Talk** to discuss the topic and questions from the textbox on page 104.

**Is this the individual's fault?** *no*
**Is this someone who was not diligent enough with their diet after all?** *No, this person did the best he or she could with diet and lifestyle choices.*
**Did God not see his or her just motives and righteous goal?** *Of course, God saw the just motives and righteous goal of the person who came down with cancer. God doesn't prevent all evil, calamity, and results of the Fall from harming humans, even His children (2 Cor. 12:9–10). God is just and righteous in how He works out His will for His glory. And God gives grace in the trial. Diligence, faithfulness, and courage remain part of a Christian's character and practice, even during the hard times of life.*

### DILIGENCE, FAITHFULNESS, AND COURAGE

Use **Activity 6.3** on pages 33–34 to apply the information in the section.

### SCHOOLWORK AND ETHICS

Use a **Think-Pair-Share** for students to work out their answers to this section's essential question.

**How should I respond when a friend asks to copy my homework?** *While this issue is one of honesty and integrity, it is also a question of courage. It takes courage to say no to a friend, especially if this friend is struggling in the subject area in question. But the principle is simple: each student is required to do his or her own work. Presenting one's work as one's own when someone else did it is lying, dishonest, deceptive, and is considered cheating. You need courage to say no, whereas your friend needs diligence to do the best that one can on the assignment.*

## Assess

### MEASURING PERSONAL VIRTUE

Use a **Ticket out the Door** to assess understanding of the virtues by allowing students to apply them to the examples below.

**What is an example of how diligence can help you make ethical decisions regarding schoolwork and extracurricular activities?** *Possible answer: Diligent study and preparation or diligent practice and training will keep you from cutting corners or being tempted to cheat when presented with opportunities to qualify for an honors class or the varsity sports team. Hard work and honest effort don't always pay off with the results that we want. But hard work and honest effort are the right things to do, and they lead to better ethical choices and result in a better lifestyle because diligence is the moral and godly choice.*
**What is an example of how faithfulness can help you make ethical decisions regarding your use of social media?** *Possible answer: Following viral trends on social media has a strong pull on young people. When the next viral trend is sensual, crude, or degrading, you should be faithful to God and the lifestyle He calls believers to. Other virtues are also called upon, but allegiance to the Lord and a godly lifestyle manifest as faithfulness, especially when faithfulness requires one to refrain from doing what everyone else is doing.*

The virtue of courage isn't a one-time stand against a formidable or blatantly unethical situation. Courage is required for common, frequent situations where it is challenging to make the right stand and say the right thing at the right time.

**What is an example of how courage can help you make an ethical decision that impacts your ethical living?** *One example is when your peers want to engage in an activity that is either sinful or offending to your conscience, whether watching a certain movie*

of faithfulness, is when any commitment to remain faithful and loyal to something or someone is disregarded (without a legitimate ethical reason). To answer the question above, where does your primary loyalty lie? To God and His ethical standards (which include not participating in cheating on assignments) or to your friend and your friendship? Actually, to not allow a friend to copy your homework isn't disloyalty to him or her; it is the right, ethical response. Real loyalty to true friendship sometimes means being willing to do or say the hard thing for the good of the other person. Your friend needs to accept the repercussions of not getting his or her homework done, whatever the reason might be.

How should I respond when a friend asks to copy my homework?

While faithfulness says, "Yes, I will be true to a righteous commitment no matter what self-sacrifice there may be," disloyalty says, "I'm out. This isn't convenient for me anymore." Disloyalty should be entirely unattractive to Christians because it stands in such contrast to the loyal faithfulness of God (Lam. 3:22–23).

Engaging in culturally acceptable sins (such as telling small lies or being impatient) and falling into apathy toward the things of the Lord—these mark the path of disloyalty to God. Watch out! It is "the little foxes" (Song of Sol. 2:15), seemingly insignificant displays of willful disloyalty, that wreak havoc on your faithfulness to God. Faithfulness won't let go of what it knows to be true and good. Disloyalty ignores all virtue and selfishly and foolishly settles for vice.

Courage can easily be twisted in two different directions—recklessness or cowardice. **Recklessness** throws all caution to the wind and acts or reacts impulsively. Recklessness parades as courage, but it acts imprudently and therefore doesn't consider the outcome of its rash actions. **Cowardice**, on the other hand, runs away from danger and won't stand up to defend what is true and right when threatened. Cowardice is the polar opposite of courage. The Bible is clear that fools and unbelievers are both reckless and cowardly (Prov. 14:16; Rev. 21:8). There is no worth, no goodness, in the vices.

Whenever you hear a friend answer the question, "Why did you do that?" with, "I wasn't thinking," recklessness is partly to blame. And when you are asked about your response to an immoral situation and you reply, "I just didn't say anything," cowardice likely had a role. Pay attention! Most of us aren't as courageous as we think we are. The test of your courage is how you respond when doing the right thing will be costly. Even with good intentions, a lack of prudence can turn courage into recklessness. And fear can easily cause courage to fail at a crucial moment. Dutch pastor and author Wilhelmus à Brakel illustrated godly courage this way:

> As someone who in a storm finds himself too weak to remain standing takes hold of a post or a tree and remains standing due to its immobility, the courageous person likewise takes hold of the strength of the Lord, and thus remains strong and unyielding.[12]

The truth is, we need the Lord's wisdom and strength to make us what we are not.

### PRACTICING DILIGENCE, FAITHFULNESS, AND COURAGE

Overcoming sloth, disloyalty, recklessness, and cowardice is essential to practicing diligence, faithfulness, and courage. Scripture teaches that believers are to put off the old self and then put on the new self (Eph. 4:22–24). Unfortunately, to sin by engaging in the vices rather than the virtues can come all too naturally to us (Rom. 7:15–19). We not only need God's help to practice these three virtues, but we also need a plan to make sure that we do.

Where do you find yourself lacking in diligence? What top priorities in your life are you struggling to be faithful to? In what circumstances do you habitually lack courage? The answers to these questions will help you set up a plan to live ethically. Ask God to help you see where you are lacking in diligence, faithfulness, and courage. And ask God to help you grow in these virtues as you depend on Christ to make them part of how you think and who you are.



*or video, skipping church for a leisure activity, or using certain vulgar or crass language. Courage is required in each case to be bold and stand firm against any opposition, not backing down or compromising due to peer pressure.*

VIRTUES, PART 1 105

### Thinking It Through 6.3

1. Define *diligence*, *faithfulness*, and *courage*.
2. In what ways can diligence, faithfulness, and courage be misapplied to wrong goals?
3. Contrast the virtues of diligence, faithfulness, and courage with the vices of sloth/laziness, disloyalty, recklessness, and cowardice.
4. Give examples of how diligence, faithfulness, and courage relate to ethical decision-making and ethical living.
5. Outline a plan for growing in diligence, faithfulness, and courage.

## 6.4 Self-Control, Temperance, and Patience

What defines a person with a chill personality? Easygoing? Never rushed? Maybe you know someone slightly introverted or shy. They don't get into trouble. They're fairly even-tempered. Is someone who doesn't blow their top at the slightest provocation necessarily practicing self-control, temperance, and patience?

### DEFINING SELF-CONTROL, TEMPERANCE, AND PATIENCE

This trio of virtues has to do with a believer's relationship to temptations and handling of hardship. Jerry Bridges explains that "***self-control*** *is the exercise of inner strength under the direction of sound judgment that enables us to do, think, and say the things that are pleasing to God.*"[13] The focus of this definition lies with the ideas of inner strength and sound judgment when a believer is faced with temptation (Gal. 5:23; 1 Cor. 9:25–27; Titus 2:2). **Temperance** is closely related to self-control and refers to one's moral conditioning and the avoidance of excessive behavior. And **patience** is a believer's faithful and hopeful endurance under long-lasting difficult circumstances. Patience carries the idea of steadfastness, longsuffering, and forbearance. A sampling of the New Testament's use of the term for patience demonstrates the expectant waiting and endurance that typifies patience (Rom. 12:12; 2 Thess. 1:4; 2 Tim. 2:10).

### MOTIVATING SELF-CONTROL, TEMPERANCE, AND PATIENCE

"Don't give in!" "Don't overdo it!" "Hang in there!" These three exhortations summarize what you might think of when you think of self-control, temperance, and patience respectively. But what motivates you to not give in? It could be pride. It could also be a legalistic mentality. What motivates you to not overdo it? It could be to avoid shame and embarrassment. It could also be to avoid trouble at home or at school. And what motivates you to hang in there? It could just be pride.

All the motives mentioned above might sound natural, but that doesn't mean they're virtuous. In fact, those motives represent what is typical for unbelievers. Refusing to binge on desserts or snacks for the third night in a row is a demonstration of self-control. The result is obviously positive, but what motivated you to show self-control in this area is also important. A general answer might be to be healthy. A non-Christian motive might be solely to look more physically attractive. A Christian motive would be to better worship God with all areas of one's life (Rom. 12:1). Attractiveness, in this case, can be a natural result or bonus, but it should not be the primary or sole motivation.

Moderating how much of your free time in the evenings is consumed by your mobile device or by a streaming platform is a demonstration of temperance. Doing this

106 VIRTUES

Guide a **summative assessment** by directing students to answer the questions in Thinking It Through 6.3.

### Thinking It Through 6.3

1. Diligence: "*The exertion of the spiritual and physical powers of a believer whereby he willingly, joyously, and earnestly executes that task which God assigns him, doing so because it is the will of God*" (Wilhelmus à Brakel, *The Law, Christian Graces, and the Lord's Prayer*, vol. 3 of *The Christian's Reasonable Service*, ed. Joel R. Beeke, trans. Bartel Elshout [Grand Rapids, MI: Reformation Heritage Books, 2015], 103–4; italics in the original).

   Faithfulness: Steadfast loyalty to that which is morally acceptable and good, despite difficulty and conflict.

   Courage: Spiritual strength to unashamedly do the right thing at the right time even at risk of one's own harm (Berg, *Essential Virtues,* 164).
2. You could be extremely diligent in being as healthy as you can. But that isn't your highest calling in life, so strict diligence in this area can become problematic.

   You might get a job, so you want to be faithful to it and make a good impression. Your faithfulness to your job might conflict with gathering with your church each Sunday morning if you get scheduled to work then.

   You might courageously confront the sin, or what you might deem imprudence, in the lives of your friends and church members. This is a commendable goal, but to consistently do this at every turn becomes problematic and could feed pride in your own life.
3. Sloth is not only the opposite of diligence, but it is a vice for which the following excuses are commonly given: "I'm tired," "I can do that later," "Someone else will do that," "I need to do something else," "I need to rest."

   The opposite of faithfulness is disloyalty. All sin is wrong, but especially conscious, purposeful sin is being disloyal to God. This is the worst form of disloyalty because it is sinning against the Creator and Savior.

   The opposite of courage is recklessness and cowardice. Courageous people are careful to plan ahead. They aren't reckless; they defend what is right even when it gets hard. And they aren't cowards.
4. Diligence comes into play when the temptation is to procrastinate or make excuses for failing to fulfill one's obligations. Faithfulness comes into play when the temptation is to be disloyal even in small, seemingly harmless ways with white lies or culturally acceptable sins. Courage comes into play when the temptation is to use the excuse of good intentions when causing a bad outcome or trying to blame something else for one's own cowardice.
5. prayer; meditating on Scriptures that teach these virtues; identifying areas where I easily succumb to the vices that are counterfeits of these virtues; getting an accountability partner to assess my actions and reactions when these virtues are in play; being aware of the areas in my life that require more diligence, faithfulness, and courage

## 6.4 Self-Control, Temperance, and Patience

How do I become an emotionally stable person?

### Objectives

**6.4.1** Define *self-control*, *temperance*, and *patience*.

**6.4.2** Compare and contrast Christian and

will help you develop a taste for a better use of your time and a distaste for wasting too much time on social media, videos, or shows. You might set those boundaries and be careful to respect them during the school year just to keep your parents from getting on your case all the time. This would be a limited, even non-Christian, motive. You should, however, be motivated to redeem the time the Lord has given you to accomplish the things He expects you to accomplish (Eph. 5:15–17).

Waiting till some point in college to seriously date someone might be a demonstration of patience. Exercising this virtue in this scenario would require many other virtues as well, but a desire to date and the availability of a good prospect would increase the need for patience. However, you might put off dating seriously because you want to live for yourself, doing whatever you want without having to worry about another's preferences. This seems more like a non-Christian motive. A Christian's motive for patience in this area might be to focus more on his or her walk with the Lord (1 Cor. 7:32–35) or to grow in the maturity necessary for marriage and possible parenthood. Often believers must patiently wait in order to see their hopes fulfilled (Rom. 8:24–25).

#### OPPOSING SELF-CONTROL, TEMPERANCE, AND PATIENCE

As you have learned by now, the opposites of virtues are vices. Two vices that stand directly opposed to self-control and temperance are self-indulgence and addiction. **Self-indulgence** is having no inhibitions, a total letting go of oneself to do as one pleases. Scripture calls this kind of behavior by various names, but what commonly comes of it are sexual sin and sin related to drunkenness (Rom. 13:13; 1 Pet. 4:3–4). **Addiction** is when an individual has become entirely dependent on getting pleasure from a substance or behavior regardless of the negative consequences. Scripture portrays the folly and danger of this vice in both testaments (Prov. 23:33–35; 1 Cor. 6:12).

Another vice that opposes the virtue of temperance is the seemingly pious vice of **asceticism**, which is the severe denial of the normal physical needs of the body, usually for the purpose of gaining spiritual merit. Rather than being the explicit opposite of temperance, asceticism stretches temperance past its breaking point. Robert Roberts explains the proper and improper use of temperance by saying the following:

> Temperance is an important virtue because food, drink, and sex, if desired improperly, can be sources of disruption, corruption, misery, and ill being both to the intemperate or weak-willed person and to others in his or her social world; but if properly loved and pursued, they can be sources of joy and wellbeing. We all want happiness, and the wise person sees that pleasure without temperance is like money without justice, generosity, and gratitude; it does not bring happiness because it upends an order of values that is normative for human nature. The temperate person is one who understands these connections between bodily pleasures and the larger human good, and whose understanding actually tempers the desires and pleasures.[14]

The issue which separates asceticism from temperance is this: there is a major difference between mortifying* sin (part of the practice of temperance) and refraining from enjoying legitimate physical pleasures (compare Rom. 8:13 with Col. 2:18–23 and 1 Tim. 4:1–5).

Strife works against patience. **Strife** is adversarial contention that leads an individual to verbally disagree with, ideologically break away from, or physically engage the conflicting party. Patience endures hardship and even hostility and doesn't end up in an altercation over every minor disagreement (see Rom. 12:18). Strife is found throughout the New Testament in lists of common sins of godless people (2 Cor. 12:20; Gal. 5:20).

Neither self-indulgence nor addiction supports the Christian's duty to practice consistent self-control (Titus 2:12). And neither self-indulgence nor addiction nor

**mortifying:** putting to death





non-Christian motives for self-control, temperance, and patience.

**6.4.3** Contrast the virtues of self-control, temperance, and patience with the vices of self-indulgence, addiction, asceticism, and strife.

**6.4.4** Give examples of how self-control, temperance, and patience relate to ethical decision-making and ethical living.

**6.4.5** Develop a plan for growing in self-control, temperance, and patience.

### Printed Resource

- Activity 6.4: A Dynamic Duo: Self-Control and Temperance

### Suggested Reading

- Berg, Jim. *Essential Virtues: Marks of the Christ-Centered Life*. Greenville, SC: JourneyForth, 2008. Pages 55–69, 199–203.
- Bridges, Jerry. *The Practice of Godliness*. Colorado Springs, CO: NavPress, 2008. Pages 131–46, 164, 169–82.
- ———. *Respectable Sins*. Colorado Springs, CO: NavPress, 2007. Pages 105–16.
- Timpe, Kevin, and Craig A. Boyd. 2014. *Virtues and Their Vices*. Oxford: Oxford UP, 2014. Pages 93–114.

## Engage

### HAVING IT ALL TOGETHER

Guide a **discussion** to illustrate how the virtues of self-control, temperance, and patience are often perceived. Growing in the virtues isn't about "having it all together."

**What comes to mind when you think of someone who is self-disciplined?**

To be self-disciplined requires self-control, temperance, and even patience. But self-discipline isn't a goal in and of itself. It isn't a virtue. Self-discipline can offer many benefits, especially to students, such as managing time to get assignments done on time, resting enough, eating a well-balanced diet, or avoiding conflicts or hot-tempered arguments. Self-control, temperance, and patience are virtues that someone possesses and, when implemented, allow for one to be self-disciplined in the right ways for the right reasons.

## Instruct

### THE DISTINCTION BETWEEN SELF-CONTROL AND TEMPERANCE

Use **direct instruction** to clarify the reasons for nuancing self-control and temperance as presented in the textbook.

The chapter makes a distinction between the virtues of self-control and temperance. It focuses on the nuances present in the two virtues. As a matter of fact, these two words are used interchangeably in older and newer versions of the Bible to describe the same virtue (see Acts 24:25; Gal. 5:23; 2 Pet. 1:6). Self-control does not give in to the urge to sin when faced with temptation, whereas temperance conditions one to desire for righteousness in order to minimize the urge to sin before it occurs. Both ideas are found in both virtues throughout the passages where they are discussed.

First Corinthians 9:25–27 is a helpful passage illustrating self-control or temperance. Paul highlights the conditioning or tempering required to resist temptation. Paul does not rely on the strength of his character or on his knowledge of right and wrong to resist temptation. But when he encounters temptations, he employs self-control. And all along he is training or conditioning his character so that temptations don't faze him because he is growing in temperance, which keeps him focused on his goal.

### HOW THE VICES OPPOSE THE VIRTUES

Use a **Socratic seminar** to discuss each virtue paired with its vice. Divide the students in up to four groups, assigning one of the following pairs to each group: self-control and self-indulgence; temperance and

asceticism enable the believer's call to a life marked by thoughtful temperance (1 Cor. 9:25). Strife flies in the face of the Christian's grace-infused desire to express his or her faith, love, and hope through patience (1 Cor. 13:7). Be careful not to view the vices as "all or nothing." In other words, a little self-indulgence, a "harmless" addiction, a little experimentation with asceticism, and temporary strife are still sinful and still need to be avoided. You might not be caught up in habitual practice of a vice to the consistent neglect of certain virtues. But every vice starts out slowly and sporadically until it grows into a damaging way of life.

#### APPLYING SELF-CONTROL, TEMPERANCE, AND PATIENCE

It has been said that buying things on sale is saving money by spending money. If the personal rule is to save money on something you know you need to buy soon anyway, then by all means get it while it is on sale! But if the personal rule is to not spend money, period, then saving by spending isn't even an option. If you are a spender, then this section's virtues can help you. If you are not a spender except for when something is on sale, this section is also for you. And if you are extremely frugal and don't like to spend a dime, you can still learn from these applications.

First, let's spell out a distinction between self-control and temperance, even though the two are interrelated. Self-control is reactive. It is used in the moment. Temperance seeks to avoid reactive situations. When presented with a temptation to sin or to indulge, a believer practicing self-control will resist that temptation and not give in to sin. Notice that the Christian is put under pressure and has to make a quick decision whether to practice self-control or concede to self-indulgence.

The moral conditioning of temperance, however, prepares the believer to be less affected by those same temptations. Temperance often reflects our human, physical appetites (for things like sleep, food, and sex) and passions (strong desires) in general. To temper metal, for example, is to heat it and cool it in such a way that the metal becomes harder and more resistant to bending or breaking. So one's desires, legitimate and illegitimate, can be tempered appropriately so that their direction and use is ethical. Both self-control and temperance are critical for believers. Just think of self-control as adjusting the way you are playing a sport so that you can keep playing even when a cramp seizes your leg. And think of temperance as all the conditioning, warming up, and stretching you do that help prevent your legs from cramping up.

self control vs. temperance

Now, back to our shopping example. Self-control is shopping at one specific store for one specific item and resisting the urge to buy multiple items that you love from the displays in the checkout line. Temperance could result in shopping for the same gift in the same store and not even noticing or being drawn to items that you know you neither need nor have the money for. Think of something more serious, such as blowing up at people online over a political issue or current event topic. You need to practice self-control when tempted to do so, but you also need to grow in temperance to use social media without being incited to even engage with incendiary* topics.

As for applying patience, there is no lack of scenarios that require us to be patient. You have undoubtedly heard many say that patience is a virtue or even the mother of all virtues. Have you ever thought about why that is? Part of our definition of patience is endurance under long-lasting difficult circumstances. The fallen and sin-stricken world we live in affords us with innumerable instances of difficult circumstances. The patience required is often greater than the version of patience needed any time you must wait for something—waiting for your sibling to finish getting ready in the bathroom, driving behind a slow-moving vehicle, or waiting for a friend to return your text.

**Incendiary:** tending to stir up strife



addiction; temperance and asceticism; and patience and strife.

Offer questions such as the following for students to consider about their virtue and vice.

**To analyze the virtue and the vice, why is it necessary to have the correct definition of them?** *See pages 106–7. It isn't possible to consider their relationship to each other without knowing exactly what the virtue and vice are.*

**How does the vice work against the virtue?** *See pages 107–8. Where there is a vice in action, or at least tolerated, the virtue can't survive, let alone be practiced. And if the vice is tolerated and practiced often, the believer runs into the danger of getting used to sinning rather than practicing righteousness.*

**In what ways does having the virtue as a motive help to avoid practicing the vice?** *Our motives are either right or wrong, coming from a moral or immoral place, or ethical or unethical. The fruit of the Spirit and the rest of the virtues displace vices in that there is no room in the heart for evil vices when righteous virtues are present and working. A believer practicing self-control will avoid splurging in self-indulgence. A believer practicing temperance will stay away from addictions and won't be drawn to asceticism. And a believer practicing patience will avoid strife in handling a problem.*

## Apply

### SCENARIOS WHERE SELF-CONTROL, TEMPERANCE, AND PATIENCE ARE NEEDED

Use a **Think-Pair-Share** to encourage students to develop example scenarios where they would need to utilize self-control, temperance, and patience. Students should come up with at least one example for each virtue.

Guide a **discussion** for the groups to share their examples with the class.

**When would you need to use self-control?** *Possible answers: When I need to resist the urge to sin when tempted; these temptations to sin (such as a racy ad or video on social media, hearing the latest gossip, or overreacting to a frustrating situation) might come suddenly. Self-control is also necessary to not slothfully oversleep on the weekend when you are pressed with other obligations. In those moments, either virtue or vice will well up inside and come out.*

**When would you need to use temperance?** *Possible answers: When I need to condition myself morally so that I can be relatively unaffected by sudden temptations; examples include using social media or browsing the web responsibly without searching for or wanting to click on racy ads or videos, calmly defusing stressful situations, and getting sufficient rest on the weekends without neglecting responsibilities. Temperance is used daily, and the results look like obedient, faithful submission to Christlike living.*

**When would you need to use patience?** *Possible answers: When I need to endure a difficult circumstance for a long or indefinite period of time; the easy option would be to give in, give up, or vent. Patience is needed in the following scenarios: when you suffer ridicule or bullying, whether online or in person, or when you don't get the scholarships you wanted or don't get into the college of your first choice. You need patience for these big scenarios, as well as for small, daily inconveniences.*

### SELF-CONTROL AND TEMPERANCE

Use **Activity 6.4** on pages 35–36 to apply the information in the section. You may also group the students and direct them to present a role-play of the scenarios.

### FINDING EMOTIONAL STABILITY

Ask students this section's **essential question.**

**How do I become an emotionally stable person?** *Answers should reflect the truths found in the passages below.*

But how does one show patience when the situation is serious? If an unmarried girl gets pregnant and she or the father considers an abortion, what role does patience play? Assuming responsibility for our actions includes patiently accepting the consequences of those actions. Patience is required to endure a less-than-ideal pregnancy and all the hardships that might come in the years following the baby's birth. Getting an abortion isn't just impatience, it is to strive against an innocent life at a lethal level. Another situation that might require patience is our country's current immigration policies. You might strongly disagree with some aspects of those policies and feel that much wrong is being done to our nation or to those trying to enter it. You need patience as you exercise faith in the sovereign God while being hopeful that certain politicians will be voted into office and will commit to improving those policies.

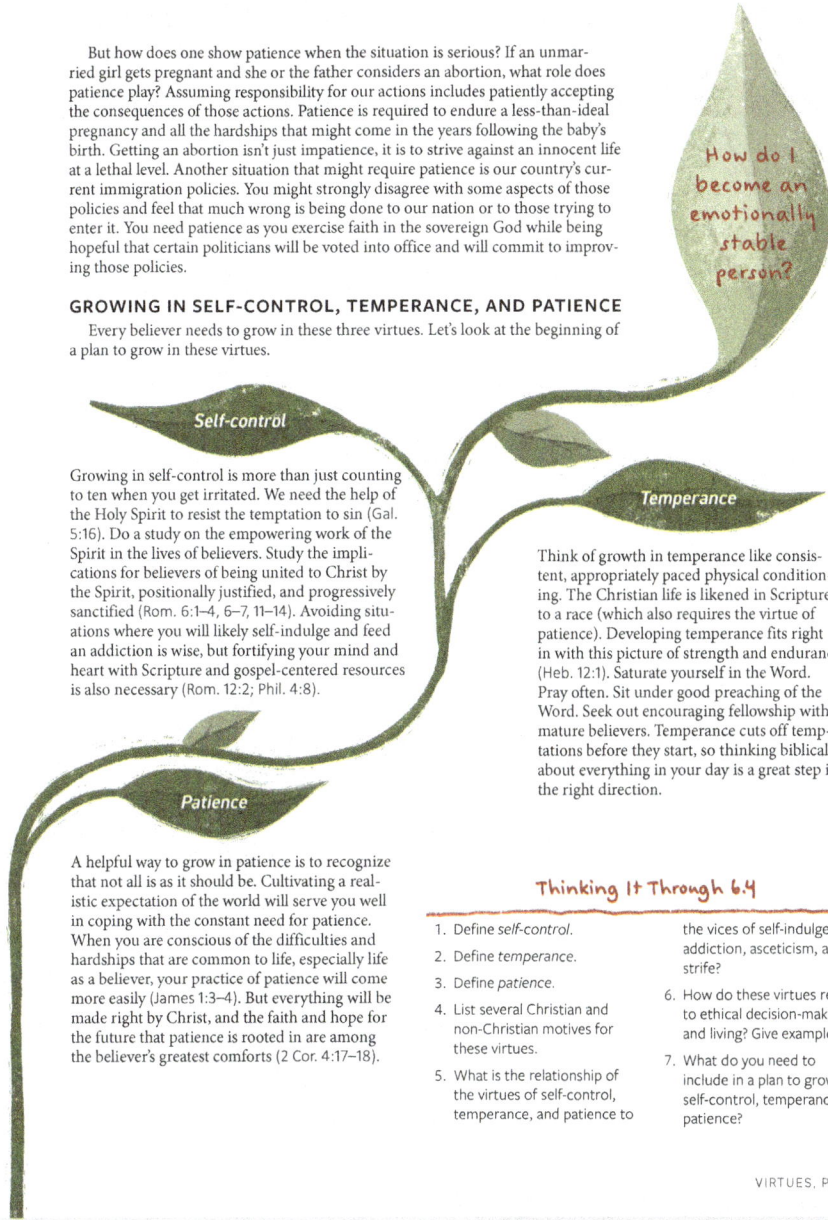

How do I become an emotionally stable person?

### GROWING IN SELF-CONTROL, TEMPERANCE, AND PATIENCE

Every believer needs to grow in these three virtues. Let's look at the beginning of a plan to grow in these virtues.

**Self-control**

Growing in self-control is more than just counting to ten when you get irritated. We need the help of the Holy Spirit to resist the temptation to sin (Gal. 5:16). Do a study on the empowering work of the Spirit in the lives of believers. Study the implications for believers of being united to Christ by the Spirit, positionally justified, and progressively sanctified (Rom. 6:1–4, 6–7, 11–14). Avoiding situations where you will likely self-indulge and feed an addiction is wise, but fortifying your mind and heart with Scripture and gospel-centered resources is also necessary (Rom. 12:2; Phil. 4:8).

**Temperance**

Think of growth in temperance like consistent, appropriately paced physical conditioning. The Christian life is likened in Scripture to a race (which also requires the virtue of patience). Developing temperance fits right in with this picture of strength and endurance (Heb. 12:1). Saturate yourself in the Word. Pray often. Sit under good preaching of the Word. Seek out encouraging fellowship with mature believers. Temperance cuts off temptations before they start, so thinking biblically about everything in your day is a great step in the right direction.

**Patience**

A helpful way to grow in patience is to recognize that not all is as it should be. Cultivating a realistic expectation of the world will serve you well in coping with the constant need for patience. When you are conscious of the difficulties and hardships that are common to life, especially life as a believer, your practice of patience will come more easily (James 1:3–4). But everything will be made right by Christ, and the faith and hope for the future that patience is rooted in are among the believer's greatest comforts (2 Cor. 4:17–18).

#### Thinking It Through 6.4

1. Define *self-control*.
2. Define *temperance*.
3. Define *patience*.
4. List several Christian and non-Christian motives for these virtues.
5. What is the relationship of the virtues of self-control, temperance, and patience to the vices of self-indulgence, addiction, asceticism, and strife?
6. How do these virtues relate to ethical decision-making and living? Give examples.
7. What do you need to include in a plan to grow in self-control, temperance, and patience?

VIRTUES, PART 1 109

Some biblical texts that address the factors necessary for emotional stability are Isaiah 26:3, Galatians 5:22–23, Philippians 4:7–9, and 2 Timothy 1:7. Allow students time to read through these passages before formulating an answer.

Pursuing Christ and, through the Spirit, renewing one's mind and heart in the Word aid the pursuit of the virtues (Rom. 12:1–2; Eph. 1:17–18). These virtues, by God's grace and power, are the path to emotional stability. It is true that physical, psychological, mental, or emotional issues greatly affect emotional stability. But the power of God through one's submission to the will of God in pursuing and practicing the virtues will assist one's efforts toward emotional stability and Christlikeness.

## Assess

Guide a **summative assessment** by directing students to answer the questions in Thinking It Through 6.4.

### Thinking It Through 6.4

1. "the exercise of inner strength under the direction of sound judgment that enables us to do, think, and say the things that are pleasing to God" (Bridges, *The Practice of Godliness*, 164)
2. self-control and the avoidance of excessive behavior
3. a believer's faith-filled and hopeful endurance under long-lasting difficult circumstances
4. Christian motives: to worship God better with all areas of one's life, to redeem the time that the Lord has given you to accomplish the things He expects you to accomplish, and to prepare oneself for the task of being a spouse and potential future parent

   Non-Christian motives: pride, legalism, avoiding shame and embarrassment, avoiding trouble at home or school, selfishness, physical attractiveness
5. The vices of self-indulgence and addiction are the opposite of the virtue of self-control. Self-control seeks to curb sinful desires and limit harmful behaviors, whereas self-indulgence seeks to indulge in sinful or harmful pleasures, and addiction enslaves one to harmful behaviors.

   The vices of addiction and asceticism are the opposite of the virtue of temperance. Temperance uses moderation, avoiding excessive behavior, for godly ends, whereas addiction is repeated and excessive engagement in harmful behavior. The vice of asceticism twists temperance by refusing to partake in legitimate and good things, assuming that such deprivation is spiritual and beneficial.

   The vice of strife is the opposite of the virtue of patience because, rather than enduring with faith and hope, one stirs up conflict and contention.
6. When shopping and trying not to overspend, splurge, or waste money, the believer is guarded by self-control, temperance, and patience. The same is true when using social media and guarding against lashing out or being argumentative. The same is also true when someone has to deal with an unplanned pregnancy before being married. Even though in this last case self-control and temperance were not practiced, resulting in the pregnancy, one must be patient because getting an abortion is wrong.
7. the help of the Holy Spirit, regularly reading the Word and hearing the Word preached, prayer, an encouraging church family, and a realistic expectation of what can happen when living in this world as a Christian

# Chapter 6 Review

## Terms to Remember

- **righteousness:** The conformity of an individual's life to God's standards of moral perfection.
- **goodness:** Generously seeking others' happiness and well-being, as determined by God's righteous standards.
- **ungodliness:** Anything that is contrary to God's nature or opposed to God's ways.
- **corruption:** Any harm done to God's good design and moral will for His creation.
- **prudence:** The ability to choose the best course of action, having considered all the constraints of the situation, to obtain the most righteous and beneficial outcome.
- **cunning:** Involves shrewdness as well as deception. Like prudence, cunning employs a thorough analysis of the situation, but it does so in order to obtain something through immoral means or to an unethical end.
- **rashness:** Acting in the moment with no regard for whether one's actions are the best way, or even a good way, to reach a desired end.
- **diligence:** "*The exertion of the spiritual and physical powers of a believer whereby he willingly, joyously, and earnestly executes that task which God assigns him, doing so because it is the will of God*" (Brakel, *The Law, Christian Graces, and the Lord's Prayer*, 103–4; italics in the original).
- **faithfulness:** Steadfast loyalty to that which is morally acceptable and good, despite difficulty and conflict.
- **courage:** Spiritual strength to unashamedly do the right thing at the right time even at risk of one's own harm (Berg, *Essential Virtues,* 164).
- **sloth:** Laziness; a lack of motivation to do necessary and productive work.
- **workaholism:** Excessive engagement in work that leaves no room for and gives no attention to the other good and necessary parts of life that aren't work.
- **disloyalty:** Disregard (without a legitimate ethical reason) for any commitment to remain faithful and loyal to something or someone.
- **recklessness:** Throwing all caution to the wind and acting or reacting impulsively.
- **cowardice:** Running away from danger; refusing to stand up to defend what is true and right when threatened.
- **self-control:** "The exercise of inner strength under the direction of sound judgment that enables us to do, think, and say the things that are pleasing to God" (Bridges, *The Practice of Godliness*, 164).
- **temperance:** Self-control and the avoidance of excessive behavior.
- **patience:** A believer's faith-filled and hopeful endurance under long-lasting difficult circumstances.
- **self-indulgence:** Having no inhibitions, a total letting go of oneself to do as one pleases.
- **addiction:** Dependence on getting pleasure from a substance or behavior regardless of the negative consequences.
- **asceticism:** The severe denial of the normal physical needs of the body, usually for the purpose of gaining spiritual merit.
- **strife:** Adversarial contention that leads an individual to verbally disagree with, ideologically break away from, or physically engage the conflicting party.

## Understanding Ethics

1. Righteousness relates to ethics in that the foundation for all righteous behavior is the righteousness of God. God's standards of righteousness govern our interactions. So to be ethical it is necessary to pursue the virtue of righteousness.

# Review 06
VIRTUES, PART 1

### Terms to Remember

- righteousness
- goodness
- ungodliness
- corruption
- prudence
- cunning
- rashness
- diligence
- faithfulness
- courage
- sloth
- workaholism
- disloyalty
- recklessness
- cowardice
- self-control
- temperance
- patience
- self-indulgence
- addiction
- asceticism
- strife

### Scripture Memory

Philippians 4:8

### Understanding Ethics

1. How do the virtues of righteousness and goodness relate to ethics?
2. How does the virtue of prudence relate to ethics?
3. How do the virtues of diligence, faithfulness, and courage relate to ethics?
4. How do the virtues of self-control, temperance, and patience relate to ethics?

### Practicing Ethical Decision-Making

5. What role does prudence play when one turns eighteen, becoming a legal adult?
6. What role does patience play in abiding by the rules set by your parents and by your school administrators?

### Analyzing and Evaluating Ethical Claims

7. Why isn't it sufficient for people to identify what is right and what is good based solely on situations starting and ending well?
8. Why does social media use require prudence?
9. Why is it unethical to allow a friend to copy your homework?
10. Does doing what is best for myself mean that I'm an emotionally stable person? Explain.

### Creating My Own Position Statements on Ethics

11. Formulate a position regarding the role of the Holy Spirit and regeneration in the proper practice of the virtues. Include scriptural support.
12. Defend your use of the virtues to chart the right path to ethical decisions through all the obstacles of life.

110 VIRTUES

Goodness relates to ethics in that all the good that we can and must do flows from the character of God. God is good and a giver of good gifts. Therefore, it is necessary to develop goodness to be ethical.

2. Prudence relates to ethics in that much thought and wisdom must go into making morally right decisions and having ethical behavior. Hurried decisions and those focused only on the present are an ethical liability. Prudence helps to correct that.
3. Diligence relates to ethics in that much of ethical decision-making and behavior requires hard, consistent effort. Faithfulness relates to ethics in that remaining loyal and committed to God and His righteous standards is paramount to a right ethic. Courage relates to ethics in that believers must press forward and weather the consequences of doing what is morally right, despite the innumerable obstacles and temptations of the vices.
4. Self-control relates to ethics in that a lack of it leads directly into unethical decision-making and behavior. Temperance relates to ethics in that a believer needs to be consistently working on a plan to fight and avoid temptation so that ethical decisions and behavior result. Patience relates to ethics in that one's lack of patience leads one to make wrong choices. These are attempts to take into one's own hands a matter that belongs in God's hands.

## Practicing Ethical Decision-Making

5. There are many privileges and obligations most young people receive when they turn eighteen. Prudence is required to decide whether to engage in certain activities or not, even though they are legally permissible. Furthermore, if an activity is undertaken, how to wisely participate in the new activity requires prudence. For example, should I vote? If so, whom should I vote for? Should I join the military? open a bank account? apply for a loan? get married? move out of my home?
6. Certain rules or policies are not necessarily likable but are reasonable, such as bedtimes at home or obligatory uniforms at school. You still need to abide by the rule even if you don't like it. Having a good attitude and outlook does require patience for all. The maturity process takes time; there are no shortcuts. Trust must be earned over time. Even smart, gifted, and reasonable teenagers are still teenagers and must wait to engage in certain activities.

## Analyzing and Evaluating Ethical Claims

7. The righteousness or goodness of plans and outcomes is never the full picture for any given situation. There are motives and desires that fuel and guide any plan and any outcome. A situation that is only partially righteous or partially good can't then be truly righteous and good. Christians are called to look at the whole of a situation, not just be pragmatic.
8. Social media is pervasive. Most people use it daily, whether for communication or entertainment. Believers must use prudence to determine when they get on social media, how long they spend there, the content of what they post and watch, the discussions they join, the connections they make, and how one's social media affects and impacts them.
9. The person asking to copy your homework is asking to do something unethical, even if that person casts it as "helping" him or her. Because diligence is required for all students, it is unethical for one to be slothful and then cheat by taking advantage of the diligence of the honest student. And since faithfulness is expected of all believers, the honest student should stay faithful to being honest and to obeying the teacher's instructions. Courage is also required to kindly confront this fellow student's unethical request.
10. No; emotional stability is not simply self-fulfillment. Self-control, temperance, and patience are needed for emotional stability. Self-control protects you from your selfish, sinful, and enslaving desires and temptations. Temperance brings moderation and balance. An emotionally unstable person lacks the stability that temperance offers. Patience is vital because without it frustration, disappointment, depression, or anger might take hold of an emotionally unstable person. These three virtues, along with others, contribute to emotional stability.

## Creating My Own Position Statements on Ethics

11. The virtues, including the fruit of the Spirit, are all connected and all flow from God's work through the Spirit (beginning at regeneration) in the life of a believer (Gal. 5:22–23; 2 Pet. 1:5–7). Without the Spirit's work of regeneration, sanctification, and empowerment in the lives of believers, even something that seems to come close to God's standards is still sin-tainted (Isa. 64:6; Phil. 3:9). Only believers are able, because of the Holy Spirit's work, to practice the virtues in a way that brings glory to God.
12. Christian virtues are building blocks for a believer's motives, desires, thoughts, goals, and behaviors. The virtues flow from God's character and are revealed in the Word. As the Lord works in your life, you will grow in your ability to discern which virtue will help you with each obstacle that you come across. The virtues are the tools to overcome those obstacles. And the more you use them, the better you will endure the obstacles of life.

# Lesson Plan Overview

**CHAPTER 7:** Virtues, Part 2

**EV** ExamView
**PPT pres.** PowerPoint presentation

| PAGES | OBJECTIVES | RESOURCES | ASSESSMENTS |
|---|---|---|---|
| **7.1 Humility, Meekness, and Gentleness** (3 DAYS) | | | |
| 112–16 | **7.1.1** Define *humility, meekness,* and *gentleness.*<br>**7.1.2** Compare and contrast Christian and non-Christian conceptions of humility, meekness, and gentleness.<br>**7.1.3** Contrast the virtues of humility, meekness, and gentleness with the vices of pride, anger, and harshness.<br>**7.1.4** Give examples of how humility, meekness, and gentleness relate to ethical decision-making and ethical living.<br>**7.1.5** Develop a plan for growing in humility, meekness, and gentleness. | **ACTIVITIES**<br>• 7.1 Virtues over Vices<br>**BJU PRESS TROVE***<br>• PPT pres.: Chapter 7 | **STUDENT EDITION**<br>• Thinking It Through 7.1 |
| **7.2 Kindness and Compassion** (3 DAYS) | | | |
| 116–21 | **7.2.1** Define *kindness* and *compassion.*<br>**7.2.2** Compare and contrast Christian and non-Christian motives for kindness and compassion.<br>**7.2.3** Contrast the virtues of kindness and compassion with the vices of cruelty and indifference.<br>**7.2.4** Give examples of how kindness and compassion relate to ethical decision-making and ethical living.<br>**7.2.5** Develop a plan for growing in kindness and compassion. | **ACTIVITIES**<br>• 7.2 Modern-Day Good Samaritans<br>**BJU PRESS TROVE**<br>• PPT pres.: Chapter 7 | **STUDENT EDITION**<br>• Thinking It Through 7.2 |
| **7.3 Gratitude, Joy, and Peace** (3 DAYS) | | | |
| 122–26 | **7.3.1** Define gratitude, joy, and peace.<br>**7.3.2** Compare and contrast Christian and non-Christian sources of joy and peace and objects of gratitude.<br>**7.3.3** Contrast the virtues of gratitude, joy, and peace with the vices of ingratitude, despair, and worry.<br>**7.3.4** Give examples of how gratitude, joy, and peace relate to ethical decision-making and ethical living.<br>**7.3.5** Develop a plan for growing in gratitude, joy, and peace. | **ACTIVITIES**<br>• 7.3 The Vice of Worry<br>**BJU PRESS TROVE**<br>• PPT pres.: Chapter 7 | **STUDENT EDITION**<br>• Thinking It Through 7.3 |

*Digital resources for homeschool users are available on Homeschool Hub.

| PAGES | OBJECTIVES | RESOURCES | ASSESSMENTS |
|---|---|---|---|
| | | **7.4 Honesty** (3 DAYS) | |
| 126–32 | **7.4.1** Define *honesty*.<br>**7.4.2** Relate the character of God to truth and the character of Satan to falsehood.<br>**7.4.3** Explain direct biblical teaching about truth and falsehood.<br>**7.4.4** Analyze Scripture narratives that seem to approve of deception.<br>**7.4.5** Apply the biblical teaching about truth and falsehood to difficult ethical choices. | **ACTIVITIES**<br>• 7.4 Don't Tell Yourself Lies<br>**BJU PRESS TROVE**<br>• Link: When Is It OK to Tell a Well-Meaning Lie?<br>• PPT pres.: Chapter 7 | **STUDENT EDITION**<br>• Thinking It Through 7.4 |
| | | **Review** | |
| 133 | Recall concepts, terms, and Scripture memory from Chapter 7. | | **STUDENT EDITION**<br>• Chapter 7 Review |
| | | **Test** | |
| | Demonstrate knowledge of the material from Chapter 7 by taking the test. | | **ASSESSMENTS**<br>• Chapter 7 Test<br>**BJU PRESS TROVE**<br>• EV: Chapter 7 test bank |

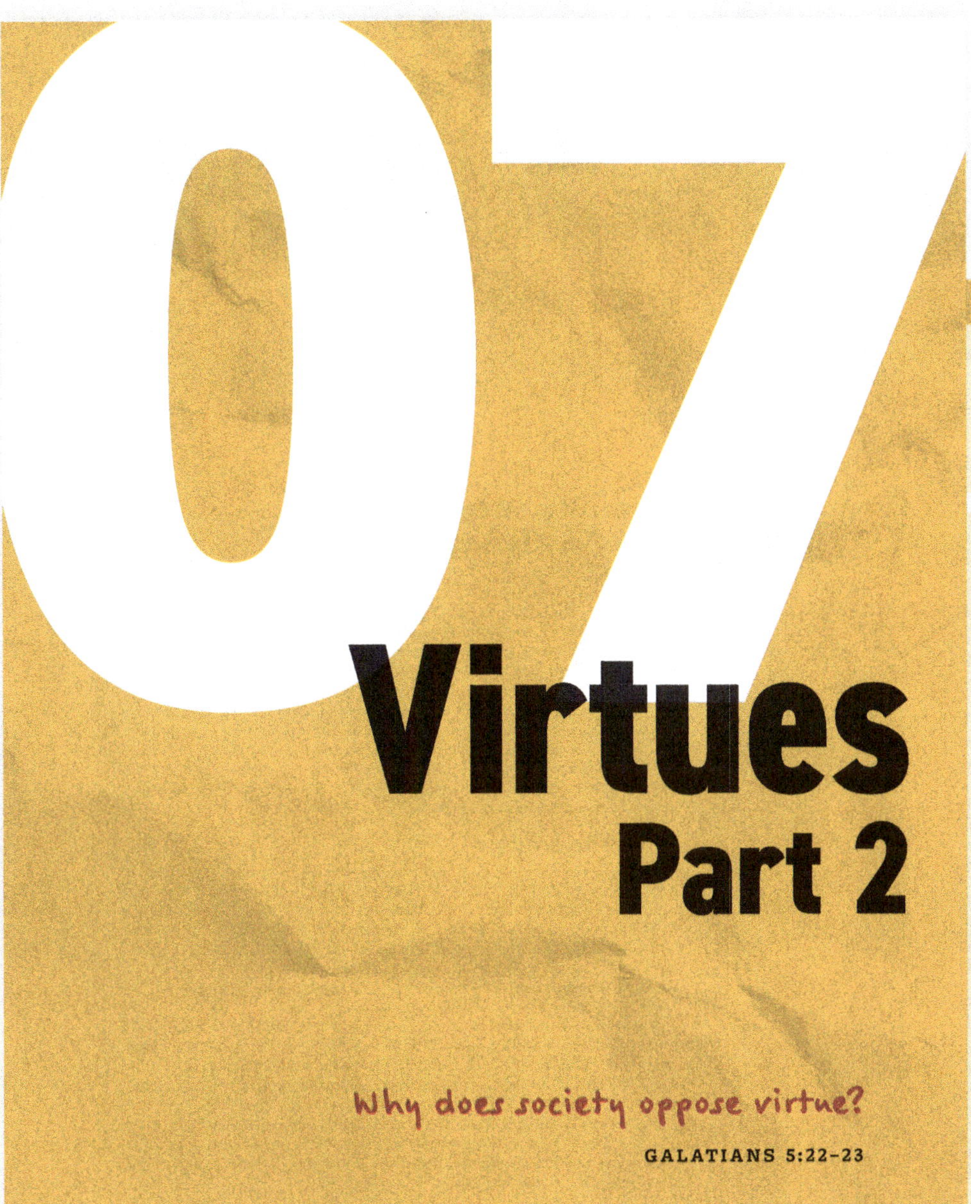


CHAPTER 7

# Overview

Why does society oppose virtue?

## Objectives

**7.1** Analyze Christian and non-Christian conceptions of each virtue.

**7.2** Evaluate Christian and non-Christian applications of each virtue.

**7.3** Formulate plans for growth in each virtue.

## Terms to Remember

- humility
- meekness
- gentleness
- pride
- anger
- harshness
- kindness
- compassion
- cruelty
- indifference
- gratitude
- joy
- peace
- ingratitude
- despair
- worry
- lying
- honesty
- falsehood

## Scripture Memory

- Galatians 5:22–23

# 7.1 Humility, Meekness, and Gentleness

How do I become great in the eyes of God?

## Objectives

**7.1.1** Define *humility*, *meekness*, and *gentleness*.

**7.1.2** Compare and contrast Christian and non-Christian conceptions of humility, meekness, and gentleness.

**7.1.3** Contrast the virtues of humility, meekness, and gentleness with the vices of pride, anger, and harshness.

**7.1.4** Give examples of how humility, meekness, and gentleness relate to ethical decision-making and ethical living.

**7.1.5** Develop a plan for growing in humility, meekness, and gentleness.

### Printed Resource

- Activity 7.1: Virtues over Vices

### Suggested Reading

- Bridges, Jerry. *The Practice of Godliness*. Colorado Springs, CO: NavPress, 1996. Pages 72–84, 180–88.
- MacArthur, John. *The Quest for Character*. Nashville: Thomas Nelson, 2006. Pages 16–19, 23–25, 101–3.

## Engage

### NOT WHAT YOU EXPECT

Guide a **discussion** of common misconceptions surrounding strength, size, and intimidation.

**What is a "gentle giant"?** *a large, strong individual whose size and intimidating features betray the heart of gold or gentle ways he actually has*
**What are some popular "gentle giant" characters from stories or movies?**
**Do you think strong, large, and mean-looking people struggle to be humble, meek, or gentle?**

The virtues of humility, meekness, and gentleness have nothing to do with the size or strength of a person. God calls believers of every size and personality to practice all the virtues. It isn't only giants who can surprise others by their gentle nature, but believers who are gifted, powerful, influential, or intimidating can also surprise others by their humble, meek, and gentle spirits.

"Humility opens the way to all other godly character traits. It is the soil in which the other traits of the fruit of the Spirit grow." JERRY BRIDGES


## 7.1 Humility, Meekness, and Gentleness

Have you ever been to one of those Japanese restaurants where the chef prepares the food in front of you on a teppanyaki grill? The chef shows off and entertains you with various antics while preparing your meal. Compare that experience to a meal prepared in a slow cooker. A slow cooker takes hours and hours to prepare a meal. It simply works in the background. But when the slow cooker has been going all day, the delicious smell of dinner permeates the house.

In a way, the virtues of humility, meekness, and gentleness are like that meal prepared in the slow cooker. Some virtues, such as faith and love, get a lot of attention. Humility, meekness, and gentleness, however, support these and other virtues by being "on," though in the background. These three virtues are godly and should be pursued by all Christians. And they are critical for avoiding one of the oldest and most pervasive of all the vices—pride.

### PROPER DEFINITIONS

Meekness and gentleness flow from humility. **Humility** is a lowly view of one's own importance, resulting from "a high view of God's person"[2] and a profound sense of one's own weakness and sinfulness. **Meekness** is a humble and calm disposition in situations that can lead to pride or anger. **Gentleness** is tender care for others even when they are hard to deal with. Jerry Bridges offers a helpful distinction between meekness and gentleness: "Gentleness is an active trait, describing the manner in which we should treat others. Meekness is a passive trait, describing the proper Christian response when others mistreat us."[3]

The Bible gives us examples of these three virtues in action. The best example of humility is seen in Christ's incarnation and crucifixion (Phil. 2:3–8). Meekness takes one's sober estimation of oneself and applies it with the proper restraints and responses to difficult circumstances. Moses exemplifies this virtue in how he endured with the children of Israel from Egypt to the brink of the Promised Land (Num. 12:3). The gentleness of Christ is closely related to His humility and meekness (Matt. 11:29; 2 Cor. 10:1) and is seen in His tender care for His people. A proper view of ourselves that leads to a patient and merciful response to sinful, imperfect people allows us to show others the gentleness of Christ.

112 VIRTUES

## Instruct

### MISCONCEPTIONS ABOUT HUMILITY, MEEKNESS, AND GENTLENESS

Guide a **discussion** regarding the misconceptions of the virtues and their corresponding vices.

**What are some misconceptions that many associate with humility, meekness, and gentleness?** *naivete, weakness, and cowardice, respectively*
**What are the vices for these three virtues?** *pride, anger, and harshness, respectively*
**Why are the misconceptions and vices poor substitutes for their corresponding virtues?** *Christians aren't to choose the easy or the sinfully natural choice when humility, meekness, or gentleness are called for. The misconceptions are bad excuses, and the vices are sins that could dangerously become habits.*
**In light of the misconceptions and the vices mentioned, what makes humility, meekness, and gentleness truly virtuous according to the Scriptures?** *To remain naive or to seek the attention that pride provides twists the virtue of humility (see Prov. 29:23; Matt. 23:12; 1 Pet. 5:5–6). Humility pursues adequate knowledge and understanding. It also seeks to love others and seek their well-being over one's own (see Phil. 2:3–8).*

*To confess weakness or lash out in anger does nothing to solve a problem or meet a need (see Matt. 11:29). Meekness, on the other hand, provides the necessary strength with patience that avoids heated situations and makes a difference (consider Moses and his dealings with the disgruntled and rebellious Israelites, Num. 12:3).*

*Rather than thinking* less of yourself, *humility leads to thinking* less about yourself. BRIAN ROSNER[4]

### PROPER CONCEPTIONS

One sure way to verify that society at large is standing on its head morally is to notice what it thinks of Christian virtues. According to many non-Christians, if you are humble, you are naïve; if you are meek, you are weak; if you are gentle, you are cowardly. These three virtues are unpopular among some unbelievers because they appear to them to hinder advancement in the face of opposition. Even Christians can be tempted to minimize or avoid these virtues because of society's influence and because they misunderstand what these virtues really are. Humility, meekness, and gentleness don't get in the way of a successful life. But these virtues definitely don't play into the selfish mindset that many people have.

#### How do I become great in the eyes of God?

Can Christians also see humility as naïveté, meekness as weakness, and gentleness as cowardice? Unfortunately, yes. Does every achievement and every fashionable outfit or hairstyle need a picture posted to social media? Is there room for humility when you do that? Do you vocally oppose every individual or organization that supports abortion and the LGBTQ agenda? How about your tirades against all those perceived injustices that are your hobbyhorses or soap boxes? Where does meekness fit in? Do you view a gracious, tender heart as contrary to a tough, steely mindset needed for this fallen world? What place does gentleness have in the life of a believer, then?

Consider humility and pride. Whom do you seek recognition from to satisfy your ego? Who must know what you have done and what you possess to give you fulfillment? Receiving due recognition and healthy encouragement is not what we are addressing here. True humility counters any notion of bragging or boasting. A Christian conception of humility considers the fact that believers are sinners saved by grace and anything good about them comes from God's hand (Eph. 2:8–9; James 1:17). Believers should, therefore, constantly point others to God and His goodness rather than themselves.

Does meekness have anything to do with weakness? Not really. The Christian conception of meekness involves a combination of patience and faith. Being hot-headed and getting even with someone flies in the face of true meekness. Meekness sees the believer entrusting the situation and outcome to God while humbly enduring the adverse circumstances (Isa. 11:4; Matt. 21:5; Eph. 4:2). Early church father Chromatius described meekness this way: "The meek are those who are gentle, humble and unassuming, simple in faith and patient in the face of every affront. Imbued with the precepts of the gospel, they imitate the meekness of the Lord, who says, 'Learn from me, for I am meek and humble of heart.'"[5] Remaining meek in the face of adversity is real strength—a far cry from weakness.

Do you enjoy following the rules and making sure everyone else does too? Do you seek justice at any cost? It is challenging to maintain righteous responses and just reactions to evil done to us or to those we care about. Gentleness shouldn't get in the way of justice and courage. But neither can gentleness be forgotten altogether. The Christian conception of gentleness seeks to bring heart and understanding to the implementation of justice. Gentleness is not cowardly; it does the right thing while tenderly caring for the individuals involved in the situation (Gal. 6:1; 2 Tim. 2:24–25).



*To excuse one's lack of gentleness because one is fearful or to blame harshness on a knee-jerk reaction is utterly lacking in virtue. Gentleness offers loving and kind assistance even when the recipient is hard to deal with or there are multiple easy ways out.*

## MOVING FROM ANGER TO MEEKNESS

Guide a **discussion** about Moses as an exemplary meek man who imperfectly displayed this virtue.

**Who in the Bible is described as "very meek, above all the men which were upon the face of the earth" (Num. 12:3)?** *Moses*

**What indications from Scripture are there that Moses practiced the virtue of meekness?** *Moses patiently and gently, for the most part, put up with a complaining and often rebellious people for forty years as they wandered in the wilderness (Num. 11, 12, 14, 16, 20, 21, 25).*

**At what points did Moses cease being meek while succumbing to the vice of anger?** *when Moses killed the Egyptian abusing his fellow Israelite (Exod. 2:11–12); when he failed to control his temper and in anger broke the stone tablets of the law (Exod. 32:19); when he complained rather strongly to the Lord about the difficulty of putting up with the Israelites (Num. 11:10–15); when he struck the rock in anger, disobeying God's command (Num. 20:2–12)*

Instruct students to **compare and contrast** these examples of Moses' anger with Christ's positive examples of righteous anger in Matthew 21:12–13 and John 2:13–17.

**How is righteous anger different from anger as a vice?** *Righteous anger is motivated by the truth and God's standards of justice and righteousness. Righteous anger toward falsehood and injustice must be carried out righteously. Anger as a vice is marked by recklessness, selfish motives, and the breaking of God's laws.*

**Can you tell whether someone is virtuous based on his or her practicing certain virtues or vices?** *No, only God knows the person's heart, motives, and how he or she is progressing in the virtues and seeking to avoid the vices.*

**What hope does the example of Moses' practice of both meekness and anger give you?** *We will practice the virtues imperfectly, but God desires a consistent and faithful pursuit of virtues. God patiently gives grace as we struggle with vices along the way. Though merciful, God does deal with us justly, as He did with Moses by not letting him into the Promised Land.*

## HONORING AUTHORITIES IS AN ACT OF HUMILITY

Use a **one-minute essay** for the students to record answers to the following question.

**Who does God command us to honor in Scripture (include Bible references as able)?** *Parents (Exod. 20:12; Eph. 6:2-3), the elderly (Lev. 19:32; Job 32:4; 1 Tim. 5:1), faithful pastors (1 Tim. 5:17), employers (1 Tim. 6:1), and civic or governmental leaders (Matt. 22:17–21; Rom. 13:7; 1 Pet. 2:17) are some of the main categories.*

Consider allowing students to use their Bibles or do online searches to find more passages or categories.

Follow up with a **discussion** so students do not confuse gifting, talents, and honorable deeds with the vice of pride.

**Should receiving appropriate honor from others cause one to feel guilty of pride? Why or why not?** *No; receiving honor is simply a way for others to show their appreciation for the good deeds or helpful contributions of the one being honored (see 1 Sam. 18:6–8).*

**Do Christians display the virtue of humility by refraining from doing something well because one is fearful of others noticing? Explain your answer.** *No; humility is not maintaining a low view of one's God-given abilities or position but instead using those gifts with a focus on God and others. God calls all to do excellent work, so performing to the highest degree of one's abilities and gifts is right and good. Thanking God while doing one's best is a mark of true humility (see Phil. 3:3–11).*

## CONFUSING GRATITUDE, LOVE, AND JOY FOR PRIDE

Use a **Turn and Talk** to begin a discussion about feelings that are commonly called *pride* but which are appropriate for Christians. Note that there are two kinds of pride: a selfish, self-focused pride and a God-and-others-focused pride. The latter can be used for a mixture of gratitude, love, and joy.

**What are some examples of things commonly called pride that are acceptable for the Christian?** *Examples could include having gratitude for, loving, and finding enjoyment in one's close family members, one's country, and one's favorite sports teams.*
**Why are these categories not a form of a selfish kind of pride?** *We should be thankful for the things that we love and enjoy. Our loyalty to those things God has given us is partly expressed by our gratitude, love, and joy in them. God is the giver of all good gifts, and He expects His children to thank Him for them and to enjoy them (Matt. 7:7–11; James 1:17).*

## Apply

## SEEKING GREATNESS

Use a **Think-Pair-Share** to discuss this section's essential question and related questions.

**How do I become great in the eyes of God?** *Through humility, meekness, and gentleness; it is the desire for and practice of these virtues that sets a believer up for greatness in the eyes of God. But both the path to and the greatness itself are the opposite of what the world expects. Christ taught that it is those who serve (humble, meek, and gentle ones) who are truly great in God's kingdom (Matt. 20:25–27; 23:8–12). Peter taught the same principle: God makes great those who humble themselves before Him and others (1 Pet. 5:5–6).*
**Why does the world see the path to greatness differently than believers?** *In general, the world sees those with the most money, power, influence, achievements, and followers as the greatest. This is a type of greatness, yes. But biblically, believers pursue greatness by humbly submitting to God by serving Him and others out of love.*
**According to Proverbs 27:2, should we let others know how great we are even though we have done certain great things? Why or why not?** *No; humility requires performing faithfully and letting others praise us, whether we get praise or not.*

### PERVERTING THE VIRTUES

Pride
self-pity
boasting
Humility

#### *Pride*

If there is one prevalent sin that Christians often fail to identify in their own hearts, it is the vice of pride. **Pride** is an inflated estimation of oneself, which attempts to rob God of His rightful place as sovereign Lord of all. Pride is the nemesis of humility. This can be seen in Scripture's descriptions of the proud being brought low and the humble being raised up (Prov. 29:23; Matt. 23:12; 1 Pet. 5:5–6). God despises the proud (Prov. 6:16–17; Ezek. 28:6–8, 17). It is ironic that pursuing what pride seeks, personal glory and self-exaltation, actually results in the destruction of the proud person (e.g., Nebuchadnezzar [Dan. 4:30–33] and Herod [Acts 12:21–23]). That doesn't always happen in this life. But the vice of pride in unbelievers will surely lead to their eternal demise (Prov. 16:18; 1 John 2:16–17).

Pride fills the void where humility should reside. If autonomy and selfishness rule a person's mind, there is no room left for a humble recognition of frailty and fallibility (Prov. 3:7). The vice of pride cancels any acknowledgement of and submission to God's wisdom, power, and sovereignty.

Anger
Meekness

#### *Anger*

The vice of anger stands opposite the virtue of meekness. **Anger** is intense displeasure arising from strong disagreement with a situation. Moses was meek, but not perfectly so. Look at these passages to see examples of Moses' anger, stirred for the right reasons but poorly expressed: Exodus 2:11–12; 32:19; Numbers 11:10–15; 20:2–12. Just as meekness is closely related to humility, anger can be closely connected to pride, as seen in the history of Haman in the book of Esther (for example, see Esther 3:5). It is too easy to let unimportant things get under our skin, and then we unleash anger. Even short outbursts of anger, if they happen often enough, can point to the vice of anger. Proverbs attributes "great understanding" (Prov. 14:29) to those who know how to control their tempers but calls quickness to anger foolish (Prov. 14:17). James memorably conveys the folly of anger by saying, "The wrath of man worketh not the righteousness of God" (James 1:20). James also relates wisdom to meekness (James 3:13). Meekness measures up to God's righteous standards and is the wiser choice over anger.

Harshness
Gentleness

#### *Harshness*

Where gentleness should thrive in the heart of a believer, harshness seeks to assert itself. The vice of **harshness** is to be unpleasant, rough, or mean toward someone. Harshness can come across through spoken or written words and nonverbally through looks and body language—and even through silence when gentleness demands verbal communication. In Scripture, the vice of harshness is described by various terms that stand against gentleness—violence, quarrels, strife, brawling (1 Tim. 3:3; 2 Tim. 2:23–24; Titus 3:2). Whereas gentleness is a fruit of the Spirit (Gal. 5:23), harshness is involved in several of the works of the flesh—"hatred, . . . wrath, strife" (Gal. 5:20). Where curt, rude responses take place, the vice of harshness is present. Gentleness encourages, de-escalates, and soothes. Harshness discourages and aggravates, making problems worse.

### PERSONALIZING HUMILITY, MEEKNESS, AND GENTLENESS

All the virtues, but especially these three, are like a cellular network that operates in the background, enabling a device to communicate properly. Just as the network your cell phone uses to communicate with other devices is always active, so must humility, meekness, and gentleness be constantly active in governing your personal interactions. In any conversation, either the virtue of humility is helping the relationship, or the vice of pride is spoiling the relationship. Meekness must counter anger, and gentleness must thrive instead of harshness. Season your success stories with humility. Blend meekness into discussions of frustrating topics. Sprinkle your defense of the truth with gentleness.

114 VIRTUES

## VIRTUES OVER VICES

Use **Activity 7.1** on pages 37–38 to bolster students' ethical decision-making.

## CUTTING THROUGH THE VENEER

Ask a **question** about the following virtues.

**Humility: How would you respond to a friend who fishes for compliments?** *Don't feed your friend's appetite for this type of attention. Rather, with loving but appropriate boldness, appeal to the person to mend his or her ways.*
**Meekness: How would you respond to a friend who always wants to be the center of attention?** *Outgoing or extroverted people can and must still exercise the virtue of meekness. Meekness is also required when this boisterous individual needs to be confronted on some level.*
**Gentleness: How would you respond to a friend who takes a stance on every issue on social media in unwise or borderline sinful ways?** *You might have a friend who spends time on social media "correcting" all the wrong posts and comments he or she encounters. You must decide whether to intervene privately or publicly to help this person see his or her folly. When you intervene, you need gentleness to do so. To correct someone with the virtue of gentleness is to show tender care for that person.*

God didn't intend humility to be the virtue that squashes all expressions of personal success and accomplishment, but humility will keep such things from being our focus. We all know the individual who wants to give off an appearance of modesty and humility but finds ways to name-drop* or boast in an indirect, nonchalant way. The fact that you have had a 4.0 all through high school or that your new car is way cooler than all your friends' cars doesn't entitle you to bring those things up at any moment in every context. Humility helps us keep everything in perspective—God is the giver of all good things, and we aren't better than anyone else, especially based on our performances or possessions (Luke 18:10–14; 1 Cor. 4:7). Pride infects all of us with great ease. Be motived by humility in all your conversations.

Do you have a short fuse? Do you get angry easily about every single thing that goes against what you believe in and support? Many things should make believers angry, in a righteous way: the far-left agenda shaping educational materials, abortion, the normalization of pornography use, rampant fornication among young people, any sort of abuse against the innocent and vulnerable, and many other expressions of evil in the world. Practicing meekness will help you keep your righteous anger from turning into sinful irritableness and brashness. Meekness is also paramount during times when pride attempts to seduce you to accept flattery. When you feel like someone is flattering you with ulterior motives, meekness will help you duck out of the way of that temptation. All believers are commanded to "put on . . . meekness" (Col. 3:12)—in other words, to practice it.

It's not only muscular or passionate individuals who need to practice the virtue of gentleness. Yes, the six-foot-four pediatrician can and should be extremely gentle with the infant patient he is treating. Gentleness presupposes the power to do damage, to be harmful or harsh. But we are all capable of that, at least with our words.

> *Meekness . . . is where humility and self-control meet. It is one of the most attractive and indispensable aspects of truly Christlike character.*
>
> JOHN MACARTHUR[7]

Think of your intellectual, athletic, or spiritual opponents. You might think they have it coming to them! You can be tempted to win at any cost because you have the right knowledge, the better team, or the right interpretation of the Word. Practicing gentleness isn't passivity or compromise. Not harming or embarrassing an opponent unnecessarily, even though it would be easy to do, is practicing gentleness. The apostle Paul makes the point that, when dealing with people who present challenging situations in the church, gentleness must reign (Eph. 4:2; 2 Tim. 2:24–25; Titus 3:2). The truth is, God deals with us with perfect gentleness (Ps. 18:35; 2 Cor. 10:1). The Almighty chooses to deal with His people with gentle tenderness (Isa. 40:10–11). These truths must permeate believers' ethical decision-making processes.

## PRACTICING HUMILITY, MEEKNESS, AND GENTLENESS

Like many of the virtues, it might seem a daunting task to actually develop these three in your life. Do you find it embarrassing if people know that you are weak in certain areas of the Christian life? Don't be afraid that people might find that out. All believers are in the same boat—all need to grow in their relationship with Christ!

The fruit of the Spirit is just that, *fruit* in the singular. The different aspects of that fruit are distinguishable—meekness and gentleness included (Gal. 5:22–23)—but each fruit comes with the rest as believers respond to the work of the Spirit in their lives. Be encouraged that God's work in the hearts of believers is comprehensive and not limited. The fruit of the Spirit is a single unit, and the virtues are interconnected (2 Pet. 1:5–7).

**name-drop:** to introduce names of important or famous people into a conversation, implying a personal connection to them



VIRTUES, PART 2 115

Do you have a plan to grow in these virtues? When was the last time you specifically prayed to God asking for His help to be less proud and more humble, less angry and more meek, or less harsh and more gentle? Praying to grow in humility, meekness, and gentleness is the right place to start. Praying taps into the Lord's power and cultivates an awareness of your need for these virtues. If you aren't aware of these virtues and their vices, then you won't be thinking of ways to practice the virtues like you should.

Another aspect of a plan to grow in these three virtues is to ask a friend, perhaps an older mentor who knows you well, to assess your humility, meekness, and gentleness. Be honest and then submissive to the report the friend gives about you. You can practice humility by graciously accepting what he or she says and repenting, if necessary, from any traces of pride, anger, and harshness in your life. Thank your friend and ask him or her to keep you accountable in these areas.

We all need God's grace to be humble, practice meekness, and treat others gently. Look to Christ, who is the supreme model of humility, meekness, and gentleness (Matt. 12:20).

### Thinking It Through 7.1

1. Define *humility*.
2. Define *meekness*.
3. Define *gentleness*.
4. How do Christian and non-Christian conceptions of humility, meekness, and gentleness differ?
5. How do the vices of pride, anger, and harshness contrast with humility, meekness, and gentleness, respectively?
6. Give examples of how humility, meekness, and gentleness relate to ethical decision-making and ethical living.
7. What are some actions you can take that can help you grow in humility, meekness, and gentleness?

## 7.2 Kindness and Compassion

You have been told to smile for the camera since you were a child wrinkling your nose in a cheesy grin. Your parents constantly reminded you to say, "Thank you" and "Please." They also taught you not to laugh at someone if they tripped or got hurt. Were all those smiles, words, and acts genuine? If you only look and sound nice at the appointed times, are you truly kind? And can compassion be faked?

True kindness is much more than being nice or polite, and compassion is much more than feeling sorry for someone.

### DEFINING KINDNESS AND COMPASSION

**Kindness** is an internal sentiment, cultivated by the Holy Spirit, that motivates believers to indiscriminately do good to others. **Compassion** is an external manifestation of loving-kindness that sympathetically and indiscriminately meets a need. Whereas kindness is primarily a disposition of one's character, compassion activates that kindness by sympathizing with someone and meeting their need.



## Assess

Guide a **summative assessment** by directing students to answer the questions in Thinking It Through 7.1.

### Thinking It Through 7.1

1. a lowly view of one's own importance, resulting from "a high view of God's person" and a profound sense of one's own weakness and sinfulness (Bridges, *The Practice of Godliness*, 91)
2. a humble and calm disposition in situations that can lead to pride or anger
3. tender care for others even when they are hard to deal with
4. Non-Christians believe that if you are humble, you are naive; if you are meek, you are weak; if you are gentle, you are cowardly. Christians pursue humility because they receive grace and mercy and all things from God. Christians know that meekness should be practiced because God expects patience and faith in Him in challenging situations. And Christ's example of being gentle, despite having infinite power and always being in the right, guides Christians to be gentle with one another.
5. Pride, the opposite of humility, is an inflated estimation of one's own self that robs God of His rightful place as sovereign Lord of all. The vice of anger stands opposite the virtue of meekness. Anger is intense displeasure arising from strong disagreement with a situation.

   The vice of harshness is unpleasant, rough, or mean toward someone. Gentleness encourages and soothes. Harshness discourages and aggravates the problems.
6. The only way to live ethically is to make it a habit to make ethically sound decisions. The virtues of humility, meekness, and gentleness help believers do that. Even when tempted with a smidgen of pride, a bit of "righteous" anger, or some well-deserved harshness, Christians must be careful to make sure they submit to God and faithfully apply humility, meekness, and gentleness. How you treat others whom you disagree with is a common testing ground for these three virtues. This happens often in person and in online engagement. You can point out error and demonstrate what the truth is without disparaging and disrespecting whomever you are addressing. And when faced with immoral government mandates, it takes humility and meekness to navigate obedience to God rather than men in the situation, without coming across as proud or cavalier.
7. committed, specific prayer and getting an older, wiser accountability partner

## 7.2 Kindness and Compassion

How should I respond to those who are hurting?

### Objectives

**7.2.1** Define *kindness* and *compassion*.

**7.2.2** Compare and contrast Christian and non-Christian motives for kindness and compassion.

**7.2.3** Contrast the virtues of kindness and compassion with the vices of cruelty and indifference.

**7.2.4** Give examples of how kindness and compassion relate to ethical decision-making and ethical living.

**7.2.5** Develop a plan for growing in kindness and compassion.

### Printed Resource

- Activity 7.2: Modern-Day Good Samaritans

### Suggested Reading

- Berg, Jim. *Essential Virtues: Marks of the Christ-Centered Life*. Greenville, SC: JourneyForth, 2008. Pages 115–29, 174–88.

Can you identify which central virtue (faith, love, or hope) is most at work behind kindness and compassion? Kindness and compassion are an outflow, a demonstration, of love. Believers can love because of God's love for them (Eph. 2:4–5; 1 John 4:19). It is also the case, then, that believers can show kindness and compassion to others because that is how God has dealt with them (Rom. 2:4; Eph. 4:32). Love always plays a role when kindness and compassion are shown.

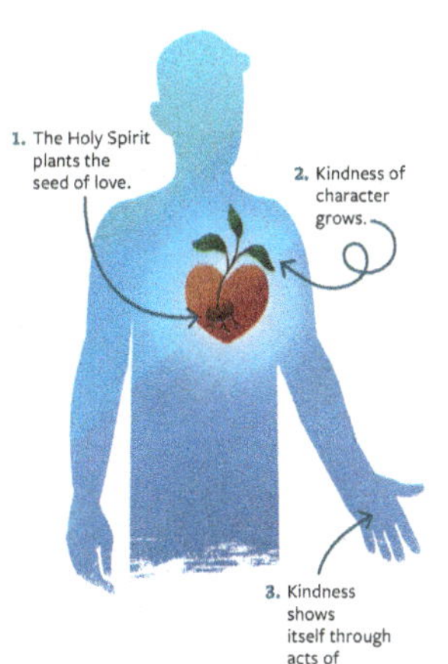

1. The Holy Spirit plants the seed of love.
2. Kindness of character grows.
3. Kindness shows itself through acts of compassion.

#### MOTIVATING KINDNESS AND COMPASSION

When discussing ethical difficulties, we should pause to consider why we do what we do. When do you stop to carefully think through decisions? Maybe it's when you stand in front of your closet or dresser deciding what to wear. Maybe it's when you decide what to spend your birthday or Christmas money on. These types of decisions may have ethical ramifications involving any number of virtues, but even then, you probably don't contemplate your motives too extensively. Determining whether the virtues of kindness and compassion are part of your normal, everyday motives as you interact with people is well worth your consideration.

A great scriptural description of these virtues motivating righteous actions is Christ's parable of the Good Samaritan (Luke 10:30–37). Though Jesus used this teaching to make a point about how to love our neighbors, it is clear that neither the priest nor the Levite showed compassion for their fellow Jew. Only the Samaritan, a non-Jew, "had compassion" (Luke 10:33) and "shewed mercy" (Luke 10:37) (which flows from compassion). Do you think we can infer from this text that the priest and Levite were kind men? What kindness did they feel that then translated into helping the man in desperate need? None. A kind heart, a disposition of kindness, leads a person to demonstrate compassion to the needy (Luke 6:45).

Kindness and compassion treat people with dignity—recognizing the enormous value of humans created in the image of God. Do you refuse to say "Hi," "I'm sorry," or "Thank you" to friends or classmates? Do you hear of physical or spiritual needs of people within your community and immediately shift your thoughts elsewhere? If you help some people out of self-interest and refuse to help others out of prejudice, then you are no different than the partial, indifferent priest and Levite in Christ's parable of the Good Samaritan.

> *Brotherly kindness is not limited strictly to physical siblings and spiritual brethren. . . . [The Bible] commands us to show kindness to strangers.*
>
> JOHN MACARTHUR[7]

Christians should be motivated—compelled even—to be aware of situations that require kindness in their area of influence. If a new student joins your class or a new kid moves onto your street, realizing that you need to be kind to him or her should be automatic. As a rule—the golden rule—as well as by conscious choice, Christians should show kindness to others (Matt. 7:12). Christians should be motivated by a desire to live according to the new life they have in Christ and according to the fruit that the Spirit produces in them (2 Cor. 5:17; Gal. 5:22).

Believers should be motivated to demonstrate compassion based on an honest examination of their own need for God's compassion. Where would sinful, rebellious humans be if it weren't for God's merciful and generous compassion (Lam. 3:22–23, 32)? Practical compassion, in which one sympathetically cares for someone in need, is expected of believers (James 1:27). Faithful obedience to the Savior is a strong motivation and should be the primary one.

- Bridges, Jerry. *The Practice of Godliness.* Colorado Springs, CO: NavPress, 1996. Pages 189–200.
- MacArthur, John. *The Quest for Character.* Nashville: Thomas Nelson, 2006. Pages 30–33, 70–73, 93–95.

## Engage

### THE REAL DEAL

Use a **misconception check** to preassess familiarity with the virtues of kindness and compassion. Invite students to label the following as true or false.

- **The person in violation of biblical standards gets to define what kindness and compassion are when confronted with his or her sin.** *False*
- **Never offending someone else is the goal of the ethical practice of kindness and compassion.** *False*
- **Christians can be kind and compassionate to individuals who practice sinful lifestyles.** *True*
- **Kindness that endorses a sinful lifestyle or compassion that supports sinful behavior is contrary to the practice of biblical kindness and compassion.** *True*

## Instruct

### BIBLICALLY DEFINED

Guide a **discussion** to direct students to a biblical definition of kindness and compassion.

**According to the textbook's definition of kindness (an internal sentiment, cultivated by the Holy Spirit, that motivates believers to indiscriminately do good to others), what is the relationship between kindness and goodness?** *When kindness is acted out, good is done to someone. In essence, the person who is kind can also be called good. Kindness does good to others. Goodness demonstrated is the result of kindness.*

**What do Romans 2:4 and 1 Peter 2:3 contribute to the definition of kindness?** *We know that God is kind because of the good He does to sinful, undeserving humans.*

**How does Ephesians 4:32 apply to our ability and responsibility to show kindness to others?** *We can and must be kind to others, even when they are unkind to us, because God has shown kindness to us in Christ.*

**According to the textbook's definition of compassion (an external manifestation of loving-kindness that sympathetically and indiscriminately meets a need), what is the relationship between compassion and kindness?** *Compassion is stirred up within a believer when one is made aware of a need, and that internal desire to help is externally manifested through acts of kindness. Compassion is also motivated by one's love for God and others that results in showing kindness, regardless of the challenges one might suffer in doing so.*

Instruct the students to look up the following passages: Matthew 9:35–36; 14:14; 15:32; 20:34.

**What elements do all four passages have in common?** *Christ was moved to compassion due to the serious needs of the people, and Christ miraculously alleviated the people's needs.*

**Referencing only these four passages, what is a biblical definition of compassion?** *According to Christ's example in Matthew's Gospel, compassion is a loving reaction to the plight of another that moves one to do all in one's power to meet that need, regardless of the efforts necessary or the effect on the one showing compassion.*

## WRONG STARTING POINT, WRONG DESTINATION

Use a **Think-Write-Pair-Share** to identify various non-Christian motives for kindness and compassion and how those motives lend themselves to the vices of cruelty and indifference.

**Why are all people deserving of kindness and compassion?** *Every person is made in the image of God and, therefore, has inherent dignity and worth. Both kindness and compassion show the dignity and worth of each image-bearer.*

**Is it ethical to show kindness or compassion to a coworker or boss, even though you loathe them internally, as a means to a personal end?** *This pragmatic and ingenuine approach to virtuous action is unethical because the loathing sentiment is sinful. The fact that the coworker or boss benefits from one's kindness or compassion doesn't erase the sinful loathing. Believers aren't to live sinful or hypocritical lives, even though there is supposed benefit to both parties.*

**What is wrong with the young person who is kind to almost everyone, always smiling, but also tends to gossip and habitually brag about his or her accomplishments?** *True kindness wouldn't harm others and their reputations through gossip. Neither would the virtue of kindness draw attention to oneself, because pride and selfishness hinder one's desire and ability to do good to others.*

**How can the absence of a proper motivation for kindness and compassion lead to the vices of cruelty and indifference?** *When there is no proper motivation to be kind or compassionate, then the opposite of these virtues, the vices, becomes readily justifiable. If people can be treated as a means to an end or without taking into account their image-bearing status, then a little cruelty or indifference isn't a big deal.*

52 likes
servant_sam puttin in the good work!
#someonesgottaserve ...
alex_the_great Love this.

There are also non-Christian motives to be kind and compassionate. Unfortunately, most of them are self-serving. For instance, you might make a kind comment on a friend's post on social media even though your friend's post was flaunting selfish, vain, or proud characteristics. Your affirmation of a friend's problematic post does not actually help him or her; the result of your action is wrong and harmful. And if your comment was motivated by the expectation that your friend will also affirm your posts, then your motive was selfish too. True kindness never uses selfish means to an end, nor does it affirm someone in their sin.

Social media can fuel non-Christian motives to display compassion. Take the young person doing inner-city community work or foreign missions work who chronicles every activity on his or her social media. These pictures and videos show this individual doing compassionate things for down-and-out people. But the sheer volume of media shared and the captions that accompany each post betray a proud and self-interested motive for showing compassion. Those posts can be therapeutic to this person's self-esteem while crafting an endearing image to friends, family, and even potential future employers. True compassion doesn't plan for people to be watching its works, nor does true compassion serve an ulterior motive (Matt. 6:1–4).

### OBSTRUCTING KINDNESS AND COMPASSION: CRUELTY AND INDIFFERENCE

If someone isn't nice, we say they are mean. If someone isn't loving, we say they are coldhearted. How mean does someone have to be to be considered cruel? How coldhearted does someone have to be to be considered indifferent? The virtues of kindness and compassion have corresponding vices of cruelty and indifference, respectively. These vices go further down the path of ungodliness than merely being mean or coldhearted. The vice of **cruelty** is the willful causation of distress or discomfort in others. The vice of **indifference** is apathy toward others and utter lack of concern for the ethical good of a situation. Cruelty enjoys being mean. Indifference finds comfort in coldheartedness.

It isn't just psychopathic criminals and totalitarian dictators who are cruel. Cruelty, like all vices, can find ways to sneak into believers' hearts and actions. Although you might not have been the one to cause someone pain or embarrassment, if you see it and could alleviate it but don't because it's entertaining, that is being cruel. It might be a little uncomfortable to let someone know about an unnoticed wardrobe malfunction or a dirty spot on his or her clothes. But it would be cruel to see either of these and chuckle to yourself or laugh with your friends about it, not making the person aware of the situation. Even more patently cruel is the killing of unborn babies or being racist against another human being. It's also sometimes tempting to make fun of the way people look, but people come in a variety of shapes and sizes; it is cruel to make fun of someone for the way God made them. There is zero room for cruelty in the heart and actions of a Christian (Eph. 4:29–32).

The vice of indifference is a blind spot for many Christians. Believers can all too easily excuse inaction due to indifference by saying, "I have too much going on to help," or "I'm not prepared, so I won't be of any real help." Have you found your heart turning to those excuses rather than warming up to act compassionately? Indifference can too easily be passed off as legitimate or even righteous. God warns us in His Word not to be deceived by our own reasoning, which so easily leads to sin (James 1:13–16)—reasoning that can drive us to a lack of compassion. What do you first think when you hear of a request at school or church for volunteers to help with a need in your school, church, or community? Your Saturdays are generally free, and the need requires someone with your profile—young, available, and able. The virtue of compassion and the vice of indifference lock horns as you contemplate how to respond to that call. There is a danger in saying no to showing compassion. You don't want to create a habit so that it becomes automatic for you to be indifferent when you need to be compassionate.

### Sympathy Tethered to Truth Versus Sympathy Severed from Truth

So far, we have established that, to display the virtue of compassion, you must possess sympathy. Sympathy is to emotionally suffer with someone who is suffering. The term itself conveys this, but Scripture further illustrates its meaning: Christ's incarnation, life, death, and ongoing priestly work are the greatest expression of true sympathy (Phil. 2:7–8; Heb. 2:17–18; 4:15).

The use of sympathy becomes problematic when someone's reactions to a situation and the resultant feelings are placed above determining the morality of the situation. For instance, if you know someone who is angry, sad, frustrated, or offended, a wrong use of sympathy would tell you to join them in their experience without asking any questions. That would be like jumping in to save someone who is drowning without considering the depth of the water or the strength of the current or size of the waves. The person in need desperately wants someone to sympathize with how they are feeling. But leaving the stability and safety of the shore leaves the one joining the person in need without a solid foundation from which to help. To truly help the one drowning would mean safely rescuing the person from the shore or at least carefully entering into the situation with wisdom, vigilance, and skill. A successful rescue produces zero casualties, not two. And to truly help someone spiritually, your sympathy and compassion must be guided by the truth of God's Word, not mere emotion. Wisdom, vigilance, and the skillful application of truth can keep both you and your struggling friend from disaster, even as you sympathize with his or her suffering.

You have seen that kindness and compassion require sympathy. Yet all virtues are tied to the character of God as revealed in Scripture. If someone is wallowing in self-pity and selfishly seeking approval of unbiblical behaviors or reactions, is sympathy the ethical approach? Simply affirming how someone is feeling is not necessarily helping them. Believers must maintain their practice of sympathetic compassion (1 Pet. 3:8) while applying the truth of God's Word to someone's situation (Gal. 6:1). How can we "rejoice with them that do rejoice, and weep with them that weep" (Rom. 12:15) and also be truthful? In what ways can sympathy severed from truth actually be harmful?

### PRACTICING KINDNESS AND COMPASSION

It's easy to be kind to those who are kind to you. This social phenomenon can be observed in the drive-through when a long chain of customers "pay it forward." You weren't expecting the person ahead of you to pay for your order, but it feels great. That kindness you were shown usually motivates you to follow suit and pay for the person behind you. This example, however, doesn't necessarily involve the Christian virtue of kindness. It is a form of kindness or generosity, but it is hard to know the motives or goals of each person who participates. The Christian virtue of kindness manifests itself when you politely and calmly interact with the drive-through workers who get your order wrong and drag their feet to fix it. Kindness is watching your words and tone when you express your disappointment about a decision your parents made. Kindness looks like respect and honor for your parents even when deep down you feel tempted to be unkind to them.

*While biblical compassion is tenderhearted (it feels deeply the distress others are in), it is never sentimental (governed by emotionality rather than spiritual purposefulness).* JIM BERG[3]

Compassion comes more easily to those who have developed a genuine kindness and love for others. But whereas kindness is a virtue you express every day, compassionate acts aren't necessarily daily activities. We can assume that the Good Samaritan didn't find mugged Jewish men alongside the road every day. But if he did, it would be unethical for him to choose indifference on some days and compassion on others. The fact that kindness is more of a constant whereas compassion is demonstrated occasionally when needs arise doesn't mean that compassion is not as big a deal as kindness. No, all virtues are important for believers and are necessary for them to live ethically (2 Pet. 1:5–10).

If one of your classmates suffered a loss in the family, reaching out to him or her with a note would be an act of compassion. Compassion would also motivate you to pray for the student and his or her family. If you were really close to this person, compassion would motivate you to support and care for your friend in even more tangible ways.



## Apply

### OBJECTS OF KINDNESS AND COMPASSION

Direct students to do a **one-word summary** to identify a category of relationships in which they need to practice more kindness or compassion.

*Possible answers: strangers, parents, siblings, friends, classmates, teammates, and neighbors*

### VIRTUES FOR THE HURTING

Use a **Quick Write** for the students to answer this section's essential question.

**How should I respond to those who are hurting?** *Answers should include situations in which the student practices the virtue of compassion primarily, as well as kindness (e.g., a friend whose parent has terminal cancer, a friend who has lost a loved one, a friend whose dad lost his job and he or she needed to move away suddenly).*

### SHORING-UP LACKING VIRTUES

Use a **journal entry** for students to analyze where they habitually lack kindness and compassion and their plan to remedy the lack of these two virtues. Encourage students to use specifics.

### MODERN-DAY GOOD SAMARITANS

Use **Activity 7.2** on pages 39–42 to apply the information in the section.

How should I respond to those who are hurting?

Ask yourself the question, How should I respond to those who are hurting? Let's take a few steps back to consider how growing in kindness and compassion can answer this question. You can't give what you don't have. This is an extremely basic principle! You might have a desire to get a gift for a friend. Your friend won't get a gift from you based on your desire alone. You must make it or buy it before you can give it. The same principle applies to the virtues—in this case to kindness and compassion. You must have a tree of kindness and compassion planted in your heart before you can pick its fruit and give it to others who need it.

By following these guidelines to engage those who are hurting, you will be well prepared to show true kindness and demonstrate genuine compassion:

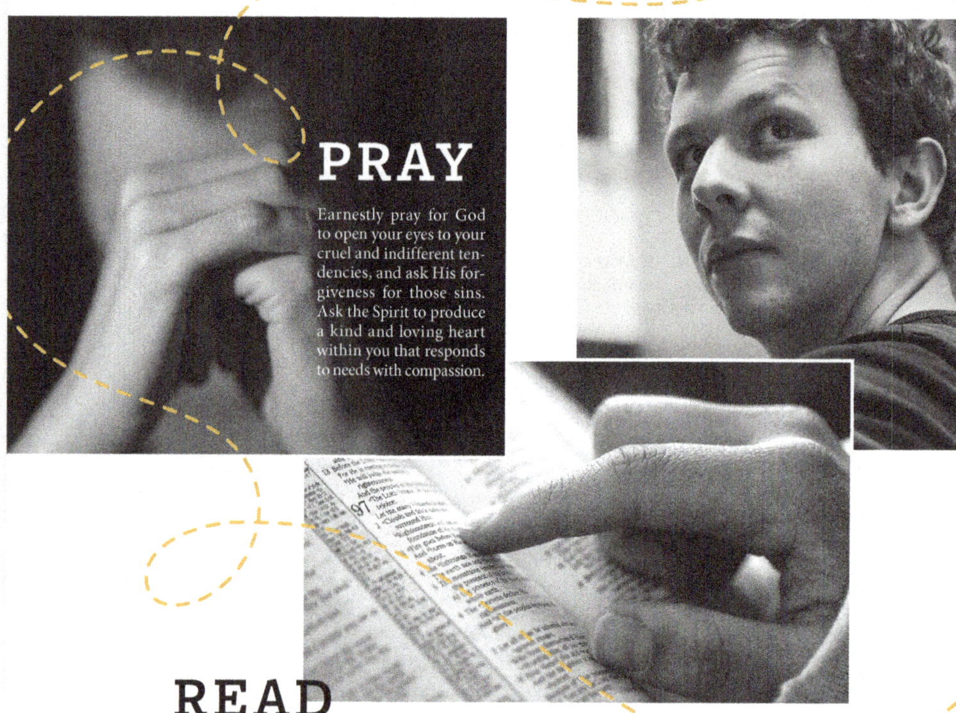

## PRAY

Earnestly pray for God to open your eyes to your cruel and indifferent tendencies, and ask His forgiveness for those sins. Ask the Spirit to produce a kind and loving heart within you that responds to needs with compassion.

## READ

Faithfully read God's Word to learn what God is like and learn more about godly kindness and compassion. Find specific verses and passages to read and study that will help you grow in kindness and compassion.



120 VIRTUES

## PRACTICE

This is where the rubber meets the road. This is where you have to step up and show kindness and compassion, even if you are nervous or uncertain how you will be received. Include those who wouldn't expect kindness or compassion from you.

## LOOK

Consciously look around for opportunities to be kind and compassionate. Purposefully look for new ways to be kind, ways you haven't shown kindness in the past. Look for a meaningful way to demonstrate compassion to someone in need, even if it is a very small way.

## REPEAT

Keep practicing kindness and compassion. Stay aware of needs around you. Continue reading and studying the Word. And keep praying for God to increase your desire to be motivated by kindness and compassion in all you do.

Allow the virtues of kindness and compassion to influence your ethical decisions. Love has many manifestations and applications. But kindness is a virtue that takes a little love and makes it go a long way. And compassion comes from a deep-seated and sympathetic love that reflects the heart of God Himself (Exod. 34:6–7; Matt. 11:28–30; Titus 3:4). What a privilege and what an opportunity!

### Thinking It Through 7.2

1. Define *kindness*.
2. Define *compassion*.
3. List various Christian and non-Christian motives for kindness and compassion.
4. Contrast the virtues of kindness and compassion with the vices of cruelty and indifference.
5. List several examples of how kindness and compassion relate to ethical living.
6. What is the difference between sympathy tethered to truth and sympathy severed from truth? Why does this difference matter?
7. List aspects of a plan for growing in kindness and compassion.



## Assess

Guide a **summative assessment** by directing students to answer the questions in Thinking It Through 7.2.

### Thinking It Through 7.2

1. an internal sentiment, cultivated by the Holy Spirit, that motivates believers to indiscriminately do good to others
2. an external manifestation of loving-kindness that sympathetically and indiscriminately meets a need
3. Christian: treating people with dignity because they are created in the image of God, a desire to live for Him who saved me, faithful obedience to God's will, gratitude for God's kindness and compassion

   Non-Christian: selfish self-advancement, self-interested gain or pleasure
4. Cruelty enjoys being mean. Indifference is cold-heartedness. Kindness seeks the good of others, while cruelty seeks to harm others. Compassion seeks to help others in need, while indifference ignores the suffering of others. These vices can go unnoticed in the lives of Christians.
5. Even in everyday interactions with people, the virtues of kindness and compassion are necessary. While kindness is needed daily, actual acts of compassion might not be possible every day. How you treat a challenging drive-through experience or a frustrating interaction with your parents requires kindness.

   Compassion requires that you do not neglect opportunities where you can practice compassion. Deciding whether to or how to reach out to a friend who suffered a loss in his family involves compassion.
6. Sympathy tethered to truth seeks to understand someone's suffering alongside them. Sympathy severed from truth seeks to get as close as possible to feeling the same suffering as that person without asking any questions. Sympathy severed from truth is dangerous because it strips any counsel, confrontation, and reasoning from Scripture from the situation. This difference between these two expressions of sympathy matters because the virtues of kindness and compassion utilize sympathy tethered to truth.
7. Pray: Earnestly pray for God to open your eyes to your cruel and indifferent tendencies and ask His forgiveness for those sins. Ask the Spirit to produce a kind and loving heart within you that responds to needs with compassion.

   Read: Faithfully read God's Word to learn what God is like and to learn more about godly kindness and compassion. Find specific verses and passages to read and study that will help you grow in kindness and compassion.

   Look: Consciously look around for opportunities to be kind and compassionate. Purposefully look for new ways to be kind, ways you haven't shown kindness in the past. Look for meaningful ways to demonstrate compassion to someone in need, even if it is in a very small way.

   Practice: This is where the rubber meets the road. This is where you have to step up and show kindness and compassion, even if you're uncertain of how you will be received. Include those who you think wouldn't expect kindness or compassion from you.

   Repeat: Keep practicing kindness and compassion. Stay aware of needs around you. Continue reading and studying the Word. And keep praying for God to increase your desire to be motivated by kindness and compassion in all you do.

# 7.3 Gratitude, Joy, and Peace

How can I be a biblically happy person?

## Objectives

**7.3.1** Define *gratitude*, *joy*, and *peace*.

**7.3.2** Compare and contrast Christian and non-Christian sources of joy and peace and objects of gratitude.

**7.3.3** Contrast the virtues of gratitude, joy, and peace with the vices of ingratitude, despair, and worry.

**7.3.4** Give examples of how gratitude, joy, and peace relate to ethical decision-making and ethical living.

**7.3.5** Develop a plan for growing in gratitude, joy, and peace.

### Printed Resource

- Activity 7.3: The Vice of Worry

### Suggested Reading

- Bridges, Jerry. *The Practice of Godliness*. Colorado Springs, CO: NavPress, 1996. Pages 100–19, 155–66.
- MacArthur, John. *The Quest for Character*. Nashville: Thomas Nelson, 2006. Pages 38–41, 84–89.

## 7.3 Gratitude, Joy, and Peace

Do you know Steady Freddy? How about Roller Coaster Roger? Roger is all over the place emotionally. Some call him moody. The weather, how many hours of sleep he got the night before, whether he has food in his stomach or not, and how he did on his last test all greatly influence his current temperament. Freddy, on the other hand, is calm, cool, and collected. He is nice to be around, and he even lifts the spirits of those he interacts with.

The virtues of gratitude, joy, and peace have much in common with Freddy. Gratitude should be a natural and consistent trait for believers because Christians are the most blessed people on the planet (Eph. 2:1–7). Joy looks to God and to the reasons believers have to rejoice in His salvation and provision (Eph. 1:3–8). And peace comes from God, who Himself is "the Lord of peace" (2 Thess. 3:16). If He can and will give peace, then His people can experience it. Gratitude, joy, and peace offer believers a steady outlook on life—something Roger lacks and desperately needs. A firm understanding of gratitude, joy, and peace contributes to a steady, vibrant faith.

### DEFINING GRATITUDE, JOY, AND PEACE

Another common term for the Christian virtue of gratitude is *thankfulness*. The two terms, though, are essentially interchangeable. **Gratitude** is an attitude of thanksgiving to God for His provision and governance of all things. Gratitude requires faith and hope for Christians, the only ones who fully express this virtue, to believe God's promises and trust in His care for them. Gratitude goes beyond being thankful for just the good or pleasant things in life. Believers know that God knows best, He knows all things, and His will is perfect for their lives (Rom. 8:28). This virtue is as much a mindset as it is individual instances of thanking God for His marvelous ways.

The Christian virtue of joy isn't the same thing as happiness. **Joy** is a confident delight in God's sovereign work in all of life's circumstances. Joy is more of a governing mindset than a fleeting emotion. In other words, joy doesn't ebb and flow as happiness and sadness do. Joy is firmly rooted outside the circumstances of life; joy is rooted in God, in His provision of salvation, and in His sovereign purposes (Rom. 5:1–5). Joy, for believers, coexists with trials and suffering (Acts 5:21; Heb. 10:34). In many cases, joy isn't put to the test in the life of a Christian *until* the arrival of difficult circumstances (James 1:2–4).

The Christian virtue of peace is much more than the absence of war or conflict. Peace also goes beyond a mere personal internal tranquility.[9] **Peace** is a harmonious wholeness produced when God's design of the world, including human relationships, is rightly ordered. There is no peace outside of God because any peace we can have with God and with others comes through Christ (Rom. 5:1; Eph. 2:13–19). Just like joy, peace coexists with trials and sufferings (John 16:33). The virtue of peace describes the mindset and character of a believer, even during difficult and unpleasant circumstances.



## Engage

### TWO PERSONALITIES

Use a **Turn and Talk** for students to evaluate their similarities or differences with Steady Freddy and Roller Coaster Roger.

The following are sample questions for the students to ask their partners:

- In what ways are you like Roller Coaster Roger?
- In what ways are you like Steady Freddy?
- What are some drawbacks you can identify in your own life of being like Roller Coaster Roger?
- What are some advantages you can identify in your own life of being like Steady Freddy?

The responses of those who identify with Roger should show a recognition of the need to pursue the virtues that Freddy practices because virtues are essential to Christian living. The responses of those who identify with Freddy should show a recognition of the need to pursue gratitude, joy, and peace as Christian virtues rather than just assuming they are "wired that way."

## Instruct

### PROPER DEFINITIONS

Use a **one-minute essay** for students to quickly answer one question about each of the virtues in this section.

Even though overlap exists between joy and happiness, the textbook uses happiness in the sense where it contrasts with the virtue of joy.

The student answers will reveal how well they know the definitions of gratitude, joy, and peace.

**Though at times synonymous, what is the main difference between gratitude and thankfulness?** *The virtue of gratitude is an overarching attitude that governs one's outlook on all of life (Ps. 100:4; 1 Thess. 5:18). Thankfulness occurs at a moment in time when one expresses thanks for receiving something.*

**Is joy the same as happiness?** *No, because joy is a confident delight in God's sovereign work in all of life's circumstances, including hard times (Ps. 16:11; Phil. 4:4). Happiness is an emotion that results from a pleasurable experience.*

**Is peace equal to the absence of conflict?** *No, because peace endures in both positive and negative circumstances. Peace is a harmonious wholeness produced when God's design of the world, including human relationships, is rightly ordered (Phil. 4:7–9; 2 Thess. 3:16).*

## CHRISTIAN GRATITUDE, JOY, AND PEACE

### How can I be a biblically happy person?

At least fifteen countries including America commemorate their own version of Thanksgiving.[10] However, the United States of America's celebration of it is the best-known to most of us. Can unbelievers express gratitude? Sure they can. Everyone is thankful, or at least happy, for good weather, for not getting badly injured in an accident, and for babies that sleep through the night. The objects of gratitude for unbelievers and for believers are very different though. But as with the original Thanksgiving Day in the United States, the primary object of gratitude should be God. Non-Christians, who refuse to come to the Creator and Sustainer of all on His terms, can't be properly grateful to Him. They simply enjoy the abundance that God graciously provides (Matt. 5:45; Acts 14:17). Sadly, unbelievers don't recognize who God is and what He does for them: "They glorified him not as God, neither were thankful" (Rom. 1:21). Non-Christians attribute the good things in their lives to things like luck, fate, destiny, cosmic energy, science, the evolutionary process, or themselves. How empty and unfulfilling!

> *Thanksgiving is a normal result of a vital union with Christ, and a direct measure of the extent to which we are experiencing the reality of that union in our daily lives.*
> JERRY BRIDGES[11]

But Christians have endless reasons to be grateful, reasons that include but go well beyond physical blessings. When was the last time you considered how much you have to be grateful for? How is a Christian's gratitude for life, health, good friends, or the opportunity to go to college different from a non-Christian's gratitude for the same things? Knowing that God is the giver of all these things, plus all the spiritual blessings in Christ, makes all the difference (Eph. 1:3; James 1:17)! Gratitude breeds more gratitude. Once you begin to thank God for His work in your life in so many ways and on so many levels, you find more and more reasons to continue to be grateful. Christians and non-Christians can be grateful for a good job and steady income. But a Christian recognizes that both of those are from God. He or she, therefore, is generous with that income and gives to his or her church and helps to meet other needs out of sheer gratitude for all that God has done on his or her behalf.

When you investigate the sourcing of a product, you are looking to see not only where a product comes from but how it is produced. In our culture, people are interested in sourcing products for a variety of reasons: allergies to certain ingredients, dietary preferences (organic, vegetarian, vegan),

#### Biblical Peace

When it comes to the idea of peace in Scripture, both Testaments have helpful terms that aid our understanding of what biblical peace is. The Hebrew word for peace is *shalom*, and it has a rich and broad meaning. *Wholeness*, *blessing*, and *prosperity* are some terms that help explain *shalom*. Three passages in Isaiah illustrate what *shalom* encompasses. First, the Messiah is called the "Prince of Peace" in Isaiah 9:6, and peace will characterize the reign of His kingdom (9:7). Second, Isaiah 32:15–18 relates peace to righteousness, quietness, and rest in God's kingdom. And third, Isaiah 52:7 describes the announcement of God's kingdom; notice how peace is a key part of that reign along with good news, happiness, and salvation.[13] When God reigns in the hearts of His people and humans live for their King, there is peace.

**εἰρήνη**

In the New Testament, the Greek term *eirēnē* is used for peace in a similar way to its Old Testament counterpart.[14] *Rest* and *harmony* are two terms that help explain *eirēnē*. Jesus is introduced at His incarnation as one whose coming signaled peace (Luke 2:14). Jesus not only spoke peace, He brought peace (Luke 7:48–50). God grants peace to those He saves (Col. 1:20). And believers can live lives of peace because of the work of Christ and the Spirit (Rom. 14:17; Phil. 4:9).[15] How divine is this biblical peace, and how necessary! Peace with God, which results in peace with others and oneself, can only come from God Himself.

> *We can go through life bored, glum and complaining, or we can rejoice in the Lord, in our names being written in heaven, in the hope of an eternal inheritance.* JERRY BRIDGES[12]



## DECIDEDLY CHRISTIAN GRATITUDE, JOY, AND PEACE

Use **one comment and one question** for small groups of students to create from the heading Christian Gratitude, Joy, and Peace on pages 123–24. Direct students to address non-Christian sources of joy and peace as well as non-Christian objects of gratitude.

Good health and the right amount of material things aren't Christian sources of peace and joy or Christian objects of gratitude. One example question: Should I deprive myself of physical comforts to increase and sanctify my gratitude, joy, and peace?

Guide the subsequent discussion pointing the students to Christian sources and expressions of joy and peace as well as Christian objects and expressions of gratitude.

God gives all good gifts, and they are meant to be enjoyed. True joy and peace that last and genuine gratitude are not the product of our physical comforts. There are bountiful spiritual blessings in God through Christ, and God's sovereign work in our lives enables our gratitude, joy, and peace and fills us with them.

## THE SIGNS OF THE VICES

Guide a **discussion** of the telltale signs of when the vices of ingratitude, worry, and despair are beginning to rear their ugly heads.

**How can you tell if ingratitude has taken hold of someone?** *Whining and complaining are two common features of someone who is ungrateful. Someone who receives much and benefits from the efforts of many but never verbalizes gratitude to anyone is giving in to ingratitude (Rom. 1:20–21).*

**What signs indicate that joy is missing and despair is on the horizon?** *Joyful people can be described as satisfied, confident, at ease under pressure, and encouraging (Neh. 8:10; 2 Cor. 8:2). And so, when you or someone you know begins to be down, pessimistic, or anxious and ceases to be encouraging, then you know that despair is on the doorstep. This individual is probably trying to improve his or her lot in life in his or her own strength too.*

**What extinguishes peace and makes restlessness and worry catch on fire?** *At its core, a failure to trust God in any situation leads to restlessness and then worry (Matt. 6:25–34). When doubts creep in or you try to handle hard or frustrating situations yourself, worry is at the door.*

or maybe the labor involved (child workers or inhumane conditions). What if we "sourced" our virtues? What are the differences between non-Christian and Christian sources of joy and peace? Non-Christians unashamedly look within themselves to find joy and peace. There is so much focus on self-care, self-worth, and being true to oneself that it comes as no surprise that most people look to themselves to find their joy and peace. On the one hand, Christians can look at this and agree that looking to circumstances outside ourselves is a shaky and unsteady source for true joy and peace. But on the other hand, looking to ourselves is just as bad a source for joy and peace as looking to the sin-twisted and curse-afflicted world (Gen. 3:14–19; Ps. 51:5; Jer. 17:9). When the mantras of the day are "Be true to yourself" and "You create your own happiness," then the unstable source of any joy and peace is readily apparent. How can someone create joy or peace when their lives are in shambles and they are relying on themselves (or their circumstances) for joy or peace?

*[Joy] is a deep gladness that comes from within, and it's prompted partly by the knowledge that God has accepted us in Christ and partly by the delight and satisfaction we find in him.*

JOHN MACARTHUR[16]

The source of true joy and true peace is God (Rom. 15:13; Gal. 5:22). It is abundantly clear from Scripture that God is the ultimate possessor and giver of joy and peace (Pss. 16:11; 51:12; Isa. 52:7–9; Rom. 5:10–11). The virtues of joy and peace are crucial for Christian living. This can be seen by their inclusion in the fruit of the Spirit (Gal. 5:22) and by Paul's frequent mention of joy and peace when greeting or saying farewell to the recipients of his epistles (Rom. 15:32–33; Phil. 1:2, 4; 1 Thess. 1:1, 6; 5:16, 23). Since God is the source of these virtues, Christians can be confident not only that they can be joyful and experience peace but also that joy and peace can't be permanently taken away from them (John 14:27; 15:11). A bad grade shouldn't take away your joy in the Lord. A broken relationship can't take away your peace with God. Sin is the real joy-killer and peace-stealer (Ps. 32:3–4). But repentance renews joy and peace in believers (Ps. 32:5–7). God's joy is greater than your adverse circumstances (and even your sin), and God's peace is overwhelmingly comforting (Phil. 4:7; 1 Pet. 1:8).

*The starting point for authentic peace is peace with God.*

JOHN MACARTHUR[17]

### FORSAKING GRATITUDE, JOY, AND PEACE

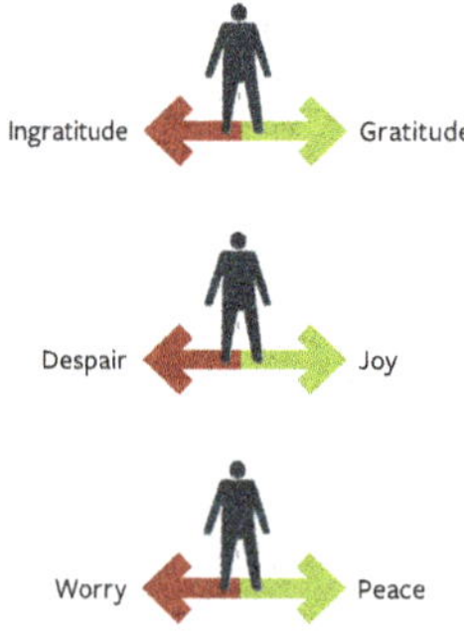


In the absence of virtue, there is vice. Out of a lack of gratitude comes ingratitude. Where there is no joy, there is despair. And no peace leads to worry. Just as the virtues are related, you should be able to see the relation between these three vices. He who thinks he has nothing to be thankful for begins to despair. This despair results from a lack of rejoicing and giving thanks for what one has. And then worry sets in because the despair builds and worsens. (Sadly, worry is often in the background of the lives of many Christians. But when despair is also present, worry comes to the fore.)

**Ingratitude** is taking things for granted, overlooking what is clearly worthy of thanks, and being unthankful for all the good one has. **Despair** is synonymous with hopelessness and describes giving up and being pessimistic about the outcome of a situation. **Worry** is emotional instability where someone rehearses all the what-ifs about a given situation and fails to trust God and His Word.

You'll recall that pride is a common vice that doesn't necessarily get called out too frequently. The same can be said for the vices of ingratitude and worry. If the average high school student rarely expresses gratitude, then the average high school student's norm is essentially ingratitude. Unchecked ingratitude can lead to a mindset of entitlement. That is a step in a very wrong direction. With entitlement comes an expectation of certain things or special treatment and then the temptation to demand what's expected. Where is the heart of gratitude in that? Stay clear of ingratitude. Express thanksgiving to God for the big and the little things in your life.

And worry is all too commonplace. In one sense it follows that unbelievers would be anxious, but worry doesn't make sense for believers (Matt. 6:25–34; Eph. 4:17). A worrisome individual thinks and acts as if God doesn't exist or at least as if He is incapable of handling a trying situation. It's easy to see how worry is also an opposite to one of the three central virtues: faith. Faith leads to hope and peace. Unbelief leads to despair and worry. What does worry accomplish? Worry is a vortex that sucks you into ungodly thinking and unbiblical behavior. God gives peace to His children for them to have and enjoy (2 Cor. 13:11). Don't settle for worry when God provides peace.

What brings you down? What causes you to despair? Life is full of one disappointing and depressing situation after another. Some are able to hold up and resist most temptations to despair when their own personal circumstances are grim. Others succumb to despair. But even when circumstances are at their worst, things like contemplating suicide or cutting oneself are sinful expressions of despair. During these times of extreme solitude, pain, sadness, and frustration, don't trade in the virtue of joy for the vice of despair. At the foundation of a Christian's joy is Christ's powerful presence (Rom. 8:31; 1 John 4:4). Believers are never without hope—Christ is willing and able to give you joy in the midst of overwhelming circumstances (Rom. 15:13). Repeated personal sin, or sin by others against you, can gnaw at you and can tempt you to despair. The vice of despair can still be crushed by the virtue of joy because you can rejoice that "where sin abounded, grace did much more abound" (Rom. 5:20).

### PRACTICING GRATITUDE, JOY, AND PEACE

Have you ever been told, "Say it like you mean it," when apologizing? Children hear this often when forced to ask their sibling for forgiveness. Words come out of their mouths, but neither their tones nor their facial expressions communicate remorse. When you are confronted with a significant ethical choice, just nodding to the pertinent virtues while operating with selfish motives for prideful gain does not equal an ethical decision. Gratitude, joy, and peace need to be deeply embedded in your head and in your heart, so those virtues can influence and guide you as you make ethical decisions.

Consider when you are tempted to cheat on a test. Cheating is dishonest and can sometimes involve stealing too, depending on how it is done. "But I need to pass this test" doesn't cut it as an excuse. That is simply pragmatic, the ends justifying the means. A believer who cheats on a test is bound to experience the following: worry that he or she will be found out, despair or regret due to resorting to cheating, and ingratitude because one can't be thankful for the results of work that isn't one's own. Doing your best on a test you haven't been able to study for, without cheating, might try your gratitude, joy, and peace. But honoring God is the virtuous choice. And it is always the right choice.

## Apply

### SOCIETAL PUSHBACK

Guide a **discussion** that answers this chapter's essential question.

**Why does society oppose virtue?** *In short, because sinners "hold the truth in unrighteousness" (Rom. 1:18) and because "there is none that seeketh after God" (Rom. 3:11). Also, "the way of a fool is right in his own eyes" directly applies to our secular society (Prov. 12:15). When believers live for the Lord with noticeable virtuous character, that light shines on the darkness of unbelievers' sin (Eph. 5:8–11). For this reason, society opposes virtue.*

### TRUE HAPPINESS

Guide a **Think-Pair-Share** to help students answer this section's essential question. Document the various answers and analyze with the class which answers qualify as being biblical.

**How can I be a biblically happy person?** *Study what the Bible says should make us happy. Pursue contentment in God. Be grateful for His abundant provisions, grace, and mercy. Rejoice in God's sovereign dealings with you and your loved ones. Promote peace through trust and confidence in God and seek to share that with your community.*

### FINDING THE BEST DECISION

Use a **Quick Write** for students to record how each virtue (gratitude, joy, and peace) practically impacts their ethical decision-making and ethical living.

**How does practicing gratitude impact your decision to be loving to a friend you are angry with or to be patient with a sibling?** *Gratitude puts the believer in a mindset to be loving toward those who are hard to get along with because God loved us while we were yet sinners (Rom. 5:8). This heart full of gratitude also influences decisions to be patient with frustrating close relatives because God is patient toward us and our rebellious ways.*

**How does practicing joy impact your decision to show meekness at a time when pride would take over?** *Being joyful cancels out pride in the sense that, even though you have done something you are proud of, taking joy in God and His gifting and His allowing you to succeed drives you to practice meekness.*

**How does practicing peace impact your decision to demonstrate diligence when you are tempted to do less than your best?** *When the peace of God reigns in your heart and mind, you have the mindset and ability to see how valuable diligence is. You are content to enjoy the empowerment that peace provides. Diligent work and effort flow more naturally as you tackle your assignments and work.*

### THE VICE OF WORRY

Use **Activity 7.3** on pages 43–44 to apply the information in the section.

## Assess

Guide a **summative assessment** by directing students to answer the questions in Thinking It Through 7.3.

### Thinking It Through 7.3

1. The textbook defines *gratitude* as an attitude of thanksgiving to God for His provision and governance of all things. Students should point out the differences they found in the online definition of this virtue.
2. The textbook defines *joy* as a confident delight in God's sovereign work in all of life's circumstances. Students should point out the differences they found in the online definition of this virtue.
3. The textbook defines *peace* as a harmonious wholeness produced when God's design of the world, including human relationships, is rightly ordered; as a virtue, it describes the mindset and character of a believer, even during difficult and unpleasant circumstances. Students should point out the differences they found in the online definition of this virtue.
4. Non-Christians source their joy and peace in themselves and in their circumstances. Christians source their joy and peace in God. Only in Him and from Him can believers truly have joy and peace. Non-Christians see themselves as the objects of their gratitude. If it isn't themselves, then it is anyone else besides the Creator who provides all things. Christians acknowledge God as the object of their gratitude. They know that all things come from His hand. Hence, they are grateful for the good and not ungrateful for the bad.
5. Gratitude requires humility that recognizes a need and graciousness to accept a gift and acknowledge it. Ingratitude ignores the good done to oneself and feeds a proud, self-sufficient disposition.

   Joy acknowledges all the reasons believers must be happy and are blessed in the Lord. Despair is giving up and failing to see all the ways God is working in one's life, community, and world.

   Peace is practiced by believers when they align themselves and those they influence with God's will and design. Worry acts as if God doesn't exist or is absent from this life. As a result, uncertainty and hopelessness set in.

What is the difference between a troublemaker and a peacemaker? One obvious answer is that peacemaking is a biblically ethical lifestyle, unlike troublemaking (Matt. 5:9). Peacemaking isn't the same thing as avoiding all confrontation; that is cowardice. If you are grateful for and rejoice in the fulfilling blessings of life in Christ, then you want others who are opposed to God to come to peaceful terms with Him. Calling others to peace with God is the duty of all believers, by the way (2 Cor. 5:18–20). And believers who are controlled by gratitude, joy, and peace will seek to return broken and disrupted relationships back to the order God created them for. When you've had a conflict with someone, do you either humbly seek forgiveness for yourself or seek reconciliation if the person wronged you? Or do you hold grudges and let the conflict remain unresolved?

Pursue growth in these three virtues through Bible reading and study, other resources (books, messages, podcasts, articles, devotionals), prayer, and encouragement from a mentor or close friend. Remember, you can't practice ethical living without a Spirit-dependent pursuit of gratitude, joy, and peace.

#### Thinking It Through 7.3

1. Find a definition of *gratitude* online. How does that definition differ from the definition of gratitude found in this chapter?
2. Find a definition of *joy* online. How does that definition differ from the definition of joy found in this chapter?
3. Find a definition of *peace* online. How does that definition differ from the definition of peace found in this chapter?
4. Do an online search for "how to be happy." Look for non-Christian ideas of happiness and contrast them with the Christ-focused virtues of joy, peace, and gratitude.
5. Contrast the virtues of gratitude, joy, and peace with the vices of ingratitude, despair, and worry.
6. List a few examples of how gratitude, joy, and peace relate to ethical decision-making and ethical living.
7. What would you include in a plan for growing in gratitude, joy, and peace?

### 7.4 Honesty

What do Abraham Lincoln, a courtroom, and the best policy all have in common? Honesty! You might have heard of "Honest Abe"; you're probably familiar with the courtroom oath to "tell the truth, the whole truth, and nothing but the truth"; and you may know the adage about honesty being "the best policy." Honesty is telling the truth, but this virtue is much more than that for Christians.

Out of all the virtues covered thus far, which virtues were practiced as far back as the Garden of Eden? What vices were present in Genesis 3 when the serpent deceived Eve and humanity fell into sin? We can identify faith, love, righteousness, faithfulness, self-control, unbelief, lust, ungodliness, cunning, disloyalty, and pride as being part of Adam and Eve's time in the garden. The vice of falsehood played a large role in the Fall. After all, the Devil is called the father of lies (John 8:44), and his first interaction with man involved his blatant lie to deceive Eve into rebellion against God (Gen. 3:4–5). The rest is history, literally.

126 VIRTUES

6. Gratitude, joy, and peace directly impact resisting the temptation to cheat on a test. Also, pursuing peace rather than tolerating or engaging in turmoil requires a firm grasp on gratitude, joy, and peace.
7. Bible reading and study, other resources (books, messages, podcasts, articles, devotionals), prayer, and encouragement from a mentor or close friend

## 7.4 Honesty

How will honesty be most challenged in my day-to-day life?

### Objectives

- **7.4.1** Define *honesty*.
- **7.4.2** Relate the character of God to truth and the character of Satan to falsehood.
- **7.4.3** Explain direct biblical teaching about truth and falsehood.
- **7.4.4** Analyze Scripture narratives that seem to approve of deception.
- **7.4.5** Apply the biblical teaching about truth and falsehood to difficult ethical choices.

### Printed Resource

- Activity 7.4: Don't Tell Yourself Lies

### DEFINING THE TERMS

Examining this first lie in human history helps us begin to define honesty as well as lying. Satan knew what God had commanded Adam, and he knew what the consequences were if the human king and queen of creation disobeyed God's clear command. The serpent was crafty and cunning, after all (Gen. 3:1). By this time Satan had already fallen from his angelic position near the throne of God (Ezek. 28:13–17). Wallowing in his hurt pride and seething with anger, Satan retaliated against God by attacking His premier creation—man. God and man were in perfect communion, and the only way Satan could interrupt that communion was by causing man to doubt God and disobey Him. As long as man trusted and followed God's commands, life in Eden was perfect. That is why Satan resorted to his original trick—lying to cause the woman to doubt God's love and care for them. Satan spoke a false assertion that he knew was untrue, contradicting God's very words. So **lying** is verbally declaring something that one knows to be false.[18] **Honesty**, on the other hand, is a devotion to truthfulness where one affirms and acts in accord with what is true and righteous. Honesty governs speech, as in truth telling instead of lying, but it also governs actions that are fair, just, and righteous. And the vice of **falsehood** is endorsing untruths to harm someone else or for one's personal gain. Ripping someone off in a transaction, slander,* and stretching the truth to one's advantage are all examples of falsehood.

#### WHAT A LIE ISN'T

We need to make room for normal types of communication that aren't violations of the virtue of honesty. An accurate understanding of honesty and falsehood is extremely important. The categories below fall outside our definition of lying.

- **Silence**
  If nothing is expressly said, then neither truth nor falsehood is stated.
- **Certain nonverbals**
  Using a noisemaker that sounds like a rainstorm to help a baby sleep isn't lying to the baby. (On the other hand, pointing to written language, like "yes" or "no," in order to deceive someone would be the same as writing or speaking it—a false verbal declaration and therefore a lie.)
- **Irony or humor**
  Jokes by their nature are fictional or made-up scenarios. (It would be lying to intentionally deceive someone and only after the fact try to excuse it by saying that it was all just a joke. That would be two lies.)
- **Fictional storytelling**
  Much literature involves telling stories that are known to be false. Parables fall under this category. Theater and filmmaking are also legitimate forms of fictional storytelling.
- **Hyperbole**
  Exaggeration to deceive or with no hint that actual hyperbole is intended is lying. But hyperbole is common in speech and is not falsehood. You might exclaim to your friends, "I'm starving! I could eat a horse!" Both sentences are instances of hyperbole.
- **Accidental misspeaking**
  There are times that we will be mistaken or share something that we didn't believe to be false information. But later what we said turns out to be false. You need to be more careful, but you didn't lie as such. For example, you might tell a friend that the game is next Monday night (you misremembered), but it actually is two Mondays away.[19]

**slander:** maliciously false accusations against someone's character and person



## Digital Resource

- Link: When Is It OK to Tell a Well-Meaning Lie?

## Suggested Reading

- Grudem, Wayne. *Christian Ethics: An Introduction to Biblical Moral Reasoning*. Wheaton: Crossway, 2018. Pages 309–41.

## Engage

### A HISTORICAL SIN: LYING

Use a **bell ringer** activity to point students to the gravity, yet relative ease, of lying.

**In Satan's arsenal of temptations, which weapon did he use to trick Eve into sinning?** *Lying. Satan caused Eve to doubt God's words by twisting them, by misrepresenting what God commanded—he lied to Eve.*
**Why are we often easily persuaded to commit the sin of lying?** *to get what we want, to avoid embarrassment or punishment, or because it is easy to get away with*

History shows the evil power of lying as well as its effectiveness in tempting people and causing them to sin. Honesty is an important virtue.

## Instruct

### NON-LIES

Guide a **Socratic seminar** to allow students to analyze what a lie isn't.

After students have read the definitions for lying, honesty, and falsehood on page 127, they will use the Socratic seminar to analyze the categories in the textbox What a Lie Isn't on that same page.

**Can you think of any Bible passages or principles that would argue either for or against these categories?** *Students should seek to use Scripture to support their cases. The main defense of these categories is that Scripture itself does not identify these categories as lying. Christians are not to be stricter than Scripture since believers are called to submit to God and obey His Word, not to add to it or to pretend to be more righteous than God.*

## THOSE BEHIND HONESTY AND LYING

Use a **Turn and Talk** for students to relate God's character to truth telling and Satan's character to falsehood.

Have students read the material on page 128 about the sources for falsehood and truth and then answer the following questions.

**How does truth telling stem from God's character and lying from Satan's character?** *Responses should include the information from the corresponding Scripture passages.* **How do these two realities affect your disposition to pursue honesty and reject lying?** *Followers of Christ should reject anything that represents Satan and his ways and carefully avoid allowing lying to be part of their lives. God's character is the standard for Christian living, including the virtue of honesty. Sanctification involves pursuing the Christlike quality of truth telling rather than the satanic vices of falsehood and lying.*

### SOURCES OF FALSEHOOD AND TRUTH

We have already briefly seen how falsehood intrinsically stems from Satan. He is the original liar, deceiver, and counterfeiter (Job 1:9–11; Rev. 3:9; 12:9–10). Peter tied Satan to this sin in his rebuke of Ananias (Acts 5:3). For Ananias and his wife, Sapphira, the consequence for lying to the Holy Spirit was extreme (Acts 5:5–6, 9–10). The book of Revelation has three lists of various sins that typify people who are hell-bound; included are lying and the vice of falsehood (Rev. 21:8, 27; 22:15). Falsehood runs in Satan's veins. Deceit oozes out of his pores (see Acts 13:10). Lying and falsehood belong to the darkness, not to the light. And the Devil's home base is the darkness (2 Cor. 11:13–15; 1 John 1:6). Falsehood and lying, categorically so, are one and the same with Satan's character and with everything that opposes God, truth, and righteousness.

It is clear from Scripture that those who are children of the Devil will live the way he lives (1 John 3:8–10). They share the same character. Just as babies imitate and look like their parents, so the children of disobedience and wrath (Eph. 2:2–3) imitate their "father the devil" (John 8:44). Should any sin that is characteristic of the lives of those outside of Christ characterize the lives of those who are in Christ? Of course not. Salvation involves an entire transformation of those who come to Christ (2 Cor. 5:17; Titus 3:5). No aspect of a believer's life is out of the Spirit's reach to conform him or her to the image of Christ (Rom. 8:29; 12:2).

So why is honesty so important for believers? What makes this virtue so valuable for Christians to pursue? Because all virtues, and therefore honesty and truth, are grounded in the character of God. God doesn't dabble in falsehoods (Heb. 6:17–18). God cannot lie (Num. 23:19; Titus 1:2). God is perfect and just in all His ways (Rev. 15:3). When God speaks, decrees, and acts, He is totally trustworthy (Prov. 30:5). In concord with such affirmations about God in general, the Scriptures also record the character of truthfulness that the Son and the Spirit exhibit (John 14:6, 17). The triune God is the source of truth and is always truthful.

In summary, the Bible clearly connects the character of Satan to falsehood and the character of God to truth. Believers, therefore, must speak the truth. Believers must be honest because truth characterizes God Himself. Lies are typically told to allow one to sin (Did you really do what you told your parents you were going to do at the place you said you were going to be?) or to cover up someone else's sin (Did you vouch for your friend who disobeyed his parents so he wouldn't get in trouble?).

Christlikeness and lying don't mix.

128 VIRTUES

## THE BIBLE ON FALSEHOOD AND TRUTH

Before considering a few passages in Scripture where deception is employed for a commendable end, we want to look at an overall picture of the Bible's teaching on lying, falsehood, honesty, and truth telling. Doing this will allow us to get a feel for the overall tone and message of the Bible on these subjects. There are dozens of passages that mention the sinfulness and dangers and consequences of lying, deceit, and falsehood. There are also many passages that praise and commend honesty, truth telling, and righteous dealings with others. Below is a mere sampling.

### *Truth and Falsehood Contrasted*

PSALM 119:163

I hate and abhor lying: but thy law do I love.

PROVERBS 11:1

A false balance is abomination to the LORD: but a just weight is his delight.

PROVERBS 14:5

A faithful witness will not lie: but a false witness will utter lies.

EPHESIANS 4:25

Wherefore putting away lying, speak every man truth with his neighbour: for we are members one of another.

EPHESIANS 4:29

Let no corrupt communication proceed out of your mouth, but that which is good to the use of edifying, that it may minister grace unto the hearers.

### *Prohibitions of Falsehood*

EXODUS 20:16

Thou shalt not bear false witness against thy neighbour.

LEVITICUS 19:11–12

Ye shall not steal, neither deal falsely, neither lie one to another. And ye shall not swear by my name falsely, neither shalt thou profane the name of thy God: I am the LORD.

EPHESIANS 4:31

Let all bitterness, and wrath, and anger, and clamour, and evil speaking, be put away from you, with all malice.

COLOSSIANS 3:9–10

Lie not one to another, seeing that ye have put off the old man with his deeds; and have put on the new man, which is renewed in knowledge after the image of him that created him.

### *The Value of Truth*

PSALM 15:1–2

LORD, who shall abide in thy tabernacle? Who shall dwell in thy holy hill? He that walketh uprightly, and worketh righteousness, and speaketh the truth in his heart.

PSALM 19:14

Let the words of my mouth, and the meditation of my heart, be acceptable in thy sight, O LORD, my strength, and my redeemer.

PSALM 120:2

Deliver my soul, O LORD, from lying lips, and from a deceitful tongue.

JOHN 8:31–32

Then said Jesus to those Jews which believed on him, If ye continue in my word, then are ye my disciples indeed; and ye shall know the truth, and the truth shall make you free.

### *The Evil of Falsehood*

PROVERBS 6:16–17, 19

These six things doth the LORD hate: yea, seven are an abomination unto him: a proud look, a lying tongue, and hands that shed innocent blood, . . . a false witness that speaketh lies, and he that soweth discord among brethren.

MATTHEW 15:19

For out of the heart proceed evil thoughts, murders, adulteries, fornications, thefts, false witness, blasphemies.

ROMANS 1:25

Who changed the truth of God into a lie, and worshipped and served the creature more than the Creator, who is blessed for ever. Amen.

ROMANS 1:29

Being filled with all unrighteousness, fornication, wickedness, covetousness, maliciousness; full of envy, murder, debate, deceit, malignity; whisperers.

1 JOHN 2:21–22

I have not written unto you because ye know not the truth, but because ye know it, and that no lie is of the truth. Who is a liar but he that denieth that Jesus is the Christ? He is antichrist, that denieth the Father and the Son.



## APPROVING LYING?

Use the **link** When Is It OK to Tell a Well-Meaning Lie? Print copies of the article for the students to read for this activity.

Direct students to do a **textual analysis** of this article to analyze whether it is OK to lie. Students should utilize the information on pages 129–30 to assist them in their analysis.

**How would you respond to the question the article asks: When is it OK to tell a well-meaning lie?** *It's never OK. It is always best to be honest. But honesty in this context doesn't mean rudeness or criticizing someone. Rather than telling a well-meaning lie, say something helpful and encouraging that is also truthful. Or avoid saying anything at all if only a lie comes to mind at that moment.*

## WHAT WOULD YOU HAVE DONE?

Guide students through a **role play** of the deception of the Hebrew midwives and/or the lying of Rahab to see how they might have responded in these critical and extreme situations without allowing innocent lives to be taken.

Assign students the roles of Pharaoh and Shiphrah and Puah as well as Rahab and the soldiers from Jericho. Without imitating what the biblical stories portray, the point is to see how they would avoid lying or creatively deceive those seeking to kill.

Guide a follow-up **discussion.**

**In these extreme examples, what factors are at play that contribute to the challenging nature of these accounts?**

- *Innocent lives were threatened by evil legislation and wicked men.*
- *Israelites, God's chosen people, were being unjustly targeted.*
- *Those who could make a difference were outranked and had few resources to physically resist those questioning their actions.*
- *Those who could make a difference understood the sanctify of life and how respecting the lives of the innocent honors God.*

**What encouragement can these two accounts offer you?**

- *God uses broken vessels who fail to practice all the virtues perfectly to accomplish His will and further His purposes.*
- *Innocent life is worth protecting even though believers might struggle to do so without compromising on morals.*

Is there any doubt about God's approval of honesty and truth and His denunciation of lying and falsehood? Some of these passages about lying, deception, and falsehood are set within descriptions of the lifestyle of the wicked and those that oppose God. Habitual cheating, deceiving, slandering, and lying are clearly condemned as the practice of the ungodly lost. Speaking the truth, being honest, and dealing fairly with others are what Christians do. But don't believers occasionally cheat, deceive, slander, and lie, thus forsaking the truth and honesty? To answer yes (and we must because believers are not-yet-glorified sinners saved by grace) is not to approve or make the sins of lying and falsehood any less serious than they are. Christians who fall into these sins should immediately seek forgiveness from all the offended parties (Matt. 5:23–24; 1 John 1:9). Be careful about dishonest behavior you might be tempted to justify. The fact that you deceived your parents once before doesn't make it acceptable or any less sinful to do so again in the future, just as one lustful thought that you quickly repented of doesn't make future lustful thoughts less sinful. Love truth telling. Hate lying. If you are a believer but have fallen into bad patterns in this area, don't excuse yourself or give up on becoming a truthful person. Instead, repent and move forward with hope in the power of the Spirit to transform you into the image of Christ.

### CHALLENGING BIBLICAL EXAMPLES

At this juncture, you might have begun to wonder about instances in Scripture where deception or lying is used to do much good. For example, Samuel had a main purpose to go to Bethlehem to anoint David as the future king of Israel. But God told him to say he was there to offer a sacrifice, which was also true (1 Sam. 16:1–5). Samuel didn't lie, nor was he guilty of falsehood for not divulging all the details of his visit—he obeyed God's direct order! God had already rejected Saul as king, and since God was the ultimate King of Israel, neither God nor His prophet was obligated to reveal all that was in God's mind regarding a successor for Saul. There are some occasions when the saying, "A partial truth is a whole lie," holds true, such as when a parent or teacher is asking for a full accounting of your wrongdoing. But there are many people who do not have a right to the whole truth, usually because of the evil they would do if they knew it.

One other initial example in which deception seems to be part of God's plan is God's judgment on the wicked in the end times. Paul records how the Antichrist will, empowered by Satan himself, lie to and deceive the wicked (2 Thess. 2:8–10). God will providentially ensure that all the wicked who loved falsehood believe what is false, sealing their judgment (2 Thess. 2:11–12). God is always above reproach, and though deception or lies will be employed by Satan and believed by wicked people, God will not be, nor is He ever, the author of evil (James 1:13). This situation is similar to how God judged Pharaoh for his hardened heart. God continued to harden Pharaoh's hardened heart (Exod. 7:3–5; 8:15).

#### *The Hebrew Midwives*

Let's turn our attention now to a seeming case of deception by two Hebrew midwives. God was blessing the Hebrew people in Egypt after the time of Joseph, but the Egyptians, fearing them, devised ways to keep them submissive to their rule (Exod. 1:8–14). A genocidal command was given to Hebrew midwives in the land—kill all the Hebrew baby boys the moment they were born (Exod. 1:15–16). Given

130 VIRTUES

## TELLING THE WHOLE STORY

Use a **Think-Pair-Share** for students to consider whether one is obligated to tell every detail one knows on a matter when questioned.

**If you know something that could harm innocent people, are you morally obligated to give that information of your own accord to the authorities?** *The virtue of honesty doesn't demand 100% transparency. Love and prudence are other related and necessary virtues to always consider. Also, volunteering information that would lead to an innocent person being harmed is evil.*

**If everyone doesn't have the same right to know something, is withholding information from those who don't have that right ethically acceptable?** *Withholding information is not the same thing as lying. Not sharing is passive. Lying is active. This is an especially critical distinction if you know the intended purpose or use of the information that they are requesting from you.*

**What category do your parents or legal guardians fall into?** *Parents and legal guardians are set in place by God to be the ones responsible for your well-being, growth, and protection. You owe them honesty and the full truth. By having that kind of trusting and open relationship, they can best care for you (Eph. 6:1–4).*

**What is an example scenario of someone who doesn't have the right to know everything when requesting information from you?** *A government official, military officer, school administrator or faculty member, or employer requesting you to divulge information about yourself or someone you know who would lose their life, their livelihood, or their freedom if you answered with that information, when you know well that you or your friend are innocent and moral in your actions.*

this evil, immoral command, the midwives disobeyed the Pharaoh because they feared God. They did all in their power to save the threatened Hebrew babies (Exod. 1:17). Word got back to Pharaoh that Shiphrah and Puah were not killing the babies as commanded. When called on to explain themselves, the women didn't reveal to Pharaoh their reasons for not killing the babies (Exod. 1:18–19). What they told him might have been at least partially true. Either way, it seemed Pharaoh believed them. But Pharaoh didn't give up his desire to see the male babies killed and turned to his own people to carry out the slaughter (Exod. 1:22). All things considered, God blessed the outcome of what these women did out of fear for Him, despite the nature of their possible deception, not because of it (Exod. 1:20–21).[20]

### *Rahab and the Spies*

And now to the most well-known passage in Scripture where God used a lie to further His sovereign will. The context of Joshua 2 is Israel's taking possession of the Promised Land. God appointed Israel to judge the wicked people who were living in the land, and Israel was supposed to clear them out and move in (Josh. 1:6, 11). Before attacking the walled city of Jericho, Joshua sent two spies into the city to do reconnaissance work (Josh. 2:1). God had apparently been graciously working in the heart of Rahab because she took the spies in and hid them rather than turn them over to the city's authorities (Josh. 2:1–11). When soldiers came to her door looking for them, Rahab lied to save the lives of the two spies and to support the attack of Israel on Jericho. She aligned herself with Israel and Israel's God and in doing so essentially put herself in the position of fighting alongside the Israelites against her own people, including the men who were looking for the spies. The passage finishes with everything working out—the spies were saved, Rahab and her family's lives would be preserved, and Joshua got the information he needed (Josh. 2:12–24).

Rahab's protection of the spies is commended in the New Testament (Heb. 11:31; James 2:25), and God sovereignly included Rahab in the direct line of the ancestry of Jesus (Matt. 1:5). The New Testament commends Rahab's faith, and her true faith showed through her works—she hid the spies. But her lie, her claim that the spies had already left Jericho, is never approved anywhere in Scripture.

What can be concluded from these challenging biblical examples above? As seen from the passages presented and considered earlier, the Bible is clear on God's approval of truthfulness and honesty. These virtues reflect God's character. And we have also seen that lying and deception are rooted in the devil and reflect his nature. The Bible contains several narratives that portray believers in God who lie or deceive. The Bible never once praises the lies or the deception as such; Scripture praises honesty and truth telling. God uses imperfect sinners saved by grace to accomplish His purposes. So, we must emulate honesty, and we must practice truth telling.

How will honesty be most challenged in my day-to-day life?

### YOUR HONESTY PUT TO THE TEST

Truth be told, you most likely won't find yourself in a work situation where you are commanded to commit infanticide. Neither will you probably ever need to hide righteous spies from a wicked government that would kill them if they found them. So there can be no case made to justify lying based on the passages examined in the previous section, since the motives, circumstances, and outcomes presented in those passages are entirely distinct from your own. Add to that the fact that the Bible never once explicitly condones lying, even in extreme circumstances. And God's Word is crystal clear on the relationship of truth to God's character and on lying's relation to evil.

The temptation to be dishonest comes at you from every direction. Sharing information known to be false that fits with your personal views is to endorse falsehood. Fact-checking has a legitimate place, especially for Christians who don't want to be dishonest. When your parents ask you whether you've completed *all* your homework and you say yes but you are actually planning to finish your last assignment on the way to school tomorrow, it is still a lie. When you are asked how you did on a test or how many points you scored in the game, and you embellish the answer, that is lying. When you minimally know someone yet you make assumptions about their character and then accuse them of some sort of wrongdoing, you are not only being mean, but you are also engaging in slander. Slander survives on falsehood. And when you peek at the answer sheet while doing your homework, even though your teacher expressly said to use it only *after* you have finished the assignment, you are cheating.

What these examples have in common is that they are normal situations you could easily find yourself in, and the actions in question are all dishonest. They all dishonor God because of the deception and falsehood involved in them. The goal or the reason why dishonesty or falsehood is used does not justify the rejection of the virtue for the acceptance of the vice. These are the everyday kinds of challenges to honesty you are likely to face. But if you ever *do* find yourself in a dire situation where a lie wouldn't cover up someone else's sin nor selfishly benefit you but could potentially save innocent life, pray that God will give you grace to do what is right.

#### Thinking It Through 7.4

1. Define *honesty*.
2. How does the character of God relate to truth, and how does the character of Satan relate to falsehood?
3. What is the Bible's direct teaching on truth and falsehood?
4. How are we to understand passages in the Bible that seem to approve of deception?
5. In what ways can you apply the biblical teaching about truth and falsehood to difficult ethical choices?



## Apply

Use a **Quick Write** to have students answer this section's essential question.

**How will honesty be most challenged in my day-to-day life?** *Honesty will be most challenged in the day-to-day life of a student when dealing with seemingly harmless and well-meaning white lies. The common danger won't be the massive lie that leads to all sorts of justifying and additional lies to keep up the falsehood. It is the little lies that eventually become part of one's personality and way of living.*

Lying is not necessary for happiness, acceptance, or success. Honesty is always the best policy, even when small and large challenges present themselves and lying would appear to offer a satisfactory solution.

### DON'T TELL YOURSELF LIES

Use **Activity 7.4** on pages 45–46 to apply the information in the section.

## Assess

Guide a **summative assessment** by directing students to answer the questions in Thinking It Through 7.4.

#### Thinking It Through 7.4

1. a devotion to truthfulness where one affirms and acts in accord with what is true and righteous
2. Scripture declares that God is true, He speaks only the truth, and all that He does is true, just, righteous, and perfect. Satan, however, is the father of lies and a liar from the very beginning of his existence. Satan deceives and promotes falsehood, devoting himself to opposing the true God and truth itself.
3. The Bible contains abundant passages on the godliness and blessedness of honesty and truth telling as well as the sinfulness and evil of falsehood. There can be no doubt that God despises and judges all untruthfulness and promotes and rewards truthfulness.
4. There are various types of deception that show up in Scripture. The context which they are in helps us determine if God approves of the deception or is simply commenting on the use of deception. The Bible doesn't always explicitly condone or condemn the instances of deception. The only time one can make a case for deception is in times of war. Outside war, deception is basically unjustifiable.
5. The automatic decision for believers must be honesty and not falsehood. Even in difficult or uncomfortable circumstances, the truth is the right answer. When dealing with authorities, in all realms, the truth is what you must give them. Extreme situations like war or the presence of an evil and immoral government disqualify certain authorities from being told the full truth. In those times where great harm would be done to the innocent, much prudence and grace from God is required to respond righteously.

# Review

VIRTUES, PART 2

### Terms to Remember

- humility
- meekness
- gentleness
- pride
- anger
- harshness
- kindness
- compassion
- cruelty
- indifference
- gratitude
- joy
- peace
- ingratitude
- despair
- worry
- lying
- honesty
- falsehood

### Scripture Memory

Galatians 5:22–23

### Understanding Ethics

1. How do the virtues of humility, meekness, and gentleness relate to ethics?
2. How do the virtues of kindness and compassion relate to ethics?
3. How do the virtues of gratitude, joy, and peace relate to ethics?
4. How does the virtue of honesty relate to ethics?

### Practicing Ethical Decision-Making

5. How do you become great in the eyes of God? Give an example of pursuing humility rather than pride.
6. How should you respond to those who are hurting? Give an example of showing kindness and compassion to someone in need rather than cruelty or indifference.

### Analyzing and Evaluating Ethical Claims

7. How would you respond to those who say that humility, meekness, and gentleness are for the weak?
8. How would you respond to those who say that kindness and compassion require us to accept someone no matter what and that Christians are required to sympathize with anybody's discomfort no matter the nature of it?
9. How would you respond to those who say that joy and peace can't be had if the circumstances are hard and discouraging?
10. Why is a "little white lie" still a lie? Defend your answer.

### Creating My Own Position Statements on Ethics

11. Formulate your own position on whether believers should constantly express gratitude. Then make a list of thirty things you are thankful for.
12. How is deception sometimes distinct from lying? What are the differences between ethical and unethical deception?

VIRTUES, PART 2 133

# Chapter 7 Review

## Terms to Remember

- **humility:** A lowly view of one's own importance, resulting from "a high view of God's person" (Bridges, *The Practice of Godliness*, 91) and a profound sense of one's own weakness and sinfulness.
- **meekness:** A humble and calm disposition in situations that can lead to pride or anger.
- **gentleness:** Tender care for others even when they are hard to deal with.
- **pride:** An inflated estimation of oneself which attempts to rob God of His rightful place as sovereign Lord of all.
- **anger:** Intense displeasure arising from strong disagreement with a situation.
- **harshness:** Unpleasantness, roughness, or meanness directed toward someone.
- **kindness:** An internal sentiment, cultivated by the Holy Spirit, that motivates believers to indiscriminately do good to others.
- **compassion:** An external manifestation of loving-kindness that sympathetically and indiscriminately meets a need.
- **cruelty:** The willful causation of distress or discomfort in others.
- **indifference:** Apathy toward others and utter lack of concern for the ethical good of a situation.
- **gratitude:** An attitude of thanksgiving to God for His provision and governance of all things.
- **joy:** A confident delight in God's sovereign work in all of life's circumstances.
- **peace:** A harmonious wholeness produced when God's design of the world, including human relationships, is rightly ordered; as a virtue, describes the mindset and character of a believer, even during difficult and unpleasant circumstances.
- **ingratitude:** Taking things for granted, overlooking what is clearly worthy of thanks, and being unthankful for all the good one has.
- **despair:** Hopelessness; describes giving up and being pessimistic about the outcome of a situation.
- **worry:** Emotional instability where someone rehearses all the what-ifs about a given situation and fails to trust God and His Word.
- **lying:** Verbally declaring something that one knows to be false (Taken from *Christian Ethics: An Introduction to Biblical Moral Reasoning* by Wayne Grudem, © 2018, p. 311. Used by permission of Crossway, a publishing ministry of Good News Publishers, Wheaton, IL 60187, www.crossway.org).
- **honesty:** A devotion to truthfulness where one affirms and acts in accord with what is true and righteous.
- **falsehood:** As a vice, describes the endorsement of untruths to harm someone else or for one's personal gain.

## Understanding Ethics

1. Humility, meekness, and gentleness relate to ethics in that they are virtues, and they stand in contrast to the unethical vices of pride, anger, and harshness. These virtues must be called upon at every juncture to make an ethical decision. These virtues give a believer the right view of oneself.
2. Kindness and compassion relate to ethics in that they are virtues, and they stand in contrast to the unethical vices of cruelty and indifference. These virtues must be called upon at every juncture to make an ethical decision. These virtues specifically display the central virtue of love.
3. Gratitude, joy, and peace relate to ethics in that they are virtues, and they stand in contrast to the unethical vices of ingratitude, despair, and worry. These virtues must be called upon at every juncture to make an ethical decision. These virtues help believers keep their eyes on God and how He is caring and will care for them.

4. Honesty relates to ethics in that it is a virtue, and it stands in contrast to the unethical vice of falsehood. These virtues must be called upon at every juncture to make an ethical decision. This virtue is a key indicator of one's moral and ethical character.

### Practicing Ethical Decision-Making

5. Examples will vary. The Bible speaks of humbling oneself before God. He is the one to recognize and reward our humility, faithfulness, and service to Him. The Bible also speaks of the first being last and the last being first. True greatness isn't measured by earthly success or material possessions. True greatness is found in aligning oneself with God's standards and expectations. Because of Christ, believers can humbly, meekly, and gently do great things for a great God and allow Him to bring attention to that faithfulness now or later in heaven.
6. Examples will vary. I should respond to those who are hurting with loving-kindness and tender compassion. This is the heart that Jesus has for sinners. Christ came to search out and save the lost at great personal cost. Imitating God's kind and compassionate heart for sinners, believers are called to come alongside to comfort and provide for the needs of those who are hurting. This exacts a price from the one showing this sort of love. That is to be expected and shouldn't even be a consideration if the virtues of kindness and compassion are to be practiced.

### Analyzing and Evaluating Ethical Claims

7. Meekness is not weakness. And humility and gentleness aren't for wimps. The sense that bold, confident personalities and charismatic leaders would be at a disadvantage if they tapped into the virtues of humility, meekness, and gentleness is entirely incorrect. The fruit of the Spirit and other lists of virtues and passages in Scripture teach that weakness is due to sin, not virtue. These virtues help Christians live in sync with the Spirit, and being united to Christ gives them true power for godly living.
8. Showing sympathy does not mean that you blindly sympathize with someone who is responding to his or her hurting in a sinful way. The Scriptures do teach to "weep with them that weep" (Rom. 12:15), but that isn't an indiscriminate call to ignore someone's gross or perpetual sinful choices. It would be unethical to console a distraught drug addict who doesn't have access to illicit drugs. It would also be unethical to sympathize with a frustrated young person at church who feels that his or her same-sex attraction is judged by those who call the person to repent of his or her apathetic attitude toward battling this sin. Kindness and compassion call for sympathy that is tethered to the truth.
9. Joy and peace, as defined biblically and expressed by believers, are not dependent on one's circumstances. If that were the case, then for believers to obey God's commands to be joyful and experience peace, God would have to calm every single rough situation. In dark times, Christ is present with believers and overseeing each situation. The Spirit Himself produces joy and peace from the inside out in the life of a Christian.
10. A white lie is admittedly a lie. It is often not regarded as one, however, because purportedly no one is harmed and it is for a good cause. A white lie is a lie that is told much more frequently than standard lies are. This is habit-forming and reflects poorly on the individual. A Christian of integrity will be above reproach and not lie at all. All sin grieves God, including white lies.

### Creating My Own Position Statements on Ethics

11. Gratitude flows from a sincere and humble examination of one's inability to do anything of worth for oneself or others without God. If the Bible is true about who God is and who we are, then gratitude should be one of the most common virtues in the life of a Christian. The recognition that all we have comes from the Father's hand should never be forgotten. Believers' appreciation for all they have in Christ is a major motive for constant gratitude.

    The contents of the lists of thirty things will vary.
12. Lying is verbally declaring something that one knows to be false (Grudem, *Christian Ethics*, 311). Deception can include lying, but it also includes various manners of withholding the truth through silence, sharing only part of the truth, and using actions that lead one to believe something other than the truth. Ethical deception is the kind found in Scripture that isn't condemned, nor condoned, but that God used in important ways. Unethical deception is any kind that involves lying to someone who deserves to know the truth, intentionally deceiving them for personal gain. War is a unique situation, where most uses of deception, assuming the side with the just cause uses it, are ethical. But they should still be carefully examined.

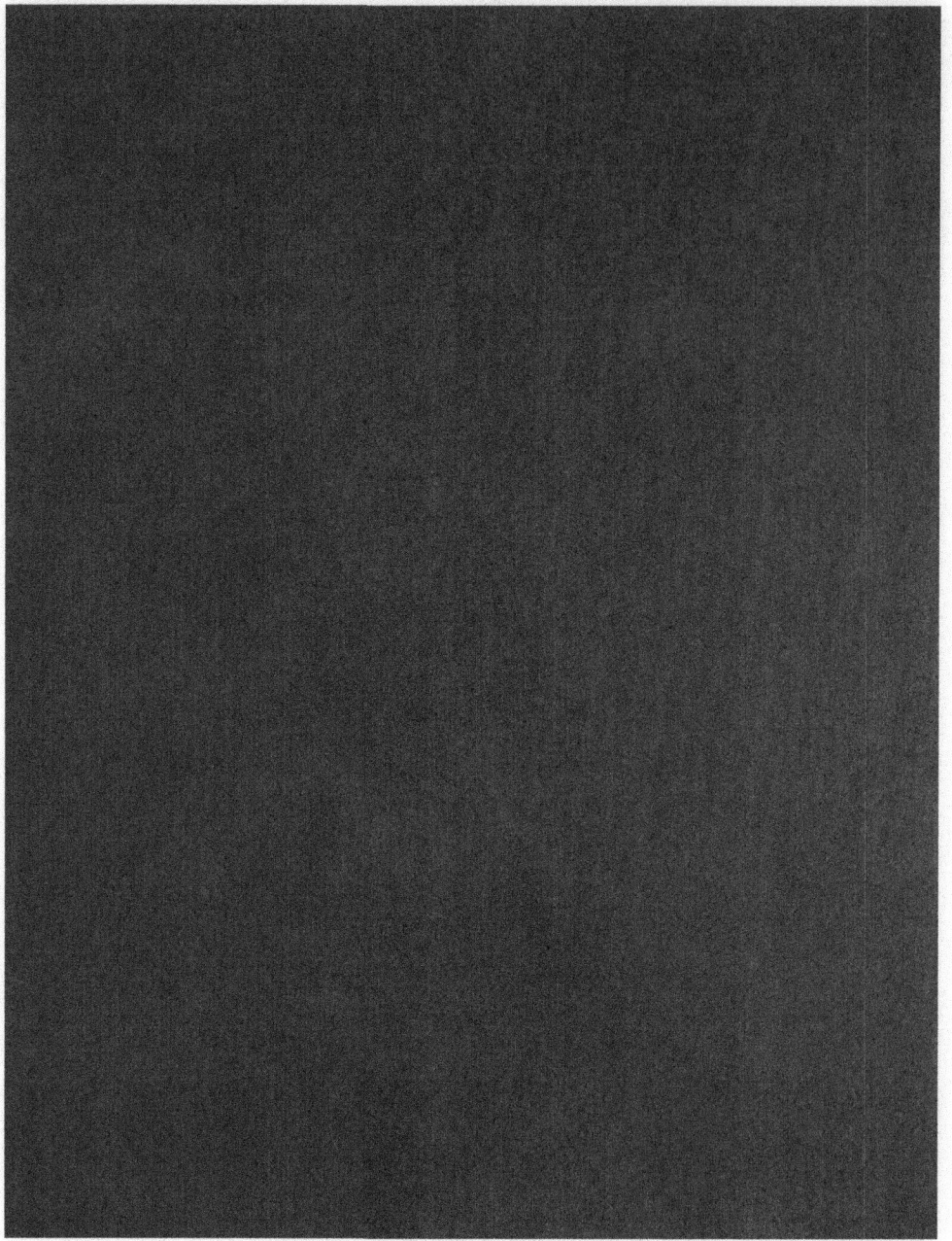

unit 3

# Issues

# Lesson Plan Overview

**CHAPTER 8:** A Method for Handling Ethical Issues

**EV** ExamView
**PPT pres.** PowerPoint presentation

| PAGES | OBJECTIVES | RESOURCES | ASSESSMENTS |
|---|---|---|---|
| **8.1 The Components of a Sound Ethical Method** (3.5 DAYS) | | | |
| 137–42 | **8.1.1** Explain acts, ends, and agents as essential components of an ethical method.<br>*BWS* Creational Order (explain); Man's Chief End (explain); Virtue (explain)<br>**8.1.2** Explain the importance of understanding the context of ethical choices.<br>*BWS* Wisdom (explain)<br>**8.1.3** Explain the necessity of each component of the ethical method working together.<br>*BWS* Authority (explain) | **ACTIVITIES**<br>• 8.1 The Components for Making Ethical Decisions<br>**BJU PRESS TROVE***<br>• Video: "Ethical Methodology"<br>• PPT pres.: Chapter 8 | **STUDENT EDITION**<br>• Thinking It Through 8.1 |
| **8.2 Using a Sound Ethical Method** (3.5 DAYS) | | | |
| 142–45 | **8.2.1** Outline a practical method for ethical decision-making.<br>**8.2.2** Relate the steps of a sound ethical method to the essential components.<br>**8.2.3** Formulate responses to various scenarios in which lost money is found. | **ACTIVITIES**<br>• 8.2 Using an Ethical Method: Test Cases<br>**BJU PRESS TROVE**<br>• PPT pres.: Chapter 8 | **STUDENT EDITION**<br>• Thinking It Through 8.2 |
| **Review** | | | |
| 146 | Recall concepts and Scripture memory from Chapter 8. | | **STUDENT EDITION**<br>• Chapter 8 Review |
| **Test** | | | |
| | Demonstrate knowledge of the material from Chapter 8 by taking the test. | | **ASSESSMENTS**<br>• Chapter 8 Test<br>**BJU PRESS TROVE**<br>• EV: Chapter 8 test bank |

*Digital resources for homeschool users are available on Homeschool Hub.

CHAPTER 8

# Overview

How do I make ethical decisions?

## Objectives

**8.1** Analyze the essential components of a sound ethical method.

**8.2** Apply this method to making ethical judgments.

## Scripture Memory

- Psalm 119:97, 101–4

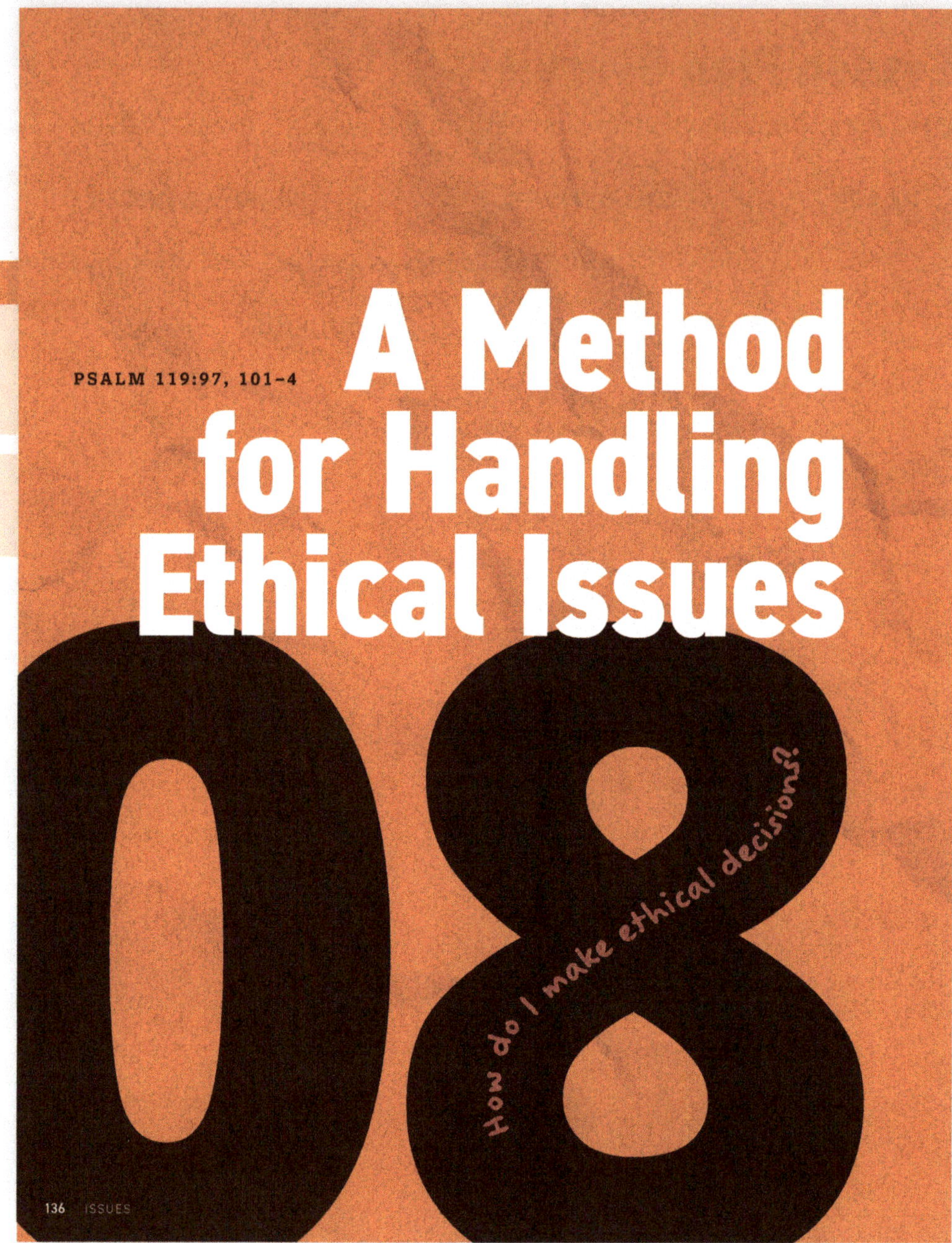

PSALM 119:97, 101–4
A Method for Handling Ethical Issues
08
How do I make ethical decisions?
136 ISSUES

## 8.1 The Components of a Sound Ethical Method

"Show me how to do it." "Coach me." When you're starting a new job or when you're learning a new skill—whether you're learning to play a sport, play a musical instrument, or use new technology—you need someone to show you the ropes. A good mentor will direct you step-by-step until you can begin working more independently. Then that person will coach you as you take more ownership. Eventually he or she will simply be in the background for support if you need it. And maybe one day you'll be the leader who takes over and mentors someone else.

Have you ever been in a position where you were given a task and nobody was there to direct you, coach you, or support you? You can feel lost when that happens. Even if you know the end result you're supposed to achieve, you have no idea how to get there. Imagine having to cook a high-class catered meal for over five hundred people. Most high-class restaurants have a hierarchy of chefs from the executive chef to the sous-chef to a host of support cooks. An executive chef can cater a high-class meal to hundreds of people only after years of experience under the guidance of others.

Ethical decision-making begins with knowledge, but it requires more than that. Even for those with a heart to please Christ, ethical decision-making is a learned skill requiring mentoring. That mentoring begins with someone showing you the ropes: the components to a sound ethical method. Then you can start practicing the skill of applying this method to issues (see Chapters 9–13).

### What do I need to know to make the right decisions?

Numerous books on Christian ethics lay out similar methods. But the most helpful method and the one we'll follow is provided by Ken Magnuson. He brings three aspects of ethics together to form a biblically based Christian ethic:

> Deontology rightly draws attention to moral acts that are grounded in moral principles. Virtue ethics rightly draws attention to moral agents, and to the communities to which they belong, and the narratives—and grand narrative—that provide the context or story of the moral life. Teleology rightly draws attention to the end or purpose of our lives, which orders and provides meaning for both acts and agents.[1]

**Remember...**

In Chapter 2 we learned that **Deontology** focuses on duty. **Teleology** focuses on results. **Virtue ethics** focuses on one's character.



# 8.1 The Components of a Sound Ethical Method

### What do I need to know to make the right decisions?

### Objectives

**8.1.1** Explain acts, ends, and agents as essential components of an ethical method. BWS

**8.1.2** Explain the importance of understanding the context of ethical choices. BWS

**8.1.3** Explain the necessity of each component of the ethical method working together. BWS

### Biblical Worldview Shaping

- **Creational Order** (explain): The acts of the ethical person need to align with the creation order. (8.1.1)
- **Man's Chief End** (explain): The goal of any ethical action must ultimately be to glorify God and enjoy Him through holy conformity to the image of Christ and the advancement of His kingdom. (8.1.1)
- **Virtue** (explain): To act ethically is not merely to do the right thing; it is to be the right kind of person doing the right thing. (8.1.1)
- **Wisdom** (explain): Ethics requires the application of God's law to specific situations. A wise person understands the ethical situation and how God's law applies to it. (8.1.2)
- **Authority** (explain): All three parts of the ethical method must work together because God must be recognized as the authority over moral standards, goals, and virtues. (8.1.3)

### Printed Resource

- Activity 8.1: The Components for Making Ethical Decisions

### Digital Resource

- Video: "Ethical Methodology"

### Suggested Reading

- Frame, John M. *The Doctrine of the Christian Life*. Phillipsburg, NJ: P&R Publishing, 2008. Pages 130–383.
- Grudem, Wayne. *Christian Ethics: An Introduction to Biblical Moral Reasoning*. Wheaton, IL: Crossway, 2018. Pages 36–265
- Magnuson, Ken. *Invitation to Christian Ethics: Moral Reasoning and Contemporary Issues*. Grand Rapids, MI: Kregel Academic, 2020. Pages 41–63.

## Engage

### THE VALUE OF SPIRITUAL MENTORS

Guide a **discussion** to help students understand their personal need for spiritual mentors.

**Why do we need spiritual mentors?** *Possible answers: to encourage us with our walk with the Lord, to keep us accountable, to help us understand scriptural truths better*

Trying to learn a new skill, such as playing a musical instrument, without the aid of an experienced practitioner can be frustrating. We're not sure what we're doing wrong and how to fix it. But with a knowledgeable teacher, we can avoid many mistakes, or at least improve quickly on the mistakes we are making. Spiritual mentors are like this when it comes to growing in ethical reasoning. Find a spiritual mentor with an uncompromising commitment to Christ and His Word, and you can sharpen your skills in ethical decision-making.

## Instruct

### ETHICAL METHODOLOGY

Show the **video** “Ethical Methodology” to introduce the subject matter to students.

### COMPONENTS OF AN ETHICAL METHOD: ACTS

Guide a **discussion** to prompt students to explain this component.

**Which ethical system (overviewed in Chapter 2) does the component of acts most closely resemble? Why?** *The deontological method; it focuses on rules that guide actions.*

**Why can’t secularists successfully find absolute principles that bind all people in all times and places? How can Christians successfully identify these principles?** *Secularists are looking for a transcendent standard in a finite world discovered by human logic. Christians have received God’s revelation, which provides such a transcendent standard in the Bible.*

**What are three ethical foundations revealed in God’s Word that provide the authoritative, universal moral absolutes for governing humans in this world? (See Chapter 1 for review.)** *God’s character, God’s wise design in creation (creational norms), and humans reflecting their Creator (the image of God in man)*

**What are the four ways that the Bible provides ethical guidance?** *(1) direct commands, (2) general principles, (3) implications, (4) descriptions and demonstrations of God’s character*

**How do passages like Matthew 19:4, 1 Corinthians 11:14, and 1 Timothy 2:13 help us to ground our ethics?** *They point to the created order (its design; creational norms) to show how we ought to direct ethical living.*

**What source of authority on ethics stands above human observations of the created world? Why?** *The Bible stands above human observations of the created world because humans are finite and fallen. God’s Word helps us to rightly understand God’s world.*

**What will a firm, courageous, and faithful commitment to God’s Word and its principles protect you from?** *It protects you from compromising to remain in step with the world around you, which undermines these principles.*

---

Magnuson recognizes how the deontological, teleological, and virtue ethics methods all pick up on needed aspects of ethics (see Sections 2.2 and 2.3).

First, God’s law, especially as presented in the Ten Commandments, provides moral principles (universals) to guide moral action. Second, the Bible is a grand story that is going somewhere; there are ends (goals). God’s goal is to glorify Himself through the establishment of His kingdom, and His goal for each person is that they glorify Him by being conformed to the image of Christ. Third, Jesus also made clear that mere external obedience without internal transformation (virtue) falls short of what God requires. The components to a Christian ethical method then, following Magnuson’s lead, can be summarized in three words: *acts*, *ends*, and *agents*.

Remember...

ETHICS

situation

agents (person, motivation)

ends (ultimate goal)

acts (principle)

#### ACTS: WHAT’S THE STANDARD?

This component most closely resembles the deontological method, which focuses on rules that guide actions. However, the secular approach seeks in vain to find an absolute principle that can bind all people in all times and places. That’s because the secularist is trying to do the impossible: find a basis for a transcendent* standard in a finite world—a basis discovered by human logic. But God alone can provide such a standard. (It’s worth noting here that this component of a Christian ethical method also contrasts sharply with the existentialist ethic and its call to be true only to oneself with no transcendent standard at all.)

Remember...

*In Chapter 2 we learned that the* **existential** ethic focuses on one’s true self.

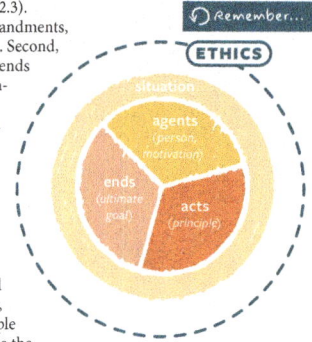

A standard is that by which something can be measured or used for comparison. If you draw a straight line freehanded and compare it to the standard of a ruler, is it perfectly straight?

Unlike the secular approach, Christians have a sure and clear transcendent standard given to them in the Bible. Since God has revealed Himself in His Word, we can know His character, we can rightly discern His wise design in creation, and we can recognize when humans are reflecting their Creator. Biblical truth (reflecting the created order) provides the authoritative, universal moral absolutes that humans need to govern themselves in this world.

First, the Bible is full of direct commands for how to live ethically in obedience to God out of love for Him and others (see Exod. 20:1–17; Matt. 22:37–40; Eph. 4:25–5:16; Col. 3:1–14). Second, the Bible contains numerous general principles that can be applied by all people in all times to a variety of situations (see Prov. 14:16; 27:6; Luke 10:27–37). Third, there are many implications to what the Bible explicitly says, meaning that believers need to make careful inferences that connect to their lives, applying the intent of God’s Word to new situations (see Matt. 5:21–48). God expects believers to mature to the point that they can discern what is pleasing to the Lord (Eph. 5:10; Heb. 5:11–14) based on the guidance of the Holy Spirit who helps them make proper inferences and applications (Rom. 8:13–14). Finally, the Bible is full of descriptions and demonstrations of God’s character (see 1 Sam. 12:7; Neh. 9:32–33; Dan. 9:14). The whole Bible is a rich resource for a Christian’s understanding of right and wrong.

**transcendent:** pertaining to the things of God beyond the earthly human experience

God’s general revelation is also a rich resource for a Christian’s understanding of right and wrong. God designed creation, including the social dimension, so that it functions a certain way. We call these principles of design *creational norms* (see Sec-

138 ISSUES

tions 1.2 and 2.1). If you read the Bible carefully, you will see that the biblical writers sometimes grounded their arguments in the authority of the created order, which is just as authoritative as a direct command from God (Matt. 19:4; 1 Cor. 11:14–15; 1 Tim. 2:13). You'll also notice in the Wisdom Literature that wise men observed God's world, seeking to discern these creational norms. Yet because we are finite and fallen, our observations of God's world must always take place in connection with what God has more clearly revealed in His written Word.

*The acts of the ethical person need to align with both the creational order and God's commands to the New Covenant believer—neither of which are subject to cultural changes.*

You'll notice that both God's wise design in the created order and God's commands are being undermined by the world around you (see Chapters 9–13 on various issues). You will have to decide where your allegiance lies if you are going to take a courageous biblical stand (Josh. 24:15). Can you trust God enough to be faithful to Him while waiting on Him to triumph in the end? Or will you twist the Bible's meaning or outright reject its clear statements to remain in step with the world around you?

#### ENDS: WHAT'S THE GOAL?

This component of a Christian ethical method most closely resembles the teleological method, which focuses on the goals or results (the ends) of a given decision or action (see Sections 2.2 and 2.3). However, the secular approach generally locates the ultimate goal of all people in themselves—in their own happiness (or freedom from pain).

Unlike the secular approach, Christians have a God-given goal: to glorify God by loving God and others. Determining exactly what this means and looks like comes from understanding the objective commands that set the standard for us. You cannot separate the goal from the standard. They work hand-in-hand. Rather than seeking self-serving happiness, Christians will even endure persecution and suffering for the sake of a greater end goal (Matt. 10:28; 2 Cor. 4:7–18). The happiness they do pursue is found in God and in His good will for them rather than in fleshly pleasures. To persevere in such commitment to God's commands in order to achieve a higher end requires the formation of inward character.

*The goal of any ethical action must ultimately be to glorify God and enjoy Him through holy conformity to the image of Christ and the advancement of His kingdom.*

Why are God's commands not burdensome to the believer (1 John 5:3)? The believer knows that God's commands are not arbitrary. God's commands have a purpose, an excellent end: God's glory and our greatest good. God's commands are not designed to get in the way of our fun; they are designed to uphold our greatest flourishing. God's commands describe what it means to love Him and others, upholding God's wise design for our best life.

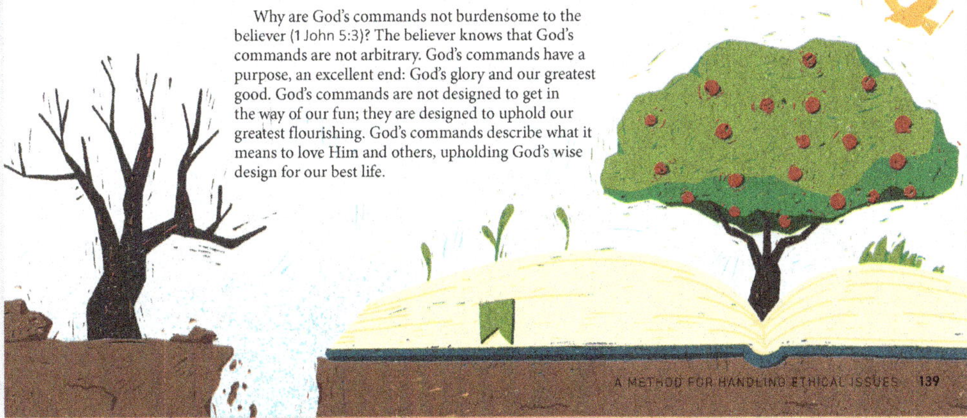



## COMPONENTS OF AN ETHICAL METHOD: ENDS

Use a **Think-Pair-Share** to prompt students to explain this component.

**Although the component of ends is teleological, why isn't it consequentialist? (See Sections 2.2 and 2.3 for review.)** *Although the component of ends does focus on the goals or results, the ends do not justify the means. The means must align with God's absolute standard, which consequentialism ignores. The goal and the standard must work hand in hand.*

**How does the ultimate goal generally identified in secular philosophies contrast with the ultimate God-given goal of Christians?** *Secularists generally locate the ultimate goal of all people in themselves, in their own happiness or freedom from pain. Christians identify the ultimate goal in glorifying God by loving Him and others.*

**What is the relationship of God's commands to this God-given goal? Why aren't these commands burdensome to the believer?** *God's commands describe what it looks like to love God and others to His glory. The commands describe what it means to glorify God. Abiding by these commands is not burdensome, because even though Christians may have to endure hardship, their ultimate happiness and flourishing comes from living in accordance with God's good commands.*

**How is the biblical worldview different from karma?** *Karma teaches that people receive good from the good things they do and bad from the bad things they do. But the Bible's teachings are far more realistic with the complexities of this world. Righteous people suffer and bad people prosper—for a time. The Bible also offers grace and forgiveness from a forbearing God toward a rebellious humanity. At the same time, the Bible does teach about sowing and reaping and provides general principles that lead to good when followed or ill when ignored, because of how God designed the world to work.*

## THE ENDS FOR WHICH BELIEVERS LIVE

Use a **journaling** activity to prompt students to expand on what it means to live according to a God-given end.

Choose one end for which believers live (see the textbox on page 140) and write two paragraphs about how that end should be directing your life in concrete ways.

## COMPONENTS OF AN ETHICAL METHOD: AGENTS

Use a **Turn and Talk** activity to prompt students to explain this component to each other.

**How should a Christian's character be shaped and evaluated?** *It should be shaped by a love for biblical truth and evaluated by one's ultimate purpose to glorify God and to carry out the Great Commission.*

**What is the importance of the component of agents?** *The component of agents emphasizes that a person cannot rightly follow God's commands apart from the inward transformation of character. One's character must be transformed to respect and obey commands or to humbly recognize one's need due to falling short of obeying them. A person must be virtuous to obey and apply commands for the right reasons.*

**Why does ethical decision-making often have little to do with one's understanding?** *It has more to do with one's desires and willingness to do the right thing. Depraved people do not have the power or the will within themselves to do what's right even when they know what the right thing is. They need an inward transformation and the grace of God toward others who fall short.*

### The Ends for Which Believers Live

Why do believers do what they do? The Bible identifies many ends for which believers live:

- to be conformed to God's image (Gen. 1:26–28)
- to rule over creation under God's greater rule (Gen. 1:26–28)
- to delight in God's law (Ps. 1:1–3)
- to fear God (Prov. 1:7)
- to trust in God with all their hearts and to know Him in all their ways (Prov. 3:5–6)
- to be blessed or to flourish (Ps. 1:1; Matt. 5:3–12)
- to walk worthy of God and do good works that glorify the Father (Matt. 5:16; Col. 1:9–12)
- to seek first God's kingdom and righteousness and to enter that kingdom (Matt. 5:20; 6:33)
- to be conformed to the Son's image for the Son's glory (Rom. 8:29)
- to be holy, blameless, pure, and righteous so that God receives glory (Eph. 1:4; Phil. 1:9–11)
- to be mature in Christ (Col. 1:28–29)
- to attain the Sabbath rest (Heb. 3–4).

All these ends can be summed up as the ultimate goal or "chief end . . . to glorify God, and to enjoy him for ever."[2]

Therefore, believers should consider the consequences of their actions (Gal. 6:7). You can only push so hard against God's norms, God's wise design, before the consequences become devastating (Prov. 1:20–33; 26:27). Although God is patient with rebellious mankind (Gen. 8:21–22; 2 Pet. 3:3–9), in the end His blessing or His judgment will be brought to bear on people's actions (Rom. 12:19; 2 Pet. 3:10–11; Rev. 20:13). The biblical worldview does allow for the suffering of the righteous and the temporary flourishing of evil people in a fallen world (Job 1:1, 8; 42:7; Ps. 73:2–14). And the Bible's teaching on grace and forgiveness (Ps. 103:10) differentiates the biblical worldview from the simplistic and fatalistic idea of karma. Nevertheless, the general principles found in the book of Proverbs hold true. Behaving a certain way does lead, in general, to good or ill because God's world generally works a certain way by His wise design and blessing.

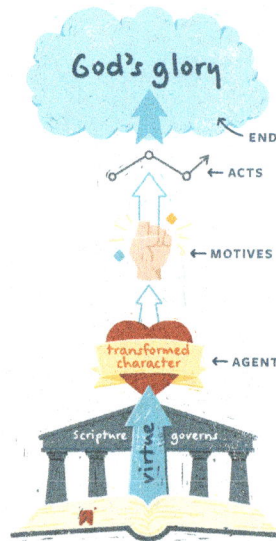

### AGENTS: WHAT'S THE MOTIVE?

This component of a Christian ethical method must correspond to virtue ethics, which focuses on the person or agent (see Sections 2.2 and 2.3). However, unbiblical approaches to virtue ethics misdefine virtue or pass off vice as virtue. Or they misapply virtue, making it fit an agenda that is at odds with the biblical ethic. (And then there is the existentialist approach, which knows *only* the agent, divorced from any virtue besides what the agent wishes to become.)

Christians' motives and virtuous characters must be governed by biblical standards (God's commands, best understood within the larger Creation, Fall, Redemption metanarrative of Scripture). And Christians' motives and virtuous characters must be evaluated in light of their ultimate purpose (to glorify and enjoy God) and mission (to carry out the Great Commission).

When biblically defined and understood, the character and motives of the agent acting to accomplish an end undergird everything else in ethics. Virtuous character is foundational to carrying out God's commands to His glory. How could God's commands be rightly followed by a person whose inward character has not been transformed? Commands mean nothing to the person who disdains authority and presumes he or she can escape consequences. On the other hand, people who imagine themselves to be inherently good can make a good show of following commands, but for all the wrong reasons. People's character determines the effectiveness of commands. More than a few countries have good laws written on paper, but the general character of the politicians and the people makes those laws next to meaningless (or by application turns the intent of those laws on its head).

God's glory
END
ACTS
MOTIVES
transformed character
AGENT
Scripture
virtue
governs

*To act ethically is not merely to do the right thing; it is to be the right kind of person doing the right thing for the right reasons.*

Ethical decision-making may relate to hard-to-solve issues. But often the issue isn't difficult to understand. Depraved people are unwilling to do the right thing. The problem isn't with their intellects but with their wills and desires. Sometimes people try to do the right thing, but they have no power to do the right thing for the right reasons and no grace toward others who fall short. They become unforgiving, perfectionistic legalists with no mercy (James 2:12–13; 4:11–12). Virtuous character and motives are vital to carrying out God's commands to His glory.

### CONTEXT: WHAT'S THE SITUATION?

The three main components—acts, ends, and agents—must all be applied to a specific ethical situation. Context is the additional element to making an ethical decision. What is the ethical issue that demands ethical decision-making? The importance of fully understanding the situation is best stated in Proverbs 18:13: "He that answereth a matter before he heareth it, it is folly and shame unto him." You must have an accurate understanding of all the factors to rightly apply God's Word and to rightly discern the proper motives and goals.

In Chapters 9–13, each section will raise an ethical difficulty (an issue or scenario). Then each section will direct you to consider the Bible's teaching on how one ought to *act*. Each section will direct you to consider the *end* consequences to an individual or a society that does or does not conform to the biblical standard. And each section will direct you to consider the virtues and vices that motivate an *agent's* (a person's or society's) response. Because we live in a world that is full of sinful responses (both your own and others' responses that affect you), each section will conclude with how to biblically respond to troubling situations you may find yourself in.

*Because of their character, persons (agents) apply norms (acts) to situations (context) for reasons (ends).*

The Bible provides the help we need to situate acts, ends, and agents in a context. The Bible isn't a dry book of rules disconnected from real-life situations. The Bible is full of narratives and parables that illustrate what is and what is not acceptable behavior in various situations. Our situation may not be identical to a situation we find in the Bible, but there are bountiful situations that we can draw analogies from in order to find guidance for our own current situation. Soaking yourself in the Word of God, from the Old Testament narratives to the New Testament imperatives, will equip you for ethical behavior (2 Tim. 3:16–17; 2 Pet. 1:3).

### CONCLUSION

All the components must work together. Magnuson summarizes the necessity and usefulness of all the components by saying the following:

> The nature and character of God (corresponding to virtue ethics) is the source from which God's commands are given (corresponding to a form of deontology), and God's purposes or ends (corresponding to teleology) flow from his character and are indicated by his commands. Likewise, a person's character (virtue ethics) provides the foundation for keeping God's commands (deontology), which work together to fulfill the purposes for which human beings are created (teleology).[3]



## AN ADDITIONAL ELEMENT: CONTEXT

Use a **group activity** in order to prompt students to explain the importance of this element.

Use the following examples to prepare the students for writing their own scenarios.

- Was it just for the Americans to fight the Mexican-American War? The answer depends on how one understands the situation. Were the Americans attacked on American territory? Did the Americans provoke the war by moving militarily into disputed territory? Or did President Polk provoke the war by sending American troops into Mexican territory? The differing understandings of the situation by Mexicans, Whigs, and Democrats led to different understandings among Mexicans and Americans regarding the justness of the war.
- Is it ever right to use certain drugs that can be (1) used as part of a chemical abortion or (2) used to deliver a stillborn baby who already died in the womb. The situation—whether the baby was already dead of natural causes or whether the drugs were used as part of an abortion to kill a living unborn child—has a bearing on whether the use of those drugs is ethical.

Then have each group choose one of the following to write and reflect on.

- Write a scenario in which a person makes a decision because he or she misjudged another person's motives in a situation. Reflect on the importance of fully understanding a situation before jumping to a conclusion.
- Write a scenario in which a person makes a decision because he or she misjudged the ultimate goals in a situation. Reflect on the importance of fully understanding a situation before jumping to a conclusion.
- Write a scenario in which a person makes a decision because he or she failed to hear all the factors and facts in a situation. Reflect on the importance of fully understanding a situation before jumping to a conclusion.

## EVERY COMPONENT IS ESSENTIAL

Guide a **discussion** to prompt students to explain and exemplify the essential nature of each ethical component.

**What is the problem with an ethic that focuses on acts detached from agents or ends (in context)?** *Obeying God's commands without a virtuous character is not acceptable in the eyes of God (Matt. 23:5).*

**What is the problem with an ethic that focuses on agents detached from acts or ends (in context)?** *Otherwise virtuous people may still fall into sin and be judged (Acts 13:22 with 2 Sam. 11).*

**What is the problem with an ethic that focuses on ends detached from acts or agents (in context)?** *Good intentions or goals do not justify violating God's commands (2 Sam. 6:1–7).*

## SPOTTING THE MISSING ETHICAL COMPONENTS

Use a **Quick Write** to assess student answers to the textbox on page 142.

Example 1: This example considers only the deontological (or acts) component while ignoring the situation, ends, and virtue (agents).

Example 2: This example considers only a kind of virtue detached from the biblical norms (acts) and ends. The virtue ends up being turned on its head.

Example 3: This example considers only the ends one wants regardless of the means according to the rules (acts) or virtuous character (agents).

Example 4: This example fails to evaluate acts, agents, and ends in light of the context or situation.

## Apply

### MAKING ETHICAL DECISIONS

Use **Activity 8.1** on page 47 to apply the information in the section.

## Assess

Guide a **summative assessment** by directing students to answer the questions in Thinking It Through 8.1.

### Thinking It Through 8.1

1. Acts refers to evaluating one's actions according to the standards of God's Word and creational norms, which reflect God's character and which provide the absolute principles that do not change culturally and that all people in all times and all places must conform their lives to.
2. Ends refers to evaluating one's purposes or goals according to glorifying God by loving Him and others in conformity to His commands. This provides the higher purpose for which a person strives to obey despite difficulties.
3. Agents refers to developing inward character according to biblically defined and applied virtues. Being the right kind of person, transformed by the Spirit, provides the power or foundation for obeying God's commands.
4. You must have an accurate understanding of all the factors in a situation to rightly apply God's Word and to rightly discern the proper motives and goals.
5. The faulty ethical approaches all emphasize one or two components to the neglect of another, and this can lead to extremes. The biblical ethic upholds the necessity of bringing together meeting God's standard according to the right goal with right motives in all of life. The Bible critiques those who have the right motive but disobey God's commands, and it also critiques those who do the right thing but for the wrong reasons or motives.

**Spotting the Missing Ethical Components**

Which components (or element) are missing in the ethical advice or evaluation in each of the following examples?

**Example 1:** "Just do your duty."

**Example 2:** "Don't judge other people. Love wins."

**Example 3:** "I know they played dirty. But they found a way to win."

**Example 4:** "No need to hear the other side. It's obvious who's wrong here."

The faulty ethical systems overviewed and critiqued in Chapter 2 were all deficient because humans tend toward one emphasis to the neglect of others. Even if they do stumble on one aspect of the truth, people tend to misuse the truth they do have by ignoring or minimizing other truths. A Christian should seek to avoid extremes by pulling all the components together.

Good intentions or goals don't justify violating God's commands (1 Sam. 15:22–23; 2 Sam. 6:1–8; Exod. 25:14). Carrying out God's commands as He has instructed is all-important (Num. 26:61; Mal. 1:6–8). And obeying God's commands with the wrong motives is not acceptable in the eyes of God (Isa. 1:11–18). A biblical ethic requires meeting God's standards to achieve the right goals with right motives—in all of life.

#### Thinking It Through 8.1

1. Explain the component labeled *acts* in a Christian ethical method.
2. Explain the component labeled *ends* in a Christian ethical method.
3. Explain the component labeled *agents* in a Christian ethical method.
4. Explain why one must understand the context of a given situation in order to properly apply the three components of a Christian ethical method.
5. Explain why acts, ends, and agents must all work together.

### 8.2 Using a Sound Ethical Method

Imagine having practiced particular skills to prepare for a big performance or a big game. Your teacher or coach assures you that you are ready. You know what you need to do, and you know how to do it. You've demonstrated it in practice. But the day arrives, and you're so nervous you're not sure you can follow through. But you finally muster up the courage and step up to the task.

How did you do? Maybe you performed well. Maybe you didn't. That's all right. That just means you get up, dust off, practice more, grow your skills, and try again. Eventually, with more dedicated effort, you are ready for the next big performance. That middle school student who forgot all his or her lines at the fine arts competition can be that high schooler who places several years later.

At this point in the year, you're ready to begin practicing the use of a sound ethical method. You'll continue to practice this method repeatedly in Chapters 9–13. And yes, you'll be tested. But the real test comes in life outside the classroom. You'll need to seek wisdom from above through prayer to put into practice what you've learned. And hopefully you'll grow into a leader who can influence others to live ethically in your church, family, workplace, and society. Today you are preparing yourself for your future—both your near and distant future.

142 ISSUES

## 8.2 Using a Sound Ethical Method

*What questions should I ask to make an ethical decision?*

### Objectives

**8.2.1** Outline a practical method for ethical decision-making.

**8.2.2** Relate the steps of a sound ethical method to the essential components.

**8.2.3** Formulate responses to various scenarios in which lost money is found.

### Printed Resource

- Activity 8.2: Using an Ethical Method: Test Cases

### Suggested Reading

- See Section 8.1.

## What questions should I ask to make an ethical decision?

### A PRACTICAL METHOD FOR ETHICAL DECISION-MAKING

In the last section, you overviewed the basic components of a biblically sound ethical method. Now it's time to put that method into use. One way to make it more useful is to boil everything down to a few basic questions to ask every time you need to make an ethical decision:[4]

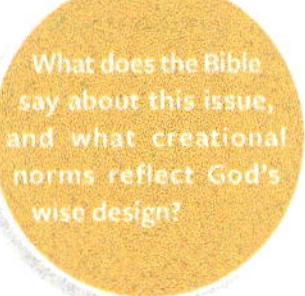


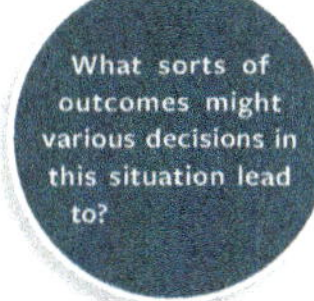


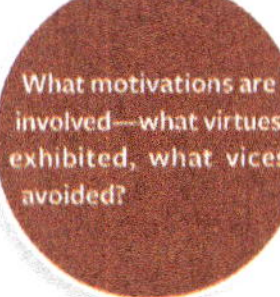


The first question relates to the situation that raises an issue. The second question relates to the standard for one's actions. The third question relates to the ends or goals being aimed at. The fourth question relates to the agents involved—their character and motives. Persons (agents) apply norms (acts) to situations (context) to achieve goals (ends). Those four basic questions encompass all that is involved in ethical decision-making.

Those questions are very general. But they break things down so you can focus on one thing at a time. They'll get you started, pointed in the right direction. They're also ordered in a way that will help guide your investigation down the right path. Then you can start filling in the details and asking more specific questions.

For example, once you ask the four major questions, you can start digging into more specifics:

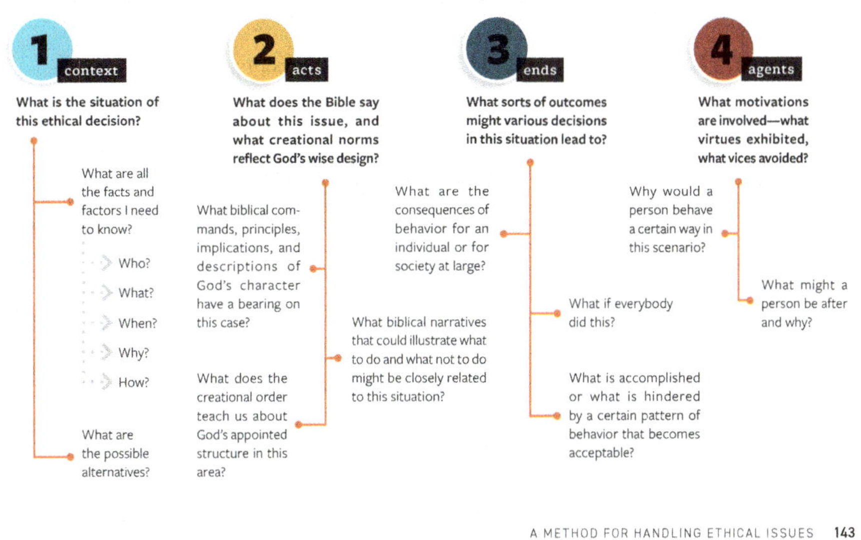

1 context
What is the situation of this ethical decision?
What are all the facts and factors I need to know?
Who?
What?
When?
Why?
How?
What are the possible alternatives?
2 acts
What does the Bible say about this issue, and what creational norms reflect God's wise design?
What biblical commands, principles, implications, and descriptions of God's character have a bearing on this case?
What does the creational order teach us about God's appointed structure in this area?
What biblical narratives that could illustrate what to do and what not to do might be closely related to this situation?
3 ends
What sorts of outcomes might various decisions in this situation lead to?
What are the consequences of behavior for an individual or for society at large?
What if everybody did this?
What is accomplished or what is hindered by a certain pattern of behavior that becomes acceptable?
4 agents
What motivations are involved—what virtues exhibited, what vices avoided?
Why would a person behave a certain way in this scenario?
What might a person be after and why?




## Engage

### PRACTICING A SKILL

Invite students to **demonstrate** skills that they have honed over the years. Prompt them to discuss the beginning stages for learning their skill and how they honed the skill over time.

**How difficult was it when you first started learning your skill? How much practice was required to hone your skill?**

Learning Christian ethics is like learning a skill; it takes time and effort. However, Christian growth also involves relying on empowerment by the Holy Spirit, not mere diligence in practicing a skill.

## Instruct

### A METHOD FOR MAKING PRACTICAL ETHICAL DECISIONS

Use a **Quick Write** to prompt students to write down the four major questions and compose additional helpful questions.

**What four questions encompass all that is involved in ethical decision-making?**

- *Context: What is the context of this ethical decision?*
- *Acts: What does the Bible say about this issue, and what creational norms reflect God's wise design?*
- *Ends: What sorts of outcomes might various decisions in this situation lead to?*
- *Agents: What motivations are involved—what virtues exhibited; what vices avoided?*

**What further questions might you ask under each of the four main categories to help you make informed ethical decisions?** *On page 143 are some examples of asking more detailed questions, but the questions need not be limited to what's in the textbook.*

### USING A SOUND ETHICAL METHOD

Use **Activity 8.2** on page 49 to apply the information in the section. Have students discuss their test cases with a classmate or with the entire class.

## Apply

### AN ETHICAL METHOD: A TEST CASE

Prompt **student reflections** to assess their understanding of making use of the practical method.

Write down one question and one comment about the test case on page 144.

Write down one alternative scenario related to any ethical issue for your classmates to reflect on.

Example: Your friends are showing you how to get social media accounts that you can hide from your parents. They insist that they aren't saying or doing anything wrong on that social media; they just want some privacy. How should you respond?

### APPLYING A BIBLICAL ETHIC

Use a **Quick Write** to provide an opportunity for the students to apply the biblical ethic to finding a lost wallet.

Suppose you are leaving the store, and as you are walking to your car you notice a wallet on the ground. Inside the wallet is the owner's driver's license, credit cards, and some cash.

**What should you do in this situation? Should you keep the wallet and tell yourself "Finders, keepers"? Should you turn the wallet in to the store manager? Or should you mail the wallet to the owner?** *Students should give their honest answers to the questions.*

The Bible supports restoring to the one you took from when you are guilty of having taken something that did not belong to you—even if some time has lapsed (Exod. 22:1). Zacchaeus is a prime example. He was the one who stole, and he returned it to the people from whom he stole (Luke 19:8).

You could probably think of a few more questions to ask under each step. And once a topic or issue is specifically identified, then your questions and research can become even more specific.

#### A TEST CASE

Are you ready to practice with a test case? As you're walking across the parking lot to school one day, you notice a wallet on the ground. Should you walk past it or pick it up? If you pick it up, should you look inside? If you find money and an ID in it, should you turn it in? To whom should you turn it in? What if there's no ID?

Let's change the scenario a little bit. As you're walking across the parking lot to the grocery store one day, you notice a ten-dollar bill near the gutter. Should you walk past it or pick it up? If you pick it up, should you pocket it or turn it in? To whom should you turn it in? How do you know that person won't just pocket it? Do you have a responsibility for what that person might do with it?

What if it were a hundred-dollar bill? What if it were more money than that? How much money would it have to be to turn it in? What if it were only a penny or a quarter? Could you just pocket it then? Why?

Before reading any more, use the four basic questions to help you make an ethical decision and discuss it. Then you can read some of the suggested answers below.

#### ANSWERING THE TEST CASE

***The Basic Scenario***

Let's think through the differences in the scenarios that might factor into different responses. Does your responsibility heighten when you can find an ID? Certainly. And does your responsibility heighten when you have a trustworthy authority at your school (who also has accountability to other staff members) to whom you can turn in that wallet? Absolutely. You have no excuse.

The Bible is clear on this matter (Exod. 20:15; 23:4; Deut. 22:1–4; Eph. 4:28). You certainly should pick up the wallet and return it to its owner or turn it in to the school office. There's no question that stealing is wrong. And there's no question that you would be stealing if you kept the wallet or took anything from the wallet before turning it in.

Even many unsaved people know in their consciences that taking something that doesn't belong to them and that someone else worked hard for is just plain wrong. They know that society as a whole is better off with honest people who do unto others as they would like others to do unto them (a creational norm and a biblical principle they borrow from a Christian worldview). Nevertheless, people's greed can cause them to do what they know is wrong (1 Tim. 6:9–10).

Additionally, there's no need to leave the wallet there in the parking lot, tempting someone else to do the wrong thing. (In fact, simply bypassing the lost item is probably not a biblical option [Deut. 22:1–3].) You may choose not to open the wallet to look inside, thus avoiding a temptation to swipe any money. You could look for an ID in the presence of the staff when you bring it in to the office, or you could let the school office staff look for the ID themselves after you turn it in to them.

Before moving on to the alternative scenarios, can you locate the four basic questions that are being answered in the above paragraphs? The first and last paragraphs are analyzing factors in the context (the first question). The second paragraph is stating what the Bible clearly says about stealing (the second question). The third paragraph is analyzing the consequences to society (the third question) and the motives of people (the fourth question). All these components fit naturally into thinking through all the factors in an ethical issue.

**NEW EVALUATING CONTEMPORARY EVENTS**

Can you find a news story involving the return of lost money or property? What took place? How did people respond? What explanations were given for why people responded the ways they did? Evaluate what took place and why. Can you spot some or all of the ethical components?

***The Scenario with Changed Factors***

Now let us consider the scenario with some of the factors changed. The buying power of an amount of money would probably determine the value lost money had to the person who lost it—which would determine the likelihood of the person returning to look for that lost money. And a person who lost any significant amount of money would expect that an honest person would seek to return that money. If someone lost just ten dollars, that amount of money has enough buying power for some small items. And an honest person would seek to locate the owner. (If you get excited over finding some money because you know it would give you buying power, then that's a clue that you should probably turn the money in so the owner can get the money back.)

However, few people would be distressed enough over one lost penny or quarter (or a handful of pocket change) to search a random grocery store parking lot. And turning a few coins in to the store manager would likely be nothing more than a contribution to that store (or to that individual) rather than a return of the coins to the person who dropped them. Someone's conscience could be constrained to turn in every penny found, based on an absolute commitment to a biblical principle not to steal. And people shouldn't violate their consciences (Rom. 14:23). Nevertheless, a God-fearing Christian could argue that the biblical principle (the letter of the law) was being pushed to the limits by the person who turned in pennies—without consideration of the context, motive, and ends. (And Deuteronomy 22:1–4 recognizes something must be of enough value that a person would come looking for it.) A rightly formed conscience should take into consideration all those elements when seeking to fulfill the spirit or purpose of God's law.

Let's say you found $100 (or more) near the gutter in a grocery store parking lot. You know it is likely that the person who lost it would want it back. But you didn't find the money in a wallet with an ID. How would you locate the person? And what if the store clerk or even the manager would be likely to pocket the money? Do these concerns justify you pocketing the money rather than turning it in? No! You have an obligation to show good faith* by trying to locate the proper authority, seeking to make sure that authority itself will be accountable, and giving an opportunity to the person who lost the money to locate it. Depending on the amount of money, this might require a police report and then communication to the community to inform them that money has been found. Then that person would have to provide some explanation or knowledge (for example, the exact amount and in what bills) of the items lost to prove ownership.

Sometimes honest people have been rewarded by the person who was able to recover a lost item(s). And sometimes when a large amount of money is never claimed after months of concerted effort by the authorities, the honest person gets to keep the money. But with or without hope for a gracious reward (which you're not entitled to), you should want to do the right thing in order to love others, obey the Lord, and be a good testimony to God's glory.

The conclusion of the matter is that you should always make a good faith effort to return lost items of value to their owner or an accountable authority. Some discernment may be required for items that have little to no intrinsic value. The context may determine what you do. Finding a quarter in a random parking lot is different from finding a quarter in the chair that your five-year-old sibling just sat in while counting piggy bank money. You have an obligation to give the money back since it has value (buying power) to your sibling and since you have enough contextual information to know who it likely belongs to and how to give it back.

Circumstances like these will reveal your character, motives, goals, and commitment to God and His Word. The issues in the coming chapters will challenge you to evaluate all these components as you make more and more ethical decisions.

**GRAPPLING WITH ETHICAL ISSUES**

What if you realize that, in the distant past, you're guilty of having taken something that did not belong to you and that you should have returned it or turned it in? What are your obligations? What if an ancestor stole something in the distant past? What are your obligations?

**Thinking It Through 8.2**

1. List the four basic questions you should ask yourself in ethical decision-making.
2. Match the three ethical components and the additional element to the four questions.
3. Practice using the ethical method you've learned in this chapter by explaining the appropriate response to a friend who wants to gossip about a classmate who has been annoying you.

**good faith:** a sincere intent to do the right thing, be honest, fulfill commitments, or carry out legal obligations



## Assess

Guide a **summative assessment** by directing students to answer the questions in Thinking It Through 8.2.

### Thinking It Through 8.2

**1.** (a) What is the context of this ethical decision?

(b) What does the Bible say about this issue, and what creational norms reflect God's wise design?

(c) What sort of outcomes may this issue or ethical decision lead to?

(d) What motivations are involved—what virtues exhibited, and what vices avoided?

**2.** Corresponding with the above answers:

(a) situation

(b) acts

(c) ends

(d) agents

**3.** Answers will vary.

First, the situation is that some kind of tension already exists and that my friend might reveal some private matter to me that I could possibly use against the other classmate. I must resist the temptation to give in to a situation that is ripe for taking revenge (Matt. 5:38–39).

Second, the Bible clearly opposes gossip and slander (Prov. 16:28; Eph. 4:31). I must resist engaging in gossip and slander.

Third, the end goal of gossip and slander is to hurt another person. But I must love others, wishing for God to transform even evil hearts of enemies that seek to do me harm (Rom. 12:17–19).

Fourth, my character will be revealed by my actions and the ends I pursue: whether I'm characterized by love, patience, humility, meekness, gentleness, and kindness or strife, pride, anger, harshness, and animosity.

The appropriate response is to refuse to listen to a friend who wants to gossip and to allow God to righteously judge or transform someone at odds against you. This does not mean a person cannot properly appeal to authorities to righteously deal with that other person or that a person cannot defend oneself against an enemy. But it does rule out taking revenge on someone—including listening to and spreading gossip. Only people who have a legitimate right to know and authorities who are a part of the solution should be involved in this kind of situation.

# Chapter 8 Review

## Understanding Ethics

1. acts, ends, agents; context
2. Acts refers to the standard one's actions ought to meet up to. Ends refers to the goals one ought to aim to achieve. Agents refers to the motives or character one ought to have. The context refers to the situation that raises an ethical issue in which these three components must be considered.
3. (a) What is the context of this ethical decision? (situation)

   (b) What does the Bible say about this issue, and what creational norms reflect God's wise design? (acts)

   (c) What sort of outcomes may this issue or ethical decision lead to? (ends)

   (d) What motivations are involved—what virtues exhibited, and what vices avoided? (agents)
4. The faulty ethical approaches all emphasize one or two components to the neglect of another, and this can lead to extremes. The biblical ethic upholds the necessity of bringing together meeting God's standard according to the right goal with right motives in all of life. The Bible critiques those who have the right motive but disobey God's commands, and it also critiques those who do the right thing but for the wrong reasons or motives.

## Practicing Ethical Decision-Making

5. Answers should include that if the objectional elements are explicit enough, gratuitous, and pervasive (situation), then a Christian should conform to the Bible's own moral tone and principles (acts) by loving God and desiring to please Him (agents) above being entertained by things that desensitize the culture to wickedness (ends).
6. Answers will vary. Regardless of the consequences of persecution to oneself (ends), a Christian should come to the defense of a fellow believer to defend his or her righteous confrontation (acts) of the unfruitful works of darkness (situation), hoping that God will reach the hearts (agents) of those who are "simple" following after scorners (ends).

### Scripture Memory

Psalm 119:97, 101–4

### Understanding Ethics

1. Identify the three components of a Christian ethical method. Identify one additional element that must be considered alongside those components.
2. Explain the meaning of each of the components and the additional element.
3. List the four main questions you should ask yourself in ethical decision-making, matching the ethical components and the additional element to the appropriate questions.
4. Why must all three components work together in the evaluation of every ethical matter?

### Practicing Ethical Decision-Making

5. Practice using the ethical method you've learned in this chapter by evaluating whether Christians should consume movies full of gratuitous and explicit objectional elements.
6. Practice using the ethical method you've learned in this chapter by explaining the appropriate response to classmates bullying or deriding another classmate for speaking up for what's right.

### Analyzing and Evaluating Ethical Claims

7. How would you respond to someone who persists in the deontological approach, denying the need to consider ends, virtues, and context? In other words, this person only cares about absolute, universal principles (what a person does)—not goals and results or personal character and motives (why and how a person acts) or careful consideration of specific circumstances.
8. How would you respond to someone who persists in the teleological approach, denying the need to consider moral rules and virtues?
9. How would you respond to someone who practices virtue ethics while denying the need to consider moral rules, ends, and context?

### Creating My Own Position Statements on Ethics

10. Defend the ethical method presented in the chapter.

146 ISSUES

## Analyzing and Evaluating Ethical Claims

7. Answers should include that the Christian should use questions and illustrations or examples to point out the ethical need to consider other factors like motives, character, consequences in society, and ultimate ends in a specific situational context.
8. Answers should include that the Christian should use questions and illustrations or examples to point out the ethical need to consider other factors like universal principles or standards, motives, and character.
9. Answers should include that the Christian should use questions and illustrations or examples to point out the ethical need to consider other factors like universal principles or standards, consequences in society, and ultimate ends in a specific situational context.

## Creating My Own Position Statements on Ethics

10. Answers will vary. Students should be able to provide biblical support for (1) the Bible being the only authoritative and sufficient standard for universal principles as well as the necessity of resting on its revelation for their ethic; (2) the importance of a God-directed ultimate end for all that they do, as well as the necessity of love for one's neighbor, including the appropriate flourishing of society as defined by God; and (3) the importance of a person's character, driven by right motives.

    All the other major ethical systems leave out one of the key factors or emphasize a factor to the neglect of another factor.

# Lesson Plan Overview

**CHAPTER 9:** The Ethics of Life and Death

**EV** ExamView
**PPT pres.** PowerPoint presentation

| PAGES | OBJECTIVES | RESOURCES | ASSESSMENTS |
|---|---|---|---|
| **9.1 Murder, Manslaughter, and Self-Defense** (4 DAYS) | | | |
| 148–54 | **9.1.1** Identify three categories of taking a human life.<br>**9.1.2** Summarize the biblical teaching on the value of human life.<br>BWS Creational Order (explain)<br>**9.1.3** Analyze the societal consequences of unbiblical views regarding murder, manslaughter, and self-defense.<br>BWS Man's Chief End (evaluate)<br>**9.1.4** Assess the virtues necessary to act ethically regarding murder, manslaughter, and self-defense.<br>BWS Virtue (formulate)<br>**9.1.5** Formulate a biblical response to scenarios in which various kinds of killing have taken place. | **ACTIVITIES**<br>• 9.1 Unethical Killing<br>**BJU PRESS TROVE***<br>• Video: "Murder, Manslaughter, and Self-Defense"<br>• PPT pres.: Chapter 9 | **STUDENT EDITION**<br>• Thinking It Through 9.1 |
| **9.2 Suicide and Euthanasia** (4 DAYS) | | | |
| 154–59 | **9.2.1** Explain common justifications for suicide and euthanasia.<br>**9.2.2** Summarize the biblical teaching on God's authority over life and death.<br>BWS Authority (explain)<br>**9.2.3** Analyze the societal consequences of unbiblical views regarding suicide and euthanasia.<br>BWS Man's Chief End (evaluate)<br>**9.2.4** Assess the virtues necessary to act ethically regarding suicide and euthanasia.<br>BWS Virtue (formulate)<br>**9.2.5** Formulate a biblical response to someone who has lost a loved one because of suicide or euthanasia. | **ACTIVITIES**<br>• 9.2 Counsel for Suicide and Euthanasia<br>**BJU PRESS TROVE**<br>• Video: "Suicide and Euthanasia"<br>• PPT pres.: Chapter 9 | **STUDENT EDITION**<br>• Thinking It Through 9.2 |
| **9.3 Abortion** (4 DAYS) | | | |
| 159–64 | **9.3.1** Explain common justifications for abortion.<br>**9.3.2** Defend the sanctity of human life from conception.<br>BWS Creational Order (formulate)<br>**9.3.3** Analyze the personal and societal consequences of unbiblical views regarding abortion.<br>**9.3.4** Assess the virtues necessary to act ethically regarding abortion.<br>BWS Virtue (formulate)<br>**9.3.5** Formulate a biblical response to someone who is considering an abortion or to someone who has already had one.<br>BWS Wisdom (apply) | **ACTIVITIES**<br>• 9.3 About Abortion<br>**BJU PRESS TROVE**<br>• Video: "Abortion"<br>• PPT pres.: Chapter 9 | **STUDENT EDITION**<br>• Thinking It Through 9.3 |

*Digital resources for homeschool users are available on Homeschool Hub.

| PAGES | OBJECTIVES | RESOURCES | ASSESSMENTS |
|---|---|---|---|
| **Review** | | | |
| 165 | Recall concepts, terms, and Scripture memory from Chapter 9. | | **STUDENT EDITION**<br>• Chapter 9 Review |
| **Test** | | | |
| | Demonstrate knowledge of the material from Chapter 9 by taking the test. | | **ASSESSMENTS**<br>• Chapter 9 Test<br>**BJU PRESS TROVE**<br>• EV: Chapter 9 test bank |

CHAPTER 9

# Overview

What is a human life worth?

## Objectives

**9.1** Evaluate various courses of action involving life and death, using a biblical ethic.

**9.2** Apply a sound ethical method to make decisions on issues of life and death.

## Terms to Remember

- murder
- first-degree murder
- second-degree murder
- manslaughter
- voluntary manslaughter
- involuntary manslaughter
- self-defense
- suicide
- euthanasia
- abortion

## Scripture Memory

- Exodus 20:13; Matthew 5:21–22

# 9.1 Murder, Manslaughter, and Self-Defense

*Is it ever right to take a human life?*

## Objectives

**9.1.1** Identify three categories of taking a human life.

**9.1.2** Summarize the biblical teaching on the value of human life. BWS

**9.1.3** Analyze the societal consequences of unbiblical views regarding murder, manslaughter, and self-defense. BWS

**9.1.4** Assess the virtues necessary to act ethically regarding murder, manslaughter, and self-defense. BWS

**9.1.5** Formulate a biblical response to scenarios in which various kinds of killing have taken place.

## Biblical Worldview Shaping

- **Creational Order** (explain): The image of God in man grounds the prohibition of murder and manslaughter and the permission for self-defense. (9.1.2)
- **Man's Chief End** (evaluate): Societies which place a low value on the life of God's image-bearers deprive God of the honor He deserves. (9.1.3)
- **Virtue** (formulate): An ethical person will be diligent about safety, courageous about defending others, prudent about when to use deadly force, self-controlled in tense situations, and willing to suffer wrong in order to preserve life (meek). (9.1.4)

## Printed Resource

- Activity 9.1: Unethical Killing

## Digital Resource

- Video: "Murder, Manslaughter, and Self-Defense"

## Suggested Reading

- Frame, John M. *The Doctrine of the Christian Life*. Phillipsburg, NJ: P&R Publishing, 2008. Pages 684–93, 717–45.
- Grudem, Wayne. *Christian Ethics: An Introduction to Biblical Moral Reasoning*. Wheaton, IL: Crossway, 2018. Pages 551–65.

*Ultimately, our chief end must be to glorify God. And we do that when we value His image-bearers.*

## 9.1 Murder, Manslaughter, and Self-Defense

The ethics of life and death includes many issues. In this section we will consider murder, manslaughter, and self-defense. Are you ready to use the four basic questions for ethical decision-making?

context 1 What is the situation requiring an ethical decision?

acts 2 What does the Bible say about this issue?

ends 3 What sorts of outcomes might various decisions in this situation lead to?

agents 4 What motivations are involved—what virtues exhibited; what vices avoided?

### YOU BE THE JURY context

The context you're in includes a basic understanding of the laws in the jurisdiction where you live. Context also includes the details of what was done by whom as well as why and how it took place.

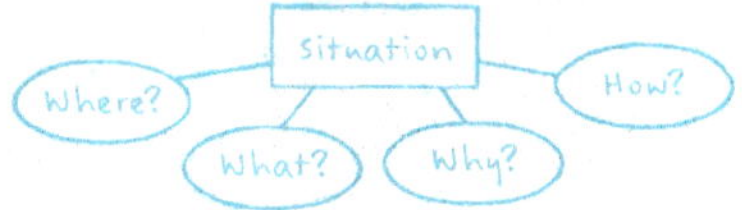


Consider some basic definitions. According to the *United States Code*, "**Murder** is the unlawful killing of a human being with malice aforethought."[1] More specifically, a charge of **first-degree murder** is usually reserved for premeditated murder or murder committed alongside another serious crime. First-degree murder is punished by the death penalty or life imprisonment. **Second-degree murder** covers any murder



## Engage

### MURDER, MANSLAUGHTER, AND SELF-DEFENSE

Show the **video** "Murder, Manslaughter, and Self-Defense" to introduce the subject to students.

that doesn't fit the definition of first-degree murder and may be punished by temporary imprisonment or life imprisonment.[2] "**Manslaughter** is the unlawful killing of a human being without malice."[3] It is considered **voluntary manslaughter** when it takes place impulsively in response to a heated exchange or serious provocation, and a person would be subject to a fine and up to fifteen years in prison. It is considered **involuntary manslaughter** when a death results from carelessness or occurs in conjunction with the commission of a minor crime, and a person would be subject to a fine and up to eight years in prison.[4]

**Self-defense** has been described this way: "The right to prevent suffering force or violence through the use of a sufficient level of counteracting force or violence."[5] Sometimes the use of deadly force and the killing of an attacker may be justifiable self-defense (generally when the attacker is using deadly force against the defender). Different US states have different philosophies for self-defense, such as a duty to retreat, the right to stand your ground, or the castle doctrine. If the circumstances of an event are deemed to fit the state's definition and philosophy of self-defense, then a person will not be criminally charged, even if the attacker is killed.[6]

Let's consider several fictional scenarios, imagining that you're on the jury. First, you need to gather the facts. Only then can the law be rightly applied.

**SCENARIO 1:**

A young woman returns to her rural home late at night. As she fumbles with her keys to enter her house, a man sneaks up behind her and points a gun at her. He starts to drag her off the porch toward his car. In the process, she begins to fight back. In the scuffle, the man pistol-whips her in the face; she falls backward off the porch and hits her head on the corner of the cement step, leading to her eventual death.

**SCENARIO 2:**

A high-rise building collapses, killing dozens of people. Soon, the public finds out there was considerable neglect in structural safety. Although inspectors raised questions and identified specific problems, these things were ignored by the owner of the building for many years.

**SCENARIO 3:**

A young man thinks he sees someone snooping around the back alley of a store. He suspects that the person might be the one involved in stealing merchandise since recent news reports had said the store was having problems. He calls out to the person, who bolts. He decides to run after him. When he catches up to the man, they get into a tussle. During the course of the tussle, the young man who chased down the suspected prowler pulls a gun and shoots the man dead.

How would you judge those who caused death in each scenario if you were on the jury? What other facts do you need? What would factor into your decision-making? What principles guide your understanding of each person's guilt or innocence, the significance of his or her actions or inaction? What consequences resulted from the actions or inaction in question—consequences for each person involved, for their families, and for society? What consequences would result from both the jury's verdict and the judge's sentence? What virtues and vices were involved that you would want to promote or punish? Although the perpetrator's intent certainly factors into the level of his or her sentencing, how would you respond to explanations for the criminal activity? What kinds of things, if any, would you consider as lessening his or her responsibility? Is there a difference between criminal guilt and moral responsibility (wisdom) in one or more of these cases?



## YOU BE THE JURY

Use a **group activity** to prompt students to discuss the three scenarios on page 149.

**How would you judge those who caused death in each scenario if you were on the jury?**

**What would factor into your decision-making?**

**What principles guide your understanding of each person's guilt or innocence?**

**What consequences would result from both the jury's verdict and the judge's sentence?**

**Is there a difference between criminal guilt and moral responsibility in one or more of these cases?**

*Answers should reflect the biblical principles discussed in this section.*

## Instruct

### EVALUATING CONTEMPORARY EVENTS

Guide a **current events** activity to help students evaluate current news stories related to life and death issues.

Do an in-class online search of news stories where a human life was taken. Choose one or two that are deemed useful for class discussion. Ask students to identify the facts in the story and to offer their critique.

**Was the taking of human life just or unjust? If it was unjust, did the governing authorities hold the person accountable? What should society do to help prevent similar situations from occurring?** *Answers should reflect the biblical principles discussed in this section.*

### THE BIBLICAL TEACHING ON VALUING HUMAN LIFE

Guide a group **Bible study** to answer this chapter's essential question. Have students gather in groups to analyze the following Bible passages. Then have them create a brief paragraph summarizing their findings.

- Genesis 1:27
- Genesis 4:10–11
- Genesis 9:6
- Exodus 21:14
- Deuteronomy 5:17
- Deuteronomy 22:8
- Psalm 22:9–10
- Psalm 106:38
- Psalm 139:13–16
- Proverbs 6:16–17
- Amos 1:13
- Matthew 5:21–22
- Matthew 6:25–26
- Matthew 15:19
- Luke 1:39–44
- Acts 17:25

### SPECIFIC BIBLICAL PRECEPTS: MURDER AND MANSLAUGHTER

Have students create a **Venn diagram** that reflects the distinctions between murder, killing, and manslaughter—differentiating the biblical principles and US law.

**EVALUATING CONTEMPORARY EVENTS**

Find a recent news story that recounts a murder, manslaughter, or self-defense case that created controversy. Evaluate the ethical reasoning in these discussions. Evaluate the approach of the news media. Evaluate the difference between popular opinions and the formal evaluation of all the evidence in a court case by an informed jury that must uphold definite laws.

God puts His image in every person He creates. Murder and manslaughter are failing to value another person who bears God's image.

*Is it ever right to take a human life?*

Act 2

#### OUR RESPONSIBILITY TO VALUE HUMAN LIFE

What universal principles does the Bible provide regarding murder, manslaughter, and self-defense?

***The General Principle***

The Bible clearly teaches that all humans are made in God's image (Gen. 1:26–27). So we have a responsibility to value the lives of all image-bearers (Gen. 9:6). God demands an accounting for the unauthorized killing of any image-bearer (Exod. 21:12; Lev. 24:17; Num. 35:33). God alone gives life and God alone takes away life (Gen. 2:7; 3:19; Job 1:21; 33:4; Ps. 104:29–30; Acts 17:28).

What the Bible reveals about the sanctity of life for all image-bearers has also been written on the consciences of all humans (Rom. 2:14–15). The created order testifies to the special, intrinsic value of all human beings. Anyone who seeks to downgrade the status of a human being to justify taking a life suppresses the truth (Rom. 1:18) and is bound to commit or condone atrocities.

> *What the sixth commandment basically says is that life and death are God's business. He is Lord of life and death, and we may not take life without his authorization.* JOHN FRAME[1]

***Specific Precepts Regarding Murder and Manslaughter***

The sixth commandment forbids murder and voluntary manslaughter (Exod. 20:13; see also Deut. 5:17). The Hebrew verb used in this commandment is more specific than the English word *kill*. The sixth commandment does not disallow *all* killing, for the Bible itself allows for the killing of plants and animals (Gen. 9:3) and demands capital punishment for a murderer (Gen. 9:6; Num. 35:31). On the other hand, this Hebrew word is also broader than the English usage of the word *murder*. The Bible demands just retribution not only for murder but also for what US law calls *voluntary manslaughter*; the Bible does not necessarily distinguish voluntary manslaughter from murder (Exod. 21:12, 18–19, 22–25). The death penalty may be appropriate in both cases as long as sufficient evidence corroborates what took place (Deut. 17:6).

The Bible does make a distinction between murder and involuntary manslaughter (Exod. 21:13–14). In these cases, the killing is certainly an accident rather than motivated by hatred (Deut. 19:5). But the person is still guilty for failing to take sufficient care to protect the other person's life (Deut. 22:8). The cities of refuge provided a means to escape the death penalty as long as a person remained within that refuge until the death of the high priest (Num. 35:6, 9–34; Deut. 19:1–13). So it was still a crime that demanded the death of another.

The New Testament repeats the intention of the sixth commandment, condemning murder (Rom. 1:29; 1 Tim. 1:9; James 2:11; 4:2; Rev. 21:8). The New Testament clarifies that hatred is murder in its seed form; murder

150 ISSUES

stems from a lack of love (Matt. 5:21–26; see also Gen. 27:41, 45; 49:6). The command not to murder is also a command to love (Rom. 13:9; 1 John 3:14–16). The sixth commandment includes more than a prohibition against unlawfully taking another person's life; it demands that we seek the well-being of others' lives as well. God's people should do all that they reasonably can to preserve life. God's people have an obligation to show great care and concern for the well-being of all image-bearers. And they are to seek reconciliation by settling matters rather than allowing hatred to grow.

#### *Specific Precepts Regarding Self-Defense*

The Bible forbids taking revenge; vengeance belongs to God (Rom. 12:14, 17–21) and to His governing authorities (Rom. 13:1–7). God's people must love their enemies when they experience persecution for their faith or when they encounter personal affronts. Christians are not to respond to insults in kind. They may have to submit to being taken advantage of in some court cases. They are to suffer and to respond by doing good (Matt. 5:38–44; 1 Pet. 3:9). The overall point is that the individual is subject to the rulings of court (even when they are unfair and unjust) and is not allowed to take justice into his or her own hands. This does not mean that you cannot seek justice in the courts (Acts 4:5–22; 5:27–42; 16:37; 25:10–12). It is a prohibition against taking vengeance.

However, if a person faces life endangerment, that person has a stewardship responsibility to preserve his or her own life and the life of other innocent people from the threats of evildoers; Scripture permits the defense of oneself and others (Exod. 22:2–3; Deut. 22:26–27; Prov. 24:11–12). Matthew 5:38–44 prohibits taking revenge. It does not prohibit self-defense. When a person does resort to self-defense, the response must be proportional to the threat. For example, the principle in Exodus 22:2–3 is that if there is a reasonable alternative (an ability to get help during the day) or a clear recognition that the crime is nothing more than thievery, then lethal force is not appropriate. But at night a person has a harder time getting help[8] or discerning thievery versus murderous intentions. In the latter case, a person has a right to self-defense with lethal force out of fear for his or her life.

### SOCIAL CONSEQUENCES WHEN LIFE IS DEVALUED

What are some common unbiblical views of murder, manslaughter, and self-defense? How do these unbiblical views affect society?

Certainly, there are evil people who believe they can get away with murder. They do not value the lives of other image-bearers (Ps. 10:8–11; Prov. 1:11, 18). The more people that are like this in a society (or neighborhood), the more dangerous that place becomes. The Bible requires that those who murder another should face the death penalty. Those who would harbor a fugitive (Prov. 28:17) or pity the murderer, in the sense of failing to give him his due penalty (Deut. 19:13), are acting contrary to Scripture. One purpose of consistently enforcing due retribution is to put fear into others to deter them from committing the same types of crimes (Deut. 19:19–20; Rom. 13:4).

On the other hand, a society may put to death innocent people. Either the death penalty is imposed when insufficient evidence is provided (Deut. 19:15), or the death penalty is used against political and religious enemies (Jer. 26:11, 15). A society that is governed in this unjust way also puts fear into people but for the wrong reasons.

The opposite kind of injustice occurs when a society is too lenient in punishing murder. A society may judge and sentence murder as if it were manslaughter. A society may accept pleas of self-defense in tenuous circumstances. To save time and expense, a society may allow for questionable plea deals in place of achieving true justice. These miscarriages of justice produce angry and discouraged citizens—some of whom may be tempted to take vengeance into their own hands rather than wait on God to set things right in the end.

Other less obvious influences in society may be at play in conforming to or working against biblical principles. Laws and social expectations can influence or incentivize



## SPECIFIC BIBLICAL PRECEPTS: SELF-DEFENSE

Use a **Think-Pair-Share** to prompt students to carefully think through the nuances of self-defense.

**How do revenge and vengeance differ from self-defense?** *Revenge takes place when a person inflicts harm on someone for a wrong done rather than appealing to the legal system for justice. Vengeance is returning evil for evil. Self-defense, on the other hand, is about using force to protect oneself and others from the physical aggression of an attacker.*
**In what situations might it be most appropriate for Christians to embrace persecution rather than find a way to escape it (see Acts 16:37)? Is self-defense ever appropriate in the face of persecution (see 1 Peter 2:23; 3:14; 4:13)?** *Christians can choose to endure persecution for the sake of their witness for Christ when they have no legal means of redress. However, physical resistance to persecution is at odds with the example of Christ and the tenor of the New Testament's instructions regarding how to respond to persecution.*
**How does the situation determine whether a person's claim of self-defense is legitimate or not?** *A person's response must be in proportion to the threat. If the threat is discerned to be less than the lethal response, then one's claim is illegitimate.*
**Why is self-defense a biblically appropriate response to a genuine threat to life?** *Stewarding God-given life, protecting it against whatever undermines the sanctity of that life, would be appropriate—whether protecting others or oneself from the evil intents of those who would make threats against that gift.*

## THE IMPACT ON SOCIETY WHEN LIFE IS DEVALUED

Assign a **writing project** of one to three paragraphs where students describe one of the unbiblical views of murder, manslaughter, and self-defense they've observed in society. Ask students to answer the following questions in their assignment.

**What are the consequences of that wrong view? How should that wrong view be addressed in society?** *Student answers should evaluate the wrong view based on the biblical principles discussed in this section.*

## VIRTUES FOR VALUING LIFE

Use a **Turn and Talk** to prompt students to assess how the virtues play into acting ethically in various situations.

Relate at least one virtue to one scenario presented on page 149. Explain how a person with such virtue may have made a difference in the scenario.

Examples include the following:

- Diligence: In Scenario 2, someone needed to follow up on the inspections more diligently.
- Prudence: Most likely, the deadly encounter in Scenario 3 could have been avoided with more prudence on the part of the young man who pursued the prowler, even if he is very likely not found guilty in a court of law for murder.
- Humility: In Scenario 2, the owner of the high rise should have submitted to the warnings raised by inspectors.

Create at least one more scenario that demonstrates the importance of one of the virtues.

Example: A father notices his son being bullied on the playground and intervenes to stop the bullies. A father of one of the bullies challenges the other father, even going so far as to physically push him and display a gun holstered to his hip. The first father feels tempted to return evil for evil, but he realizes that the situation could escalate, so he chooses instead to respond with meekness, taking his son by the hand and calmly walking off the playground.

a social order toward courageously protecting and defending the innocent from criminal threats. On the other hand, laws and social expectations can lower demands on people to avoid violence, use prudence, and take safety precautions. Both aspects of valuing life (thwarting criminal violence but also trying to prevent needless death) need to be rightly balanced. But societies tend to err in one direction or the other. How would you be able to tell whether a society places a high or low value on the life of God's image-bearers? Be careful in your evaluation. Both hindering self-defense and making it very easy to claim self-defense could work against protecting the high value of an image-bearer.

Do you live in a country that has carefully constructed laws and penalties for murder and manslaughter? Do you live in a country that has carefully crafted laws allowing for appropriate self-defense? How well are those laws enforced, and how are such acts judged in a court of law? Do your country's laws match up well with the biblical principles? Do the populace and its leaders embrace or reject good laws and proper enforcement? If a society embraces good laws and proper enforcement, it will flourish; if not, it will devolve into tyranny and anarchy. If the latter is the kind of culture in which you live, the unrest will make for a volatile atmosphere in your country.

Ultimately, our chief end must be to glorify God. And we do so when we value His image-bearers. Societies that place a low value on people's lives dishonor the God who made those people in His image.

### agents NECESSARY VIRTUES FOR UPHOLDING THE VALUE OF LIFE

What virtues are most relevant to the issues discussed in this section? How do these virtues affect a person's motives? Why does character matter?

An ethical person will be diligent about safety, courageous about defending others, prudent about when to use deadly force, self-controlled in tense situations, and willing to suffer wrong in order to preserve life (meek). Many other virtues may come to mind. But let's focus on three: courage, prudence, and meekness.

Courage is the boldness to stand up to protect something of value, even at personal risk. The courageous person overcomes fear and pain to rise to the occasion. If a terrorist is about to murder someone, we praise the self-sacrifice of courageous people who intervene to stop that murderous intent, even if lethal force is required.

Memorial at the crash site of United Flight 93. Courageous passengers prevented hijackers from reaching their intended target of Washington D.C. during the terrorist attacks of 9/11. The plane went down in a field near Shanksville, PA. All on board were killed.

Prudence is wisdom applied to careful decision-making (Prov. 8:12). This would include the diligence and foresight to ensure the safety of others. A prudent person will seek to avoid volatile situations rather than walking into them and afterward pleading self-defense. A prudent person will seek alternatives to deadly force, like escape (see 1 Sam. 19:10; Luke 4:29–30; 2 Cor. 11:32–33). A prudent person will check equipment (rather than cutting corners) to make sure workers are safe and won't be seriously injured because equipment was not maintained.

Meekness is a humble and calm disposition in situations that can lead to pride or anger. Murder stems from anger and hatred. But the meek person has the self-control and humility to resist flying off the handle when provoked to take revenge.

Virtues motivate.[9] In other words, a person will tend to respond to a situation a certain way based on the virtues that have been instilled within him or her. He or she will be trained to respond according to those virtues in the heat of the moment. The heat of the moment reveals that person for who he or she truly is—courageous, prudent, meek, and so forth.

Character matters. Many people do not commit crimes like murder or even manslaughter. Does that make them good people? Not necessarily. Someone might avoid doing wrong because he or she does not want to face the consequences. But a person with a righteous motive will do right not just to avoid bad consequences for him- or herself. A person of character truly values the lives of others and desires to glorify God.

context

### RIGHTLY RESPONDING IN THE AFTERMATH OF A TRAGEDY

We live in a fallen world, in which unethical behavior takes place all the time. And those unethical behaviors are not always justly judged or rightly sentenced. What advice would you give to someone who has been affected by murder, manslaughter, or a questionable self-defense ruling? How would you be the right kind of friend, giving biblical advice? How would you counsel someone about appropriately offering forgiveness and appropriately seeking justice? What if you found *yourself* in a situation in which a relative was murdered or killed due to someone's criminal negligence (like drunk driving)?

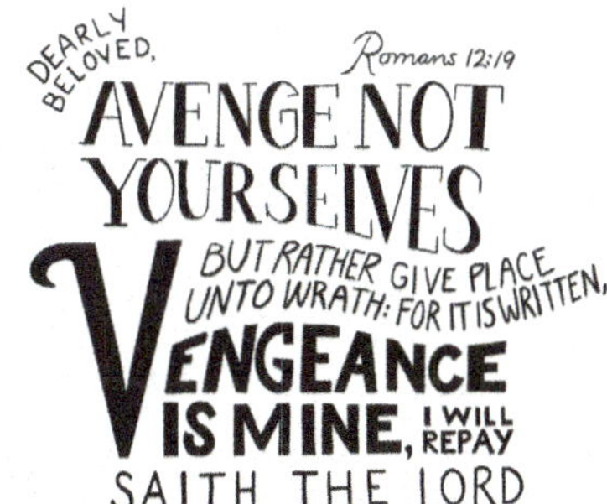

DEARLY BELOVED,
Romans 12:19
AVENGE NOT YOURSELVES
BUT RATHER GIVE PLACE UNTO WRATH: FOR IT IS WRITTEN,
VENGEANCE IS MINE, I WILL REPAY
SAITH THE LORD


Grappling with injustice in this world is hard. You may become disillusioned if you learn from the Bible the way things ought to be. If you assume that life will work out for you when you try hard to operate rightly, your world can be turned upside down by evil seemingly triumphing over good (Ps. 73; Isa. 5:20). Christians find comfort in knowing there is an ultimate Judge who will settle all things righteously in the final judgment (Isa. 26:21). The Christian must rest in the faithful Creator to sustain him or her in the meantime (1 Pet. 4:19). The Christian may desire immediate justice but need not be hopeless and despairing when justice is delayed. True justice will be done. Christians need not be bitter or vengeful in the meantime (Rom. 12:12–21).

On the flip side, if you were to end up being the one who had committed involuntary manslaughter through your own negligence (such as careless driving from texting, goofing off with friends, or driving way too fast), you would not be beyond the hope of God's forgiveness (Ps. 51:14). God's forgiveness would not remove all the consequences in this life. In fact, a person with a godly sorrow (2 Cor. 7:9–10) would willingly accept deserved consequences as appropriate (in contrast to an ungodly sorrow that simply wished to be free from consequences). But God's forgiveness could free you from the weight of eternal guilt. And you could seek to make restitution in the best way possible in order to reconcile broken relationships with others in this life.



## Apply

### RIGHTLY RESPONDING TO TRAGEDY

Guide an **internet search** for students to become better acquainted with reliable Christian resources that address tragedy.

Instruct the students to search websites such as Association of Certified Biblical Counselors, Ethics & Religious Liberty Commission, or Christian Counseling & Educational Foundation and choose a few articles about responding rightly to tragedy. Below are example articles:

- Heath Lambert, "Grieving the Loved Ones We've Lost," Association of Biblical Counselors (website), April 5, 2017.
- Dale Johnson and John Babler, "Counseling Those Impacted by Trauma," Association of Biblical Counselors (website), February 3, 2020.
- "Killing. Are There Exceptions?" Ethics & Religious Liberty Commission (website), July 15, 2014.
- Kevin DeYoung, "How Does the Sixth Commandment Speak to Our Culture?" Ethics & Religious Liberty Commission (website), November 29, 2018.

### RESPONDING TO UNETHICAL KILLING

Use **Activity 9.1** on page 51 to apply the information in the section.

## Assess

Guide a **summative assessment** by directing students to answer the questions in Thinking It Through 9.1.

### Thinking It Through 9.1

1. Murder is "the unlawful killing of a human being with malice aforethought" (18 U.S.C. 1111[a]). Manslaughter is "the unlawful killing of a human being without malice" (18 U.S.C. 1111[a]). Self-defense is "the right to prevent suffering force or violence through the use of a sufficient level of counteracting force or violence" ("Self-Defense Law: Overview," FindLaw [website]).
2. The sanctity of life applies to all people since all people are image-bearers and thus possess intrinsic value. God is the giver and taker of life, so any unauthorized taking of life demands an accounting with Him.
3. Unlike US code, the Bible seems to group murder and voluntary manslaughter together in one category. Like US code, the Bible does recognize involuntary manslaughter as a lesser crime than murder.
4. hatred
5. to love (or to seek reconciliation)
6. True; a society must be careful not to prohibit people from protecting themselves or innocent people from a deadly threat. But a society must also be careful not to allow people to act imprudently or sinfully under the guise of self-defense.
7. Possible answers:

   Courage: one must overcome fear and pain to protect oneself and others from a deadly threat.

   Prudence: one must diligently care for others' safety and must wisely avoid volatile situations.

   Meekness: one must be willing to suffer wrong in order to preserve life.
8. Justice is appropriate in God's hands and in the hands of His appointed rulers. If justice is not done in this life, then vengeance will surely be in the hands of God in the final judgment. We are not to take revenge.

   Forgiveness is appropriate when a person is repentant. But that does not mean that the consequences are wiped away in this life. A person would need to demonstrate the willingness to receive what he or she rightly deserved to demonstrate repentance. Yet, a person can rest in God's eternal forgiveness that will one day release him or her from any guilt and final eternal penalty.

**NEW EVALUATING CONTEMPORARY EVENTS**

Find a real-life news story that focuses on the response of the victim's family to a wrongful killing. Find a real-life news story that focuses on society's response to a justified self-defense killing. Evaluate the responses according to a biblical ethic.

#### Thinking It Through 9.1

1. Differentiate murder, manslaughter, and self-defense.
2. What general principle is written on everyone's conscience and clearly enunciated in the Bible as our responsibility regarding life?
3. How does the sixth commandment (and further biblical explanations of that command) slightly differ from US code on the matters of murder and manslaughter? How do the Bible and these laws agree?
4. What does the New Testament identify as murder in its seed form?
5. The command not to murder is also a command to do what?
6. True or False: A society may subtly undermine the value of life by either making it nearly impossible for someone to exercise self-defense or by making it far too easy for someone to claim self-defense. Explain your answer.
7. Identify one of the three virtues highlighted in this section that are necessary for upholding the value of life. Explain why the virtue is important.
8. If you found yourself the victim of a tragedy involving a wrongful death or if you found yourself the victimizer of someone else by murder, manslaughter, or accidental killing, how would a biblical view of justice and forgiveness be rightly applied to such a situation?

### 9.2 Suicide and Euthanasia

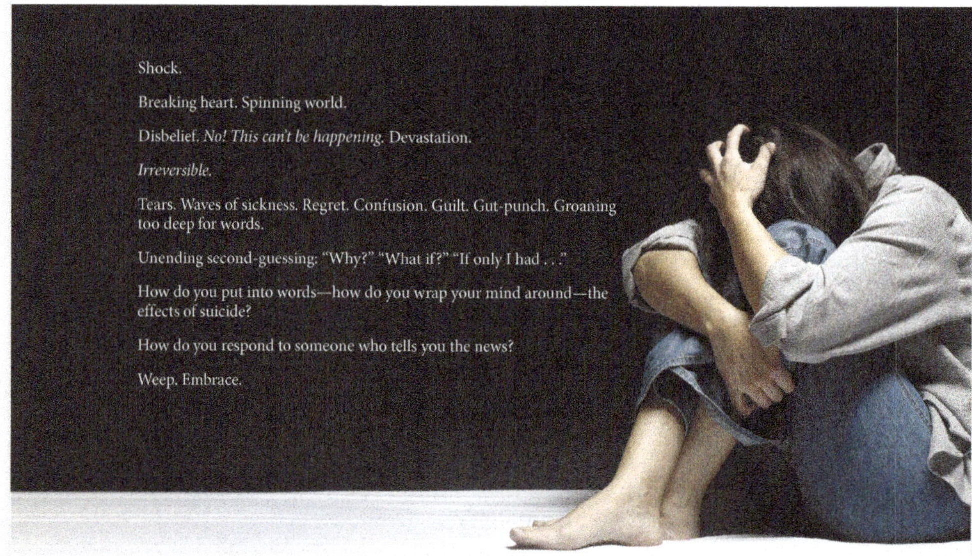

Shock.
Breaking heart. Spinning world.
Disbelief. *No! This can't be happening.* Devastation.
*Irreversible.*
Tears. Waves of sickness. Regret. Confusion. Guilt. Gut-punch. Groaning too deep for words.
Unending second-guessing: "Why?" "What if?" "If only I had . . ."
How do you put into words—how do you wrap your mind around—the effects of suicide?
How do you respond to someone who tells you the news?
Weep. Embrace.




## 9.2 Suicide and Euthanasia

*How can I help a friend who is struggling with thoughts of self-harm?*

### Objectives

**9.2.1** Explain common justifications for suicide and euthanasia.

**9.2.2** Summarize the biblical teaching on God's authority over life and death. BWS

**9.2.3** Analyze the societal consequences of unbiblical views regarding suicide and euthanasia. BWS

**9.2.4** Assess the virtues necessary to act ethically regarding suicide and euthanasia. BWS

## JUSTIFICATIONS AND MOTIVATIONS FOR SUICIDE AND EUTHANASIA

**Suicide**, the intentional and voluntary taking of one's own life, is tragic, and yet it happens far too often. The Centers for Disease Control and Prevention found that in 2019, 6,488 people between the ages of ten and twenty-four took their lives by suicide, and it was the second leading cause of death for this age range.[10] What motivates people to commit or attempt to commit suicide?

The specific circumstances can vary widely, but the common thread tends to be despair and hopelessness due to some kind of suffering, emptiness, or guilt and shame. When someone is unable to cope with pressures, that person seeks a way out. Convincing themselves that there is no other way to find relief, many people overcome (or seek to overcome) the self-preservation instinct God built into each and every one of us.

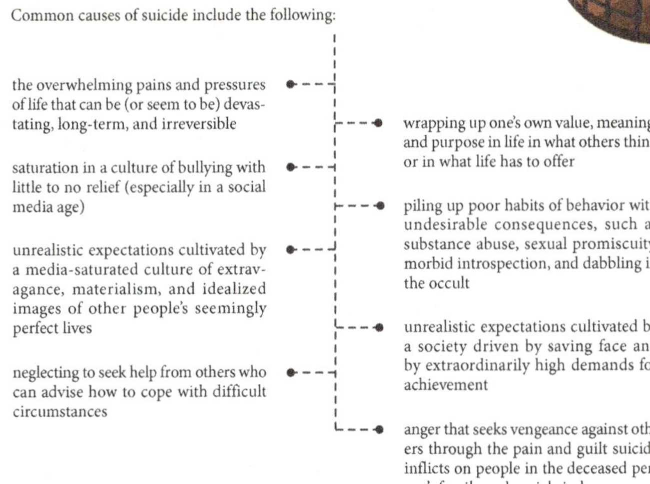

Common causes of suicide include the following:
the overwhelming pains and pressures of life that can be (or seem to be) devastating, long-term, and irreversible
wrapping up one's own value, meaning, and purpose in life in what others think or in what life has to offer
saturation in a culture of bullying with little to no relief (especially in a social media age)
piling up poor habits of behavior with undesirable consequences, such as substance abuse, sexual promiscuity, morbid introspection, and dabbling in the occult
unrealistic expectations cultivated by a media-saturated culture of extravagance, materialism, and idealized images of other people's seemingly perfect lives
unrealistic expectations cultivated by a society driven by saving face and by extraordinarily high demands for achievement
neglecting to seek help from others who can advise how to cope with difficult circumstances
anger that seeks vengeance against others through the pain and guilt suicide inflicts on people in the deceased person's family and social circles


**Euthanasia** closely relates to the topic of suicide. This term refers to "the act of intentionally ending the life of a person who is elderly, terminally ill, or suffering from some incurable injury or disease."[11] It can be voluntary: at the request of a patient, a physician takes lethal action. (It is often called physician-assisted suicide when the patient is in control of a lethal act and the doctor simply facilitates.) It can be nonvoluntary: unwanted people who are severely debilitated are put to death without their consent.

How does a person get to the point that he or she desires a physician's help to end his or her own life? Usually, the person is suffering from a terminal disease. And the person does not want to endure the suffering or the degradation, or the cost and burden on others, that comes from the loss of independence and need for ongoing care.



**9.2.5** Formulate a biblical response to someone who has lost a loved one because of suicide or euthanasia.

### Biblical Worldview Shaping

- **Authority** (explain): Only God ultimately has the authority to take a human life. (9.2.2)
- **Man's Chief End** (evaluate): A society that creates an expectation for certain kinds of people to end their lives is contrary to the biblical vision of flourishing in the midst of hardship. (9.2.3)
- **Virtue** (formulate): Hope in God can sustain those who despair of life, providing a foundation for the cultivation of gratitude for life. Compassion should sustain those tempted to kill themselves rather than support their death. (9.2.4)

### Printed Resource

- Activity 9.2: Counsel for Suicide and Euthanasia

### Digital Resource

- Video: "Suicide and Euthanasia"

### Suggested Reading

- Frame, John M. *The Doctrine of the Christian Life*. Phillipsburg, NJ: P&R Publishing, 2008. Pages 684–93, 717–45.
- Grudem, Wayne. *Christian Ethics: An Introduction to Biblical Moral Reasoning*. Wheaton, IL: Crossway, 2018. Pages 587–615.
- Magnuson, Ken. *Invitation to Christian Ethics: Moral Reasoning and Contemporary Issues*. Grand Rapids, MI: Kregel Academic, 2020. Pages 434–73.

## Engage

### FEELING AS THOUGH LIFE IS HOPELESS?

Use a **Ticket in the Door** to preassess student experiences with suicidal friends, family, or acquaintances.

True or False: I, a close friend, or a family member has seriously contemplated ending one's own life.

The True answers will give you a quick idea of who may need to be gently helped through the discussion of these issues even more purposefully and carefully.

## Instruct

### COMMON CAUSES OF SUICIDE

Guide a **discussion** that relates the common causes of suicide to the relevant, underlying spiritual issues in a way that is biblically faithful and emotionally sensitive.

**What are some common causes of suicide, and how might you respond biblically to them?** *Possible answers:*

- *Cause: wrapping up one's own value, meaning, and purpose in life in what others think or in what life has to offer*

  *Response: turning to what God says about you in Scripture to find value, meaning, and purpose*
- *Cause: piling up poor habits of behavior with undesirable consequences, such as substance abuse, sexual promiscuity, morbid introspection, and dabbling in the occult*

  *Response: humbly acknowledging these things for what they are (sin against God) and asking for His grace to pardon and empower a new life*

## REFUTING COMMON ARGUMENTS FOR EUTHANASIA

Use a **Think-Pair-Share** to prompt students to trace how worldview assumptions lead people to different conclusions about the value and purpose of suffering.

**What are some of the most common justifications for euthanasia?** *Possible answers:*

- *the obligation to show mercy to people who are going to die anyway and who are currently suffering so terribly that they themselves greatly desire an end to their lives*
- *the poor quality of life for a severely mentally or physically disabled individual, sometimes accompanied by an appeal to what the person "would want" if able to express himself or herself*

**What does support for euthanasia imply about one's view of human value? What should be the basis in society for valuing human life (Gen. 1:26–27)?** *Support for euthanasia implies that human value is based on a person's contribution to society or the cost or benefit to others. An individual may view euthanasia as a legitimate means to escape suffering, but the person is devaluing his or her own life in the process. From a biblical standpoint, human value should be based on a person's inherent status as an image-bearer, a God-granted value regardless of circumstances.*

**What does the desire to escape suffering by means of euthanasia reveal about people's view of suffering and their view of God's sovereignty in that suffering (James 1:2–4)?** *They view suffering as purposeless, and therefore the notion that enduring it is of some value to their soul is nonsensical. They dismiss God's purposes and oversight and seek to take things into their own control.*

## EVALUATING CONTEMPORARY EVENTS

Assign a **writing project** of one to three paragraphs based on the instructions in the Evaluating Contemporary Events textbox on page 156. Based on the cases, the students should evaluate the arguments for and against euthanasia.

## ONE ULTIMATE AUTHORITY OVER LIFE AND DEATH

Guide a **discussion** to provide an overview of the Bible's teaching on suicide. Ask volunteers to read the relevant biblical passages for each question. Then have the class answer based on the passages read.

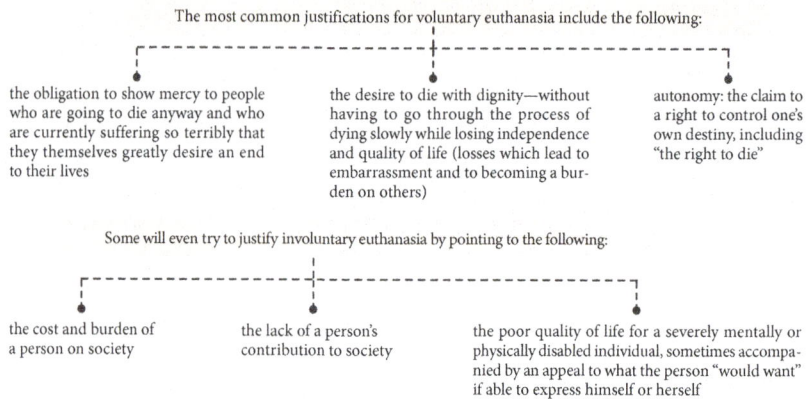

The most common justifications for voluntary euthanasia include the following:

- the obligation to show mercy to people who are going to die anyway and who are currently suffering so terribly that they themselves greatly desire an end to their lives
- the desire to die with dignity—without having to go through the process of dying slowly while losing independence and quality of life (losses which lead to embarrassment and to becoming a burden on others)
- autonomy: the claim to a right to control one's own destiny, including "the right to die"

Some will even try to justify involuntary euthanasia by pointing to the following:

- the cost and burden of a person on society
- the lack of a person's contribution to society
- the poor quality of life for a severely mentally or physically disabled individual, sometimes accompanied by an appeal to what the person "would want" if able to express himself or herself

NEW

**EVALUATING CONTEMPORARY EVENTS**

Research the cases involving Karen Ann Quinlan, Nancy Cruzan, Terri Schiavo, and Brittany Maynard to find out how people have argued for and against euthanasia. You can also look up other current events involving new cases. How would you evaluate the arguments on both sides of the debate?

If you were in a situation involving excruciating pain leading to a certain death, wouldn't you want someone to help you end your life? If it were in the best interests of you and others, wouldn't that be the moral thing to do? These are powerful-sounding arguments to many people, as demonstrated by the fact that 81 percent of young adults supported physician-assisted suicide in a 2015 poll.[12] If you have a right to live, don't you also have the right to die on your own terms—to die with dignity? Who has any right to interfere with such a personal decision?

### GOD'S AUTHORITY OVER LIFE AND DEATH

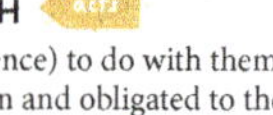

Humans cannot claim autonomy (complete independence) to do with themselves whatever they wish. They are created beings dependent on and obligated to their Creator. Their Creator made them with intrinsic value, whether they or anyone else recognizes it or not. That value forever remains because its basis is in a God-given status: the image of God (Gen. 1:26; 9:6). Who a person is can never be overturned or taken away as long as that person exists.

People who support euthanasia or who succumb to suicide have fundamentally misunderstood or rejected the true basis of human value. They tend to locate value in a person's contribution to society, in achieved desires, in status in the eyes of themselves or others, or in some kind of positive impact on others. While these are often good and desirable outcomes, none of these things determine the fundamental value of a human being.

The sixth commandment forbids murder (Exod. 20:13; Rom. 13:9). The commandment is not limited—as in, you are merely not to murder *others*. No, the command is not to murder, period. The command applies to self-murder, which is what suicide is (whether helped by a physician or not). Since no human owns himself or herself (Ps. 100:3; see also 1 Cor. 6:19–20), a person must care for the body, and a person who takes his or her own life is taking God's prerogative (Ps. 90). This is an affront to God's lordship and a denial of God-granted value (Job 14:5).

*Taking your own life is a direct challenge to the One who created it and reflects the actions of someone who does not value God's authority over the number of our days.* JULIE LOWE[13]

156 ISSUES

**What's the biblical basis of human value that suicide undermines (Gen. 1:26; 9:6)?** *the image of God in man—a status that can never be removed*

**What direct biblical command does suicide violate?** *Exodus 20:13 and Romans 13:9 forbid murder (the unlawful taking of life); this includes self-murder.*

**Why doesn't a person have a right to do with himself or herself whatever he or she wishes (Ps. 100:3; 1 Cor. 6:19–20)?** *No person ultimately owns himself or herself. All people are ultimately owned by their Creator God.*

**Who is the only person who has the prerogative over the number of our days (Ps. 90; Job 14:15)?** *God*

**When you don't feel that you have value, how can passages like Psalm 139:17–18 and Matthew 10:31 correct such thoughts and emotions?** *These passages remind you that God is an ever-present, personal God who is always attuned in the most caring way to the smallest detail of all aspects of your own thinking and living. Wrong emotions follow from flawed thinking or disconnecting what we know to be true with how we feel.*

**What's a major factor in the rise of suicide from the influence of our secular world?** *The lie that humans should happily pursue autonomy, seeking to fulfill self-made dreams; when those efforts become futile, then people who have put stock in only themselves will have nothing left to live for or rely on.*

**Can people go to heaven if they commit suicide (1 Cor. 10:13)? Do we have assurance that those people are in heaven (1 John 5:16–18)?** *Nothing in the Bible*

If you exist, you have extraordinary value, particularly in the eyes of the one who matters most: your Creator (Ps. 139:17–18; Matt. 10:31). As long as you are fooled into believing that your value comes from something other than your status as an image-bearer, you are in danger of devaluing what God has made and declared to be of immeasurable value. One of the most dangerous messages of our day is that you can be anything you dream to be—that your life is all about fulfilling self-made dreams, following your heart, and being true to yourself. Is it any wonder that suicide has skyrocketed? People find out that they are not in control of their lives, and then what happens to them? They run into futility and failure. They can't make life work the way they dreamed. This false message (that through self-determination you can do anything) backfires, resulting in a massive amount of suicide when life doesn't seem to be working out for so many.

Although suicide is not the unpardonable sin (1 Cor. 10:13), it is a fruit of a person's life that gives rise to questions about that person's spiritual condition (1 John 5:16–18). It is never appropriate to take this route to get to eternity faster. God can provide another way; God can sustain you through all the shame, pain, and difficulties in this life (Ps. 42; Rom. 8:25–39; 1 Cor. 10:13). The Bible does approve of self-sacrifice in the sense of laying down one's life for another (John 15:13). But nearly every biblical narrative that describes suicide describes it in a negative light (1 Sam. 31:3–5; 2 Sam. 17:23; 1 Kings 16:18–19; Matt. 27:3–5; Acts 16:28).

### ends THE SOCIAL CONSEQUENCES OF SUICIDE AND EUTHANASIA

Many of the motives for suicide relate to wrong ends: wrapping up one's own meaning and purpose in oneself and in what one can get out of life in this world. This is not to downplay the real suffering many have endured. But living for a correct end will provide the strength and hope one needs to endure and to overcome suffering in this life. When your meaning and purpose in life are found in God's glory (1 Cor. 10:31; Col. 3:17; 1 Pet. 4:11) and in God's purposes for the suffering in your life (Gen. 50:20; Rom. 8:28; 2 Thess. 1:5–6), then His grace will be sufficient (2 Cor. 4:16–18; 12:9).

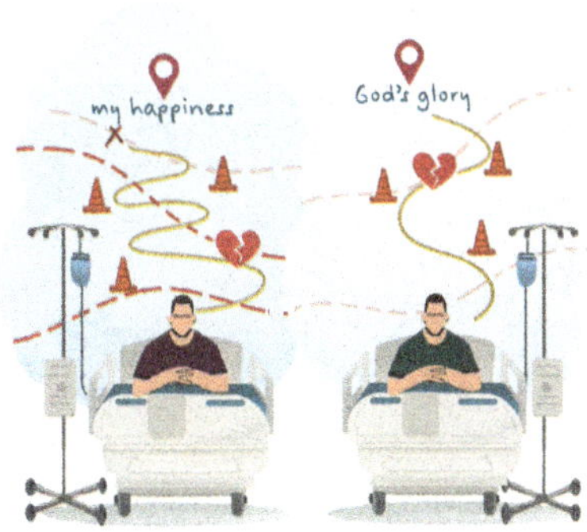


Many of the justifications for euthanasia relate to freeing someone from having to endure serious pain. But such reasoning ignores the alternatives that can successfully relieve pain and the value that can come from enduring pain. Many of the other justifications relate to wrong views of one's relationship to society: contribution, not draining resources, not being a burden to others. But what if society (and especially family) is supposed to set aside some of its resources, planning to care for people once they are in great need? What if society was designed to take care of people out of a great love for who those people are, regardless of their perceived contribution? Maybe a person's contribution is to humble us, to make us less selfish, to grow our compassion, to engender gratitude (so we won't take for granted our own abilities), and to inspire us with their endurance against all odds.

Wrong ends (whether in relation to suicide or euthanasia) have consequences on the operation of the social order, mainly expressed in a culture's expectations and laws. A society that excuses or even glamorizes suicide and euthanasia undermines the sanctity of life for all people and thus endangers individual lives—by pressuring people to end their own lives, opening up that option as acceptable, or even determining when others no longer deserve to live.

Another tragic effect on society (especially on friends and families) takes place when a person decides to take his or her own life. What happens in a church or school community when someone takes his or her own life? Excruciating sadness sweeps over the whole community. Sometimes this effect is the final vengeance



*indicates that suicide definitely sends a person to hell; we are all subject to potentially committing every kind of sin. However, whenever suicide occurs, we are left wondering about a person's standing before God. Ultimately, we can't know for sure; God is the only one who can be the ultimate judge of that.*

**Instead of seeking escape from shame, pain, and difficulties by way of suicide, what should Christians seek instead (Ps. 42; Rom. 8:25–39; 1 Cor. 10:13)?** *Christians should seek God's grace to help them endure, overcome, and get through their difficulties. They can find forgiveness and sustaining grace to find a way out of the temptations and trials.*

**How would you differentiate suicide and self-sacrifice?** *Suicide is an attempt to selfishly escape responsibility; self-sacrifice is giving oneself in the place of another.*

**What do the biblical narratives demonstrate regarding God's attitude toward suicide (1 Sam. 31:3–5; 1 Kings 16:18–19; Matt. 27:3–5)?** *The Bible consistently describes suicide in a negative light.*

**Does the account of Samson provide a positive example of suicide, contradicting the other biblical narratives?** *No, although the interpretation of this account can be controversial. Many would not define what Samson did as suicide. Or if they define it as suicide, they would not hold up Samson's suicidal act as a positive example.*

## SOCIAL CONSEQUENCES OF SUICIDE AND EUTHANASIA

Use a **mock debate** to prompt students to seek to persuade others of the negative effects of physician-assisted suicide and to argue for preferable alternatives to suicide.

## VIRTUES THAT OVERCOME DESIRES FOR SUICIDE AND EUTHANASIA

Use a **Turn and Talk** to prompt students to answer this section's essential question with the information on page 158.

**How can I help a friend who is struggling with thoughts of self-harm?**

Instruct students to partner with someone to create a scenario where the other is going through some difficult situation.

**How would you give advice based on the following three virtues?**

- Hope (Lam. 3:24)
- Gratitude (1 Thess. 5:18)
- Compassion (Gal. 6:2)

A helpful model to follow includes

- listening and gathering information to understand the situation or context;
- identifying how emotions have been formed by wrong behavior or how wrong thinking has been rooted in wrong commitments or both;
- offering the hope of the gospel for its power to encourage the downcast by reminding them of God's free gift of grace and acceptance through the person and work of Christ.

For more detailed help on a biblical counseling model, see Jeremy Pierre, *The Dynamic Heart in Daily Life: Connecting Christ to Human Experience* (Greensboro, NC: New Growth Press, 2016).

desired by the person who takes his or her own life. This in itself is sad—that a person could be driven by such hurt and hate rather than seeking reconciliation. Yet, such an event is indeed a wake-up call for all of us to reexamine how we treat others and how we can better listen to, love, and encourage those who are facing overwhelming circumstances (which is not to say those things haven't happened in some cases where a person still decides to commit suicide). These tragedies remind us to go beyond superficial friendliness to truly befriend people and to speak the truth of the gospel into their lives.

agents

### VIRTUES NECESSARY TO OVERCOME DESIRES FOR SUICIDE AND EUTHANASIA

How can I help a friend who is struggling with thoughts of self-harm?

What does a person need in order to overcome his or her desires for suicide? Hope. Gratitude. What does a society need in order to overcome its desires to get rid of people deemed undesirable? Compassion. People and societies filled with hope, gratitude, and compassion will flourish in upholding the sanctity of life and in sustaining people who have given up on life.

Have you seen any shows or read accounts about extreme rescues? Someone falls into an icy crevice while skiing or gets caught in a sinking ship but survives in an air pocket until a rescuer comes. Would you rather live in a society that all too quickly just lets people die or one that against all odds makes extraordinary efforts to rescue people? We should support a society that is bent on extreme rescues for those who lose heart and want to give up on life.

People contemplating suicide or euthanasia need hope. They need a confident expectation, not that their circumstances will change for the better, but that Christ and His unfailing promises will sustain them through suffering and complete a perfect work in them (Rom. 5:1–5; James 1:2–4).

People contemplating suicide or euthanasia need gratitude. Instead of focusing on all that has gone wrong, a person needs to focus on all that has been granted. In the climax of his passage on suffering, James points us to the unchanging God who gives us every good and perfect gift, best exemplified by the Word of God that brings us eternal salvation (James 1:16–18 in the context of James 1:2–15). Sadly, many people treasure the things of this world and worry themselves to death over those passing things. Instead, we can rest in the care of the Father while we seek first His kingdom (Matt. 6:19–34). Living with gratitude for the basic necessities of life will sustain us and keep us from anxiety.

People contemplating suicide or euthanasia need compassion. A compassionate society plans to spend its time and resources to care for others. Only a selfish society spends all its time and resources prioritizing entertainment and pleasure in place of caring for others. A compassionate society seeks to make a suffering person as comfortable as possible through pain management. Very few cases cannot be managed in this way. A compassionate society seeks to encourage and to help those who go through the process of deterioration and experience shame from losing independence. A compassionate society communicates how much it respects those who are suffering and persevering through it.

158 ISSUES

## Apply

### SUICIDE AND EUTHANASIA

Show the **video** "Suicide and Euthanasia" to help students apply the lessons learned.

### COPING IN THE AFTERMATH OF TRAGEDY

Use a **Quick Write** to allow students to describe some unhelpful ways and some biblical ways to respond to someone coping with tragedy.

**What responses would be unhelpful to a person who has just experienced a friend or loved one taking his or her own life?** *Possible answers:*

- *If you had only a distant relationship, then prying into the details of what exactly happened and why would be unhelpful.*
- *If you had a friendly relationship, then ignoring what happened and distancing yourself from that person out of fear or because you don't know what to say would also be unhelpful.*
- *Trying to minimize the reality of what took place and its consequences or expressing biblical truths in a trite way wouldn't be helpful.*

**What responses would be both biblical and helpful?** *Possible answers:*

- *Initially, simply affirm the reality of the tragedy and its saddening effect. Assure the person of your compassionate care in both words and actions.*
- *Although you never want to be trite in how biblical principles are communicated to someone, reaffirming the truths of Scripture are vital for giving others a sure hope in the promises of God. Encourage Bible reading, prayer, and meditation on those promises to counter the natural sinful responses of doubt, fear, anger, and so forth.*
- *Although truly bad things happen that we cannot change, we can choose to dwell on things in which we can be full of gratitude. It is appropriate to mourn for someone lost in such a tragic way. However, it shouldn't overshadow the many ways God continually takes care of us and blesses us. However, God's continual care is being demonstrated in all things.*

### RESPONDING TO SUICIDE AND EUTHANASIA

Use **Activity 9.2** on page 53 to apply the information in the section.

### COPING WITH SOMEONE'S DECISION TO END THEIR OWN LIFE

In a fallen world, we are sure to face circumstances in which a person decides to take his or her own life. How should we respond in the face of suicide or euthanasia?

There are many practical things you can do to show compassion and to offer help. But the most important thing you can do is to point yourself and others to the Lord and His gospel for grace and hope. Know that God cares (Ps. 34:17–18) even when you may not see or feel that He does. Look for meaning and fulfillment in eternal things. Encourage yourself and others to persevere, to continue in hope. Find your identity in Christ. And be grateful for all that God has given you, particularly life.

### Thinking It Through 9.2

1. Explain at least three common justifications for suicide.
2. How does euthanasia relate to physician-assisted suicide?
3. Explain at least three common justifications for euthanasia.
4. Does the Bible give a person the right to take his or her own life? Explain your answer using Bible passages used in the chapter.
5. What are some reasons (wrong ends) that lead a person to contemplate suicide or that lead a society to promote euthanasia?
6. What are some of the consequences of these wrong ends?
7. List and explain three virtues that would head off the desire for suicide and euthanasia.
8. What is the most important response after experiencing the devastation of someone committing suicide?

## 9.3 Abortion

**Abortion** can be defined as "any action that intentionally causes the death and removal from the womb of an unborn child."[14] Is your heart tender enough to grieve over what has been done for decades to innocent babies? Do you know the magnitude of the death count? Are you aware of the horrific and callous processes that are involved in disposing of so many helpless little ones? Few atrocities could give you more cause to weep.

> *Rivers of waters run down mine eyes, because they keep not thy law.* PSALM 119:136
>
> *Horror hath taken hold upon me because of the wicked that forsake thy law.* PSALM 119:53

God's law is clear: we must not murder (Exod. 20:13). We must protect the most innocent and vulnerable among us (Pss. 72:12–14; 82:3–4). Why would the psalmist weep and become righteously angry toward lawbreakers? He had such a love for God and the goodness of His law that he was heartbroken and dismayed by those who would act so wickedly. God is a God of life; it is Satan who seeks to destroy it (John 8:44).

And yet, there are many in our society who would balk at the charge that abortion is murder. Society has conditioned people for decades to redefine this sin.



## Assess

Guide a **summative assessment** by directing students to answer the questions in Thinking It Through 9.2.

### Thinking It Through 9.2

1. See the bulleted points on page 155.
2. Euthanasia is "the act of intentionally ending the life of a person who is elderly, terminally ill, or suffering from some incurable injury or disease" (Taken from *Christian Ethics: An Introduction to Biblical Moral Reasoning* by Wayne Grudem, © 2018, p. 587. Used by permission of Crossway, a publishing ministry of Good News Publishers, Wheaton, IL 60187, www.crossway.org). When the patient is in control of the lethal act that the doctor facilitates, then it is called physician-assisted suicide.
3. See the bulleted points on page 156.
4. The Bible commands us not to murder (Exod. 20:13; Rom. 13:9), which would include forbidding us to murder ourselves. God is the giver and taker of life (Job 14:5; Pss. 90; 100:3). Our value is a God-given status that cannot be lost or taken away (Gen. 1:26; 9:6; Ps. 139:17–18).
5. Possible answers: wrapping up one's own value, meaning, and purpose in life in oneself and in what one can get out of life in this world; contribution to society, not draining resources, not being a burden to others
6. Expectations or laws can undermine the sanctity of life and pressure people to end their own lives. Excruciating sadness sweeps over the whole community. It can also be a wake-up call on how we treat others and how well we speak the gospel into their lives.
7. Hope is a confident expectation in God and His promises to sustain one through suffering and to complete His perfect plan in a Christian.

   Gratitude shifts the focus from all that has gone wrong to all that God has granted, resulting in thankfulness for His greatest eternal gifts (such as His Word and salvation) that ought to overshadow all our temporary earthly suffering.

   Compassion drives a society to spend its time and resources to care for others, to make a person as comfortable as possible through pain management and palliative care, to encourage and to help those who go through the process of deterioration and even shame, and to communicate how much it respects those who are suffering and persevering through it.
8. Point yourself and others to the Lord and His gospel grace for hope.

## 9.3 Abortion

Does abortion take the life of a person?

### Objectives

**9.3.1** Explain common justifications for abortion.

**9.3.2** Defend the sanctity of human life from conception. BWS

**9.3.3** Analyze the personal and societal consequences of unbiblical views regarding abortion.

**9.3.4** Assess the virtues necessary to act ethically regarding abortion. BWS

**9.3.5** Formulate a biblical response to someone who is considering an abortion or to someone who has already had one. BWS

### Biblical Worldview Shaping

- **Creational Order** (formulate): The creation order testifies to new life beginning at fertilization. (9.3.2)

- **Virtue** (formulate): Love for God and others means that it is never right to take an innocent life. Courage and gratitude need to be cultivated for situations in which abortion is a temptation. (9.3.4)
- **Wisdom** (apply): The wise person can compassionately counsel people to live in light of the reality of God's Word. He or she can offer God's message of grace and reconciliation to those who have already sinned in this matter. (9.3.5)

### Printed Resource

- Activity 9.3: About Abortion

### Digital Resource

- Video: "Abortion"

### Suggested Reading

- Frame, John M. *The Doctrine of the Christian Life*. Phillipsburg, NJ: P&R Publishing, 2008. Pages 717–32.
- Grudem, Wayne. *Christian Ethics: An Introduction to Biblical Moral Reasoning*. Wheaton, IL: Crossway, 2018. Pages 566–86.
- Magnuson, Ken. *Invitation to Christian Ethics: Moral Reasoning and Contemporary Issues*. Grand Rapids, MI: Kregel Academic, 2020. Pages 394–433.

## Engage

### ABORTION

Show the **video** "Abortion" to introduce the subject to students.

### FEELING GUILT FROM AN ABORTION?

Use a **Ticket in the Door** to preassess student experiences with abortion in the life of a friend, family member, or acquaintance.

True or False: I, a close friend, or a family member has either contemplated an abortion or had an abortion.

The True answers will give you a quick idea of who may need to be gently helped through the discussion of these issues even more purposefully and carefully.

## Instruct

### CIRCUMSTANCES LEADING TO ABORTION

Guide a **discussion** to prompt students to think through the difficult circumstances that lead to abortions taking place. You may also have students do further research, using the instructions in the textbox on page 161.

**Why do people get abortions (including mothers who go through with it and fathers or others who pressure the mother to do so)?** *See the ten most common reasons displayed in the graphic on pages 160–61 for possible student answers.*

**Of those reasons, which are the least common?** *to save the life of the mother (doesn't register on the statistics), incest (less than 0.5 percent), and rape (1 percent)*

**Why would pro-life advocates allow for laws that permit abortion for reasons of rape or incest?** *Although most pro-lifers do not, in principle, support allowing abortion in cases of incest and rape, it is very hard politically to convince others to completely ban abortion. So, some attempt to ban abortion, except for these more difficult cases, with the hope that they could ban 98.5 percent of abortions. Most, however, hope to persuade voters that exceptions in the case of rape and incest are not moral.*

Note also that the pro-choice movement tends to argue for allowing all abortions by scaring people into thinking that an abortion ban would mean that mothers' lives would not be saved and so forth.

**Do you think that it should be considered an abortion when doctors must choose between saving the life of the mother or the baby?** *Many pro-lifers would not even want to categorize such an event as an abortion. The doctor's intent is not to murder the baby. The doctor is simply limited as a finite*

Abortion is described as medical care, a woman's choice to do with her own body what she will. Many do not regard the fetus in the womb as a person, so they do not consider the removal of the fetus by abortion to be murder. Many women who have believed the lie that abortion is not murder get pressured into making a sinful decision to abort. Nevertheless, a God-given conscience causes many of these women to suffer from guilt, especially if they realize later that they have taken the life of an unborn baby. Further complicating the situation, many women (for example, those caught in sex slavery) are victims of the wickedness of others who pressure or force them to undergo abortions.

What should be the Christian assessment of and response to a culture that promotes abortion? Rather than soften the reality of what abortion is and of one's personal responsibility for choosing it (with the recognition that people may have varying levels of complicity and guilt based on the situation), Christians magnify the gospel hope of God's great grace and forgiveness. God's great love shines brighter in the darkness; thus, we do not uphold the greatness of God's love by downplaying the wickedness or by excusing it (Luke 7:47).

Do you have a heart that reflects the character of God—full of righteous indignation against wickedness while at the same time extending grace, mercy, and love toward those who would repent and be transformed?

context **APPEALS TO DIFFICULT CIRCUMSTANCES**

Doing the right thing seems so easy until you find yourself in a situation of great pressure and fear. Suddenly, you find yourself justifying the unimaginable.

Abortion is commonly justified for the following reasons:

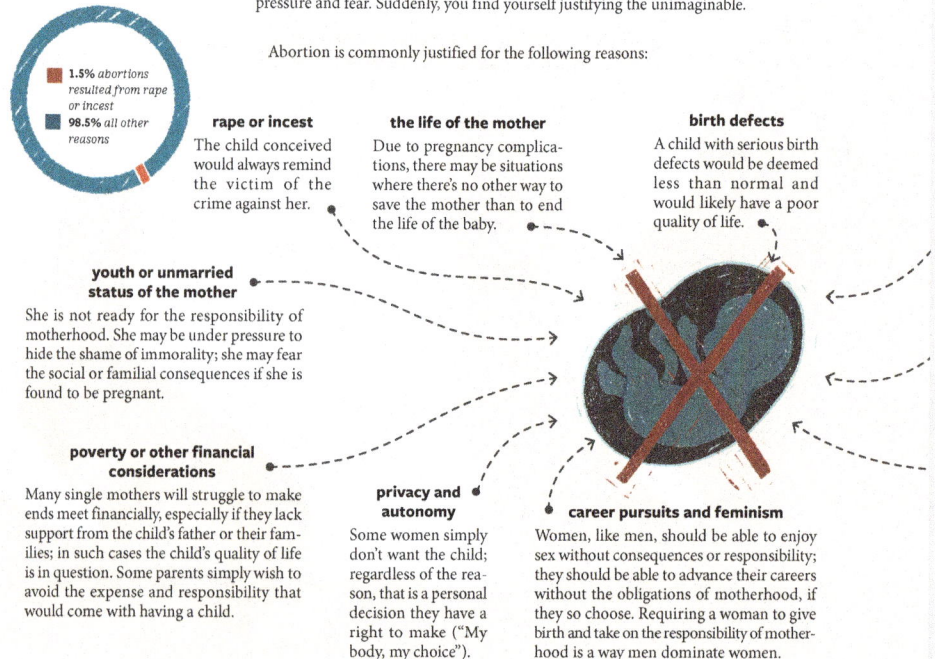

**1.5%** *abortions resulted from rape or incest*
**98.5%** *all other reasons*

**rape or incest**
The child conceived would always remind the victim of the crime against her.

**the life of the mother**
Due to pregnancy complications, there may be situations where there's no other way to save the mother than to end the life of the baby.

**birth defects**
A child with serious birth defects would be deemed less than normal and would likely have a poor quality of life.

**youth or unmarried status of the mother**
She is not ready for the responsibility of motherhood. She may be under pressure to hide the shame of immorality; she may fear the social or familial consequences if she is found to be pregnant.

**poverty or other financial considerations**
Many single mothers will struggle to make ends meet financially, especially if they lack support from the child's father or their families; in such cases the child's quality of life is in question. Some parents simply wish to avoid the expense and responsibility that would come with having a child.

**privacy and autonomy**
Some women simply don't want the child; regardless of the reason, that is a personal decision they have a right to make ("My body, my choice").

**career pursuits and feminism**
Women, like men, should be able to enjoy sex without consequences or responsibility; they should be able to advance their careers without the obligations of motherhood, if they so choose. Requiring a woman to give birth and take on the responsibility of motherhood is a way men dominate women.

160 ISSUES

*Nearly one out of four women in the United States will have had an abortion by the time they are 45.*[15]

**ADVOCATING AND OPPOSING ABORTION**

If you search online on the topic of abortion, you will find numerous articles advocating for or opposing abortion. Look for the reasons given to support abortion, and look for other articles that oppose abortion and the reasons they give. Are there reasons in addition to the ones listed here in your textbook? What are the most common reasons in support of abortion?

What reasons do you think would be the most persuasive? Saving the life of the mother (even for most pro-lifers) and rape or incest (for some pro-lifers) are the most persuasive arguments for many people. How often do the most persuasive reasons motivate the abortions that actually take place in our society? Magnuson, citing research, concludes, "One percent claimed to be a victim of rape, less than 0.5 percent became pregnant as a result of incest, and statistics did not register anyone who claimed to have an abortion to save their life."[16] (This statement is not suggesting abortions are never done to save the life of a mother, but these are so rare that they are not even reflected in the statistics.)

In other words, the most compelling reasons for abortion are those that motivate abortions *least* frequently. It's safe to say that most abortions do not take place in the context of a moral dilemma.[17] Many pro-lifers will allow for abortions for these reasons in an effort to ban all other abortions, though in principle many recognize it's wrong to kill an innocent human being regardless of the circumstances. But the majority of abortions are sought to make life easier for the mother—to avoid financial pressures, to maintain respectability, to avoid inconvenience. Abortion, though it takes the life of an innocent person, relieves such pressures. But for believers, God provides a path forward without having to resort to sin (1 Cor. 10:13).

**other priorities**
A child would interfere with plans (travel, lifestyle, career, education, or finance) for some people, including some married couples. Abortion can be used for family planning if contraception fails.

**body image**
Some women want to avoid the permanent changes to their bodies and appearances that will come from pregnancy and delivery.

**population control and eugenics***
The world is headed for an overpopulation crisis, and abortion is a means of avoiding that. Or abortion should be used to eliminate from the gene pool characteristics deemed undesirable for a society. (These justifications are less common today than they once were.)

## THE FUNDAMENTAL PRINCIPLE: THE SANCTITY OF LIFE

In the debate on abortion, one crucial question must be answered:

### Does abortion take the life of a person?

First, understand the key arguments on both sides of the debate. The pro-choice side will argue that a woman has the fundamental freedom to pursue her own self-interest and the rights to privacy and to control over her own body. Thus, she must be allowed to end a pregnancy deemed to be detrimental to her own well-being and health (broadly defined to include both physical and psychological factors).[18] The 1973 *Roe v. Wade* case guaranteed legal abortion in the United States through the first two trimesters of pregnancy. Over the years, various modifications and clarifications have been made, usually in response to state or federal attempts to regulate abortion.[19] One key point of contention is the question of fetal viability[20]—the time during a pregnancy after which a baby can survive outside the womb. Roe seems to define viability as the point at which a fetus "has the capability of meaningful life outside the mother's womb."[21] The timing of viability changes with advances in medical technology.

In 2021, the *Dobbs v. Jackson* case rose to the Supreme Court, in part because of arguments over viability.[22] As a result of the Supreme Court's review of the alleged constitutional right to an abortion, the court overturned *Roe v. Wade* in 2022. And now the determination of abortion rights is in the hands of the states.[23]

**eugenics:** the quest to bolster human genetics by preventing people with traits deemed undesirable from reproducing, while encouraging people with traits deemed desirable to procreate; often associated with the idea that some races are superior to others.

THE ETHICS OF LIFE AND DEATH 161

*being. Theoretically she does the best she can to save both, and practically she must make a wise choice on where to focus all her efforts by weighing chances and her own capabilities. In some instances (e.g., ectopic pregnancies), there's little, if any, chance of saving the baby if the mother is to be saved. This need not be considered an abortion. The doctor simply does what she can to save the mother and allows the baby to pass because medically it is impossible to save the fetus.*

**Of the remaining reasons, which ones seem most common?** *Possible answers: birth defects, poverty, young and unwed mothers, career pursuits*

**What are some biblical responses to those reasons for choosing an abortion?** *The biblical response can begin with compassionate understanding of the great difficulties of each of those circumstances. However, the biblical response will always point people to the sanctity of all life, including life in the womb, and God's authority over that life. It will point people to biblical resources for enduring and overcoming hardship with the help of the Lord and His people. There are obligations to preserve life and alternatives to taking innocent life even in the difficult circumstances that motivate people to contemplate abortion. (This could be a good segue into the gospel since many people are driven by fear or shame rather than trusting the Lord and resting in Him.)*

## THE SANCTITY OF LIFE

Guide a **group writing assignment** on this section's essential question.

Instruct students to look for various news articles or video clips in which the question below is being debated. Ask students to evaluate the responses of pro-life advocates versus those in favor of abortion.

After the writing assignment, guide a **town hall** or **mock debate** on how students would answer the essential question.

**Does abortion take the life of a person?** *Students should enunciate in their answers the biblical principles summarized on page 162. Since personhood begins at conception, as taught by Scripture (Gen. 25:22–23; Exod. 21:22–25; Judg. 13:5; Job 31:15; Pss. 51:5; 139:13–18; Jer. 1:5; Luke 1:41, 44), then it is undeniable that abortion takes the life of a person.*

## A SOCIETY ACCUSTOMED TO ABORTION

Use a **Quick Write** to reinforce the main problems and solutions.

**What are three major consequences to the culture of death that has overtaken societies in which abortion is rampant? What is the impact of those three consequences?**

- *Guilt: Many women who undergo an abortion admit to overwhelming feelings of guilt and remorse, even to the point that they contemplate suicide.*
- *Desensitization: Some are proud that they chose to do away with an unwanted life, shameless that it was indeed a life they had the power to nurture or dispose of. They're desensitized to the evil.*
- *Polarization: The social order has been locked into a polarizing battle for decades now. Not only have lines been drawn between the pro-choice and pro-life positions, but differing strategies set pro-lifers at odds with each other.*

**How can pro-lifers impact the society they live in?** *First, they must contend for the sanctity of all life. Second, they must present people with the hope of the gospel and its grace for those who repent. Third, they can offer various kinds of measures to help those suffering difficulty by providing alternatives to abortion (e.g., adoption, financial help, biblical counseling).*

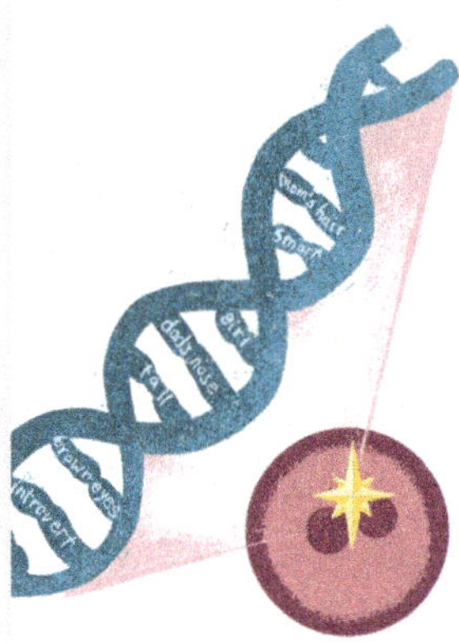


From the moment of conception, God crafts an individual human being in His image.

Pro-life supporters will argue that there is no fundamental right to end the life of another person (since the fetus's life is distinct from the mother's body, having its own unique DNA from the time of fertilization) and that there *is* a fundamental obligation to sustain the life of another human being. The disagreement is over the sanctity of life versus the freedom of a woman to maintain her own pursuits without the burden of an unwanted pregnancy. The pro-lifer is not dismissive of the difficult circumstances many women face. Crisis pregnancy centers alleviate some of these burdens and counsel alternative options for dealing with troubling circumstances. But they cannot concede that killing a human being is appropriate for relieving a burden or freeing someone to pursue other priorities in life.

Pro-lifers appeal to a variety of principles:

- The Bible reinforces the personhood of all those in the womb (Gen. 25:22–23; Exod. 21:22–25; Judg. 13:5; Job 31:15–18; Pss. 51:5; 139:13–18; Jer. 1:5; Luke 1:41, 44). The creational order testifies that life begins at conception (in other words, at fertilization). That life may develop and mature, but it is the same unique individual from the time of fertilization onward. Advancements in science support this reality[24] so that few abortionists today can argue that what's in the womb is only a blob of tissue or a part of the mother's own body. Many honest abortion advocates have had to admit that abortion takes a human life.[25] Yet, supporters of abortion still try to justify it as appropriate based on whether that life is viable. They favor the rights of the mother by allowing her to decide how *her* life will be affected.
- The taking of any innocent human life cannot be justified, even if that life is dependent on another for viability (Gen. 1:26–27). Dependency only increases the responsibility to care for life (Pss. 72:12–14; 82:3–4). If dependency were a legitimate reason to end someone's life, scores of human beings outside the womb could lose their lives, and "the sanctity of life" would be meaningless.
- God is the giver of life from conception (Gen. 4:1; Ps. 113:9). He alone has authority over life and death (Gen. 9:6).
- Children are a blessing, not a burden (although the Fall makes childrearing challenging, to be sure). The blessing of children (Pss. 127:3–5; 128:3–4) far outweighs the struggles involved in rearing them, even if a parent's circumstances may be difficult.
- Personal responsibility requires us to consider and accept the consequences of our actions. If someone consents to sexual relations (i.e., in all circumstances other than rape or sex slavery), then that person must be willing to take responsibility for caring for any children that may result (1 Thess. 4:3–5; 1 Tim. 5:8; 2 Tim. 2:22). If the parents cannot care for a child, adoption is an alternative, even in a case of sexual assault. God is able to bring about a positive outcome from any circumstances that produce human life (Gen. 50:20).

Although the debate may seem complex at times (particularly in legal arguments), the fundamental issue should be clear for the Bible-believing Christian. God holds everyone morally responsible to make every effort to preserve the life of an innocent person. If a situation arises in which a doctor has no choice but to remove a baby who would die anyway, to save the life of a mother (as in an ectopic pregnancy*), then that surgical removal should not be construed as murder. The doctor is unable to save both, so he or she concentrates on saving the mother. The doctor's intent is not to end a life that could otherwise be saved; even if he or she put all his or her efforts into saving the baby, those efforts would be futile.

**ectopic pregnancy:** a pregnancy in which the fetus never implants in the uterus but begins to develop elsewhere, usually in a fallopian tube; the baby cannot survive, and the mother will likely also die without intervention.[26]

### THE IMPACT OF ABORTION ON SOCIETY ends

What does the loss of over sixty million lives in a few decades mean to American society? What does a culture of abortion—a culture of death—mean for people living in that culture? Guilt. Desensitization. Polarization.

Many women who undergo an abortion admit to overwhelming feelings of guilt

162 ISSUES

and remorse, even to the point that they contemplate suicide.[27] Abortion hurts not just the unborn baby but also the mother, the father, the family unit, and the community. There are those, however, who boast in their callousness. They're proud that they chose to do away with an unwanted life, shameless that it was indeed a life they had the power to nurture or dispose of. They're desensitized to the evil they boast of. And the social order has been locked into a polarizing battle for decades now. Not only have lines been drawn between the pro-choice and pro-life positions, but differing strategies set pro-lifers at odds with each other.

A culture of abortion normalizes medical procedures like embryonic stem cell research, in vitro fertilization (see Chapters 12 and 13), and the use of abortifacients* for birth control. Although the number of surgical abortions has been dropping according to statistics, those statistics are based on what is known and reported. Although surgical abortions are decreasing, chemical abortions (by means of pills) are increasing. Whatever the means of ending a pregnancy, life begun at fertilization is being snuffed out.

How can pro-lifers impact the society they live in? They must reckon with the pressures many women face and offer alternatives to abortion: adoption, financial assistance during and after pregnancy, counseling that encourages right priorities and upholds children as a blessing, and support systems such as crisis pregnancy centers. Underlying all the resources should be an effort to inculcate respect for innocent children as image-bearers of inestimable value, regardless of whether they are intentional additions to a family or the result of sexual assault. It's important to educate people about how certain kinds of birth control work (those that prevent fertilization versus abortifacients that terminate life after fertilization) and to point people to the gospel for forgiveness and transformation.

### THE NEED FOR A CHANGE OF HEART

Ultimately, any change in a society's stance on abortion must come from a change of heart. The proper virtues must be cultivated. Only a virtuous people will uphold virtuous laws and practices. Certainly, the transforming work of the gospel is the fundamental need. But by God's common grace, some cultures, though filled with unconverted people, tend to be more virtuous than other cultures. Three virtues stand out above the rest in these cultures: love, courage, and gratitude.

Every kind of murder is rooted in a lack of love for God and others. True love will never consider taking innocent life. By God's common grace, people should recognize that compassionate love for the unborn would be the most natural response of a mother toward her own child. But our culture has moved away from God's creational order, which protects and values the lives of those made in His image. We are left with a society that does not uphold and value the God-given instincts of a woman to nurture and protect her child. Life-affirming virtues have been replaced by self-love—demanding autonomy, privacy, freedom, and "the right to choose," even at the expense of the most helpless among us.

Tough situations like unwanted or unexpected pregnancies will always be present in a fallen world. And when people get desperate in those situations, they are naturally tempted to take what has been falsely advertised as the easy way out (abortion). It takes courage to do the right thing—to bring a new life to birth. What if a culture supported an ethical view of enduring hardship and of steadfastness in the face of temptation? Christians should be there to help instill this courage and point women to its source: Christ, who alone forgives sin, frees from guilt, and empowers His children to lead godly lives.

Gratitude engenders satisfaction with the basic blessings of life, God's provision of "our daily bread" (Matt. 6:11). The result of gratitude is selflessness and contentment. Ironically, the most prosperous societies, which have the greatest reasons for gratitude, tend to justify abortion based on supposed financial needs. God's people should model contentment for their cultures and give generously to support those in need.

**abortifacients:** drugs that cause an abortion



## Apply

### VIRTUES NEEDED TO CHANGE HEARTS

Use a **group discussion** activity where each small group comes up with ideas to expand on the textbook's suggestions.

**How would the Christian virtues of love, courage, and gratitude transform a culture of death into a culture of life?** *Answers should reflect how the virtues of love, courage, and gratitude uphold the sanctity of life.*

## RESPONDING TO ABORTION

Use **Activity 9.3** on page 55 to apply the information in the section. Have students complete the activity with a partner.

## Assess

Guide a **summative assessment** by directing students to answer the questions in Thinking It Through 9.3.

### Thinking It Through 9.3

1. See the bullet points under the heading Appeals to Difficult Circumstances on pages 160–61 for potential student answers.
2. The key argument centers on the woman's freedom. The pro-choice side will argue that a woman has the fundamental freedom to pursue her own self-interest and the rights to privacy and control over her own body. Thus, she must be allowed to end a pregnancy that is deemed to be detrimental to her own well-being and health (broadly defined to include both physical and psychological factors). The only limitation conceded is that the decision to abort must be made before the viability of a fetus: its ability to live a meaningful life independently from the mother's body.
3. The key argument centers on the sanctity of life. The pro-life side will argue that there is no fundamental right to end the life of a helpless, innocent person (a distinct and unique life from the mother's body) but that we all have an obligation to sustain the life of another human being.
4. See the bullet points under the heading The Fundamental Principle: The Sanctity of Life on page 162 for potential student answers.
5. Possible answers: guilt, desensitization, polarization, procedures medically practiced and normalized
6. Answers may include one of the following: love because all murder is rooted in hate and abortion is murder; courage because it overcomes pressures of circumstances to do the right thing; gratitude because it is content with the basics of life and won't prioritize materialistic pursuits over the life of an innocent person.
7. An inappropriate response could be either assuring someone that she could get an abortion and not to worry about it since God is forgiving or telling someone that they have committed an unpardonable sin by getting an abortion. A wise response is to lay out the biblical truth about the sanctity of life as well as to provide hope for God's forgiveness if a sin has already been committed.

context **UNCOMPROMISED COMPASSIONATE COUNSEL**

How would you respond to women who admit they're considering an abortion or have had an abortion? You should respond wisely with truth in love. Truth and love should not be pitted against one another. The truth should be conveyed in love, and real love must be truthful. What does a wise response look like?

First, no one should go away from your counsel thinking it would be okay to opt for an abortion and rely on a gracious God for forgiveness later. That would be a complete misunderstanding of God's grace (Titus 2:11–12) and would reveal a careless attitude toward sin (Rom. 6:1–2; Jude 1:4).

Second, you should communicate clearly to any repentant person who is suffering from the guilt of having had an abortion that she should rest in God's mercy and grace for forgiveness; abortion should never be seen as an unpardonable sin. Although some consequences are irreversible in this life, God can use these kinds of circumstances to draw people to Himself, and God's mercy and grace can sustain people through any difficulty. Despite regret for the loss of relationship in this life, a woman who has had an abortion may find comfort in the knowledge that the baby enjoys eternal life in heaven with the Lord.

### Thinking It Through 9.3

1. Summarize three of the common justifications for abortion.
2. Identify and explain the key arguments for the pro-choice position in the abortion debate.
3. Identify and explain the key arguments for the pro-life position in the abortion debate.
4. What are two of the principles pro-lifers appeal to in opposition to abortion? How would you use these principles when talking to a person who is unsure about the morality of abortion?
5. What's at least one personal or social consequence of abortion?
6. What is one key virtue that orients a person away from getting an abortion and a culture away from advocating abortion? Explain why.
7. What would be an inappropriate response to someone who is contemplating having an abortion or who confesses to having had an abortion? What would be a better alternative response?

164 ISSUES

# Chapter 9 Review

## Terms to Remember

- **murder:** "The unlawful killing of a human being with malice aforethought" (18 U.S.C. 1111[a]).
- **first-degree murder:** Premeditated murder or murder committed alongside another serious crime (see 18 U.S.C. 1111[a]).
- **second-degree murder:** Any murder that does not fit the definition of first-degree murder (see 18 U.S.C. 1111[a]).
- **manslaughter:** "The unlawful killing of a human being without malice" (18 U.S.C. 1112[a]).
- **voluntary manslaughter:** Manslaughter that takes place impulsively in response

## Review THE ETHICS OF LIFE AND DEATH

### Terms to Remember

- murder
- first-degree murder
- second-degree murder
- manslaughter
- voluntary manslaughter
- involuntary manslaughter
- self-defense
- suicide
- euthanasia
- abortion

### Scripture Memory

Exodus 20:13; Matthew 5:21–22

### Understanding Ethics

1. What does the Bible teach about the source of a person's value?
2. What does the Bible teach about who has the authority over life and death?
3. What does the Bible teach about the sanctity of life from conception?

### Practicing Ethical Decision-Making

4. How should you respond when you learn that a classmate is contemplating self-harm?
5. What are some practical ways you can involve yourself in the fight against abortion?

### Analyzing and Evaluating Ethical Claims

6. How would you respond to someone claiming that a husband and father ought not use lethal force to protect his wife and children from an armed home invader?
7. How would you respond to someone claiming that suicide might not always be sinful? Conversely, how would you respond to someone claiming that suicide is an unforgivable sin that guarantees someone who committed it is in hell?
8. How would you respond to someone claiming that withholding food and water from a dependent is the same as removing artificial life support and allowing someone to pass naturally?
9. How would you biblically respond to the pro-choice slogan "My body, my choice"?

### Creating My Own Position Statements on Ethics

10. Write a one- to two-page paper that summarizes your understanding of a biblical position on the sanctity of life as it applies to the issues in this chapter. Or write a pro-life pamphlet that you could share with friends, co-workers, and family members.



to a heated exchange or serious provocation (see 18 U.S.C. 1112[a]).

- **involuntary manslaughter:** Manslaughter that results from carelessness or occurs in conjunction with the commission of a minor crime (see 18 U.S.C. 1112[a]).
- **self-defense:** "The right to prevent suffering force or violence through the use of a sufficient level of counteracting force or violence" ("Self-Defense Law: Overview," FindLaw [website]).
- **suicide:** The intentional and voluntary taking of one's own life.
- **euthanasia:** "The act of intentionally ending the life of a person who is elderly, terminally ill, or suffering from some incurable injury or disease" (Grudem, *Christian Ethics*, 587).
- **abortion:** "Any action that intentionally causes the death and removal from the womb of an unborn child" (Taken from page 202 of *Invitation to Christian Ethics: Moral Reasoning and Contemporary Issues* © Copyright 2020 by Ken Magnuson, Invitation to Theological Studies Series. Published by Kregel Publications, Grand Rapids, MI. Used by permission of the publisher. All rights reserved).

## Understanding Ethics

1. The source of a person's value comes from their status of being made in God's image.
2. God has authority over life and death. He authorizes the taking of life by appointed authorities for certain crimes.
3. The Bible upholds the personhood of those in the womb and teaches us to protect life, which begins at conception (fertilization).

## Practicing Ethical Decision-Making

4. I should alert mature adults to intervene, and I should seek to encourage the classmate with biblical principles that uphold the sanctity of life. I should point them to the hope that comes from the gospel and the virtues that can be cultivated from that hope-giving gospel.
5. Answers will vary. Examples might include financially supporting or volunteering at a crisis pregnancy center. Other examples might include writing or speaking in defense of the sanctity of life to influence peers.

## Analyzing and Evaluating Ethical Claims

6. Answers should provide biblical support for self-defense for the vulnerable against someone who would do evil.
7. Answers should support the biblical ethic that God has the only authority over life and death; if He has not delegated the authority to take a life, then nobody has the right to take life, even one's own. Even Christians can fall prey to any and every temptation (1 Cor. 10:12–13). The Bible identifies only one unforgivable sin: the blasphemy against the Holy Spirit.
8. Answers should differentiate between refusing to feed someone, essentially starving someone to death, and allowing someone to pass naturally because they're unable to remain alive off a machine artificially forcing some bodily processes to work.
9. Answers should clarify that the baby in the womb is its own unique life within the body of a woman—the baby is not a part of the woman's body but separate from it.

## Creating My Own Position Statements on Ethics

10. Papers should reflect principles enunciated in this chapter and from other supporting resources.

# Lesson Plan Overview

**CHAPTER 10:** Ethical Government

**EV** ExamView
**PPT pres.** PowerPoint presentation

| PAGES | OBJECTIVES | RESOURCES | ASSESSMENTS |
|---|---|---|---|
| **10.1 Capital Punishment** (4 DAYS) | | | |
| 167–72 | **10.1.1** Summarize different views regarding capital punishment.<br>**10.1.2** Summarize the biblical teaching on capital punishment.<br>BWS Creational Order (explain)<br>**10.1.3** Analyze the societal consequences of unbiblical views regarding capital punishment.<br>**10.1.4** Evaluate motives for supporting capital punishment.<br>**10.1.5** Formulate a biblical response to a family member of someone who suffered injustice related to capital punishment. | **ACTIVITIES**<br>• 10.1 The Justice of the Death Penalty<br>**BJU PRESS TROVE***<br>• PPT pres.: Chapter 10 | **STUDENT EDITION**<br>• Thinking It Through 10.1 |
| **10.2 Just War** (4 DAYS) | | | |
| 173–78 | **10.2.1** Summarize viewpoints regarding warfare.<br>**10.2.2** Evaluate pacifism and realism based on biblical teaching.<br>BWS Creational Order (explain)<br>**10.2.3** Analyze the societal consequences of unbiblical views regarding warfare.<br>BWS Man's Chief End (evaluate)<br>**10.2.4** Analyze the virtues necessary to act ethically regarding warfare.<br>BWS Virtue (evaluate)<br>**10.2.5** Formulate a biblical response to be used if called upon to go to war.<br>BWS Wisdom (apply) | **ACTIVITIES**<br>• 10.2 Serving in the Military versus Serving in Combat<br>**BJU PRESS TROVE**<br>• PPT pres.: Chapter 10 | **STUDENT EDITION**<br>• Thinking It Through 10.2 |
| **10.3 Immigration** (4 DAYS) | | | |
| 178–85 | **10.3.1** Identify important questions regarding immigration.<br>**10.3.2** Summarize the biblical teaching on the national and individual treatment of immigrants.<br>BWS Creational Order (explain)<br>**10.3.3** Analyze the societal consequences of unbiblical views regarding immigration.<br>BWS Man's Chief End (evaluate)<br>**10.3.4** Formulate a biblical position regarding immigrants and ethical immigration policy.<br>BWS Virtue (formulate)<br>**10.3.5** Formulate a biblical response to current immigration policy.<br>BWS Wisdom (apply) | **ACTIVITIES**<br>• 10.3 Evaluating Current Immigration Policy<br>**BJU PRESS TROVE**<br>• Video: "Immigration"<br>• PPT pres.: Chapter 10 | **STUDENT EDITION**<br>• Thinking It Through 10.3 |

*Digital resources for homeschool users are available on Homeschool Hub.

| PAGES | OBJECTIVES | RESOURCES | ASSESSMENTS |
|---|---|---|---|
| **10.4 Christian Disobedience to Authority** (4 DAYS) | | | |
| 185–90 | **10.4.1** Compare and contrast Christian disobedience to authority with rebellion.<br>**10.4.2** Summarize the biblical teaching on Christian disobedience to authority and rebellion.<br>*BWS* Creational Order (explain)<br>**10.4.3** Analyze the societal consequences of unbiblical views regarding Christian disobedience to authority and rebellion.<br>**10.4.4** Assess the virtues necessary to act ethically regarding Christian disobedience to authority.<br>*BWS* Virtue (formulate)<br>**10.4.5** Formulate a biblical response to situations where Christian disobedience to authority would be ethical.<br>*BWS* Wisdom (apply) | **ACTIVITIES**<br>• 10.4 Ethical Christian Disobedience to Authority<br>**BJU PRESS TROVE**<br>• PPT pres.: Chapter 10 | **STUDENT EDITION**<br>• Thinking It Through 10.4 |
| **Review** | | | |
| 191 | Recall concepts, terms, and Scripture memory from Chapter 10. | | **STUDENT EDITION**<br>• Chapter 10 Review |
| **Test** | | | |
| | Demonstrate knowledge of the material from Chapter 10 by taking the test. | | **ASSESSMENTS**<br>• Chapter 10 Test<br>**BJU PRESS TROVE**<br>• EV: Chapter 10 test bank |

CHAPTER 10

# Overview

How should a government act?

## Objectives

**10.1** Analyze the biblical ethic regarding governance and proper responses to governance.

**10.2** Apply a biblical ethic to issues of governance and responses to governance.

## Terms to Remember

- capital punishment
- militarism
- pacifism
- realism (on war)
- just war doctrine
- immigrant
- realism (on immigration)
- cosmopolitanism
- communitarianism
- Christian disobedience to authority
- rebellion

## Scripture Memory

- Romans 13:1, 4

## 10.1 Capital Punishment

The government is people. Have you ever thought about the government this way? You might think of buildings, courtrooms, laws, or politicians when you hear the word *government*, but those in charge of running a country are people. They will either pursue justice and righteousness (thus meeting God's approval and blessing the citizens) or they will deal out injustice and unrighteousness (earning God's disapproval and leading to the citizens' loss and frustration).

This chapter addresses four government-related issues (capital punishment, just war, immigration, and Christian disobedience to authority) that impact believers. In our fallen world, there will be unethical aspects in any government, but that reality doesn't make room for believers to respond unethically. Even in the area of government, Christians must live ethically, as unto the Lord, no matter how complicated or costly it might be to do so.

### VIEWS ON CAPITAL PUNISHMENT

The previous chapter covered the ethics of life and death. Capital punishment is certainly an issue of life and death. But we are covering this topic in this chapter because **capital punishment** is a government's use of execution as a criminal penalty. Capital punishment is not becoming any less controversial. People on both sides of the issue argue passionately for their position. So, what are some different views on capital punishment?

#### *Oppose—Abolish Entirely*

Those who advocate for the abolishment of capital punishment do so for a variety of reasons. Below is a brief description of these arguments.[1]

Secular advocates ignore the Bible's teaching on capital punishment. Christians who hold this view interpret biblical texts to fit with secular thinking about capital punishment.

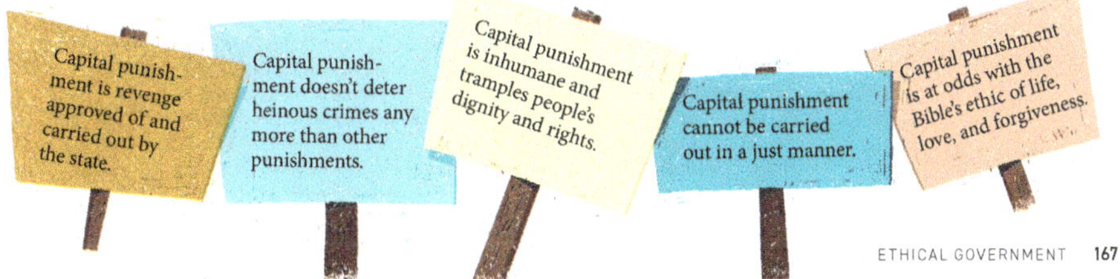

Capital punishment is revenge approved of and carried out by the state.
Capital punishment doesn't deter heinous crimes any more than other punishments.
Capital punishment is inhumane and tramples people's dignity and rights.
Capital punishment cannot be carried out in a just manner.
Capital punishment is at odds with the Bible's ethic of life, love, and forgiveness.




# 10.1 Capital Punishment

How seriously does God view murder?

### Objectives

**10.1.1** Summarize different views regarding capital punishment.

**10.1.2** Summarize the biblical teaching on capital punishment. BWS

**10.1.3** Analyze the societal consequences of unbiblical views regarding capital punishment.

**10.1.4** Evaluate motives for supporting capital punishment.

**10.1.5** Formulate a biblical response to a family member of someone who suffered injustice related to capital punishment.

### Biblical Worldview Shaping

- **Creational Order** (explain): God requires capital punishment of those who wrongly take the life of a person who bears God's image. (10.1.2)

### Printed Resource

- Activity 10.1: The Justice of the Death Penalty

### Suggested Reading

- Frame, John. *The Doctrine of the Christian Life*. Phillipsburg, NJ: P&R Publishing, 2008. Pages 701–4.
- Magnuson, Ken. *Invitation to Christian Ethics: Moral Reasoning and Contemporary Issues*. Grand Rapids, MI: Kregel Academic, 2020. Pages 393–421.

## Engage

### CHILDLIKE JUSTICE

Use a **bell ringer** activity to introduce the topic of appropriately correlating the punishment with the infraction.

Encourage students to think of a time in their childhood when they attempted to apply a fitting punishment for an offense committed against them. Direct the students to consider why their solution was not just.

Elicit that responding in a like manner (a scratch for a scratch, a slap for a slap, marking someone's paper if he or she marked yours, etc.) might seem fair to a child. But to properly carry out justice for an infraction or an offense, the proper authority must apply the appropriate punishment.

**How should children make sure the infraction is given its appropriate punishment?** *A child would need to go to a parent or teacher (the authority figure) and make him or her aware of what happened. The parent or teacher would then apply the just punishment.*

## Instruct

### CAPITAL PUNISHMENT DISCUSSION

Guide a **Think-Pair-Share** where the three views on capital punishment are distributed among groups of students. Each group should highlight the pros and cons and the strengths and weaknesses of each position before sharing those with the class.

After the activity, guide a **discussion** of the following questions.

**What other crimes might be worthy of capital punishment, other than murder?** *Possible answers: espionage, treason*

**What about these significant crimes qualifies them to potentially be worthy of capital punishment?** *These two categories are along the same lines as murder when the purpose for the espionage or treason is to facilitate gaining advantage over one's enemy, which often results in loss of life. Even during war, espionage and treason can lead to more assassinations or more deaths.*

## THREE BIBLICAL CASES

Assign a one-sentence summary for the following three categories from pages 168–69.

**Respect for the Image of God in Man (Gen. 9:6):** *Murder is deserving of capital punishment because humans are made in God's image and murder defaces the image of God Himself.*

**Enforcing the Sixth Commandment (Exod. 20:13):** *Punishing murder with capital punishment is entirely within the context of keeping God's commands, including the sixth commandment.*

**Responsibility of the Government (Rom. 13:4; 1 Pet. 2:13–14):** *The government fulfills its God-given role by punishing evildoers, which undeniably includes meting out God's wrath on murderers.*

The term *kill* used in the sixth commandment communicates premeditated murder as well as that of the "manslayer" who takes someone's life accidentally. Almost half the occurrences of this term occur in Numbers 35 which discusses instances of taking innocent life intentionally or accidentally. This use of the term *kill* indicates that the sixth commandment prohibits the taking of innocent life. But the sixth commandment doesn't prohibit capital punishment, which punishes the guilty party because the person did something deserving of his or her own death.

## TWO EXTREME VIEWS

Guide the completion of a **T-Chart** to critique the two extreme views: the outright abolition of capital punishment and the immediate application of capital punishment for those found guilty of murder.

- Outright abolition: contradicts the teaching of Scripture; leaves the family of the victim without justice; abdicates the most powerful deterrent to murder
- Immediate application: may contradict the teaching of Scripture about needing two or three witnesses for a fair and just carrying out of justice; would tend to encourage false testimonies to see someone executed; facilitates the perversion of justice in being more likely for an innocent person to be sentenced to death

**How then should capital punishment be viewed?** *Students will likely choose one of the two views introduced earlier in the section: support for significant crimes or support only for murder. Students should use the biblical material in support of capital punishment presented in this section.*

### *Support—For Significant Crimes*

Those who advocate for this position appeal to biblical evidence of God's approval of capital punishment (Gen. 9:5–6; Exod. 21:12; Rom. 13:4). The Mosaic law prescribed capital punishment for approximately twenty different sins.[2] Advocates also point to the God-appointed role the government plays in carrying out punishments like capital punishment (Rom. 13:1–7; 1 Pet. 2:13–14).

### *Support—Only for Murder*

This third view is similar to the second one, but it is slightly more nuanced and specific. It also builds a strong biblical case and highlights God's disapproval of and due consequence for murderers (Gen. 9:5–6). The main difference is that advocates of this view are most comfortable limiting capital punishment to those who commit exceptionally violent murders.[3]

American Adults in Favor of Capital Punishment

2006 71%

55% 2022

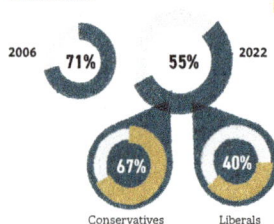

67% Conservatives

40% Liberals

## SCRIPTURE'S VERDICT ON CAPITAL PUNISHMENT

We have already briefly mentioned a few passages that support or command the use of capital punishment. Now we want to dig a little deeper into those and other passages that will help believers get a handle on what the Bible teaches on this topic. Public opinion, which is always fluctuating, is not the authority for determining the ethics of capital punishment, but it does help us to understand a culture's character. In 2022, 55 percent of American adults were in favor of capital punishment. This is down from the 71 percent who viewed the death penalty as morally acceptable in 2006. Interestingly, but not surprisingly, there was lower support for the death penalty among liberals (40 percent) than support from conservatives (67 percent).[4]

How seriously does God view murder?

### *Respect for the Image of God in Man—Genesis 9:6*

The first and main reason murder is a grievous sin is because the unjustified taking of someone's life is highly offensive to God. God made man and woman in His image, to bear His likeness (Gen. 1:26–27). So every human being intrinsically has value because of whose image he or she bears. To murder someone is to destroy one who reflects God Himself. That is a capital offense by any measure! But it is God's measure that matters, and He has determined that the just penalty for murder is capital punishment (Gen. 9:5–6). After the global Flood, God told Noah a remarkable three times that He would "require" (demand retribution for) the lifeblood of slain humans (Gen. 9:5). This is just, reciprocal retribution foreshadowing the future "eye for eye" principle in the law of Moses (Exod. 21:24). God's message to us is essentially, "If you dare take a life when you shouldn't, you must forfeit your own life for this highly offensive sin."

Life is so valuable to God that He even provided protection for those who killed someone unintentionally (Num. 35:9–34). But the only condition that freed the one who accidentally took a life was the (eventual) death of another, the high priest (Num. 35:25). Even in this situation involving manslaughter, the death of another (in this case, a substitute) was the price to pay for the death of the innocent—only a loss of life covers another loss of life (Num. 35:33).

### *Enforcing the Sixth Commandment—Exodus 20:13*

Believers today are part of the New Covenant announced by the prophets and inaugurated by Christ (Jer. 31:33; Ezek. 36:26–37; Luke 22:19–20). The Mosaic Covenant isn't binding on Christians since they are part of the New Covenant. But just as two different states can have the same law, some of the laws in the Mosaic Covenant are the same under the New Covenant. This is the case with the sixth of the Ten Commandments. Exodus 20:13 says, "Thou shalt not kill." This Hebrew word for *kill* refers to murder or to an unintentional killing (the same term is used for both a manslayer and a murderer in Numbers 35). This verb never refers to killing when done in warfare. This detail is important, especially considering the next section on just war. So, the sixth commandment isn't a universal prohibition against taking someone's life, but a prohibition against taking innocent life.

Part of the instruction God gave Moses included the repeated command to sentence murderers to death (Exod. 21:12, 14; Lev. 24:17, 21; Num. 35:16–21, 30–31). The sixth commandment codified a principle that already existed, and so it endures till today. The command of a life for a life and blood for blood was first given to Noah, the father of all nations after the Flood, way before the time of Moses. This means it was intended for all people in all places for all time. A violation of the sixth commandment was, is, and will always be serious to God.

### *Responsibility of the Government—Romans 13:4; 1 Peter 2:13–14*

In the New Testament, Scripture teaches that the government is in charge of punishing those who do wrong and rewarding those who do right (Rom. 13:1–7; 1 Pet. 2:13–14). Romans 13:4 is very similar in principle to the passage in Numbers 35 discussed above. But rather than a family member of the slain doing the avenging, the government is God's servant, "a revenger to execute wrath upon him that doeth evil." This verse teaches the government's responsibility to use "the sword" in punishing wrongdoing, an image which surely suggests the death penalty (Rom. 13:4). Along these lines, Paul himself said he was ready to suffer the death penalty if he deserved it (Acts 25:11). He was guilty of no crime, so his eventual execution was actually an injustice. But Paul never questioned his government's authority to use the death penalty. In a fallen world, governments can and sometimes do misuse their authority and rule unjustly, but that is not an argument against the *legitimate* authority God has given them.

Punishing crimes other than murder with the death penalty is an ethically challenging proposition. There is precedent in the biblical text, as seen above, for this approach. Historically, the United States did apply the death penalty more broadly. An example is that of the Rosenbergs, sentenced to death during the Cold War after being convicted of espionage.[5] But only people convicted of murder have been executed since 1976.[6] Examination and prudence are needed to apply capital punishment for crimes that aren't directly related to murder, but Scripture seems to support its broader use.

> *Christians may therefore affirm government's authority to use the death penalty in response to murder, but must also hold the government accountable to justice in its administration.* KEN MAGNUSON[7]

## CONSEQUENCES OF WRONG APPROACHES TO CAPITAL PUNISHMENT

For almost every situation or concept, there are two extreme positions. The number is commonly two because on a linear graph there is a line that forms a spectrum having two ends that are opposite one another; these ends represent the extremes. Consider the use of a turn signal while driving. You could never use it. That's one extreme. Or you could overuse the turn signal by using it for every bend in the road and by turning it on two blocks too early before each turn. Both are wrong approaches. Both could cause an accident.

What would happen if society took one extreme or the other regarding capital punishment? Are there consequences for a society that takes a wrong approach to this important issue? Consider the complete abolishment of capital punishment for any crime. If the death penalty is not a legal resource, how do you punish the worst



ETHICAL GOVERNMENT 169

and the most dangerous criminals? (There is considerable disagreement on the advantages and disadvantages of our current prison system, including sentences of life in prison.)

Look at the example of a Norwegian political extremist turned mass murderer, Anders Breivik. He killed seventy-seven fellow Norwegians in Oslo in one day back in 2011 before surrendering to the police. He was given the maximum sentence

2011 Oslo bombing

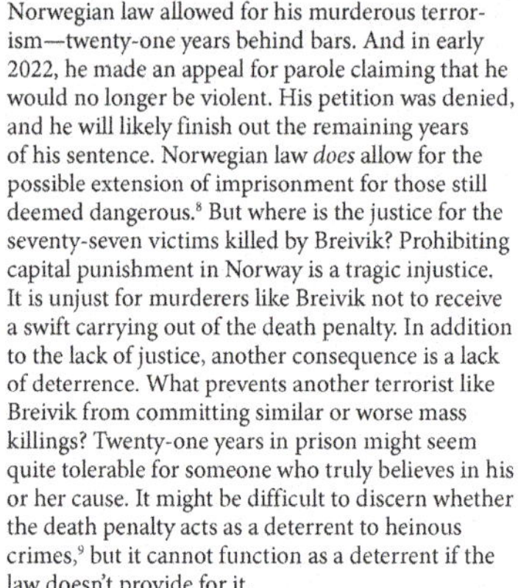

Norwegian law allowed for his murderous terrorism—twenty-one years behind bars. And in early 2022, he made an appeal for parole claiming that he would no longer be violent. His petition was denied, and he will likely finish out the remaining years of his sentence. Norwegian law *does* allow for the possible extension of imprisonment for those still deemed dangerous.[8] But where is the justice for the seventy-seven victims killed by Breivik? Prohibiting capital punishment in Norway is a tragic injustice. It is unjust for murderers like Breivik not to receive a swift carrying out of the death penalty. In addition to the lack of justice, another consequence is a lack of deterrence. What prevents another terrorist like Breivik from committing similar or worse mass killings? Twenty-one years in prison might seem quite tolerable for someone who truly believes in his or her cause. It might be difficult to discern whether the death penalty acts as a deterrent to heinous crimes,[9] but it cannot function as a deterrent if the law doesn't provide for it.

On the other end of the spectrum is the immediate application of capital punishment for any and all heinous crimes upon conviction. The implications of this position might sound fair enough, considering the biblical evidence for the validity of capital punishment for murder and other crimes. But a swift carrying out of capital punishment assumes a just conviction. It also assumes that capital punishment is a just sentence for the crime a person has been convicted of. If there is confidence in the evidence, eye-witness testimonies, and any confessions, then it *is* unethical to have a criminal guilty of such a crime sit on death row for decades. However, delay in carrying out justice may benefit those who are truly innocent if the judicial system wrongly convicted them. An example is the case of Donald Gates, who was wrongly convicted of rape and murder before being exonerated twenty-eight years later.[10] But what is the truly just solution to such wrongful convictions? Is it decades on death row while years of appeals wind their way through the court system? No (although there should be a reasonable time window to appeal). Is it abolition of the death penalty since someone might be wrongly convicted? No. The solution (in any society) is criminal justice reform, such that (1) the standard for conviction is high; (2) the death penalty applies only for crimes worthy of it; and (3) those who give false evidence, coerce confessions, and fabricate evidence are punished with the punishment they would have brought on the innocent (see Deut. 19:15–21). Hard, irrefutable evidence needs to be obtained prior to sentencing someone to death. If that case can be made justly, then the lethal punishment is also just.

As seen in the Scripture passages treated earlier, capital punishment (for murder, at the very least) is a biblical and just mandate. Abolishing capital punishment provides no justice for the victim or relief for the victim's family. Abolishing capital punishment removes a possible deterrent from those considering committing heinous crimes. But failing to obtain accurate and just convictions damages the just purpose of capital punishment. Society needs a legal system it can count on to enforce just laws justly. And the government needs laws with just consequences for crimes—laws that also help keep potential criminals in check.



170 ISSUES

*That severe punishment underscores the severity of murderous violence and of God's wrath against evil, which will ultimately be carried out in the final judgment by God directly, but which for now is administered by governing authorities as God's servants.* KEN MAGNUSON[11]

### MOTIVES FOR CAPITAL PUNISHMENT 

How do love and forgiveness and justice go together? Some proponents of abolishing capital punishment will appeal to their understanding of the Bible's ethic of life, love, and forgiveness. But the Bible's ethic on these topics isn't without sacrifice and loss of life. Just think of the whole sacrificial system God gave to the Israelites so they could live in fellowship with Him (Lev. 1–7); death for sin was central to that system. Most Christians and many non-Christians are familiar with one of the most popular verses in the Bible, John 3:16: "For God so loved the world, that he gave his only begotten Son, that whosoever believeth in him should not perish, but have everlasting life." This verse combines (eternal) life, love, and forgiveness in one sentence. But Christ, being innocent, had to give up His life so those guilty and deserving of death could live! This is a beautiful picture of God—His mercy and justice simultaneously on display.

LOVE + FORGIVENESS ≠ JUSTICE

But isn't the death of a murder victim enough violence already? What could motivate someone to add death upon death? These questions assume that executing a murderer is another unjust homicide. But the opposite is true; what is at stake is whether the person who committed the actual unjust homicide will be brought to justice. Those who oppose capital punishment purportedly believe the highest goal is the preservation of life. John Frame discusses the realities and effects of capital punishment this way:

> Objectors often assume, furthermore, that death is the absolute end of human existence, whereas Scripture teaches that there is a life to come. Murderers who repent of their sins and embrace Christ will spend an eternity in glory. Capital punishment is not an absolute deprivation of existence. It is rather a means of turning a person over to God for final judgment.[12]

Those who oppose capital punishment have an idea of justice that doesn't match with God's determination of the value of human life and the (corresponding) consequences for murder. Christians need to follow God's declaration of what justice looks like and let God's ways motivate them to support a just carrying out of capital punishment.

Many would like to substitute capital punishment with reformation and rehabilitation. Instead of a life-for-a-life biblical framework, they want to see the murderer be reformed and possibly rehabilitated back into society. But this idea is motivated by a wrong understanding of the morality of human nature. For some crimes, like theft or vandalism, restitution can be made where the guilty party pays for what he or she stole, broke, or damaged. In the case of murder, however, the murderer cannot restore the life taken; the person who committed the murder must forfeit his or her own life. Restitution cannot be done in the case of murder. Murder demands retribution since each crime must be punished in proportion (Lev. 24:17–23). Restitution and rehabilitation for certain crimes have their place. Capital punishment should be motivated by just retribution. Those guilty of murder must face the consequences of their actions—only another life can pay for the sin of murder.

CAPITAL PUNISHMENT FOR MURDER = JUSTICE

If we desire to value what God values and treat sin like God treats it, capital punishment won't sound immoral or unfair to us. Sin is tragic, and so are its consequences. Believers are motivated by faith in God and His ways and by the



## RIGHTEOUS MOTIVES FOR CAPITAL PUNISHMENT

Use a **Quick Write** for students to analyze why the two statements in the margin on page 171 are true.

Because God values human life, He has given society directions for justly dealing with murderers. The fact that God loves and forgives sinners doesn't negate the necessity of punishing criminal behavior. Murder is serious, and biblical justice calls for an appropriate retribution.

# Apply

## THE SERIOUSNESS OF MURDER

Ask this section's **essential question**.

**How seriously does God view murder?** *Extremely seriously; to murder someone is to destroy one who reflects God Himself.*

## THE JUSTICE OF ANDTHE DEATH PENALTY

Use **Activity 10.1** on page 57 to emphasize that love, forgiveness, and justice can be maintained while supporting capital punishment.

## GETTING INVOLVED

Use a **Think-Pair-Share** for students to share ideas for their involvement regarding the topic of capital punishment.

**How might you respond to someone whose loved one was murdered or sentenced to death?** *Pray with them and for them, comfort them, and direct them to the truths of Scripture and the ministry of a local church.*

**How can you influence government policy so that its laws surrounding this topic align more closely with biblical teaching?** *You can contact your state representatives, sign petitions to see new legislation stopped or passed, or interact with the district judge's office in your county. Praying and trusting God should always go along with acting in these and other ways.*

## Assess

Guide a **summative assessment** by directing students to answer the questions in Thinking It Through 10.1.

### Thinking It Through 10.1

1. a government's use of execution as a criminal penalty
2. Oppose—Abolish Entirely: Capital punishment is inhumane, violent, antithetical to Scripture, and tragic, and it doesn't reduce murders.

   Support—For Significant Crimes: Capital punishment is just and good and can be used for any number of atrocious and heinous crimes.

   Support—Only for Murder: Similar to the previous view, but capital punishment is to be used only for murder.
3. Genesis 9:6 teaches that we must respect the image of God in man. The most serious way to disrespect God is to murder someone, destroying the image-bearer that God made that person to be.

   Exodus 20:13 validates capital punishment because capital punishment is a response to someone breaking the sixth commandment.

   Romans 13:4 and 1 Peter 2:13–14 describe the responsibility of the government as God's servants to punish evil and reward good.
4. Where no capital punishment exists, the evildoers receive no justice and there is no serious threat to keep potential evildoers at bay. Also, the families of the victims would have no resolution to their losses. Where capital punishment is carried out too hastily or applied to minor crimes, the danger of putting to death the wrong person or being excessive in punishment is high.
5. Aligning one's sense of justice with that of God's should be a believer's primary motivation. Believers don't rejoice in the death of another, even if the person is guilty and deserving of death. Faith in God and the rightness of His ways motivates a Christian to trust Him while doing one's best to encourage the government to apply capital punishment justly.
6. Pray for him and for the situation. Advocate wherever and however possible to correct the wrong. Trust in the Lord through the whole thing, resting in His wisdom and grace.

---

understanding that implementing capital punishment responsibly and justly is what is best for society.

#### MURDER HITTING HOME

*Capital punishment is not perfect justice, but it is part of the process by which God brings his judgments to bear on a sinful world.* JOHN FRAME[13]

To be affected by murder, a miscarriage of justice, or the execution of a loved one on death row is extremely difficult. Even in these tragic scenarios, God is sovereign and gives His grace to those where murder hits home. Probably the most difficult of those three scenarios is to see justice being trampled on and twisted. This could be where someone you know is wrongly convicted or where someone who murdered your loved one doesn't receive the death penalty. How do you respond when you are helpless to effect any change, being at the mercy of what the state or federal government decides?

| *Pray* | *Advocate* | *Trust* |
|---|---|---|
| When you pray for local, state, and federal leaders, pray specifically that they would make just laws and decisions and fix the wrong decisions brought to their attention (1 Tim. 2:1–3). If faced with injustice, pray that God would give you grace and the boldness to have a faith-filled testimony during such a difficult time (1 Thess. 1:3, 6). | Reach out to your elected representatives and use processes for legal appeals. You might have limited power to appeal to the judge or authorities that were involved in the miscarrying of justice, but there is usually a process for appeal and review by higher authorities. Find out how you can appeal and keep pursuing justice. | Trust in the Lord and in His will for you and your family, even when you don't understand His purposes. This sin-laden world is hard and frustrating. Turn to the Lord, keeping your faith and trusting Him to work in and through this terrible situation. Even when murder hits home, the Shepherd is with His people to comfort and guide them (Ps. 23:4). |

#### Thinking It Through 10.1

1. Define *capital punishment*.
2. List and briefly explain the three views presented above regarding capital punishment.
3. Summarize the biblical teaching on capital punishment.
4. What are some societal consequences of unbiblical views regarding capital punishment?
5. What motives should undergird supporting capital punishment?
6. How would you help a friend who suffered injustice related to capital punishment?

## 10.2 Just War

Courage, strength, determination—these three words can describe the popular image of a soldier. Soldiers protect our freedoms. But soldiers can also be used as pawns in the hands of tyrannical leaders. Have you ever considered becoming a soldier or joining the military? For many, the thought of defending their homeland trumps the thought of the pain and suffering they might experience fighting a war.

Is it permissible for Christians to engage in warfare? Governments declare war and use their citizens to fight those wars. Before we can discuss the virtues a believer needs if called upon to fight in a war, we must consider the various views on war, what the Bible has to say about engaging in warfare, and both the goals and consequences of war.

### PERSPECTIVES ON WAR

One end of the spectrum views war through **militarism**. This perspective sees war as the means to fulfilling the desires of a country or its leaders. Think about the empires of the distant past (e.g., Greek and Roman) that expanded their territories to display their military prowess and to prosper financially. For more modern times, think of Hitler's Germany around the mid-twentieth century. The mentality of militarism is "I want it, and I will go to war to get it."

On the other side of the spectrum is pacifism. **Pacifism** in its most extreme form opposes all forms of violent action, even those which would avoid great harm or promote a great good. For the first three hundred years of the church's existence, Christians weren't keen on fighting even in just wars because that would have meant joining forces with a pagan government who persecuted them.[14] When Christianity became the official religion of the Roman Empire, the hesitancy of Christians to serve in the military lost most of its influence.[15] At the time of the Reformation in Europe, the Anabaptist movement emerged and was well-known for including pacifism as one of their tenets.[16] Groups like the Plymouth Brethren and the Mennonites have perpetuated pacifism in the United States.[17] The mentality of the most extreme pacifism is "Avoid war, and especially killing someone in war, at all costs."

Christian pacifists support their beliefs by appealing to various teachings in Scripture. From the Old Testament they interpret the sixth commandment, "Thou shalt not kill" (Exod. 20:13), as prohibiting taking a life even in war. From the New Testament they appeal to Jesus' teaching about believers as peacemakers (Matt. 5:9), to a believer's responsibility to turn the other cheek when slapped (Matt. 5:39), and to



### Printed Resource

- Activity 10.2: Serving in the Military versus Serving in Combat

### Suggested Reading

- O'Donovan, Oliver. *The Just War Revisited*. Cambridge: Cambridge University Press, 2003. Pages 1–18.
- Walzer, Michael. *Arguing about War*. New Haven and London: Yale University Press, 2004. Pages ix–22.

## Engage

### PERSPECTIVES ON WAR

Use a **Four Corners** activity where each corner of the room represents one of the four perspectives on war: pacifism, just war doctrine, realism, and militarism. After students have gathered in their chosen corners, direct them to discuss the merits of the perspective they have chosen to represent.

Briefly elicit evaluations from the students about each position to conclude the activity.

## 10.2 Just War

When is it right to go to war?

### Objectives

**10.2.1** Summarize viewpoints regarding warfare.

**10.2.2** Evaluate pacifism and realism based on biblical teaching. BWS

**10.2.3** Analyze the societal consequences of unbiblical views regarding warfare. BWS

**10.2.4** Analyze the virtues necessary to act ethically regarding warfare. BWS

**10.2.5** Formulate a biblical response to be used if called upon to go to war. BWS

### Biblical Worldview Shaping

- **Creational Order** (explain): God instituted government to ensure justice. Just warfare is one way for a government to ensure justice. (10.2.2)
- **Man's Chief End** (evaluate): Refusing to fight in a just war is an abdication of the responsibility to rule over God's world. Fighting without adherence to a righteous standard is an abdication of the responsibility to rule with justice. (10.2.3)
- **Virtue** (evaluate): Warfare should be an act of love toward one's neighbor, entered into only with prudence and courage. (10.2.4)
- **Wisdom** (apply): A Christian called upon to fight for his country needs to assess whether the war and the way he is being asked to fight are just. (10.2.5)

## Instruct

### THE JUSTNESS OF JUST WAR

Guide a **discussion** to defend the approach of just war doctrine as a valid position.

**Given the horror of war, does it seem oxymoronic to speak of a just war?** *Depending on where on the spectrum of perspectives on war a student falls, responses will be yes, no, or maybe. The point is that, though the phrase* just war *might sound oxymoronic, it is a term for a balanced and biblically supported position on war.*

**Because war involves death and suffering, can we really call war just?** *War is inevitable in a fallen world. That doesn't automatically make it just, but the reality of war forces believers to consider how they will engage in it when war impacts their lives directly.*

pacifism
just war doctrine
realism
militarism

the commandment for believers to love their neighbors as themselves (Matt. 22:39). Also, Matthew 5:43–44 is combined with what Romans 12:14 says to support loving and blessing the enemy instead of engaging him in battle.

There are two perspectives on war toward the middle of the spectrum. The first is realism. **Realism** is utilitarian and pragmatic, viewing wars as necessary evils, where any moral considerations either don't exist or are very flexible. The mentality of realism is "All is fair in love and war."

The final view on war is the teaching of just war doctrine. **Just war doctrine** sets ethical parameters on when war is ethically viable and how to conduct oneself in war because war is a moral matter—human life is at stake.[18] A just war is used by a government to ensure justice for its own country or close allies.[19] Just war doctrine has a biblical basis, not just a philosophical one. Each tenet of just war doctrine can be supported from various scriptural principles. Human government is entrusted with the power of the sword to punish those who do wrong (Rom. 13:4). The mentality of just war is: "War should be fought ethically and only when necessary to defend one's country and seek justice for one's own people and close allies."

**THE TENETS OF JUST WAR DOCTRINE[20]**

Over time, the just war ethic has developed a common set of criteria that can be used to decide if going to war in a specific situation is right. These include the following:

1. **just cause**
is the reason for going to war a morally right cause, such as defense of a nation?... [cf. 2 Kings 19:32–35];
2. **competent authority**
has the war been declared not simply by a renegade band within a nation but by a recognized, competent authority within the nation? cf. Rom. 13:1;
3. **comparative justice**
it should be clear that the actions of the enemy are morally wrong, and the motives and actions of one's own nation in going to war are, in comparison, morally right; cf. Rom. 13:3;
4. **right intention**
is the purpose of going to war to protect justice and righteousness rather than simply to rob and pillage and destroy another nation? cf. Prov. 21:2;
5. **last resort**
have all other reasonable means of resolving the conflict been exhausted? cf. Matt. 5:9; Rom. 12:18;
6. **probability of success**
is there a reasonable expectation that the war can be won?... [human life is valuable and shouldn't be needlessly spent; cf. Gen. 9:6];
7. **proportionality of projected results**
will the good results that come from a victory in a war be significantly greater than the harm and loss that will inevitably come with pursuing the war? cf. Rom. 12:21 with 13:4;
8. **right spirit**
is the war undertaken with great reluctance and sorrow at the harm that will come rather than simply with a "delight in war," as in Ps. 68:30?

In addition to these criteria for deciding whether a specific war is "just," advocates of just war theory have also developed some moral restrictions on how a just war should be fought. These include the following:

1. **proportionality in the use of force**
no greater destruction should be caused than is needed to win the war; cf. Deut. 20:10–12;
2. **discrimination between combatants and noncombatants**
insofar as it is feasible in the successful pursuit of a war, is adequate care being taken to prevent harm to noncombatants? cf. Deut. 20:13–14, 19–20;
3. **avoidance of evil means**
will captured or defeated enemies be treated with justice and compassion, and are one's own soldiers being treated justly in captivity? cf. Ps. 34:14;
4. **good faith**
is there a genuine desire for restoration of peace and eventually living in harmony with the attacking nation? cf. Matt. 5:43–44; Rom. 12:18.

## PACIFISM AND REALISM UNDER BIBLICAL SCRUTINY

What does the Bible teach about Christians participating in war? We want to elaborate on a few passages that pacifists use to support their position. We will also look at the arguments that realism offers. (Realism is much more common in our day than straightforward militarism. The empires of centuries and millennia past that were won and maintained through military might are no longer the way of our modern times. Militarism is essentially an extreme version of realism in that it actively and unashamedly uses military force when the powers at be deem it appropriate.)

### *Pacifism*

Some who hold the pacifist position believe that killing someone in war or self-defense is off the table. Others would make allowances for lethal force in limited circumstances.[21] Some pacifists might simply look for non-lethal ways to defend themselves and others. Christian pacifists support their beliefs by appealing to certain Scripture passages. Their interpretations of these passages tend to ignore the surrounding context, and little effort is made to synthesize these passages with other teachings in Scripture. For example, Exodus 20:13 isn't a universal prohibition against all taking of life. The sixth commandment prohibits individuals from taking the life of a person through murder, voluntary manslaughter, or negligence. It also prohibits taking justice into one's own hands. Individuals, therefore, are not on their own terms to hate, attack, kill, or threaten the life of even a legitimate personal enemy. In just war, however, a government responds to an invasion or an attack and righteously defends its people and their livelihood. Pacifists would oppose even preemptive attacks,* which may save much loss of life by avoiding a full-out conflict altogether. But preemptive attacks which hinder injustice from happening can be accommodated in just war doctrine. A government that refuses to defend and protect its people by engaging in a just war renounces its responsibility to rule over God's world.

*Love for one's neighbor does not nullify the requirement to carry out God's justice on wrongdoers.* WAYNE GRUDEM[22]

### *Realism*

War is a part of life. Someone will be the victor. The victor gets the spoils. And all people want spoils. This, in part, is the mindset of those who see war as a real part of life. But realists are very utilitarian in that any war that gives the greatest amount of good to the greatest number of people is justified. Realists also use this mindset to justify how they fight a war. A lack of morality affects how pragmatic realists are in doing what it takes to win a war. Why does this viewpoint violate a biblical worldview on what constitutes a just war?

← Sound familiar? With what ethical approach is realism most closely associated?

Even if a nation has a just reason for entering a war, that doesn't mean those fighting the war are allowed to do anything and everything that ensures victory. Humane conduct during warfare has been codified by international agreements, beginning in 1864 at the initial Geneva Convention and continuing through the Rome Statute in 1998, which created the International Criminal Court.[23] Even secular states realize that war crimes and atrocities of war are immoral and should be prevented and prosecuted where possible. Morality is found in God and in His revelation (Exod. 34:5–7; Matt. 22:37–40). All humans, including soldiers and civilians involved in war, should pursue that morality, not a morality of their own creation. A soldier fighting for the side who started the war can still fight in a way that qualifies as just.

Just war doctrine gives peace its proper place as preferable to bloodshed and loss of life on both sides. But even when pulled into war, believers can be confident that just war doctrine provides superior guidance to that of either pacifism or realism. Knowing that God has given governments authority to punish evil and provide justice for their citizens (Rom. 13:3–4; 1 Pet. 2:13–14) should be a great comfort. Yet punishing evil doesn't make room for immoral and unethical behavior in how one makes war against an aggressor nation or its civilians.

**preemptive attack:** a military attack intended to avoid a full-out war or to protect from an imminent attack from the enemy



## EVALUATING PACIFISM

Use a **Take and Pass** for students to interact with one of the following Scripture passages used by some Christians to defend pacifism.

- Matthew 5:9: This isn't a call to a nonviolence, anti-war position. This passage, like the two others in Matthew 5, is part of Jesus' Sermon on the Mount. Just wars don't break the peace of a nation; they are designed to protect and restore the peace. And so, participants and supporters of a just war are indeed peacemakers.
- Matthew 5:38–39: The context of these passages relates to interpersonal relationships, condemning vengeance; the context isn't related to self-defense or governments declaring or responding to war. Believers are not to personally seek retaliation or revenge on those who persecute them.
- Matthew 5:43–46: This passage in the Sermon on the Mount also focuses on an individual and not on governments responding to threats or attacks. Love is the greatest distinguishing feature for believers and is a key motivator for participating in a just war. This passage teaches how believers should imitate God in loving difficult people, even those who are undeserving of our love.
- Matthew 22:39: The second Great Commandment does not invalidate the justness and righteousness of punishing evil. Unlawful and immoral behavior has consequences, and it is loving to correct a person's sinful behaviors and patterns. Loving others, according to the second Great Commandment, is a motivation for participating in a just war. Love motivates defending and protecting the innocent target of an attacking country.

## EVALUATING REALISM

Guide a **discussion** on realism as it pertains to war.

**How would you respond to the statement "All is fair in love and war"?** *The statement itself, along with its assumptions, leaves no room for a sense of justice if there is no moral standard for how one behaves in love and war. Rightness or justness of a war ends up being whatever contributes to one winning the war, regardless of how it was started or fought.*

**Why is realism's approach to war misguided, and why should it be resisted?** *Living in a fallen world will at times necessitate a just war because sinful aggression must be opposed. But this attitude toward war is different from realism, which treats war as though moral considerations either do not apply or are subordinate to consequentialist considerations.*

**What is wrong with realism's pragmatic philosophy of "the ends justify the means" as a motivation for war?** *Scripture is the standard by which we measure the motivations for fighting a war. By biblical standards, realism falls short because it promotes an ethic that justifies using sinful means to accomplish one's goals. Realism is an abuse of humanity's rule and power given in the Creation Mandate. Rulers are responsible for how they exercise their rule, including when and how they call their nation to war.*

## THE DANGER OF THE EXTREMES

Use a **one-minute essay** for students to summarize the major drawbacks for pacifism and realism regarding how they affect society in general.

- Pacifism: It has no answer to the abuse and mistreatment of other nations fighting unjust wars. The well-being, including the lives, of innocent people are jeopardized.
- Realism: It threatens the lives of those on both sides of a war by launching into wars focusing solely on a nation's self-interest at the expense of morality. Realism lacks morality when entering a war and while fighting that war.

When is it right to go to war?

ends

## THE EFFECTS OF WAR ON SOCIETY

We need to look more closely at war and its effects on society when viewed from pacifist and realist perspectives. When a war is over, the hardship and challenges for many are just beginning. The leaders of nations might sign a peace treaty and go back to their homes, but the devastated soldiers, their families, and the communities directly affected by the war must begin the process of healing and restoration. Michael Walzer addresses the ethical obligations of the victor of a just war:

> Once we have acted in ways that have significant negative consequences for other people (even if there are also positive consequences), we cannot just walk away. Imagine a humanitarian intervention that ends with the massacres stopped and the murderous regime overthrown; but the country is devastated, the economy in ruins, the people hungry and afraid; there is neither law nor order nor any effective authority. The forces that intervened did well, but they are not finished.[24]

Since every war leads to devastation that must be addressed, the reasons for going to war must be just and worthy of the immense sacrifice.

For pacifism, warfare is never justified. Since many nations go to war for unjust reasons, commit genocide, and disrupt a country's infrastructure, who would make sure that the spread of oppression and injustice by a nation making unjust war didn't go unchecked? These are thorny questions for pacifism. It is unfortunate that wars have to be fought to end wars and avoid future wars. But they are necessary and can and should be fought justly. The Cold War between the United States and the Soviet Union (1947–91) shows how pacifism would have been disastrous for the world. At the end of World War II, communism began to slowly spread into various regions across the world. Even if the Soviet Union didn't fight many wars directly, it supported the furtherance of its ideologies in each nation where it maintained a foothold. The United States was directly involved in fighting against or supporting resistance to the Soviet Union in these countries, with mixed levels of success:



176 ISSUES

Greece, China, Korea, Vietnam, Cuba, and Afghanistan.[25] Pacifism would have meant little to no participation in these conflicts, and the spread of communism would have been much greater and much stronger as a result.

For realism, the pragmatic benefits or advantages of war mean that war may be waged whenever a nation deems it wise and beneficial for them. A nation would count the cost, but this calculation doesn't invoke the principles of just war doctrine. A more pragmatic, and ultimately self-serving, approach to war is taken. This results in more powerful nations increasing their power and influence while weaker nations struggle to survive and do what they can to avoid being attacked by a powerful opponent in war. Without the right reasons for going to war and the right goals, realism can't achieve righteous ends. Realism produces an unstable world order where the playground bully is justified in pushing everyone around.

### FIGHTING A WAR JUSTLY

So how can a Christian engage in a war in a just manner? What virtues do Christian combatants need as they participate in a just war? Love, courage, and prudence are needed to fight a just war. Even though love seems antithetical to war, some Christian thinkers as far back as Augustine have associated just war with love for neighbor.[26] Love, because those who fight a just war do so out of love for the people and values they are defending. Love, because loving God and others means that believers value what God values. Governments will need to go to war to defend their citizens' well-being and freedoms. But while at war, love governs how Christians treat non-combatants, enemies who surrender, and the natural resources of the enemy. It would be unloving to cause unnecessary short-term and long-term harm to non-combatants and their communities.

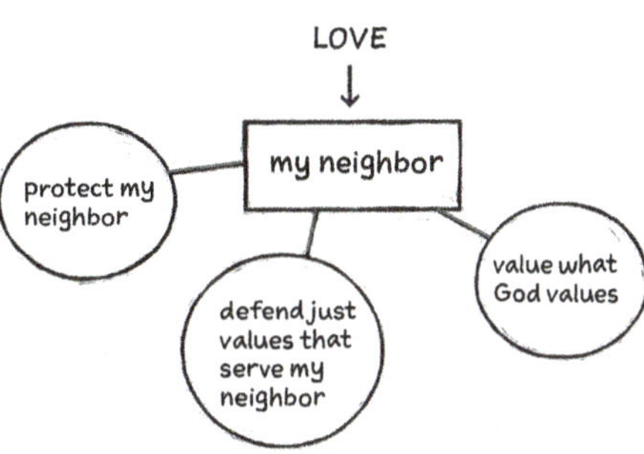


If a Christian must fight in a war, then he or she will need courage. Courage for the right causes is virtuous. The Scriptures use various warfare analogies to charge believers to live for the Lord (for example, see Eph. 6:10–17; 2 Tim. 2:3–4; 2 Cor. 10:1–6). Opposing sin, temptation, and all sorts of evil takes real spiritual courage. Thankfully, believers trust in an almighty God who fights for them (Ps. 24:8). The same truth applies to a physical battle. God gives the courage Christian combatants need to fight a just war even in the face of defeat and death.

And Christians need prudence to help them determine if a war their government is entering is just for them to participate in. This prudence could lead to hardship if those required to fight decide to oppose their government by refusing to take up arms in an unjust conflict. Prudence guides the believer to determine what aspect of a war effort (perhaps behind the front lines in a supporting, non-combat position) he or she can participate in. Prudence also guides the soldier in making good decisions, though potentially at great cost, while fighting on the front lines.

### JUST WAR HITTING HOME

How would you respond if your government drafted you into the military to fight a war? Could you apply a biblical worldview to everything surrounding the war? Would you be able to demonstrate the virtues of love, courage, and prudence as you waded into the situation? Always remember God's purpose for government. And always remember your responsibilities as a citizen of heaven and as a citizen on earth.



## VIRTUE IN WAR

Use a **Socratic seminar** for pairs of students to discuss the virtues of love, courage, and prudence in (1) the context of engaging in a just war and (2) how to conduct oneself in fighting that just war.

- Love: Love is necessary to protect the well-being and livelihood of the citizens of one's country. And in war, love for the enemy is shown by discerning between combatants and civilians and by treating captives humanely.
- Courage: Courage is necessary to take up arms even when one doesn't desire to. In the thick of war, courage motivates the fighter to sacrifice even one's life for the just cause and the defense of the innocent.
- Prudence: Prudence is necessary to make the right call of starting a war or even doing preemptive attacks. Additionally, prudence helps one determine what aspect of war he or she is comfortable participating in. During a war, prudence aids the fighter in making decisions that align with just war doctrine.

## Apply

## GOING TO WAR

Use a **Think-Pair-Share** to answer this section's essential question.

**When is it right to go to war?** *Students should utilize The Tenets of Just War Doctrine textbox on page 174 to formulate their answers. Students might choose a few of the tenets that make the most sense to them. Elicit discussion on those tenets that don't seem as clear.*

## MANDATORY MILITARY SERVICE

Use **Activity 10.2** on page 59 for students to formulate a biblical response should they get called upon to go to war.

## Assess

Guide a **summative assessment** by directing students to answer the questions in Thinking It Through 10.2.

### Thinking It Through 10.2

1. Militarism sees war as the means to fulfilling the desires of a country or its leaders. Pacifism in its most extreme form opposes all forms of violent action, even those which would avoid great harm or promote great good. Realism is utilitarian and pragmatic, viewing wars as necessary evils, where any moral considerations either don't exist or are very flexible. Just war doctrine recognizes that war is a moral matter (Walzer, *Arguing about War*, 22) and a legitimate way for governments to ensure justice (O'Donovan, *The Just War Revisited*, 5). It sets ethical parameters on when war is ethically viable and how to conduct oneself in war.
2. Pacifism can't be supported biblically because God has approved of war throughout the Old Testament. Just wars mete out, though partially, God's justice while protecting and defending the innocent or oppressed.

   Realism cannot be supported biblically because, even though the Fall and its sinful effects pervade everything, the current state of the world doesn't determine the morality of all actions done in the world. Also, the ends do not justify the means. Right intentions and moral ends must both be considered.
3. Society faces more evil, more oppression, more poverty, and more suffering if pacifism is the dominant view of the world's major nations. Wars fought justly contribute to a greater well-being of the world, not just of the winning country. Evil must be kept in check and evildoers must be dissuaded from committing great evil. And if realism were the dominant view, the more powerful nations would grow even more powerful. More countries would lose their independence and freedom. Justice wouldn't prevail because morality wouldn't be rooted in biblical principle but in the strength of one's army.
4. Love guides those who fight a just war because it is loving and just to defend the innocent and endangered people of one's country. Love will also guide individual soldiers to treat enemy captives or non-combatants ethically.

   Courage guides those who go to war because war comes with a cost. But if the cost is just and worth it, then soldiers need courage to do the right thing, even at great cost.

   Prudence guides government officials who determine whether they should or must go to war. The citizens also need to determine their level of involvement in the war, if any. Prudence also guides how to make war and how to treat the defeated enemy after the war ends.
5. Knowing that Romans 13:3–4 and 1 Peter 2:13–14 address the government's responsibility to use the sword to punish evil and evildoers, one uses love, courage, and prudence to determine one's participation in a specific war. Using Scripture passages (see textbox on page 174) that seem to support a just war doctrine will help one come to a good decision.

## 10.3 Immigration

### How should I treat foreigners in my community?

**Objectives**

**10.3.1** Identify important questions regarding immigration.

**10.3.2** Summarize the biblical teaching on the national and individual treatment of immigrants. BWS

---

### Thinking It Through 10.2

1. Define the four perspectives on war.
2. Evaluate pacifism and realism according to Scripture.
3. What consequences does society face if pacifism or realism are practiced?
4. Why are the virtues of love, courage, and prudence required for believers to act ethically regarding warfare?
5. How would you respond to being called to go to war? Defend your answer biblically.

## 10.3 Immigration

"Home is where the heart is" goes the popular saying. But what happens when your heart yearns for a place where you no longer live? Uprooting oneself or one's family to move to a new country is no small undertaking. Chances are someone in your family's not-too-distant history immigrated to the country where you live. And you may know an immigrant or the child of an immigrant. An **immigrant** is someone who relocates to a country other than his or her own. Assessing the ethicality of a nation's immigration policy is not easy. But it is a relevant issue for Christians to consider.

### WHY IS IMMIGRATION A HOT TOPIC?

Immigration is a hot topic, and not only in the United States. Why do so many people feel so passionately about immigration and immigration policy? Countries that offer consistent employment, good wages, political freedom, law and order, a comfortable standard of living, and educational opportunities are desirable for millions of people who live in countries that don't offer these things. Many are willing to leave their homelands for countries with greater opportunities. But even countries that receive only a few immigrants still struggle to treat them ethically when they do arrive. Ethnic, cultural, and religious differences; stereotypes; language barriers; and socioeconomic disparities make it difficult for immigrants to adapt quickly or easily. When the host nation rejects immigrants or when immigrants refuse to respect the ways of the host nation, these difficulties are compounded.

So what policies should govern our borders? What are we to do with the unauthorized immigrants* who are currently living in our country? What should the enforcement of our borders and immigration laws look like? Since immigration is such a hot topic that raises challenging questions with complicated answers, what light can the Bible shed on this issue?

### THE BIBLE ON IMMIGRATION

We will examine three main approaches to immigration. The Bible, however, doesn't contain a handbook on how the United States should issue visas to foreigners or secure its borders. Before mentioning the three philosophical frameworks that may describe a society's general approach to the topic of immigration, let's examine the biblical teaching on the two main disputed topics.

**unauthorized immigrants:** those who have entered a foreign country without proper permission or who remain in a foreign country after their official documentation has expired

#### *Borders—Laws*

The Bible demonstrates that since the beginning of civilization, there have been borders that separate groups of people from each other (Gen. 4:16–17; 15:18–21). God created nations, and as such they can regulate their borders (Gen. 10:31–32; Judg. 11:16–20). Edom is an example of a nation wrongly governing its borders in

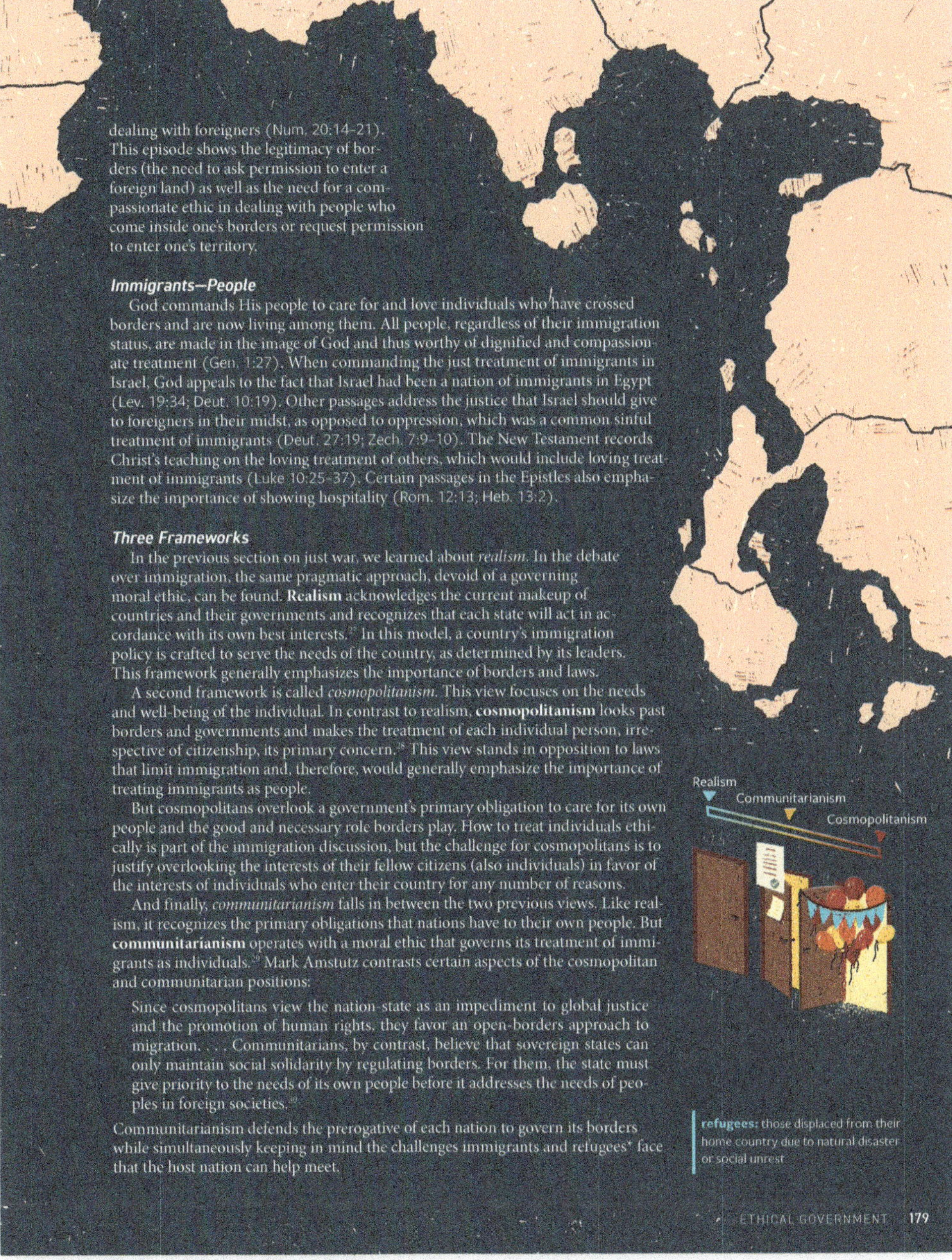

dealing with foreigners (Num. 20:14–21). This episode shows the legitimacy of borders (the need to ask permission to enter a foreign land) as well as the need for a compassionate ethic in dealing with people who come inside one's borders or request permission to enter one's territory.

*Immigrants—People*

God commands His people to care for and love individuals who have crossed borders and are now living among them. All people, regardless of their immigration status, are made in the image of God and thus worthy of dignified and compassionate treatment (Gen. 1:27). When commanding the just treatment of immigrants in Israel, God appeals to the fact that Israel had been a nation of immigrants in Egypt (Lev. 19:34; Deut. 10:19). Other passages address the justice that Israel should give to foreigners in their midst, as opposed to oppression, which was a common sinful treatment of immigrants (Deut. 27:19; Zech. 7:9–10). The New Testament records Christ's teaching on the loving treatment of others, which would include loving treatment of immigrants (Luke 10:25–37). Certain passages in the Epistles also emphasize the importance of showing hospitality (Rom. 12:13; Heb. 13:2).

*Three Frameworks*

In the previous section on just war, we learned about *realism*. In the debate over immigration, the same pragmatic approach, devoid of a governing moral ethic, can be found. **Realism** acknowledges the current makeup of countries and their governments and recognizes that each state will act in accordance with its own best interests.[27] In this model, a country's immigration policy is crafted to serve the needs of the country, as determined by its leaders. This framework generally emphasizes the importance of borders and laws.

A second framework is called *cosmopolitanism*. This view focuses on the needs and well-being of the individual. In contrast to realism, **cosmopolitanism** looks past borders and governments and makes the treatment of each individual person, irrespective of citizenship, its primary concern.[28] This view stands in opposition to laws that limit immigration and, therefore, would generally emphasize the importance of treating immigrants as people.

But cosmopolitans overlook a government's primary obligation to care for its own people and the good and necessary role borders play. How to treat individuals ethically is part of the immigration discussion, but the challenge for cosmopolitans is to justify overlooking the interests of their fellow citizens (also individuals) in favor of the interests of individuals who enter their country for any number of reasons.

And finally, *communitarianism* falls in between the two previous views. Like realism, it recognizes the primary obligations that nations have to their own people. But **communitarianism** operates with a moral ethic that governs its treatment of immigrants as individuals.[29] Mark Amstutz contrasts certain aspects of the cosmopolitan and communitarian positions:

> Since cosmopolitans view the nation-state as an impediment to global justice and the promotion of human rights, they favor an open-borders approach to migration. . . . Communitarians, by contrast, believe that sovereign states can only maintain social solidarity by regulating borders. For them, the state must give priority to the needs of its own people before it addresses the needs of peoples in foreign societies.[30]

Communitarianism defends the prerogative of each nation to govern its borders while simultaneously keeping in mind the challenges immigrants and refugees* face that the host nation can help meet.



**refugees:** those displaced from their home country due to natural disaster or social unrest

ETHICAL GOVERNMENT 179

**10.3.3** Analyze the societal consequences of unbiblical views regarding immigration. BWS

**10.3.4** Formulate a biblical position regarding immigrants and ethical immigration policy. BWS

**10.3.5** Formulate a biblical response to current immigration policy. BWS

## Biblical Worldview Shaping

- **Creational Order** (explain): God created nations, which can regulate their borders. God requires His people to act with love especially toward the immigrants in their midst. (10.3.2)
- **Man's Chief End** (evaluate): Christians should press for immigration policies that are righteous, that advance God's kingdom, and which are worthy of the calling to good works to which He has called us for His glory. (10.3.3)
- **Virtue** (formulate): As Christian citizens influence immigration policy, they should be motivated by compassion, guided by righteousness, and characterized by prudence. (10.3.4)
- **Wisdom** (apply): Prudence requires reforms that take into account the realities of the present situation; righteousness requires formulating policy changes that lead to effective enforcement of the law; compassion involves generosity toward those in need. (10.3.5)

## Printed Resource

- Activity 10.3: Evaluating Current Immigration Policy

## Digital Resource

- Video: "Immigration"

## Suggested Reading

- Amstutz, Mark R. *Just Immigration: American Policy in Christian Perspective*. Grand Rapids, MI: Eerdmans, 2017. Pages 1–15, 49–79, 110–33.

## Engage

### THOUGHTS ON IMMIGRATION

Use a **one-word summary** for each student in the class to describe his or her thoughts on the topic of immigration.

Follow up with a **discussion** on the reasons for the most recurring words.

**Why do you think _____ came up as the most frequent word? Would you categorize most words mentioned as positive or negative? Why?**

*Takeaways for Christians from the Three Frameworks*

Without necessarily subscribing to everything communitarianism believes, we can say that this perspective seems closest to balancing the biblical concerns of justice on this issue. A biblical assessment of immigration policy must balance the two concerns highlighted earlier. On the one hand, laws and borders are important, and nations have the responsibility to construct their immigration laws in a way that prioritizes the needs of their own citizens. On the other hand, love and compassion for those fleeing poverty and instability should also motivate immigration policy. Offering opportunities for uncomplicated *legal* immigration to those willing to start over, work hard, and integrate into their new homeland is consistent with *both* biblical concerns—laws and people. When a country has a strong economy with a healthy infrastructure, it can be generous with its resources and benefit from immigration.[31] A government that provides well for its own citizens is also able to provide in good measure for immigrants that it welcomes into its country.

A great example in Scripture of how all these concerns can work together is that of Abraham securing a burial site for his wife Sarah (Gen. 23). Abraham was a foreigner in the land of the Hittites. He followed all the proper legal proceedings to purchase the land and cave for the burial site. Abraham was the outsider, and he willingly followed all the customs and laws of the land he was living in, insisting on paying the full price for the field rather than accepting a handout from the Hittites (Gen. 23:9, 11, 13, 15–18). The Hittites, for their part, did not attempt to take advantage of the foreigner among them. Instead, in Abraham's time of grief, they even offered to give him a tomb in their land free of charge; eventually, far from fearing the influence of a foreigner, they gave Abraham the dignity of purchasing and the legal status of owning property in their own land.

Christians should make much of the Bible's teaching that God cares for those who are at risk of being mistreated, including immigrants, and the fact that God doesn't show partiality to or favoritism for one group of people over another (Deut. 19:17–18; Ps. 146:9; Acts 10:34). Christians should also recognize a country's right to control its borders and the responsibility of immigrants to respect the laws and appropriately adapt to the customs of the land in which they are trying to live.

#### IMMIGRATION DONE WRONGLY IN SOCIETY

A government's policies on immigration can have positive or negative effects on society. But a greater concern, one more fundamental, is whether a government's immigration policies are biblically just. Realism isn't a plausible option for believers because this view picks and chooses which morality serves its purposes best rather than seeking to follow God's prescribed morality. But someone calls the shots and affects the policies that are implemented in society. Who is running the show? For the realist the answer is whoever is in charge at a given moment. And those in charge might want any version of open or closed borders. For a time, either option might be advantageous. The political parties in charge of the White House, the Senate, and the House of Representatives favor immigration policies that further their agendas. This is acceptable to a good number of people in the nation. But if certain immigration policies are supported out of mere loyalty to one's party or to sway voters, then morality is not the goal. Realism has no objective ethical guidelines to shape immigration policies into something biblical and beneficial to a nation and those who immigrate to it.

We have so much to offer!
But we can't let in EVERYONE.


But cosmopolitanism also comes up short in terms of ethical immigration policies. Advocates would say that immigrants are people, and we should love all people. But governments that adopt this view can end up making decisions that are unloving to their own people! Consider the impact on a country's limited resources if they must be shared with millions of immigrants,



## Instruct

### MISCONCEPTIONS ABOUT IMMIGRATION ENFORCEMENT

Use a **misconception check** to highlight that advocates of immigration enforcement and border security should not be presumed to be xenophobic or racist.

**Why should advocates of immigration enforcement and border security not be presumed to be xenophobic or racist?** *Although some advocates are xenophobic and racist, not all are. Many advocates of secure borders and immigration enforcement are willing to welcome immigrants of every ethnicity, but they believe in welcoming them in a lawful and orderly fashion.*

### TESTIMONY OF AN IMMIGRANT

Show the **video** "Immigration" to expose students to the testimony of a legal immigrant and the negative effects of illegal immigration.

### A BIBLICAL ALTERNATIVE TO REALISM AND COSMOPOLITANISM

Guide a **scenario** where two halves of the class both prepare a briefing for a congressional committee seeking to frame a new immigration policy. One half represents the Bible's teaching on borders and laws, while the other half represents the Bible's teachings on immigrants. The entire class acts as the committee and formulates a policy at the end.

**What does the Bible teach on borders and laws that govern those borders and a nation's treatment of immigrants?** *See pages 178–79.*

**What does the Bible teach on the treatment of immigrants as people who enter or who need to enter a foreign country?** *See page 179.*

Include one final question for the class as part of the final policy.

**How can a nation who seeks to follow God's instruction on this matter combine respect for laws and borders and care for immigrants into one cohesive whole?** *First, since both are true, both must be embraced. Borders are good and necessary, and citizens and foreigners should abide by the laws of the land unless the laws are immoral. But people do leave their homelands and immigrate to other countries for multiple reasons and should be respected as people. There are moral and humane ways to treat even those who purposefully entered a country illegally. Governments are also responsible for preventing this and punishing those who violate the country's laws.*

### DANGERS OF REALISM AND COSMOPOLITANISM FRAMEWORKS

Use a **Think-Pair-Share** for students to elaborate on why realism and cosmopolitanism are two frameworks on immigration that are harmful to society.

**If realism represents a country that exclusively attends to the needs and wants of its own people, how then is realism harmful to society at large?** *First, God references Israel's duty to be kind and meet the needs of foreigners and immigrants multiple times in Scripture (Lev. 19:34; Deut. 10:19). Though Christians are not directly under the Mosaic Covenant, they should uphold the character traits and desire to be hospitable and understanding of immigrants since those traits are moral expectations that remain true under all the covenants (Heb. 13:2–3). Second, hospitality is practiced and received by believers, and this practice is godly and good (Acts 2:44–45; Rom. 12:13). All people have needs that others can meet with their hospitality. Even nations should be willing to extend a measure of hospitality to others in need.*

*Realism leads a country to be reticent to take in refugees or those seeking asylum, as well as immigrants who contribute to and enrich society.*

many of whom are in the country illegally. The allocation of taxpayers' dollars (health services, education, food and housing assistance, etc.) could be stretched thinner than necessary, which might mean citizens with legitimate needs would struggle to see those needs met. The negative effects of this view aren't limited to economic issues.

Another important end to consider is the effect of immigrants on a society's cultural identity. Every nation has its own cultural identity built by its history, traditions, and values. The fabric of many societies' cultures was woven by many generations of heavy immigration as well as by certain core principles—the United States of America is a prime example. The question for any nation is how much immigrants should be allowed to contribute to and change that culture.

Answering that question with one extreme or another is bound to be detrimental to a culture. This is because most cultures have aspects that are positive, biblically defensible, and in line with God's creational design. Conversely, all cultures also have aspects that are negative, unbiblical, and opposed to God's creational design. A society that is too proud and ultranationalist might embrace a closed border, no immigration. But that isolation would limit good influences from other cultures that might make a society stronger. It is arguable that immigrants from cultures with strong family ties could possibly help the current American society, where the family is in decay. On the other hand, a society that dismisses its traditions and distinct national identity might embrace an open border policy. But that society would soon lose its own identity and open itself uncritically to bad influences from other cultures that might destroy human flourishing. In the process, it could lose the positive distinctives that made it attractive to immigrants in the first place.

There are other concerns regarding the societal consequences of unbiblical views of immigration. Is there any correlation between lax border enforcement and an increase in crime? The data say no,[32] but not being able to track down a terrorist group or individual as he or she enters and exits the country is a problem. Would very restrictive immigration policy turn a blind eye to oppressed and persecuted foreigners in need of asylum or refugee status in a safe country? What criteria should be used to screen those applying for a visa, and how many visas should be issued per year? Adopting a strict position for open or closed borders can bring on serious negative societal consequences.

NEW

**EVALUATING CONTEMPORARY EVENTS**

And what about the challenge of illegal immigration? In the United States, this is a serious and divisive issue. What are the best ways to secure the country's borders against unlawful crossings? How can the government ensure that those who come in via visas renew them appropriately or return to their countries when their authorized stay expires? What is the just and compassionate way to handle the millions of unauthorized immigrants who are living and working in the country now, especially immigrant children who have grown up in the United States? Does the cheap labor that comes from unauthorized immigrants benefit American businesses so much that serious change is hindered? Does encouraging illegal immigration enable the exploitation of unauthorized immigrants? Is it possible both major political parties use the controversial issues of illegal immigration and border security to their own advantage instead of providing real, helpful solutions?

Christians need to pay attention to all of these issues so they can be citizens who contribute to ethical solutions while caring for the real needs of immigrants they encounter.

**If cosmopolitanism openly accepts and cares for all who come into one's country, how is that treatment of foreigners harmful to society at large?** *While the welfare of others should be a concern to everyone, to a nation even, the welfare of one's own nation, like a larger extension of one's family, is primary (Gal. 6:10). If nothing is being done to keep immigrants from entering a country and living as they want, without responsibilities or accountability, then the host society has lost control of its self-governance and of propagating what it holds most dear. Immigration is helpful and beneficial on many levels, but uncontrolled immigration without a meaningful structure put in place by the host nation leads to problems.*

## Apply

### BIBLICAL IMMIGRATION FOR TODAY

Use a **journal entry** for students to begin to formulate a biblical position regarding immigrants and what they imagine an ethical immigration policy would look like. This is a synthesis of the material covered thus far. Guide students to consult and incorporate the following passages and virtues:

- Deuteronomy 10:18–19
- Deuteronomy 24:14–22
- Matthew 25:34–40
- Galatians 6:9–10
- Compassion
- Righteousness
- Prudence

Christian citizens are motivated to show compassion to needy individuals around them. Christians should be influenced by God's kind and generous heart toward those in hard situations. Christians love God by loving others, including immigrants. The United States has generous (moral) policies for receiving refugees and those with legitimate requests for asylum. Christians also see the necessity to follow the country's laws and enforce them appropriately. Christians need prudence to decide how to influence lawmakers, where possible, with suggestions for improving current unethical immigration policies or creating new ethical immigration policies. Preserving the integrity of families should be a central consideration in the just treatment of the large number of unauthorized immigrants of all ages in the United States. Mass deportations, therefore, are out of the question. At the same time, prudence is needed to know how to interact with immigrants of all statuses in one's own community.

### CHRISTIAN TREATMENT OF FOREIGNERS

Guide a **discussion** on this section's essential question.

**How should I treat foreigners in my community?** *On the one hand, believers should treat all people, regardless of their nationality or visa status, with dignity, respect, and love. Many times, we are ignorant of a foreigner's legal status. Believers aren't required to determine a person's legal status. Assuming the worst of someone or being nosy or rude by asking questions to determine a foreigner's immigration status fails to show kindness and goodness to that person. On the other hand, if knowledge of a person (authorized to be in the country or not) committing a crime arises, then it is appropriate to report that activity to law enforcement.*

The following are suggested follow-up questions:

**What role does the church have in evangelizing and discipling unauthorized immigrants?**

**Should a Christian employer hire workers that he or she knows are unauthorized to work in the country?**

agents

### ATTEMPTING TO GET IMMIGRATION RIGHT

Believers need to pursue and be motivated by various virtues as they encounter ethical difficulties (2 Pet. 1:5–8). Immigration has to do with people, and many times immigrants are trying to provide themselves and their families with a better life, new opportunities, or a fresh start. Compassion, righteousness, and prudence are three virtues that should motivate the humane treatment of immigrants and the development of ethical immigration policy.

#### How should I treat foreigners in my community?

***Compassionately***

Those who hold to cosmopolitanism are likely to be accused of being too compassionate. They care so much about immigrants that they can't think of a good reason to turn any away. To them, that would be missing the mark of showing compassion. However, this way of thinking can be misdirected sentimentalism rather than true compassion. On the other hand, a realist could go to the extreme of limiting immigration so much that even legitimate refugees are turned away—this would be a gross display of indifference.

How can a believer show compassion in a fair but loving way? First, as you come across any immigrants in your neighborhood, workplace, school, or church, you can treat them with loving compassion without jumping to conclusions about their legal status (Matt. 7:12). The immediate response of a believer to foreigners should be to welcome them (see Gen. 18:2–8; 24:18–20, 31–33; Exod. 2:20; Ruth 2:8–10; 1 Kings 17:9–15; Job 31:32; Matt. 25:34–39; Heb. 13:2), not to judge them (Matt. 7:1–2; John 7:24). They are fellow image-bearers of God! Second, you can support legislation that resolves some of the current immigration problems. It is not compassionate to allow people to break the law without consequences or to ignore a scenario in which millions of immigrants are vulnerable to exploitation. Third, you can appeal to your elected representatives for the humane and fair treatment of immigrants. Fourth, you could give to trustworthy agencies that can facilitate the distribution of financial aid to refugees who haven't been given asylum in the United States yet. Fifth, you can show compassion by praying for and helping immigrants you come into contact with who have been displaced and have acute needs.

***Righteously***

Even though the topic of immigration is complicated, believers should apply the virtue of righteousness to this topic. The laws that govern who is allowed to immigrate, the visa process, the treatment of immigrants, and the expectations for immigrants should all be governed by God's righteousness. For example, this could include streamlining the approval process for family-sponsored visas by giving priority to immediate family members over extended family members.[33] God's righteousness (as seen in both justice and mercy) should also be applied to the steps unauthorized immigrants are legally required to take to correct their undocumented status.

We know that God deals justly with humanity in every way (Rev. 15:3). Believers need to pursue justice and equity with those who come looking to live in their country. There should be accountability for those who fail to obtain authorized permission to enter a country. But it would be ungodly, the opposite of righteous, to demean, ridicule, or discriminate against immigrants. There is no room for hatred or mockery of people who are of a different ethnicity, who have foreign cultural customs, or who have an unstable financial footing. Believers should seek to align their sentiments toward immigrants with God's righteous care and concern for those facing the challenges of immigration (Exod. 22:21; Lev. 23:22).

182 ISSUES

### *Prudently*

Just as it is true that the fairer the skin, the more sunblock is necessary, more prudence is required for more complicated issues (like immigration). This is not just because most politicians and lawmakers hold to various forms of realism, cosmopolitanism, or communitarianism. Immigration requires prudence because the public and national opinion is divided on what the best approach to immigration is. This problem is compounded by the fact that the government has allowed illegal immigration by not taking steps to prevent or deter it effectively. The government sends a mixed message by communicating one thing to immigrants through laws but in practice essentially allowing for the opposite by ineffective and inconsistent enforcement. Prudence is required to know how to effectively enforce current policies, how to develop future policies, and who to prioritize when implementing immigration policies.

One way to implement prudence on a local, personal level is how you vote once you turn eighteen. Voting for local, state, and federal officials impacts the development of your country's policies on immigration. You need prudence to vote for the candidates who best reflect biblical principles on immigration. You cannot fail to consider that every political candidate also holds other positions of varying ethical merit. You also need prudence to decide whether, or to what extent, you might involve yourself in meeting the needs of legitimately needy immigrants. Is there a need you can fill, or do community programs sufficiently help immigrants get on their feet and see that their basic needs are met? Serving immigrants could provide great gospel opportunities as well as clear chances to show love to your neighbors.

Christians can never go wrong showing wise compassion for the needy, engaging in righteous interpersonal conduct, and constructing prudent priorities. This is true for interacting with unauthorized immigrants just as much as with legal immigrants. You might not be called to develop immigration policy, but you are called to relate to others virtuously, including immigrants in your community.

### EVALUATING CURRENT IMMIGRATION POLICY

What reform, if any, should the government of the United States submit its immigration policies to? That is a big question for a high school student! You cannot assume that the current policies regarding immigration or the security of your nation's borders are ethical. Most presidents make changes to their predecessor's immigration policies. You need to consider some current statistics on immigration in the United States. Refer to the infographic in this section to see some of those numbers.

Nations typically place annual limits on the number of visas they may issue and the number of refugees they may accept. What matters more than the limits is the number of immigrants actually allowed entrance into the country on any given year. Nations also regulate who gets approved: family members of current residents or citizens, specialized

RECENT IMMIGRATION STATISTICS IN THE UNITED STATES

**Rate that non-US citizens are becoming lawful permanent residents**

Lawful permanent residency means a person is allowed to live, study, work, and do business in the United States as well as be protected by and be held responsible for the laws of the land.[34]

= 38,000 people

**1,063,000**
**immigrants per year gained permanent residency.**[35]
*(2010–19)*

**2/3** those approved for permanent residency based on family ties to people already lawfully in the United States[36]
*(2018–20)*

**Immigrants becoming US citizens**
*(2017–20)*

= 38,000 people

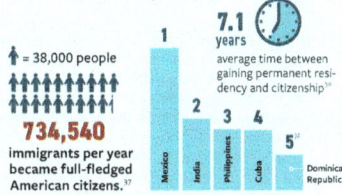

**734,540**
**immigrants per year became full-fledged American citizens.**[37]

1 Mexico
2 India
3 Philippines
4 Cuba
5[38] Dominican Republic

**7.1 years**
average time between gaining permanent residency and citizenship[39]

**Unauthorized immigrants residing in the United States**
*(as of January 1, 2018)*[40]

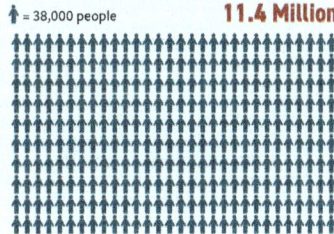

= 38,000 people

**11.4 Million**

**People admitted as refugees or granted asylum**
*(2019)*

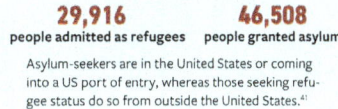

**29,916**
**people admitted as refugees**

**46,508**
**people granted asylum**

Asylum-seekers are in the United States or coming into a US port of entry, whereas those seeking refugee status do so from outside the United States.[41]



## EVALUATING IMMIGRATION POLICY

Use **Activity 10.3** on page 61 for students to formulate a biblical response to current immigration policy.

## Assess

Guide a **summative assessment** by directing students to answer the questions in Thinking It Through 10.3.

### Thinking It Through 10.3

1. What policies should govern our borders? What are we to do with the unauthorized immigrants that are currently living in our country? What should the enforcement of our border and immigration laws look like?
2. Realism: Countries can govern their borders (Gen. 4:16–17; 10:31–32; 15:18–21; Judg. 11:16–20). But it is not right for countries to violate God's moral laws when governing their borders (Num. 20:14–21), which realism would allow. Though realism aligns with the biblical teaching on the main point, realism's treatment of immigrants isn't biblical. Therefore, it remains an erroneous position as a whole.

   Cosmopolitanism: Believers should treat individual immigrants well because God taught the Israelites to do that in their day (Deut. 27:19; Zech. 7:9–10). But loving an immigrant neighbor (Matt. 25:35, 40; Rom. 12:13; Heb. 13:2) doesn't cancel out the responsibility of the government to oversee its immigration policies, as cosmopolitanism believes. Though cosmopolitanism aligns with the biblical teaching on the main point, it isn't a fully biblical position and, therefore, remains an erroneous position as a whole.

   Communitarianism: This view appeals to the Scripture passages in the previous two views but tries to harmonize them. Genesis 23 shows Abraham abiding by and submitting to the host nation's requirements of him as an immigrant in the land of the Hittites. God truly does care for all and shows no partiality to anyone (Ps. 146:9; Acts 10:34).
3. Realism wouldn't see justice or righteousness applied to immigration policies because it has no governing morality but operates on pragmatism. Cosmopolitanism would disrupt the economy and well-being of the citizens of a country if immigrants with no restraints entered and settled down in the country, sharing in all its benefits. Also, this view would see the rapid decline of the parent country's values and distinctives since no system would be in place to facilitate the assimilation of immigrants into society.

   Some other possible societal consequences would be allowing terrorists or immigrants who may commit crimes into the country or not allowing immigrants into the country who may add value to society.
4. The virtues of compassion, righteousness, and prudence need to be considered in decisions concerning the treatment of immigrants and the development of immigration policies. Compassion helps people with real needs. Righteousness is required for those in government to govern their country and the interests of their people rightly and justly, according to God's moral standards. And prudence is necessary to know how to make the right and best decisions when navigating issues of immigration policy.
5. Answers will vary. The government is the servant of God and should act as compassionately, righteously, and prudentially as it can regarding immigrants and immigration policy. Citizens of a country should submit to their government unless it causes them to sin against God. Immigration policy should seek appropriate compassion, righteousness, and prudence for immigrants while each government seeks to provide for the needs of its own people first and foremost.

workers, public figures, and so on. Depending on your view of how a nation should regulate immigration, you might decide that there shouldn't be caps on visas at all, that they should be lowered considerably, or that the distribution between visa categories should be altered. But what should be considered when evaluating the current immigration policy of your country?

Christians thinking through the ethical difficulties of immigration policy can come at the task from various angles. Since governments will always have to deal with immigration, the subject is always relevant. Believers should keep the following points in mind:

> *Immigration is social engineering. . . . You're building the population of the future.*
> JUSTIN GEST[42]

- The second Great Commandment, "Thou shalt love thy neighbour as thyself" (Matt. 22:39), summarizes all the Old Testament laws relating to how we should treat people, including the laws on the treatment of immigrants (see Matt. 22:36–40; Lev. 19:18, 33–34). It is hard to love people you don't come into contact with. The neighbors that believers are called to love are those they encounter who need help (for example, see Luke 10:29–37). Men are called to provide for those under their immediate care (1 Tim. 5:8), and all believers are called to "do good unto all men, especially unto them who are of the household of faith" (Gal. 6:10). In sum, the priority is to care well for those closest to you, but you should expand the reach of your compassion and generosity as you have the ability and opportunity. Providing well for those closest to us prepares us to help our immigrant neighbors in need. Remember that immigration policy involves current immigrants (our present neighbors) as well as future immigrants (our future neighbors).
- A country is healthy when its economy is stable and growing. Thousands of jobs require specialized workers that authorized immigrants willingly and capably fill. This setup is ideal because the immigrants, the companies, and the nation's economy all benefit from this arrangement. But stable and growing economies often benefit from cheap, unskilled labor. One question is whether unauthorized immigrants are taking jobs from citizens; a government needs to prioritize opportunities for its own citizens. However, if unauthorized immigrants are filling jobs citizens don't want and businesses are willing to employ them because that saves them money, then our society has to ask itself whether we're really just content to benefit from the status quo. If the market needs inexpensive unskilled labor, a more ethical solution would be to meet that need with current citizens or legally permit more such laborers to enter the country, but to pay them reasonable wages. On the other hand, it is helpful to train authorized immigrants in our institutions of higher education since the host nation benefits from the contributions of excellent students and future workers. An immigrant shouldn't be considered for citizenship based solely on the value of his or her contribution to society. But new citizens should be encouraged to be valuable contributors to the society they are joining.
- There should be compassion and sympathy for the immediate family members of immigrants (both legal and unauthorized) who are here or are desiring to come to the United States. Children should be raised by both of their parents whenever possible. Immigration policy that seeks to unite extended family members seems ethically defensible since family members need one another for care and support.
- There should be consequences for lawbreaking. The penalties unauthorized immigrants receive when apprehended upon illegal entry into the country or when they commit certain crimes should be carefully considered and just. Deportation should be an option, especially once unauthorized immigrants get on the radar of government officials by committing some other offense. But the situation should still be considered. What penalty applies best to this specific individual? Would an immediate deportation separate a parent from a dependent child, for example? Nevertheless, since the unauthorized immigrant entered the country illegally, a case can often be made for eventual deportation of one who commits a serious crime.

The fact that the United States offers a more comfortable life than many other countries doesn't mean the US government must accommodate every visa applicant. But immigration is real, and immigrants are people. Compassion, righteousness, and prudence are needed in great quantities for believers, their fellow citizens, and lawmakers alike. On the subject of immigration, pray for wisdom and pray for gospel opportunities.

### Thinking It Through 10.3

1. What are a few of the important questions regarding immigration?
2. Compare and contrast the biblical teaching on the national and individual treatment of immigrants with the three frameworks discussed in this chapter.
3. Analyze possible societal consequences of unbiblical views regarding immigration.
4. Explain how the three virtues discussed above are important for a biblical position regarding immigrants and ethical immigration policy.
5. What is your biblical response to current immigration policy?

## 10.4 Christian Disobedience to Authority

Many people avoid disobedience, some at any cost. Christians usually lead the way opposing disobedience. But disobedience can't always be sidestepped, nor should it always be. Disobedience, though not entered into lightly, is a very real option when a citizen is confronted by a government that requires immorality or forbids morality.

But what should a citizen's normal and expected disposition to government be? Citizens should respect, honor, obey, and submit to the God-given authorities in their land (Acts 23:5; Rom. 13:1; Titus 3:1–2; 1 Pet. 2:13–14, 17). Christians should also pray for their leaders (2 Tim. 2:1–2). Even though citizens should expect the government to fulfill its roles of punishing evil and protecting its citizens, Scripture teaches the obligations of citizens to their governments.

But governments don't always govern well—even when they have good intentions. Since this is true, a category of careful yet convictional disobedience to authority becomes viable for believers. Governments don't have absolute authority and shouldn't command blind allegiance from their people. The rest of this section will explain the ins and outs of affirming that at times citizens can and must disobey their government or other authorities.

### CHRISTIAN DISOBEDIENCE TO AUTHORITY VERSUS REBELLION

What is the difference between a protest and a riot? A riot involves violence and damage to property. But a protest is a non-violent gathering of people to call attention to a specific issue. What is the difference between a reformation and a revolution? A revolution topples the current government and builds another one from the ground up. A reformation takes what exists and pushes for change, improving it.

Now, think of the difference between Christian disobedience to authority and rebellion in a similar way. A protest and a reformation correspond somewhat to Christian disobedience to authority, while a riot and a revolution correspond to rebellion. **Christian disobedience to authority** is a refusal to obey a legitimate authority's laws or commands that contradict the commands of God. Christians engage in disobedience to governmental authorities out of moral obligation and not simply to see an immoral law changed, though that is a valid outcome. A **rebellion** rejects the current government's authority and, through violence, asserts its own opposing agenda.

An example of Christian disobedience to authority is Chinese Christians disobeying the mandate that all churches must be registered with the government. Every time unregistered churches meet, they run the risk of seeing their services interrupted and their properties raided because they are operating outside the law. It is not uncommon for the authorities to shut down churches and arrest members and pastors. But the Christian church in China is growing by leaps and bounds, and

ETHICAL GOVERNMENT 185

## 10.4 Christian Disobedience to Authority

*Is it ever right to disobey the government?*

### Objectives

**10.4.1** Compare and contrast Christian disobedience to authority with rebellion.

**10.4.2** Summarize the biblical teaching on Christian disobedience to authority and rebellion. BWS

**10.4.3** Analyze the societal consequences of unbiblical views regarding Christian disobedience to authority and rebellion.

**10.4.4** Assess the virtues necessary to act ethically regarding Christian disobedience to authority. BWS

**10.4.5** Formulate a biblical response to situations where Christian disobedience to authority would be ethical. BWS

### Biblical Worldview Shaping

- **Creational Order** (explain): God created the institution of government and requires citizens to obey it unless government is requiring them to disobey God. Good systems of government will include checks on tyranny and avenues of appeal in cases of injustice. (10.4.2)
- **Virtue** (formulate): A Christian living under unjust rule needs faith that God is in control, patience to endure injustice, courage to live for truth under pressure, and prudence to know if civil disobedience is warranted and how to best practice it. (10.4.4)
- **Wisdom** (apply): Christians who engage in civil disobedience should be confident that the law they are violating either is contrary to what God requires of them or is itself unlawful. Christians should also be prudent in how they disobey the law and be willing to accept the consequences of their disobedience. (10.4.5)

### Printed Resource

- Activity 10.4: Ethical Christian Disobedience to Authority

### Suggested Reading

- Frame, John M. *The Doctrine of the Christian Life*. Phillipsburg, NJ: P&R Publishing, 2008. Pages 618–21.
- Littlejohn, Bradford. "Christian Citizenship and the Rule of Law." The Gospel Coalition (website). December 9, 2020.

## Engage

### THE ANTI-AUTHORITARIAN

Use a **bell ringer** activity to encourage students to answer the following question about supposed anti-authoritarianism.

**How is refusing to pay taxes not an example of justified Christian disobedience to authority?** *God has given governments the authority to collect taxes. When Jesus was asked whether it was lawful to pay taxes to Caesar, He noted that Caesar's likeness was on Roman coinage and said citizens should render unto Caesar what was Caesar's (Luke 20:22–25). Therefore, refusing to pay taxes is opposing God-sanctioned authority (Rom. 13:5–6).*

Christian disobedience to authority is not a license for Christians to refuse to cooperate with any law or demand from an authoritarian or immoral government. Christian disobedience to authority shouldn't be done lightly or carelessly. Dislike for a government policy or governor doesn't make it ethical to refuse to cooperate with the specific law.

## Instruct

### REBELLION IS NOT AN OPTION

Guide students to create a **T-Chart** with "Christian disobedience to authority" on one side and "rebellion" on the other.

See pages 185–86 to gather the information for the T-Chart.

## THE BIBLICAL APPROACH TO CHRISTIAN DISOBEDIENCE

Use a **Think-Write-Pair-Share** for students to study the relevant biblical passages concerning a Christian's relationship to the government and its officials.

**What does each passage teach regarding how citizens are to relate to their government and its officials?**

- **Acts 23:5:** *Quoting Exodus 22:28, Paul confessed his disrespectful response even while acknowledging that his inappropriate words were said in ignorance of who the man, Ananias, was. It is sinful to speak with contempt about one's government officials, for God has put them in that position.*
- **Romans 13:1:** *A believer recognizes that God has ordained the existing government and submits to it. This is God's good creational design for governments and their citizens.*
- **Titus 3:1–2:** *This passage combines the principles of the two following passages: respect and obedience.*
- **1 Peter 2:13–14:** *The realm of obedience, repeated here, gets delineated a bit more: the purposes of government are to punish evildoers and to protect those who do good.*
- **1 Peter 2:17:** *Honoring everyone includes honoring those in power in one's country.*
- **Acts 5:29:** *This verse doesn't contradict the previous ones. The previous passages remain true, but when a government demands or requires a Christian citizen to disobey God or commit sin, disobedience to that human authority is necessary and just.*

this is in part due to the consistent practice of Christian disobedience to authority by many Christians.[43]

An example of rebellion is what happened in Russia in 1917. There were two revolutions, one in March and one in November. The Russian monarchy, in power for over three hundred years, was overthrown by revolutionaries (industrial workers on strike, hungry peasants, and fed-up soldiers) in Petrograd in March. The monarchy was replaced by a provisional government. In November of that same year, Vladimir Lenin's revolutionary Bolshevik Party replaced the provisional government, with hardly any bloodshed, with his communist government and its long-reaching influence.[44]

In both examples, people are taking matters into their own hands. Chinese Christians are in the right because the government mandates are immoral and restrict what God has commanded. The Russian Revolution of 1917 was a rebellion in which the people, having been mistreated by their government, used force to see that their demands were met.

It should be clear which option is valid for Christians to engage in, when necessary. Christian disobedience to authority shouldn't be entered into lightly. Mario Morelli offers a helpful insight that applies to Christian disobedience to government authority. (What Morelli says about "the civil disobedient" would also apply to a Christian forced to disobey the government.)

> Unlike the ordinary criminal, motivated by self-interest or malice, the civil disobedient is often moved by moral or conscientious motivation, in the sense that a moral belief prompts the illegal act. The revolutionary aims, at least ultimately, at overturning the existing political or legal order.[45]

An arrogant attitude is the wrong approach to any type of Christian disobedience to authority. A mere dislike for certain officials in the government doesn't justify breaking any law you disagree with. That would be rebellion. And Christian disobedience to authority isn't limited to governments. Other authorities are also in view and can include employers, teachers, and even parents.

### A BIBLICAL DEFENSE FOR CHRISTIAN DISOBEDIENCE TO AUTHORITY AND AGAINST REBELLION

Christian disobedience to authority isn't the norm for believers today. Neither was it the norm for God's people in the Old and New Testaments. But there were still many times when those in positions of authority were evil or demanded their subjects to sin. We'll look at some of those examples below. There is only one absolute authority in the world—God (Rev. 4:11; 5:12–13). Only God can be fully trusted. And rebelling against God, directly or indirectly, is consistent with the lives of unbelievers, not believers (Rom. 1:21, 25, 32). So even in the face of governmental pressure to sin against God or others, rebellion isn't an option for believers (Matt. 5:3–12, 43–48). God demands that His people do justice and that they let Him repay evil as He sees fit (Deut. 16:20; Rom. 12:17–19). That sounds nothing like rebellion. What passages in Scripture teach on this topic, and what are some examples of Christian disobedience to authority from Scripture?

*Romans 13:1–7 and 1 Peter 2:13–17 are decidedly antirevolutionary in their emphasis.*

JOHN FRAME[46]

#### *Foundational Passages*

Romans 13:1–7 and 1 Peter 2:13–17 are foundational passages for civil *obedience* and make a case against rebellion. That's what also makes them foundational for our current topic! Romans 13 describes obeying the governing authorities as equal to obeying God who appointed them. 1 Peter 2 essentially says the same thing while referencing the reality of higher (national) authorities and lower (local) authorities that both require our submission. These two passages guide Christians how to live as good citizens of the nations where they reside (see also 1 Tim. 2:2). Christians shouldn't develop an unruly or haughty attitude toward their government because they think they are above the laws of their land. That kind of attitude fuels rebellions. Christians should consistently pray for their local and national government authorities (1 Tim. 2:1–2, 8). Paul also gave instruction for all believers to submit to the established authorities in a respectful and ethical manner (Titus 3:1–2).

The beginning of the book of Acts provides two foundational passages for the exception to the rule—Christian *dis*obedience to authority. In Acts 3, Peter healed a lame beggar. The religious leaders became upset because Peter and John were preaching in the name of Jesus after this miraculous healing. Their solution was to command Peter and John to stop preaching and teaching about Jesus (Acts 4:18). Peter and John were Jews and, like the rest of the Jewish people, had a certain obligation to follow their leadership's instruction. The two apostles responded by stating, "Whether it be right in the sight of God to hearken unto you more than unto God, judge ye. For we cannot but speak the things which we have seen and heard" (Acts 4:19–20). The second passage is even clearer. With a memorable declaration, the apostles committed to do God's work by obeying God's commands rather than those of human authorities: "We ought to obey God rather than men" (Acts 5:29).

The apostles were not bluffing or bucking the established system for the fun of it. They were committed to truth and righteousness; they were obligated to fulfill their God-given mission. They preached and performed miracles and served the Lord faithfully even to the point of death or imprisonment (Acts 12:1–4). They willingly accepted the consequences of their faithfulness to God. They didn't take matters into their own hands and overthrow Rome's appointed leaders. Since God has absolute authority over all spheres of life, His commands supersede any human commands (Matt. 28:18–20; Acts 1:8). But when human commands align with government laws and God's revelation, those human commands must be obeyed in order for us to be faithful to the commands of God. In the case of the apostles in the book of Acts, Christian disobedience to authority meant showing their worship of and devotion to Christ instead of obeying human commands that were opposed to Christianity. Christ is above the state. Christ is over all (Col. 1:16–17).

Is it ever right to disobey the government?

### *Primary Examples*

Are there other examples in Scripture where God's people had to disobey man in order to obey God? Yes, there are. And none of these cases turned into a rebellion or hinted at the need for one. The Pharaoh of Moses' infancy commanded the Hebrew midwives to kill the baby boys that were born to the Hebrew women. But the midwives feared God; their disobedience to Pharaoh's command proved their obedience to God (Exod. 1:15–17). Esther disobeyed the laws of the land where she lived, risking her own life. She went before the king without an invitation to plead for the lives of her people (Esther 4:16). Daniel disobeyed the king's commands and didn't even adjust his already-established custom of prayer (Dan. 6:7–10). And Daniel's three friends violated the clear command to worship the idol of the king and in their integrity were willing to suffer the consequences of obeying God rather than man (Dan. 3:10–12, 16–20).

Because of the stark contrast between good and evil in these examples, the Christian disobedience to authority practiced on an individual level almost seems obvious or even easy. But that didn't make it easy for these saints to disobey their governing authorities, especially because they could have lost their lives (and many did) for their courageous stances! Rebellion wasn't even on the table. In our day opposing unrighteous laws seems much more complicated. Rebellion is tempting since so many anti-God policies are being made into laws (e.g., abortion, gender and sexuality issues, teaching evolution in public schools). Refraining from rebellion in favor of Christian disobedience to authority (when warranted) is an act of faith!

But Christian disobedience to authority is not the only solution. For example, during the Divided Kingdom, Ahab was Israel's most wicked king, and his extended family followed his example. His daughter Athaliah tried to murder all the rightful royal heirs in order to take the throne in Jerusalem for herself (2 Chron. 22:10).



ETHICAL GOVERNMENT 187

## NEITHER TYRANNY NOR ANARCHY

Guide a **discussion** for students to explain when Christian disobedience to authority can avoid the societal upheaval of tyranny and anarchy.

**When is Christian disobedience to authority beneficial to a society?** *Christian disobedience to authority counters tyranny and rejects anarchy because it seeks to act justly for the benefit of others. A society benefits from all participants in a nation relating to one another in a just, ethical, and moral manner. Even when a society chooses to act immorally by supporting and passing unethical laws, Christian disobedience to authority allows believers to operate within the bounds God has appointed by peacefully disobeying the immoral human authority and obeying God as the higher authority.*

Rather than rebelling through a military operation, one of former king Ahaziah's sisters saved young Joash so he could one day rightly replace Athaliah and her unjust rule (2 Chron. 22:11–23:15). Another example is Paul, who experienced an unjust imprisonment at the hand of the Jews and Romans (Acts 24:27; 25:7–10). Paul didn't rally a band of friends and supporters to overthrow the local Jewish or Roman authorities. Paul used the available legal channels to make and defend his case (Acts 25:11). Straightforward godly disobedience to authority (other than hiding Joash) was avoided in both of these examples. But rebellion was purposefully avoided as well. Ahaziah's sister and Paul prudently chose the best ethical and legal options available to them. Christian disobedience to authority is valid when necessary, but at times other legal options, still in opposition to and in disagreement with a government mandate or action, are more prudent.

### ANARCHY VERSUS TYRANNY

Have you ever had to care for a houseplant? If so, you might have learned that too much of a good thing (water or sunlight) can be a bad thing. And then maybe the next time you cared for a houseplant, you provided it with too little of a good thing, with similar consequences. Let's face it, not everyone has a green thumb!

What are the societal consequences of unbiblical views of Christian disobedience to authority and rebellion? We are making the case that Christian disobedience to authority can be good and necessary, when done properly, with the right motives, and for the right goals. We are also making the case that rebellion is not an alternative Christians should turn to. How do Christians discern when disobedience to authority is the appropriate response? Christian disobedience to authority *can* get out of hand and be harmful to society. When too much focus is placed on the *disobedience to authority* part and not enough focus is placed on the *Christian* part, rebellious behavior can raise its ugly head. And if that happens, an actual rebellion could break out, which could lead to anarchy. Anarchy throws the baby (an organized government) out with the bath water (the abuses and shortcomings of the government), leaving chaos and disorder to rule. If every citizen took it upon himself or herself to determine which laws he or she deemed constitutional and unconstitutional (and thus non-binding for him or her), we would find ourselves in the days of the judges when "every man did that which was right in his own eyes" (Judg. 17:6; 21:25). If you know anything about the book of Judges, you probably know this: no king in Israel meant unprecedented levels of sinful behavior and societal decay.

Christian disobedience to authority should not be the Christian's first recourse when thinking that the government has overstepped its proper biblical bounds. There are many other avenues that should be attempted before Christian disobedience to authority. In addition to prayer, Christians living under republican forms of government should first challenge unconstitutional laws in court or seek to overturn such laws legislatively. There are some laws that would overstep a biblical understanding of the rightful authority government has been given by God and yet are not causes for Christian disobedience to authority. The governments that Daniel, Ezra, Peter, and Paul lived under used their God-given authority for evil. Indeed, these governments were foreign rulers of the Jews. Yet they were the existing governmental power of their day, and God's people were expected to submit to them.

Believers need to proceed with care when considering whether Christian disobedience to authority is justified and necessary and suffering persecution is the godly and ethical option to choose. Tyranny and anarchy are not situations which believers should be comfortable with. But it's important to remember that good citizeship will use the proper governmental channels and representatives to push back against an immoral government.

In a wisely framed government, citizens have recourse against tyranny. The reformer John Calvin observed that, in many governments, there are government officials who have the responsibility for resisting the tyranny of other governmental officials when it occurs. When these other governmental officials, or magistrates, are

Hananiah, Mishael, and Azariah resisted the command to bow down before an idol of a pagan king, choosing to obey God instead (Dan. 3:10-12, 16-20).

in place, it is their solemn responsibility, within the legal scope granted to them, to resist unjust laws and protect citizens from them.[47]

These officials, also known as lesser magistrates, are a legitimate and helpful resource for believers to oppose unjust government mandates. Bradford Littlejohn clarifies that "there is a crucial difference between an *unjust law* and a law that *requires us to do injustice*."[48] He also reminds us that we can appeal to the lesser magistrates even concerning laws that may seem unjust:

> For Christians convinced that certain government actions represent an overreach of the government's own laws, the proper course of action is to appeal to the courts—the "lesser magistrates"—for protection. (To be sure, sometimes the most straightforward way to do so is to disobey in a pointed fashion so as to force the legal issue, but this should be done with great care and humility.)[49]

For example, Paul wasn't afraid to take advantage of his rights under the Roman rule of his day in demanding justice and fairness (Acts 16:35–39; 22:25–29). But Paul's employment of his rights wasn't a personal, subjective, or violent resistance to laws he deemed unrighteous. He rightfully and publicly pushed back against the illegal injustices he was receiving.

### THE VIRTUES REQUIRED FOR CHRISTIAN DISOBEDIENCE TO AUTHORITY

To be involved in Christian disobedience to authority is no small matter. But if your government does require you to engage in behavior God has forbidden or to refrain from doing what God has commanded, then Christian disobedience to authority is your duty. There are several virtues that need to guide and influence the Christian who finds himself in this situation: faith, patience, courage, and prudence.

Faith is needed because you must trust in God's designed purpose for government (Rom. 13:3–4, 6; 1 Pet. 2:14). And you need faith to rest in God's timetable for punishing evildoers. This is exactly what Jesus did through suffering an unjust trial and crucifixion (1 Pet. 2:23). Christians must tolerate the uncomfortable consequences of having wicked people in government who revel in opposing God and His standards. It takes faith to rest in God's plan for the world and in His protection of His people.

Patience is needed because if you engage in Christian disobedience to authority hoping for change, the desired change might not happen when you would like to see it happen or might not happen at all. You need patience as a citizen because the candidates you vote for might not get elected, and if they are elected, they might not be able to do as much good as you hoped. The virtue of patience helps believers battle the urge to rebel or start a revolution when things aren't going their way politically. It also takes patience to endure pressure and persecution from the wicked. God keeps an account of all the wicked's deeds, and believers are called to live for the Lord and patiently wait for Him to accomplish His will (Ps. 37:34).

Courage is needed because it is difficult to defend and live by godly convictions. It takes courage to live by a biblical ethic and do your part to hold accountable those who make and enforce policy. Even though a government might not force its citizens to offer sacrifices to any idols, it takes godly courage to denounce ungodliness in society (e.g., abortion, LGBTQ+ agenda). The psalmist encourages believers by saying, "Be of good courage, and he shall strengthen your heart" (Ps. 31:24). Much courage and strength from the Lord will be required to do what is right if your freedom to live according to biblical convictions is threatened.

And prudence is needed to determine when Christian disobedience to authority may be necessary and to discern the wisest way to proceed. It takes prudence to understand what is at stake and then pursue the appropriate, God-honoring strategy to exercise Christian disobedience to authority (or pursue a legal alternative).



## VIRTUOUS CHRISTIAN DISOBEDIENCE TO AUTHORITY

Use a **one-minute summary** for students to briefly elaborate on why believers need faith, patience, courage, and prudence when disobeying authority.

- Faith: Believers need faith in God because He has designed the government to be an authority over them (Rom. 13:3–4, 6; 1 Pet. 2:14). Although God requires that those in charge act ethically, faith acknowledges that God is in control and trusts in His timing for judging those who are acting unjustly.
- Patience: Patience is required because God works out His will according to His timetable (Ps. 37:34). Disobedience to authority may achieve short-term goals; patience is required to wait and see how God will work in the short- and long-term even while enduring injustice.
- Courage: Courage is needed because the leaders of a corrupt or immoral government won't always respond with humility or repentance when confronted. God helps believers have courage in difficult situations while under pressure (Ps. 31:24).
- Prudence: Prudence is necessary while a believer is considering all the details surrounding the commitment to obey authorities or to disobey in order to obey God, who has the ultimate authority. One should consult and exhaust various alternatives, using prudence, before deciding to disobey government in order to obey God.

## Apply

### THE MILLION DOLLAR QUESTION

Ask this section's **essential question**.

**Is it ever right to disobey the government?** *It depends. Peter says in Acts 5:29 that "we ought to obey God rather than men." If the government requires you to do what God forbids or if it forbids you from doing that which God requires, disobedience to authority is the ethically justified response. However, if possible, believers must utilize the legal and proper channels to avoid direct civil disobedience. If that is not possible, believers must patiently and courageously accept whatever consequences occur when they disobey the civil government.*

### A GOVERNMENT'S RESPONSIBILITY

Ask this chapter's **essential question**.

**How should a government act?** *The most succinct answer to this question is found in two passages: 1 Peter 2:14 and Romans 13:4. They indicate that governments should punish evildoers, even executing lawbreakers worthy of death, and do good to or protect law-abiding citizens. Every decision governments make and every action they take, they do as God-ordained ministers. Governments are required to act justly and follow God's righteous standards.*

### INSTANCES OF ETHICAL DISOBEDIENCE

Use **Activity 10.4** on page 63 for students to formulate a response to situations where Christian disobedience to authority would be ethical. Have students complete this either individually or in groups.

## Assess

Guide a **summative assessment** by directing students to answer the questions in Thinking It Through 10.4.

### Thinking It Through 10.4

1. Christian disobedience to authority shares common traits with a protest and a reformation. Rebellion shares common traits with a riot and a revolution. Christian disobedience to authority is a refusal to obey a legitimate authority's laws or commands that contradict the commands of God. Rebellion is the rejection of a current government's authority and the assertion of an opposing agenda through violence.
2. Romans 13:1–7 and 1 Peter 2:13–17 show the legitimacy of Christian disobedience to authority. Acts 4:19 and Acts 5:29 are the foundational passages for disobeying one's civic leaders.

   Primary examples of disobedience to authority include the Hebrew midwives (Exod. 1:15–17), Esther (Esther 4:16), Daniel (Dan. 6:7–10), Daniel's three friends (Dan. 3:10–12, 16–20), Joash's escape from Athaliah (2 Chron. 22:11–23:15), and Paul's appealing to Caesar (Acts 25:11). None of these involved rebellion, but the citizens of the countries did take a personal stand against the evil of those governments.
3. Anarchy or tyranny. With anarchy the citizens rebel, and chaos and disorder result. With tyranny the government overreaches and abuses its power, oppressing its people.
4. Believers need faith in God's designed purpose for government and faith in God's provision for them as they suffer at the hands of immoral governments. Believers need patience to wait for God's judgment of the wicked, according to His timetable.

   Believers also need patience as they pray for righteous elected officials to influence the government. Believers need courage to initiate and follow through with disobedience to authority. This requires going against the flow of culture, and believers will be attacked for pushing against evil.

   Believers need prudence to discern when a government demands that they sin or overreaches its prescribed authority. They also need prudence in how best to practice disobedience to authority, including how and if they should make that disobedience known to others.
5. Proceed with faith, patience, courage, and prudence. Even though suffering and persecution might ensue, noncompliance from the beginning, followed by appealing to a lesser magistrate or government official is the answer, all the while entrusting one's self, family, and church to the Lord.

Knowledge of laws and legislation isn't sufficient for believers to make ethical decisions. The virtues of faith, patience, courage, and prudence all interact with one another as believers wrestle with challenging issues that might require Christian disobedience to authority. Do you have patience to suffer and an enduring faith in God's ways that would help you courageously and prudently confront government-sanctioned evil?

### RIGHTEOUS CHRISTIAN DISOBEDIENCE TO AUTHORITY

How would you respond to a government mandate that required you to put your children in the public school system? If that happened, private Christian schools and homeschooling would be illegal. Since the Bible doesn't give us commands to only homeschool our children or only put them in Christian or public schools, the best way to answer this question is to use the Scriptures to discover if the state or the parents are responsible for educating children. If a husband and wife know that it is their God-given right and responsibility to guide their children's education (Deut. 6:4–9; Eph. 6:4), then opposing such a mandate could be a prudent course of action that doesn't necessarily have to turn into Christian disobedience to authority. Even if a government decided to mandate obligatory schooling in solid, conservative Christian schools, it would still interfere in a sphere of society that doesn't belong to it. Local and state governments, along with community-based advocacy groups, should be able to legally question and oppose unethical and manipulative mandates. Christians can use the lesser magistrates to push back against inappropriate government mandates.

But how would you handle a government mandate that criminalized the biblical teaching on gender and sexuality? This would mean that any teaching that opposed the LGBTQ+ agenda and sensibilities would be outside the scope of what is lawful. Based on your knowledge of the Bible's teaching on this topic, you know that your church could not comply with such a mandate. The process of Christian disobedience to authority would need to start right away. Certainly, churches should appeal to all the appropriate lesser magistrates, including fighting the mandate in the courts. But also, you and your church should be prepared for any consequences of not complying with this mandate. Your church shouldn't even consider agreeing to the demands of such a mandate, nor should your church remain silent about certain sins—because "we ought to obey God rather than men" (Acts 5:29).

In any instance of potential Christian disobedience to authority, pray that your faith would be strong, that your patience would endure, that your courage wouldn't falter, and that your prudence would be sharp. As a rule, submit to the government. But never disobey God's commands in your pursuit of obedience to human government. Be vigilant about where your government is headed and how it seeks to impact its citizens, believers especially, with its laws and regulations.

### Thinking It Through 10.4

1. Compare and contrast Christian disobedience to authority and rebellion.
2. What is the biblical teaching on Christian disobedience to authority and rebellion?
3. What are some of the societal consequences of unbiblical views regarding Christian disobedience to authority and rebellion?
4. Assess the virtues necessary to act ethically regarding Christian disobedience to authority.
5. What would your biblical response be to situations where Christian disobedience to authority would be ethical and necessary?

10 ETHICAL GOVERNMENT **Review**

#### Terms to Remember

- capital punishment
- militarism
- pacifism
- realism (on war)
- just war doctrine
- immigrant
- realism (on immigration)
- cosmopolitanism
- communitarianism
- Christian disobedience to authority
- rebellion

#### Scripture Memory

Romans 13:1, 4

#### Understanding Ethics

1. How seriously does God view murder?
2. When is it right to go to war?
3. How should I treat foreigners in my community?
4. Is it ever right to disobey the government?

#### Practicing Ethical Decision-Making

5. Two friends ask your opinion of their job choices. One will be a prison guard, overseeing lethal injections when capital punishment is administered. The other is joining the military. He will have a frontline battle position if your country goes to war. What do you tell them?
6. You have a classmate or friend on your street who came to the United States with his parents illegally as a baby. His father was recently deported, and his mother is struggling to make ends meet at home. How do you respond when he asks to carpool with you and asks for other favors that would help meet real needs that he is currently experiencing? How does his legal status affect your treatment of him?

#### Analyzing and Evaluating Ethical Claims

7. How would you counter the following claim? "Capital punishment only adds violence to violence. Christians should seek to break the cycle of violence, not commit more of it."
8. Based on the tenets of just war, do you think it's possible to defend any war from the past or present? Do you think a Christian can participate in a war with a clean conscience? Explain.
9. How would you respond to a friend who says, "Entering the United States illegally is breaking the law, so all illegal immigrants should be imprisoned or deported immediately"?
10. How would you respond to a friend or church member who says, "I answer to God alone, so I choose which federal and local laws I obey"?

#### Creating My Own Position Statements on Ethics

11. How should a government act? Write a brief statement answering this question as it applies to the four topics in this chapter.
12. How should you relate to your government's laws and policies regarding the four topics of this chapter?

ETHICAL GOVERNMENT 191

# Chapter 10 Review

## Terms to Remember

- **capital punishment:** A government's use of execution as a criminal penalty.
- **militarism:** A perspective on war that sees war as the means to fulfilling the desires of a country or its leaders.
- **pacifism:** A perspective on war that, in its most extreme form, opposes all forms of violent action, even those which would avoid great harm or promote a great good.
- **realism (on war):** A utilitarian and pragmatic perspective on war that views wars as necessary evils, where any moral considerations either don't exist or are very flexible.
- **just war doctrine:** A perspective on war that recognizes war as a moral matter (Walzer, *Arguing about War*, 22) and also recognizes that war can be a legitimate way for governments to ensure justice (O'Donovan, *The Just War Revisited*, 5); sets ethical parameters on when war is ethically viable and how to conduct oneself in war.
- **immigrant:** Someone who relocates to a country other than his or her own.
- **realism (on immigration):** A framework that when applied to immigration recognizes that each government will act according to its best interests in relation to its own people. Borders and immigration laws feature positively in this framework (Amstutz, *Just Immigration*, in the introduction to Chapter 4).
- **cosmopolitanism:** A framework that when applied to immigration focuses on the needs and well-being of the individual regardless of a person's immigration status (Amstutz, *Just Immigration*, in the introduction to Chapter 4).
- **communitarianism:** A framework that when applied to immigration defends the prerogative of each nation to govern its borders with moral appropriateness, keeping in mind the challenges immigrants and refugees face that host nations can help overcome.
- **Christian disobedience to authority:** A refusal to obey a legitimate authority's laws or commands that contradict the commands of God.
- **rebellion:** The rejection of a current government's authority and the assertion of an opposing agenda through violence.

## Understanding Ethics

1. God assigned capital punishment to murderers as early as Genesis 9:6. The reason is that humans, and only humans, are made in God's image. To destroy an image-bearer of God is a capital offense because it is a direct offense against the Creator God.
2. This question gets at the legitimacy of war or how ethical going to war is. According to just war doctrine, Christians can go to war when these eight criteria are met: (1) there is a "just cause"; (2) the war is carried out under a "competent authority"; (3) "comparative justice" is used; (4) there is a "right intention"; (5) the war is used as a "last resort"; (6) there is a "probability of success"; (7) there is a "proportionality of projected results"; and (8) the war is conducted in the "right spirit" (Taken from page 2555 of *The ESV® Study Bible* [The Holy Bible, English Standard Version®], Copyright © 2008 by Crossway, a publishing ministry of Good News Publishers. Used by permission. All rights reserved.).
3. Treating immigrants ethically requires Christians to combine and apply numerous things at the same time: Christian virtues, good motives, just ends, and responsibilities as a neighbor and citizen of the country where the immigrant and citizen reside. Love and compassion are part of the treatment of any person, including immigrants. There should also be a desire to help the immigrant adjust well in society. The treatment of a legal

immigrant will look a little different than the treatment of one who is in the United States illegally. Love and compassion will be part of both interactions though.

4. Yes, but only when the government either commands us to do what God prohibits or forbids us from doing what God requires. In practicing Christian disobedience to authority, all the right channels with the right attitudes should be employed to change the law or get an exemption from the law where possible. But believers must obey God when government officials demand that they disobey God.

## Practicing Ethical Decision-Making

5. To the friend who is working as a prison guard I would say: Be assured that the Bible warrants capital punishment for murderers. Consider getting involved in prison reform, at least in your state, so you can work in an environment where you know justice is being carried out as it should be.

   To the friend joining the military I would say: You might never get sent off to war. If you do find yourself in direct conflict with enemy combatants, behave justly as a soldier, avoiding any temptations to commit war crimes. The higher your rank in the military, the greater responsibility you have to assess and respond to the justness, or lack thereof, of a specific war.

6. This friend did not choose to come to the United States illegally. His parents brought him. While lovingly and compassionately helping to meet the real needs that he has, you can help him look into options to correct his legal status. Neither his legal status nor that of his parents changes the way you should treat him as your neighbor and as a fellow image-bearer of God.

## Analyzing and Evaluating Ethical Claims

7. Murder is violence against the victim and against God. Not applying capital punishment to the murderer violates explicit teachings in Scripture (Gen. 9:6; Deut. 19:21). Because of the gravity of the crime of murder, God has given government the responsibility to make murderers pay this ultimate price (Rom. 13:4). God doesn't have any aversion to violence when it is righteous judgment on wicked sinners.

8. Some wars erupt between nations where there have been ongoing skirmishes and political maneuvering. In these cases it is hard to determine who the aggressor is and who is fighting the war justly. However, when an unprovoked nation invades or attacks another nation, it is easier to determine which side is the guilty party. The best way to fight in a war with a clean conscience is to abide by the eight tenets of just war doctrine and the four points of how to conduct oneself justly in war.

9. The scenarios surrounding the illegal nature of an immigrant's presence in the United States are complicated. Not all people who enter the United States illegally or who overstay their visas are guilty of a felony. But both scenarios are a crime. Imprisonment, deportations, and fines are some of the tactics used to combat illegal entry into the United States. A case needs to be made for the best solution. However, tactics like mass deportations can have negative effects on families and would therefore be unjust.

10. Christian disobedience to authority isn't about following the laws that suit you the most. Romans 13 and 1 Peter 2 teach the Christian's responsibility to submit to one's government. The norm is to practice civil obedience. The posture for any believer practicing civil disobedience is one of faith, patience, courage, and prudence. Unless the government is forcing us to disobey God or forbidding us to obey Him, then we should submit to the government.

## Creating My Own Position Statements on Ethics

11. Governments should operate as closely to God's standards of justice and righteousness as possible. This is the ideal, and it is God's design for governments. Regarding capital punishment, governments should ensure with utmost care that only those guilty of qualifying crimes (e.g., murder) receive capital punishment. Regarding just war, governments should be responsible in how they preserve the interests of their nation. Following just war doctrine helps nations stay away from sinning against other nations, one's own people, and God Himself. Regarding immigration, governments should look to the interests of their own people before compromising those interests by doing too much for those who want to immigrate to the United States. This leaves room for limited, compassionate, and prudent immigration policies that benefit both one's nation and certain foreigners. Regarding civil disobedience, governments should make room for its citizens who have a conscientious objection to some of its policies. Governments should behave righteously and justly to provide the greatest benefit for the people they serve.

12. As a citizen, I should support my government's careful and responsible use of the death penalty for murderers, if not also for other aggravated or egregious crimes. I should fully support all just wars my country participates in. When my government sanctions a war unjustly, then I should call attention to that injustice through the proper channels and even through peaceful protests. I shouldn't contribute to the complications of current immigration policies. I should treat all people with dignity, meeting needs that I can meet. All immigrants are people, and I should treat all my foreign neighbors as such, regardless of their legal status. I should obey my government, and when disobedience to authority is required, I should do it using the proper channels and willingly accept any consequences for my continued disobedience. In all four cases, prudence is an important virtue to pursue.

# Lesson Plan Overview

**CHAPTER 11:** Ethical Society

**EV** ExamView
**PPT pres.** PowerPoint presentation

| PAGES | OBJECTIVES | RESOURCES | ASSESSMENTS |
|---|---|---|---|
| **11.1 Racial Discrimination and Inequality** (4 DAYS) | | | |
| 194–201 | **11.1.1** Define *race*, *racism*, and *inequality*.<br>**11.1.2** Summarize the biblical teaching regarding race and racism.<br>BWS Creational Order (explain)<br>**11.1.3** Evaluate the societal consequences of unbiblical views of race.<br>BWS Man's Chief End (evaluate)<br>**11.1.4** Assess the virtues necessary to act ethically toward all who are made in the image of God.<br>BWS Virtue (formulate)<br>**11.1.5** Formulate a biblical response to racist attitudes and actions. | **ACTIVITIES**<br>• 11.1 Responding to Racism with Grace and Truth<br>**BJU PRESS TROVE***<br>• Video: "Racial Discrimination"<br>• PPT pres.: Chapter 11 | **STUDENT EDITION**<br>• Thinking It Through 11.1 |
| **11.2 Addictions** (4 DAYS) | | | |
| 201–6 | **11.2.1** Describe common addictive vices.<br>**11.2.2** Summarize the biblical teaching regarding substance abuse and gambling.<br>BWS Creational Order (explain)<br>**11.2.3** Evaluate the consequences of a society that normalizes these vices.<br>**11.2.4** Assess the virtues necessary to resist these vices.<br>BWS Virtue (formulate)<br>**11.2.5** Formulate a biblical response to peer pressure to engage in these vices. | **ACTIVITIES**<br>• 11.2 Pressure to Engage in Substance Abuse or Gambling<br>**BJU PRESS TROVE**<br>• Video: "Addictions"<br>• PPT pres.: Chapter 11 | **STUDENT EDITION**<br>• Thinking It Through 11.2 |
| **11.3 Communication and Media Use** (4 DAYS) | | | |
| 206–10 | **11.3.1** Describe ethical issues related to communication and media use.<br>**11.3.2** Summarize the biblical teaching regarding communication and media use.<br>**11.3.3** Evaluate the personal and social consequences of unethical communication and media use.<br>BWS Man's Chief End (evaluate)<br>**11.3.4** Assess the virtues necessary for ethical communication and media use.<br>BWS Virtue (formulate)<br>**11.3.5** Formulate a biblical response to cultural pressure to engage in unethical communication and social media use. | **ACTIVITIES**<br>• 11.3 Ethical Challenges with Social Media<br>**BJU PRESS TROVE**<br>• PPT pres.: Chapter 11 | **STUDENT EDITION**<br>• Thinking It Through 11.3 |

*Digital resources for homeschool users are available on Homeschool Hub.

| PAGES | OBJECTIVES | RESOURCES | ASSESSMENTS |
|---|---|---|---|
| | **11.4 Business Ethics** (4 DAYS) | | |
| 210–14 | **11.4.1** Identify common ethical issues related to business practices.<br>**11.4.2** Summarize the biblical teaching on business practices.<br>*BWS* Creational Order (explain)<br>**11.4.3** Evaluate the consequences of unethical business practices.<br>**11.4.4** Assess the virtues necessary to act ethically regarding business practices.<br>*BWS* Virtue (formulate)<br>**11.4.5** Formulate a biblical response to pressure from coworkers or employers to engage in unethical business practices. | **ACTIVITIES**<br>• 11.4 Business Ethics<br>**BJU PRESS TROVE**<br>• Video: "Business Ethics"<br>• PPT pres.: Chapter 11 | **STUDENT EDITION**<br>• Thinking It Through 11.4 |
| | **Review** | | |
| 215 | Recall concepts, terms, and Scripture memory from Chapter 11. | | **STUDENT EDITION**<br>• Chapter 11 Review |
| | **Test** | | |
| | Demonstrate knowledge of the material from Chapter 11 by taking the test. | | **ASSESSMENTS**<br>• Chapter 11 Test<br>**BJU PRESS TROVE**<br>• EV: Chapter 11 test bank |

CHAPTER 11

# Overview

How does a Christian ethic form a good society?

## Objectives

**11.1** Analyze various ethical issues in society.

**11.2** Apply a biblical ethic to various issues in society.

## Terms to Remember

- race
- racism
- inequality
- abstinence
- recreational drugs
- bribery
- extortion
- exploitation
- commercialism

## Scripture Memory

- Matthew 7:12

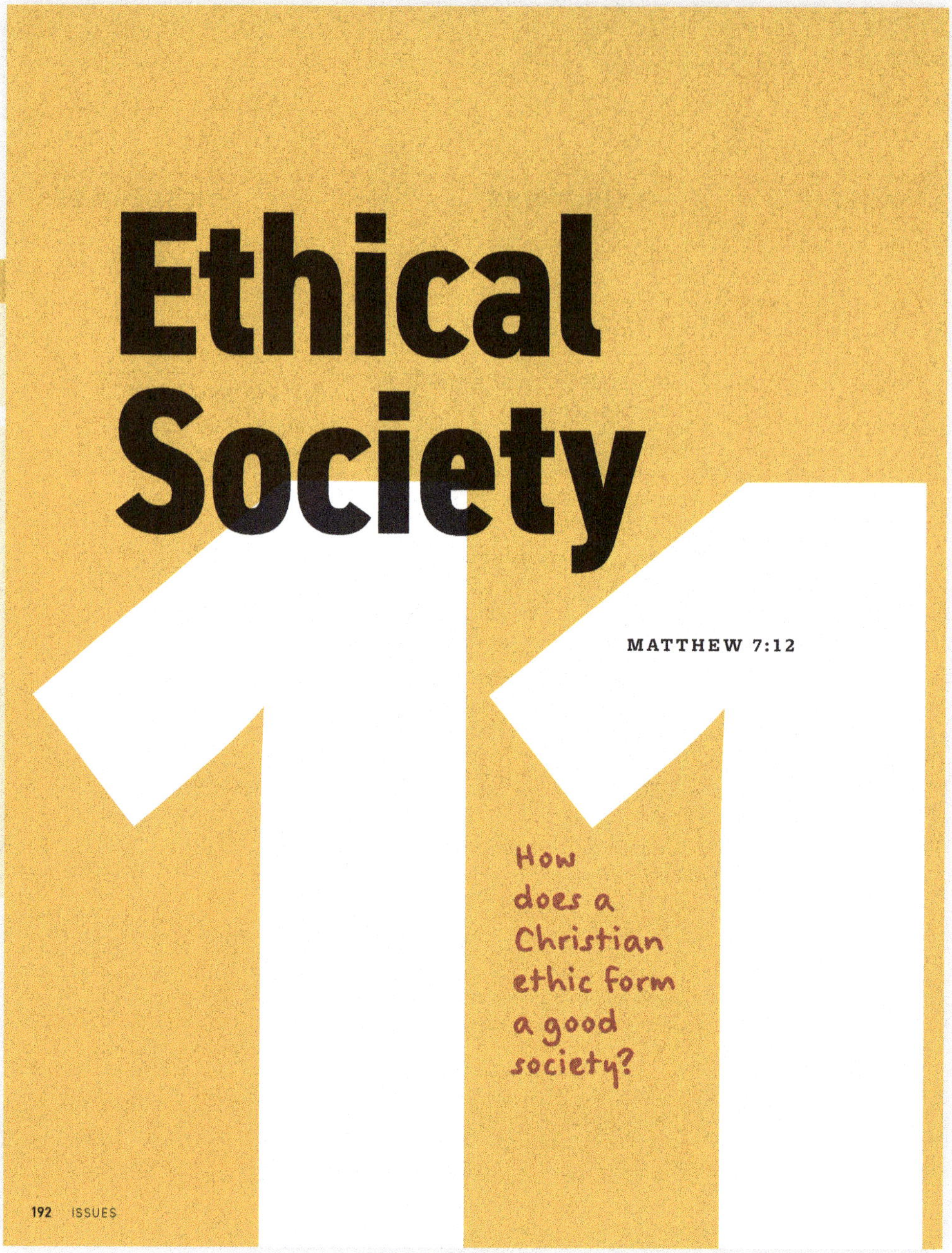

# Ethical Society

11

MATTHEW 7:12

How does a Christian ethic form a good society?

192 ISSUES

The ripple effects of our choices extend further than we realize. Our immediate circle of family and friends are obviously impacted by the choices we make, but the larger society is also affected, even if it is less obvious. Every choice has ethical implications for society.

Framing our choices in terms of their impact on society can be a bit overwhelming. The point, however, isn't to overwhelm but to debunk the myth that what people do in private is of no consequence to society. Popular sentiment says, "I can do whatever I want as long as I'm not hurting anyone." The assumption is that it's possible to seal off the impact of one's choices, as if foolish decisions only hurt the one making them. Take, for instance, drug abuse. While clearly hurting the individual abuser, drug abuse also hurts society.

Given the fallen human condition, we understand that not everyone in society will embrace the Christian ethic (John 3:19–20). But if the book of Acts and church history teach us anything, it is that corruption in society is no match for the power of the gospel (for example, see Acts 1:8; 13:47; 17:6). With God's blessings, the gospel can spread like leaven throughout society, giving people a new appetite for true justice and deeds of love (Acts 2:37–47). As more hearts in society are changed, the ethical character of society is also changed. A society shaped by Christianity is a society where people generally treat others as they want to be treated (Matt. 7:12).

One way to think of Christian ethics as it relates to society is to think of it in terms of Christians pressing the claims of Christ's lordship over all reality. Our study in this chapter is concerned with what that might look like with respect to some of the social problems of our day. What does Christian ethics have to say about racial discrimination and inequality? Does Christian ethics have an answer to the problem of substance abuse? Is Christian ethics capable of restoring decency to our communication and media use? And how can Christian ethics improve business practices? Even if Christians cannot bring cultural change in these areas, they still live within culture and need to think about how a Christian should address these issues.



ETHICAL SOCIETY 193

# 11.1 Racial Discrimination and Inequality

How should I foster racial reconciliation?

## Objectives

**11.1.1** Define *race*, *racism*, and *inequality*.

**11.1.2** Summarize the biblical teaching regarding race and racism. BWS

**11.1.3** Evaluate the societal consequences of unbiblical views of race. BWS

**11.1.4** Assess the virtues necessary to act ethically toward all who are made in the image of God. BWS

**11.1.5** Formulate a biblical response to racist attitudes and actions.

### Biblical Worldview Shaping

- **Creational Order** (explain): Both the unity of the human race and ethnic diversity are creationally normative. Effective responses to racism must align with creational norms. (11.1.2)
- **Man's Chief End** (evaluate): In a fallen world humans have made themselves or their group the center of their chief end. (11.1.3)
- **Virtue** (formulate): Those who are seeking racial reconciliation need humility as they address a complex problem, prudence to find the better solutions, love for those impacted by racism, and hope that racism can be effectively addressed. (11.1.4)

### Printed Resource

- Activity 11.1: Responding to Racism with Grace and Truth

### Digital Resource

- Video: "Racial Discrimination"

### Suggested Reading

- Adams, Isaac. *Talking about Race: Gospel Hope for Hard Conversations*. Grand Rapids, MI: Zondervan, 2022.
- Ware, Charles. "Grace Relations." Answers in Genesis (website). January 22, 2009.
- ———. "Racial Reconciliation That Matters." Answers in Genesis (website). September 25, 2016.
- ———. "Racial Reconciliation: The Grace Relations Way." Answers in Genesis (website). June 4, 2019.
- Yancey, George. *Beyond Racial Gridlock: Embracing Mutual Responsibility*. Downers Grove, IL: InterVarsity Press, 2006.

## 11.1 Racial Discrimination and Inequality

A society consistently shaped by a Christian ethic would not discriminate against people because of their race or ethnicity. Race-based slavery, as seen in American history, is a clear example that the Christian ethic has sadly not been consistently applied. Although many white Americans misused the Bible to justify discrimination against black Americans, there were other courageous voices who appealed to Scripture in order to end racial discrimination. Therefore, we maintain that a consistent application of a Christian ethic produces real justice and real equality for all people.

### DEFINING RACE, RACISM, AND INEQUALITY

To get a handle on this subject, we need clear definitions. Unfortunately, there's disagreement on how to define terms such as *race*, *racism*, and *inequality*. If we had common definitions in society, it would make it easier for people to have a conversation about race.

#### *Race and Ethnicity*

The term *race* has commonly been defined in terms of skin color and other features such as kind of hair or the shape of various facial characteristics. However, there is no biblical or creational basis for this definition of race. The selection of which characteristics define a "race" is arbitrary, and a different selection would result in different racial groupings. As one author notes,

> All racial taxonomies—whether popular or scientific—are the product not of nature but of the imagination combined with inherited cultural stereotyping as well—to be fair—as the empirical observation of genuine (though superficial, trivial and inconsequential) biological differences.[1]

Sometimes it's unavoidable to speak of *race* in this manner since this is how many people still understand the term, but this definition cannot be supported by an examination of creation through the lenses of Scripture. Apart from God's revelation regarding the human race, people groups have historically made their "racial" differ-



## Engage

### RACIAL DISCRIMINATION

Show the **video** "Racial Discrimination" to introduce the subject to students.

### THE BIBLICAL BASIS FOR HUMAN EQUALITY

Conduct a **Think-Pair-Share** to allow students to discuss the biblical basis for human equality.

**What is the biblical basis for human equality? Why is secularism unable to consistently uphold human equality?** *The image of God in man and our common descent from Adam (Acts 17:26) make the biblical basis for human equality. No matter what differentiates one person from another or one group of people from another group, all people are equally valuable by virtue of being made in God's image. Therefore, all people deserve to be treated with equal worth and dignity. Secularism affirms human equality, but it denies that humans are created in the image of God and thus lacks a rational basis to consistently uphold human equality.*

## Instruct

### UNDERSTANDING RACE AND ETHNICITY

Guide a **discussion** about the terms *race* and *ethnicity* to explain their meaning and usage.

ences an occasion for prideful division.[2] Being a believer does not guarantee racial harmony with others. The history of racism in the United States among professing evangelical Christians is proof of that. But Christian acts of unbelief in the area of race do not change the truth that racial harmony is impossible apart from God's revelation about the human race.

There are two other definitions of *race* that do conform to biblical teaching and creational norms. *Race* can be used to refer to the one human race—the Bible speaks of all humanity in its unity as descended from Adam (Acts 17:26). By starting with what unites all people as *one* race, we set the stage for a constructive conversation about ethnic diversity as part of God's good design.

On the other hand, *race* in the sense of ethnicity is also a biblical concept. Paul said that God made the nations, meaning ethnic groups (Acts 17:26). The diversity of nations is a creational norm worked out over time. While the origin of diverse human languages traces back to the Tower of Babel, the origin of ethnic diversity does not. If it did, ethnic diversity would be a result of the Fall instead of God's creational intention.

Nations or ethnic groups will continue to exist in the eternal state (Rev. 7:9; 21:24–26). We should celebrate God's amazing creativity manifested in the ethnic diversity of the human race. We should also recognize that ethnicity is broader than the term *race* as commonly used to refer to skin color and other features. People of different biological ancestry can be incorporated into a different ethnic group, as in the case of biblical figures like Rahab, Ruth, and Uriah. Though not biologically Jewish, they became part of ethnic Israel. Thus, nations are not static; they include people from different and mixed biological backgrounds who come together to form nations or ethnic groups.

#### *Racism and Inequality*

Proper definitions for *racism* and *inequality* help provide clearer conversation and therefore a higher probability of successful communication. The *Oxford English Dictionary* defines **racism** as

> prejudice, antagonism, or discrimination by an individual, institution, or society, against a person or people on the basis of their nationality or (now usually) their membership of a particular racial or ethnic group, typically one that is a minority or marginalized. Also: beliefs that members of a particular racial or ethnic group possess innate characteristics or qualities, or that some racial or ethnic groups are superior to others; an ideology based on such beliefs.[3]

Since an attitude of racial superiority can reside in anyone's heart, anyone may be guilty of racism. Honesty requires us to acknowledge that historically when a majority ethnic group views itself as superior to a minority ethnic group within a culture, the minority ethnic group has suffered the brunt of racist behavior. This has often resulted in laws and customs that deprive minority groups of equal treatment. **Inequality** before the law and within society occurs when certain groups are treated as less worthy of respect and dignity than other groups.

#### UNDERSTANDING RACIAL PREJUDICE, DISCRIMINATION, AND ANTAGONISM

Racial prejudice is a dehumanizing attitude toward a group of people based on their physical features. Racial prejudice may then produce discrimination in the laws or customs of a society. People who are the objects of racial prejudice may be denied certain rights and privileges that the more powerful ethnic group enjoys in that society. This denial of rights and privileges is what constitutes discrimination. On the other hand, a society might afford everyone the same legal protections and thereby outlaw discrimination. But even in this situation, racial prejudice and antagonism (personal hostility) could still exist in a society because there may be some who view those of a different ethnicity as inferior to them. A just society should ensure that its citizens are not, on the basis of physical characteristics, denied the rights and privileges that other law-abiding citizens enjoy. A just society should also discourage racial antagonism—because all people have equal value as bearers of God's image.



**Why is it unhelpful to define *race* in terms of skin color and other features such as hair or the shape of various facial features?**

- *Although biological differences exist within humanity, the selection of certain physical features for the purpose of grouping people into one race or another is arbitrary. A selection of different biological characteristics could just as easily result in a different grouping of people.*
- *Grouping people based on an arbitrary selection of physical features lacks biblical support. Scripture speaks of one human race.*
- *Grouping people based on an arbitrary selection of physical features has historically led to prideful division.*

**How does the denial of Adam as humanity's common ancestor (Acts 17:26) confuse our understanding of race?** *Without Adam as humanity's common ancestor, it is impossible to argue for one human race. If we have no support for a unified human race, we are left with no choice but to make biological differences the determinate factor in our understanding of race. This confusion results in dividing humanity into competing races with separate ancestral roots.*

**How does a biblical view of ethnicity differ from secular definitions of race?** *The biblical view of ethnicity hinges on the idea that within the one human race there exists a diversity of nations and cultures. This diversity of nations is a creational norm worked out over time and is not a result of the Fall. Whereas the biblical view of ethnicity celebrates God's creativity in the ethnic diversity of the human race, secular definitions of race fail to synthesize human diversity with the unity of the human race.*

**What do we learn about the concept of ethnicity from the fact that non-Jewish biblical figures like Rahab, Ruth, and Uriah became part of ethnic Israel?** *We learn that nations are not static. They include people from different and mixed biological backgrounds who come together to form nations or ethnic groups.*

## UNDERSTANDING RACISM AND INEQUALITY

Use **direct instruction** to present the problem of racism and inequality in America.

Although inequality is not always a sign of racism, there is plenty of historical evidence that it can be an indicator of racism or the effects of racism. One example of the ongoing impact of racism in America regards housing patterns. In the past, black citizens couldn't use FHA loans to buy affordable housing from a white neighborhood (Yancey, *Beyond Racial Gridlock*, 91). Although there is no longer this prohibition for black citizens using FHA loans, the lingering effects of racism can still be seen in current housing patterns (Yancey, 92).

Residential segregation is evidenced when whites tend to relocate if blacks move into their neighborhoods (Yancey, 92). As Yancey says,

> Residential segregation influences school financing because most school districts rely heavily on property taxes. If the homes in a school district have a high economic value, then the schools in that district are likely to receive the money they need. If the homes are not worth a great deal of money, then the schools will struggle to find adequate resources. Because of white flight, money has fled the minority communities.
>
> . . . Are we to believe that none of the gap in academic scores between whites and nonwhites is due to the educational segregation of our children, when whites are able to send their children to better-funded schools? Is it not clear that at least part of the reason why people of color do not reach the economic level of whites is that they receive an inferior education? (93–94).

Many gains have been made over the years to make America a more just and equal society. Black Americans have progressed economically but still lag behind white Americans, and black unemployment is still a huge problem (Adapted from *Christian Ethics: An Introduction to Biblical Moral Reasoning* [First Edition] by Wayne Grudem, Copyright © 2018, p. 639. Used by permission of Crossway, a publishing ministry of Good News Publishers, Wheaton, IL 60187, www.crossway.org).

Consider what one author says:

> Think for a moment about how different race relations would be today if white churches during the period of Reconstruction and Jim Crow would have excommunicated unrepentant segregationists within their congregations. Consider how different the racial makeup of churches would look today if churches would have simply *declared the truth* about racial equality instead of perpetuating the lie of racial hierarchy. (Isaac Adams, *Talking about Race: Gospel Hope for Hard Conversations*, 128–29; italics in original)

Top left, clockwise: segregated gas station restrooms, South Carolina, 1965; Japanese Americans arriving at an internment camp during World War II; *The Indian campaign-prisoners captured by General Custer* by Theodore R. Davis; political cartoon during the Chinese Exclusion Act, 1882.

### RACISM AND INEQUALITY IN AMERICAN HISTORY

Americans are today wrestling with controversies over race because racism and inequality have been part of the legal and social structure of America. For example, at various times, laws protected the slave trade (contrary to Exod. 21:16), required the return of runaway slaves (contrary to Deut. 23:15–16), and treated black Americans as second-class citizens (contrary to Lev. 24:22). Laws were used to prevent black Americans from voting. Under the guise of "separate but equal," black children were forced into schools with facilities and educational materials that were not equal to those of white schools. There was a time when the Federal Housing Administration would not grant loans to black citizens that it was granting to white citizens. Such laws and policies were supported by and gave cover to racist customs such as businesses that would not serve black Americans. These examples have focused on the plight of black Americans, but additional examples of racism in America include the removal of American Indians from their lands, the Chinese Exclusion Act, or the internment of Japanese Americans during World War II.

Most Americans would now condemn these aspects of our history. However, controversy exists regarding whether there are enduring effects from past racism that need to be addressed, whether racism remains a significant problem in current American culture, and what the best ways are to achieve racial reconciliation in the present.

196 ISSUES

## UNBIBLICAL SOLUTIONS TO RACISM

Secular solutions to racism tend to exacerbate racial problems because they misidentify something that is creational as evil and live contrary to the way God made His world to work. They also look to something in God's creation for "racial salvation," rather than looking to God. As Christians evaluate secular approaches, they should not expect them to be wrong on every point. These approaches have often correctly grasped one or more creational norms. Nevertheless, Christians cannot simply adopt the view of one or another secular approach to racism because all secular approaches have been warped by the Fall and are rival worldviews to a biblical one.

Thus, in evaluating false systems of thought, we will (1) look at the creational structure that is identified as part of the problem, (2) look at the creational structure that is idolized as the means of salvation, (3) look at the aspects of the Fall that a view has neglected, and (4) acknowledge the creational norms that a given view has recognized, at least in part. We will survey two popular secular approaches to addressing racism. One approach could be called the *white responsibility* model, though today the term *antiracism* is often used. Another approach could be called *majority conformity*. Both descriptions below are brief generalizations of viewpoints held by many people with many different variations. While space requires us to be brief, we have sought to be fair and accurate in our summaries.

### *White Responsibility*

This approach sees racism as structural (that is, it is embedded in the structures, laws, and customs of a society) and places the responsibility for solving racism on the white majority group. Racism is defined as "the effort by the majority to maintain economic and emotional advantages over the minority."[4] By this definition, minorities can be prejudiced, but they cannot be racist.[5] According to this view, racism in America continues for two reasons. One, the historic impact of slavery and discrimination is still with us. Two, though white individuals may not personally be racist, their participation in a social system that benefits them and hurts minorities is ongoing racism.

White people, therefore, need to change the social systems so that they no longer have economic and emotional advantages over minorities. To be antiracist, whites need to dismantle their privilege and the social structures that sustain it. There are numerous proposals for how this is to be done. One controversial approach is through payment of reparations.* These could take various forms: financial investments in more conscious efforts to promote equity (e.g., in government, business, and various industries), trust funds to support minority community improvement, or investment targeted toward minority business development.

This view identifies "whiteness" as the problem at the root of racial conflict. *Whiteness* is used to describe the ways in which whites maintain their dominance. We should acknowledge that there have been social systems created by whites to maintain social dominance and that the effects of these systems are still present in society. But the charge to dismantle "white social systems" is so broad that too often it includes systems that are creationally normative such as the family, diligence in education, or hard work. It is also wrong and counterproductive to use *whiteness* as a tag for what is racially wrong in the world because white ethnic groups are also part of God's created order. "Whites" are not monolithic; to negatively stereotype a group of people on the basis of physical characteristics is itself racism. In addition, while it is undoubtedly true that some people are born more privileged than others, the Bible does not permit this to be a point of prejudice or resentment (Lev. 19:15; Eph. 4:31) even while it requires those who have been blessed to help those in need (Gal. 6:10; 1 Tim. 6:17–19; James 2:16; 1 John 3:17). Many white abolitionists (before and during the Civil War) and integrationists (during the civil rights movement) leveraged their privilege to promote justice.

**reparations:** "monetary or other compensation payable by a country to an individual for a historical wrong"[6]



## EVALUATING UNBIBLICAL SOLUTIONS TO RACISM

Guide a **discussion** about unbiblical solutions to racism.

**How do secular solutions to racism mishandle what is creational, and where do they look for "racial salvation"?** *They treat what is creational as though it is evil (e.g., "whiteness"), or they look to something in God's creation for racial salvation (e.g., requiring minority groups to conform to the majority culture).*

**What does the white responsibility approach to racism get wrong?**

- *It is wrong to speak of dismantling "white social systems" because this phrase includes creationally normative things such as the family, diligence in education, and hard work.*
- *It is wrong to use "whiteness" as a tag for what is racially wrong in the world because white ethnic groups are also part of God's created order. "Whites" are not a monolithic group; to negatively stereotype a group based on physical characteristics is itself racism.*
- *It is wrong to think that elevating minority groups to positions of power can achieve racial salvation, because it assumes that minorities are not sinners too.*

**What does the white responsibility approach to racism get right?**

- *It recognizes that sin can be institutionalized and systemized, as it was with slavery and segregation.*
- *It recognizes that sins committed by nations or families, or leaders who represent them, have corporate consequences.*
- *Though the reparations schemes promoted by advocates of this view tend to be unbiblical and unjust, Christians should recognize that restitution for past wrongs is part of a biblical principle, but it needs to be applied wisely. This biblical principle includes that the direct descendants of those who wronged others should make restitution to the descendants of the ones who were wronged. Likewise, institutions that have wronged others should make restitution to those who were directly harmed or to their descendants.*

**What do the majority conformity and colorblindness approaches to racism get wrong?**

- *It is wrong to deny the ongoing effects of the long-term national sin of racism.*
- *It is wrong to think that requiring minority groups to conform to the majority culture can achieve racial salvation.*
- *It is wrong to think that we can achieve racial salvation by merely focusing on the oneness of humanity because it ignores repenting for past sins of racism.*

**What do the majority conformity and colorblindness approaches to racism get right?**

- *They recognize the unity of the human race and the ideal of treating all people fairly regardless of their ethnicity.*
- *They recognize the danger (and the dehumanizing effect) of treating minority people primarily as victims.*

## CHRISTIANS AND RACISM

Assign a brief **writing assignment** (or **Quick Write**) to defend a biblical view of race and racism. Students may work individually or in groups.

Utilize the biblical framework of Creation, Fall, and Redemption to defend a biblical view of race and racism.

**How should biblical creation inform our view of different ethnic groups?** *Biblical creation provides the foundation for understanding the unity and value of all humanity with its diverse ethnicities. Acknowledging the one true God as Creator is foundational. Each human derives his or her intrinsic worth from being created in the image of God. Anyone who rightly understands this cannot view one ethnicity as inferior to another. Furthermore, no view of human origins other than the biblical doctrine of creation can rationally and vigorously maintain the notion of one human race in which diverse ethnicities are treated with equal worth. It should be stressed that those professing Christians in the past who failed in this area did so not as a logical consequence of biblical teaching but in contradiction to it.*

**What is the biblical view of racism, and why are all people capable of racism?** *The Bible treats racism as sinful partiality (James 2:1–4). Therefore, racism is not a consequence of God's creative diversity within humanity, but a consequence of the Fall. Man's sinful heart is full of pride, including racial pride. White supremacy is racial pride. So is Black Power. Racism may exist in any individual and in any society dominated by a particular race. Thus, the possibility of individual or structural racism is not limited to one race. All ethnicities are capable of racism because the single race of humanity equally shares the corruption inherited from Adam. To say that one ethnicity is capable of racism and another ethnicity is incapable of racism is itself an expression of racial pride and is therefore racist. Apart from the biblical doctrine of the Fall, this view of racism is impossible to understand.*

**How does the redemptive work of Christ in the formation of the church address the problem of racism?** *Christ's work of redemption restores God's original intention in creation. Where sin separated humanity along the lines of different ethnicities, redemption unites diverse ethnicities into a new humanity called the church. While redemption does not unite all humanity (some people choose to remain in their sin), it does unite believers from every ethnicity. With Christ as the head of the church and all believers united as His body, we have a sufficient answer to racism. No other ideologies alien to biblical Christianity are necessary to address the problem of racism.*

White Responsibility Approach

This view also elevates minority groups, seeing their attainment of social power as the means of salvation from racial conflict. This, however, neglects the truth that all humans are sinners. It neglects the fact that some of the problems ethnic minorities face are due to their own sins. This approach also relies on giving ethnic minorities a great deal of power without acknowledging that any sinner with unchecked power is liable to abuse it. In fact, this view often exacerbates racial conflict because white citizens feel that this power is already being misused and that the charges against whites are so sweeping as to be unfair.

While this approach is unbiblical, Christians should not dismiss the idea that sin can be institutionalized and systematized, as it was with slavery and segregation. Likewise, the idea that sins committed by nations or families, or leaders who represent them, have corporate consequences is well attested in Scripture (1 Kings 11:31–35; 14:9–14; 2 Kings 24:3; Zech. 8:14; Neh. 9:2). Finally, though the reparations schemes promoted by advocates of this view tend to be unbiblical and unjust, Christians should recognize that restitution for past wrongs is part of the biblical pattern (Exod. 21:23–27, 33–36; 22:1–17; Luke 19:8–10). If an institution or family can track down descendants of people they wronged, it would be in keeping with the spirit of Scripture to attempt some kind of restitution for the wrong done.

### *Majority Conformity and Colorblindness*

The majority conformity approach operates from an individualistic definition of racism, though with acknowledgement of past structural injustices. The responsibility for solving unequal outcomes for various ethnicities lies primarily with the minority groups. This approach holds that racism is no longer a significant problem in the United States and that racial discrimination no longer holds ethnic minorities back from achievement. The problem as it now exists is a class problem, not a race problem. If people would stop talking about race and if minority groups would conform to majority norms, they would become upwardly mobile.

Colorblind Approach

The colorblind approach thinks the whole idea of seeing multiple ethnic groups instead of one humanity is the fundamental problem. On the one hand, this view is correct in seeing all humans as part of a unified human race; on the other hand, the Bible sees ethnic diversity as part of God's good creational design. To view oneness as salvation from our racial conflicts is to idolize that aspect of God's creational design.

The problem with these approaches is they tend to deny the ongoing effects of long-term national sins. This can lead to an unwillingness to even consider historical and contemporary accounts of such injustice on the grounds that we must move past such things. In advocating conformity to majority norms, the first approach ignores or downplays the effects of sin on all cultures, including majority cultures. Because the Fall has corrupted cultures, there is no aspect of any culture untouched by the Fall. All cultures, majority and minority, must be measured by the standard of Scripture rather than serving as the measurement for other cultures. Thus, while it would be good for Americans of all ethnicities to forge a unified, shared culture, this project is likely to fail if minority cultures are required to abandon what is positive in their own cultures.

While these approaches are unbiblical, Christians should be careful not to dismiss what they get right. They rightly recognize the unity of the human race and the ideal of treating all people fairly regardless of their ethnicity. They also recognize the danger (and the dehumanizing effect) of treating minority people primarily as victims.

acts

## A BIBLICAL VIEW OF RACE AND RACISM

The various secular models have all failed to bring about racial reconciliation, and Christians, insofar as they have adopted secular viewpoints, have also failed in this project. However, the Bible is sufficient for providing us with the wisdom needed to address the issues of racial controversy (2 Tim. 3:16–17). The biblical doctrine of creation makes Christian ethics uniquely qualified to speak to racial discrimination. All people are descendants of the historical Adam and Eve and are therefore physically united in one human race, and all the ethnic groups that have emerged since Adam and Eve were "made" by God (Acts 17:26). The biblical doctrine of creation accounts for both human unity and human diversity.

Racism is a form of sinful partiality, which the Bible forbids (Lev. 19:15; James 2:1–4). It is a fundamental denial of our shared equality as God's image-bearers (Gen. 1:26; 5:3; 9:6; James 3:9). A biblical approach to racism recognizes that all people bear God's image and that all people are sinners. Thus, a biblical approach would recognize that both majority and minority groups have incentives to slant conversations on race to their own advantage. A biblical approach would encourage people from all groups to build respectful, enduring, cooperative, and equal relationships across ethnic lines. It would encourage those groups who have historically faced oppression, and who continue to face racism, to speak constructively about injustices but to avoid a life focused on grievances.

Christians should not be surprised if much of the racial conflict in the United States today is the direct result of the nation's sins regarding racial discrimination and segregation. Churches, institutions, and organizations that have contributed to racism could follow a biblical model of corporate repentance by making statements that their past actions were wrong and by demonstrating change (Ezra 9; Neh. 1:6–7; Dan. 9:3–19), with the offended extending forgiveness according to the pattern of God's forgiveness.

The biblical model of reformation (not revolution) is the best way to promote true racial justice. Instead of tearing down existing societal structures and thereby leading to greater injustice, we should seek to align societal structures with the creational norms of a just society (for example, see Ps. 37:30; Prov. 31:8–9). A biblical approach would not accept the idea that all racial disparities are a sign of racism. However, it would recognize that some racial disparities may point to problems that need addressing. It would be open to appropriate reforms to policies and laws. It would also seek to promote creationally and biblically sound social norms among all groups (e.g., the importance of intact families).

A biblical approach would involve gratitude for the progress that has been made in repudiating racism, while also recognizing that sin problems like racism will stubbornly persist in a fallen world. Christians can work on addressing racial problems on the national level, but they should also advance solutions on the personal, organizational, and local levels—arenas in which they may have more influence and responsibility (for instance, see Acts 20:28). Finally, Christians should not depend on their own efforts for success. Dependance on God through prayer will be essential to progress in this matter.

The goal for the nation should be to unify all ethnic groups around core values (biblically understood) while allowing all groups to continue to value and practice the creationally normative traditions of their own ethnic heritage.

Within the church, Scripture's teaching on the unity of believers is essential in overcoming racial animosity. It's impossible to overcome racial divisions in the church in any meaningful fashion without the concept of the body of Christ. John 17 calls for unity in the body, implying that ethnic divisions that disrupt that unity are a contradiction of our shared union in Christ. Ephesians 2:11–3:10 indicates that the bringing together of people from different ethnic backgrounds into a unified Christian body is something that brings glory to God because it bears witness to the world that we are the one people of God.

## Apply

### PROMOTING RACIAL RECONCILIATION

Use a **Turn and Talk** to answer this section's essential question and to prompt students to assess how the virtues of humility, prudence, love, and hope can enable them to promote racial reconciliation. Use the following scenarios for this activity.

**How might the virtues of humility and prudence guide you in responding to the following scenario? An African American student, Tim, shares with his Caucasian classmates about his family's experience with racism in the South. Tim remembers his grandfather telling him about the racial insults he endured and how he was denied certain employment opportunities because of his skin color. Tim says that his grandfather refused to grow bitter and vengeful. His grandfather taught him that all people are created equal. Tim is grateful that life in the South is better for him than it was for his grandfather, but he admits that he too has experienced forms of racism. On two occasions Tim was pulled over by police, who searched his person and his vehicle. Tim is convinced that the search was racially motivated, because in both cases Tim was respectful and cooperative and the police officers offered no reason for the search.** *If you're Caucasian, the virtue of humility can lead you to listen to Tim's story with a sympathetic ear, being open to learning from his experience. If you're African American, humility can guard you against making sweeping judgments about all police. The virtue of prudence might lead all students to research the issue of racial profiling in law enforcement to become better informed.*

**How might the virtues of love and hope guide this church in choosing a solution to racial reconciliation in the following scenario? A church has recently experienced controversy regarding how best to promote racial reconciliation in the larger society. Although the church is racially diverse and the membership is united in the desire for racial harmony, a serious disagreement has erupted over the idea of "white social systems." A racially diverse group on one side maintains that these systems must be dismantled before racial reconciliation is achieved in society. Another racially diverse group in the church views this proposal as divisive and incompatible with Scripture.** *Love should compel the church to pursue righteous solutions that are compatible with Scripture, knowing that such solutions may require long-term effort. The church must guard against secular notions that creationally normative structures like the family are considered "white social systems." Hope will guard the church against the temptation to adopt secular solutions, pursuing instead the kind of racial reconciliation rooted in the reconciling power of the gospel of Jesus Christ.*

### RESPONDING TO RACISM WITH GRACE AND TRUTH

Use **Activity 11.1** on page 65 to have students formulate a biblical response to racist attitudes and actions.

Wayne Grudem summarizes the ultimate expression of ethnic diversity, found among the worshipers of God in heaven. "If we skip to the end of the Bible, we see the same emphasis on racial and ethnic unity, because the innumerable multitude of people worshiping before God's throne in heaven includes people from every tribe and nation of the earth:"[7]

> After this I beheld, and, lo, a great multitude, which no man could number, *of all nations, and kindreds, and people, and tongues*, stood before the throne, and before the Lamb, clothed with white robes, and palms in their hands; and cried with a loud voice, saying, Salvation to our God which sitteth upon the throne, and unto the Lamb. (Rev. 7:9–10, emphasis added)

 ends

### THE EFFECTS OF RACISM ON SOCIETY

There is an inevitable breakdown in a society where racism exists. For example, we can look back to the days of Jim Crow laws in America and recognize this period as one characterized by enormous social upheaval. Treating a minority group as second-class citizens is not only immoral, but also bad social policy. It is only natural for that minority group to rise up in defense of their dignity and demand from the larger society equal treatment and equal opportunities. The long struggle for civil rights in America challenged the white majority to acknowledge the racial injustice enshrined in the law and to admit how poisonous this was for the entire body politic.

Many voices of the civil rights movement appealed to the conscience of the nation, calling the country to live up to the ideals of America's founding documents, which were influenced by a biblical worldview. If America is described as a nation of people "endowed by their Creator with" the "unalienable Rights" of "Life, Liberty, and the pursuit of Happiness,"[8] then this principle must equally apply to black Americans. The efforts of the civil rights movement led to crucial legislative changes and court decisions. In following years, making good on the promises of the US Constitution has struck a chord with many white Americans, and the tide has turned toward a more just society.

How should I foster racial reconciliation?

 agents

### VIRTUES THAT PROMOTE RACIAL RECONCILIATION

Discussing race relations can be difficult because emotions run high on this issue, but Christians should be eager to enter the conversation with humility and hope (see Acts 10–11). Our humility and hope stem from several biblical realities, not least of which is the unifying power of the gospel of grace that reconciles a repentant and believing humanity both to God and to one another. Focusing on biblical solutions to the problem of racial discrimination neither minimizes the complexity of the issue nor surrenders to the status quo. Those seeking racial reconciliation need *humility* as they address a complex problem (Phil. 2:3–4); *prudence* to find better solutions (Ps.



## Assess

Guide a **summative assessment** by directing students to answer the questions in Thinking It Through 11.1.

### Thinking It Through 11.1

1. First, race can refer to the one human race, and the Bible does speak of all humanity in its unity as descended from Adam (Acts 17:26; cf. Gen. 6:5). Second, race in the sense of ethnicity is also a biblical concept. Paul said that God made the "nations," meaning ethnic groups (Acts 17:26).
2. The *Oxford English Dictionary* defines racism as "prejudice, antagonism, or discrimination by an individual, institution, or society, against a person or people on the basis of their nationality or (now usually) their membership of a particular racial or ethnic group, typically one that is a minority or marginalized. Also: beliefs that members of a particular racial or ethnic group possess innate characteristics or qualities, or that some racial or ethnic groups are superior to others; an ideology based on such beliefs" (*Oxford English Dictionary* online, s.v. "racism," last modified March 2022).
3. The charge to dismantle "white social systems" is so broad that it often includes creationally normative systems such as the family, diligence in education, or hard work. It is wrong and counterproductive to use *whiteness* as a tag for what is racially wrong in the

37:30; Prov. 14:15); *love* for those impacted by racism (Phil. 2:1–2); and *hope* that racism can be effectively addressed (Rom. 15:13).

Humility is necessary in dealing with racial problems because it will enable us to consider arguments that challenge our preconceived ideas about race. This doesn't mean we will always agree with opposing arguments, but it does mean we will give them a fair hearing before deciding. In some cases, we may recognize an element of truth in another person's critique of our own attitudes about race. The key is to sift all arguments about race—our own arguments as well as those of others—through a biblical lens of Creation, Fall, Redemption.

Prudence enables us to develop constructive ways of pursuing racial reconciliation where it is genuinely needed. This is in contrast to the destructive path of revolution, which is typically the impatient person's way of dealing with social problems. Prudence should not be mistaken for apathy toward racism, because prudence does not stand alone from the virtues of love and hope.

Love for those impacted by racism should lead us to vigorously pursue righteous solutions, knowing that such solutions may require long-term effort. As we nurture the hope that the Christian ethic can prevail in producing a more just society for all people, we not only guard against the temptation to adopt secular solutions, but we also promote the kind of racial reconciliation rooted in the reconciling power of the gospel of Jesus Christ.

*To have a truly integrated church (reflecting the demographic profile of the neighborhood in which it is found) takes hard work, very substantial forbearance, self-sacrificing winsomeness, patience—in a word, love.* D. A. CARSON[9]

### Thinking It Through 11.1

1. How should we define race and ethnicity from a biblical perspective?
2. How does the *Oxford English Dictionary* define racism?
3. What is wrong with the white responsibility view of race?
4. What is wrong with the majority conformity and colorblind views of race?
5. How does a biblical model of reformation promote racial justice?
6. How do the virtues of humility, prudence, love, and hope promote racial reconciliation?

## 11.2 Addictions

One of the signs of Christianity's waning influence upon Western societies is the removal of restraints on addictive behaviors. Though alcoholism and drug abuse are still regarded as social problems to be solved, there's been a moral shift in our society's attitude toward harmful, intoxicating substances. The legalization of marijuana is evidence of this. Societies whose governments profit from the taxation of recreational drugs and addictive behaviors (like gambling) reveal an ethical and social erosion. Individuals are not served well when their government risks their well-being for the sake of monetary gain.

For our society to recover from this ethical erosion, we will need to recover certain Christian virtues. Honesty, hope, and self-control would be a good place to start.

ETHICAL SOCIETY 201

world because white ethnic groups are also part of God's created order. "Whites" are not monolithic. While it is undoubtedly true that some people are born more privileged than others, the Bible does not permit this to be a point of resentment (Eph. 4:31) and requires those who have been blessed to help those in need (Gal. 6:10; James 2:16).

4. The problem with these approaches is that they tend to deny the ongoing effects of long-term national sins. This can lead to an unwillingness to even consider historic and contemporary accounts of such injustices on the grounds that we must move past such things. The majority conformity approach ignores or downplays the effects of sin on all cultures, including majority cultures. Because the Fall has corrupted cultures, there is no aspect of any culture untouched by the Fall. All cultures, majority and minority, must be measured by the standard of Scripture rather than serving as the measurement for other cultures. Thus, while it would be good for Americans of all ethnicities to forge a unified, shared culture, this project is likely to fail if minority cultures are required to abandon their own cultures.
5. The biblical model of reformation (not revolution) is the best way to promote true racial justice. Instead of tearing down existing societal structures, we should seek to align societal structures with the creational norms of a just society (cf. Ps. 37:30; Prov. 31:8–9). A biblical approach would not accept that all racial disparities are signs of racism. However, it would recognize that some racial disparities may point to problems that need addressing. It would be open to appropriate reforms to laws. It would also seek to promote creationally and biblically sound social norms among all groups (e.g., the value of intact families).
6. Those seeking racial reconciliation need humility as they address a complex problem (Phil. 2:3–4), prudence to find better solutions (Ps. 37:30; Prov. 14:15), love for those impacted by racism (Phil. 2:1–2), and hope that racism can be effectively addressed (Rom. 15:13).

## 11.2 Addictions

*What is controlling me?*

### Objectives

**11.2.1** Describe common addictive vices.

**11.2.2** Summarize the biblical teaching regarding substance abuse and gambling. BWS

**11.2.3** Evaluate the consequences of a society that normalizes these vices.

**11.2.4** Assess the virtues necessary to resist these vices. BWS

**11.2.5** Formulate a biblical response to peer pressure to engage in these vices.

### Biblical Worldview Shaping

- **Creational Order** (explain): God created man to rule over creation, but at present fallen creation often rules over man. (11.2.2)
- **Virtue** (formulate): Those who struggle with addictions are in need of honesty as they assess their enslavement, hope that God can provide them deliverance, and Spirit-empowered self-control to think and act rightly. (11.2.4)

### Printed Resource

- Activity 11.2: Pressure to Engage in Substance Abuse or Gambling

### Digital Resource

- Video: "Addictions"

### Suggested Reading

- Jaeggli, Randy. *Christians and Alcohol: A Scriptural Case for Abstinence*. Greenville, SC: BJU Press, 2014.
- Rosengren, John. "How Casinos Enable Gambling Addicts." The Atlantic (website). December, 2016.

## Engage

### ADDICTIONS

Show the **video** "Addictions" to introduce the subject to students.

### HOW SHOULD WE THINK ABOUT VAPING?

Conduct a **Think-Pair-Share** in which students answer the following questions.

**Why is vaping addictive? Is vaping a safer option than smoking?** *Nicotine, which is extremely addictive, is present in many vape products. Withdrawal symptoms are so difficult that many people struggle to stop once they begin. Many young people mistakenly believe that vaping is a safer option than smoking. Research is still underway about possible heart and lung damage, but one thing is certain: nicotine addiction from vaping is still a destructive addiction.*

## Instruct

### UNDERSTANDING THE NATURE OF ADDICTION

Guide a **discussion** about the nature of substance abuse, particularly the abuse of alcohol.

**How would you describe the nature of addiction?** *something that enslaves and exercises paralyzing control over a person*
**How do many addicts delude themselves with respect to their addiction?** *by thinking they can quit anytime they choose*
**How does genuine recovery begin?** *by admitting one has a problem and by asking for help*
**What is the most common substance addiction?** *alcohol abuse*
**What are the two common positions held by Christians with respect to drinking alcohol?** *the moderation position and the abstinence position*

We need to be honest about the personal and social devastation caused by addictive vices. At the same time, we need to offer hope to those trapped in various forms of addictions. And finally, instead of mocking the virtue of self-control, we need to elevate self-control as an essential part of our human dignity. Indulging oneself in intoxicating substances may seem cool to some people, but when it costs them their dignity and even their lives, it doesn't look cool at all.

What is controlling me?

context

### THE NATURE OF ADDICTION

Addiction is by definition enslaving; it exercises paralyzing control over the addict. Once enslaved to a particular addiction, many live in denial about the seriousness of their problem. While addicts bear personal responsibility for their behavior, they delude themselves by thinking they can quit anytime they choose. Genuine recovery begins by admitting one has a problem and by asking for help.

Alcohol abuse is by far the most common addiction. The pressure on young people to conform to their worldly peers is part of the problem. At the average secular university, excessive drinking at raucous parties is virtually a rite of passage for young people. Our culture sends mixed signals with regard to drunkenness. On the one hand, it glorifies debauchery and unrestrained freedom. On the other hand, it spends millions of dollars on alcohol rehab.

Given the biblical prohibitions against drunkenness, you might think that all Christians would agree on a biblical response toward alcohol. However, there are at least two common positions among Christians. The **abstinence** position emphasizes both the necessity of avoiding drunkenness and the wisdom of abstaining from that which gets someone drunk. Other Christians who are equally opposed to drunkenness argue that the problem is not alcohol *per se* but the abuse of alcohol. Responsible, moderate drinking, they argue, is biblically permissible.

#### *The Moderation Position*

One advocate for moderate drinking offers the following considerations. First, while wine in the ancient world was often diluted with water, the fact that drunkenness was a problem as far back as Noah and Lot indicates that alcohol was not always diluted (Gen. 9:21; 19:30–36). Therefore, Scripture's allowance for wine, coupled with its prohibition of drunkenness, assumes a moderation position (Ps. 104:14–15; Eph. 5:18). Second, while abstinence certainly guarantees that drunkenness will be avoided, it is also true that many Christians practice moderation without becoming drunk. Third, given the biblical celebration of wine, it seems the abstinence position requires a stricter position than does Scripture (Prov. 3:9–10; Eccles. 9:7; John 2:9–10).[10]

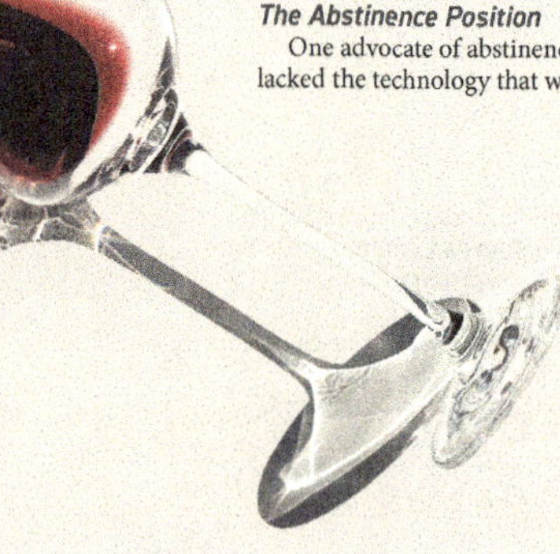

#### *The Abstinence Position*

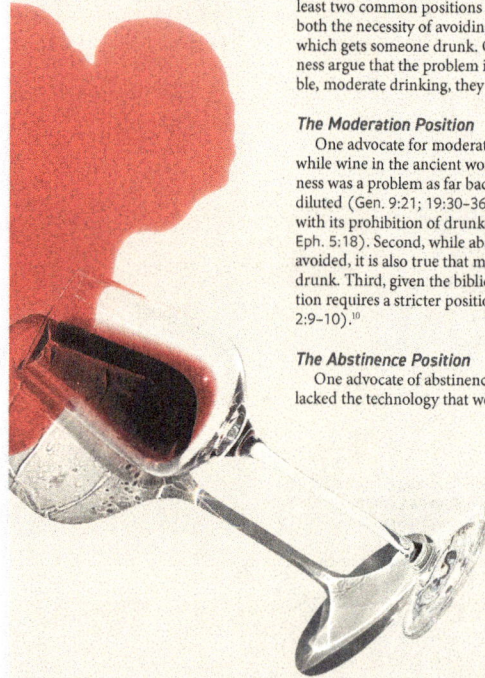

One advocate of abstinence provides four considerations. First, the ancient world lacked the technology that we possess today to prevent the fermentation of grape juice. Second, the ancient practice of diluting wine with water means that wine in biblical days doesn't compare to the high alcohol content of modern alcoholic beverages; the "wine" of today is not the same as the wine the Bible refers to. In other words, we should avoid modern alcohol because of its significantly higher alcohol content. Third, Scripture's warnings against the dangers of alcohol (coupled with the serious danger of addiction) mean that abstinence would be the most appropriate biblical application today (for example, see Prov. 20:1; 23:29–35; Isa. 5:22; 28:7–8). Fourth, even if drinking alcohol could be construed as a matter of Christian liberty, believers should avoid it because it (a) is especially prone to enslaving people, (b) offers nothing in terms of edification, and (c) poses a stumbling block to others (1 Cor. 6:12; 8:9, 13; Rom. 14:17, 21).[11]

Proponents of abstinence respond to the first moderation argument by pointing out that, in the ancient world, those who wanted to become intoxicated would seek out the wine before it was mixed. In response to the second moderation argument, when people drink modern alcoholic beverages, the alcoholic content is significantly higher than the alcoholic content of the beverages drunk by those in Scripture. In response to the third moderation argument, in biblical times wine was a staple, like bread. The rejoicing associated with it was not tied to its alcoholic content but to the fact that God was supplying the basic needs of His people. Proponents of this form of abstinence reject the claim that their position is stricter than Scripture.

Everything the Bible says about drunkenness can be applied to drug addiction. Scripture has nothing positive to say about **recreational drugs**.* Recreational drugs like marijuana have proven to have harmful consequences even in low doses. Claims of marijuana's medicinal value are not an argument for recreational use but rather an argument for continued scientific research to create new medicines that do not have the addictive or intoxicating effects of marijuana use.[12]

#### *Gambling*

Gambling is included in this discussion because it, too, can have a controlling influence on people, with devastating social consequences. Gamblers talk about the rush of winning; this rush has effects on the human brain similar to those of illicit drugs. And like a drug that requires higher doses to get the same effect over time, gambling requires more bets to maintain the rush. As the losses continue to mount, the gambler is under compulsion to gamble more.[13] How else is he supposed to recover his losses except from a huge win? That's how a gambling addict reasons.

### A BIBLICAL RESPONSE TO ADDICTION

Being under the control of alcohol, drugs, or a vice like gambling is incompatible with the Christian life, where the controlling influence is supposed to be the Holy Spirit (Eph. 5:18). Whereas self-control is the fruit of the Spirit (Gal. 5:22–23), lack of control is the fruit of addiction. God created man to rule over creation, but at present the fallen creation often rules over man. Addiction is an example of creation ruling over man.

Numerous biblical texts condemn drunkenness and by extension the intoxication from other drugs (for example, see Prov. 23:20–21; 1 Cor. 6:10; 1 Pet. 4:3). Additionally, the biblical view of wise stewardship argues against any form of gambling (Luke 16:11).

#### *Responding to Substance Abuse*

Because secular notions of bodily autonomy pervade our society, many people justify substance abuse on the grounds that they can do with their bodies as they please. The biblical doctrines of creation and redemption provide a correction to this outlook. When we remember that our bodies are a gift from our Creator and that they ultimately belong to Him, we come to understand that there are some good and necessary limits to what we should do with our bodies. Scripture amplifies this point when speaking of Christian redemption (1 Cor. 6:19–20). Christians are to glorify God in their bodies because they've been bought with the price of Christ's own blood (Eph. 1:7; 1 Pet. 1:18–19). As Christians weigh what they do with their bodies, they should always consider whether their choices will glorify the Savior who bought them.

We could apply this principle to the practice of vaping. Nicotine (present in many vape products) is extremely addictive, and the withdrawal symptoms are so difficult that many people struggle to stop once they begin. Many young people mistakenly

**recreational drugs:** drugs "that some people take occasionally for enjoyment, especially when they are spending time socially with other people."[14]

ETHICAL SOCIETY 203

## WHAT DOES SCRIPTURE TEACH ABOUT ALCOHOL?

Guide a **Bible study** to help students evaluate the two positions regarding alcohol consumption. Check the following biblical passages and answer the assigned questions.

**How would you respond to advocates for moderation who cite the following passages in defense of their position?**

- Genesis 9:21; 19:30–36
- Psalm 104:14–15
- Ephesians 5:18
- Proverbs 3:9–10
- Ecclesiastes 9:7
- John 2:9–10

**How would you respond to advocates for abstinence who cite the following passages in defense of their position?**

- Proverbs 20:1; 23:29–35
- Isaiah 5:22; 28:7–8
- 1 Corinthians 6:12; 8:9, 13
- Romans 14:17, 21

## RESPONDING TO ADDICTION

Use a **Turn and Talk** activity to answer this section's essential question and to prompt students to collaborate on a biblical response to substance abuse and gambling based on the textbook.

**How does living under the control of the Holy Spirit enable a Christian to resist addictive behavior?** *The Holy Spirit implants new desires (godly ones) within the heart of the believer. These new desires to please God and live for Him enable believers to battle against sinful desires. Though the temptation toward addictive substances may exist for believers, Christians can be confident that the indwelling Spirit is more powerful than the temptation. By living in daily surrender to the Spirit, believers can resist any other controlling influence and thereby live free of addictive behaviors.*

**How would you respond to the argument that people can do with their bodies whatever they choose as long as they're not hurting others?** *First, our bodies do not ultimately belong to us; they belong to God. Since God created us, He has rights over our bodies. To say we can do whatever we want with "our" bodies fails to recognize this fact. Second, it is impossible to abuse our bodies with addictive behavior without hurting others. We hurt our loved ones and friends when we abuse ourselves.*

**How can a Christian's desire for God to be glorified in his or her body help the Christian fight the temptation to use drugs?** *Simply put: God is better than any drug. Enjoying God empowers one to fight the temptation to use drugs. When we choose pleasure in God over the pleasure of drugs, God is glorified in our bodies. This choice demonstrates that God is more valuable to us than the fleeting pleasures of sin.*

**How would you respond to someone who justifies buying a lottery ticket on the grounds that he is helping to support public education?** *This is a clear example of justifying sin under the guise of doing good. No one buys a lottery ticket because he wants to support public education. He buys the ticket because he wants a quick and easy path to financial wealth. If a person wants to support public education, he can do so through a financial donation.*

**How does Scripture's warning about taking advantage of poor people apply to gambling (Prov. 22:22–23; Phil. 2:4)?** *Statistics show that the people harmed most by gambling are poor people. Scripture teaches that we are not to take advantage of the poor but to protect them from such stumbling blocks.*

## THE SOCIAL CONSEQUENCES OF ADDICTION

Guide a **discussion** on the consequences of a society that normalizes addictive behavior.

**Why does society need its members to function ethically?** *It needs its members to exercise their God-given abilities for the well-being of the larger society.*

**How does addiction deprive society of certain positive goods that an individual might offer?** *Addictions incapacitate individuals, robbing them of the dignity of work and of serving others. The societal benefit that might have accrued from the individual's contribution is lost to the addiction.*

**How does addiction harm society with extra burdens and problems?** *Addictions add problems for families, governments, economies, health care systems, and employers.*

**How does alcohol abuse cause problems for society?** *It leads to physical abuse in the home, causes thousands of deaths each year from drunk driving, and results in various health problems, including mental illness.*

**How does marijuana use adversely impact individuals and society?** *It deprives people of sound judgment, motivation, and mental alertness. Like drunkenness, marijuana use has led to traffic accidents and fatalities.*

**How does a gambling addict financially injure his or her family?** *The addict deprives his or her family of daily necessities, such as food and money for rent, as well as a better financial future.*

**What do studies indicate regarding the relationship between gambling and crime?** *Where gambling is legalized, crime goes up.*

**How are governments complicit in gambling's destructive effects upon individuals and society?** *State-sponsored lotteries, which use deceptive advertising regarding the odds of a big win, prey on the poorest and most vulnerable.*

believe that vaping is a safer option than smoking. Research is still underway about possible heart and lung damage, but one thing is certain: nicotine addiction from vaping is still a destructive addiction. Glorifying God with our bodies precludes such an addiction.

#### *Responding to Gambling*

The idea of gaining money without work is contrary to the Creation Mandate (Gen. 1:28). Yet that's exactly what gambling falsely promises: the ability to reap financially without contributing to the improvement of society. Comparing gambling with investing in the stock market is a red herring that proponents of gambling often use. Scripture encourages wise investing because it provides opportunities to produce something that benefits society (Deut. 28:12; Eccles. 11:2; Matt. 25:14–30). Gambling, on the other hand, is strictly a game of risk, one that heavily favors the house.* It's a poor stewardship of one's resources (Prov. 21:5; 28:20). Unlike investments, where people on both sides have the potential of winning, gambling requires some people to lose in order for others to win.

Christians can debate the wisdom of a school raffle. (Most people recognize it as a benefit to the school. Basically it's a donation.)[15] But the gambling industry has no redeeming qualities. Gambling is based on the love of money, is accompanied by an array of immoral and criminal behavior, and is proven to be addictive (1 Tim. 6:9–10; James 1:15–17). Our concern for gambling addicts is heightened when we realize that the gambling industry preys on the poorest and most vulnerable among us. The false promise of striking it rich is like setting a trap for the poor. Therefore, Scripture's warning about taking advantage of the poor applies to the gambling industry (Prov. 22:22–23; Phil. 2:4).

### THE SOCIAL CONSEQUENCES OF ADDICTION

An ethical society depends, among other things, on its members exercising their God-given abilities for the well-being of the larger society. But addictions incapacitate individuals, robbing them of the dignity of work and of serving others. The societal benefit that might have accrued from the individual's contribution is lost to the addiction. This is the negative cost of addiction, the good it *removes* from society.

#### *The Social Cost of Substance Abuse*

Addictions also cause positive social harm; they *add* problems for families, governments, economies, health care systems, employers, and more. Alcohol abuse has been particularly devastating, often leading to physical abuse in the home, causing thousands of deaths each year from drunk driving, and resulting in various physical problems, as well as being associated with mental illness.[16] Drug addictions take a similar toll on families and society. Marijuana deprives people of sound judgment, motivation, and mental alertness. It, too, has led to traffic accidents and fatalities. It is also known as a gateway drug.[17] Many cocaine and heroin addicts started with marijuana.

We can add to these social costs the criminal activity often associated with substance abuse and addiction. Some addicts engage in illegal behavior to fund their addiction. And some people profit from the addictions of others through drug trafficking. Drug cartels are notoriously violent, frequently at war with each other and with government authorities. This dark underbelly of the drug world is both a cause and a consequence of addiction.

#### *The Social Cost of Gambling*

Money wasted on gambling is money that could have been spent on food and rent, a reality many families experience firsthand from having a gambling addict in the family. Having a gambler for a parent deprives many children of daily necessities as well as a better financial future. In some cases, gambling tragically deprives children of the life of a parent. Suicide is not uncommon for gambling addicts. The

**the house:** the casino running the gambling operation

self-inflicted humiliation and despair that stems from squandering everything on a roll of the dice leads many people to end their lives.[18]

Studies indicate that, wherever gambling is legalized, crime goes up. Governments that profit from this corrupt enterprise are complicit in gambling's destructive effects upon individuals and society. This includes state-sponsored lotteries, which use deceptive advertising regarding the odds of a big win.[19] Raising funds for public education with a lottery is like raising funds for health care by taxing marijuana. It is self-contradictory and self-defeating.

## VIRTUES THAT COUNTERACT ADDICTION

Honesty, hope, and self-control are three Christian virtues well-suited to counteract addiction. Honesty is necessary to counteract the lies that people tell themselves about their addictions. Hope is necessary to counteract the despair that addicts experience. And self-control is necessary to counteract the out-of-control nature of addiction itself.

### *Getting Honest about Addiction*

Admitting that one has a problem with addiction is difficult for a couple of reasons. First, it's a blow to one's pride. You have to be honest about having made poor choices and about needing help. Second, it means giving up something you love, namely the pleasure that comes from whatever you're addicted to. An honest addict will not fool himself or herself; withdrawals will be painful, and victory over the addiction will be costly.

Honesty is a virtue that grows in the soil of the gospel. In other words, the offer of forgiveness in the gospel means the addict does not have to hide in shame. He or she can bring his or her sin to Christ with honest confession and repentance to receive a complete pardon from God. Although this first step does not impart immediate victory over the addiction, it's a necessary step on the long road of recovery.

### *Gaining Hope over Addiction*

Relapse among addicts is extremely high. Drug and alcohol rehab centers will attest that many of their patients will graduate from their program only to return again. This can increase the sense of despair and hopelessness an addict may experience. Believers struggling with addiction need constant reassurance that no matter how strong their addiction is, the power of Christ is even stronger.

Some addicts have heard the gospel message many times and have grown numb to it. Others, however, have found real hope in the gospel, especially as they were surrounded by loving and patient Christians who shouldered their burden with them. This gave the addicts hope that, as they relied on Christ for help, He would not abandon them to their addictions.

> *When you call addiction a sin issue of the heart rather than . . . a disease, then you have biblical words, biblical language, to offer them . . . the hope of the gospel for the heart of addiction.* MARK SHAW[20]

### *Growing in Self-Control and out of Addiction*

Addiction robs a person of control over himself or herself. Reversing this situation is stressful but not impossible. Exercising self-control is like exercising a muscle; the more one exercises self-control, the more one grows in self-control. The virtue of self-control arises from the Holy Spirit's work in a believer's life. Nevertheless, self-control must be exercised for a believer to become proficient in it.



## Apply

### BATTLING ADDICTION WITH VIRTUE

Use a **Quick Write** to allow students to create a plan for counteracting addiction with Christian virtues.

**How would you apply the virtue of honesty in the following scenario? You discover that your older brother, Bob, has become addicted to alcohol. Even though his drinking has cost him his job and his relationship with his girlfriend, Bob doesn't think that he has a problem. He also insists that he can quit drinking any time he chooses, though he refuses to do so. How can the virtue of honesty help Bob?** *Without being honest about his choices regarding alcohol and his need for help, Bob will not overcome his addiction. He needs to be honest about his addiction, instead of deceiving himself about quitting whenever he chooses. Most importantly, Bob needs honesty to confess and repent of his addiction so that he can experience Christ's forgiveness and the grace to deal with his problem.*

**How would you apply the virtue of hope in the following scenario? Your cousin Nick has admitted that he has a gambling problem and that he has been fighting it for several months. Although Nick recently became a Christian, he confides in you that he yielded again to temptation and squandered his paycheck betting on a football game. Nick is feeling defeated and doubting whether he will ever overcome his addiction because he views it as a disease that will not let him go. How can the virtue of hope help?** *Nick needs reassurance that no matter how strong his addiction is, the power of Christ is even stronger. For Nick to live in the liberating power of the gospel, he needs to view his addiction as a sin rather than a disease. Also, Nick needs greater accountability with Christian friends. All these things will give Nick hope in his ongoing battle with gambling.*

**How would you apply the virtue of self-control in the following scenario? Your friend Nancy admits to you that she recently has been vaping, and she is afraid that she is becoming addicted to it. Nancy is a Christian and does not want to be controlled by an addiction. She reaches out to you for help. Why is the virtue of self-control needed for Nancy to counteract this temptation to become addicted to vaping?** *Nancy needs to be reminded that self-control is a fruit of the Spirit that grows stronger with exercise. As she grows in self-control, she will not be controlled by vaping. She can resist the cravings by relying on the Spirit's help and by replacing her craving for vaping with greater pleasure in being a child of God, chosen and loved by Him.*

### DEALING WITH PEER PRESSURE

Use **Activity 11.2** on page 67 to help students consider ways of responding to pressure from others to abuse substances or to engage in gambling.

## Assess

Guide a **summative assessment** by directing students to answer the questions in Thinking It Through 11.2.

### Thinking It Through 11.2

1. An addiction is enslaving; it exercises paralyzing control over the addict. Once enslaved to a particular addiction, many live in denial about the seriousness of their problem. While addicts bear personal responsibility for their behavior, they delude themselves by thinking they can quit anytime they choose. Genuine recovery, however, begins by admitting one has a problem and by asking for help.
2. Being under the control of alcohol, drugs, or a vice like gambling is incompatible with the Christian life where the controlling influence is supposed to be the Holy Spirit (Eph. 5:18). Whereas self-control is the fruit of the Spirit, lack of control is the fruit of addiction (Gal. 5:22–23). God created humans to rule over creation, but the present fallen creation often rules over humans. Addiction is an example of creation ruling over man. Numerous biblical texts condemn drunkenness and by extension the intoxication from other drugs (Prov. 23:20–21; 1 Cor. 6:10; 1 Pet. 4:3). With respect to gambling, the biblical view of wise stewardship argues against it (Luke 16:11).
3. Answers should reflect the biblical principles discussed in this section.
4. You have to be honest about having made poor choices and about needing help. An honest addict will not fool himself or herself; withdrawals will be painful, and victory over the addiction will be costly. Honesty is a virtue that grows in the soil of the gospel. In other words, the offer of forgiveness in the gospel means the addict does not have to hide in shame. The addict can bring his or her sin to Christ with honest confession and repentance to receive a complete pardon from God.
5. Drug and alcohol rehab centers will attest that many of their patients will graduate from their program only to return. This can increase the sense of despair and hopelessness that an addict may experience. Some addicts have found real hope in the gospel, especially as they were surrounded by loving and patient Christians who shouldered their burden with them. This gave the addicts hope that as they relied on Christ for help, He would not abandon them to their addiction.
6. Exercising self-control is like exercising a muscle: the more one exercises self-control, the more one grows in it. Of course, the virtue of self-control arises from the Holy Spirit's work in a believer's life. What does it look like to exercise self-control regarding addiction? It looks like the daily habit of "putting off the old man" and "putting on the new man" as described in the book of Colossians (Col. 3:1–14). Given that believers have been raised with Christ to walk in newness of life, they're no longer enslaved to their former addiction. Their flesh may still crave the addiction, but they're able to resist these cravings in the power of the Spirit. Putting off the old man means accepting the pain of addiction withdrawals. Putting on the new man means finding pleasure in being a child of God, chosen and loved by Him (Col. 3:12).

## 11.3 Communication and Media Use

*How can I please God in my communication and media use?*

**Objectives**

**11.3.1** Describe ethical issues related to communication and media use.

**11.3.2** Summarize the biblical teaching regarding communication and media use.

---

What does it look like to exercise self-control with regard to addiction? It looks like the daily habit of putting "off the old man" (Col. 3:9) and putting "on the new man" (Col. 3:10) as described in Colossians 3:1–14. Given that a believer has been raised with Christ to "walk in newness of life" (Rom. 6:4; see Col. 1:1–3), that person is no longer enslaved to his or her former addiction (Rom. 6:16–23). The flesh may still crave the addiction, but a believer is able to resist these cravings in the power of the Spirit. Putting off the old man means accepting the pain of addiction withdrawals. Putting on the new man means finding one's pleasure in being a child of God, chosen and loved by Him, and adding new virtues and habits to one's life (Col. 3:12–17).

### Thinking It Through 11.2

1. What is the nature of addiction?
2. What is the biblical response to substance abuse?
3. Do a search for "Is it okay to gamble?" How would you biblically respond to an article defending gambling?
4. How does the virtue of honesty help a person to resist or defeat these vices?
5. How does the virtue of hope help a person to resist or defeat these vices?
6. How does the virtue of self-control help a person to resist or defeat these vices?

## 11.3 Communication and Media Use

Everything about our social interaction with one another is of ethical significance, including our communication. What we say, how we say it, and even what we refuse to say reveals much about ourselves individually and culturally. The verbal as well as the non-verbal messages that people exchange every day are value laden, though most of us are unaware that our values rest on the surface of everything we say.

The forms of communication that our society finds acceptable and unacceptable can be difficult to evaluate. As we've done in previous lessons with other topics, we need to apply some biblical worldview thinking to the subject at hand. Our model (Creation, Fall, Redemption) has real advantages for evaluating communication and media use; it gives us wisdom to distinguish that which is consistent with creational norms and that which is fallen.

In addition, we need to look at certain Christian virtues that directly relate to this subject. If we want to please God in our communication and media use, we will need to grow in the virtues of honesty, gentleness, and righteousness. Each of these virtues is a necessary correction to the vices that characterize so much of our society.

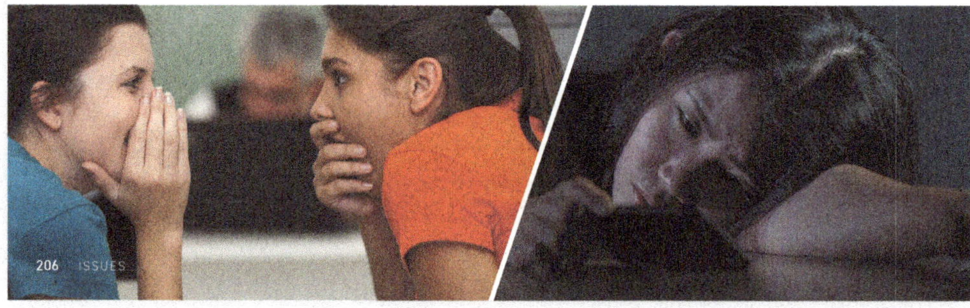

## COMMUNICATION AND MEDIA: WHAT ARE THE ETHICAL ISSUES?

What ethical issues come to mind when you think of communication and media use? Social media bullying? Virtue signaling? Trolling? Forcing politically correct speech? These are common problems in our current media environment. In addition, there are ethical problems that have been with us for much longer—profanity,* crude joking, gratuitous violence in entertainment, and a loss of modesty.

Such things have always been part of our fallen culture. There was a time, however, when debased forms of communication caused the general public to blush. As our society continues its moral decline, we're witnessing an increase in vulgarity* and a decrease in blushing. There seems to be a race to the bottom when it comes to communication and media use.

While communication is creational, the worldviews embedded in the current social media platforms assume that humans are basically good and that giving every human a voice will have beneficial consequences. But in actuality, social media tends toward pride, narcissism, and the idea that we can construct our own realities. It has also loosened certain restraints. Many people who express themselves inappropriately on social media might think twice if they were face-to-face with a person. Bullying has become rampant on social media. The pressure to present a picture-perfect life leads some to embellish their lives on social media. And regret from posting explicit images or video of oneself on social media has become such a huge problem that companies now exist to do reputation repair. Many Christians speak and share falsehoods online because they don't take the time to check whether what they read is true or not.

Although the medium by which we communicate is important, the nature of our communication is more important. Where social media and entertainment are being used effectively to communicate messages consistent with a biblical ethic, we should be thankful and follow those examples.

## COMMUNICATION AND MEDIA: HOW SHOULD WE THINK?

What proceeds from our mouths (and our keyboards) reveals the moral condition of our hearts (Matt. 12:34). Corrupt communication flows from fallen hearts, and clean communication flows from redeemed hearts. This is true whether our communication is spoken or written, whether our interactions are face-to-face or on Instagram. What we post on social media is just as revealing and consequential as the words we speak.

### *The Origins of Communication*

Human communication is a gift from God, and we have a responsibility before Him to steward this gift well. It was originally designed as a reflection of God's nature and God's character. A biblical understanding of communication must begin here. To think of communication as a mere social convention rather than a reflection of the Creator deprives society of the richness and fullness of communication. We'll never be able to elevate our communication in society until we understand its elevated origins.

God is a speaking God. There once was a time when no one existed but God. No angels. No humans. No created speaker. Yet communication has always existed. It existed by virtue of the fact that God is a triune God. The communication between Father, Son, and Holy Spirit is eternal and perfect. There never was a time when they were not speaking to one another, and there never was a time when their speech was inappropriate. Divine communication, therefore, is synonymous with fellowship in the Godhead.

**GRAPPLING WITH ETHICAL ISSUES**

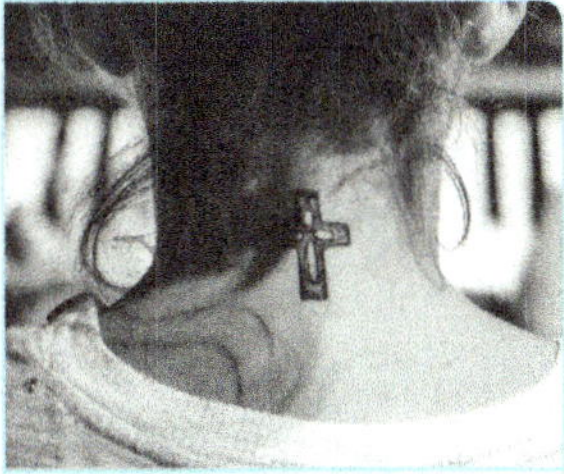

Ink and Communication

Tattoos are another form of communication worthy of ethical consideration. The Bible addresses tattoos in Leviticus 19:28: "Ye shall not make any cuttings in your flesh for the dead, nor print any marks upon you: I am the Lord." These instructions come as part of a series of instructions for the Israelites to not follow the pagan practice of disfiguring the body in various ways. Since humans are made in God's image, disfiguring the body dishonors God. Some Christians defend tattoos on the grounds that they no longer have pagan associations. Other Christians observe that the pagan connotations of tattoos have persisted across cultures for thousands of years. These connotations will not easily be lost—especially in an increasingly paganized Western culture. The existence of tattoos reflecting devotion to God does not negate the numerous non-Christian tattoos that don't communicate devotion to God. In addition, the more fundamental principle behind Leviticus 19's prohibition of tattoos is a refusal to deface the body since humans bear the image of God. The fundamental question for the Christian to ask is: What does inking the body communicate about the Creator of the body?

**profanity:** "a type of language that includes dirty words and ideas"[21]

**vulgarity:** "the quality of being crude and lacking refinement. Many people consider swearing to be a form of vulgarity."[22]

ETHICAL SOCIETY 207

**11.3.3** Evaluate the personal and social consequences of unethical communication and media use. BWS

**11.3.4** Assess the virtues necessary for ethical communication and media use. BWS

**11.3.5** Formulate a biblical response to cultural pressure to engage in unethical communication and social media use.

## Biblical Worldview Shaping

- **Man's Chief End** (evaluate): Christian communication and media consumption should further a life of purity and righteousness. By thus walking worthy of the gospel, Christians glorify God. (11.3.3)
- **Virtue** (formulate): Christian communication should be characterized by honesty, gentleness, and righteousness. (11.3.4)

## Printed Resource

- Activity 11.3: Ethical Challenges with Social Media

## Suggested Reading

- DeYoung, Kevin. "The One Indispensable Rule for Using Social Media." The Gospel Coalition (website). June 13, 2012.

# Engage

## BULLYING AND SOCIAL MEDIA

Use a **Ticket in the Door** to preassess student experiences of bullying and social media.

True or False: I have experienced, or a close friend of mine has experienced, bullying on social media.

Invite students to discuss with a teacher or another trusted adult if they need help handling the impact of being bullied on social media. Students need to know that they do not have to suffer in silence. Help is available.

# Instruct

## BIBLICAL COMMUNICATION

Use **direct instruction** to reinforce the importance of a biblical worldview regarding communication.

To understand the power of human communication for good or for ill, we need to think of it from a biblical worldview. Secular worldviews tend to regard human communication as a power play between humans, a socially constructed way for one person (or a particular group of people) to gain power over another person (or group of people). A biblical worldview, however, informs us that the Fall has not destroyed God's good intention for language. While it is true that fallen people often misuse language to manipulate and deceive others, a biblical worldview can guard us from becoming cynical about human communication.

Because communication finds its origin in the triune God who spoke the world into existence and who has begun to restore all that sin has broken, human language is still capable of reflecting what is good, true, and beautiful about the world around us in ways that bless people rather than harm them. Therefore, truthful communication is possible in a world of deception because communication originates with the God of truth who has called His people to speak the truth (Eph. 4:15). Words of healing are possible in a hurting world because communication originates with the God of comfort who has called His people to comfort the hurting (2 Cor. 1:3–4). Wise communication that builds people up is possible in a world that foolishly slanders because communication originates with the God of life who has called His people to speak words of life (Prov. 15:4; 18:21).

As these examples indicate, a biblical worldview of human language has practical value in our everyday lives. It helps us appreciate the power of human language as well as recognize its limits. It helps us discern helpful communication from harmful ones. It helps us to evaluate whether the motives behind our communication align with the character of God. And it helps us remain confident that one word of truth can conquer a world of lies.

## EVALUATING UNETHICAL COMMUNICATION AND MEDIA USE

Use a **Turn and Talk** to prompt students to evaluate unethical communication and media use based on the Scripture provided.

**What does Psalm 141:3 imply about unethical communication?** *It implies that unethical communication is a problem for humans, and it necessitates God's help if we are to refrain from it.*

**According to Proverbs 13:3, why should a person be careful about the kind of communication that comes from his or her mouth?** *The kind of communication that comes from someone's mouth has serious ramifications for his or her own life.*

**What does Proverbs 11:11 imply about the kind of speech that tears down a society?** *When wicked people give full expression to their thoughts and attitudes in public conversation, they poison the discourse and bring ruin upon society.*

**What can you infer from James 1:19 about responding too quickly to an insult on social media?** *Quick responses are prone to arise from anger and cause further problems. It is better to slow down and think about one's response so that one may speak in a measured way.*

**What does 1 Peter 2:22–23 teach us about the ethical nature of uttering threats when others revile us?** *Christ's example makes clear that the ethical response to being reviled is to avoid uttering threats.*

**According to Colossians 4:5–6, why is it wrong to engage in gossip?** *Our conversation is always to be seasoned with grace, and gossip is ungracious speech.*

## ETHICAL CHALLENGES WITH SOCIAL MEDIA

Use **Activity 11.3** on page 69 to help students respond biblically to ethical challenges with social media.

## Apply

## VIRTUES NECESSARY FOR ETHICAL COMMUNICATION AND MEDIA USE

Use a **Quick Write** to assess the virtues necessary for ethical communication and media use.

It was by divine communication that God created the world. When God turned His attention to human beings, He designed our communication to facilitate fellowship with Him and with other people. Fellowship occurs when our speech is truthful, righteous, honorable, gracious, and peaceable. Speech that reflects God's character also promotes human flourishing. Society functions more efficiently and effectively when communication is ethical.

### *The Fall and Restoration of Communication*

Ever wonder why people misunderstand one another, why they twist the meaning of each other's words, and why they sometimes cease to communicate with certain people? The answer lies in the fact that we live in a world marred by sin. Although communication still facilitates human fellowship and human flourishing, it is at best a frustratingly poor reflection of what it once was. At its worst, communication is misused to dishonor God, to deceive other people, and to destroy relationships.

James warns that the tongue (and we can extend this to online speech) "is a fire" (James 3:6) and "an unruly evil" (James 3:8). He also warns against bitter envy, strife, and boasting deceit—and says such things are demonic (James 3:13–18). Galatians 5:15 warns about speech that devours others. Proverbs 6:19 says that God hates those who sow discord. Exodus 20:16 prohibits bearing false witness.

Redemption is God's answer to broken communication. The righteous judgment that fell upon human communication at the Tower of Babel has its redemptive parallel at the Day of Pentecost. Whereas the former incident resulted in confused human languages to frustrate man's sinful goal, the later incident overcame those barriers to advance God's redemptive goal. Redemption enables believers to encourage others with wise and helpful words instead of destroying them with foolish and hurtful words.

ends

### COMMUNICATION AND MEDIA: WHAT HAS HAPPENED TO US?

Living in this present evil age is difficult for the redeemed because the world treats unethical communication as normal and ethical communication as prudish. Corrupt uses of media are more common than noble uses. Christian communication and media consumption, however, should further a life of purity and righteousness. This means Christians will have to go against the tide of culture in their communication and media use.

Profanity, crude joking, lying, gossiping, and the general promotion of messages that dishonor God and debase human beings have not served our society well. Words are powerful, and when they're misused, they do not cease to be powerful. Their power is merely directed to destructive ends rather than constructive ones. Individual families suffer from harsh words spoken in the home, from the undiscerning use of media, and from the absence of reassuring words of love. Multiply this situation in families throughout society, and the culture becomes desensitized to the coarsening of communication.

Unethical communication and media use not only reveals the character of our society, but it also plunges society into an unsustainable situation. Just as ethical communication is essential to building trust in society, so unethical communication guarantees the erosion of trust. Gossip and slander erode the trust necessary for hurting people to confide in others, pushing them into the shadows of society. The hopeless ones often resort to self-harm or harming others in part because of



**How do you think the virtue of honesty should guide Charlotte in her communication in the following scenario? Charlotte is a Christian student attending a secular university. She is confronted with transgender ideology in the classroom when her professor instructs the class to refer to fellow classmates by each person's preferred pronouns. Charlotte is not sure what she should do. She doesn't want to be disrespectful to students who identify as a gender different from their biological sex, but neither will her Christian convictions allow her to speak words that she genuinely believes contradict reality.** *Even though non-Christians will not agree, the fact is that Charlotte can simultaneously be respectful and honest by letting the person know that she understands how important it is to be affirmed and that she wants to affirm the worth and dignity of every person, but she also believes that our worth and dignity are not determined by us but by the God who made us. Therefore, by affirming God's creational design in each person's gender, Charlotte respects the person but is honest about the person's gender based on the person's fixed biological sex.*

**How do you think the virtue of gentleness should guide Robert in his communication in the following scenario? Robert enjoys debating fellow classmates who hold different positions from him on certain biblical points. While Robert's classmates respect his knowledge of the issues and his debating skills, many of them are concerned about Robert's communication style. When arguing for his positions,**

bullying. The normalization of profanity and vulgarity produces a society of cynics who no longer trust that the sacred is real and worthy of respect. Deception in news media and misinformation on social media create an environment of distrust. The loss of trust spells the loss of social cohesion. This is the price that a society pays for tolerating unethical communication.

When the overuse of technology is mixed into the equation, the result is a society of people unable to properly interact with one another. Human beings in such a society become hollow, a shell of what they were meant to be. Just think of a family sitting around the table at a restaurant—dad, mom, brother, and sister all looking at their smartphones and unable to enjoy the company of their family. The negative social impact of all these behaviors may take time to notice, but eventually people realize their relationships are deficient.

## COMMUNICATION AND MEDIA: WHERE DO WE GO FROM HERE?

How can I please God in my communication and media use?

The biblical reality of our world is this: we currently live in the overlap of two ages. The age of redemption has invaded this present evil age, and that should give every Christian hope. The devastating cultural effects of unethical communication and media use should not be minimized, but neither should they be given the last word.

For all the destructive words on social media and in our personal lives, God's final word to us in Christ will prevail in the end. The triumph of righteous communication was initiated when the eternal Word became flesh, communicated words of grace and truth throughout His life on earth, and then nailed to the cross every sinful word from our hearts and lips.

Union with Christ transforms our communication. It replaces dishonesty with honesty, harshness with gentleness, and vulgarity with righteousness. Our honesty should proceed from a love for the truth and a willingness to speak the truth, even when it is unpopular. Our gentleness should arise from a consciousness of the power of our words and the obligation to use that power for the good of our listeners. Our righteous speech should spring from a desire to reflect our righteous God, knowing that it pleases Him and blesses others.

Believers should take care that their speech influences society for the better and that their media use influences themselves for the better. As our communication and media use is suffused with the virtues of honesty, gentleness, and righteousness, we can promote God's intention for human fellowship and human flourishing. A society that values these virtues is a society whose members can trust one another.

> *You represent Christ in a real way even if it is in the virtual world.*
>
> KEVIN DEYOUNG[23]

**Robert often comes across as abrasive and belittling toward those with whom he disagrees. Some classmates have ceased to engage Robert any further, causing Robert to reevaluate his communication style. He doesn't want to compromise his biblical positions, but neither does he want to unnecessarily offend his classmates.** *Robert can be encouraged that he desires to change from being abrasive to being more gracious in his communication style. Robert would do well to make sure his motivations for defending his position on certain biblical points are the glory of God and the good of his neighbor, rather than winning an argument or being thought clever. Robert can then engage in a mutually respectful conversation that listens well to the other person. Robert does not have to compromise his position, but neither does he have to have the last word.*

**How do you think the virtue of righteousness should guide George in his media use in the following scenario? George is careful to avoid pornographic websites. He even uses filtering software on his computer, and he has accountability partners that can review his daily internet activity. Even with these precautions in place, George has noticed that many news sites that he visits show sensual images in the margins of the websites. He doesn't want to see these images, but neither does he want to avoid his favorite news sites because of the information they provide.** *As valuable as the news information may be on these various websites, George should be encouraged to value purity more than the news. Other reliable news sites are available that refuse to allow sensual images. George may need some help identifying these sites so that he can continue to stay informed while simultaneously protecting his heart from unwanted images.*

## Assess

Guide a **summative assessment** by directing students to answer the questions in Thinking It Through 11.3.

### Thinking It Through 11.3

1. Virtue signaling, trolling, and politically correct speech are common terms in our current media environment. Other problems include profanity, crude joking, gratuitous violence in entertainment, and a loss of modesty. Social media tends toward pride, narcissism, and the idea that we can construct our own realities. Bullying has also become rampant on social media. And regret from posting inappropriate material of oneself on social media has become such a huge problem that companies now exist for the purpose of doing reputation repair. Many Christians speak and share falsehoods online because they don't take the time to check whether the statements they read are true or not.
2. God originally designed human communication to reflect His nature and character. It was by divine communication that God created the world. When God turned His attention to human beings, He designed our communication to facilitate fellowship with Him and with other people. Fellowship occurs when our speech is truthful, righteous, honorable, gracious, and peaceable. Speech that reflects God's character also promotes human flourishing.
3. James 3:6–8 warns that "the tongue is a fire" and "an unruly evil." Galatians 5:15 warns about speech that devours others. Proverbs 6:19 says that God hates the sowing of discord. Exodus 20:16 prohibits bearing false witness. James 3:13–18 warns against bitter envy, strife, boasting, and deceit because such things are demonic. Redemption is God's answer to broken communication. Redemption enables believers to encourage others with wise and helpful words instead of destroying them with foolish and hurtful words.
4. Unethical communication plunges society into an unsustainable situation. Gossip and slander erode the trust necessary for people who hurt to confide in others. The hopeless ones often resort to self-harm in part because of the bullying. The normalization of profanity and vulgarity produces a society of cynics that no longer believes that the sacred is worthy of respect. Deception in news media and misinformation on social media creates a distrusting environment. The loss of trust spells the loss of social cohesion.
5. Trusting Christ transforms our communication. It replaces dishonesty with honesty, harshness with gentleness, and vulgarity with righteousness. Our honesty should love the truth and be willing to speak the truth, even when it is unpopular. Our gentleness should motivate us to use our words for the good of our listeners. Our speech should reflect God, knowing that it pleases Him and blesses others.

Thinking It Through 11.3

1. What are the ethical issues related to communication and media use?
2. How does a biblical view of God and creation shape our understanding of communication and media use?
3. How do the biblical concepts of the Fall and redemption shape our understanding of communication and media use?
4. What are the personal and social consequences of unethical communication and media use?
5. How can the virtues of honesty, gentleness, and righteousness improve our communication and media use?

11.4 Business Ethics

Perhaps you've had your own lawn-mowing service or babysitting service. If so, you understand the value of hard work and the mutual benefit of serving others. Exchanging a product or a service for money is a blessing because it improves the quality of life for everyone involved. A farmer feeds the community, a teacher educates the children in the community, and a police officer protects the community. Each receives compensation for their skill and their labor, thereby enabling them to secure the products and services of others.

Christian ethics is qualified to give meaning and purpose to the business enterprise because it honors the dignity of people and the dignity of work. It also equips society with principles for addressing corruption in business (such as greed, theft, and laziness). In addition, Christian ethics promotes the virtues necessary for conducting business in an ethical society (such as love, diligence, and righteousness).

context

**ETHICAL PROBLEMS RELATED TO BUSINESS**

Money is not the root of all evil. The love of money is (1 Tim. 6:10). This distinction is important to keep in mind when thinking about the ethics of business. Currency is an efficient and effective way of making economic transactions. It's impossible for the car mechanic to trade his services for everything he needs and wants. With currency, however, he can earn money and trade it for goods and services.

Problems with money arise because of misplaced priorities and misdirected trust. Jesus said, "No man can serve two masters: for either he will hate the one, and love the other; or else he will hold to the one, and despise the other. Ye cannot serve God and mammon" (Matt. 6:24). Mammon (or money) is a suitable servant. But as a master it corrupts the workplace and the marketplace through the vices of greed, theft, and laziness.

***Corruption in the Workplace***

While the employer-employee relationship should be honored as a creational norm, we should also identify and correct instances of corruption that may arise in the workplace. Greed corrupts this business relationship when employers overwork their employees, demanding that they prioritize the company over their families. Theft and laziness corrupt this business relationship when employees neglect their work and receive compensation for work not done. More egregious forms of theft occur when employees steal money, supplies, or products from their company.

**Bribery*** and **extortion*** are also forms of corruption. A company paying a government official to secure a contract is an example of bribery. An employee blackmailing an employer guilty of something illegal or embarrassing is an example of extortion. In each case, the love of money is the driving motivation behind these corrupt practices.

**bribery:** "an attempt to make someone do something for you by giving the person money, presents, or something else that he or she wants"[4]

**extortion:** "the act of getting something, especially money, by force or threats"[5]

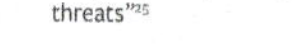

210 ISSUES

## 11.4 Business Ethics

*Is a business practice right just because it is legal?*

### Objectives

**11.4.1** Identify common ethical issues related to business practices.

**11.4.2** Summarize the biblical teaching on business practices. BWS

**11.4.3** Evaluate the consequences of unethical business practices.

**11.4.4** Assess the virtues necessary to act ethically regarding business practices. BWS

**GRAPPLING WITH ETHICAL ISSUES**

### Hiring and Firing

Jeffrey Moriarty addresses some key issues in hiring and firing: "Ethical issues in hiring and firing tend to focus on the question: What criteria should employers use, or not use, in employment decisions?"[26] What distinguishes legitimate job qualifications from unfair discrimination? Must an employer always hire the most qualified candidate for a given job opening? Should an employer be able to fire an employee "at will," or should an employer have to demonstrate "just cause" for a firing?[27] How would you answer these questions?

#### *Corruption in the Marketplace*

The marketplace consists of various players (producers, distributors, advertisers, consumers, etc.). In short, there are those who have something to sell and those who wish to purchase what's being sold. Greed and theft corrupt this otherwise beneficial economic arrangement too.

For instance, producers who use unsafe materials to save money risk their customers' health and safety. Advertisers who misrepresent a product deceive the buying public. Businesses that engage in price gouging during times of emergency take advantage of the helpless and needy (e.g., during natural disasters when water, gasoline, and other supplies are in high demand).

Consumers also corrupt the marketplace when they steal from business establishments. Some thefts are blatant smash-and-grab larcenies. Others are more subtle. Switching the price tag of an item with a lower price tag is theft. Purchasing an item of clothing with the full intention of returning it for a refund after wearing it once is also theft. These thefts eat into business profits, and the cost is then passed on to honest customers in the form of higher prices.

### BIBLICAL PRINCIPLES REGARDING BUSINESS

The purpose of business is for human beings to fulfill the Creation Mandate in the most efficient and effective way for the glory of God and for the flourishing of human society. To achieve this goal, societies must conduct business according to the ethical principles set forth in Scripture. Christian ethicist Wayne Grudem identifies six core principles.

First, since God is the God of truth and requires truthfulness from us, our business practices should be conducted in all truthfulness (Eph. 4:25). This means companies should honestly advertise their product or service, not claiming more for them than is accurate. It also means candidates for a job should be truthful on their resumes, not embellishing their accomplishments.

Second, private property is a key creational norm that underlies business ethics. Scripture's prohibition against stealing is predicated on the notion that God has entrusted individuals with the right of ownership (Exod. 20:15). Therefore, for example, "you should never put personal (nonbusiness-related) items on a business receipt and claim more reimbursement than is due to you."[28] Taking what belongs to another person (or company) is wrong.



**11.4.5** Formulate a biblical response to pressure from coworkers or employers to engage in unethical business practices.

### Biblical Worldview Shaping

- **Creational Order** (explain): Private property is a key creational norm that underlies business ethics. (11.4.2)
- **Virtue** (formulate): Ethical businesspeople should be motivated by love for others, should be diligent in all their work, and should be righteous in all their dealings. (11.4.4)

### Printed Resource

- Activity 11.4: Business Ethics

### Digital Resource

- Video: "Business Ethics"

### Suggested Reading

- Grudem, Wayne. *Christian Ethics: An Introduction to Biblical Moral Reasoning*. Wheaton, IL: Crossway 2018. Pages 1060–72.

## Engage

### BUSINESS ETHICS

Show the **video** "Business Ethics" to introduce the subject to students.

### A BIBLICAL VIEW OF MONEY

Conduct a **Think-Pair-Share** in which students answer the following questions.

**Why does the Bible warn us against the love of money? Why should we not conclude from this warning that money is evil?** *God does not want anything to compete with Him for our highest affections. Therefore, Scripture warns about the love of money because money is often a rival competitor with God. This is not because money is inherently evil, but because the human heart in its fallen condition tends to trust money rather than God for the provisions and security needed in life. Money is a suitable servant but a terrible master. As a servant, money is an efficient way of making transactions with other people. Money is not contrary to a biblical worldview; it is consistent with the Creation Mandate.*

## Instruct

### BIBLICAL PRINCIPLES REGARDING BUSINESS

Guide a **discussion** about the biblical teaching on business practices.

**Some businesses profit from being dishonest, and some people advance in their career through misrepresenting their accomplishments. What does Ephesians 4:25 say in regard to honesty in business and personal careers?** *Because God is the God of truth, He requires truthfulness from us in our business practices and careers.*

**Most people agree that employees should not steal from their employers. According to Exodus 20:15, how does the creational norm of private property uphold this ethical principle?** *Scripture's prohibition against stealing is predicated on the notion that God has entrusted individuals with the right of ownership. Taking what belongs to another person (or company) is wrong.*

**Given that the work environment consists of men and women helping one another with various business responsibilities, what biblical principle should businesses consider in the way they arrange for their employees to interact with those of the opposite sex?** *Since God requires faithfulness in marriage, companies should establish reasonable boundaries for their male and female employees so that they are not tempted with infidelity.*

**How does the biblical principle of loving our neighbor relate to our business practices?** *Loving our neighbor can guide our business practices by making us consider how a particular transaction will benefit not only us but also our neighbor. We should desire the transaction to be good for our neighbor.*

**According to James 1:5–6 and 1 Corinthians 10:13, how might belief in God's guidance in our business dealings prevent us from choosing a sinful option in a business transaction?** *Since God provides wisdom and direction for His people, we can be confident that a righteous solution is available when facing difficult business decisions. This principle refutes the notion that some business situations present us with nothing but sinful options. This is never the case because, no matter how difficult the decision, God promises to provide a way of escape from sin and invites us to ask for the wisdom to see it.*

**Philippians 4:19 teaches us that God supplies our needs. What heart attitude toward God does a person need in order to make ethical decisions in all of one's economic transactions?** *One needs the attitude of dependence upon God, seeking to please Him in every transaction and trusting Him to "supply all [our] need according to his riches" (Phil. 4:19).*

## HOW ABUSING BUSINESS PRACTICES IMPACTS SOCIETY

Assign a brief **writing assignment** to answer this section's essential question and to allow students to determine how abusing business practices impacts society. Students may work individually or in groups.

Several examples of abusive business practices were identified on pages 212–13. Ask the students to identify another abusive business practice that they think dehumanizes people or destabilizes society or both.

**What are the consequences of that abusive practice? How might that abuse be corrected in society?** *Answers should reflect the information discussed in this section.*

Third, since God requires faithfulness in marriage, companies should establish reasonable boundaries for their male and female employees. For example, sending two employees of the opposite sex on a business trip without safeguards is inviting temptation. To mitigate temptation, the employees should never be alone together during the business trip.

Fourth, love of neighbor extends to the people with whom we conduct business. "In bargaining for a price, love for neighbor means understanding a 'good deal' is one that is not only good for you but also allows the other person to make some money and to have some benefit from the transaction."[29] A simple way to apply this principle is to treat others the way you want to be treated (Matt. 7:12).

Fifth, since God provides wisdom and direction for His people, we can be confident that a righteous solution is available when facing difficult business decisions. This principle refutes the notion that some business situations present us with nothing but sinful options. This is never the case because, no matter how difficult the decision, God promises to provide a way of escape from sin and invites us to ask for the wisdom to see it (1 Cor. 10:13; James 1:5–6).

Sixth, every business decision should be made in dependence upon God, seeking to please Him in every transaction and trusting Him to "supply all [our] need according to his riches" (Phil. 4:19). This means that it is better to make less money on an honest deal than it is to make more money on a dishonest deal (Prov. 16:8). Practicing biblical principles in business is not an automatic guarantee of financial success, but it does guarantee personal integrity, which is far more valuable in the eyes of God.[30]

Is a business practice right just because it is legal?

ends

### CONSEQUENCES OF ABUSING BUSINESS

In general, businesses cannot survive without advertising, making a profit, and competing against other businesses. Instead of abandoning what is morally good about these business practices,[31] we should ensure that the above-mentioned biblical principles guide our practice. Otherwise, society becomes locked in an economic battle where unethical means are justified by sheer profit. The consequences of abusing legitimate business practices are that people are dehumanized and society is destabilized. Consider the following abuses.

#### *Abuse of Advertising*

The purpose of advertising should be to inform the public about the benefits of a company's product. However, certain kinds of advertising dehumanize people. For example, the use of sensual images to attract attention to a product is crass **exploitation*** of people. A company may justify the practice on the grounds that they couldn't compete otherwise. Though this form of advertising is legal, it's not right. It debases the people being exploited, and it desensitizes society to the exploitation of others, as well as causing many who view it to fall into sexual sin (Matt. 5:27–28; Mark 9:42).

Unbridled pragmatism in advertising has a destabilizing effect on the moral foundation of society. If advertisers concern themselves only with increasing sales without also concerning themselves with righteousness, they reinforce a consequentialist ethic for their audience. They contribute to an atmosphere of moral compromise, making it more difficult for society to define and defend moral norms. Dishonesty in advertising is one way marketers frequently manifest this pragmatism.

#### *Abuse of Profit*

**Commercialism** is the abuse of profit-making that dehumanizes people by reducing them to cogs in an economic machine. Making reasonable profits and making wise purchases are both morally good. The problem arises when businesses intentionally appeal to the covetousness of potential customers. One result is a society of affluent yet ungrateful individuals who are not content with what they have.

**exploitation:** "the use of something in order to get an advantage from it"[32]

Abusing the practice of profit-making also destabilizes society by obscuring the deeper and more fundamental priorities of human existence (e.g., raising children within stable families). Because our society places economic pressure on both parents to work outside the home, many children are raised by someone other than a parent. Even more tragic is how abortion advocates insist that a woman's success in her career depends on her ability to be free from the responsibility of children. The negative social consequences of sacrificing children on the altar of economic prosperity are a sad and present reality in Western society.

#### *Abuse of Competition*

In an ethical society, competition motivates companies to innovate and avoid stagnation. Earning a customer's business should be about honestly providing the best product at the lowest cost. However, unrestrained competition dehumanizes people because it allows businesses to treat competitors as mere rivals to be crushed. Businesses that lie about their competitors violate their dignity. Businesses that steal their competitors' ideas or designs violate their property rights.

These things have a destabilizing effect on society. First, they weaken consumer confidence in the marketplace. Consumers are not quite sure which businesses they can trust. Second, honest people are discouraged from starting their own businesses. Starting a business is risky even in the best of ethical environments. But if a society tolerates a company breaking the rules of fair play, honest people face a disincentive for taking a business risk.

### agents VIRTUES FOR ACTING ETHICALLY IN BUSINESS

Despite the challenges of doing business in a fallen world, people still have a responsibility to utilize their talents and skills, often either as an employee of a reputable company or as an owner and operator of one. God still rules over creation, and He is able to protect and to prosper those in business. Every legitimate business enterprise that advances the Creation Mandate has the stamp of God's approval. If God is calling you to serve Him in business, then that is also your mission field as a Christian.

To faithfully represent God in all of our business activities, we must be growing in certain virtues. Ethical Christians should be motivated by *love* for others, be *diligent* in all their work, and be *righteous* in all their dealings. These virtues are relevant for employers and employees, for business owners and for customers.

> *Business is an essential sphere in the unfolding work of God in Christ.*
>
> WILLIAM MESSENGER[31]

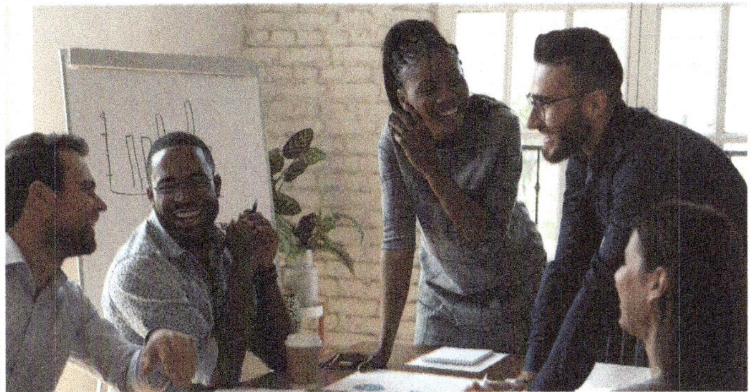



## Apply

### VIRTUES FOR ACTING ETHICALLY IN BUSINESS

Use a **Turn and Talk** to prompt students to assess how the virtues of love, diligence, and righteousness might enable them to act ethically in business.

**Why is the virtue of love among the business owners necessary in the following scenario? A coastal city in the United States has just been devastated by a hurricane. Although resources are limited, there are sufficient supplies of water and gasoline to last the community a few days. Some store and gas station owners choose to capitalize on the situation by raising prices on water, gas, and other essential items. Other business owners choose to lower their prices. Some even choose to freely give what they have until other resources arrive.** *Love is necessary if business owners are to put the needs of the community above their own personal profit. The main goal in a natural disaster is not to make a profit but to ensure the safety and well-being of others. Charging higher prices during a natural disaster is contrary to the virtue of love; it is an example of a business owner taking advantage of hurting people. Without love for others, business owners will make decisions based on what they believe will benefit only them.*

**How might the virtue of diligence guide the painter's decision to fix the mistake in the following scenario? A painter has promised his customer to finish painting his house by a specific date. The customer clearly gave the painter the name of the color of paint, but the painter accidentally used a slightly different paint color. Since the customer was away on vacation when the painting started, it was weeks later that the mistake was caught.** *The virtue of diligence might lead the painter to either hire an extra painter or work overtime to ensure that the job is finished on schedule as promised.*

**How might the virtue of righteousness guide the bank employee in her decision in the following scenario? An employee for a bank learns that her manager accidentally made a financial error. Rather than admit the error and risk losing his job, the manager engages in a cover-up. The employee is aware of the cover-up and has informed her manager that she cannot be a party to his misdeed because of her Christian convictions. The manager threatens to fire the employee if she reveals his actions. Furthermore, he tells her that he will deny any wrongdoing and insists that the company will believe him over her.** *Although the employee cannot be sure that the company will believe her over her manager, she can trust that God will be honored for her righteous decision. Losing one's job in a situation like this is preferable to compromising one's biblical convictions.*

### BUSINESS ETHICS

Use **Activity 11.4** on page 71 to familiarize students with difficult ethical decisions in business.

## Assess

Guide a **summative assessment** by directing students to answer the questions in Thinking It Through 11.4.

### Thinking It Through 11.4

1. Greed corrupts the business relationship when employers demand that employees prioritize the company over their family. Theft and laziness corrupt the business relationship when employees get paid for work not done. More egregious forms of theft occur when employees steal from their company. A company that pays a government official to secure a contract is an example of bribery. An employee that blackmails an employer guilty of impropriety is an example of extortion. In each case, the love of money is the driving motivation behind these corrupt practices.
2. Producers who use unsafe materials to save money risk their customers' health and safety. Advertisers who misrepresent a product deceive the buyers. Businesses that engage in price gouging during times of emergency take advantage of the helpless and needy (e.g., natural disasters when water, gasoline, and other supplies are in high demand).

   Consumers also corrupt the marketplace when they steal from businesses. Some thefts are blatant snatch-and-grab robberies. Others are more subtle. Switching the price tag of an item in a retail store with a lower price tag is theft. Purchasing an item of clothing with the intention of returning it for a refund after wearing it a few times is also theft. These thefts eat into business profits, and the cost is then passed on to honest customers in higher prices.
3. First, since God is the God of truth and requires truthfulness from us, we should conduct our business practices in all truthfulness. Second, private property is a key creational norm that underlies business ethics. Third, since God requires faithfulness in marriage, companies should establish reasonable boundaries for their male and female employees. Fourth, love of neighbor extends to the people with whom we conduct business. Fifth, since God provides wisdom and direction for His people, we can be confident that a righteous solution is available when facing difficult business decisions. Sixth, every business decision should be made in dependence upon God, seeking to please Him in every transaction.
4. The use of sensual images to attract attention to a product is crass exploitation of people. Though it is legal, it's not right because it debases the people being exploited and desensitizes society to that exploitation. If advertisers think only of effectiveness without also thinking about righteousness, they reinforce a consequentialist ethic. They contribute to an atmosphere of moral compromise, making it more difficult for society to define and defend moral norms.
5. Commercialism (i.e., the abuse of profit-making) dehumanizes people by reducing them to cogs in an economic machine. The abuse of profit-making also destabilizes society by obscuring the more fundamental realities of human existence (e.g., raising children within stable families).
6. Love ensures that we profit by doing good to others and that we avoid profiting from the harm of others. Diligence undergirds excellence in business. Righteousness guards against compromises in our business dealings. Doing what is right must always take precedence over earning money or achieving success. A Christian takes seriously the words of Jesus: "What shall it profit a man, if he shall gain the whole world, and lose his own soul?" (Mark 8:36). Being righteous in business is about learning how to succeed without losing your soul.

#### *Love Promotes Ethical Business Practices*

It would be incorrect to view love and profit as competing motives in business, as though an ethical person should be disinterested in personal profit. Instead, we should think of love for others as the virtue that properly directs our profit motive. Love ensures that we profit by doing good to others and that we avoid profiting from the harm of others.

For instance, a business owner who loves his employees will share his company's profits with them by paying them a fair wage as opposed to paying them meager wages to enrich himself. Conversely, an employee who loves his employer will work diligently to help grow the company's profits as opposed to doing the bare minimum with no other concern than getting a weekly paycheck.

Love is also essential in promoting an ethical relationship between business owners and customers. For example, a restaurant owner motivated by love will serve his customers the kind of food that has been advertised, not deceptively serve an inferior substitute. Similarly, a customer motivated by love for a restaurant owner will not dishonestly complain about a good meal in order to manipulate the owner into canceling his bill, because that would be stealing.

#### *Diligence Promotes Ethical Business Practices*

Diligence is the virtue that undergirds excellence in business. Employers recognize diligence in those employees who strive to perform their duties to the best of their abilities. Customers recognize diligence in a business that goes the extra mile to provide friendly customer service.

On the other hand, slothfulness is a vice that leads to poverty (Prov. 10:4; 13:4; 20:4). For those who are capable of working but refuse to do so, Scripture has this to say: "If any would not work, neither should he eat" (2 Thess. 3:10). Fallen people often look for ways to satisfy their desires for daily necessities without expending much effort.

Although the creational norm of labor has been frustrated by the Fall, Christians understand the importance of diligence in overcoming certain frustrations. For example, builders face frustration with their building projects (e.g., getting permits, returning defective material, facing delays). Nevertheless, a diligent builder overcomes these frustrations. The builder's work ethic produces a building that is structurally sound and within budget as much as possible.

#### *Righteousness Promotes Ethical Business Practices*

Righteousness is the virtue that guards against unethical compromises in our business dealings. Doing what is right must always take precedence over earning money, achieving success, and the thrill of competition. A Christian takes seriously the words of Jesus: "What shall it profit a man, if he shall gain the whole world, and lose his own soul?" (Mark 8:36). Being righteous in business is about learning how to succeed without losing your soul.

There will always be some wins and some losses for everyone in business. Righteousness is a virtue that enables Christians to accurately weigh the wins and losses. It evaluates each business decision by what matters for eternity. Sometimes an employee loses a job because of a righteous stand. Sometimes a business loses a customer because of a moral position on a cultural issue. But these are minor losses compared to the eternal losses some businesspeople will experience.

Of course, acting ethically in business can lead to success in this world. This is a good thing, and Christians should be thankful when God prospers them. Some of the most successful businesses have also been the most ethical. The world needs more businesspeople who are motivated by love for others, diligent in all their work, and righteous in all their dealings. Having an ethical society depends upon it.

#### Thinking It Through 11.4

1. What are some common ethical problems in the workplace?
2. What are some common ethical problems in the marketplace?
3. What are the six core biblical principles for ethical business practices?
4. How does sensuality in advertising dehumanize people and destabilize society?
5. How does commercialism dehumanize people and destabilize society?
6. How do the virtues of love, diligence, and righteousness promote ethical business practices?

# Review 11

ETHICAL SOCIETY

### Terms to Remember

- race
- racism
- inequality
- abstinence
- recreational drugs
- bribery
- extortion
- exploitation
- commercialism

### Scripture Memory

- Matthew 7:12

### Understanding Ethics

1. What does the Bible teach about the origin of communication?
2. What does the Bible teach about substance abuse?
3. What does the Bible teach about truthfulness with respect to business practices?

### Practicing Ethical Decision-Making

4. How should you respond when you hear a friend make a racist comment?
5. What are some responsible ways you can use social media?

### Analyzing and Evaluating Ethical Claims

6. How would you respond to someone claiming that white responsibility is the solution to racial discrimination?
7. How would you respond to someone claiming that profanity and vulgarity are ethically neutral forms of communication?
8. How would you respond to someone claiming that gambling is a harmless activity?
9. How would you respond to the claim that love and profit are incompatible motives for Christians engaged in business?

### Creating My Own Position Statements on Ethics

10. Write a one- to two-page paper that summarizes your understanding of a biblical position on racial discrimination. Explain why a biblical solution is more just than secular solutions.



# Chapter 11 Review

## Terms to Remember

- **race:** The single race of humans (all descended from Adam and distinct from animals) or a distinct cultural, ethnic, social, or people group within the human race.
- **racism:** "Prejudice, antagonism, or discrimination by an individual, institution, or society, against a person or people on the basis of their nationality or (now usually) their membership of a particular racial or ethnic group, typically one that is a minority or marginalized. Also: beliefs that members of a particular racial or ethnic group possess innate characteristics or qualities, or that some racial or ethnic groups are superior to others; an ideology based on such beliefs" (*Oxford English Dictionary* online, s.v. "racism," last modified March 2022).
- **inequality:** The treatment of certain groups as less worthy of respect and dignity than other groups.
- **abstinence:** With respect to alcohol use, the position that emphasizes both the necessity of avoiding drunkenness and the wisdom of abstaining from that which gets one drunk.
- **recreational drugs:** Drugs "that some people take occasionally for enjoyment, especially when they are spending time socially with other people" (*Collins COBUILD Advanced Learner's Dictionary* online, s.v. "recreational drug," accessed April 4, 2023).
- **bribery:** "An attempt to make someone do something for you by giving the person money, presents, or something else that he or she wants" (*Cambridge Dictionary* online, s.v. "bribery," accessed July 29, 2022).
- **extortion:** "The act of getting something, especially money, by force or threats" (*Cambridge Dictionary* online, s.v. "extortion," accessed July 29, 2022).
- **exploitation:** "The use of something in order to get an advantage from it" (*Cambridge Dictionary* online, s.v. "exploitation," accessed July 30, 2022).
- **commercialism:** The abuse of profit-making that dehumanizes people by reducing them to cogs in an economic machine, by appealing to their covetousness.

## Understanding Ethics

1. Human communication is a gift from God, originally designed as a reflection of His nature and His character. Communication has always existed because God is a triune God.
2. Substance abuse is incompatible with the Christian life, where the controlling influence is supposed to be the Holy Spirit (Eph. 5:18). God created humans to rule over creation, but at present the fallen creation often rules over humans. Addiction is an example of creation ruling over man.
3. God is the God of truth and requires truthfulness from us, so we should conduct our business practices in all truthfulness (Eph. 4:25).

## Practicing Ethical Decision-Making

4. Students should consider how the virtue of love would apply to their response. Love for one's friend and love for people of other ethnicities should lead you to correct your friend for making a racist comment.
5. Students should apply the virtues of honesty, gentleness, and righteousness to their answer. Honesty should compel one to speak truthfully, but truth should also be presented in a humble and righteous way.

### Analyzing and Evaluating Ethical Claims

6. It will not work because often it wrongly treats the family, diligence in education, and hard work as part of "whiteness." Furthermore, "whites" are not monolithic; to negatively stereotype a group of people based on physical characteristics is itself racism.
7. There are no neutral forms of human communication. All communication either reflects God's character or humanity's fallen character. Profanity and vulgarity are in the latter category.
8. Gambling is based on the love of money and is proven to be addictive (1 Tim. 6:9–10; James 1:15–17). It deprives many families of daily necessities. Studies indicate that wherever gambling is legalized, crime goes up.
9. We should think of love for others as the virtue that properly directs our profit motive. Love ensures that we profit by doing good to others and that we avoid profiting from the harm of others.

### Creating My Own Position Statements on Ethics

10. Papers should reflect principles enunciated in Section 11.1 and from other supporting resources.

# Lesson Plan Overview

**CHAPTER 12:** Ethical Science

**EV** ExamView
**PPT pres.** PowerPoint presentation

| PAGES | OBJECTIVES | RESOURCES | ASSESSMENTS |
|---|---|---|---|
| **12.1 Stem Cell Research, Cloning, and Gene Editing** (4 DAYS) | | | |
| 217–23 | **12.1.1** Identify scientific research methods that raise ethical questions.<br>**12.1.2** Summarize the biblical teaching on repairing the effects of the Fall through medical science.<br>BWS Creational Order (explain)<br>**12.1.3** Defend the need for discernment regarding the consequences of scientific research and applications.<br>BWS Wisdom (evaluate)<br>**12.1.4** Assess the virtues necessary to ethically pursue advances in medical science.<br>BWS Virtue (formulate)<br>**12.1.5** Formulate a biblical response to those who favor editing the human germline.<br>BWS Wisdom (apply) | **ACTIVITIES**<br>• 12.1 Editing the Human Germline<br>**BJU PRESS TROVE***<br>• Video: "Stem Cell Research, Cloning, and Gene Editing"<br>• Link: Should We Edit the Human Germline?<br>• PPT pres.: Chapter 12 | **STUDENT EDITION**<br>• Thinking It Through 12.1 |
| **12.2 Organ Donation and Transplantation** (4 DAYS) | | | |
| 223–28 | **12.2.1** Identify scenarios where organs are donated or transplanted.<br>**12.2.2** Summarize the biblical teaching regarding the nature of personhood and the care of the body.<br>BWS Creational Order (explain)<br>**12.2.3** Evaluate the societal consequences of exploitative organ harvesting.<br>**12.2.4** Assess the virtues necessary to discern when organ donation is appropriate.<br>BWS Virtue (formulate)<br>**12.2.5** Formulate a biblical response to the practice of paying people for organ donation.<br>BWS Wisdom (apply) | **ACTIVITIES**<br>• 12.2 Paying for Organ Donations?<br>**BJU PRESS TROVE**<br>• PPT pres.: Chapter 12 | **STUDENT EDITION**<br>• Thinking It Through 12.2 |

*Digital resources for homeschool users are available on Homeschool Hub.

| PAGES | OBJECTIVES | RESOURCES | ASSESSMENTS |
|---|---|---|---|
| **12.3 Conservation, Environmentalism, and Animal Rights** (4 DAYS) | | | |
| 228–34 | **12.3.1** Identify various ethical issues regarding the environment and animals.<br>**12.3.2** Summarize the biblical teaching regarding the Christian's relationship to the natural world.<br>*BWS* Creational Order (explain)<br>**12.3.3** Evaluate the consequences of unbiblical views of creation stewardship.<br>*BWS* Man's Chief End (evaluate)<br>**12.3.4** Assess the virtues necessary to motivate appropriate care for the earth and animals.<br>*BWS* Virtue (formulate)<br>**12.3.5** Formulate biblical responses to those who abuse the creation and to those who idolize the creation. | **ACTIVITIES**<br>• 12.3 Mishandling Creation<br>**BJU PRESS TROVE**<br>• Link: Creation Care<br>• PPT pres.: Chapter 12 | **STUDENT EDITION**<br>• Thinking It Through 12.3 |
| **Review** | | | |
| 235 | Recall concepts, terms, and Scripture memory from Chapter 12. | | **STUDENT EDITION**<br>• Chapter 12 Review |
| **Test** | | | |
| | Demonstrate knowledge of the material from Chapter 12 by taking the test. | | **ASSESSMENTS**<br>• Chapter 12 Test<br>**BJU PRESS TROVE**<br>• EV: Chapter 12 test bank |

**CHAPTER 12**

# Overview

How do I know when science has gone off the rails?

## Objectives

**12.1** Analyze various ethical issues regarding the role of science in society.

**12.2** Apply a biblical ethic to the role of science in society.

## Terms to Remember

- stem cells
- embryonic stem cells
- cloning
- gene editing
- germline
- organ donation
- organ transplantation
- conservation
- environmentalism
- animal rights

## Scripture Memory

- Genesis 1:28–30

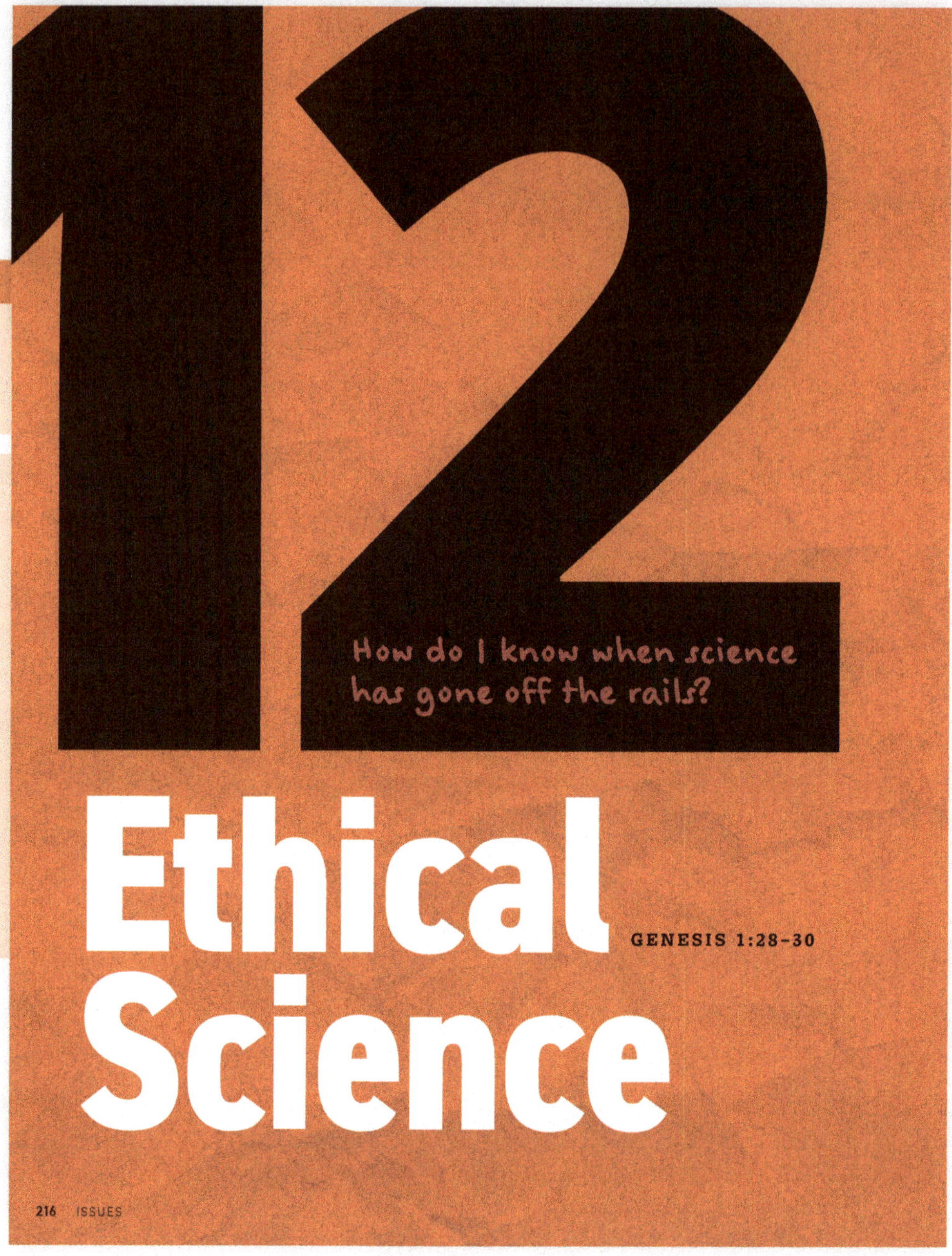

12
How do I know when science has gone off the rails?
Ethical Science
GENESIS 1:28–30
216 ISSUES

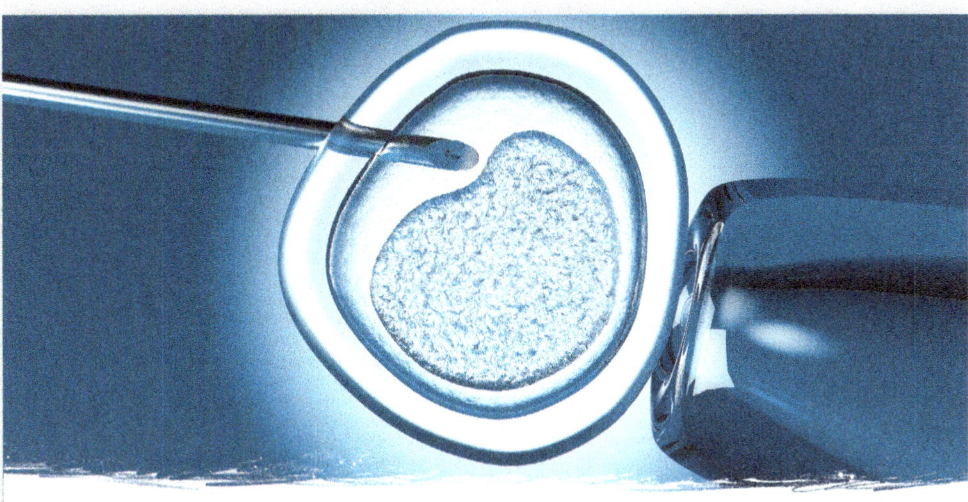

## 12.1 Stem Cell Research, Cloning, and Gene Editing

Have you noticed that sci-fi movies give technology a dominant role in the future? Technology—and its related field of science—features heavily in the undoing of society in end-of-the-world-type scenarios. Typically, it is a zombie apocalypse or computers or robots (artificial intelligence achieving a life of its own) taking over and oppressing humans. Futuristic sci-fi scenarios aside, technology is pressing forward at breakneck speed and in areas that directly impact human flourishing. What are Christians supposed to make of advances in medical science?

context

### INNOVATIONS IN MEDICAL SCIENCE

The study of the human body, on the cellular level specifically, is a field that has exploded in the past few decades. According to the Mayo Clinic, "Stem cell therapy, also known as regenerative medicine, promotes the repair response of diseased, dysfunctional or injured tissue using stem cells or their derivatives. It is the next chapter in organ transplantation and uses cells instead of donor organs, which are limited in supply."[1]

Stem cells were identified in the 1960s in mice,[2] and by 1981, embryonic stem cells were identified for the first time, also in mice.[3] One article explains,

> The human body contains more than 200 types of cells. Most of the cells are of a particular type and have a specific function. . . . **Stem cells** are different, though, in that they are relatively undifferentiated and unspecialized, meaning they have not yet obtained a special structure and function."[4]

**Embryonic stem cells**, available in embryos in their first few days of development, are the most versatile and valuable for medical scientific research because they can develop into any type of cell in the body.[5] But these gold mines of medical science research usually originate from mere days-old human embryos. The potential benefits of using embryonic stems cells seem to be tremendous. They may have great potential for treatment of serious diseases, injuries, and conditions. But the cost of those benefits is horrendous. Embryonic stem cells are normally derived from a destroyed human embryo.



# 12.1 Stem Cell Research, Cloning, and Gene Editing

*How should science improve my quality of life?*

## Objectives

**12.1.1** Identify scientific research methods that raise ethical questions.

**12.1.2** Summarize the biblical teaching on repairing the effects of the Fall through medical science. BWS

**12.1.3** Defend the need for discernment regarding the consequences of scientific research and applications. BWS

**12.1.4** Assess the virtues necessary to ethically pursue advances in medical science. BWS

**12.1.5** Formulate a biblical response to those who favor editing the human germline. BWS

## Biblical Worldview Shaping

- **Creational Order** (explain): Righteous dominion over creation involves using science to press toward the restoration of creational order in a fallen world. It does not involve seeking to transcend the creational order. (12.1.2)
- **Wisdom** (evaluate): A wise person understands the limits of his knowledge and takes into account that his actions may bring unforeseen dangers. (12.1.3)
- **Virtue** (formulate): Kindness toward others should motivate medical research. However, such research must be conducted prudently, with humility and righteousness. (12.1.4)
- **Wisdom** (apply): The virtues of prudence and humility and the fact that humans should not seek to transcend the creational order argue against editing the human germline. (12.1.5)

## Printed Resource

- Activity 12.1: Editing the Human Germline

## Digital Resources

- Video: "Stem Cell Research, Cloning, and Gene Editing"
- Link: Should We Edit the Human Germline?

## Suggested Reading

- Carter, Joe. "The FAQs: Chinese Scientists Create First Monkey-Human Embryos." The Gospel Coalition (website). April 19, 2021.
- ———. "The FAQs: What Christians Should Know about CRISPR Genetic Scissors." The Gospel Coalition (website). October 14, 2020.
- ———. "9 Things You Should Know about Human Cloning." The Gospel Coalition (website). May 17, 2013.
- "Cloning Fact Sheet." National Human Genome Research Institute (website). Last updated August 15, 2020.
- Frame, John. *The Doctrine of the Christian Life*. Phillipsburg, NJ: P&R Publishing, 2008. Pages 789–95.
- "How Does Genome Editing Work?" National Human Genome Research Institute (website). Last updated August 3, 2017.
- Magnuson, Ken. *Invitation to Christian Ethics: Moral Reasoning and Contemporary Issues*. Grand Rapids, MI: Kregel Academic, 2020. Pages 269–96.

## Engage

### INNOVATION AT ANY COST?

Use a **bell ringer** activity for students to interact with a series of questions that introduce this chapter.

**Should anything that is legally permissible be done just because it is possible?** *No, the ethical nature of the activity must also be considered, not just the legality.*

**Should robots be employed for all the jobs that they could reasonably do?** *Whereas some situations profit from automation done by a robot (e.g., mass production), in no way is employing robots as widely as possible ethical by default. It is ethical for societies to grow and be healthy, and much of that involves citizens working and providing for their own needs and for the needs of others in their communities. If robots replace most jobs of those trying to provide for their families and contribute to their communities, there is an ethical problem.*

**Regarding scientific innovations and advancement, is it ethical to pursue stem cell research, cloning, and gene editing as far as possible?** *No, stem cell research and cloning can involve tampering with how human life is conceived and gestated, and they often involve the destruction of embryos. Gene editing is questionable when permanent alterations are made to one's sex cells, thus affecting future generations.*

## Instruct

### QUESTIONABLE SCIENTIFIC RESEARCH METHODS

Use a **Think-Write-Pair-Share** for students to identify scientific research methods that raise ethical questions.

During the Write phase, instruct students to record at least one reason why the following research methods raise ethical questions.

**embryonic stem cell research:** *the destruction (death) of embryos (living humans)*

**human cloning:** *altering God's good design of having children born into a family with a father and a mother; the degradation of human life to potential lab experimentation or medical use*

**editing the germline:** *permanently altering one's sex cells (germline) which impacts all future generations born to a person; the motivations for such enduring alterations*



Cloning is a related method of medical science research and itself is an area of ethical difficulty. **Cloning** is a form of reproduction, but instead of the natural method of using a sperm and an egg, genetic material from a single person is used to manufacture a new, almost identical, but separate, individual.[6] Joe Carter provides a helpful explanation of how cloning takes place:

> Human cloning is achieved by a technique referred to as somatic cell nuclear transfer (SCNT). The process involves introducing material from the nucleus of a human somatic cell (any biological cell forming the body of an organism, though for the purposes of SCNT, usually a skin cell) into an oocyte (a female egg cell that has not yet gone through the process to become an ovum) whose own nucleus has been removed or inactivated. The oocyte becomes an ovum that now no longer needs to be fertilized, because it contains the correct amount of genetic material. This new entity begins dividing and growing, yielding a cloned human embryo.[7]

Dolly the sheep, the world's first cloned adult animal

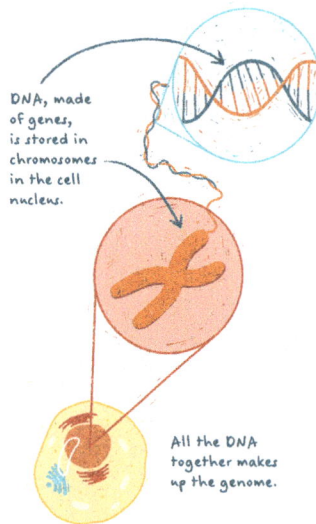

There are three types of cloning: gene, reproductive, and therapeutic. Gene cloning is the least ethically problematic since it involves only copying certain genes or parts of DNA rather than producing a whole animal or person. This type is used for researching diseases and treating diseases in the laboratory. We will focus on the other two types of cloning. Reproductive cloning involves taking a cloned embryo and implanting it in a surrogate womb to produce a live offspring. This is how the famous groundbreaking animal clone, Dolly the sheep, was produced. And therapeutic cloning involves the creation of embryos from a donor's DNA with the intention of using embryonic stem cells to develop treatments for the donor or another person.[8]

Reproductive cloning of humans is riddled with ethical challenges and red flags. God's design for and blessing on human procreation is through a man and a woman within the covenant of marriage. Cloning eliminates the need for two parents and requires so much trial and error—the deaths of many human embryos—that trying to justify it biblically or ethically is impossible.

DNA, made of genes, is stored in chromosomes in the cell nucleus.

All the DNA together makes up the genome.

Therapeutic cloning has been envisioned to create "spare parts"[9] for individuals who need certain treatments. There appear to be significant obstacles to successful cloning and to using embryonic stem cells to treat disease in humans.[10] Additionally, the National Human Genome Research Institute says, "Despite several highly publicized claims, human cloning still appears to be fiction."[11] But just like embryonic stem cell research, therapeutic cloning would create life to extinguish it within days. That would be barbaric because it would be the sinful murdering of days-old people in the name of the advance of medical science. Cloning's sense of mystery, its reputation as a technological advancement, and its potential benefits don't remove its scientific, medical, legal, and ethical difficulties and ramifications. Christians must be aware of how a medical treatment was developed before being able to accept or support its use.

A final ethical difficulty in the field of medical science is gene editing. This innovative approach is just one more medical breakthrough that allows humans to manipulate the genetic makeup of a person's DNA. Joe Carter defines **gene editing** as "a form of genome engineering in which DNA is inserted, replaced, or removed from the genetic material of a cell using artificially engineered enzymes, or 'molecular scissors.'"[12] According to Gabriella Beer, "A genome is an organism's complete set of DNA." She continues by comparing it to a paper's structure by saying the following: "If the DNA code is a set of instructions that's carefully organised into paragraphs (genes) and chapters (chromosomes), then the entire manual from start to finish would be the genome."[13]

Another important term in this field is **germline**. Once again Joe Carter offers a definition:

> Our genes, the basic physical and functional unit of heredity, are passed on from generation to generation through our sex cells (i.e., ovum [egg] and sperm). These sex cells are part of the germline. The term germline can refer to these cells in an individual or to the lineage of cells spanning generations of individuals. The other cells in the body that are not part of the germ line (and hence do not pass on traits to other generations of people) are called somatic cells.[14]

To date, the most profitable and efficient process to perform gene editing is the use of CRISPR. This acronym stands for clustered regularly interspaced short palindromic repeats. With this method, scientists insert engineered strands of DNA into the nucleus of a cell and use the protein Cas9 to cut the cell's DNA. The process ensures that the new DNA binds with the cell's DNA, essentially editing the cell's DNA sequence and creating a modified blueprint for producing future DNA.[15] The potential for gene editing is far reaching and includes gene therapy, where defective or diseased genes can be swapped out for healthy versions of the same gene. Even cancer is a target for treatment through developments of gene editing.

The key questions with gene editing (especially as its uses expand) are (1) why a modification is being made and (2) whether a modification will have enduring effects on future generations. Are genetic modifications being made to treat a real disease or condition that resulted from the Fall, or are they being made to boost characteristics we consider desirable? An alteration of a person's *somatic* cells to treat a disease in that person seems ethically acceptable. On the other hand, editing a person's *sex* cells (changing his or her germline) to permanently alter characteristics for following generations of offspring seems more questionable. Does God expect us to permanently reengineer certain aspects of the way He made us? Do we know all the consequences of such fundamental changes to our programming, especially if we pass those changes on to our posterity? Curing injuries and diseases is one thing. But to alter DNA God sovereignly gave us when we were just a single cell, merely for our own preferences, is to oppose the wisdom of His creative purposes.[16]

Each of these innovations in medical science raises multiple ethical concerns. Is it ethical to pursue long-term benefits for millions of people with harmful or life-threatening diseases by killing unborn babies? Is it ethical to create a life in a laboratory in a way that diverges from God's established norm of a husband and wife conceiving within the covenant of marriage? Is it ethical to permanently alter someone's genetic makeup for any reason (either a pragmatic enhancement or to correct hereditary diseases)?

## BIBLICAL GUIDANCE FOR MEDICAL SCIENCE

Christians can't allow themselves to blindly follow technology wherever it takes them. People are made in God's image and therefore can achieve remarkable feats. Reading up on records people hold in all areas of athletics, art, and engineering proves this. Browse scientific and medical journals to learn of the most recent achievements in those fields. But the fact that people are *capable* of building supersonic jets, landing men on the moon, putting robots on Mars, exploring the deepest trenches in the ocean, creating babies in test tubes, and permanently altering someone's DNA doesn't automatically make each endeavor ethically valid. What teachings in Scripture provide foundations for our beliefs regarding advancements in medical technology and science?

### *God Is Sovereign over Life and Death*

The first chapters in Genesis give us a look at who the Creator is, how He made man, and what expectations He gave to mankind. At the end of God's creation of all things, He capped it off with the creation of man and woman (Gen. 1:26–27; 2:7, 21–22). He also determined that all future generations of humans were designed



## REPAIRING SOME EFFECTS OF THE FALL

Use a **journal entry** for students to summarize the biblical passages that support believers pushing back against the effects of the Fall in the context of medical science. The passages fall under the two headings below.

### *God Is Sovereign over Life and Death*

- Genesis 2:24, 4:1: God created marriage as the institution that would bring about new life and nurture it to adulthood. Creating human embryos in test tubes, coupled with the subsequent handling of those embryos, is outside of God's good design.
- Job 1:21; 12:10; Hebrews 9:27: God alone is the giver of life and, therefore, He alone is also the taker of life. Human embryos aren't tools of science; they are new human lives.
- Genesis 9:6, Exodus 20:13: Man's life is valuable because of the dignity each human being has (from conception) from being made in the image of God. So, to take someone's life is a clear and serious violation of God's righteous standards.
- Matthew 9:18–33: Jesus cared about people and about healing their physical problems. Modern medicine must accept its limitations and the danger of sacrificing ethics on the altar of the blind pursuit of health, happiness, and long life.

### *Humanity Rightly Pushes Back against the Effects of the Fall*

- Genesis 1:26–30: Humans have been charged with subduing and having dominion over the earth and what it contains. But this Creation Mandate isn't an open-ended command to do whatever it takes to achieve the prime for human health by employing secular notions of well-being.
- Romans 8:18–23, Revelation 21:1: We must recognize that all things are under the Curse and the effects of the Fall. The complete reversal and full restoration of all things is promised in the age to come, not this present age. We must be careful not to try to transcend, to go beyond, the creational order.

## WISDOM PUTS ON THE BRAKES

Guide a **discussion** of the relationship between the refrain of this textbook, "the ends don't justify the means," and the *application* of scientific research.

**Why are discernment and wisdom necessary to sift through the ends and the means when considering the application of scientific research?** *Like any endeavor in life, believers need to know God, His Word, and His will to do what is right (Prov. 9:10). And believers need to explicitly ask God for wisdom in order to make wise decisions about the applications of stem cells, cloning, and gene editing. These are complicated, unavoidable, and relevant topics Christians must consider. And they can't rightly discuss the means or the ends of applying this scientific research without discernment and God's wisdom.* **But the ends of creating cures for deadly diseases or lasting treatments for chronic illnesses is honorable, right? Why wouldn't those highly commendable ends justify the destruction of weeks-old human embryos, the development of human clones, or the permanent altering of one's germline?** *Yes, it is honorable and loving to help our neighbors by creating cures and better treatments. But violating God's law by killing unborn babies, creating new life in a way and for a purpose outside of God's design, and permanently altering one's God-given genetic makeup (with risky side effects and many questions remaining about long-term effects) can never be justified for any end, no matter how lofty. Scientific research should continue, but the means must be as ethical as the ends.* **Why can't medical scientific research be trusted on face value even if the goal and result are successful treatments for sick adults?** *Overall, the scientific community doesn't operate out of a fear of God nor by seeking His wisdom. All advances in any technology and its applications should be evaluated in light of Christian ethics, which requires much discernment and wisdom.* **Why is pressing into the unknown in these three fields dangerous and unwise overall?** *A wise person understands the limits of his or her knowledge and takes into account that one's actions may bring unforeseen dangers. And these dangers include death, either of human embryos or of grown patients. There are real and serious risks with many of these developments, and they have to be considered for what they are. Progress for progress's sake easily ends in unethical situations.*

to come through procreation by the joining together in marriage of one man with one woman (Gen. 1:28; 2:24; 4:1). We see in Scripture that God alone gives life and grants authority to take it away (Job 1:21; 12:10). God is sovereign over the life span of every human (Ps. 90:3; James 4:14–15). Because of the Fall, all people must die (Rom. 5:12; Heb. 9:27), yet God detests murder (Exod. 20:13). Even killing a newly formed, unborn baby in the womb or in a laboratory extinguishes the life of a person made in God's image (Gen. 9:6).

It is sinful and unethical to nurture the formation of a new life to serve a purpose (embryonic stem cell research or therapeutic cloning) that results in the guaranteed death of a human embryo. Francis Beckwith presents a case comparing the protection of a ten-year-old's life to protecting a fetal clone:

> If it is wrong to kill a 10-year-old as a result of taking his kidneys and giving them to people the government thinks will benefit society (e.g., scientific geniuses on the verge of curing cancer or AIDS), it is wrong to kill a 20-week-old fetal-clone as a result of taking his kidneys and giving them to his genetic progenitor, a scientific genius, who needs them to survive so that he may continue his work on cures for cancer and AIDS.[17]

Since life begins at conception, "farming" human embryos for research, stem cell collection, or even therapeutic use is appalling to the Christian ethic and devoid of any alignment with God's standards. This loss of life is the primary objection to these methods of medical science research. A righteous dominion over creation does not include the heartless formation and destruction of human embryos for the purpose of research or treatment. In response to sin's destructive effect on all creation, believers should seek the restoration of fallen creation rather than contribute to the worsening of its broken condition.

#### *Humanity Rightly Pushes Back against the Effects of the Fall*

There is good news for stem cell research: not all treatments derived from stem cells have to be from embryonic stem cells. There have been developments in stem cell research where certain types of valuable stem cells are collected from placentas[18] or developed from adult skin cells.[19] The Fall and the Curse corrupted every aspect of creation, including the cells and genes in the human body, and man still has to fulfill the God-given mandate to subdue and have dominion over the earth and everything in it (Gen. 1:28). Gene cloning is being used to this end. Stem cell research is revealing many insights and treatments that in effect help reverse the decay and disease brought on by the Fall. Scientists are hoping to use stem cells to research disease, treat a variety of conditions, and test drugs.[20]

God is in the business of restoring His creation by pushing back against the evil and damaging effects of the Fall. Prophets of the Old Testament, apostles of the New Testament, and Christ Himself engaged in many miracles of healing sickness, removing disease, and reversing death. These were real reversals of the effects of the Fall but only happened occasionally and on a very small scale. One day in the future, God will permanently restore all that the Fall has tarnished and twisted (Rom. 8:18–23; Rev. 21:1). But for now, what is the standard for knowing when humanity has gone beyond the bounds of what pushing back against the effects of the Fall is supposed to look like? What limits does developing therapeutic treatments have? Is there an



## QUESTIONABLE SCIENTIFIC RESEARCH METHODS

Show the **video** "Stem Cell Research, Cloning, and Gene Editing" to familiarize students with scientific research methods that raise ethical questions.

**Apply**

## VIRTUOUS MEDICAL SCIENCE

Use a **one-minute essay** for students to elaborate on how the virtues of kindness, humility, and righteousness need to be applied to medical scientific research and those affected by it.

- Kindness: All people are human beings created in the image of God, regardless of their age or stage of development. It is

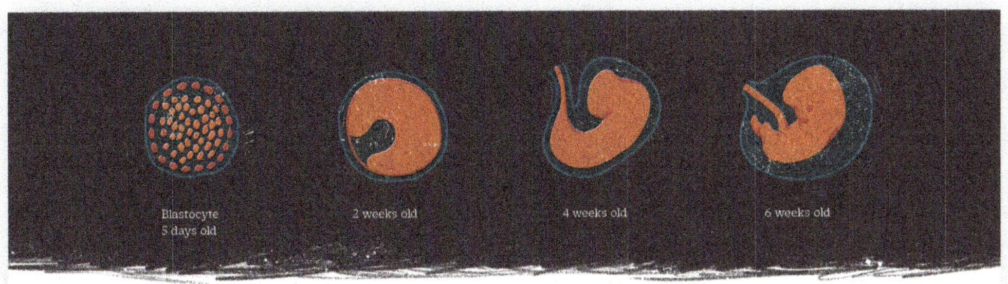


ethical line that is crossed when we go from medical therapy to elective enhancement?

What limit does the Bible's teaching place on this type of medical science research? When the death of human embryos (immediately or after a few days or weeks) is the expected or unavoidable result, we have passed the limit. We can't accept a utilitarian approach where the focus is the advancement of technology for the betterment of future people at the cost of killing unborn people in the form of countless human embryos. That is unacceptable from a biblical worldview; it is a position that cannot be compromised.

Gene editing involves using technology and detailed knowledge of the human genome to attempt to treat diseases in people or prevent their children from inheriting certain diseases. Treating someone's current condition has fewer ethical question marks than preventing diseases in someone's descendants would. Neither therapy is free from serious potential side effects, including death.[21] But gene editing has other possible uses. Are cosmetic changes—enhancements rather than therapies[22]—pushing back against the effects of the Fall, or are they merely serving someone's conception of beauty? Restoring the creation order is noble. But trying to improve on the creational order by permanently altering what humans look like and can physically do is a problematic idea that carries with it unforeseen consequences. God did design man to create, develop, and cultivate technologies to be used for taking dominion over and subduing creation. But God's rule and power and design of all things, including human appearances and abilities, remain God's prerogative and right (Job 40:6–42:4).

How should science improve my quality of life?

### What about Elective Cosmetic Surgery?

Plastic surgeons can alter virtually any part of the human body. Elective cosmetic surgery is the non-therapeutic enhancement or alteration of a body part. This can include things like a facelift or a nose job. The purpose of elective cosmetic surgeries is often to satisfy the person's sense of beauty or worth. But not all plastic surgeries are of this nature. For example, those who suffer the loss of a limb or severe scarring due to an accident require plastic surgery to regain (as close as possible) the function and appearance their bodies had prior to their traumatic accident.

But what about physically changing the way one looks, in a surgical and essentially permanent fashion, based on feelings or perception rather than health? Regularly visiting the dentist to ensure good tooth and gum health is different than going for sessions of teeth whitening. Similarly. wearing contact lenses to correct one's poor vision is different from getting colored contact lenses to change one's eye color. These cosmetic changes aren't automatically unethical or sinful. But you should evaluate your priorities, motivations, and goals when considering whether to change your appearance, no matter how minor or major the change.

Gene editing might be able to produce a tall, green-eyed, slender-nosed, muscular boy. Even if that were realistically possible, how ethical would it be for parents to choose how their offspring look when God alone has had that prerogative since Eden? From the beginning, God has formed and fashioned humans, and that includes governing the way each gene and chromosome shapes the unborn

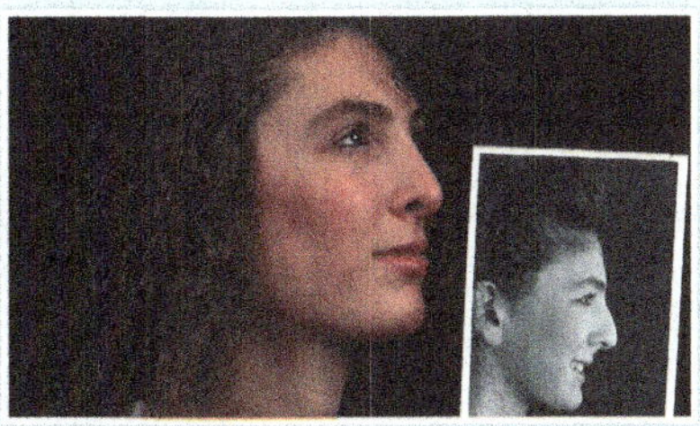

baby (Ps. 139:13–16). Shortness, brown eyes, big noses, and slender frames don't fall outside God's sovereignty and wisdom in how He creates each human being.

When one's physical appearance becomes an idol, Christians struggle to discern ethical choices from unethical ones. There is room to want to be attractive and to appreciate the inherent beauty in each image-bearer of God. But attractiveness keeps getting redefined by our culture, and it commonly becomes an end in itself. God is the ultimate standard for beauty and, therefore, what He does bears the marks of the beauty that He determines (Pss. 19:1; 27:4; 96:6). Our physical appearance isn't unimportant. But we need to stop to consider our underlying motivations and the long-term effects when considering elective cosmetic surgery.



unkind, and therefore unethical, to kill human embryos (babies in their earliest stages of development) for the sake of potentially helping others. Medical scientific research should create solutions and innovations to help all people, unborn and born alike. (See Romans 12:10 and Ephesians 4:32.)

- Humility: The scientists, philosophers, and sociologists involved in this discussion need humility before God. This is a recognition that God is sovereign over life and death and that, regardless of the value of the ends pursued, we can't make unjust and unrighteous means just or righteous. Even recipients of what the research in medical science produces must demonstrate humility by rejecting the notion that they deserve treatments at the expense of the lives of countless unborn human babies. (See Psalm 8 and Isaiah 45:18.)
- Righteousness: God's standard of righteousness is the only standard that can govern this topic. For all parties involved, the motivations, means, and ends all are subject to the scrutiny of God's standard of righteousness. It is never righteous to consider only the greatest good for the greatest number of people (utilitarianism). This notion implies much wrong done to many lives. Human life must be preserved before it is helped or improved. (See Matthew 6:33 and 1 John 3:10.)

Prudence is required to evaluate and assess the multiple dimensions of each treatment option produced at least in part by stem cell research, cloning, or gene editing.

## ETHICAL QUALITY OF LIFE

Ask this section's **essential question** to discuss how science should improve our quality of life.

**How should science improve my quality of life?** *We all want to improve our quality of life. Science, together with technology, helps us do that. But there are limits to the way that quality of life can be improved. Those limits are ethical and moral and are fixed by God and His perfect character. God designed the world to function and flourish, and science can help that to happen. To step over God's creational design, reverse it, or buck against it doesn't improve one's quality of life. To pursue science to improve one's quality of life unethically is not an improvement. Science that ethically pursues cures for diseases or treatments for ailments improves our quality of life in a right way.*

## EDITING THE HUMAN GERMLINE

Use **Activity 12.1** on pages 73–74 for students to formulate a biblical response to those who favor editing the human germline.

## KEEPING SCIENCE IN CHECK

Ask this chapter's **essential question** to discuss when science has gone off the rails.

**How do I know when science has gone off the rails?** *Not all scientific innovation is wrong or close to moral disaster. To assess whether a certain scientific endeavor has gone off the rails, one must compare the following to the ethical standards of God's Word: the ends (the purpose or goal of a certain application of science), the means (how a certain application of science is being pursued), and the motives (why a certain application of science is being pursued). Science doesn't get a pass just because humans can come up with amazing technology or medical breakthroughs. All life is subject to the standards established by the Creator.*

ends

## THE PATH OF MEDICAL SCIENCE

Medical scientists today must feel like kids in a candy shop. Compared to just a few decades ago, the possibilities for treating diseases with stem cells, cloning, and gene editing are mind-boggling. From a Christian perspective, this reality increases the need for believers (as patients, doctors, or scientists) to use discernment as they engage with these aspects of medical science. Believers can only find wisdom and discernment by submitting to God's ways and by seeking His help to make hard decisions (Prov. 9:10; James 1:5). It is wise to recognize the limitations humans have. We aren't God, and even though we can't truly usurp His role, we should beware of trying to. In contrast to those who want to live as if their actions have no consequences and they are responsible to no one (Rom. 1:18–23), believers should recognize and honor God's power and authority.

Prudence works side-by-side with discernment and wisdom to not only assess a challenging situation correctly and intelligently but also carefully choose the best righteous alternative and seek a just outcome to the ethical difficulty. Discernment about the topics of this section will lead to confidence in your acceptance or rejection of treatments that are derived from stem cells, cloning, or gene therapy. Knowledge of the ins and outs of each of these subjects is extremely important in learning to discern their morality or immorality. It is worth repeating, especially with this topic, that the ends don't justify the means.

If medical scientific research can make leaps and bounds going forward without harvesting human embryos, the outlook will be much more positive. Altering the creational order through editing the germline is where gene editing technology may be heading. The Bible is full of instances of physical suffering and all the challenges of living in a fallen world in imperfect, dying bodies. And the teaching is that believers are to trust God and care for one another as they make their pilgrim journey to God's eternal kingdom (Rom. 8:23; 2 Cor. 5:2; James 5:13–14). The elimination of disease and sickness is promised for all believers in the new heaven and earth (Rev. 21:4)—not in the here and now. This truth must stay in the forefront of our minds when considering the trajectory of gene editing and the frontiers of medical science.

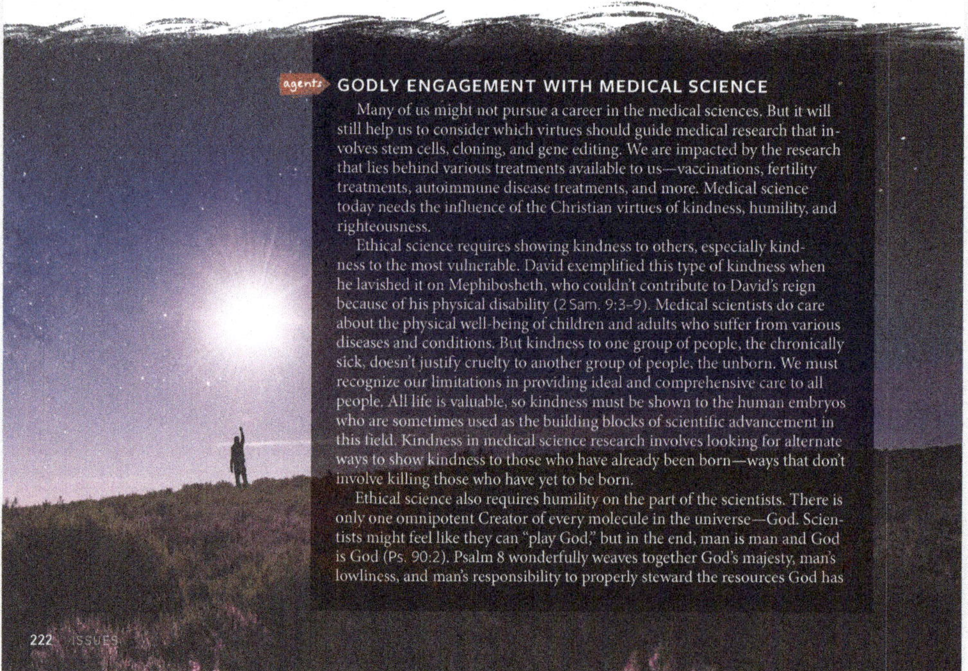

agents

## GODLY ENGAGEMENT WITH MEDICAL SCIENCE

Many of us might not pursue a career in the medical sciences. But it will still help us to consider which virtues should guide medical research that involves stem cells, cloning, and gene editing. We are impacted by the research that lies behind various treatments available to us—vaccinations, fertility treatments, autoimmune disease treatments, and more. Medical science today needs the influence of the Christian virtues of kindness, humility, and righteousness.

Ethical science requires showing kindness to others, especially kindness to the most vulnerable. David exemplified this type of kindness when he lavished it on Mephibosheth, who couldn't contribute to David's reign because of his physical disability (2 Sam. 9:3–9). Medical scientists do care about the physical well-being of children and adults who suffer from various diseases and conditions. But kindness to one group of people, the chronically sick, doesn't justify cruelty to another group of people, the unborn. We must recognize our limitations in providing ideal and comprehensive care to all people. All life is valuable, so kindness must be shown to the human embryos who are sometimes used as the building blocks of scientific advancement in this field. Kindness in medical science research involves looking for alternate ways to show kindness to those who have already been born—ways that don't involve killing those who have yet to be born.

Ethical science also requires humility on the part of the scientists. There is only one omnipotent Creator of every molecule in the universe—God. Scientists might feel like they can "play God," but in the end, man is man and God is God (Ps. 90:2). Psalm 8 wonderfully weaves together God's majesty, man's lowliness, and man's responsibility to properly steward the resources God has



## Assess

Guide a **summative assessment** by directing students to answer the questions in Thinking It Through 12.1.

### Thinking It Through 12.1

1. Embryonic stem cell research, cloning, and gene editing. These three scientific research methods raise ethical questions because they involve the creation and destruction of a human embryo, risky procedures that lead to the death of the embryo or fetus, or the birth of a baby with severe defects. Also, gene editing that edits the germline results in permanent genetic change with unknown long-term effects.

given him. Beware of the proud attitude captured in an interview with in vitro fertilization pioneer Robert Edwards:

> "I wanted to find out exactly who was in charge, whether it was God Himself or whether it was scientists in the laboratory."
>
> And what did he conclude? "It was us."[23]

Since God is the giver and taker of life, we must approach these issues with great humility.

Ethical science also requires one to pursue righteousness. Researching and producing life in a laboratory still needs to meet God's standard of righteousness. Death is unnatural to God's original creation and is the enemy of mankind. However, that doesn't give man a free license to do everything and anything possible to slow down the process of death or lengthen the human life span (Ps. 90:10; 1 Cor. 15:26). Preserving life is generally good, as is improving one's quality of life. But both must be held in check by righteousness. Prudence plays the role of assisting the scientist, patient, citizen, or lawmaker to choose the righteous decision rather than the utilitarian one.

### THE NEXT STEP FOR INNOVATIVE SCIENTIFIC RESEARCH METHODS

Everyone would like to see Alzheimer's disease, Parkinson's disease, and cancer eradicated. To see these diseases go the way of smallpox and rinderpest,* total eradication,[24] would provide relief to millions of people and their families. Medical researchers must ask whether human embryos are being sacrificed to reach this goal and whether the creational order established by God is being disturbed. Believers need to ask these two questions as they watch society take the next steps in innovative medical science.

### Thinking It Through 12.1

1. What scientific research methods raise ethical questions? Why do they?
2. What is the Bible's teaching on repairing the effects of the Fall through medical science?
3. Why do we need discernment regarding the consequences of scientific research and applications?
4. Which virtues are necessary to pursue advances in medical science ethically? Why these specific virtues?

## 12.2 Organ Donation and Transplantation

You have likely heard praise for athletes who suffer physical harm while exerting themselves to score a point or win the game. "No pain, no gain" is a popular motto. Athletes suffer bruises, scrapes, cuts, concussions, sprained joints, dislocated joints, pulled muscles, and broken bones, all for the sake of beating their opponents. But what is the ultimate sacrifice a person could give *for another person*? Their life. Images of soldiers dying in battle might come to your mind. Maybe your thoughts go to a parent saving his or her children from an attack and dying in the process. Christ's death for sinful humanity is the best example of ultimate sacrifice (Rom. 5:7–8).

**rinderpest:** a deadly disease affecting cattle in the 18th through 20th centuries[25]



2. Under God's sovereign design, humans are to steward and have dominion over all creation. We aren't called to leave sickness and disease untreated. Modern medicine is the result of God's grace upon the human race. So, responsibly and ethically, humans push back against and repair the effects of the Fall. We must remember our place as created and finite persons and that God has set up creation with a specific order.
3. It is easy to get excited about new and groundbreaking treatments for serious medical conditions. Discernment guides believers to look at the whole picture of a treatment or medical option. Christians should ask the following questions: Are embryonic or adult stem cells utilized? Is cloning of human embryos used? What effects will the treatment have on the patient? Medical science definitely isn't neutral.
4. Kindness, humility, and righteousness. Kindness to human embryos is practiced when they aren't harvested for stem cell research, cloning, or gene editing. The accusation of cruelty can't be made against those showing kindness to unborn humans just because those who suffer from serious medical conditions could benefit from actual cruelty shown to unborn human beings. Killing days- or weeks-old human embryos is purposeful. Not treating a sick patient with a risky treatment does not seek their death. Humility is needed for scientists and doctors so they don't try to "play God." There must be an acknowledgment of human limitations and our place in God's creational order. And righteousness is needed because unless God's standard for righteousness is pursued and met, those sinning against God incur His judgment. What is humanly convenient and expedient must be analyzed and held to God's righteous standards.

## 12.2 Organ Donation and Transplantation

*How should Christians view organ donation?*

### Objectives

**12.2.1** Identify scenarios where organs are donated or transplanted.

**12.2.2** Summarize the biblical teaching regarding the nature of personhood and the care of the body. BWS

**12.2.3** Evaluate the societal consequences of exploitative organ harvesting.

**12.2.4** Assess the virtues necessary to discern when organ donation is appropriate. BWS

**12.2.5** Formulate a biblical response to the practice of paying people for organ donation. BWS

### Biblical Worldview Shaping

- **Creational Order** (explain): Because humans are created in God's image, they are to be treated with respect even after death. Because humans are created in God's image, we should seek to save human lives. (12.2.2)
- **Virtue** (formulate): Compassion motivates organ donation, prudence guides when it is best pursued, and righteousness guides how it is done. (12.2.4)
- **Wisdom** (apply): Citizens need wisdom for determining what should and shouldn't be treated as commodities to avoid bringing moral harm. (12.2.5)

### Printed Resource

- Activity 12.2: Paying for Organ Donations?

### Suggested Reading

- "Living Donation." Unos: Transplant Living (website).
- Meilaender, Gilbert. *Bioethics: A Primer for Christians*. 4th ed. Grand Rapids, MI: Eerdmans, 2020. Pages 105–24.
- "Organ Transplant." Unos.org.

## Engage

### THE MORAL GOODNESS OF ORGAN DONATION AND TRANSPLANTATION

Use a **Quick Write** to record student reactions to the following statement.

"If you accept blood transfusions as ethical, then you should accept, on the same grounds, organ donations and transplantations."

Follow up with a **discussion** for students to defend the position they take regarding this statement.

## Instruct

### THE NEED FOR ORGAN DONATION

Use a **misconception check** for students to determine why there is a valid need for organ donation. Students may work individually or in groups to explain why they agree or disagree with the statement below.

"Organ transplantation is simply medical professionals trying to play God when it would be best for society to acknowledge the limits of medical scientific innovation."

Answers dispelling this misconception would include the recognition that organ transplantation is similar to blood transfusions or other ethical medical interventions. The logic of the statement in question would rule out most, if not all, medical interventions. God has called humanity to subdue and have dominion over all the earth (Gen. 1:28), and in order to do that in a fallen world, ethical medical interventions are often required for diseased or injured individuals.

### THE BIBLE ON ORGAN DONATION AND TRANSPLANTATION

Use a **Think-Write-Pair-Share** for students to explain what the Bible teaches on organ donation and transplantation.

**Into what two categories does the textbook divide the biblical support of organ donation and transplantation?** *the personhood of man and the care of the body*

**Using scriptural support, how does the personhood of man relate to organ donation and transplantation?** *Man is created in the image of God and has material and immaterial parts (Gen. 1:26–27; 2:7, 21–22). Man's personhood isn't disrespected in organ donation and transplantation because man's body isn't man's ultimate earthly form. Every person's body will be resurrected and reunited with his or her soul to either live or perish forever (John 5:28–29). Also, one's personhood isn't wrapped up in one's body alone. Ethical organ donation respects the personhood of the one receiving the donated organ or tissue while not disrespecting the donor.*

**Using scriptural support, how does the care of the body relate to organ donation and transplantation?** *To care for one's body does not mean to avoid any and all potential and actual discomfort. Jesus even used hyperbole related to harming oneself physically in order to save oneself spiritually and eternally (Matt. 5:29–30). Paul embraced physical harm to his body for the sake of the gospel and commends believers for doing the same (1 Cor. 4:11–16; 2 Cor. 6:4–5). The point is that one's body isn't to be preserved at all costs when greater matters arise. Ethical organ donation and transplantation cares for the body and well-being (many times as a matter of life or death) of another human made in the image of God (Matt. 22:39).*

---

Are there other contexts in which people would sacrifice their bodies for the good of others? Choosing to die for someone when there are non-lethal options available would be ethically wrong and is a form of suicide. Organ donation for transplantation is a great example of someone sacrificing his or her body, while alive or upon death, for the good of others. **Organ donation** is when a person willingly makes available certain organs or tissues to replace someone's defective or damaged organs or tissues. **Organ transplantation** is the replacement of a defective or damaged organ or tissue in one person with a healthy organ or tissue taken from another person. How should Christians view organ donation and transplantation?

#### THE REALITY OF ORGAN DONATION AND TRANSPLANTATION

How should Christians view organ donation?

Organ transplantation is a relatively new medical wonder. In 1954 the first organ transplantation occurred—a kidney from a living donor.[26] Kidneys and lungs are paired organs, and as such living patients can donate one of their kidneys or all or part of one of their lungs. Other organs, parts of organs, and tissues such as the liver, pancreas, intestines, skin, bone, bone marrow, and blood can also be donated by living patients.[27] But for most organ transplants (e.g., heart transplants), a donation from a deceased donor is required. In a world of such advanced medical research and technology, why are organ transplantations even necessary?

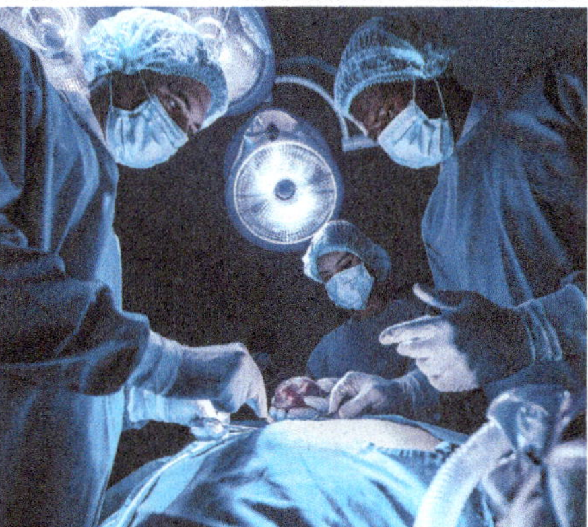

Doctors performing a heart transplant procedure

Organ transplantations are necessary for people who have organs that have ceased to operate normally. Organ failure can be brought on by a hereditary condition. Sometimes lifestyle issues (e.g., habitual smoking, excessive drinking, poor diet) hasten the deterioration of certain organs. Injuries, diseases, or birth defects can also cause organ failure.[28]

This fallen world is an environment where brokenness and pain flourish like wildfire in a dry field (Gen. 3:16–18). Medical science pushes back against the unrelenting destructive effects of the Fall. Organ donation is a tool used by thoughtful and loving people to attempt to give someone the gifts of health and life. Organ donation is truly a matter of life or death. Over 106,000 people were on the national transplant waiting list in early 2022. At that time, every nine minutes a new individual was added to that waiting list. But sadly, around seventeen people waiting for a transplant die each day.[29]

#### THE BIBLICAL TEACHING ON ORGAN DONATION AND TRANSPLANTATION

What are the ethical red flags raised when discussing organ donation and transplantation? Does the teaching of the Bible oppose or support organ donation and transplantation?

##### *The Personhood of Man*

Some might equate the issues surrounding organ donation to the issues surrounding cremation.* The belief is that the body is disrespected if it is disturbed (reduced to ash or has organs removed) after death. The belief is that the personhood of man is affronted and the image of God in man is defaced if cremation or organ donation takes place. The Bible shines some light on the practices of burial and cremation—believers in both testaments exclusively practiced burial. But Scripture doesn't directly address the topic of organ donation and transplantation.

**cremation:** reducing a corpse to ashes by fire

Surely, God has made man in His image (Gen. 1:26-27). And man is body and soul. His personhood isn't wrapped up in either just the body or just the soul. It is the unity of these two parts of man, one material and one spiritual, that makes man the person he is. The body isn't a prison house for the soul, nor is the body an object of worship. People who undergo serious, life-altering surgeries (including amputations and the removal of injured or diseased organs) don't become any less of a person, nor is their personhood disrespected. Organ donation and transplantation are like other lifesaving surgeries. There must be a realistic understanding of what respect looks like when dealing with the body that the soul of a person has left behind at death. This realistic understanding must be rooted in the Bible. And a biblical understanding of man's personhood is critical in evaluating organ donation from a biblical worldview.

The biblical doctrine of bodily resurrection also impacts our understanding of the personhood of man. At Christ's return, all people will be resurrected either to life or to death (John 5:28-29; Rev. 20:6, 12-15). The bodies of all people, regardless of where or how they died, will be restored and reunited with their souls to spend eternity in the new creation or in the lake of fire (Rev. 21:1-3, 8). The effects of organ donation and transplantation are no obstacle to the power of God to reconstitute the bodies of all human beings. The same omnipotent God who created each atom in the universe out of nothing will reunite each person's soul with his or her resurrected body.

### *The Care of the Body*

The overall tenor of Scripture regarding how we should use our bodies is responsible, faithful work, not sloth or entertainment (Eccles. 9:10; Matt. 24:45-46; 2 Thess. 3:10). Caring for or respecting our bodies doesn't mean isolation from anything that might endanger them. Believers are called to endure the hardships and physical sufferings that accompany a life in service of Christ (Luke 9:23; Rom. 12:1).

Is there a verse that teaches us to care for the bodies of others? What about Matthew 22:39, "Thou shalt love thy neighbour as thyself"? This verse doesn't teach believers to actively love and care for and pamper themselves. It teaches believers to go to the same extremes to which we love ourselves in loving others. We are already highly interested in our own well-being, including the well-being of our bodies. While we shouldn't be self-consumed, we should care for the well-being of others (including the well-being of their bodies) to the same extent we care for our own. Ethical organ donation is a selfless act of love for someone with a dire physical need.

Caring for our own bodies or for the bodies of others requires prioritizing the well-being and life of each person made in God's image. The following points express the biblical priority of life as well as the dignity of everyone in life or death:

- It is wrong for someone to donate an organ if he or she knows that the donation would lead to his or her own death.
- It is wrong to take an organ from a terminally ill but living person if taking that organ would result in that person's death.
- It might be unwise for a living donor with health risks to donate an organ, because that donation could result in serious harm to the donor. But as a rule, organ donations from living donors aren't wrong.
- It is wrong to disrespect the body of the deceased when legally procuring the donor's organs.

An ethical approach to organ donation and transplantation provides people with the opportunity to show loving care for the body of the organ donor and for the body of the organ recipient.

#### Jehovah's Witnesses and Blood Transfusions

Jehovah's Witnesses, an unorthodox religion with a global following, believe that any introduction of blood into their bodies violates Scripture. They abstain from blood, including blood transfusions, based on their interpretation and application of texts like Genesis 9:4, Leviticus 17:14, and Acts 15:20. They say, "God commands that we abstain from blood because what it represents is sacred to him."[30] Though the organization did oppose organ transplants in the 1960s–70s,[31] Jehovah's Witnesses aren't entirely opposed to organ transplants now, provided all the blood is drained from the organ. But in their attempt to respect the sanctity of life, they elevate blood to a position that is not based in faithful exegesis of Scripture. And in doing so, they deprive themselves or others of life when a necessary blood transfusion is rejected.[32] Bible-believing Christians can submit to God's teaching in the three passages mentioned by abstaining from eating or drinking blood. Blood transfusions and organ transplantations are distinct practices from making a meal out of animal blood.



ETHICAL SCIENCE 225

## EXPLOITING ORGAN DONATION AND TRANSPLANTATION

Guide a **discussion** regarding the ethical merits of the three positions.

- Organ donation is critical to tens of thousands of people (including infants who need vital organs, such as a heart, liver, or kidney, donated from infants), so harvesting organs and tissues from live but dying infants or adults is necessary to save the lives of those who *can* live with a donated organ from a live donor who will die anyway.
- Organ donation is critical to tens of thousands of people, so harvesting viable organs and tissues from anyone who dies from natural causes (including fatal traffic accidents), *regardless of consent*, is ethical.
- *Prior consent must always be given* by the donor or by the immediate family (including those non-family members who hold power-of-attorney rights) for organ donation to be ethical.

The first approach is ethically reprehensible because it involves killing a person, be it a newborn baby or dying elderly person, for the sole purpose of harvesting organs. When living people are viewed as the prime sources for harvesting organs for transplantation, regardless of their quality of life or impending death, an ethical line has been crossed. It is always unethical to medically accelerate the death of any patient, including using the patient's organs to attempt to save the life of another patient with better chances of living.

The second position plays on the emotions because it is a sad reality that people who could survive their condition if they received a donated organ die for lack of donated organs. But this is a utilitarian approach because it disrespects someone's dignity by using unethical means for a good end.

The third approach is the ethical and biblical approach. True love for others is demonstrated in the golden rule (Matt. 7:12) and in treating fellow image-bearers as such (Gen. 1:26–27) and not merely as potential organ donors whom no one cares about. Or even worse, they are pushed to an early death in order to utilize their organs and tissues for donation.

### ends THE ETHICAL LIMITS OF ORGAN DONATION

What happens when you push a good thing too far? The saying "Too much of a good thing is a bad thing" is usually true. An occasional bowl of ice cream before bed (or any time of day for that matter) is a good thing. But multiple bowls of ice cream every day would be bad for anyone's health. Working a job you enjoy to make an income you need is a good thing. But to put in forty-plus hours per week on top of finishing high school would be a bad thing. You would begin to give up other obligations and activities that are good and necessary (personal, educational, familial, religious, social).

Organ donation and transplantation are good, in that people who would otherwise die or live in chronically poor health can benefit from the organs donated to them. But if these life-saving medical practices are pushed too far, then ethical lines are crossed. This can result from a consequentialist approach in which the end seems so beneficial that the way one accomplishes that goal is nearly irrelevant. How could this go wrong with organ transplantation? Consider the following scenarios:

- Organs are taken from individuals who said no to organ donation.
- Organs are taken from individuals who were silent on the question of organ donation, but consent isn't sought from family members.
- Organs and tissues are harvested from aborted unborn babies.
- Organs and tissues are harvested from laboratory-created human embryos or fetuses.
- Organs and tissues are harvested from cloned human embryos or fetuses.
- Organs are taken from those who have chosen physician-assisted suicide to end their suffering.
- Organs are taken from elderly or disabled people who are euthanized.

Organ donation veers into questionable territory when consent isn't given or can't be given by the individual whose organs or tissues are taken. Organ donation is abused when an unethical practice is encouraged directly or indirectly for the sake of obtaining useful organs and tissues. Taking organs should be off the table if a person would be brought into existence for the purpose of harvesting their stem cells, tissues, or organs. Abortion, suicide, and euthanasia are all murder and are entirely unethical, regardless of any possible benefit of taking and transplanting healthy organs.

*When death becomes simply an obstacle on the way to organ procurement, we permit our desire to mitigate the organ shortage to undermine our attempts to keep company with the dying.* GILBERT MEILAENDER[33]

The scarcity of viable organs from deceased individuals adds pressure to the temptation to push the ethical limits of organ donation. Only three people out of one thousand die in a way where their organs are salvageable for organ donation.[34] Typically, those who suffer an accident involving serious head trauma die in a way that their heart and lungs can be artificially supported, even though they are dead, to preserve the organs until they arrive at a hospital where they are removed.[35]

Having no ethical limits or boundaries for those who desire more widespread organ donation and transplantation would quickly turn into a futuristic science-fiction horror film. Similar to the serious ethical violations involved in embryonic stem cell research, cloning, and germline gene editing, harvesting organs from the most vulnerable in society is extremely problematic. Believers are called to demonstrate virtuous character while following a careful decision-making process regarding organ donation and transplantation.

### Animal Organ Transplantation?

How ethical is using organs or tissues from animals to supplement the limited availability of human organs for transplantation? Medical scientists and doctors collaborated and successfully transplanted a heart from a genetically-modified pig into a man with terminal heart disease in early 2022. He died two months later,[36] but the science behind animal organ transplantation is continuing to develop.

It is one thing to use animal tissues or organs to replace defective or damaged human tissues or organs. Since as far back as 1838, pig skin has been used to graft on humans who had serious burns.[37] However, it is an entirely different thing, having serious ethical ramifications, to alter a human or animal embryo in such a way that a hybrid is created. To produce an embryo that has animal and human genes, DNA, organs, and features is to cross the line of human and animal differentiation. God established this division when He created all things (Gen. 1:20–30). Although both man and beast are described as having "the breath of life" (Gen. 2:7; 7:15), only man is created in the image of God (Gen. 1:26–27). Blurring or erasing this distinction is a direct affront to God's wise and purposeful creational order.

## AN ETHICAL APPROACH TO ORGAN DONATION

Christians need to have reasons for their convictions for or against organ donation. They need to ground their beliefs in Scripture and, when confronted with challenging ethical situations, be ready to make the right decisions. You might think one way about organ donation when looking at it from afar, considering it theoretically. But you might change your mind when you or someone close to you requires an organ transplant to continue living. Virtues serve as guardrails to keep believers on the right ethical and moral path when navigating this challenging topic.

Compassion, prudence, and righteousness are necessary for discerning when organ donation is appropriate. A common scenario is when a live donor is required to provide one of his or her kidneys to someone experiencing kidney failure. Compassion plays the role of seeing a legitimate need; a donor who is a perfect match could offer his or her kidney, out of loving compassion, to meet that need. But prudence also plays a role in determining whether the donor can assume the risks of the surgery and of living the rest of life with only one kidney. Life situations, health issues, and other factors all demand prudence to help determine whether this is a good choice for the donor. And righteousness is also necessary in this situation because the motive, means, and ends all have to be righteous by God's standards for Christians to participate in organ donation. It would be ungodly for a person to knowingly put his or her life at great risk by donating a kidney. Changing which person is seriously ill is not the purpose of organ donation, nor does it really solve the problem. Offering payment for an organ to a living donor clouds judgment and opens the door for abuse and pressure. This would be a total lack of prudence as well as being unrighteous.

What if a person who expressed a desire to donate his or her body or organs passes away without any written record of personal wishes, but the closest family members don't want to go through with it? Prudence is required to discern whether the deceased person's wishes were well-informed and definitely expressed. But if the person's wish to donate is confirmed, wouldn't it be righteous for the family to respect the wishes of the deceased and allow the organ donation to take place? Compassion for their loved one and for all who would benefit from the donation should also make the right decision clear. Prudence may also be required by medical professionals to navigate the wishes of the deceased and the wishes of the family. Righteousness plays the role of making sure that the motives, means, and outcomes in such scenarios conform to God's righteous standards.

On the other hand, prudence is also involved in making sure a loved one who wishes to donate isn't pressured or neglected in receiving care before he or she dies. It would be unrighteous for the doctors to prematurely and purposefully reduce the number of the loved one's final days or adjust his or her care simply to hasten an organ donation.



## VIRTUOUS ORGAN DONATION

Guide a **Think-Pair-Share** to assess the virtues necessary to discern when organ donation is appropriate. Form three groups and assign to each group one of the virtues covered in this section—compassion, prudence, and righteousness.

Organ donation is not a requirement for believers to show compassion or righteousness. Prudence helps determine whether organ donation is righteous or not. And compassion can be shown in any number of ways.

**How do compassion, prudence, and righteousness affect a living donor, a deceased donor, and family members of a deceased donor?**

- *Compassion: A living donor can choose to show compassion and reap the benefits of seeing someone live, or live with a vastly improved quality of life, because of the fruits of one's compassion; a deceased donor also showed compassion by being hopeful that upon death his or her organs can benefit others; family members of a deceased donor can show compassion if called upon to make a decision about a deceased family member who didn't specify if he or she wanted to be an organ donor if a good match is found for one of his or her organs.*
- *Prudence: A living donor must exercise much prudence in determining how well one would fare (physically and in other ways) given the health risks from donating an organ, part of an organ, or certain tissues; prudence is required for those desiring to donate upon death because some family members might object to one's desire; family members of a deceased donor should exemplify prudence by carefully considering everything involved in organ donation upon death, because many times much time passes between a family member's wish to donate upon death and when that death actually occurs.*
- *Righteousness: For all three categories of people, righteousness guides the motives, means, and goals so that, at every step of the way, the right decision is made; there should be no pressuring, lying, or carelessly entering into organ donation, because doing so is unrighteous.*

## Apply

### PAYING FOR ORGAN DONATIONS?

Use **Activity 12.2** on pages 75–76 for students to formulate a biblical response to the practice of paying people for organ donations.

### A CHRISTIAN APPROACH TO ORGAN DONATION

Ask this section's **essential question**.

**How should Christians view organ donation?** *First, the Bible doesn't command Christians to donate organs, nor does it prohibit organ donation. Second, organ donation fits within the Christian worldview; it doesn't pollute the Christian faith, nor does it detract from a Christian's testimony. Third, organ donation is essentially giving the gift of a life to either a family member, loved one, or total stranger who needs what someone has to survive. Organ donation is a clear way to practice compassion, though it is to be done with prudence and righteousness.*

## Assess

Guide a **summative assessment** by directing students to answer the questions in Thinking It Through 12.2.

### Thinking It Through 12.2

1. Organ failure is the underlying reason for the need for organ donation and transplantation. Birth defects, accidents, and disease are all reasons behind organ failure.
2. Humans are people made in God's image. One's person isn't limited to just the body or just the soul. One's person is found in his or her whole being, which includes both the material and immaterial parts. Donating an organ or accepting a donated organ does not deface the image of God in a person. Caring for the body involves surgery and invasive and extreme procedures at times. Donating an organ is extreme but very loving, and accepting a donated organ is caring for one's own body if that is the only available treatment that will potentially work.
3. There are massive consequences in society when organs are exploitatively harvested. When individuals or family members are pressured either by intimidation or through remuneration, ethical lines are crossed. When consent isn't given, then abuse is bound to happen and worsen. The sanctity of life is in danger of being violated for human embryos created in a lab through natural fertilization or cloning, for the comatose, the elderly, the chronically ill, and anyone who is remotely suicidal. Abortion, euthanasia, and physician-assisted suicide would be more rampant than they already are. And the genetic modification of human and animal embryos by combining them with each other in some way is an affront to God's design and purpose for humans and animals.
4. Compassion is needed to do what is ethically necessary to care for people with dire physical needs. Prudence is needed to make the decision to be an organ donor and to determine who should handle the organ donation discussions after a loved one passes away. Righteousness is needed to guide every step of the process so that the motives, means, and ends are morally ethical.

context **CONCLUSION**

Take care not to force organ donation and transplantation. Done ethically, organ donation and transplantation are great benefits of modern medical science. Even an ethical use of animal-derived organs or tissues holds some promise to contribute to preserving human life. The need for donated organs is overwhelming, but that doesn't eliminate the ethical approach required for this endeavor. Remember the virtues of compassion, prudence, and righteousness as you engage with this challenging topic.

#### Thinking It Through 12.2

1. List various scenarios that require the donation and transplantation of organs.
2. What is the biblical teaching regarding the nature of personhood and the care of the body?
3. List various societal consequences of exploitative organ harvesting.
4. In what ways are compassion, prudence, and righteousness necessary to discern when organ donation is appropriate?

### 12.3 Conservation, Environmentalism, and Animal Rights

Why do homeowners post No Trespassing and Private Property signs at the edges of their property? Is it simply because they like their privacy? Most do, but the main reason homeowners post these kinds of signs is because they don't want trespassers stealing, vandalizing, or messing with their stuff. Most people enjoy a clean, organized, and attractive home and yard. However, unless measures are taken to protect and maintain the place we live, chaos and ruin tend to follow.

Christians point to Adam and Eve's fall into sin as the reason for everything bad and wrong in the world (Gen. 3:6, 16–19; Rom. 5:12; 8:20–22). Unbelievers point to the second law of thermodynamics that states entropy is inevitable, that energy is being spent and therefore the material world is running down, not getting better. But beyond natural decay, many believe that, if the earth is the Titanic, then mankind has already rammed into the iceberg and the ship is sinking. Describing a 2019 United Nations General Assembly meeting, an article from the UN's website carried this title: "Only 11 Years Left to Prevent Irreversible Damage from Climate Change, Speakers Warn during General Assembly High-Level Meeting."[38] According to this position, by 2030 we will have compromised the earth in such a way that catastrophe and global harm will be the unavoidable reality.

Society has come up with three main approaches to deal with the current and future state of our planet. Conservation, environmentalism, and animal rights are offered as solutions to the damage man has inflicted, and is inflicting, upon the earth and its non-human inhabitants. **Conservation** is the effort to preserve or improve certain resources so that they remain available for use in the future. This applies to natural resources such as water, trees, plants, and animals; to air quality; and to the climate overall. **Environmentalism** seeks to protect the environment from human destruction and improve the conditions of the environment through social and political action. **Animal rights** is the idea that animals are entitled to the same rights and privileges that humans are entitled to—no exploitation and no abuse—and generally includes the notion that any killing or prolonged caging of animals to benefit humans is unethical.

228 ISSUES

## 12.3 Conservation, Environmentalism, and Animal Rights

*How involved should I be in caring for God's creation?*

### Objectives

**12.3.1** Identify various ethical issues regarding the environment and animals.

**12.3.2** Summarize the biblical teaching regarding the Christian's relationship to the natural world. BWS

**12.3.3** Evaluate the consequences of unbiblical views of creation stewardship. BWS

**12.3.4** Assess the virtues necessary to motivate appropriate care for the earth and animals. BWS

**12.3.5** Formulate biblical responses to those who abuse the creation and to those who idolize the creation.

### Biblical Worldview Shaping

- **Creational Order** (explain): Wise rule over God's earth means treating creation well both because God made it and all the creatures in it and because God intended it to be beautiful and useful for every human generation. (12.3.2)
- **Man's Chief End** (evaluate): Ruling over God's world to bring Him glory is the first commission God gave to mankind. (12.3.3)
- **Virtue** (formulate): The virtues of prudence and humility lead people to think about the consequences of their impact upon creation. The virtue of gratitude inspires people to conserve parts of creation with great beauty and value for others. (12.3.4)

context

### ETHICAL ISSUES IN CREATION

Is the human race on the verge of extinction? We're not talking about extinction from an asteroid or nuclear holocaust but from humans overpopulating the earth, polluting it, and depleting its resources beyond repair. Organizations like the World Economic Forum take the data they have and make projections and predictions about the next ten, twenty, or one hundred years. Their presentation is apocalyptic when describing the floods, fires, droughts, and destruction they say await the earth if major changes are not made.[39] Ken Magnuson summarizes the worries by saying the following:

> Many concerns are raised about the environment and its future. The most prominent concern, and one that relates to many of the others, is global warming or climate change. . . . Related concerns include rise in sea level, overpopulation and the earth's "carrying capacity," biodiversity loss and species extinction, deforestation, air and water pollution, human consumption and waste, and sustainable farming, to name a few.[40]

So, should Christians join the ranks of those predicting the earth's impending demise? Is humankind really set on a path to ruin our planet unless drastic measures are taken?

One organization called The Partnership Project partners with several environmental groups "addressing the climate crisis, accelerating the transition to clean energy, reducing the use of fossil fuels, and amplifying the work of environmental justice."[41] In this organization's own words: "We are the Partnership Project, your partner to save the planet."[42] Notice how they end their list with climate.

Why has The Partnership Project gotten behind the specific issues it has outlined? The environmental and climate research done by scientists includes gathering data from the atmosphere, water, and ice caps and comparing that information to data from previous decades. It is true that no one benefits from nor enjoys a damaged climate or polluted environment. But one's understanding of the source and purpose of creation also directs one's use and stewardship of that creation. Those who don't have Christ only have this world. Many of the ethical issues on conservationism's and environmentalism's agendas are hot-button issues for unbelievers for this very reason. At the same time, Christians can put forth helpful questions and endeavor to answer them:

- Is the earth warming?
- Are humans contributing to the warming of the earth?
- Are the consequences of a warming earth good, bad, or mixed?
- What are the proposed solutions?
- What is the impact of those solutions?

Christians can't ignore accurate data and statistics gathered from the environment. Even so, believers must carefully distinguish a secular and worldly interpretation of the data from a biblically informed interpretation, one that incorporates God's design for the earth and man's responsibility to use and protect the earth and its resources. The significant environmental issues brought about by man's irresponsibility must be dealt with biblically and ethically. A proper biblical worldview is necessary for this endeavor.

Another ethical issue in creation is that of animal rights. According to PETA (People for the Ethical Treatment of Animals), one of the most outspoken and proactive defenders of animal rights, people are animals, and all animals are beings and should thus be afforded the same treatment as human beings.[43] Make sure you notice that their use of the term "ethical" by no means implies a biblical ethic. The founder of PETA, Ingrid Newkirk, made this statement that clearly explains this organization's view on human and animal life: "When it comes to pain, love, joy, loneliness, and fear, a rat is a pig is a dog is a boy. Each one values his or her life and fights the knife."[44]

Is a vegan lifestyle the only option for people who care about animals? Has humanity been abusing and exploiting animals, either out of ignorance or purposefully, for millennia? The question of animal rights affects farming, food production, medical research, scientific research, pharmaceutical research, clothing, accessories, entertainment, pets, and even how one treats unwelcome animals in one's home. The issues raised touch on how we live every day of our lives! There must be a biblical response to how we can properly and ethically treat animals and care for creation.

> *The earth is the habitat not only for human beings but for other creatures as well, and human beings have the responsibility to manage it well for our own sake, for our descendants, and for other creatures.*
>
> KEN MAGNUSON[45]



## Printed Resource

- Activity 12.3: Mishandling Creation

## Digital Resource

- Link: Creation Care

## Suggested Reading

- Frame, John. *The Doctrine of the Christian Life*. Phillipsburg, NJ: P&R Publishing, 2008. Pages 269–70, 743–45.
- Grudem, Wayne. *Christian Ethics: An Introduction to Biblical Moral Reasoning*. Wheaton, IL: Crossway, 2018. Pages 1095–169.
- Magnuson, Ken. *Invitation to Christian Ethics: Moral Reasoning and Contemporary Issues*. Grand Rapids, MI: Kregel Academic, 2020. Pages 501–32.

## Engage

### ENVIRONMENT AND ANIMAL ETHICAL ISSUES

Use a **bell ringer** activity to promote a brief discussion, in pairs or small groups, about popular topics regarding conservation, environmentalism, and animal rights.

**What is your initial response or reaction to the following popular topics? Add two or more to the list.**

- **global warming**
- **fossil fuel emissions**
- **overpopulation**
- **veganism**

*Answers might include climate change, rising sea levels, pollution, clean energy, deforestation, sustainable farming, and so forth.*

**Why do you think these topics are important to many people today?** *Generally, people care about the world they live in and the condition of the earth that their children and grandchildren will inherit. There are multiple factors at play affecting what people know about the environment and why they feel strongly about these issues or not, including exposure to the media coverage of these topics, national and global politics, and what people experience firsthand regarding the health or lack thereof of the environments around them.*

There is a level of disagreement about the issues outlined above, even among Christians. Much of this disagreement comes down to different interpretations of the data or the proposed solutions. For example, depending on one's interpretation of the rate that the earth is warming or the long-term effect of fossil fuel emissions, one will approve of one proposed solution over another.

This section will provide biblical answers and a biblical worldview to these and related topics.

## Instruct

### BIBLICAL INSIGHT ON CARING FOR THE NATURAL WORLD

Use a **Quick Write** for students to develop the biblical teaching from key passages on caring for the natural world.

**Read Genesis 1. How would you summarize the condition of creation and humanity's relationship to it?** *God made all things good, every inanimate object and every plant and animal (vv. 4, 10, 12, 18, 21, 25). God called His creation of man and woman "very good" (v. 31). God tasked Adam and Eve with subduing and having dominion over the earth and what filled it (vv. 26–29). Their use of creation was inherently coupled with their care of it.*

**Read Genesis 2:15–16 and Psalm 8:6–8. With the Fall happening in Genesis 3, what is significant about both passages?** *Humans are responsible to utilize creation for their well-being and flourishing, even after the Fall and its negative effects on creation and on humanity.*

**Read Genesis 9:1–3. What is the direct teaching of this passage, and how does it affect our care for creation, specifically animals?** *This passage includes similar commands that Adam and Eve received in the Garden of Eden. But God commanded Noah and his descendants to eat animals and fish, no longer just plants.*

**Read Colossians 1:16 and 1 Corinthians 10:31. Given humanity's responsibility to use creation for its needs, what do these passages contribute to this understanding?** *Humans must steward, or use well, the creation for their needs. God is glorified when He is recognized as the Giver of all, and He is disrespected when His creation is abused or used for other purposes than that which He gave it.*

### CONSEQUENCES OF UNBIBLICAL VIEWS OF CREATION STEWARDSHIP

Guide a **Think-Pair-Share** to evaluate various consequences of unbiblical views of creation stewardship.

Extreme limitations to and extreme abuses of the use of creation are unbiblical views of creation stewardship.

**What are the consequences of prohibiting any extraction or use of fossil fuels, and why is this an unbiblical view of creation stewardship?** *While the excessive use and improper disposal of fossil fuels and their byproducts can be harmful to the environment, to completely restrict the use of fossil fuels poses a threat to humanity's freedom and livelihood. The alternative resource must be proven to be superior, and therefore more ethical, to the widespread use of fossil fuels. Other limitations and restrictions could be implemented without banning fossil fuels outright, seeking a more responsible use of them. The restrictive measures implemented shouldn't be more harmful than the lack of restrictions though. Any biblical approach requires prudence that the measures being taken are ethical on all fronts, beginning with assessing the studies of the effects of using fossil fuels and the long-term effects and advantages of using a cleaner alternative. The Bible calls for a responsible use of whatever resource is being used (Gen. 1:28; Deut. 8:7–10).*

**What are the consequences of restricting the use of animals for food and other products for human consumption, and why is this an unbiblical view of creation stewardship?** *To prohibit the use of animals for food goes directly against God's permission and command to Noah, which is still ongoing, to use animals for food. Animals are an important food source for people. Only people are made in the image of God, and so it is they who need to take advantage of the abundant food source God has provided them (Acts 10:10–16).*

**What are the consequences of using creation without any thought of the impact on the environment or future generations, and why is this an unbiblical view of creation stewardship?** *This foolish approach would cause the ruin and destruction of current resources while making it nearly impos-*

#### BIBLICAL CARE FOR CREATION

Do you step on ants that cross your path? Do you swat flies in your kitchen in the summer? Do you kill or trap pests on your property? If so, that would imply a certain dominance or advantage that humans have over animals. Animals do attack and sometimes kill people. Many insects, reptiles, and fish bite or sting in self-defense or as a reflex, and many of these animals are venomous or are otherwise capable of lethal attacks. The Bible explains why humanity's relationship to animals went from peaceful coexistence to fearful dread—sin (Gen. 2:19–20; 9:2). Even man's relationship to plants and the natural world in general changed as a result of the Fall and the Curse (Gen. 2:8, 15; 3:17–19).

We need biblical guidance to know how to relate to creation in general and to animals in particular. We can't just do what has always been done if there isn't a biblical basis for those habits. Psalm 104 describes God's greatness and how that is shown in His governing all of creation. God is praised for His unfathomable wisdom in creating everything (104:24). This psalm serves as a guide for how man, made in God's image, should care and provide for and govern over creation. And man needs wisdom—wisdom God provides—to care for creation well.

In the United States, states have specific hunting seasons and game laws to control animal populations. How might this be good dominion over animals?

*Responsible Stewardship of Resources*

God created everything for His own glory (John 1:3; Col. 1:16). But God delegated to man the responsibility of stewarding all the resources that He made (Gen. 1:26–31). This was a very good creation, all of it, and man had the privilege to work and tend the garden where God placed him (Gen. 2:15). Dutch theologian Abraham Kuyper reinforces this by noting some biblical reasoning which explains why we should apply good stewardship of creation to animals specifically:

> Only because God gives the animals to us and further grants us permission to slaughter and eat them do we human beings have the right to use animals in this way. . . . The commonly accepted view that people may do with an animal just as they please "because it is only an animal" must for that reason be resisted by all Christians, because the animals are not ours but God's. We do not have the least right to them, because we did not create them. . . . Without God's permission we have no right to haul even one fish out of the water and kill it, to shoot down and pluck a single bird, or hunt and slay any game.[16]

No part of creation was off-limits from man's subduing and having dominion over it (Ps. 8:4–8). Only man was made in God's image, which made him the only being capable of having a relationship with God and governing creation.

Man was designed to use the earth and its natural resources to flourish, resulting in praise to God for His gift of creation (Deut. 8:7–10). Nevertheless, God instructed the people of Israel to be responsible and wise when besieging an enemy city. He told them not to cut down the fruit trees (Deut. 20:19–20). It wasn't a ban on cutting down any tree, because some could be used for their wood, but they were not to cut down the trees that would continue to produce fruit after the battle was over.

John 6:12 contains an interesting short phrase that impacts our current discussion: "that nothing be lost." Jesus had just fed more than five thousand people with five loaves of bread and two fish. But Jesus didn't want to see the extra twelve baskets full of leftovers go to waste—even though He was able to miraculously produce more food. We can't know for sure what the disciples did with the extra food. It was likely given to the poor or maybe even consumed by them as they continued their journey. The point is, God expects us to be good stewards of the resources (e.g., food, water, energy, clothes) He has provided for us, so we should not be wasteful.

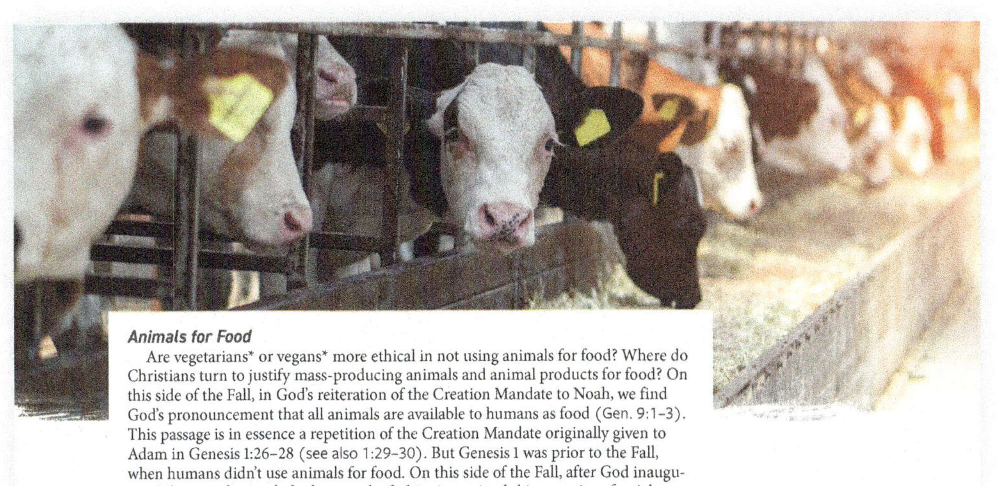

### Animals for Food

Are vegetarians* or vegans* more ethical in not using animals for food? Where do Christians turn to justify mass-producing animals and animal products for food? On this side of the Fall, in God's reiteration of the Creation Mandate to Noah, we find God's pronouncement that all animals are available to humans as food (Gen. 9:1–3). This passage is in essence a repetition of the Creation Mandate originally given to Adam in Genesis 1:26–28 (see also 1:29–30). But Genesis 1 was prior to the Fall, when humans didn't use animals for food. On this side of the Fall, after God inaugurated the use of animals for humans by fashioning animal skin coverings for Adam and Eve (Gen. 3:21), animals serve the purpose of feeding humans and providing for their needs. Mankind is free to enjoy scrambled eggs, milkshakes, and hamburgers.

The New Testament contains a few mentions of the good use of animals for food (Acts 10:10–16; Rom. 14:14; 1 Tim. 4:3–4). These examples already assume that man has been eating meat, at least certain kinds, all along. God didn't change His position on giving us animals for food (although He did regulate clean and unclean foods for Israel for a season). What He revealed to us in His Word, in both testaments, remains true.

*The humane use of animals for human well-being and flourishing isn't pragmatic or consequentialist. It is obedience to God's command to do so.*

### Treatment of Animals

The fact that God has given humans animals to use for food doesn't mean that we may mistreat, abuse, or torture animals. Since man is made in the image of God, man is still to accurately reflect the image of his kind Creator as best as he can. To mistreat an animal for fun or sport is cruel and evil. A proverb teaches us on this topic: "A righteous man regardeth the life of his beast: but the tender mercies of the wicked are cruel" (Prov. 12:10). In the fourth commandment on keeping the Sabbath day, God made provision for work animals to rest (Exod. 20:10; Deut. 5:14). Other laws in the Old Testament also take into account the considerate and good treatment of animals (Deut. 22:4, 6; 25:4). God even allowed Balaam's donkey to call out Balaam for beating her unjustly (Num. 22:23–32)!

Despite today's advancements in scientific research and technology, the use of animals for experimentation remains critical. The fact that an animal subject might suffer some pain during the experimentation doesn't invalidate the use of an animal for that trial. The alternative would be to use a human subject or to release a product for consumption that could be harmful if not lethal to the customer or patient. This is an unfortunate reality due to the fallen world we live in. How we treat other people and how we treat animals tells a lot about us, for good and for bad. God cares for the creatures He created (Ps. 147:9; Matt. 10:29, 31). His people should show them equally humane treatment in all normal circumstances.

*The humane treatment of animals used to contribute to human well-being and flourishing is ethical because God placed animals under human stewardship.*

**vegetarian:** does not eat any type of meat

**vegan:** does not eat any meat or animal-based product of any kind



*sible for future generations to utilize the great resources we now have today. To be careless, wasteful, or slothful flies in the face of biblical virtue. One wouldn't use the well that supplies the water to one's home as a latrine. Along those same lines, we should use God's resources carefully and responsibly (Deut. 20:19–20; John 6:12).*

## VIRTUOUS CARE FOR CREATION

Guide a **Socratic seminar** for students to dig deeply into how prudence, humility, and gratitude aid believers in caring for creation.

Start with the following questions for each virtue and continue until each virtue has been sufficiently probed and discussed.

**In what ways is prudence critical to caring for creation?** *Prudence is required to know how to interact with the data and statistics that exist regarding the impact of humans on the earth, the climate, and so forth. Prudence is necessary to make decisions about one's use or avoidance of various energy sources and products.*

**How does humility influence one's care for creation?** *Humility allows one to acknowledge that God is Creator and Sovereign over all things. His knowledge and wisdom are greater than ours, so His Word to us is necessary to help govern our care of creation.*

**Why is gratitude necessary for proper care for creation?** *God made all things good, and even after the Fall, God has blessed us with so many good gifts including plants, animals, and natural resources. Gratitude for these things as we use them allows us to honor and glorify the Giver.*

## Apply

### MISHANDLING CREATION

Use **Activity 12.3** on pages 77–78 for students to formulate biblical responses to those who abuse creation and to those who idolize it.

### PERSONAL INVOLVEMENT IN CREATION CARE

Ask this section's **essential question**.

**How involved should I be in caring for God's creation?** *Each Christian can and should employ the virtues of prudence, humility, and gratitude in creation care. This is always good and right. Also, each person is called to follow the Creation Mandate of Genesis 1, meaning that subduing and having dominion over the earth begins on an individual level. One's own lifestyle and treatment of plants, animals, and the earth's resources impact the world we live in. Our example, for good or for bad, influences others. Involvement in local initiatives to correct pollution or extreme restrictions is one way to get involved personally.*

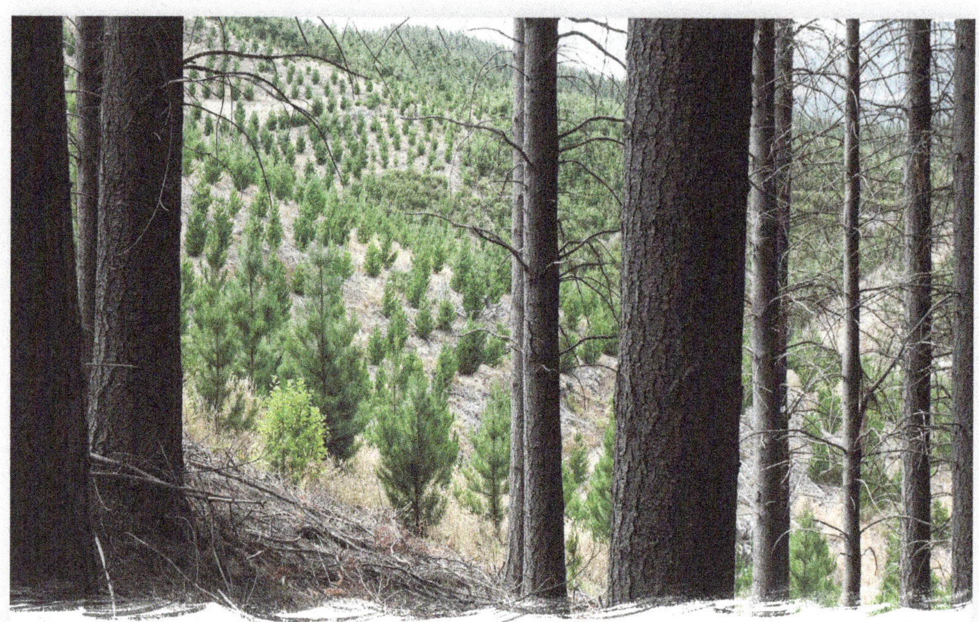

***Caring, Not Worshiping***

In prioritizing the worth of humans, animals, and creation in general, humans come out on top every time. Christ reaffirmed this truth in His parable about doing good on the Sabbath—man is better than a sheep (Matt. 12:12). Although man is the pinnacle of God's creation, he is still a created being, and we shouldn't worship anyone except God (Exod. 20:3). God alone is deserving of our worship (Exod. 20:4–6). In discussing the extent to which man rebels against God and sins against Him, Paul pointed out the idols man makes out of creation instead of worshiping his Creator (Rom. 1:22–25). We must take great care not to elevate any part of God's creation, be it animals or stars, higher than God Himself. Believers are obedient stewards of God's creation when they care for it well and use it for the purposes God has intended.

The support of human life through fishing, farming, mining, and processing in factories is according to God's design. The ultimate goal of humanity isn't to have as many untouched and undeveloped natural landscapes as possible. The Bible gives humans the responsibility to steward creation, and believers should take seriously what wise stewardship of creation looks like. That might well include things like recycling, conserving energy and resources, and safely disposing of waste. There is a balance that must be struck. Future generations need to use this planet and its resources, but we don't get there by worshiping creation. We need to care for creation without elevating it above the Creator.

### CONSEQUENCES OF MISUSING CREATION

The fact that God entrusted man with the Creation Mandate at the outset of creation doesn't mean that man does a good job subduing and having dominion over creation. Because of the Fall, abuses and excesses in using creation became not only possibilities but realities. The media does a good job at presenting doom and gloom photos and videos of our broken planet. Skinny polar bears, turtles skewered



### CREATION CARE

Use the **link** Creation Care to access the video that the students will watch.

After that, guide a **discussion** using the following questions.

**What two reasons does the speaker give for caring for creation?** *Earth is our home; the relationship between the Lord and His creation is highlighted in Genesis 1.*

**What two points does the speaker give describing the relationship of creation to the Lord?** *Creation belongs to the Lord, and creation brings the Lord joy and pleasure.*

**What motivations does the speaker give for caring for creation?** *We don't want to damage the earth in a way that diminishes God's joy in it; we want to please the Father; we seek to please the Father by taking care of the earth which He receives joy and pleasure from.*

by plastic straws, and seagulls floundering in oil slicks combine with aerial or satellite imagery of melting ice caps, retreating glaciers, dwindling rainforests, and growing deserts. These images might all be realities, but what is presented as causing all these tragedies and what responses are proposed reveal one's worldview concerning conservation, environmentalism, and animal rights.

Most agree on what qualifies as a blatant misuse of creation. Examples might include destroying magnificent natural rock formations, cutting down emblematic trees, pumping toxic waste straight into a body of water, or releasing harmful factory gases and smoke straight into the atmosphere. The two former examples are misuses of creation by someone raising a hand against God and His beautiful creative abilities. The latter two examples are misuses of creation because they affect millions of people and multiple generations of people. Air and water pollution are serious and growing problems in many parts of the world. You don't have to be a biblical scholar, tenured professor, or acclaimed scientist to know that we need clean air to breathe and clean water to drink to survive.

Is it the end of the world if you occasionally litter small pieces of trash? Water treatment plants can handle a few toxins in the ground water, right? Leaving lights on in your home and letting the water run a long time in the shower aren't that big a deal, are they? There is a principle that's also the title of a children's book: *If Everybody Did.*[47] You can imagine the consequences of certain actions if everybody (billions of people) did them repeatedly. On the flip side, if everyone planted a few trees to make up for all that are being cut down, you can imagine the positive benefits that might result. A concerted effort goes a long way in either direction! Loving one's neighbor and doing unto others as you would want them to do to you are biblical principles (Luke 6:31; 10:27). A biblical view of creation care results in positive outcomes for creation and our neighbors, not negative consequences.

There are negative consequences to misusing creation in two different ways that are on opposite ends of a spectrum. On one end of the spectrum is an unhindered, short-sighted, and careless use of energy sources, food sources, and other natural resources. This approach would not take into account the effects on the environment of obtaining and using energy sources and other natural resources. Neither would this approach consider the side effects of depleting a food source and the chain effect that would have on the rest of the food chain and ecosystem. On the other end of the spectrum would be eliminating or severely limiting the use of certain energy sources, to the extent that there would be an energy crisis resulting in no access to energy or extremely high prices for that energy. Outlawing or severely limiting certain food sources would have a similar effect—food shortages or extremely high prices for some foods.

Most environmentalists don't like the extraction, refining, and burning of fossil fuels (e.g., petroleum, natural gas, coal). They consider carbon emissions to be one of the lead factors in what they describe as climate change. Others propose the use of nuclear energy, but the potential for leaks in the plants (e.g., the Fukushima Daiichi accident, March 2011) and the disposal of radioactive waste are both problematic. But hydraulic, wind, and solar energies aren't sufficient for the current usage of the world population. There must be wisdom and balance in the pursuit of clean energy. Regarding animal species, Adam named land animals and birds as one of the ways he ruled over the creation God made and put him in charge of (Gen. 2:19–20). When an animal species disappears forever, that specific reflection of God's creative power and genius disappears as well. Even when plant species go extinct something is lost. To poach an animal to extinction or to wipe out an animal completely that is a perceived nuisance is a gross misuse of creation.

The western rhinoceros and the passenger pigeon are two examples of extinct species.

ETHICAL SCIENCE 233

## Assess

Guide a **summative assessment** by directing students to answer the questions in Thinking It Through 12.3.

### Thinking It Through 12.3

1. Climate change is the biggest issue, but Ken Magnuson also lists the following: "rise in sea level, overpopulation and the earth's 'carrying capacity,' biodiversity loss and species extinction, deforestation, air and water pollution, human consumption and waste, and sustainable farming" (Taken from page 504 of *Invitation to Christian Ethics: Moral Reasoning and Contemporary Issues* © Copyright 2020 by Ken Magnuson, Invitation to Theological Studies Series. Published by Kregel Publications, Grand Rapids, MI. Used by permission of the publisher. All rights reserved.). Each entry on this list requires a careful definition of the issue and thorough treatment. The secular influences and their corresponding worldviews need to be distinguished from Christian influences and their corresponding biblical worldview. A purely secular worldview doesn't, however, have an understanding of God's plan for humans and the earth and humanity's responsibility to govern creation. There are actual issues concerning the environment and animals. These issues affect everyone; but one's understanding of them and how they affect the environment, animals, and people is why they're on this list.
2. The Creation Mandate and what God promised Noah in the Noahic Covenant ground believers on their responsible use of animals for food and harnessing the earth's resources for their well-being. Humans are made in God's image and so should be thoughtful, careful, loving, and wise users of creation for their own good as well as the good of generations to come. Creation is to be used responsibly, not worshiped as deity.
3. On the one hand, an unhindered, short-sighted, and careless use of energy and food resources results in an environmental mess and a depletion of resources that might not be able to be replaced. On the other hand, an outright restricting or severe limiting of energy and food resources causes shortages or extremely high prices.

How involved should I be in caring for God's creation?

agents

### CHRISTIANS CARING FOR CREATION

When you stayed the night at a friend's house, did your parents ever tell you to leave the place better than you found it? This teaches a principle that we can apply to caring for creation. Improving what you use and replacing what you have consumed or broken expresses the virtue of gratitude. Being truly thankful for the creation God has entrusted us with should motivate us to take care of, even improve, the parts of creation we come into contact with. To mistreat or exploit aspects of creation, spoiling those aspects for anyone else now or in the future, shows ingratitude and selfishness.

Christians should also exhibit humility in caring for creation. God has entrusted us with a great task—to govern creation in a way that imitates God's governance of all things. Any comparison of yourself or your work to God and His work should cause you to be humble. And it takes humility to not think we are entitled to waste resources and pollute the environment irresponsibly and unnecessarily. It takes humility to see the other people who are affected by our actions when it comes to our use or abuse of God's creation. Humility also submits to God's power to sustain the earth and all He has created until He brings judgment and restoration—rather than believing humanity has power to either save the world or destroy it.

Lastly, Christians need to approach caring for creation with prudence. Issues concerning the environment and shared resources that every human needs and uses call for wisdom and discernment. Much of the decision-making is done by governments and community leaders, but individuals can have a say in certain local decisions as well. The virtue of prudence allows Christians to determine whether a certain choice is helpful in the long run as well as the short run. A certain course of action might have ramifications that must be studied and addressed. Prudence helps Christians apply their biblical worldview to guide their interpretation of the latest conservation effort or environmental concern. Whether to speak up regarding a restrictive or permissive measure calls for prudence.

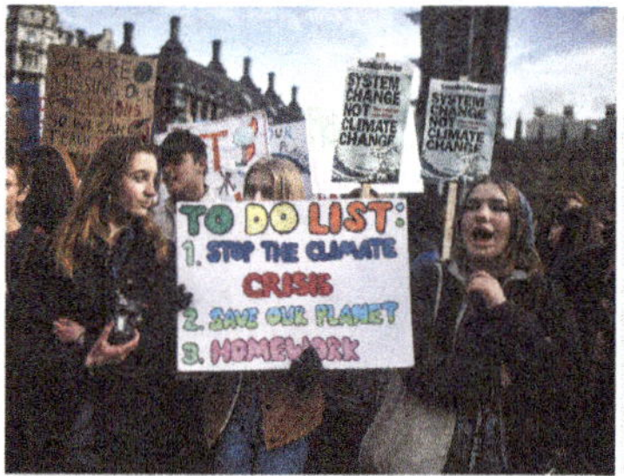

Teen Climate Crisis activists in London, England, strike from school as part of the global movement started by Swedish teen Greta Thunberg, demanding climate action from political leaders.

### RESPONDING TO EXTREME VIEWS OF CARING FOR CREATION

context

How would you respond to individuals with extreme responses to the current state of our world's climate, energy production, and food consumption? Start thinking about the short- and long-term effects of those who abuse creation. Also consider the short- and long-term effects of those who idolize creation. Do you personally have a tendency either way? To what areas of your daily routine should you apply gratitude, humility, and prudence in order to care for creation better? When it comes to conservation, environmentalism, and animal rights, strive to be a responsible and obedient steward of what God has generously blessed you with.

#### Thinking It Through 12.3

1. List the main ethical issues regarding the environment and animals. Why did these make the list?
2. What is the biblical teaching regarding the Christian's relationship to the natural world?
3. What are some consequences of unbiblical views of creation stewardship?
4. How do the virtues of gratitude, humility, and prudence motivate appropriate care for the earth and animals?
5. How would you respond to someone who abuses creation?
6. How would you respond to someone who idolizes creation?



4. Gratitude motivates believers to take care of the earth and its resources so others can enjoy them in the present and future. Humility motivates believers to gladly accept God's provision of the earth and its resources. No part of creation is exalted or more important than it should be because humans recognize their role and creation's role in this world. Prudence motivates Christians to carefully consider local and short-term decisions and their impact, and they carefully assess the long-term and global effects of their use of creation and animals. There are many moving pieces and at times conflicting information regarding the impact on the earth and animal populations. Much prudence is required.
5. Answers should reflect the biblical principles discussed in this section. Answers are also developed further in Activity 12.3.
6. Answers should reflect the biblical principles discussed in this section. Answers are also developed further in Activity 12.3.

# Review

ETHICAL SCIENCE

### Terms to Remember

- stem cells
- embryonic stem cells
- cloning
- gene editing
- germline
- organ donation
- organ transplantation
- conservation
- environmentalism
- animal rights

### Scripture Memory

Genesis 1:28–30

### Understanding Ethics

1. How do you know when science has gone off the rails in the areas this chapter covers?
2. How should science improve your quality of life?
3. How should Christians view organ donation?
4. How involved should you be in caring for God's creation?

### Practicing Ethical Decision-Making

5. How would you respond to a family member who asked whether becoming an organ donor (live or upon death) was an ethical thing to do? How would you respond to a family member who needed an organ to survive but wasn't sure whether receiving an organ transplant was right for a Christian?
6. Suppose an employee of the power company in your town visits your home and gives your family a box of energy-saving LED lightbulbs that he recommends you substitute for the incandescent bulbs you currently use. At the dinner table that evening, what suggestion do you offer if most in your home prefer the warmer feeling of incandescent light?

### Analyzing and Evaluating Ethical Claims

7. How would you respond to someone who says that the Bible has nothing to say about science, much less ethical science and how it applies to a whole society?
8. How would you respond to someone who justifies using embryonic stem cells to save the lives of many people and improve the lives of many more?
9. Medical students and scientific researchers need to practice and study the human body in detail. The use of a cadaver is the best way to do this, as it gives the closest parallel to doing the same procedures and seeing the same anatomy on a live patient. Do you think Christians should be able to donate their bodies to science? Explain.
10. Does the assumption that those who recycle follow a liberal agenda and those who sacrifice the environment to benefit business follow a conservative agenda hold true? Explain your answer while discussing the value of recycling and the significance of industry's impact on the environment.

### Creating My Own Position Statements on Ethics

11. Based on your understanding of the image of God in man and the personhood of all human beings, how would you respond to the ethical questions raised by stem cell research, cloning, and gene editing?
12. Apply the Creation Mandate and the virtues of gratitude, humility, and prudence to the ethics of a Christian's obligation to care for creation.

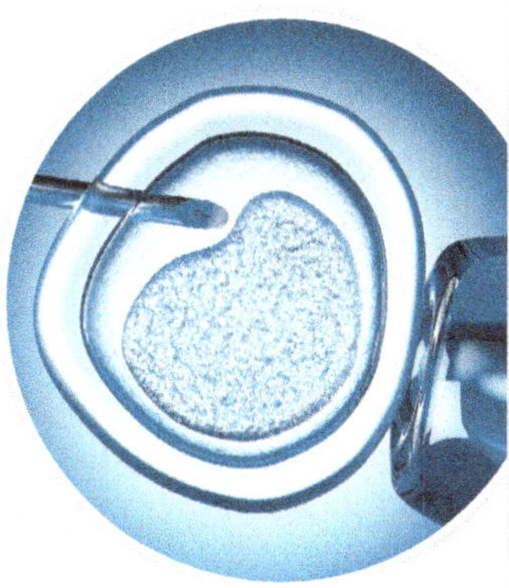

ETHICAL SCIENCE 235

# Chapter 12 Review

## Terms to Remember

- **stem cells:** Cells that "have not yet obtained a special structure and function" (Carter, "The FAQs: Chinese Scientists Create First Monkey-Human Embryos").
- **embryonic stem cells:** A type of stem cell found in embryos in their first few days of development that can develop into any type of cell in the body (Carter, "The FAQs: Chinese Scientists Create First Monkey-Human Embryos").
- **cloning:** A form of reproduction that does not use a sperm and an egg but takes genetic material from a single person to manufacture a new, almost identical, but separate, individual (Carter, "9 Things You Should Know about Human Cloning").
- **gene editing:** "A form of genome engineering in which DNA is inserted, replaced, or removed from the genetic material of a cell using artificially engineered enzymes, or 'molecular scissors'" (Carter, "The FAQs: What Christians Should Know about CRISPR Genetic Scissors").
- **germline:** An individual's sex cells (ovum or sperm) or "the lineage of [sex] cells spanning generations of individuals" (Carter, "The FAQs: What Christians Should Know about CRISPR Genetic Scissors").
- **organ donation:** Voluntarily giving one's organs or tissues to replace someone else's defective or damaged organs or tissues.
- **organ transplantation:** The replacement of a defective or damaged organ or tissue in one person with a healthy organ or tissue taken from another person.
- **conservation:** The effort to preserve or improve certain natural resources so that they remain available for use in the future.
- **environmentalism:** A movement that seeks the protection of the environment from human destruction and the improvement of the conditions of the environment through social and political action.
- **animal rights:** The idea that animals are entitled to the same rights and privileges that humans are entitled to—no exploitation and no abuse; generally includes the notion that any killing or prolonged caging of animals to benefit humans is unethical.

## Understanding Ethics

1. For science to be ethical, to not have gone off the rails, the motivations, means, and goals of science need to be rooted in commands, truths, and principles found in Scripture. Circumstances can be unique, extreme even, but when the end justifies the means or only the greatest good for the greatest number of people is considered, then science has become unethical and has gone off the rails. One must lay the scientific ethical question alongside the rule of God's Word to determine how ethical the issue is. In stem cell research, cloning, gene editing, organ donation and transplantation, and issues with the environment and animal rights, science goes off the rails when God's creational norms are ignored and God's creation is elevated over the Creator. If a human is killed, even at the embryonic or terminally ill stages, then science has flown off the rails.
2. Science improves the quality of life of essentially everyone on the planet. The resources doctors and nurses use to monitor pregnancies, assist mothers in childbirth, and help people live healthy lives are a huge blessing. When science crosses the line of taking the life of the unborn or of prematurely ending the lives of the sick or elderly, regardless of

how much someone else's life might be improved, then Christians shouldn't use or support those "advances" to improve someone's quality of life.

3. Christians should count it as a blessing that a live donor would be willing to risk his or her own health to give health or life to someone else. Christians should also count it as a blessing to see one's organs donated to a needy recipient. To see the gift of life (a true blessing) come after someone passes away (a true tragedy) is a powerful gift. Organ donation can be more emotionally troubling than morally problematic as it is generally understood and rightly practiced.

4. Christians should be very involved in caring for God's creation, at least on a personal and local level. Not everyone will have an influential voice to address this topic with higher-up government officials or politicians. Small choices and little adjustments to one's lifestyle, if everyone did them, can have a big impact in caring for creation around the world. Christians understand that creation is God's but that He has charged humanity with governing it through subduing it and having dominion over it. That does not equal abuse or exploitation. Humans should imitate God's sovereign care over creation.

## Practicing Ethical Decision-Making

5. The situation of a live donor is complicated because many factors must be considered to arrive at a safe and right decision. But live donating, just like donating upon death, is a legitimate and ethical option for believers. Family members might face emotional and psychological turmoil, but ethically and scientifically it is a legitimate decision. Man is made in God's image, and that image of God in man remains intact even when organs are taken or transplanted. Humans have a body and soul, so even when someone commits a grave sin, the image of God in that person isn't lost.

6. The family might make the following cases to reject the gift of the energy-saving lightbulbs: a distrust of the thinking behind the gift of the energy-saving lightbulbs, the difference in the color and brightness of the new lightbulbs, and thinking that a little change in energy consumption is not a big deal.

   A helpful suggestion would include these points: less power consumption means a cheaper power bill, certain critical incandescent bulbs can be retained while replacing the rest, and individuals contribute to a collective impact of saving power. These efforts see benefits from less waste being produced, including gas emissions.

## Analyzing and Evaluating Ethical Claims

7. The Bible is inspired by God and useful for every aspect of life (2 Tim. 3:16–17). It is also inerrant and sufficient for salvation and Christian living. Christians live together and in society, so the Bible is relevant for how people relate to all that God created. Though the Bible isn't, strictly speaking, a science handbook or textbook, it reveals how God has created humans to discover, invent, create, and cultivate. The Bible shows us the closeness of God to His creation and how in His sovereign power He relates to it.

8. Those who justify this case have to confess that the ends (curing the sick, prolonging the life of those already born, or both) justify the means (killing unborn, days-old embryos). To kill the most vulnerable of all human beings, who have no say in what happens to them, to save human beings who do have a say in the decisions that they can make is a gross violation of the dignity of life of the unborn human beings. Since even the unborn are people, we must show sympathy and love for all lives, not merely the ones we value the most according to our own standard. God gives us the standard in His Word (Exod. 20:13).

9. The dignity of man being made in God's image isn't exclusively tied to the physical form. And since God will resurrect from ash and dust the physical bodies of all people prior to the eternal state, the condition or placement of our bodies and organs is irrelevant to God's full plan of redemption. The ethical challenge is emotional and psychological since most people are most comfortable giving their loved one a proper burial. This provides them peace of mind knowing that the loved one is "resting peacefully" in the grave. Agreement as to what happens to one's body should be sought out while the individual is still living and able to come to an agreement with the family.

10. Assumptions, associations, and presuppositions will always be attached to controversial topics. Recycling makes sense on all levels unless the hassles (cost, effectiveness, short- and long-term benefits) outweigh the burden placed on individuals and societies. Environmental issues shouldn't be presented falsely or deceptively to serve ulterior motives. Industry impacts the environment—there is no question about that. Much of the negative impact can be mitigated, but some of it can't be avoided. Even if measures to avoid temporary or permanent damage to the environment surrounding the industry are costly to implement, a real attempt should be made. Even large businesses need to consider how their actions affect others, both in the present and in the future. Christians have an obligation to care for creation, not destroy it irresponsibly.

## Creating My Own Position Statements on Ethics

11. Stem cell research can be ethical if the stem cells are extracted from persons whose lives aren't endangered or whose health is not compromised in the process. But embryonic stem cell research harvests stem cells from embryos used specifically for this purpose, killing the days-old unborn person. Cloning violates God's design for the creation of life—one man and one woman physically and sexually producing an offspring—by leaving out one of the parents. Gene editing violates God's sovereign control over each person's life and death. Even with the effects of the Fall on all creation, God's will is untouched and unmoved regarding His purposes for humanity. Gene editing that alters the germline puts humans in charge of aspects of future generations. Humans are created in the image of God and thus have dignity and worth in the sight of God. All people, regardless of their level of development or how they arrived at the tiny embryonic stage, have personhood and thus their life is sacred.

12. Christians shouldn't shy away from caring for creation in balanced and respon-

sible ways. Humans have been entrusted with the governance of creation from the beginning of their existence. The Creation Mandate humans received requires them to be grateful for what God has created and entrusted to them. They must be humble in their knowledge and ability of how to best care for creation and those who share it with them. They must be prudent in making the best decisions that align with Scripture and its principles, allowing as many as possible to flourish. We aren't the only generation to live on this planet. What humans do now and in the future surely impacts the earth and everything in it.

# Lesson Plan Overview

## CHAPTER 13: Sexual Ethics

**EV** ExamView
**PPT pres.** PowerPoint presentation

| PAGES | OBJECTIVES | RESOURCES | ASSESSMENTS |
|---|---|---|---|
| **13.1 Marriage and Divorce** (4 DAYS) | | | |
| 237–41 | **13.1.1** Summarize common views of marriage.<br>**13.1.2** Summarize the biblical teaching on marriage, divorce, and remarriage.<br>BWS Creational Order (explain)<br>**13.1.3** Evaluate the personal and societal consequences of divorce.<br>**13.1.4** Assess the virtues necessary to act ethically regarding marriage, divorce, and remarriage.<br>BWS Virtue (formulate)<br>**13.1.5** Formulate a response to a loved one who is planning to get a divorce. | **ACTIVITIES**<br>• 13.1 When Faced with Divorce<br>**BJU PRESS TROVE***<br>• PPT pres.: Chapter 13 | **STUDENT EDITION**<br>• Thinking It Through 13.1 |
| **13.2 Fornication, Adultery, and Marital Purity** (4 DAYS) | | | |
| 242–46 | **13.2.1** Define *fornication, adultery*, and *marital purity*.<br>**13.2.2** Summarize the biblical teaching on appropriate sexual activity.<br>BWS Creational Order (explain)<br>**13.2.3** Assess the personal and societal consequences of rejecting a biblical ethic of sexuality.<br>BWS Man's Chief End (evaluate)<br>**13.2.4** Assess the virtues necessary to act ethically regarding sexuality.<br>BWS Virtue (formulate)<br>**13.2.5** Formulate a plan for maintaining sexual purity before and during marriage. | **ACTIVITIES**<br>• 13.2 A Vigil against Fornication and Adultery<br>**BJU PRESS TROVE**<br>• PPT pres.: Chapter 13 | **STUDENT EDITION**<br>• Thinking It Through 13.2 |
| **13.3 Homosexuality, Bisexuality, and Transgenderism** (4 DAYS) | | | |
| 247–55 | **13.3.1** Identify recent LGBTQ+ trends.<br>**13.3.2** Summarize the biblical teaching regarding human sexuality and gender.<br>BWS Creational Order (explain)<br>**13.3.3** Assess the personal and societal consequences of rejecting God's design for human sexuality and gender.<br>BWS Man's Chief End (evaluate)<br>**13.3.4** Assess the virtues necessary to embrace God's design for human sexuality and gender.<br>BWS Virtue (formulate)<br>**13.3.5** Formulate a response to a friend who is considering a same-sex relationship or a transgender transition.<br>BWS Wisdom (apply) | **ACTIVITIES**<br>• 13.3 A Biblical Response to LGBTQ+<br>**BJU PRESS TROVE**<br>• Video: "Homosexuality, Bisexuality, Transgenderism"<br>• Link: An Interview with Rosaria Butterfield<br>• PPT pres.: Chapter 13 | **STUDENT EDITION**<br>• Thinking It Through 13.3 |

*Digital resources for homeschool users are available on Homeschool Hub.

| PAGES | OBJECTIVES | RESOURCES | ASSESSMENTS |
|---|---|---|---|
| | **13.4 Birth Control, Reproductive Technologies, and Eugenics** (4 DAYS) | | |
| 256–60 | **13.4.1** Explain various ethical issues regarding procreation and birth control.<br>**13.4.2** Summarize the biblical teaching on procreation and birth control.<br>*BWS* Creational Order (explain)<br>**13.4.3** Assess the personal and societal consequences of unbiblical views regarding procreation and birth control.<br>**13.4.4** Assess the virtues necessary to live in accordance with a biblical view of procreation and birth control.<br>*BWS* Virtue (formulate)<br>**13.4.5** Formulate a response to a couple struggling to decide whether to have children.<br>*BWS* Wisdom (apply) | **ACTIVITIES**<br>• 13.4 Childless Couples Wanting Children<br>**BJU PRESS TROVE**<br>• PPT pres.: Chapter 13 | **STUDENT EDITION**<br>• Thinking It Through 13.4 |
| | **Review** | | |
| 260–61 | Recall concepts, terms, and Scripture memory from Chapter 13. | | **STUDENT EDITION**<br>• Chapter 13 Review |
| | **Test** | | |
| | Demonstrate knowledge of the material from Chapter 13 by taking the test. | | **ASSESSMENTS**<br>• Chapter 13 Test<br>**BJU PRESS TROVE**<br>• EV: Chapter 13 test bank |

CHAPTER 13

# Overview

When is the gift of sex to be enjoyed?

## Objectives

**13.1** Analyze various ethical issues related to human sexuality.

**13.2** Apply a biblical ethic to issues related to human sexuality.

### Terms to Remember

- compatibility
- cohabitation
- no-fault divorce
- immodesty
- pornography
- masturbation
- fornication
- prostitution
- incest
- sexual abuse
- bestiality
- adultery
- polygamy
- marital purity
- homosexual
- LGBTQ+
- bisexual
- transgender
- birth control
- assisted reproductive technology (ART)
- artificial insemination from a husband
- artificial insemination from a donor
- in vitro fertilization (IVF)
- surrogacy
- eugenics

### Scripture Memory

- 1 Thess. 4:3–5

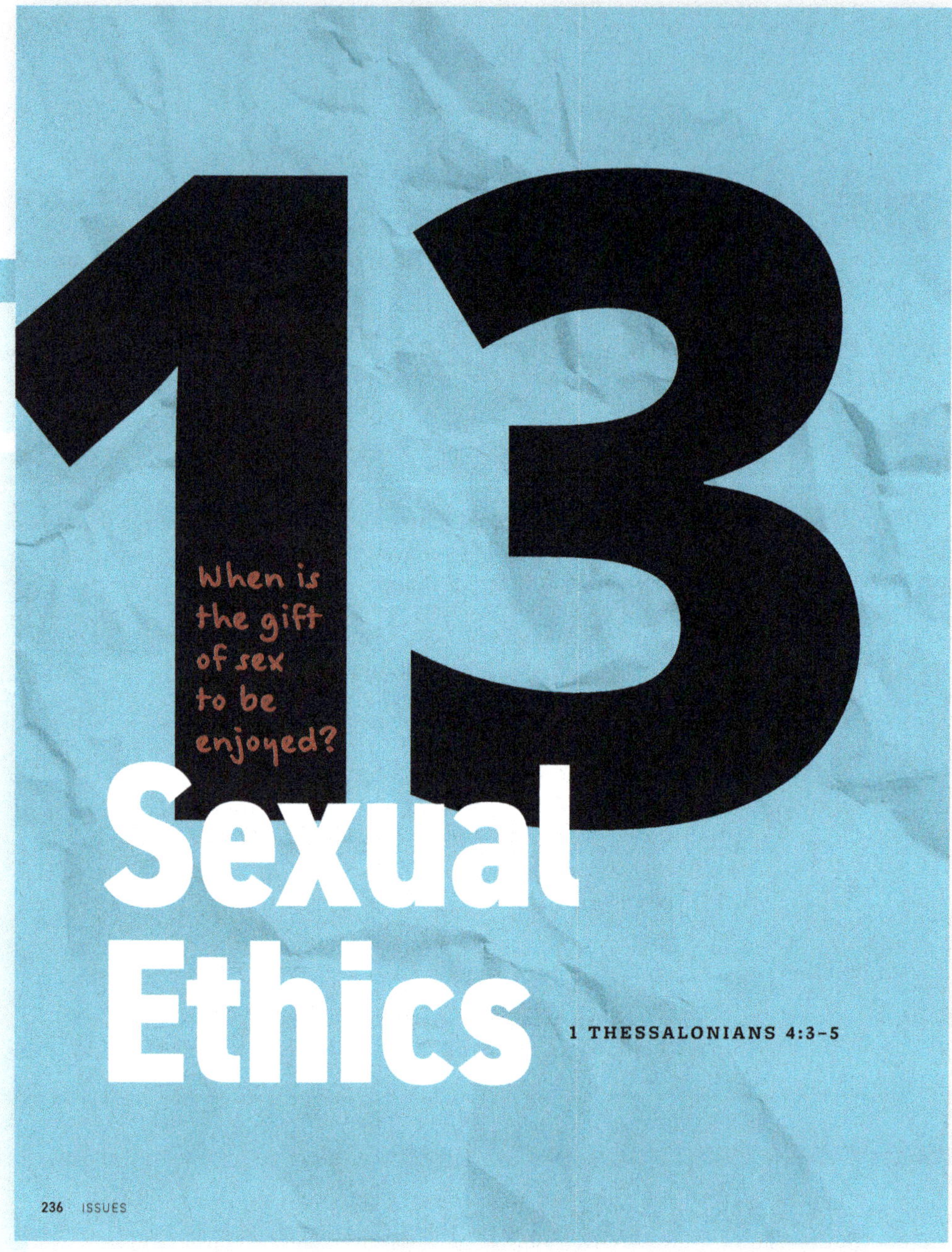

13
When is the gift of sex to be enjoyed?
Sexual Ethics
1 THESSALONIANS 4:3–5
236 ISSUES

## 13.1 Marriage and Divorce

How do you view marriage? What has shaped your view?

Maybe you've always dreamed of the perfect wedding and of getting married to the "one and only." You can just imagine what a satisfying life of enjoyment lies ahead of you as you fulfill all your dreams alongside your soulmate. Or maybe your experiences in real life have led you to be more cynical. You've mostly observed heartbreak, conflict, and betrayal. You think it's best to avoid taking the chance of getting hurt.

Or perhaps you want to avoid either idealism or cynicism regarding marriage. You know that marriage is a lifelong commitment and that there are many trials along the way. But you also know that a good marriage is worth fighting for because marriage was beautifully designed by God. And maybe you have been privileged to observe the faithful efforts, if not of your own parents, of godly men and women in your church.

### COMMON ATTITUDES TOWARD MARRIAGE

Our world has normalized disregard for marriage. Marriage is still common—though less so than in the past. For the most part, it's viewed as optional and easily dissolved. Far from being seen as an essential institution, marriage seems to many to be an unnecessary formality. It's now hard for many young people to imagine a world in which marriage—the lifelong commitment of spouses until death parts them—was the norm for the majority of people.



# 13.1 Marriage and Divorce

*What are the keys to staying married when it is difficult?*

### Objectives

**13.1.1** Summarize common views of marriage.

**13.1.2** Summarize the biblical teaching on marriage, divorce, and remarriage. BWS

**13.1.3** Evaluate the personal and societal consequences of divorce.

**13.1.4** Assess the virtues necessary to act ethically regarding marriage, divorce, and remarriage. BWS

**13.1.5** Formulate a response to a loved one who is planning to get a divorce.

### Biblical Worldview Shaping

- **Creational Order** (explain): God created marriage to be a lifelong covenant of love between one man and one woman. (13.1.2)
- **Virtue** (formulate): Sacrificial love and faithfulness are the foundation for all healthy marriages. Patience is a necessary virtue in all marriages. (13.1.4)

### Printed Resource

- Activity 13.1: When Faced with Divorce

### Suggested Reading

- Frame, John M. *The Doctrine of the Christian Life*. Phillipsburg, NJ: P&R Publishing, 2008. Pages 769–81.
- Grudem, Wayne. *Christian Ethics: An Introduction to Biblical Moral Reasoning*. Wheaton, IL: Crossway, 2018. Pages 799–842.
- Magnuson, Ken. *Invitation to Christian Ethics: Moral Reasoning and Contemporary Issues*. Grand Rapids, MI: Kregel Academic, 2020. Pages 232–65.

## Engage

### THE PROSPECT OF MARRIAGE: EXCITEMENT OR DREAD?

Use a **Likert scale** to preassess student proclivities toward idealism or cynicism regarding their presumptions about marriage.

Ask students whether they strongly agree, agree, remain neutral, disagree, or strongly disagree with the following statements.

- Most marriages are happy.
- Most marriages are unhappy.
- I'm likely to find a soulmate within the next five years.
- I'm unlikely to find someone who can meet up to my expectations.
- The person I plan to marry will fulfill my dreams.
- I'm not sure about marriage; most spouses end up being abusive.
- I'm afraid that my future marriage will likely end in a divorce.
- I think I'll be careful enough and likable enough to prevent a divorce from ever happening to me.
- I'm considering cohabiting in order to prevent a bad marriage.
- There's nothing anybody can do to prevent a divorce from happening to them.

## Instruct

### COMMON ATTITUDES TOWARD MARRIAGE

Use a **web search** to initiate some discussion regarding the concept of compatibility and its impact on the assumptions of most people in society. Then prompt a **group discussion** to see whether students can relate the assumptions of the culture to its common practices.

Ask students to research "Tim Challies, The Problem with Love Languages." Instruct students to watch the video or read the transcript. Encourage them to discuss the relationship between the concept of love languages and compatibility. Then they should enunciate one key takeaway from the video or transcript.

**What is *compatibility*? How are cohabitation and no-fault divorce connected to compatibility?** *The idea of compatibility has made possible our current situation of "no-fault divorce." The prevailing idea of compatibility is that couples must be able to get along well to remain together. To discern whether they are compatible, couples need to try each other out to find out how well they work together. This may include cohabitation: living together before marriage. Only after testing each other out (sometimes long-term) might a couple decide to get married. The legal reality of no-fault divorce allows for the dissolution of a marriage for as minor a cause as one person's claim of incompatibility.*

Christians who recognize the problems with cohabitation and no-fault divorce may unwittingly accept an assumption that leads to those problems: the concept of compatibility. Christians should be concerned about having similar beliefs, values, and philosophy of life. But they should not create non-biblical or selfish standards for potential marriage prospects (e.g., this person must earn a very high yearly income, have this kind of personality, maintain this level of health).

**How would you critique the underlying philosophy of most dating apps? What is the biblical view of relationships?** *Many dating apps or websites presume compatibility as the key to making the right matches. But this search for compatibility often has a hidden undercurrent. The quest is to find someone who will suit you and satisfy you. In contrast, the biblical posture is that of being a servant to others. Instead of seeking self-gratification, you seek the other person's highest good as God defines it. In fact, that is what true love is. True love involves denying oneself, overcoming difficulties and difficult people, and maintaining a heart that seeks their good. Such love will be tested through the difficulties of life.*

## THE MARRIAGE COVENANT

Guide a **discussion** to reinforce the biblical teachings on marriage and divorce.

**According to Malachi 2:14, who governs the marriage relationship? What key purpose ought to characterize this relationship?** *God is the key witness to the covenant that binds a husband and wife together. The relationship should be characterized by companionship.*

**What is a covenant? What does the Bible teach regarding the permanence of the marriage covenant?** *A covenant is a solemn commitment that ought to be kept; the marriage covenant is a commitment to companionship that changes two individuals into one flesh so that they no longer see themselves as separate individuals living according to self-interest (Matt. 19:4–6). This joining together is until death (Rom. 7:2).*

**What role did God give to the man in this relationship (1 Cor. 11:3; Eph. 5:22–33)? What role did God give to the woman in this relationship (Gen. 1:27; 2:18, 21–23; Eph. 5:22–33)?** *God created man to lead, as God's representative; the husband is to love and self-sacrificingly serve his wife just as Christ loves and serves the church to present it blameless. God created woman to complement and complete what was lacking in man; the wife is to respectfully submit to the headship of her husband in order to be his helper.*

**In what way is marriage a picture of Christ's relationship with the church (Eph. 5:23, 31–32)?** *The permanence of the relationship and the roles in the relationship mirror Christ's commitment to the church.*

**How important is the institution of the family to the social order?** *The family is the most fundamental unit in God's design of the social order; marriage must be protected for a society to grow and flourish.*

**Why should Christians not marry unbelievers (1 Cor. 7:39; Exod. 34:16; 1 Kings 11:4)? Why should Christians remain married to an unbeliever (1 Cor. 7:12–14, 16; 1 Pet. 3:1–2)?** *They should seek to marry "in the Lord" in order to be joined in partnership with someone who is dedicated to the Lord. Nevertheless, believing spouses can be a witness and righteous influence on children and unbelieving spouses.*

How has our society been transformed with respect to marriage in recent decades? Although there may be many factors, one idea and one legal reality undergird what has become the "new normal" in recent generations. The one fundamental idea that seems so common-sense that most people couldn't fathom thinking otherwise is the idea of compatibility. The one legal reality that has made possible our current situation is the introduction of "no-fault divorce" laws.

The prevailing idea of **compatibility** is that couples must be able to get along well to remain together. To get along well requires couples to share similar interests, goals, temperaments, likes and dislikes, enjoyable intimacy, continuing attraction, and so on. To discern whether they are compatible, couples need to try each other out to find out how well they work together. This involves recreational dating (with generally low moral boundaries) and may include **cohabitation**: living together before marriage. Only after testing each other out (sometimes long-term) might a couple decide to get married. Of course, many couples don't see much point in getting married if they were able to cohabit for so long without marriage. Nonetheless, many couples end up getting married if that is deemed advantageous to both parties involved.

The legal reality of **no-fault divorce** allows for the dissolution of a marriage for as minor a cause as one person's claim of incompatibility. In other words, a divorce can happen at will for almost any subjective reason one person gives for desiring that divorce. Not much can stop it. This means that individuals remain viewed as individuals even in a marriage: self-interest can rip such a marriage apart at a whim. The marriage relationship is never legally viewed as a one-flesh relationship that should never be torn apart.

### GOD'S CREATION OF THE MARRIAGE COVENANT

In contrast to what has been normalized in society, the Bible stands as a witness to God's original design for marriage. God created marriage to be a lifelong covenant of love between one man and one woman. God created woman to be a counterpart to man, to complement and complete what was lacking in him when he was alone (Gen. 1:27; 2:18, 21–23). God created man to lead, as God's representative (1 Cor. 11:3). God's design was to join a man and a woman together as one (Gen. 2:24), inseparably bound to each other until death (Matt. 19:4–6; Rom. 7:2; 1 Cor. 7:39).

According to this original design, the joining of a man and woman was formally recognized by a covenant: a solemn commitment to companionship that ought to be faithfully kept (Mal. 2:14). And this kind of unity and unbreakable commitment was designed by God to be a picture of Christ's relationship with the church (Eph. 5:31–32; see also 5:23). Furthermore, the institution of the family was the first and most fundamental unit in God's design of social order. For a society to grow and flourish, marriages must be protected.

**Marriage Joins Together in Partnership**

Should a Christian ever date or marry an unbeliever? The Bible is clear that believers should not join themselves to unbelievers in partnerships that would compromise their commitment to God. Believing widows who remarry are told to marry "in the Lord" (1 Cor. 7:39). The Old Testament is full of warnings not to intermarry with idolaters (Exod. 34:16; Deut. 7:3–4; Josh. 23:12–13; Ezra 9:14), and Solomon exemplifies what happens when such warnings are ignored (1 Kings 11:4). Too many people are deceived into thinking they have the power in themselves to change someone else, to convince the other person to live for the Lord. They end up in marriages where the spouses find themselves at odds in many areas. Nevertheless, if one spouse trusts Christ after marriage, the Bible encourages maintaining that marriage and striving to be a good witness to the unbelieving party (1 Cor. 7:12–14, 16; 1 Pet. 3:1–2).

God is grieved by divorce because divorce breaks apart God's good design. Marriage is one of His greatest blessings for men and women on this earth (Mal. 2:16). When Jesus was asked about divorce, His response was to reinforce God's original design: the permanence of marriage (Matt. 19:3–6). Jesus made clear the general rule that divorce followed by remarriage is no different than committing adultery (Matt. 19:9). That's a serious charge. This teaching was so shocking to Jesus' disciples that they could hardly fathom anyone's risking marriage in the first place without the option to divorce and remarry (Matt. 19:10). The commands against adultery and the consequences for adultery highlight the seriousness of this sin and are meant to protect the sacred covenant of marriage (Exod. 20:14, 17; see also Lev. 20:10; Prov. 6:29–32; Rom. 13:9; James 2:11). Christians are encouraged to seek reconciliation (1 Cor. 7:10–16; see also Hosea 3:1–5).

> *The fundamental question is not to ask when divorce is justified, but to ask what God's will is for marriage, and whether divorce is ever justified.*
>
> KEN MAGNUSON[1]

There are indeed two possible biblical exceptions to the general principle; these exceptions make an allowance for divorce (and likely remarriage) in two situations: the case of sexual immorality or the case of abandonment (Matt. 5:32; 19:9; 1 Cor. 7:15; see also Hosea 1:9; Jer. 3:8). However, the exceptions should not overshadow the general rule. The reason for these allowances has to do with God's mercy in the face of the hardness of sinful people's hearts (Matt. 19:8; see also Deut. 24:1–4). God cares for those who must cope with life in a broken world in which a spouse fundamentally breaks the marriage covenant and refuses to repent. When the innocent person is abandoned by or trapped with a perpetually fornicating, unrepentant spouse, God makes a way of escape.

### THE CONSEQUENCES OF BROKEN COVENANTS

While people generally divorce to escape a seemingly unbearable situation, statistically, second marriages rarely work out much better.[2] That's because most people's biggest problem is not the circumstances they find themselves in but their own responses to those circumstances. Sadly, too many people simply weigh the perceived positives and negatives of a divorce and convince themselves that the positives outweigh the negatives. Have they really reckoned with the negative outcomes of divorce?

As much as society would like to normalize divorce, it cannot escape divorce's negative consequences. Both adults and children suffer greatly from the resulting broken relationship.[3] Divorce has negative emotional effects on all involved, and these effects may lead to struggles with life's normal responsibilities. God's grace can help people better cope with challenges to their quality of life in the face of the instability caused by a divorce. Knowing the grief and hardship that follow, Christians should step in to lend their support to those going through divorce, particularly to innocent children affected by it.

Since the family unit formed by marriage is the building block of society, the breakdown of the family leads to the breakdown of society. To reverse this trend in society and repair the family unit, people need to reexamine their goals in marriage. The goal of any marriage according to a biblical model is loving, self-sacrificial service to one another for the glory of God. God provided the gift of marriage to enable people to be fruitful and multiply and to be stewards of this world together. God designed marriage so that a man and a woman could give to one another as they serve God and others together.

**When unbiblical means and ends lead to rampant divorce, how does divorce commonly impact both individuals and society?** *Both adults and children suffer from the brokenness that results from relationships being torn apart. Coping emotionally and fulfilling responsibilities can become difficult, leading to dysfunction in society. (Students may be more specific based on personal experience, depending on how much they wish to share. Offering biblical counseling and mentorship in light of these difficulties would be helpful for some students.)*

**How should Christians respond to innocent children affected by divorce, regardless of whether the divorce is biblical or not?** *Christians should reach out with compassion to support those affected by divorce.*

**What is the general principle regarding divorce and remarriage (Mal. 2:16; Matt. 19:3–6, 9–10)?** *Divorce and remarriage (apart from the two possible exceptions noted below) should be viewed the same as adultery.*

**What are the two possible biblical exceptions to the general principle that make an allowance for divorce followed by remarriage without it being viewed the same as adultery (Matt. 5:32; 19:9; 1 Cor. 7:15; see also Hos. 1:9; Jer. 3:8; Matt. 1:19)?** *sexual immorality and abandonment*

## THE EFFECT OF BROKEN COVENANTS

Use a **Quick Write** to prompt students to enunciate the effects of divorce on people and on society.

Create a **T-Chart** that contrasts the unbiblical and biblical ends for which people get married and the means that people seek to achieve through that marriage.

Answers may include the following:

- Biblical means and ends: to be fruitful and multiply; stewarding the earth together to fulfill the Creation Mandate; companionship; a means of serving God together; loving; self-sacrificing service to one another for the glory of God
- Unbiblical means and ends: achieving one's own personal ambitions; self-fulfillment; self-serving romance and intimacy; self-oriented achievements

## MAINTAINING THE MARRIAGE COVENANT

Use a **Turn and Talk** to prompt students to give examples of the necessary virtues required to maintain the marriage covenant.

**What three virtues are key to staying married when it is difficult?** *love, faithfulness, and patience*

**What is biblical love, and how do you think it should be fostered in marriage?** *Biblical love is defined by God and His commands. It is directed by God's moral norms, and its source is in God's grace. One example of fostering love might include a spouse who learns to overcome the daily annoyances of the other spouse's failures in time management. The annoyed spouse must be understanding of the other one who simply fails in that regard—loving the spouse more than loving the ease or benefits that come from good time management.*

**What is faithfulness, and how do you think it should be fostered in marriage?** *Faithfulness is a steadfast commitment that overcomes the difficulties in marriage. When two people pass a difficult test, they grow in their confidence, trust, and love for one another. One example might include a spouse who has a life-transforming physical loss, but the healthy spouse refuses to leave his or her side. The spouse is committed to care, proving unwavering commitment.*

**Why is patience a key virtue for maintaining a marriage, and how do you think it should be fostered in marriage?** *Many problems cannot possibly be fixed quickly; mending hurt and fixing problems will take patient cultivation. Spiritual growth, biblical counseling, and demonstrating fruits of true repentance all take time. Spouses must wait on God to sanctify hearts. Living with one another in an understanding way requires people to be longsuffering and forgiving. One example might include a spouse who is willing to extend forgiveness repeatedly as the other spouse seeks to put off a besetting sin.*

Marriage covenants are prone to break when marriage is entered into with the wrong ends in mind: self-fulfillment, self-serving romance and intimacy, and self-oriented life achievements (seeking a so-called soulmate who satisfies one's own selfish desires). In this approach, marriage is reduced to the means of fulfilling personal ambitions.

But marriage covenants will remain intact only through fidelity to the right ends: mutual love and permanent covenant companionship in service to God. By God's grace, spouses can fulfill their duties through self-sacrificial fidelity. In this approach, marriage is a means to serve God. That service is richer when performed by the two becoming one than if each person tried to do so individually.

### agents MAINTAINING THE MARRIAGE COVENANT

For people to maintain a godly marriage, they will need to be people of virtue. The most relevant virtues for a lifelong commitment include love, faithfulness, and patience. These virtues produce other virtues, like truthfulness and open communication. Maintaining the marriage covenant depends on the grace of God, which teaches us to turn away from ungodliness and to cultivate virtues (Titus 2:11–12).

#### What are the keys to staying married when it is difficult?

Love is one key to staying married when marriage is difficult. But love must be rightly defined, rightly directed, and rightly sourced. Marriage breaks apart when love is understood as nothing more than sentimentalism or emotionalism, when it is directed by one's feelings and the definitions of popular culture, and when it is sourced in one's own imagined ability to be loving. Marriage grows strong when love is understood as a heart of great affection for another person, manifested through fulfilling self-sacrificial duties. True love is directed by God's moral norms (John 14:15); God's commands describe what it means to love the other person in a marriage relationship. All this is made possible by God's love transforming our own hearts.

Faithfulness is another key to staying married when marriage is difficult. This shows itself in one's steadfast commitment to keep the covenant promises made at the commencement of the marriage. The waves can pound the rocks, but the rocks remain firm. Such faithfulness stems from the empowerment of the Holy Spirit that enables a person to respect the seriousness of the marriage commitment and the God-given design for marriage. This covenant should not be entered into flippantly, nor should it be easily forsaken. Faithfulness perseveres through great hardship rather than bailing when life gets tough. Instead of taking the easy route of escapism, faithfulness leads people to work through their difficulties and come out stronger, closer, and more loving.

Patience is a key to staying married when marriage is difficult. There's often no quick fix to major problems. As a tender plant must be cultivated over time to grow, so also marriages revive only after patient effort to nourish the marriage with the right inputs. Counseling, biblical teaching, and cultivating new selfless patterns in response to another's needs all take time. Demonstrating the fruits of true repentance may take time. Marriages cannot last without a willingness to wait on God to sanctify one's own heart and the heart of one's mate. Patience is key for living with one another in an understanding way, giving honor and respect to one another (1 Pet. 3:1–7).

### GRAPPLING WITH HARDNESS OF HEART

Most likely, we all know someone who has been touched by divorce. You may know someone who is experiencing it or contemplating it right now. How should you respond to someone contemplating a divorce? How should you respond to someone who has already gotten a divorce, especially if that divorce did not fit within the parameters of the biblical exceptions and allowances?

The right response depends on your relationship with that person and your appropriate role in that person's life. You may not have the authority or the closeness to give advice, but you may be able to point him or her to a trusted friend or authority who can give biblical counsel.

If you have a friend who is being affected by the decisions of others, be compassionate. Point your friend to the guidance and comfort of the Scriptures. But in seeking to show compassion, avoid justifying wrongdoing. Truth about sin in God's Word cannot be set aside or overshadowed by our own desires to solve things in our own way or to avoid offending someone. The solution is not to avoid recognizing sin but to learn how to rightly respond to sin. God's Word provides counsel on how to respond to the unbiblical actions of others. It gives us the resources we need for encouragement and for perseverance in the face of the sinful decisions of others.

Those touched by divorce often feel shocked when it occurs. Divorce was not the plan. And it's hard to fathom how it could have happened, especially if those involved thought they were doing all the right things. Such circumstances demonstrate that we are not in control of life or the decisions others make. We are challenged to trust in God's good sovereignty to uphold us through the trials of life. Every tragedy He allows in our lives has as its purpose to test and refine us. In your own life and in the lives of those with whom you interact, the best advice is to look to Christ for wisdom and for comfort (James 1:1–18).

#### Thinking It Through 13.1

1. What common idea about marriage and what legal reality have led to marriage being viewed as optional and easily dissolved?
2. What did God create marriage to be? Explain God's design in marriage (Gen. 1:27; 2:18, 21–24; Matt. 19:4–6; Rom. 7:2; 1 Cor. 7:39).
3. According to God's design, the joining of a man and woman is to be formally recognized by what? Explain its significance (Mal. 2:14; Eph. 5:31–32; see also 5:23).
4. What should be our general attitude toward divorce, based on God's will for marriage (Matt. 19:3–6)?
5. What are two possible biblical exceptions to the general rule, which make an allowance for someone to divorce (and likely to remarry without being charged with adultery) (Matt. 5:32; 19:9; 1 Cor. 7:15; see also Hosea 1:9; Jer. 3:8)?
6. What are the wrong ends or goals for marriage that often lead to divorce? What should be the ultimate goals of any marriage?
7. What three virtues are keys to remaining married?
8. How should you respond to a friend whose parents have decided to divorce?

SEXUAL ETHICS 241

## Apply

### WHEN FACED WITH DIVORCE

Use **Activity 13.1** on page 79 to help students respond with biblical wisdom to various situations regarding divorce.

## Assess

Guide a **summative assessment** by directing students to answer the questions in Thinking It Through 13.1.

#### Thinking It Through 13.1

1. the idea of compatibility and the legal reality of no-fault divorce
2. Marriage is a lifelong covenant of love between one man and one woman. God created woman to be a counterpart to man, to complement and complete what was lacking in him when he was alone (Gen. 1:27; 2:18, 21–23). God's design was to join a man and a woman together as one (Gen. 2:24) so that they would never be separated from each other until death (Matt. 19:4–6; Rom. 7:2; 1 Cor. 7:39).
3. A covenant. It is a solemn commitment to companionship that ought to be faithfully kept (Mal. 2:14). And this kind of unity and expected unbreakable commitment was designed by God to be a picture of Christ's relationship with the church (Eph. 5:23, 31–32).
4. We should not desire divorce since marriage is to be permanent (Matt. 19:3–6).
5. sexual immorality or abandonment
6. Wrong ends: self-fulfillment, self-interested romance and intimacy, and self-oriented life achievements (seeking a so-called soulmate who coddles one's own selfish desires)

   Correct ends: self-sacrificial service to one another to the glory of God; a permanent commitment to covenant companionship in service to God
7. love, faithfulness, and patience
8. with compassion and by pointing to the resources found in God's Word

# 13.2 Fornication, Adultery, and Marital Purity

Why is sex only for marriage?

## Objectives

- **13.2.1** Define *fornication, adultery,* and *marital purity.*
- **13.2.2** Summarize the biblical teaching on appropriate sexual activity. BWS
- **13.2.3** Assess the personal and societal consequences of rejecting a biblical ethic of sexuality. BWS
- **13.2.4** Assess the virtues necessary to act ethically regarding sexuality. BWS
- **13.2.5** Formulate a plan for maintaining sexual purity before and during marriage.

### Biblical Worldview Shaping

- **Creational Order** (explain): Sexual activity is a creational good within a covenant of marriage. God intends for children to be raised by both a father and a mother. (13.2.2)
- **Man's Chief End** (evaluate): God's kingdom and its righteousness, rather than personal pleasure, should be the chief pursuit of the Christian. (13.2.3)
- **Virtue** (formulate): True love is self-controlled and faithful. (13.2.4)

### Printed Resource

- Activity 13.2: A Vigil against Fornication and Adultery

### Suggested Reading

- Frame, John M. *The Doctrine of the Christian Life.* Phillipsburg, NJ: P&R Publishing, 2008. Pages 622–47, 746–81.
- Grudem, Wayne. *Christian Ethics: An Introduction to Biblical Moral Reasoning.* Wheaton, IL: Crossway, 2018. Pages 698–745; 784–842.
- Magnuson, Ken. *Invitation to Christian Ethics: Moral Reasoning and Contemporary Issues.* Grand Rapids, MI: Kregel Academic, 2020. Pages 169–265.

## Engage

### A COMMITMENT TO PURITY

Use a **Quick Write** to reinforce the appropriate manner of engaging in the topic of purity. Instruct students to read Titus 1:15 and Ephesians 5:4 in context.

# 13.2 Fornication, Adultery, and Marital Purity

*Sex*! Is that a dirty word?

Sex is good and wonderful! The Bible does not condemn *sex* as dirty or wrong (Prov. 5:18–19; see also Song of Solomon). The Bible condemns *immorality* (Prov. 5:15–17, 20; 1 Thess. 4:3–5). God created sex (Gen. 2:24–25); He blessed humans with this gift of companionship to be exercised within the lifelong covenant of marriage (Heb. 13:4).

The word *sex* and other words associated with it should not be thrown about carelessly or coarsely (see Section 11.3). The world often degrades what God made to be beautiful. Society shamelessly vulgarizes* things out in the open that should be treated with respect and sobriety in their proper contexts. (For example, talking about body parts in the privacy of a doctor's office due to a medical necessity—with safeguards of accountability in place even in that situation—is far different than yelling out those same words in public to get attention.) Demonstrate maturity, godliness, and purity as you think through, talk about, and respond to the content in this chapter (Titus 1:15; see also Eph. 5:4).

### INAPPROPRIATE SEXUAL ACTIVITY

Perhaps you've been asked a series of questions such as: "Why won't your parents let you see the latest R-rated movie? Sure, there are some sex scenes, but do they really think it's all that bad?" "Why can't you join us for the party we've been planning? Your parents don't have to know." "Don't you keep up with the latest celebrities?"

Peer pressure—even in Christian schools and churches—can lead to feeling beat-up for trying to walk worthy of the Lord. Or it can lead to feeling like you need to break out and have a little freedom and fun. Which way are you inclined? There's one good answer to all that peer pressure: Proverbs 14:16. If you fear God, you won't fit in with the "norms" of the fleshly, indulgent society around you, and neither will you want to. If you routinely seek to fit in, that fruit reveals who you really are and what your end will be (Prov. 1:20–33).

Rampant sexual immorality in the surrounding culture is nothing new; it marks most cultures, ancient and modern (Gen. 6:5; Lev. 18:3; Eph. 4:17–21). Yes, the Christian ethic has influenced many societies, providing some restraint at times. Many societies may cover their wickedness in darkness and hypocrisy for a time (John 3:19–20; Eph. 5:11–13), but eventually they grow bolder, parading perversions out in the open for all to see (Rom. 1:24–32; 2 Tim. 3:13; 1 Pet. 4:3; see also Jer. 13:27). You live in a morally corrupt culture. But what you face is not unique. God has always called believers to live transformed lives, distinct from the depraved cultures surrounding them (1 Cor. 6:9–11). And God calls on you to do the same (Eph. 2:1–5). He can empower you by His Spirit and sanctify you so that you can put off the works of the flesh (Eph. 4:22–24).

**vulgarize**: to make lower or to debase

context: What kinds of inappropriate sexual activity are discussed, excused, or even celebrated in our society?

acts: What does the Bible have to say about each of these activities?



**What are the implications of these verses for how you should engage in discussions of sex?** *Possible answers:*

- *Talking about sex should be done with dignity and respect, never in crude and debasing ways. Sex is not a dirty word; sex is not wrong. God created sex as a good gift within the appropriate bounds of His design.*
- *Talking about sex can be done in a manner that is pure and mature, but those with defiled minds will twist the discussion toward impurity.*
- *The Bible clearly commands believers not to engage in dirty talk, even in a joking manner. Followers of God, His children, will avoid doing such because they seek to walk in love toward God and others.*

Encourage the students to commit themselves to striving toward purity and maturity during the discussions of Chapter 13, both inside and outside the classroom.

## Defining Inappropriate Sexual Activity:

### Context and Acts

**sexual immorality**
a phrase often used by modern Bible translations to express the Greek word *porneia*, which is a general word for any kind of sexual perversion (something that twists God's intended design)

**immodesty**: *drawing attention to one's sexuality or sexual parts through the cut of clothing, the fit of clothing, or a lack of clothing*

*acts*

God designed the function of clothing to cover nakedness (Gen. 3:7, 10–11, 21; see also Gen. 2:25); it is not fitting to expose one's nakedness to others (Gen. 9:20–27; Lev. 18) or to dress and behave in a manner intended to evoke sexual desire outside the bounds of marriage (Prov. 7:10; 1 Tim. 2:9). Christians are responsible to refrain from lustful gazing (Job 21:1; Ps. 101:3; Matt. 5:27–30; see also 2 Sam. 11:2) and to not purposefully seek to attract lustful gazing (Prov. 6:25–26; 7:10 and context).

**pornography**: *pictures, videos, or graphic descriptions intended to stimulate sexual desire*

*context*

We live in a pornographic world; you don't have to go to a pornographic website—these kinds of images inundate mainstream advertising and entertainment and contribute to styles and fads embraced by the culture.

The principles that address immodesty apply even more emphatically to pornography. Feeding one's lust by pictures, videos, or descriptions of nudity and of people performing sexual acts is a blatant sin against God's holy design for sex. Pornography takes something beautiful and turns it into something dirty.

**masturbation**: *sexual self-stimulation*

The purpose for sex is not isolated personal enjoyment, but giving yourself to your spouse and receiving pleasure from your spouse. Sexual self-stimulation results from and leads to lust, physically harming oneself, sexually defrauding a spouse, and misusing the purpose of sex (1 Thess. 4:4). It can also burden you with guilt, negatively affecting your general spiritual walk.

Biblical principles regarding the purpose of sex within marriage (for procreation and the mutual giving of pleasure between spouses) as well as those forbidding lust (Col. 3:5) would seem to forbid this practice even without a specific text of Scripture on this matter.

**sexual activity outside of marriage**

This includes the stoking of sexual desires (lust) through sexting (texting sexual content), intimate touching, making out, dirty talk, and other types of sexual stimulation that don't involve intercourse but may lead to it.

Multiple passages in Scripture warn against this (Prov. 7:10–20; Matt.15:19; Acts 15:20, 29; 1 Cor. 7:2; 1 Thess. 4:3; Rev. 21:8) as well as the lust (the inward desire) and seduction that draw people into sexual activity forbidden in God's law (Matt. 5:27–28; Gal. 5:19; Eph. 5:3; Col. 3:5).

**fornication**: *sexual intercourse between two unmarried people*
*(The KJV sometimes uses this word more broadly to indicate sexual immorality in general.)*

Though it doesn't involve breaking marriage vows, sexual intercourse before marriage twists God's design (Gen. 2:24–25; Exod. 22:16–17; Deut. 22:20–21), and sexually joining oneself to another apart from a marriage covenant harms many.

**prostitution**: *providing sex acts for pay or in return for some benefit*

The Bible clearly forbids and warns against prostitution (Lev. 19:26; Prov. 23:27–28; 1 Cor. 6:13–18). Turning the most intimate act of unity into a commodity to be sold cheapens and defiles the Lord's gift.

**incest**: *sexual relations among family members*

People from the same general family unit (siblings and half-siblings, parents and children or stepchildren) are to be protected from turning a family relationship into a sexual relationship. Failing to provide a safeguard leads to twisted relationships, broken trust, trauma, and abuse.

Both the Old (Lev. 18:6–18) and New Testaments (Luke 3:19; 1 Cor. 5:1) clearly forbid incest. (Early on, before the Mosaic law, brothers and sisters would have married. But the lifespans of people were much longer, and marriage may have taken place later in life, so it is unlikely these brothers and sisters grew up in the same household at the same time.)



## Instruct

### INAPPROPRIATE SEXUAL ACTIVITY

Instruct students to **write** a two-page paper discussing various violations to God's design for sexual activity and the cultural pressures related to it. They should also formulate a plan for maintaining sexual purity among cultural pressures. Students can use the chart on pages 243–44 to help answer the following questions in their papers.

- What constitutes a violation of God's design for sexual activity? What happens when a society celebrates these violations?
- Why is sexual sin enticing?
- What does the Bible say about each subcategory?
- What is marital purity? How is it cultivated?

Further biblical wisdom and solutions will be offered throughout the chapter.

SEXUAL ETHICS 243

## CONSEQUENCES FOR REJECTING THE BIBLICAL ETHIC

Ask this section's **essential question** and guide a **discussion** to prompt students to assess the consequences of rejecting the biblical ethic.

**Why is sex only for marriage?** *One of the purposes for marriage is procreation, with the intent that children would be raised by a father and a mother committed to one another for life. Second, marriage creates a unique, one-flesh union between a husband and a wife. Sexual relations picture this marriage union and thus should not occur outside it.*

**Why are God's commands good?** *God's commands reflect His character, which we were designed to mirror. Abiding by our design is the only way to flourish in God's world. His commands describe what it means to love Him and others for our and their greatest good.*

**How can a Christian's desire to glorify and enjoy God guard him or her from sexual promiscuity?** *Defeating the pleasures of sin requires an even greater pleasure. Knowing God is the greater pleasure. By prizing the pleasure of knowing God above the pleasures of sin, Christians can guard themselves from sexual promiscuity.*

**In what three ways can promiscuity be damaging?**

- *Spiritual damage: Feelings of shame and guilt for violating God's design for sex are real. Some people describe feeling "dirty" after committing sexual sin. Although sex itself is not dirty, sexual sin, as all sin, pollutes the soul. Spiritual destruction does not mean someone committing sexual sin is beyond hope of restoration; it means that sexual sin leaves a devastating impact upon the soul. Therefore, it should serve as a warning not to abuse God's gift of sex.*
- *Physical damage: Immoral sex is dangerous to one's health. Sexually transmitted diseases are clear indications that God disapproves of sexual sin. Lifelong monogamous sexual relations within marriage pose no threat to one's health. Some sexual diseases can be fatal too. This danger should serve as an incentive to keep oneself sexually pure.*
- *Societal damage: A society that revels in sexual sin sows the seeds of its own demise. Broken families, fatherless or motherless children, abortion, and a rising healthcare burden are all heavy costs upon society for disregarding God's design for sex. God's mercy in calling that society to repent should not be ignored.*

| sexual immorality *(continued)* | |
|---|---|
| **sexual abuse**: *any criminal activity that forces any kind of sexual perversion on another person; includes rape and pedophilia* | |
| This is both a criminal and moral matter, so it must be addressed both as a crime by the appropriate governmental authorities and as sin by the appropriate authorities in the church. Many of the same arguments that have been used to persuade society to embrace homosexuality as a person's identity are being used to defend pedophilia. | Under the Mosaic law, rape was a serious offense (Deut. 22:25–29); the New Testament makes clear that someone who would harm a child deserves the harshest of punishments (Matt. 18:6). |
| **homosexuality**: *sexual desires and actions between people of the same God-given sex (males with males or females with females)* | |
| Both homosexual desires and behavior are clearly condemned (Gen. 19 with Jude 1:7; Lev. 18:22; Rom. 1:24–27) and must be turned away from in repentance (1 Cor. 6:9–11). The Bible does not condone treating | sinful desires as an unchangeable part of a person's identity. True, the sin nature is part of who we are after the Fall, but it must be repudiated and put to death (Rom. 8:13; Col. 3:5–10).<br>This will be discussed in detail in Section 13.3. |
| **bestiality**: *sexual behavior with animals* | |
| This is a form of abuse toward an animal and is unfitting for a human being, who should be matched with his or her own kind. | This practice, though rare, is flatly condemned (Exod. 22:19; Lev. 18:23; see also Gen. 2:20). |
| **adultery**: *marital unfaithfulness; lust or sexual activity that violates the marriage covenant of one or both people involved* | |
| Such infidelity breaks trust and deeply damages what is supposed to be a special, unique, and valuable companionship. | The Bible strongly prohibits a married person from engaging in sexual activity with someone outside his or her marriage and condemns those who violate someone else's spouse (Exod. 20:14, 17; Lev. 20:10; Prov. 6:23–35; Matt. 5:27–30; 15:19; 19:9, 18; Rom. 2:22; 13:9; James 2:11). It upholds the importance of marital faithfulness (Mal. 2:14–15). |
| **polygamy**: *having multiple spouses at one time* | |
| Although this practice is currently less common in Western culture, discussions for allowing it have recently increased, and it has been portrayed on television. | God's original design was for an exclusive relationship between one man and one woman (Gen. 2:24). Many Old Testament narratives describe tensions and negative consequences that resulted from polygamous relationships. Elders in the church, who are exemplars of what all Christians ought to be, are not to be in polygamous relationships (1 Tim. 3:2). Nevertheless, this practice was tolerated but limited in the Old Testament (Exod. 21:10–11; Deut. 17:17), and it seems that if a practicing polygamist in our day is converted to Christ, he or she should fulfill familial obligations. |

Inappropriate sexual activity is often fueled by carousing and revelry. Partying often includes drinking, drugs, suggestive clothing, certain types of music, and carnal dancing that all promote a sexually loose atmosphere that lowers inhibitions and fuels lust (Rom. 13:13; 1 Pet. 4:3). The world loves to party, arousing the lusts of the flesh and the eyes (1 John 2:15–17). Don't be deceived by the promises of freedom and fulfillment dangled before you by perversions of God's design for sex (Rom. 7:11). Listen to the instructions of the wise and godly people in your life, and be willing to submit to their attempts to protect you from yourself (Prov. 5:1, 20; 7:1; Heb. 3:13).

**Marital purity** can be defined as forsaking all forbidden sexual activity and partaking in the sexual activity God designed for a man and woman within the bounds of marriage (1 Cor. 7:2–5). Appropriate sexual activity has been limited by God to the marriage relations of one man and one woman for life (Gen. 2:24–25; Prov. 5:18–21; Song of Sol. 1–8; Heb. 13:4).

> We should cultivate purity of heart in sexual matters, avoiding occasions of temptation.
>
> JOHN FRAME[4]

Cultivating purity of heart gets to the root of the problem: lust (Rom. 6:12; Col. 3:5; 2 Tim. 2:22; James 1:14–15). The Bible teaches us to make no provision for the flesh—avoid things that will stoke your lust (Rom. 13:14; 1 Pet. 2:11). Instead, we must walk in the Spirit and by God's grace turn from worldly lusts (Gal. 5:16; Titus 2:11–12; 1 Pet. 4:2–3). This endeavor is diametrically opposed to the spirit of our age (Jude 1:18). Even false teachers within the church will downplay and excuse sexual sin (2 Pet. 2:18–22). Don't be deceived; sexual perversion cannot be excused or toyed with (Prov. 6:27–28; Gal. 6:7). And someone who has engaged in these sexual perversions while in pastoral ministry should never be quickly restored to such a position since he cannot be trusted as an exemplar to lead the church (1 Tim. 3:2). The fruits of true repentance must be demonstrated over a long period of time (2 Cor. 7:10).

### THE DAMAGE OF PROMISCUITY

Why is sex only for marriage?

God's commands describe what it means to love both Him and others. God's commands also reflect the good design of the creation, which in turn reflects God's perfect character. Living according to that design promotes the flourishing of our lives (although we will still suffer in a fallen world). Therefore, we should not view God's restrictions as hampering our fun and freedom. Rather, God's commands are designed for our well-being and the well-being of others. That's why we can delight in God's commands (Pss. 1:2; 119:174; Rom. 7:12, 22; 1 Tim. 1:8). God's commands are not burdensome (Matt. 11:30; 1 John 5:3). They give us true freedom—freedom from the deceptive slavery of sin (Rom. 6:15–16; Gal. 5:13). God reserved sex for marriage to preserve its exquisiteness, creating a unique covenant bond of companionship. By promoting our flourishing, God's commands protect us and others from being used, abused, and thrown away. That's why sexual immorality often leaves people feeling broken, dirty, and traumatized.

The consequences of promiscuity can be greatly damaging in several ways: spiritually, physically, and societally. First, sexual promiscuity damages our relationship with God, who has called us to purity (Eph. 1:4; 4:1). A pattern of promiscuity characterizes those who have been separated from God and do not have a true saving relationship with Him (2 Pet. 2:18–22; Rev. 21:8), and it harms the souls of God's people (Ps. 51:3, 8). Second, sexual promiscuity often causes sexually transmitted diseases (STDs) and other medical problems for those who use and abuse their bodies contrary to God's creational design for sexuality. Third, sexual promiscuity has a ripple effect of disaster that extends from the promiscuous person (guilt and harmful addictions) to his or her family (distrust, shame, hurt, broken relationships), to his or her social circles (disruptions to work, removal from positions, shock and dismay or worse among friends and at church), and to society as a whole (destabilization of communities, negative effects on education, financial costs of broken homes).

In contrast, Christians must be driven by their chief end to glorify and enjoy God by living for God's kingdom and His righteousness (Matt. 6:33). Their pursuit of pleasure should be aligned with God's commands (Ps. 37:4). When pursuit of pleasure runs contrary to God's commands, that pursuit will eventually lead to ruin and judgment. Such deceitful pleasures will never truly satisfy. Considering all the guilt, shame, and ruin caused by sin, people need the hope of the gospel with the forgiveness it offers (1 Cor. 6:11). When a person has felt the full force of the destructiveness of sin, he or she may come to his or her senses and realize the value of serving a loving Father (Luke 15:11–32). But the opportunity for such repentance doesn't last indefinitely (Prov. 1:20–33; Heb. 3:12–15). The wise person learns from instruction rather than through personal destructive experience (Prov. 5:7–14; Eccles. 12:1, 13).

### VIRTUES NECESSARY FOR SEXUAL PURITY

Sexual purity requires the cultivation of virtues from within. Three virtues stand out. *Love* is one. And true love is *self-controlled* and *faithful*. In fact, if someone claims to love but lacks these other virtues, that person is most likely being controlled by lust. And such so-called love will likely fizzle out (2 Sam. 13:15).

A person who has cultivated the virtue of true love will recognize the damage done to oneself and others by engaging in inappropriate sexual activity. Therefore, a person who truly loves another will refrain from sexual activity outside marriage. This is important to understand, because one of the main excuses for extramarital sex is how much two people supposedly love each other and just can't help expressing that love sexually. This is patently false and based on a false sense of love. True love is self-controlled and faithful.

Faithfulness binds a person to another person in a commitment that will be steadfastly maintained. Faithfulness rules out even a consideration of inappropriate sexual activity. Instead, faithful couples cultivate a deep love, focusing on remaining loyal to each other and to their unconditional commitment promised in the marriage ceremony before God and witnesses.



## KEY VIRTUES FOR ACTING ETHICALLY

Use a **Think-Pair-Share** to prompt students to assess the virtues necessary to act ethically regarding sexual purity.

**What three virtues are necessary to act ethically sexually? How and why should these virtues be cultivated?**

- *Love: Couples engaging in sexual sin will often use the word* love *while embracing their non-spousal partner, never realizing that the word* selfishness *more accurately describes their behavior. True love seeks the good of others, but engaging in sexual sin with others is not good for them. Therefore, it cannot be love. Those who love will not take from others what does not belong to them. And if we are not married to someone, that person's body does not belong to us for sexual union. Cultivating love is necessary to see people as people rather than objects for our selfish gratification. We cultivate the virtue of love for others by abiding in Christ's love for us, and by His Word abiding in us.*
- *Faithfulness: When two people vow to one another in marriage to forsake all others, they promise to keep their sexual union free from the intrusion of other partners. Faithfulness is the lifelong fulfillment of that promise. To break one's promise and commit adultery is to be unfaithful to one's spouse. Faithfulness is cultivated by the constant reminder of God's covenant faithfulness to believers. Even single people can be faithful to their potential future spouse by remaining sexually pure before marriage. The golden rule can help here. If you want your future spouse to be sexually pure, then do unto your future spouse what you're hoping he or she will do for you.*
- *Self-control: The Bible never underestimates the power of the sexual drive. On the contrary, the Bible is very realistic about the strength of sexual desire, hence all the biblical warnings not to play fast and loose with it. But as strong as sexual desires are, Christians are not at their mercy. The spiritual fruit of self-control means that believers are able to keep their desires in check. Be honest about your desires. Cultivating self-control is done in the context of accountability to other believers committed to Christ and the biblical ethic.*

## Apply

### PLANNING TO LIVE WITH CONVICTIONS

Use **Activity 13.2** on page 81 to help students respond with biblical wisdom to the issues of fornication and adultery.

## Assess

Guide a **summative assessment** by directing students to answer the questions in Thinking It Through 13.2.

### Thinking It Through 13.2

1. sexual intercourse between two unmarried people; sexual immorality
2. marital unfaithfulness; lust or sexual activity that violates the marriage covenant of one or both people involved
3. forsaking all forbidden sexual activity and partaking in the sexual activity God designed for a man and woman within the bounds of marriage
4. See the chart on pages 243–44 for potential student answers.
5. Promiscuity damages in three ways. Spiritually, it hurts one's relationship with God. Physically, it hurts one's own body. Societally, it hurts other people.
6. Self-control: not allowing lust to direct sexual desires in violation of God's commands and purposes for those God-created desires
7. See the speech bubbles on page 246 for potential student answers.

If the heart of the problem is lust (out-of-control sexual desire), then one of *the* key virtues to cultivate within yourself would be self-control. In clarifying what exactly lust is, John Frame makes these helpful comments:

> Lust is not sexual desire as such. That is something good, a God-given incentive to marriage, to intimacy within marriage, and to reproduction. . . . First Corinthians 7:9 does not condemn the desire itself, but only a desire that cannot be controlled.[5]

Self-control is not the only thing that will keep you sexually pure. But it is certainly one virtue that will keep you from being foolish. How many teens could have prevented their lives from being turned upside down if they had waited only a few more years for marriage? Exercise of self-control (and willingness to submit to the safeguards of accountability) could save much destructive living and heartache.

### PLANNING TO LIVE WITH CONVICTION

context

How can you plan to maintain sexual purity before and during marriage? Read Proverbs 7:1–6, and then consider these guidelines drawn from the rest of Proverbs 7.

Don't be naive, thinking you're above sin and its consequences. Stay on guard (7:7).
Don't approve of or practice immodesty; both men and women can be culpable of enticing by what they wear and of lusting when enticed (7:10).
Don't approve of or practice double-entendre (veiled dirty talk) or brazen impure talk (7:10–11; 16–18, 21).
Don't put yourself in compromising situations (7:8–9, 12).
Don't be alone with someone of the opposite sex without accountability; welcome the oversight of others who will help protect you (7:19–20).
Don't play around with physical intimacy that draws you into more and more physical intimacy (7:13).
Don't be duped by flattery and enticements to sin (7:13–21).
Count the cost of immorality: it leads to ruin (7:22–27).


### Thinking It Through 13.2

1. Define *fornication*.
2. Define *adultery*.
3. Define *marital purity*.
4. Identify and explain at least three types of inappropriate sexual activity. Provide biblical support.
5. Summarize three consequences of sexual promiscuity.
6. Identify and explain one virtue that would address the root problem of sexual promiscuity.
7. Provide at least three guidelines that would help you plan to avoid sexual impurity.

## 13.3 Homosexuality, Bisexuality, and Transgenderism

The discussion in this section demands a lot from you: maturity, humility, a commitment to truth and righteousness, and compassion. If you love God, then you will have an unwavering commitment to His righteous character, His created order, and His Word. If you love others, you will display compassion informed by God's view of what is good and right for people's well-being according to His wise design.

We all need to have compassion without compromise. That means that we will not accept, accommodate, or approve of *unethical desires and behavior.* We also will not deride or act in ungodly ways toward *a person made in God's image*. The difficulty in walking this fine line is that our culture is confused about what is ethical and what is creational (the essence, or objective reality, of who a person is, regardless of feelings). You may be accused of hating the person whose unethical desires and behaviors you oppose because those desires and behaviors are made out to be that person's identity.

For example, a baker has baked cakes for a customer who identifies as a homosexual, even cultivating a friendship over the years. (The baker has no problem treating the customer well as an image-bearer of God.) But that same baker refuses to bake a wedding cake for a homosexual wedding ceremony, due to religious and moral convictions. (He cannot participate in, promote, or help with what he considers to be sin.) That baker gets sued for discriminating *against those persons*. Our culture has blurred the lines between opposing a person and opposing what a person stands for and wants everyone else to support.

Before continuing our evaluation of our culture and the biblical teaching and virtues that drive an ethical response, we need to understand some basic terms. The term ***homosexual*** (which includes both lesbian and gay categories, the *L* and the *G* in the **LGBTQ+** abbreviation) refers to someone with sexual desires for a person of the same sex or who engages in sexual behavior with a person of the same sex (male with male or female with female). The term ***bisexual*** (the *B* in the LGBTQ+ abbreviation) refers to someone with sexual desires for or who engages in sexual behavior with both men and women. The term ***transgender*** (the *T* in the LGBTQ+ abbreviation) refers to someone who thinks of him or herself as having a gender different from his or her sex. This category is based on an assertion that people can choose gender for themselves rather than genders being determined by God-granted biology and genetics (males have XY chromosomes and females have XX chromosomes). The Q in the acronym can refer to *queer* or *questioning*. The + is shorthand for more letters that are sometimes included to represent the growing spectrum of invented gender identities.



## 13.3 Homosexuality, Bisexuality, and Transgenderism

*Is the Bible's sexual ethic unloving?*

### Objectives

**13.3.1** Identify recent LGBTQ+ trends.

**13.3.2** Summarize the biblical teaching regarding human sexuality and gender. BWS

**13.3.3** Assess the personal and societal consequences of rejecting God's design for human sexuality and gender. BWS

**13.3.4** Assess the virtues necessary to embrace God's design for human sexuality and gender. BWS

**13.3.5** Formulate a response to a friend who is considering a same-sex relationship or a transgender transition. BWS

### Biblical Worldview Shaping

- **Creational Order** (explain): God created mankind male and female, and God designed all sexual activity to take place between a man and a woman within a covenant of marriage. (13.3.2)
- **Man's Chief End** (evaluate): God calls on all people to delight in His law because it is good and for their good. (13.3.3)
- **Virtue** (formulate): Faithfulness to God's design for sexuality requires commitment to righteousness, Spirit-empowered self-control in the face of temptation, and steadfastness in the face of cultural pressure. (13.3.4)
- **Wisdom** (apply): Helping a friend in this area requires dependence upon God's work in one's heart and a loving commitment to speak the truth, which can set the friend free from slavery to sin. (13.3.5)

### Printed Resource

- Activity 13.3: A Biblical Response to LGBTQ+

### Digital Resources

- Video: "Homosexuality, Bisexuality, Transgenderism"
- Link: An Interview with Rosaria Butterfield

### Suggested Reading

- Frame, John M. *The Doctrine of the Christian Life*. Phillipsburg, NJ: P&R Publishing, 2008. Pages 622–47, 757–63.
- Grudem, Wayne. *Christian Ethics: An Introduction to Biblical Moral Reasoning*. Wheaton, IL: Crossway, 2018. Pages 843–93.
- Magnuson, Ken. *Invitation to Christian Ethics: Moral Reasoning and Contemporary Issues*. Grand Rapids, MI: Kregel Academic, 2020. Pages 266–320.

## Engage

### HOMOSEXUALITY, BISEXUALITY, TRANSGENDERISM

Show the **video** "Homosexuality, Bisexuality, Transgenderism" to introduce the subject to students.

### COMPASSION WITHOUT COMPROMISE

Use a **group activity** in which students discuss the following questions in order to preassess their understanding of the biblical principles as well as the culture in which they live.

**How would you discern whether a professing Christian is wrongly compromised or rightly compassionate in response to LGBTQ+?** *A Christian has wrongly compromised if the compassion is based on a secular approach toward tolerance and coexistence or a sentimental understanding of love. A Christian is rightly compassionate if the compassion is based on a biblical ethic, which is concerned about God's righteousness and law. A biblical ethic also seeks to rescue people from God's judgment by calling them to repent from the destructiveness of their sin.* **What does it mean to have biblical compassion toward sinners?** *Biblical compassion will be demonstrated in one's respect for* *people as image-bearers while being saddened over their embrace of destructive lifestyles rather than approving or equivocating on the sins that they identify with and embrace.*

**Why is it important to not compromise biblical morality in one's efforts to show compassion to sinners?** *Christians ought not to accept, accommodate, or approve of unethical desires or behavior, because they love God and His righteousness. Christians ought to be more concerned about pleasing God and standing for Him than pleasing the culture and not offending people with God's standard of righteousness.*

**Why is showing compassion without compromise most often misconstrued as hatred?** *Currently, the culture has confused the categories of what is creational and what is ethical so that they will not accept the distinction between God's created order and a person's unethical (sinful) deviation from that created order. If you oppose that which is unethical, you are viewed as opposing that person as a person.*

**Can you provide examples of the confusion in our culture between that which is ethical and that which is creational? How does this confusion cause problems in society for convictional Christians?** *Our culture has blurred the lines between people and their immoral lifestyles. Multiple examples from the past decade or so in American culture illustrate people's efforts to distinguish between serving people, which they will willingly do, versus serving those people's immoral stances and events, which they do not wish to do. However, our culture judges those who do not wish to support LGBTQ+ stances and events.*

context

### LGBTQ+ TRENDS

Same-sex sin and gender confusion aren't anything new. The Bible dealt with these issues in ancient Israel (Gen. 1:27; 19:4–8 with Judg. 19:20–30 and Jude 1:7; Lev. 18:22; 20:13; Deut. 22:5) and in the first century (Rom. 1:26–27; 1 Cor. 6:9–11; 1 Tim. 1:10). Humans from every era and in every place have the same sinful heart (Ps. 51:5; Rom. 3:23).

However, cultures in different times and places can manifest different kinds of sinfulness to a greater or lesser degree (2 Tim. 3:13). In fact, when a culture spirals deeper into depravity, it blatantly manifests these kinds of sins (Rom. 1:24, 32). Through the restraining work of the Spirit, the influence of Christians and Christian ethics, and even the consciences of unsaved people, these kinds of sins may be uncommon or at least hidden—due to a cultural recognition that such behaviors should be viewed as depraved. Recognition of this kind of depravity used to be the common understanding of much of the Western world, highly influenced by a biblical ethic—until recently. Denny Burk and Heath Lambert summarize the staggering change that has taken place in America:

> Most Christians have been surprised by the velocity of cultural change on the issue of homosexuality. Just one measure of that change is the acceptance of homosexual marriage. In 2005, same-sex marriage was illegal in every state in America. In 2015, the Supreme Court of the United States has declared same-sex marriage to be a constitutional right nationwide. That is a tremendous amount of change for one decade.[6]

In addition to the changed perspective in society, the church has also grappled with challenges to the biblical ethic on this matter as never before. Wayne Grudem says,

> To my knowledge, no evangelical Christian pastors or Bible scholars in previous generations ever claimed that the Bible gives moral approval to any kind of homosexual conduct. The unanimous consensus of centuries of Christian teaching on such a major moral issue cannot be dismissed lightly.[7]

More recently, however, self-professed evangelicals have been trying to find ways to accommodate the Bible to homosexuality, bisexuality, and transgenderism. Bible-believing pastors, counselors, and scholars have had to write numerous, detailed defenses of the biblical ethic in response to challenges to its clarity.

What led to this hypersonic change in sexual ethics? The changed perspective in society didn't come out of nowhere. Ideas have consequences. And some key philosophical influences on our society have produced this changing ethic. Just one of those influences can be traced back to a philosopher you were introduced to in Chapter 2: the existentialist Jean-Paul Sartre. This philosopher is famous for teaching that existence precedes essence.[8] That means that you exist first as a person. Then you create for yourself the essence of who you want to be. You're in charge of the very essence of your being. In other words, you are in charge of who you want to be or become.

The complexities of philosophy get translated into the simplistic sayings of popular culture: "Follow your heart." "Be true to yourself." "You can become anything you want to be."[9] And by "anything," our culture means *anything*: a man can choose to become a woman, and a woman can choose to become a man. Society increasingly rejects the idea of a God-created, God-designed, and God-granted essence to one's existence that is objectively real, regardless of one's feelings.



## Instruct

### WHAT'S NEW ABOUT LGBTQ+?

Use a **Quick Write** to prompt students to reckon with the reality of the shifts that have taken place in their culture only recently and why such a shift occurred.

**In what sense are the LGBTQ+ issues nothing new?** *Humans in every era have the same sinful hearts, though they may manifest that sin in different ways. The Bible addresses these issues in both ancient Israel and in the first-century church.*

**In what sense are the LGBTQ+ issues relatively new to our culture?** *Western culture used to be highly influenced by the Christian ethic. For instance, in all of the United States, same-sex marriage was outlawed as recently as 2005, but by 2015 same-sex marriage was codified into law as a constitutional right (Adapted from page 14 of* Transforming Homosexuality: What the Bible Says about Sexual Orientation and Change *by Denny Burk and Heath Lambert. Copyright 2015, P&R Publishing, Phillipsburg, NJ). Western culture has now shifted away from respecting God and His Word. Furthermore, Christianity used to unanimously recognize that homosexuality was unbiblical (Adapted from page 202 of* Invitation to Christian Ethics: Moral Reasoning and Contemporary Issues *© Copyright 2020 by Ken Magnuson, Invitation to Theological Studies Series. Published by Kregel Publications, Grand Rapids, MI. Used by permission of the publisher. All rights reserved.). Now even evangelical Christians are wrestling over the clarity of the Bible on this matter.*

**What's one idea that underlies this massive shift in the culture?** *the existentialist idea that humans are in charge of determining their own essences rather than recognizing the creational design and God-granted essence given to them*

## THE CLARITY OF THE BIBLE ON GENDER AND SEXUALITY

### *Gender*

We are not our own, and this reality should cause us to rejoice (Ps. 100:3)! Because God created us, we belong: we have purpose. We are not lost, left to figure out who we are and what we should be doing. We don't need to find ourselves. We find security and stability in our lives by joyfully submitting to our Creator and His perfect created order designed for human flourishing.

God's created order includes two distinct genders (male and female) in one human race, labeled *man* (Gen. 1:26–27; 5:1–2). Gender is not a psychological construct—with endless ideas about where one might fit on a spectrum between male and female. Gender corresponds with biological reality. The so-called gender spectrum is rooted in distorted thinking arising from fallen desires that must be repudiated as untrue and wrong. Regardless of what a person does cosmetically to hide or change appearances, genetic realities define one's essence as designed by God.

Scripture never distinguishes gender from biology; Scripture presumes that it is readily apparent who is a male or female based on biological observations. It addresses men as men and women as women with the assumption that nobody is truly confused over who is who. Scripture condemns men who portray themselves as women and women who portray themselves as men (Deut. 22:5). The Mosaic law includes commands like this that reflect an application of creational norms that transcend the Old Covenant. Thus, this command would, in principle, also apply to us today. Nature itself teaches appropriate gender distinctions (1 Cor. 11:14–15); our rebellious culture makes it difficult to distinguish between men and women. Our culture is also rebelling against gender roles. The Bible distinguishes the roles of men and women in society (Gen. 3:16; Isa. 3:12), the family (1 Cor. 11:3), and the church (1 Tim. 2:11–15).

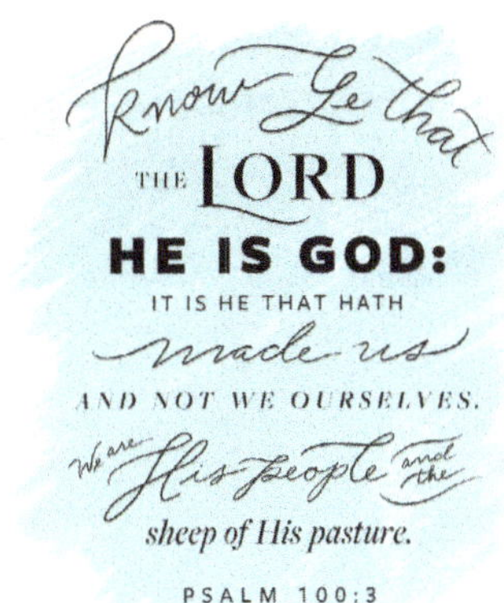

Know Ye that
THE LORD
HE IS GOD:
IT IS HE THAT HATH
made us
AND NOT WE OURSELVES.
We are His people and the
sheep of His pasture.
PSALM 100:3


*Every person's sense of his or her own 'gender identity' should be the same as that person's biological sex.*

WAYNE GRUDEM[10]

### *Sexuality*

The biblical pattern for appropriate sexual desires and behaviors is given in Genesis 2:22–24 and reinforced by Jesus Himself in Matthew 19:4–6: one man and one woman joined by covenant for life. God designed this sexual union for two distinct, complementary individuals who are joined together as one flesh, often resulting in procreation. Deviations from that pattern are flatly condemned in both the Old (Gen. 19:4–8; Lev. 18:22; 20:13) and New Testaments (Rom. 1:21–32; 1 Cor. 6:9–11; 1 Tim. 1:10; Jude 1:7).

Both the biblical pattern and Scripture's verdict on deviations from that pattern should be clear enough if you take the time to read each text. However, each text has been challenged by those who support homosexual desires or behavior while seeking to retain some adherence to the Bible. As weak as these arguments are, they have influenced many who have a superficial understanding of Scripture or a feeble commitment to its authority. You need to be equipped with answers to some of their most popular arguments.

## IS THE BIBLE CLEAR ON GENDER?

Use a **misconception check** to make the connection between the created order and ethical living.

Ask the students whether the following statements are True or False. Instruct the students to explain their answers.

**True or False: A part of the natural process of growing up includes finding yourself and establishing your own identity—including deciding which gender you want to be.** *False*

*God has told us who we are, what our purpose is, how to function according to His creational order, and where to find our core identity—in Christ. The created order defines our gender, and God's Word guides how we should function within our God-given gender. And this provides stability, confidence, and true freedom from slavery to sin and the anxieties that accompany it.*

**True or False: True freedom is found in being an autonomous, independent person who gets to create his or her own essence and identity.** *False*

*True freedom is found in fulfilling one's created design and purpose. Anything contrary to this leads to disorder and ruin due to rebellion and its consequences.*

**True or False: Rather than being a psychological or social construct, gender is a biological and genetic reality rooted in the created order that the Fall never overturned—one race of humans, male and female.** *True*

*The feelings or ideas that contradict this truth are evidence of the Fall that cause people to think or feel in distorted and disordered ways contrary to reality.*

**True or False: People are successfully changing their genders today through the advancements of medical therapies and surgeries.** *False*

*People may be changing and distorting their appearances, but such changes cannot override biological and genetic realities.*

**True or False: Deuteronomy 22:5 is part of the Old Testament law that is archaic and no longer applies to us today.** *False*

*The Old Testament law reflects God's creational norms, and its principles carry over to New Covenant believers even in their new context—especially when the same creational norm is explicitly repeated in the New Testament (1 Cor. 11:14–15).*

**True or False: The Bible distinguishes the roles of men and women in the home, church, and society. These distinctions are all-encompassing because the reason for them is rooted in the created order.** *True*

*These roles are not culturally defined or haphazard; they are purposefully designed into the fabric of the created order for all time. "In Christ" there are no gender distinctions regarding one's righteous standing before God. But the distinctions remain in the society, where God has designed specific purposes for men and women (e.g., Titus 2:1–8).*

## IS THE BIBLE CLEAR ON SEXUALITY?

Use a **Turn and Talk** to prompt students to enunciate to each other what the Bible clearly says.

**What is the biblical pattern for appropriate expressions of sexual desires and behaviors (Gen. 2:22–24; Matt. 19:4–6; Heb. 13:4)?** *God designed the marriage covenant, including sexual relations within it, between one man and one woman for life, along with the blessing of procreation.*

**How does the Bible condemn deviations from this pattern in each of the following texts?** *Student answers should reflect what the following texts explicitly say.*

- Genesis 19:4–8 (see also the context of Chapter 19, including Genesis 18:20–33)
- Leviticus 18:22; 20:13
- Romans 1:21–32
- 1 Corinthians 6:9–11
- 1 Timothy 1:10
- Jude 1:7

## OBJECTIONS TO THE BIBLICAL ETHIC

Assign a **one-page essay** for the students to summarize and respond to one of the false arguments against the biblical ethic on pages 250–52.

Choose one of the six false arguments against the biblical ethic. Summarize the argument. Give the biblical counterargument to the false argument.

Students may want to expand their research by reading the relevant chapters in the Suggested Reading or one of the following recommendations:

- Burk, Denny. *What Is the Meaning of Sex?* Wheaton, IL: Crossway, 2013.
- Burk, Denny, and Heath Lambert. *Transforming Homosexuality: What the Bible Says about Sexual Orientation and Change.* Phillipsburg, NJ: P&R Publishing, 2015.
- DeYoung, Kevin. *What Does the Bible Really Teach about Homosexuality?* Wheaton, IL: Crossway, 2015.

# Are Christians wrong to use the Bible to condemn homosexuality?

Some professing Christians question whether the Bible condemns all homosexual behavior or desires. They use alternative interpretations of Scripture to challenge Christians who have traditionally interpreted and applied the Bible as wholly condemning such things. In addition, even Christians who believe homosexual behavior is wrong debate about how homosexual sin should be understood and how Christians who battle homosexual temptations should label themselves. What follows addresses these arguments and questions.

### FALSE ARGUMENT #1

***"The story of Sodom does not condemn loving, committed homosexual relationships."***

One common argument is that Genesis 19 has nothing to do with identifying homosexuality as the sin of Sodom. The claim is that the men of Sodom were guilty only of wanting to participate in a homosexual rape—the homosexual desires and behavior in general are not condemned but only the intention to rape. But this ignores both the pattern for human sexuality in Genesis 2 as well as the straightforward condemnations of homosexuality in other passages of Scripture (for example, see Lev. 18:22; 20:13). The men of Sodom were guilty of wanting to participate in homosexual rape, but *both* the rape and the homosexual desires were wrong.

Another argument claims that the men of Sodom were guilty only for inhospitality, since Ezekiel 16:49 lists pride and lack of hospitality (failing to care for the poor), not homosexual sin, as Sodom's offense. However, Ezekiel 16:50 identifies Sodom's sin as "abomination," which would have been understood to be homosexuality (see Lev. 18:22). In addition, Genesis 19 must be read in context. Sodom's sin was considered "very grievous" (Gen. 18:20) and pervasive. Not even ten righteous people existed in that city (Gen. 18:32). The sin at Lot's house was one expression of a thoroughgoing cultural depravity. Furthermore, the Bible is clear that the euphemism of wanting to "know" someone (Gen. 19:5) means sexual relations (Gen. 4:1, 17, 25; Judg. 19:22). Finally, Jude 1:7 makes abundantly clear that the sin of Sodom was sexual. Sodom's sin was multifaceted: arrogance and autonomy led to gross inhospitality (more precisely, an absence of practical love) and to twisted rebellion against God's design for sex.

### FALSE ARGUMENT #2

***"Opponents of homosexual relationships pick and choose which Old Testament laws to follow."***

Yet another charge against the biblical view is that Christians are picking and choosing which Old Testament laws to follow and which ones not to follow. The claim is that Christians eat shellfish and wear mixed fabrics (both condemned in the Mosaic law), but they still hold onto the laws against homosexuality. The implication is that Christians are inconsistent and should throw out the whole Old Testament law. This charge reflects a poor understanding of the Mosaic law and the Christian's relationship to the law. The laws regarding fabric and shellfish are unique to the Mosaic law and served a teaching purpose for Israel. Laws regarding sexual morality transcend the Mosaic law and are true in all times and places. How do we know this? First, same-sex lust and relations were contrary to God's creational design (Gen. 1–2) long before Moses gave the law to the nation of Israel. Second, the law of Moses is an application of God's creational design to His people in that nation. The underlying creational design has not changed. Third, Leviticus 18:24–25 says that God judged the Gentile nations in Canaan for these sins. Thus, these prohibitions are not unique to the Mosaic Covenant or the nation of Israel. Fourth, none of the moral principles of the law are ever overturned. While the Mosaic law contains some provisions that are in force only under that covenant, other provisions are in force in all times and places because they are rooted in God's character and the moral order built into creation. Fifth, the New Testament repeats laws from the Old Testament that believers in Christ must clearly still follow (for example, see Rom. 1:21–32; 1 Cor. 6:9–11; 1 Tim. 1:10; Jude 1:7). The laws in Leviticus 18 that condemn sexual perversions are still relevant—against adultery, incest, bestiality, and sexual relations between people of the same sex.

## FALSE ARGUMENT #3

*"The New Testament does not forbid committed homosexual relationships, only predatory ones."*

In response to the New Testament condemnations (particularly Rom. 1:21–32 and 1 Tim. 1:10), some have tried to claim that Paul was not really condemning homosexuality but homosexual predation. Others have tried to claim that Paul was telling people with a *heterosexual* orientation not to practice homosexuality; they claim Paul never said those who had a homosexual orientation by nature couldn't practice it. Still others claim that Paul was conforming to his own day's cultural expectations; they say our cultural expectations have changed, allowing for the practice of homosexuality now. All these reinterpretations of New Testament teaching are simply dishonest treatments of the text.

First, Paul was not limiting his condemnation to predation or exploitation. Both partners in the act are equally condemned, indicating that Paul was not condemning a more powerful predator while recognizing an innocent victim (by contrast, see the differentiation made in Deut. 22:25–26). Nothing in the text itself even suggests this claim; homosexuality is wholly condemned.

Second, the Bible never recognizes a homosexual orientation as an unchanging, essential part of a person's being. Rather, that kind of orientation stems from an ethical problem: sinful desires that stem from original sin. We are sinners by nature who twist God's creational design. It may be true that a person feels that he or she was born with a tendency to same-sex attraction. That tendency could exist as a manifestation of someone's sin nature and yet still be "against nature" (Rom. 1:26), that is, contrary to God's creational design.

Third, Romans 1 is not simply condemning sexual exploitation, a lack of committed relationships, or rebellion against cultural expectations of the day; it is condemning people for turning away from God's design in nature (Rom. 1:26–27). "Against nature" means contrary to the biological complementary design of male and female, a design made clear by the natural outcome of procreation that is part of God's intent for sexual relations. The point is that even pagans should know from observing the natural world that this behavior is depraved and contrary to God's design. This natural law should be evident even apart from the Mosaic law.

## FALSE ARGUMENT #4

*"The Bible does not talk much about same-sex relations and neither should the church today."*

Another popular claim is that the Bible doesn't really say much about this sin. Instead of defending same-sex relations, those who speak this way often wish the church to be silent on this matter, a first step toward compromise on this issue.

It's simply untrue that the Bible does not talk much about this sin. Plenty of biblical texts have been surveyed here in this section. In addition, whenever the Bible upholds the pattern established in Genesis 1–2, and whenever the Bible condemns sexual immorality in general, the Bible is condemning homosexuality.

Why are Christians speaking against homosexual sins so often right now? Society is currently challenging the biblical ethic on this issue especially. Society at large sees opposition to homosexuality as an outrage, and its opposition to Christianity on this point is hindering some Christians' ability to practice their faith in the public square. The prominence of this issue in today's culture has forced Christians to respond with more focused attention than ever before.

## FALSE ARGUMENT #5

*"Homosexual sins are no worse than other sins."*

It was once common to hear claims that homosexual sins were the worst possible kind of sin. It has now become popular to claim that homosexual sins are no worse than any other sin. The Bible teaches that all sin is sin—from showing partiality to unlawfully taking someone's life. A violation of God's law in a single point results in a guilty verdict before God. Nonetheless, the Bible itself teaches that some sins are greater than others (Ezek. 8:6; John 19:11). And some sins can reflect hearts that have gone from bad to worse (Rom. 1:21–32; 2 Tim. 3:13). The Bible even categorizes some sins as especially repulsive to God, calling them abominations (see Lev. 18:22, 26–27). Homosexuality is worse than many other sexual sins because it goes against the fundamental nature of God's created order[11] as expressed in the Creation Mandate. Nonetheless there are arguably worse sins than homosexuality—blasphemy of the Holy Spirit and unbelief, for example (Matt. 11:21–24; 12:31).



SEXUAL ETHICS 251

# Are Christians wrong to use the Bible to condemn homosexuality?

## FALSE ARGUMENT #6

*"Same-sex attraction is not sinful."*

Another challenge faces Bible-believing churches. How should people with same-sex attraction be counseled? There has been a lot of confusion over whether desires to sin are themselves sinful or simply temptations that fall short of being sin.

The Bible specifies that the root of sinful behavior is in the heart with its desires (James 1:13–14). The Bible warns against sinful desires: lust as well as the act of adultery is sinful (Exod. 20:14, 17 with Matt. 5:28), and covetousness as well as theft is sinful (Exod. 20:15, 17). If by *same-sex attraction* one means sexually desiring someone of the same sex, then same-sex attraction is a forbidden lust. The Bible teaches that God's goal is the transformation of the heart, not just external compliance (1 Sam. 16:7).

This is confusing to many who argue that temptations to sin are not themselves sinful. This was a matter of debate between the Protestant Reformers and Roman Catholics. The Reformers agreed with the Catholic Church that the "first stage" of temptation, an outward occasion or suggestion of sin, is not itself sin, because it is external to the person. The Reformers and Catholic Church also agreed that the "third stage" of temptation, in which a person gives in to the temptation, is sin. But they disagreed on the "second stage," in which a person desires the sin but has not yet decided to follow it. The Reformers asserted that desires to sin are themselves sinful.[12] Thus, temptations are not necessarily sin if the temptations are externally provoking us to sin, but temptations arising from our own degrading passions (Rom. 1:26) or "lust" (Rom. 1:27) entails sin because desiring to commit sinful acts is itself sinful. This is true whether those desires are heterosexual or homosexual. Everyone is born with a propensity toward sin, and that propensity is itself sinful. It is called *original sin*.

The whole point of the gospel is that, while we are unable to transform ourselves, *Christ can* transform us (Phil. 2:13). The sanctification process takes time, but Christians can put sinful desires to death (Rom. 6:12–14) through a pattern of putting off vices and putting on virtues and renewing the mind (2 Cor. 5:17; Col. 3:5–14; Ps. 51:10). Sinful desires may not be entirely eradicated in this life, but they can be more and more consistently turned away from (1 John 3:1–10) by the power of God, who transforms us through a process that includes our active submission to Him.

## GAY CHRISTIANS?

Finally, there is a debate about whether Christians who battle same-sex temptations should be identified by the label *gay Christian*. Some Christians argue that the label *gay* simply refers to their temptations. However, it is unwise for Christians to identify themselves in terms of their sins. A Christian shouldn't identify as a gay Christian any more than someone should identify as an adulterous Christian or a lying Christian. First Corinthians 6:11 puts these sinful identifications in the past: "Such *were* some of you" (emphasis added). To be sure, Christians still struggle with temptation and with their flesh. But their identity is now in Christ, rather than in their sin.

### CONCLUSION

The traditional biblical position has not been overturned by any of the arguments that seek to harmonize the Bible and homosexual practice. These arguments attempt to explain away what is clearly understood from a straightforward reading of the Scripture text in context. Bible-believing Christians should not be intimidated or moved from the biblical position by those who try to reinterpret or read into the Scriptures what has never been recognized by orthodox Christianity for thousands of years. Likewise, precision about the nature of homosexual sin and how to think about temptations in this area are important for the health of the church.

### THE CONSEQUENCES OF REJECTING GOD'S DESIGN

Both personal and societal consequences can occur from living contrary to God's design. On the personal level, there is loss as transient relationships replace lifelong commitments. There is pain as relationships that are entered into without lifelong commitments break apart. And though not everybody who is sexually immoral contracts a sexually transmitted disease, STDs are a consequence for some. Most significant, an unrepentant immoral person is under God's judgment (Rom. 1:26–32).

Societal consequences also follow as more people stray from God's design for marriage. One consequence is that fewer people are having children. While at one time some (wrongly) worried about over-population, now the worry is that a shrinking population will disrupt economic prosperity to the point at which significant social unrest becomes more likely.[13]

As homosexual relationships are mainstreamed, it becomes more difficult for same-sex friendships to be deep without having to combat the perception that they are or should be sexualized. The same tensions present in friendships between men and women may affect friendships between men and men or women and women. Hesitance to build close friendships furthers the alienation that many in society are already feeling.

Debates over transgenderism have increased societal conflicts. As transgender advocates insist that men who identify as women be allowed in women-only spaces, such as bathrooms and women's shelters, many women argue that the intrusion of men into these spaces makes them less safe. Furthermore, with the slogan "Trans women are women," transgender advocates also insist that men who identify as women be allowed to participate in women's sports. But this slogan does not capture the biological differences between men and women that give men an advantage in these sports. More significant, many children who claim to be transgender have been given puberty-blocking drugs and have undergone irreversible surgeries. They will have to live with the effects of these procedures, and as some of them grow up and realize the gravity and permanence of what has been done to them, society will have to reckon with what it has promoted. At present, those who reject transgenderism are under pressure to speak and act in ways that they believe are truly harmful to those who identify as transgender. Failing to do so—for instance, failing to use a person's preferred pronouns—can result in job loss.

One thing is clear: sexual ethics is not merely a matter for consenting adults in the privacy of their homes. Sexual ethics invariably has significant society-wide consequences. How could it be otherwise, since God created a man and a woman and gave as His first command to them, "Be fruitful, and multiply" (Gen. 1:28)?

#### What Does It Mean to Love My Neighbor If My Neighbor Rejects God's Design for Sex?

**Is the Bible's sexual ethic unloving?**

The most common accusation against those who clearly enunciate the biblical ethic is that they are unloving. That accusation seems so powerful that some Bible-believing Christians are silent or accommodating on this issue. No doubt, some speak about homosexual sin in an unloving manner and with motives other than the salvation of the sinner. But there can also be clear statements of biblical teaching regarding homosexual sin that are motivated by true, biblically defined love (2 Tim. 4:2; see also Eph. 4:15).

Most of the time, the accusation that Christians are unloving is based on a wrong definition and description of love. Love is not merely sentimental affirmation of others. Calling people to live in conformity to God's commands is loving in that God's commands are designed for our flourishing. As Psalm 1 teaches, the blessed man is the one who delights in God's law; he is like a flourishing tree. God calls on all people to delight in His law because it is good and for their good. Sin is destructive: "the way of the ungodly shall perish" (Ps. 1:6). Ultimately that destruction will occur in the final judgment, but it can also manifest itself in the present. Indeed, Paul teaches that turning a people over to homosexual lusts is itself part of God's judgment (Rom. 1:26–27). Accommodating this culture's desire for so-called sexual freedom furthers its self-destruction and accelerates its judgment, which is hardly loving. The most loving thing to do is to call upon people to repent, submit to the God who created them, and begin functioning according to His good design.

But the heart behind the call to repentance must be love for the sinner. We have all seen or heard about those who spew diatribes like "God hates fags!", implying that God wants certain people to burn in hell. That's not the gospel or biblical Christianity! Biblical Christianity recognizes that we have all been under the judgment of God, deserving of hell (Rom. 3:23; 6:23). And biblical Christianity seeks to reach people, rescuing them from such a plight (Jude 1:18–23). Those who stubbornly harden their hearts will indeed face only condemnation. But those who still have an opportunity to repent should be offered the grace that teaches them to deny ungodliness (Titus 2:11–12).

Read "An Interview with Rosaria Butterfield—A Friend of Sinners" on AnswersinGenesis.org or in *Answers Magazine*. How did the pastor and his family show her compassion without compromise as they witnessed to her when she was a lesbian activist?

SEXUAL ETHICS 253

## PERSONAL AND SOCIAL CONSEQUENCES

Use a **Think-Pair-Share** to prompt students to assess the personal and social consequences of rejecting God's design.

**What are the personal and social consequences of rejecting God's design for sexuality by embracing homosexuality or transgenderism? Can you think of consequences in addition to what was mentioned in the textbook or expand on the categories mentioned in the textbook?** *Possible answers:*

- *Personal consequences: disordered relationships, STDs, God's judgment*
- *Social consequences: the undermining of marriage and procreation; fractured relationships; threats to women's safety; undermining women's competitive sports; irreversible physical and mental harm on children; loss of freedom of speech and freedom to counsel; job loss*

# Apply

## WHAT DOES IT MEAN TO LOVE MY NEIGHBOR?

Guide a **discussion** to clarify what it means to love your neighbor.

**If I am supposed to have a God's-eye view of sin and God describes homosexual behavior as an abomination (Lev. 18:22), then what is supposed to be my view of that sin?** *Since God views such sin as an abomination, then we should view it that way too. We should have such love for God and His law that we hate sin as God does.*

**If I am supposed to have a heart like God toward sinners (2 Pet. 3:9), then how am I supposed to express love toward them even when I see them in the midst of their sin (Rom. 5:8)?** *God loves sinners so much that he sent His Son to die for them. We should imitate God in loving sinners to the point that we would be willing to die to see them saved (cf. Rom. 9:3).*

To further understand God's wrath and love in relation to sinners, see D. A. Carson, *The Difficult Doctrine of the Love of God* (Wheaton, IL: Crossway, 2000), 65–73.

**How would you contrast true biblical love with a false sentimental love that accommodates sin? How would you contrast it with the kind of hate toward sinners that the Bible condemns?** *True biblical love doesn't soften the reality of sin and the need to repent, but it does offer opportunities to receive grace and mercy by calling people to repentance. While Christians do warn about the coming judgment, they do so desiring to rescue people from the coming judgment (Jude 1:22–23).*

Use the **link** An Interview with Rosaria Butterfield to access Rosaria Butterfield's interview. Have students read the article.

**After reading the interview with Rosaria Butterfield, how do you think that the pastor and his family showed her compassion without compromise as they witnessed to her when she was a lesbian activist?** *Answers should include ideas regarding the hospitality of the pastor and his wife even while they sought to direct Rosaria to the Bible and its claims challenging Rosaria's worldview.* **Can you think of some scenarios of what it looks like to show compassion without compromise?** *One example could be responding to a relative who embraces his or her sin. You should seek to clarify to the relative that you love him or her as a human being but that you cannot approve or accommodate the relative's embrace of sin. Depending on the circumstances, you may be able to invite that person to family gatherings, but you would not be able to celebrate the same things that person celebrates in regard to sinful expressions.*

## VIRTUES FOR EMBRACING GOD'S DESIGN

Prompt students to **journal** about one of the following virtues to expand on what it means to develop the virtue and why the virtue is important: faithfulness, righteousness, self-control, steadfastness.

**How can you practically develop the virtue for the purpose of living according to God's design for human sexuality and gender?** *Possible answers:*

- *Faithfulness: Faithfulness to God's design for sexuality requires commitment to righteousness, Spirit-empowered self-control in the face of temptation, and steadfastness in the face of cultural pressure. Such faithfulness is cultivated by a commitment to God and His Word and revealed when there's pressure to compromise. You can develop this virtue through the influences of an uncompromising church and Christians who are not embarrassed by biblical stances. You can grow in faithfulness by growing closer to God, so that His opinion (His truth) is the touchstone for your responses (rather than prevailing popular opinion and fallen human reasoning).*
- *Righteousness: God's own righteousness sets the standard. Such conformity to God's righteousness is cultivated by actively getting to know your righteous God in a relational way through His Word and prayer. You can develop righteousness by committing to a deeper daily study of God's Word and specific, Scripture-filled prayers that require time and attention (rather than shallow formulas repeated once a day to check "prayer" off your list).*
- *Self-control: Christians must rely on the Spirit to help them actively put to death the desires of the flesh. Mortifying the flesh requires the fruit of the Spirit, self-control. Only God can help us to grow more consistently in saying no to desires that seem to come naturally to us. You can develop self-control by seeking accountability from mature believers and perhaps even formal biblical counseling to assist you in your battle against sin. You can read sound doctrinal and devotional books that help you effectively and actively combat sin. The Christian has made a fundamental change from living for the flesh to living for Christ.*
- *Steadfastness: Christians need to remain steadfast in their profession of new life in Christ. The pressures from within and without mean that Christians should not grow weary in well-doing. They shouldn't give up in the face of lost battles. They should keep waging war against the flesh, the world, and the devil. Christians need to wait patiently for the day when the Lord restores this broken world. You can develop steadfastness by remaining in close fellowship with other believers who will encourage you, help you, counsel you, and keep you accountable (1 Thess. 5:14). As unlikely as it seems that the biblical sexual ethic will triumph over the perverted ethic of our day, Christians should not grow weary in the face of growing oppression and persecution for their beliefs. Believers live for a goal that Scripture tells us will be our reward only through the path of great persecution (Matt. 5:10–12; 6:33; Acts 14:22; 2 Thess. 1:4–10). Our job is to remain steadfast (1 Cor. 15:58) as ambassadors for Christ (2 Cor. 5:20) while we sojourn in a foreign land (Heb. 11:13; 1 Pet. 2:11). We should not be surprised that we are persecuted in this foreign land (John 15:18–20; 1 Pet. 4:12–15). We are to be the purifying influence of salt and the bright, shining witness of light (Matt. 5:13–16; John 3:19–20; Eph. 5:8, 11).*

### THE RIGHT MOTIVES AND CHARACTER NECESSARY FOR A RIGHT STAND

What marks the character of Christians who embrace God's design for sexuality and gender? Key virtues include faithfulness, righteousness, self-control, and steadfastness. Faithfulness to God's design for sexuality requires commitment to righteousness, Spirit-empowered self-control in the face of temptation, and steadfastness in the face of cultural pressure.

Christians need to be marked by faithfulness to God and His Word. In the face of intimidation, false accusations, threats, and even legal persecution, Christians must be unwaveringly brave and confidently loyal, determined to hold fast to what is right. Such faithfulness is cultivated by a commitment to God and His Word and revealed when there's pressure to compromise. You can develop these virtues through the influences of an uncompromising church and Christians who are not embarrassed by biblical stances. You can grow in faithfulness by growing closer to God, so that His opinion (His truth) is the touchstone for your responses (rather than prevailing popular opinion and fallen human reasoning).

STAY the COURSE

What is right? God's own righteousness sets the standard. While the world tries to convince people that right is wrong and wrong is right, Christians must conform themselves to what God has revealed about Himself and His expectations in His inerrant and authoritative Word. Such conformity to God's righteousness is cultivated by actively getting to know your righteous God in a relational way through His Word and prayer. Develop this virtue by committing to a deeper daily study of God's Word and specific, Scripture-filled prayers that require time and attention (rather than shallow formulas repeated once a day to check "prayer" off your list).

But the battle we face is not simply external—pressures from the world around us. The battle is also internal—pressures from our own sinful nature. Christians must rely on the Spirit to help them actively put to death the desires of the flesh. Mortifying the flesh requires the fruit of the Spirit, self-control. Only God can help us to grow more consistently in saying no to desires that seem to come naturally to us. You can develop this virtue by seeking accountability from mature believers and perhaps even formal biblical counseling to assist you in your battle against sin. You can read sound doctrinal and devotional books that help you effectively and actively combat sin.

The Christian has made a fundamental change from living for the flesh to living for Christ. But the Christian needs to remain steadfast in his or her profession of new life in Christ. The pressures from within and without mean that the Christian should not grow weary in well-doing. Don't give up in the face of lost battles. Keep waging war against the flesh, the world, and the devil. Wait patiently for the day when the Lord restores our broken world. You can develop this virtue by remaining in close fellowship with other believers who will encourage you, help you, counsel you, and keep you accountable (1 Thess. 5:14).

As unlikely as it seems that the biblical sexual ethic will triumph over the perverted ethic of our day, Christians should not grow weary in the face of growing oppression and persecution for their beliefs. Believers live for a goal that Scripture tells us will be our reward only through the path of great persecution (Matt. 5:10–12; 6:33; Acts 14:22; 2 Thess. 1:4–10). Our job is to remain steadfast (1 Cor. 15:58) as ambassadors for Christ (2 Cor. 5:20) while we sojourn in a foreign land (Heb. 11:13; 1 Pet. 2:11). We should not be surprised that we are persecuted in this foreign land (John 15:18–20; 1 Pet. 4:12–15). We are to be the purifying influence of salt and the bright, shining witness of light (Matt. 5:13–16; John 3:19–20; Eph. 5:8, 11).

### RESPONDING BIBLICALLY TO A FRIEND

No doubt you will have conversations with friends who have adopted transgender, bisexual, or homosexual identities and relationships. Our society tries to normalize these unbiblical sexual choices, and it seeks to silence any opposition to them. You must have the character outlined in the previous section to discern how and when to address someone. There is no formula for how to do this without offending someone. But there are wise and unwise ways to approach the situation.

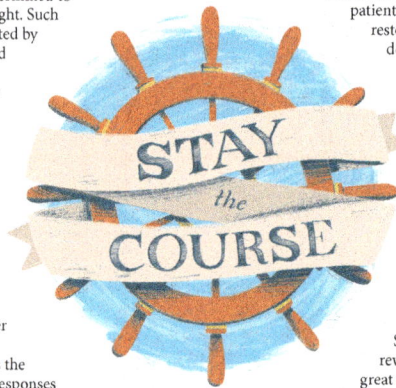



## A BIBLICAL RESPONSE TO LGBTQ+

Use **Activity 13.3** on page 83 to help students respond biblically to various scenarios related to LGBTQ+ issues.

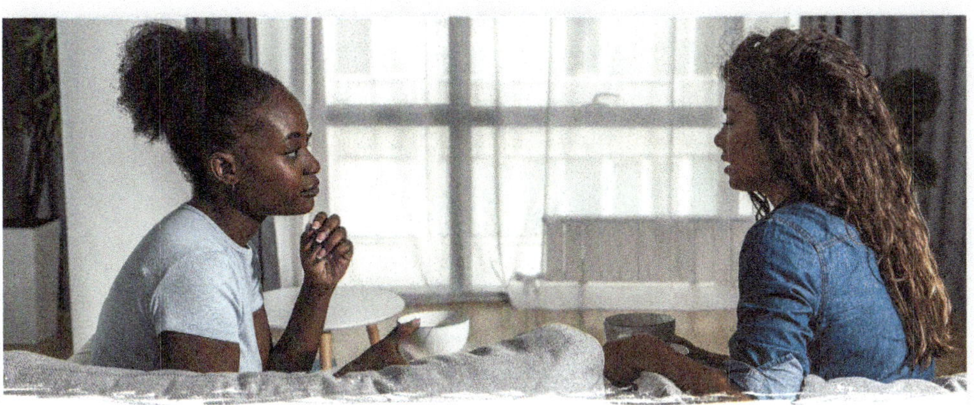

Helping a friend in this area requires dependence upon God's work in the heart and a loving commitment to speak the truth, which can set your friend free from slavery to sin. You must seek to demonstrate compassion without compromise. Compassion is demonstrated when Christians humbly recognize that we all need forgiveness and empowerment from God because we're all sinners. The question is whether we're repentant sinners actively engaged in putting sin to death by the enablement of the Spirit. Compassion is demonstrated when Christians refuse to join in belittling people made in God's image yet remain uncompromisingly opposed to that which is unethical. Christians cannot accept and enable unethical identities and behavior. But Christians can compassionately extend the grace of the gospel to those who heed the call to repent. Christians can be known for both their humble hospitality to sinful people *and* their honest and bold confrontation of sin. Both align with God's response to sin and sinners. The solutions for those trapped in sin are straightforward: salvation and sanctification—repentance and growth in Christ (1 Cor. 6:11).

As you seek to build redemptive relationships to speak the gospel into people's lives, you will have to make hard, careful decisions. For example, you may be able to go to dinner with an unsaved person who is living this kind of sinful lifestyle but not with a professing Christian in unrepentant sin (see 1 Cor. 5:9–13). Each person is made in the image of God; Christians don't reject a *person*. However, that does not mean that you can condone or support in any way that person's immoral choices. How is this put into practice? Though you might, as a Christian with a biblically informed conscience, eat a meal with an unbeliever living in open sin, should you feel free to attend a same-sex wedding? Your answer to this question will reveal your understanding of principles covered in this section.

Contemplating the possible situations you may face in your future should drive you to prayer for wisdom. It should motivate you to take the study of the Bible more seriously. It should encourage you to find joy in the fellowship of other believers in your local church, who will certainly need to uplift one another through harsh persecution in the coming days. Will you grow into the committed Christian, and perhaps leader, that the church needs?

### Thinking It Through 13.3

1. Identify and explain the terms represented by the abbreviation *LGBTQ+*.
2. What are two major indicators of recent and rapid change for society and the church on ethical perspectives regarding LGBTQ+ issues?
3. Explain the biblical teaching on gender found in Genesis 1:26–27; 5:1–2.
4. Explain the biblical teaching on expressing one's gender found in Deuteronomy 22:5 and 1 Corinthians 11:14–15.
5. Identify two key passages that present the biblical pattern for sexual desires and behaviors.
6. Refute the arguments that Genesis 19 can't be used as proof that the Bible forbids homosexual desires and behavior.
7. Refute the arguments that Romans 1:21–32, 1 Corinthians 6:9–11, and 1 Timothy 1:10 can't be used as proof that the Bible forbids homosexual desires and behavior.
8. Is the Bible's sexual ethic unloving? Explain your answer.
9. What character will be needed in the life of a Christian to conform to the biblical ethic?
10. Contrast a biblical and an unbiblical response to a friend who is contemplating or has embraced homosexual or transgender behavior and identity.



## Assess

Guide a **summative assessment** by directing students to answer the questions in Thinking It Through 13.3.

### Thinking It Through 13.3

1. The *L* and *G* refer to *lesbian* and *gay*, respectively. Both are encompassed in the term *homosexual*, which refers to someone with sexual desires for a person of the same sex and/or who engages in sexual behavior with a person of the same sex. The *B* refers to *bisexual*, someone with sexual desires for or who engages in sexual behavior with both men and women. The *T* refers to *transgender*, someone who thinks of him- or herself as having a gender different from his or her sex. The *Q* refers to someone who is *queer* or *questioning*. The + is shorthand for more letters that are sometimes included to represent the growing spectrum of invented gender identities.
2. One indicator of the quick and massive change is the fact that homosexual marriage was outlawed in all fifty states in the United States in 2005, but by 2015 it was made a constitutional right (Burk and Lambert, *Transforming Homosexuality*, 2015). Another indicator is that Christianity used to unanimously oppose LGBTQ+ issues (Grudem, *Christian Ethics*, 843–44), whereas recently self-proclaimed evangelicals are rethinking how to accommodate the Bible to LGBTQ+ issues.
3. God created the human race in His image with only two genders, male and female. Gender is a God-granted creational design (an ontological reality) that cannot be separated from someone's biology and genetics.
4. Men are to present themselves as men and women are to present themselves as women. God has made these distinctions evident in the design of nature, and cultures should seek to reflect those natural distinctions rather than blur them.
5. Genesis 2:22–24 and Matthew 19:4–6
6. Jude 1:7 identifies Sodom's sin as sexual. Ezekiel 16:50 identifies the sin as an abomination, using the same language from Leviticus 18:22, which outlaws all homosexual behavior. The context in Genesis 19 is clear enough that the sin was sexual (see also Judg. 19:22).
7. The New Testament passages do not recognize an innocent victim or different orientations or cultural expectations as any of the reasons why those passages are condemning homosexuality. Rather, those passages condemn homosexuality as against nature, stemming from sinful desires that are unnatural (not according to God's design in nature).
8. No; God's commands describe what it means to be loving, reinforcing God's good design for human flourishing.
9. Faithfulness to God's design for sexuality requires commitment to righteousness, Spirit-empowered self-control in the face of temptation, and steadfastness in the face of cultural pressure.
10. Answers will vary. Unbiblical examples include both saying that "God hates fags" and attending a gay wedding. Unbiblical responses also include using transgender pronoun preferences. A biblical response would include showing hospitality to a person (who is not an unrepentant professing Christian) by having dinner together with the purpose of seeking to share the gospel. A biblical response would be to explain biblical sanctification, putting to death sinful desires.

# 13.4 Birth Control, Reproductive Technologies, and Eugenics

Should all married couples have children?

## Objectives

**13.4.1** Explain various ethical issues regarding procreation and birth control.

**13.4.2** Summarize the biblical teaching on procreation and birth control. BWS

**13.4.3** Assess the personal and societal consequences of unbiblical views regarding procreation and birth control.

**13.4.4** Assess the virtues necessary to live in accordance with a biblical view of procreation and birth control. BWS

**13.4.5** Formulate a response to a couple struggling to decide whether to have children. BWS

### Biblical Worldview Shaping

- **Creational Order** (explain): Having children is a normal part of God's plan for marriage, though it is not the only purpose for sexual union within marriage. (13.4.2)
- **Virtue** (formulate): Those who are not able to have children need faith that God's way is best and gratitude for the good blessings God has given. Those who can have children need faith that God will provide for the needs of their family and gratitude for the gift of children. (13.3.4)
- **Wisdom** (apply): Wisdom involves living in harmony with the created order, which means that most couples should seek to have children. However, certain circumstances, such as health issues, can affect this decision. (13.4.5)

### Printed Resource

- Activity 13.4: Childless Couples Wanting Children

### Suggested Reading

- Frame, John M. *The Doctrine of the Christian Life*. Phillipsburg, NJ: P&R Publishing, 2008. Pages 782–95.
- Grudem, Wayne. *Christian Ethics: An Introduction to Biblical Moral Reasoning*. Wheaton, IL: Crossway, 2018. Pages 746–83.
- Magnuson, Ken. *Invitation to Christian Ethics: Moral Reasoning and Contemporary Issues*. Grand Rapids. MI: Kregel Academic, 2020. Pages 321–93.

## 13.4 Birth Control, Reproductive Technologies, and Eugenics

How many children do you plan to have? That might sound like a funny question to ask someone in high school. You probably have not given this topic serious consideration. But perhaps you and your friends have thrown out some numbers on how many children you think you would like to have. It's not such a far-out question for someone your age to consider. You're already projecting the kind of life you think you would most enjoy. And those desires and assumptions may affect your decisions just a few years from now regarding marriage and children. Maybe you've already formed an attitude that you would love to have lots of children, a few children, or no children. What factors into these different attitudes and desires?

Should all married couples have children? context

### TO HAVE OR NOT TO HAVE CHILDREN—THAT IS THE QUESTION

As you consider your future, you must be very purposeful in determining to be God-centered and God-submitted. Otherwise, you can quickly resort to selfishness and unethical behavior. That goes for those who want lots of children, some children, or no children. Think about the possible motivations of a husband and wife in each case, and consider some fundamental ethical questions: Should married couples seek to have as many children as physically possible? Why should a married couple want to have children? Why wouldn't a married couple want to have children? What about couples who seem to be unable to have children? Should they use modern technology to overcome infertility?

#### *The "No Children" Ideal*

Why wouldn't a married couple want to have children? Could there be a legitimate reason? Are most reasons illegitimate? Although there may be some legitimate reasons to forego having children (such as severe physical problems), the majority of married couples who view being childless as an *ideal* tend to have wrong priorities rather than a biblical view of children: career pursuits, lifestyle preferences, greed, viewing children as a nuisance, or a simple fear of responsibility may be motivating factors. Such married couples can be tempted to resort to medical technologies used to take fetal life, such as what has become known as the morning-after pill or other abortifacients (this would include the **birth control*** method known as an intrauterine device [IUD]). Any method that ends unique human life begun at fertilization should be understood to be murder (see Section 9.3 on Abortion).

**birth control:** a general term that refers to preventing pregnancy; contraception; most often birth control takes place through the use of artificial methods (such as condoms, pills, barriers, or permanent sterilization) rather than natural methods (such as avoiding sex during a woman's fertile time of the month)[14]

256 ISSUES

## Engage

### YOUR ATTITUDE TOWARD CHILDREN

Use a **Four Corners** activity to preassess student attitudes toward children. Label the corners as the following: "Children are mostly annoying"; "Children are a lot of work and responsibility"; "Children are fun and enjoyable"; "Children are a balanced mix of all these." Instruct the students to choose the corner that describes their own attitudes toward children.

**Based on your attitude, how likely do you think your future decisions will tend toward wanting a lot of children, some children, or no children?** *Students should give their honest opinion to the questions.*

**What factors might influence your decision to have children?** *Answers may include the influence of a spouse, one's growing maturity and confidence in abilities, providential factors, finances, changed pursuits, a better grasp of a biblical worldview, and so on.*

## Instruct

### SHOULD MARRIED COUPLES HAVE CHILDREN?

Use a **group activity** to answer this section's essential question and to prompt students to summarize the reasons and motives for the three ideals and the biblical guidance on whether married couples should seek to have children.

#### *The "Some Children" Ideal*

Why should a married couple want to have some children? Are all reasons to limit the number legitimate? Married couples usually want to have some children. The desire to have children is both biblical and natural. Nevertheless, most couples want to limit the number of children they have. They have at their disposal both natural and artificial birth-control methods. The reasons some have for limiting the number of children they plan to have may be just as illegitimate as those given by couples who wish to remain childless. However, others advocate birth control for reasons that may be considered legitimate (assuming the contraceptive methods used *prevent* fertilization rather than end new life after fertilization). A legitimate argument for limiting the number of children will center on stewardship of responsibilities: recognizable human limitations to physical, emotional, and financial resources and abilities (Luke 14:28; Eph. 6:4; 1 Tim. 5:8).

> *All of life consists in deciding not to do some good things in order to be able to do some other good things.*
>
> WAYNE GRUDEM[15]

Perhaps the greatest struggle for those couples who would like to have some children is the inability to have any (or any more) children due to infertility. Such married couples can be tempted to resort to medical technologies that may bring about life at the cost of jeopardizing or even killing other life in the process. To make ethical decisions, infertile married couples need to become accurately informed about how various reproductive technologies work.

#### *The "Many Children" Ideal*

Should married couples seek to have as many children as physically possible? Is this a matter of preference, or is this a biblical requirement?

First, the Creation Mandate is a blessing and a stewardship responsibility. But it should not be understood to mean that a couple must literally multiply two or three times beyond the two people they start with. Rather, the blessing and responsibility are for the human race as a whole to accomplish, not for each individual couple to accomplish. Married couples should not purposefully live at odds with the Creation Mandate, but each couple is not responsible to fill the earth themselves.

Second, a couple can embrace the blessing of children without focusing on that one blessing alone and maximizing it to the fullest possible extent. For example, food is a blessing, but consuming it to an extreme is gluttony. Rather, believers should steward and balance all their blessings with other priorities and good endeavors. What is prudent for one family may not be wise for another. There is no biblical requirement to have as many children as possible. Yet some couples may indeed be called and equipped to glorify God by raising large families. Other couples may be called to raise the children of others by fostering or adopting.

Third, God created sex for multiple purposes, not just for procreation. Procreation is one good result from sex. But the sexual relationship between husband and wife was also created for enjoyment and intimate companionship. It does not and need not always result in a child.

Finally, use of artificial birth control methods should not be understood as always usurping God's prerogatives. Artificial methods are no different from natural methods in this respect. Humans have been granted by God the responsibility of wise stewardship. Use of artificial methods (so long as they aren't ending human life) may be wise dominion—or they can be used unwisely. Each couple will have to assess its own situation and motives.

Some people will still be convinced that their family should avoid using birth control. On such matters, Christians should be able to honor the preferences of others and avoid judging each other for differing convictions (see Rom. 14:3–10).

### THE BIBLICAL TEACHING ON PROCREATION

Acts

God's Word begins by helping us to understand our roles and responsibilities in God's creational order: having children is a normal part of God's plan for marriage (Gen. 1:26–28; 9:1; Mal. 2:15), though as we've noted already it is not the only purpose for sexual union within marriage. The Bible reinforces the Creation Mandate as a blessing by emphasizing that children are a blessing, a gift from God (Ps. 127:3–5; 128:3–4). They are not to be viewed as a nuisance (Matt. 19:13–15). In addition, the Bible recognizes both the great hardship of infertility (Gen.5:2–3; 1 Sam. 1:2–18; Luke 1:7) and the great joy that results when those who were barren are able to give birth (Gen. 21; 5:7; 1 Sam. 2:1–10; Ps. 113:9). Infertility is sad because it is a result of the Fall and not the way the world was originally designed to be for married couples. The desire for children is good, and sadness when this is not possible is appropriate. God has compassion, and we should have it too when we see the heartache of those who are childless.

We can use **assisted reproductive technology (ART)*** to overcome the effects of the Fall; in all areas of life, we exercise stewardship by pushing back against the effects of the Fall and the Curse (Gen. 1:28; 3:7, 10, 16–19, 21). However, while some technologies seem appropriate, others seem questionable, and others would certainly be inappropriate.

---

**assisted reproductive technology (ART):** a broad term referring to all types of medical technology used to promote reproduction to overcome infertility



**Should all married couples have children? What are the three ideals married couples can have? And how would you evaluate biblically each ideal?** *Compare student answers to the information on pages 256–57.*

## BIBLICAL TEACHING ON PROCREATION

Use a **Quick Write** to prompt students to summarize the biblical teaching on procreation.

**What is God's intended design for the marriage relationship and procreation?** *God designed husbands and wives to fulfill the Creation Mandate by procreating (producing children).*

**What is God's description regarding how children should be viewed? Why should they be viewed that way?** *Children should be viewed as a gift from God. Answers include that children bring joy and help extend the influence and abilities of parents to the next generation.*

**What is the biblical view of infertility?** *It is a result of the Fall and causes sadness; when infertility is overcome, everyone is filled with joy because of God's graciousness.*

## BIBLICAL PRINCIPLES TO CONSIDER RELATING TO ART

Use a **Think-Pair-Share** to prompt students to evaluate assisted reproductive technologies (ART) according to biblical principles.

Identify the major ART that are available, describe how they work, and categorize the appropriateness, inappropriateness, or questionable nature of each category. Explain and defend your answers. (See page 258 to evaluate student answers.)

### Methods of Assisted Reproductive Technologies

*ART that seem appropriate*

**Artificial insemination from a husband**: collecting a husband's semen and injecting it into his wife's cervix or uterus.[16] This does not cause the death of any embryos. This mechanism also maintains the pattern of the marriage relationship by bringing together the reproductive elements of a husband and a wife rather than using a third party. This is a use of medical technology that simply helps someone overcome a physical problem.

Medical treatments that support bodily hormones or other bodily functions or surgically repair organs would also be completely appropriate.

*ART that seem questionable*

**Artificial insemination from a donor**: collecting semen from a man other than a woman's husband and injecting it into her cervix or uterus.

Although this does not cause the death of any embryos, it does not maintain the pattern of the marriage relationship by bringing together the reproductive elements of a husband and a wife. It brings in the reproductive element of a third party. While some Christians do not see this as problematic, other Christians rightly see this as troubling (see the discussion on surrogacy below).

**In vitro fertilization (IVF)**: joining together a wife's egg and a husband's sperm to form an embryo in a laboratory. This usually involves the creation of many embryos in which one or a few embryos produce a baby or babies. This technique could be appropriate if the semen and egg come from a husband and a wife (maintaining the pattern of the marriage relationship) and if all the embryos are implanted in the wife's womb so that no embryos are destroyed. However, IVF often involves the reproductive elements of third parties and the creation of many other embryos that either are destroyed or left in a frozen state, likely to be destroyed in the future. Since an embryo is human life, destroying an embryo is destroying life, which is unbiblical. Nevertheless, recent advancements in IVF treatments where only one or two embryos are created have made it possible for Christians to consider these treatments.

**Surrogacy**: using the womb of a third party (a surrogate mother) for the gestation of a baby. The surrogate mother is impregnated either by artificial insemination or by implanting an embryo formed through IVF from the reproductive elements of both parents, one parent and a donor, or two donors.[17] Using donor reproductive elements and surrogacy leads to an extremely complicated lineage and relationships. The parties involved could include multiple combinations of the following: a mother, a father (or two men and two women in a same-sex relationship), a male donor, a female donor, and the surrogate mother who carries the baby.

Many Christian ethicists cite concerns with such a complex lineage and the emotions involved in these relationships. The pattern in the Bible reflecting God's intent is for conception to follow from the marital union of a man and a woman. Surrogacy does not fit this pattern, particularly when fertilization is accomplished from the sperm or egg of someone else other than the married partners. The question is whether surrogacy violates biblical morality. Certainly, one could not say definitively that surrogacy is equivalent to adultery (because there is no sexual activity occurring between two people in this situation). But we are still introducing a third party into the marriage relationship. Surrogacy also opens the way for people to have children outside the pattern of marriage. Nevertheless, children born as the result of surrogacy are to be treated with love and respect as image-bearers; there's no place for rejecting, deriding, or shunning innocent children who result from unions or methods that were not God's ideal.

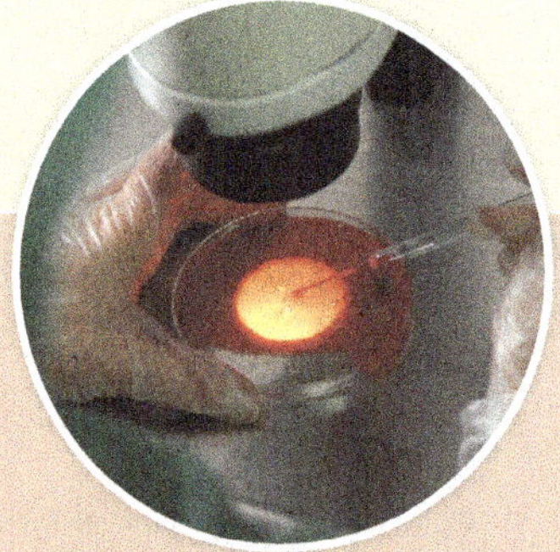

*ART that would be inappropriate*

Artificial insemination or in vitro fertilization used to impregnate a woman who wanted to raise a child outside a biblically approved marriage relationship would be a means of bypassing a God-ordained marriage to have the blessing of children despite rebellion against God's design. This would also be true for the use of a surrogate to carry a child for a male same-sex couple. Such arrangements stand in opposition to God's design for marriage.

**Eugenics** is the quest to bolster human genetics by preventing people with traits deemed undesirable from reproducing, while encouraging people with traits deemed desirable to procreate. (Eugenics has often been associated with the idea that some races are superior to others.) Today, there are those who believe that only those who are desirable to a society should be allowed to live. This view may lead to killing embryos after genetic prescreening because of predicted disabilities or other characteristics considered undesirable. Such a practice violates the biblical prohibition against murder and is antithetical to the biblical view that all humans have value because they bear the image of God.

In conclusion, Christians should seek to preserve life. Christians should seek to procreate according to God's pattern and design for marriage. Any practice that undermines these principles should be questioned, if not rejected.

ends **AVOIDING IDOLATRY**

Desiring to have children is a good thing; children are a blessing. But desiring to have children by any available means is not a good thing; it's idolatry. Christians who want to please the Lord above all will not resort to unethical means to produce children. They will rely on God to sustain them through heartache; they will wait on God to bless them with children, if it is His will, through ethical means. Though challenging to maintain, this attitude testifies of what it is to live for God's glory rather than live for something else.

Other forms of idolatry may be more obvious to us. Eugenics may lead to eliminating "undesirable" people due to idolizing certain traits or idolizing freedom from disease. There is a type of genetic prescreening that eliminates certain people from existing by screening them out, rather than by killing already-alive people. A couple considering having children may elect to be genetically screened to determine what might be passed on to the next generation. Prospective parents can thus determine the chances of their kids having various genetic disorders,[18] but in theory they could also be screened to determine their chances of having children with various other traits such as height, hair color, and the like. Parents might decide to forego having children if they don't like their chances of having their preferred kind of offspring. It's one thing to try to heal and prevent disease (an effect of the Fall). But it's another thing to try to prevent certain kinds of people from existing in the first place or to decide that certain aspects of God's good, diverse creation are undesirable.

agents **VIRTUES THAT COUNTERACT IDOLATRY**

The key to avoiding such idolatry is to cultivate the virtues of faith, gratitude, and love. Those who are not able to have children need faith in God's purposes and gratitude for the blessings God has given. Like so many in Scripture, the childless must also believe that God is sovereign over the womb and is able to provide children if He wishes, even in seemingly impossible circumstances. Those who can have children need faith that God will provide for the needs of their family, and they must be grateful for the gift of children, even when the going gets tough. And rather than despising certain people as undesirable, we ought to cultivate love for all of God's image-bearers.

SEXUAL ETHICS 259

## AVOIDING IDOLATRY

Guide a **discussion** to help students pinpoint different ways that people can pursue idolatrous ends.

**How can the desire to have children lead to idolatry? How would such idolatry be exposed?** *Idolatry occurs when someone's desire for something, even a good thing, becomes prioritized above God and His righteous ways. Such idolatry is exposed when people resort to unbiblical methods and means to achieve the desired thing at the expense of trusting and waiting on God to allow them to have it through righteous means.*

**In what two ways could idolatry be expressed in relation to birth control and reproductive technologies?** *First, couples may resort to questionable or inappropriate ART to produce children. Second, couples may resort to eugenics or prescreening to prevent certain kinds of human beings from being born.*

## VIRTUES THAT COUNTERACT IDOLATRY

Use a **Turn and Talk** to prompt students to assess the virtues necessary to live in accordance with a biblical view of procreation and birth control.

**What are three key virtues for avoiding idolatry? Why are these virtues necessary, and how can they be developed?** *Answers should reflect and expand on the information on page 259.*

## Apply

### CHILDLESS COUPLES WANTING CHILDREN

Use **Activity 13.4** on page 85 to help students strategize about the best counsel possible regarding a couple who is unable to conceive children.

## Assess

Guide a **summative assessment** by directing students to answer the questions in Thinking It Through 13.4.

### Thinking It Through 13.4

**1a.** birth control/contraception

**1b.** assisted reproductive technologies (ART)

**2.** The "no children" ideal: This position can be appropriate only in the face of a severe physical disability or other lack of ability to raise children. Most of the time couples who pursue this as the ideal have misplaced priorities rather than a biblical view of children as a blessing.

The "some children" ideal: This position can be due to misplaced priorities as in the first category. A couple might also fail to trust that God provides for the needs of the children. However, this position may align with biblical wisdom on one's stewardship of limited resources (as long as the means of limiting children does not endanger a life).

The "many children" ideal: This position can be due to personal preference and abilities to enjoy much blessing. But it can also be due to misinterpreting the Creation Mandate as a demand to literally multiply.

**3.** Procreation was designed as a blessing for married couples rooted in the Creation Mandate. Children are a blessing and gift from God. However, God has compassion on those suffering from infertility caused by the Fall.

**4.** Compare student answers to the information on page 258.

**5.** One form of idolatry can lead to desiring children by any means necessary, including unethical means to produce children, rather than relying on God to sustain or to provide through ethical means.

context

#### COUNSELING A STRUGGLING COUPLE

You never know what trials you may face in your future. The topics of this section may seem distant rather than relevant to your life. But what if someday you find yourself at a crossroads, needing to make decisions about birth control or ART? How would you counsel a married couple struggling over whether to have children or how to overcome infertility? Wisdom involves living in harmony with the created order, which means that most married couples should seek to have children. However, there are circumstances, such as health issues, that can affect this decision. Wisdom also involves a precise knowledge of birth control and ART options and the ethical questions involved.

Another option for Christian couples to consider would be the God-honoring decision to adopt or foster. Jesus Himself lived as Joseph's adopted son (Luke 2:41, 48). God is "a father of the fatherless" (Ps. 68:5); He shows tremendous care and concern for the orphan (Hosea 14:3; James 1:27). And He pictures one glorious aspect of our salvation in terms of spiritual adoption (Gal. 4:5). Many Christian parents can testify to the privilege and joy that come from rescuing, protecting, providing for, and nurturing a child in need of parents and a stable, loving home. That child becomes one of their own, a beautiful reflection of what Christ has done for us.

#### Thinking It Through 13.4

1a. In general, what do people resort to if they do not wish a pregnancy to result from sexual relations?

1b. In general, what do people resort to if they are trying to overcome infertility?

2. Summarize the pros and cons of each position on how many children to have.

3. Summarize the basic biblical teaching on procreation.

4. Describe one assisted reproductive technology (ART) that seems appropriate, one that seems questionable, and one that would be inappropriate.

5. Explain two forms of idolatry that relate to couples' views of procreation.

6. Identify three virtues highlighted in this section and explain how those virtues would help a person avoid idolatry related to procreation.

7. What is an alternative to the use of ART for infertile couples—an option that reflects what Christ has done for us in salvation?

# Review 13

SEXUAL ETHICS

#### Terms to Remember

- compatibility
- cohabitation
- no-fault divorce
- immodesty
- pornography
- masturbation
- fornication
- prostitution
- incest
- sexual abuse
- bestiality
- adultery
- polygamy
- marital purity
- homosexual
- LGBTQ+
- bisexual
- transgender
- birth control
- assisted reproductive technology (ART)
- artificial insemination from a husband
- artificial insemination from a donor
- in vitro fertilization (IVF)
- surrogacy
- eugenics

260 ISSUES

Another form of idolatry can be seen in the practice of eugenics, a willingness to kill or prevent the birth of undesirable people.

**6.** Faith, gratitude, and love are virtues that help believers to rely on God whether they can have healthy children or not.

**7.** adoption

## Chapter 13 Review

### Terms to Remember

- **compatibility:** The popular idea that, in order for a marriage to work, couples must have a lot in common.
- **cohabitation:** Living together before or apart from marriage.
- **no-fault divorce:** Divorce law that allows for divorce without the need for either party to demonstrate that the other has violated the marriage covenant.
- **immodesty:** Dress, or undress, that draws sexual attention.
- **pornography:** Pictures, videos, or graphic descriptions intended to stimulate sexual desire.
- **masturbation:** Sexual self-stimulation.
- **fornication:** Sexual immorality.
- **prostitution:** Providing sex acts for pay or in return for some benefit.
- **incest:** Sexual relations among family members aside from between a husband and wife.

**Scripture Memory**

1 Thessalonians 4:3–5

**Understanding Ethics**

1. Contrast the biblical view of marriage, divorce, and remarriage with common views found in the culture.
2. Explain the biblical teaching on inappropriate sexual activity.
3. Why is it not sufficient or appropriate to use conversion therapy to get a person to become heterosexual?
4. Should all married couples have children? Explain.

**Practicing Ethical Decision-Making**

5. How would you respond to a friend in the following situation? What virtues could have helped your friend avoid such a situation?

   Soon after graduating from high school, one of your friends moves out of his parents' house while they are gone over the weekend. Your friend moves in to cohabit with someone he met at work; both partners have had a string of previous sexual relationships. After several years of living in immorality (including having several children), your friend gets married to that same person. However, a year later your friend asks you to be a character witness in court since he is filing for divorce. He complains that his spouse is committing adultery, but he admits that he too has been unfaithful once or twice. Your friend also wants you to affirm that the divorce is biblically sanctioned.

6. How should you conduct yourself in the following situation to protect yourself (and show love for your Christian brother or sister), and what is one key virtue that you will need to live out?

   You are excited to attend your first junior-senior banquet (or prom). Although the event is chaperoned, many couples slip out of the event early and hang out afterward in groups. However, the other couple that was supposed to hang out with you afterward ditched you. You find yourself all alone with your date in a dark car. Barriers have been breaking down in the last half-hour. It's clear what's wanted.

7. How should you respond if you found yourself in the following situation?

   During high school you take up photography as a hobby. By the time you graduate from college, you've become quite skilled. You find wedding photography to be quite lucrative. However, you have nagging questions about your role in some situations. Some people dress extremely immodestly. And now you've been approached by a gay couple who wants you to photograph their wedding.

8. How should you respond if you found yourself in the following situation?

   You've just gotten married. You're both in grad school and both working full-time jobs. You have a lot of school debt. And you're trying to save up enough money to get an apartment or your first home and move out of your parents' basement. You want to use birth control, but your spouse isn't sure it's healthy or biblical.

**Analyzing and Evaluating Ethical Claims**

9. How would you respond to someone who claims divorce is the best decision they've ever made, who celebrates the benefits of divorce in general, and who scoffs at the negative consequences of divorce?
10. How would you respond to someone who claims Christianity teaches that sex is dirty?
11. How would you respond to someone who claims that committed homosexual relationships are never condemned in the Bible?
12. How would you respond to someone who claims that using the morning-after pill or an IUD is perfectly fine?

**Creating My Own Position Statements on Ethics**

13. Write a position statement on divorce and remarriage.
14. Write a position statement on homosexuality, bisexuality, and transgenderism.
15. Write a position statement on birth control and artificial reproductive technology.

- **sexual abuse:** Any criminal activity that forces any kind of sexual perversion on another person; includes rape and pedophilia.
- **bestiality:** Sexual behavior with animals.
- **adultery:** Marital unfaithfulness; lust for someone or sexual activity that violates the marriage covenant of one or both people involved.
- **polygamy:** Having multiple spouses at one time.
- **marital purity:** Forsaking all forbidden sexual activity and partaking in the sexual activity God designed for a man and woman within the bounds of marriage.
- **homosexual:** According to LGBTQ+ advocates, someone with sexual desires for a person of the same sex and/or who engages in sexual behavior with a person of the same sex.
- **LGBTQ+:** An abbreviation that stands for lesbian, gay, bisexual, transgender, queer (or questioning), and several other terms that are used to denote various types of gender identity confusion.
- **bisexual:** According to LGBTQ+ advocates, someone with sexual desires for or who engages in sexual behavior with both men and women.
- **transgender:** According to LGBTQ+ advocates, someone who thinks of him- or herself as having a gender different from his or her sex.
- **birth control:** A general term that refers to preventing pregnancy; contraception through the use of artificial or natural methods.
- **assisted reproductive technology (ART):** All types of medical technology used to promote reproduction in order to overcome infertility.
- **artificial insemination from a husband:** Collecting a husband's semen and injecting it into his wife's cervix or uterus.
- **artificial insemination from a donor:** Collecting semen from a man other than a woman's husband and injecting it into her cervix or uterus.
- **in vitro fertilization (IVF):** Joining together a wife's egg and a husband's sperm to form an embryo in a laboratory.
- **surrogacy:** Using the womb of a third party (a surrogate mother) for the gestation of a baby.
- **eugenics:** The quest to bolster human genetics by preventing people with traits deemed undesirable from reproducing, while encouraging people with traits deemed desirable to procreate; has often been associated with the idea that some races are superior to others.

## Understanding Ethics

1. The biblical view of marriage is that it should be a lifelong covenant of love between one man and one woman, who was created to be a counterpart to man. And this kind of unity and unbreakable commitment was designed by God to be a picture of Christ's relationship to the church. Marriage is to be permanent; God hates divorce. This contrasts with the idea of compatibility (leading to the promotion of cohabitation) and no-fault divorce. Remarriage is possible only if one's spouse has passed away. (Sexual immorality and abandonment are two possible biblical exceptions that could allow for remarriage while the other spouse lives.)
2. Answers should reflect the chart in Section 13.2 on pages 243–44.
3. Conversion therapy erroneously assumes that someone has an orientation (something ontological) that can be fixed like a broken machine. One's sinful sexual desires are an ethical problem rooted in the sin nature. The goal is not to get people to become heterosexual but to transform them through salvation and sanctification, putting sin to death.
4. The biblical norm would be for most married couples to seek to have children. Yet, a great physical problem or another inability may make that extremely difficult and unwise. Also, some couples will face infertility. In these cases, adoption is an option.

### Practicing Ethical Decision-Making

5. It would not be possible to be a character witness for a friend who demonstrated a gross lack of character. And it would not be appropriate to support such a divorce as biblically sanctioned even if technically the friend's wife ended up committing immorality, because the larger context is not that of an innocent party being victimized. Instead, one must call upon that friend to demonstrate the fruits of repentance rather than excusing his own sin and character flaws and playing the victim.

   Virtues that would have prevented the friend from such a situation include a correct understanding of love in contrast to lust, a commitment to faithfulness even to an unbelieving spouse, and patience to seek reconciliation before jumping on an opportunity for justifying divorce.
6. Answers should reflect the cautions enunciated in the eight speech bubbles on page 246. A person in such a situation should live out the virtue of self-control, but that will be difficult apart from returning to a place where you aren't alone. Without accountability, lust can be stoked through various means (e.g., talk, dress, touching, kissing).
7. Christians should be careful to use their artistic abilities to promote and uphold only those things that fall within the biblical parameters of truth, goodness, and beauty (all three together). Immodesty perverts beauty by doing away with goodness. And homosexuality perverts truth, goodness, and beauty in clear violation of God's commands. If God views such activity as an abomination, then the Christian should recognize that God could not approve of appearing at that event to provide services to help celebrate such an event.
8. There are several different options that would be possible and biblical. You could change priorities and not focus just on paying off the school debt or moving out of your parents' basement. Having children can still be an option, even if it might require a lot of work taking care of them. However, using birth control could be appropriate once a spouse has received biblical counsel and clarification on the biblical position on birth control.

### Analyzing and Evaluating Ethical Claims

9. It would not be possible to agree with such an assessment since the Bible never glories in divorce even though it may allow for it in a couple of exceptional circumstances. An honest assessment of divorce recognizes its detrimental effects on people and society, including but not limited to tremendous anger, sadness, stress, fear, confusion, instability, insecurity, loneliness, greater health risks, poverty, and difficulties in school as well as family breakdown leading to societal breakdown.
10. Sex is a God-given blessing within the context of biblical marriage; the Bible does not condemn sex but immorality.
11. The Bible never distinguishes between committed and uncommitted homosexual relationships. It clearly condemns all homosexual desires and behavior as against nature (God's design in creation) and identifies them wholly as an abomination in God's eyes.
12. As soon as an egg is fertilized, new and unique human life has begun, and that life must not be snuffed out (even before implantation into the uterus). The only appropriate birth control is that which prevents fertilization in the first place.

### Creating My Own Position Statements on Ethics

13. Students may research the topic in more detail. In general, answers should reflect the biblical data presented in Section 13.1.
14. Students may research the topic in more detail. In general, answers should reflect the biblical data presented in Section 13.3.
15. Students may research the topic in more detail. In general, answers should reflect the biblical data presented in Section 13.4.

# conclusion

Do you seek to know God's will? Presumably, you'd answer "Yes, of course!"

Why do you seek to know it? Have you ever asked yourself "What am I trying to gain?" Can you identify your motivations for seeking that knowledge?

Perhaps we should get the magnifying glass off ourselves for a moment and be a little less personal. Let's ask, "Why do people in general seek to know God's will?"

People might want wisdom to make a decision that is very narrow. "Should I buy this car? Should I take this job?" Others might have broader concerns; they seek to know God's will because they want to create a Christian ethical system, like this textbook seeks to do. Other people might understand God's "will" as meaning God's good pleasure in general, not just for decision making. In that case, people might seek to gain knowledge simply to know Him.

Could it be that some individuals want knowledge of God's will to use as ammunition against others, or to gain leverage on people they want to control? The patriarch Jacob did that. He deceived his blind father into thinking that he was his brother Esau, and he lied when he passed off a slaughtered goat as wild game. Jacob's father Isaac noticed how soon the food had been prepared, and he knew hunting takes a long time, so he asked, "How is it that thou hast found it so quickly, my son?" Jacob told yet another lie, but this time he enlisted God in it: "The Lord thy God brought it to me" (Gen. 27:20). At this point in Jacob's life, God was just a tool to get what he wanted.

Why do *you* seek to know God's will? Can you identify a motive of yours? Let's compare our motives with Paul's words in Colossians.

Paul prays for Christians to be "filled with the knowledge of his will in all wisdom and spiritual understanding" (Col. 1:9). Paul wants this so "that ye might walk worthy of the Lord" (Col. 1:10). That is a statement of purpose. Paul is telling us what our purpose should be in seeking to know God.

To put it simply, we are to know God's will so that we will "walk worthy of" Him. Walking is a common biblical metaphor for living one's life. We are to know God's will to live in a way that is "worthy" of God, that is, in a way that treats God as He deserves to be treated and honors Him as He deserves to be honored. That implies something tremendous: *knowledge of God must radically change one's life into a God-honoring one.*

All our seeking God, all our gaining knowledge must funnel into this goal. When knowledge doesn't lead to our honoring the Triune God, it is futile, for it is disconnected from reality, and it is abortive, for it fails to achieve its purpose. God lets us know Him so that we will glorify Him.

It is natural to wonder what a worthy walk looks like. The rest of Colossians 1:9–14 explains that, and in doing so, it provides a well-rounded Christian ethic. It answers the questions "What makes a good deed truly good?" and "What makes a good deed worthy of God, or honoring to Him?"

**A worthy walk is "unto all pleasing" (Col. 1:10).** That is, a worthy walk fully pleases God. Other texts add specifics to that. "Without faith it is impossible to please him" (Heb. 11:6). So, pleasing God always involves faith in God, for there is no pleasing God without faith. In Romans 8:7–8 pleasing God is equivalent to being subject to God's law. That's talking about obedience to His commands. So, walking worthy of the Lord means trusting Him and obeying Him. These things are fundamental to a worthy walk. You don't honor Him as He deserves when you distrust Him and dismiss His commands.

**A worthy walk is "fruitful in every good work" (Col. 1:10).** "Fruitful" refers to producing works that please God. Fruitfulness "in every good work" may mean one of two things. Paul could mean something like this: "God wants you to bear fruit in every one of His commands." So, it could mean to obey everything God has said to do. Such an idea fits well with Paul's statements elsewhere, such as where he says that keeping God's commandments is what matters (1 Cor. 7:19). Jesus said with great simplicity: "If ye love me, keep my commandments" (John 14:15).

But fruitfulness in every good work may mean "God's norms are to be used in every conceivable activity." In other words, no endeavor should be thought of as secular, or removed from a religious worldview. If this is what Paul means, he is saying that a worthy walk makes Christ the Lord over every aspect of life. Whether Paul has this in mind here in Colossians or not, it is clearly a biblical point. Elsewhere, Paul tells Christians to glorify God in whatever they do (1 Cor. 10:31) and to take every thought captive to Christ (2 Cor. 10:5).

Paul may have only one of these meanings in mind here in Colossians, but a worthy walk surely includes both of the two options. We must obey all that God has commanded, and just as clearly, we must serve Him in all our endeavors to Him. Our norms come from God, and we must apply those norms to our situations. When we do so, we let Christ be our king.

**A worthy walk means "increasing in the knowledge of God" (Col. 1:10).** This means that a worthy walk is intellectual, God-centered, and relational. A worthy walk cannot involve mere activity without deep reflection on God. And that reflection must not be inactive in the soul but should be experiential. For how can a walk be worthy without the soul's soaring home to God in prayer? How can it be worthy without abasement before His majesty, joy in His mercy, worship of His Person? A worthy walk must include theological development and relationship with God in all its richness.

Let's sum up what Paul has said so far: we should seek to know God's will to walk worthy of Him. Walking worthy of God means pleasing Him by believing in Him, obeying Him, and gaining ever more knowledge of Him in relationship with Him.

But Paul's Christian ethic isn't complete yet.

**A worthy walk means being "strengthened with all might, according to his glorious power" (Col. 1:11).** A person might seek to please God but be self-reliant instead of relying on God's empowerment. That is called moralism. Being moral isn't necessarily Christian, and moral people who rely on themselves aren't walking worthy of Christ at all, because they presume that they have the ability in themselves to please God, when God says differently. This divine strengthening leads to "all patience and longsuffering with joyfulness" (Col. 1:11). This empowerment is truly wonderful, for it helps us endure doing right with patience and joy. Who among us doesn't feel his or her need for spiritual strength such as this?

We read more about this empowerment elsewhere in Scripture. In Acts 1:8 we're told that when the Holy Spirit came, the disciples would "receive power." In Ephesians 3:16, Paul prays that God would strengthen believers "with might by his Spirit in the inner man." The strengthening that we are to rely on is that which is given by the Holy Spirit.

Sometimes talk of the Holy Spirit can seem strange and mysterious to people. Someone might wonder, "How do you gain strength from the Spirit?" It comes down to two things: first, we must believe that the Spirit really is available to believers, which amounts to simply accepting by faith the biblical statements, such as those above. Second, we must pray for the Spirit's gracious filling. It may sound strange to ask God to fill you with the Spirit so that you can bear the fruit of His Spirit in your life, but that is exactly what the Bible says to do: "If ye then, being evil, know how to give good gifts unto your children: how much more shall your heavenly Father give the Holy Spirit to them that ask him?" (Luke 11:13). Paul's statement "be filled with the Spirit" (Eph. 5:18) amounts to a command to submit yourself to Spirit-filling constantly. Spirit-filling is part of the normal Christian life, and it is crucial to a truly Christian ethic.

Do you rely on God's power imparted through the Holy Spirit? Or do you think of the Christian life as primarily a matter of willpower and self-discipline? Paul is saying that relying on God's strength is how we become enabled to persist in obedience and joy. Without reliance on God, attempting to be moral goes astray. It becomes an arrogant ode to human ability, for it says, "I have the power to love and please God in myself." It becomes hypocritical, for it professes love for God but rejects His Word about our need for the Spirit. It becomes an impossible burden, for we cannot live up to God's ideals, and sin is ever with us. It sets up a false religion, for to seek to be godly in one's own strength and without reliance on God's specified help is the soul and substance of false religion. The world is full of Christless moralism. Christianity is moral, highly moral, but it is Christ- and Spirit-centered in its ethic. A Christian approach to living right never forgets that Christ gave the Holy Spirit to His followers, and if you want to walk worthy and please God, you must rely on that supply of grace. Paul put it very succinctly: "Walk in the Spirit, and ye shall not fulfil the lust of the flesh" (Gal 5:16).

But Paul's Christian ethic still isn't complete. A person could conceivably obey God's commands and do so seeking empowerment from God, but their obedience might still have little to do with God's redemption in Christ.

**A worthy walk means "giving thanks unto the Father, which hath made us meet to be partakers of the inheritance" (Col. 1:12).** How did God make us "meet" (or *fit*) to inherit? Paul says that God has "delivered us from the power of darkness" and transferred "us into the kingdom of his dear Son" (Col. 1:13). And he says that in Christ "we have redemption through his blood, even the forgiveness of sins" (Col. 1:14). He made us fit to inherit by Jesus Christ's saving work on the cross.

Look at all the activity in those verses: God made us fit; He delivered us from darkness, transferred us into Christ's kingdom, and redeemed us by Christ's blood. That is a lot of activity, and it is all God's. There is a tendency in the heart of fallen people to emphasize their own works for God and de-emphasize God's works for them. When this happens, religion becomes like a competitive sport, full of effort, panic, and self-comparison. That is not a worthy walk. It does not treat God as He deserves to be treated or honor Him as He deserves to be honored. To take one's eyes off God's works for you means all you have left is yourself and other people.

We must recognize that we were in the domain of darkness, not just a slave there, but a willing participant. We weren't poor captives in Mordor, to use a Tolkien illustration, we were orcs in Mordor. We were part of the darkness. We contributed to it. We aren't the heroes of any story. We're villains whom, for some reason beyond our capacity to understand, God had mercy on despite our crimes. And He not only had mercy on us and saved us, but He gave us an inheritance, placed us into Christ's kingdom, and greatest of all, He sent His Eternal Son to purchase our redemption with His own blood.

As long as these things are true, and they have been in God's plan since before He made the world, there is no such thing as a worthy walk that doesn't constantly rejoice in them. This is why Paul ends his discussion of the Christian life in Colossians 1 on the note of

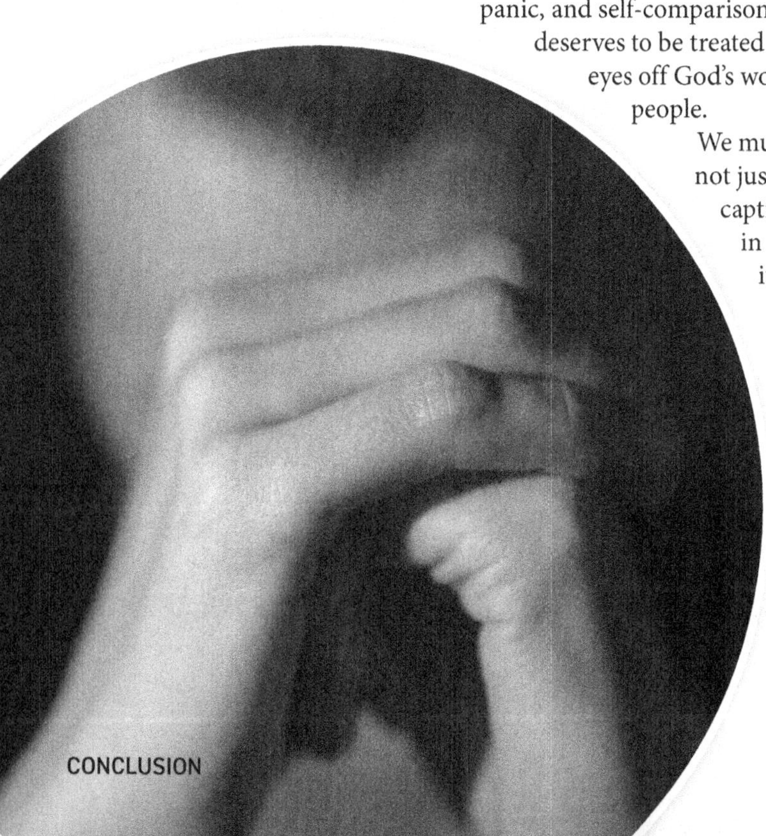

thanking the Father for His great mercy in Christ. Seeking to live a life of godliness without constant gratitude for God's salvation in Christ is not worthy of God; it is an affront to Him.

We have come to the end of Paul's discussion of Christian ethics, and we need to tie up all the strands of thought.

Here is Paul's teaching summed up, and this is a good lesson to end a book on Christian ethics. For a walk to be truly worthy, for a deed to be truly good and pleasing and honoring to God, it must be carried out by someone who has a certain state of mind and heart. Such a person must be informed by the knowledge of God's will, must carry out his works by the Spirit's power, and do them out of gratitude to the Father for His salvation in Christ. This is a consistent and fully formed Christian and Trinitarian ethic. Without these elements, good works aren't good.

Here is the teaching in the simplest terms: We must do what God wants, through God's Spirit, because of Christ, and for God's glory. Our norms, means, reasons, and purposes must be Trinitarian. Anything less is unworthy of God as He has revealed Himself to be; anything less does not treat God as He deserves to be treated and does not honor Him as He deserves to be honored.

This is how Paul conceived the broad outlines of the all the actions a Christian takes in this world. It is a comprehensive and universally applicable view of Christian ethics, and it is given in marvelous language that seems miraculously both full and concise. Paul could put an ocean of matter in a drop of language.

The final question before us is naturally applicational. "Do Paul's words describe how we live?" I would imagine that, if we've really digested what Paul says here, that we all feel quite lowly, insufficient, and wretched. We might even wonder if we've ever done a good work in our lives. What a wonderful way to finish an ethics book, make the students feel like complete wretches!

It is crucial to point out that Paul opens the paragraph by praying for this worthy walk (Col. 1:9), and he closes by referring to forgiveness of sins (Col. 1:14).

Paul seeks a worthy walk from God's gracious hand (Col. 1:9). He pursues God for it, and he relies on Him to give it. So, we see that a worthy walk takes divine power, just like any good we do. Without Christ we can do nothing, so we must seek Him for everything. If you feel convicted that you have fallen far short of Paul's view of the Christian life, follow Paul's lead and seek God for it, and for your friends and loved ones. God has promised to perform the good work He has begun in you (Phil. 1:6), but He wants you to seek Him for its progress. You must go forward on your knees all your life.

It is also crucial to point out that Paul ends this marvelous paragraph on a note of forgiveness in Christ. In Christ, "we have redemption through his blood, even the forgiveness of sins" (Col. 1:14). We see from this that if we are believers in Christ, we should not feel condemned and rejected for our many sub-Christian works. Every time the law of God comes and shows us our shortcomings, we should repent anew but also rejoice that there are no shortcomings in our High Priest who ever lives to intercede for us (Heb. 7:25). We are His, and He is ours. He bore the punishment for all our sins, and He gave us His righteousness when we believed (2 Cor. 5:21). We can look at all our failures, self-reliance, and self-glory, and we can denounce them all, knowing that we are not condemned by them. Though we have fallen far short of a worthy walk, Christ never has, and He obeyed perfectly not for Himself but for His people. A truly Christian ethic relies ultimately and joyously on the all-sufficient work of Christ that makes up for our innumerable deficiencies.

# notes

## Cover

The quotation that begins "It is never right" is from *The Chapel Sayings of Dr. Bob Jones Sr., founder of Bob Jones University* (Greenville, SC: Bob Jones University, 1976), 10.

## Introduction to Ethics/Chapter 1: Creational Foundations for Ethics

1. Taken from pages 43–47 of *Invitation to Christian Ethics: Moral Reasoning and Contemporary Issues* © Copyright 2020 by Ken Magnuson, Invitation to Theological Studies Series. Published by Kregel Publications, Grand Rapids, MI. Used by permission of the publisher. All rights reserved.
2. Jonathan T. Pennington, *Jesus the Great Philosopher: Rediscovering the Wisdom Needed for the Good Life* (Grand Rapids, MI: Brazos, 2020), 22.
3. "The Shorter Catechism" in *Westminster Confession of Faith*, rev. ed. (Glasgow: Free Presbyterian Publications, 1994), 287.
4. Albert M. Wolters, *Creation Regained: Biblical Basics for a Reformational Worldview*, 2nd ed. (Grand Rapids, MI: Eerdmans, 2005), 34–35.
5. Taken from *Christian Ethics: An Introduction to Biblical Moral Reasoning* by Wayne Grudem, © 2018, p. 43. Used by permission of Crossway, a publishing ministry of Good News Publishers, Wheaton, IL 60187, www.crossway.org.
6. Subheadings below taken from Grudem, *Christian Ethics*, 57–61.
7. Football History, "The Development of Football Rules," accessed September 28, 2021, https://www.footballhistory.org/rules.html; Travis Yoesting, "22 Incredible Changes to Soccer Rules Since 1863," The 18, August 17, 2017, https://the18.com/en/soccer-entertainment/lists/timeline-soccer-rule-changes-evolution-laws; James Sweeney, "The Rise and Fall of the Golden Goal: How It Defined Tournaments and Created Legends," These Football Times, May 12, 2019, https://thesefootballtimes.co/2019/12/05/the-rise-and-fall-of-the-golden-goal-how-it-defined-tournaments-and-created-legends/.
8. Magnuson, *Invitation to Christian Ethics*, 71.
9. "The Shorter Catechism" in *Westminster Confession of Faith*, rev. ed. (Glasgow: Free Presbyterian Publications, 1994), 287–88, 289.
10. Tom D. Crouch, Roger E. Bilstein, and Walter James Boyne, s.v. "history of flight," Encyclopedia Britannica online, last modified November 12, 2020, https://www.britannica.com/technology/history-of-flight/Construction-of-the-sustaining-wings-the-problem-of-lift.
11. Wolters, *Creation Regained*, 17; italics in the original.
12. Wolters, *Creation Regained*, 25; italics in the original.
13. Fleming James, *Personalities of the Old Testament*, The Hale Lectures (New York: Charles Scribner's Sons, 1939), 502.
14. Taken from page 34 of *The Defense of the Faith*, 4th ed., by Cornelius Van Til, ed. K. Scott Oliphint. Copyright 2008, P&R Publishing, Phillipsburg, NJ.
15. Excerpt from page 40 of *Reformed Ethics* by Herman Bavinck and John Bolt, ed., copyright © 2019. Used by permission of Baker Academic, a division of Baker Publishing Group.
16. Augustine, *City of God* 15.22, trans. Marcus Dods, with an introduction by Thomas Merton (New York: Modern Library, 1993), 511.

## Chapter 2: The Fall's Effects on Ethics

1. Jobmaster Magnets, "What Exactly Is a 'Strong' Magnet?," July 8, 2015, https://www.jobmastermagnets.com/what-is-a-strong-magnet; Thomasnet.com, "Neodymium Magnet Applications," accessed on September 28, 2021, https://www.thomasnet.com/articles/electrical-power-generation/NIB-magnet-application/.
2. Bodie Hodge, "Should We Look to the Animal World for Answers?," *Answers Magazine*, January 1, 2007, https://answersingenesis.org/morality/should-we-look-to-the-animal-world-for-answers/; Pam Sheppard, "Of Penguins and People," Answers in Genesis, October 1, 2005, https://answersingenesis.org/reviews/movies/of-penguins-and-people/.
3. Albert M. Wolters, *Creation Regained: Biblical Basics for a Reformational Worldview*, 2nd ed. (Grand Rapids, MI: Eerdmans, 2005), 59.
4. Excerpts taken from *The Doctrine of the Christian Life* by John M Frame. Used with permission from P&R Publishing, Phillipsburg, NJ.
5. Immanuel Kant, *Foundations of the Metaphysics of Morals*, trans. Lewis White Beck (New York: Bobbs-Merrill, 1959 [1785]), 39, quoted on page 25 of *Invitation to Christian Ethics: Moral Reasoning and Contemporary Issues* © Copyright 2020 by Ken Magnuson, Invitation to Theological Studies Series. Published by Kregel Publications, Grand Rapids, MI. Used by permission of the publisher. All rights reserved.
6. Frame, *Doctrine of the Christian Life*, 111.
7. Frame, *Doctrine of the Christian Life*, 112.
8. Frame, *Doctrine of the Christian Life*, 112.
9. Frame, *Doctrine of the Christian Life*, 114.
10. Magnuson, *Invitation to Christian Ethics*, 27.
11. Magnuson, *Invitation to Christian Ethics*, 27.
12. Magnuson, *Invitation to Christian Ethics*, 29.
13. Frame, *Doctrine of the Christian Life*, 116.
14. Aristotle, *Nichomachean Ethics* 4.3.1123b, trans. Terence Irwin, 2nd ed. (Indianapolis: Hackett, 1999), 56.
15. Taken from page 28 of "Greeks Bearing Gifts" in *Revolutions in Worldview: Understanding the Flow of Western Thought* by John Frame, ed. W. Andrew Hoffecker. Copyright 2007, P&R Publishing, Phillipsburg, NJ.
16. Magnuson, *Invitation to Christian Ethics*, 43–47.

## Chapter 3: The Role of Redemption in Ethics

1. Albert M. Wolters, *Creation Regained: Biblical Basics for a Reformational Worldview*, 2nd ed. (Grand Rapids, MI: Eerdmans, 2005), 40.
2. Wolters, *Creation Regained*, 40–41.
3. John Owen, *Practical Exposition upon Psalm CXXX* (1835; n.p.: Wentworth Press, 2019), 85.
4. Sinclair Ferguson, "Union with Christ in Pastoral Ministry," conference session at Basics 2010 (May 11, 2010), audio, https://www.truthforlife.org/resources/sermon/union-christ-pastoral-ministry/.
5. Taken from pages 12–13 of *The Christ of Wisdom: A Redemptive-Historical Exploration of the Wisdom Books of the Old Testament* by O. Palmer Robertson. Copyright 2017, P&R Publishing, Phillipsburg, NJ.
6. See Francis Schaeffer, "08 - The Age of Fragmentation," episode 8 in *How Should We Then Live?*, 1977, Gospel Films, last updated July 17, 2017, https://www.youtube.com/watch?v=d0eYmFOQBs0&list=PLP0lSOp9RORx7W0REI8SVK2CNIrMjhS_T&index=8.
7. Tremper Longman III, *How to Read Proverbs* (Downers Grove, IL: InterVarsity, 2002), 16–17.
8. Robertson, *The Christ of Wisdom*, 13.
9. Craig G. Bartholomew and Ryan P. O'Dowd, Old Testament Wisdom Literature: A Theological Introduction (Downers Grove, IL: InterVarsity, 2011), 89.
10. Wolters, *Creation Regained*, 59.
11. Longman, *How to Read Proverbs*, 53–54.
12. "The Shorter Catechism" in *Westminster Confession of Faith*, rev. ed. (Glasgow: Free Presbyterian Publications, 1994), 287.
13. Augustine, *The Confessions of St. Augustine* 1.1, trans. E. B. Pusey and William Benham (New York: P. F. Collier, 1909), 5.
14. *Holman Illustrated Bible Dictionary* (Nashville, TN: Holman Bible Publishers, 2003), s.v. "meekness."
15. David Mathis, "We Will See His Face: What Is the Beatific Vision?" Desiring God, March 11, 2021, https://www.desiringgod.org/articles/we-will-see-his-face.

## Chapter 4: Becoming Like Christ

1. For the understanding of virtue as excellence in moral character, see Kevin Timpe and Craig A. Boyd, eds., introduction to *Virtues and*

<Their Vices* (New York: Oxford University Press, 2014), 6.
2. See O. Bauernfeind, "ἀρετή," in *Theological Dictionary of the New Testament*, ed. Gerhard Kittel, trans. and ed. Geoffrey W. Bromiley (Grand Rapids, MI: Eerdmans, 1964), 1:457–61.
3. See Augustine, *City of God* 15.22, trans. Marcus Dods, with an introduction by Thomas Merton (New York: Modern Library, 1993), 511.
4. Taken from page 326 of *The Doctrine of the Christian Life* by John M. Frame. Copyright 2008, P&R Publishing, Phillipsburg, NJ.
5. Taken from page 37 of *Invitation to Christian Ethics: Moral Reasoning and Contemporary Issues* © Copyright 2020 by Ken Magnuson, Invitation to Theological Studies Series. Published by Kregel Publications, Grand Rapids, MI. Used by permission of the publisher. All rights reserved.
6. Frame, *Doctrine of the Christian Life*, 326.
7. Andrew M. Davis, *An Infinite Journey: Growing toward Christlikeness* (Greenville, SC: Ambassador International, 2014), 173.

## Chapter 5: Three Central Virtues

1. Oliver O'Donovan, *Self, World, and Time*, vol. 1 of *Ethics as Theology* (Grand Rapids, MI: Eerdmans, 2013), 98–99.
2. O'Donovan, *Self, World, and Time*, 98–99.
3. John Calvin, *Institutes of the Christian Religion* 3.2.7, vol. 1, ed. John T. McNeill, trans. Ford Lewis Battles, The Library of Christian Classics, vol. 20 (Philadelphia: Westminster Press, 1960), 551.
4. Charles Spurgeon, "The Trial of Your Faith," no. 2055, sermon at the Metropolitan Tabernacle (December 2, 1888).
5. THE GREATEST LOVE OF ALL. Words by LINDA CREED. Music by MICHAEL MASSER. © 1977 (Renewed) EMI GOLD HORIZON MUSIC CORP. and EMI GOLDEN TORCH MUSIC CORP. Exclusive Print Rights Administered by ALFRED MUSIC.
6. Augustine, *On Christian Teaching* 3.10.16, in William Harmless, ed., *In His Own Words* (Washington, DC: CUA Press, 2010), 170.
7. Jonathan Edwards, *The End for Which God Created the World*, in *The Works of Jonathan Edwards*, rev. ed., ed. Edward Hickman (Edinburgh, UK: Banner of Truth Trust, 1974), 1.105; italics in the original.
8. J. C. Ryle, "Christian Love!," Monergism, https://www.monergism.com/christian-love.
9. John Webster, *Confessing God: Essays in Christian Dogmatics II*, T&T Clark Cornerstones (Bloomsbury T&T Clark: 2016), 196, 204–5.
10. Wilhelmus à Brakel, *The Law, Christian Graces, and the Lord's Prayer*, vol. 3 of *The Christian's Reasonable Service*, ed. Joel R. Beeke, trans. Bartel Elshout (Grand Rapids, MI: Reformation Heritage Books, 2015), 322.
11. James T. Dennison, Jr., comp., "Calvin's Catechism (1537)," in vol. 1, *Reformed Confessions of the 16th and 17th Centuries in English Translation* (Grand Rapids, MI: Reformation Heritage Books, 2008), 378.
12. Oliver O'Donovan, *Resurrection and Moral Order: An Outline for Evangelical Ethics*, 2nd ed. (Leicester, UK: APOLLOS / Grand Rapids, MI: Eerdmans, 1994), 253.
13. Webster, *Confessing God*, 205.
14. Charles Pinches, "On Hope," in *Virtues and Their Vices*, ed. Kevin Timpe and Craig A. Boyd (New York: Oxford University Press, 2014), 351.
15. À Brakel, *The Law, Christian Graces, and the Lord's Prayer*, 327.
16. D. W. Gill, "Hope," in *New Dictionary of Christian Ethics and Pastoral Theology*, ed. David J. Atkinson, David H. Field, Arthur F. Holmes, and Oliver O'Donovan (Downers Grove, IL: InterVarsity, 1995), 456–57.
17. Frank Thielman, *Ephesians*, BECNT (Grand Rapids, MI: Baker Academic, 2010), 356–57; *Biblical Worldview: Creation, Fall, Redemption* (Greenville, SC: BJU Press, 2016), 179.
18. Gill, *New Dictionary of Christian Ethics and Pastoral Theology*, 456–57.

## Chapter 6: Virtues, Part 1

1. *Merriam-Webster.com Thesaurus*, s.v. "righteousness," accessed February 26, 2022, https://www.merriam-webster.com/thesaurus/righteousness.
2. "Deep Blue," IBM, Icons of Progress, accessed February 16, 2023, https://www.ibm.com/ibm/history/ibm100/us/en/icons/deepblue/; "Deep Blue," *Encyclopedia Britannica* online, last modified January 26, 2023, https://www.britannica.com/topic/Deep-Blue.
3. Clarke D. Forsythe, *Politics for the Greatest Good: The Case for Prudence in the Public Square* (Downers Grove, IL: InterVarsity, 2009), 24.
4. "The Fox and the Crow," *The Aesop for Children* (1919), adapted interactive book presented by Library of Congress, accessed November 11, 2021, http://read.gov/aesop/027.html.
5. W. Jay Wood, "Prudence," in *Virtues and Their Vices*, ed. Kevin Timpe and Craig A. Boyd (New York: Oxford University Press, 2014), 37.
6. Wood, "Prudence," 38.
7. Sir Walter Scott, s.v. "Sir Walter Scott on chivalry," *Encyclopedia Britannica* online, August 5, 2014, https://www.britannica.com/topic/Sir-Walter-Scott-on-chivalry-1987278.
8. Wilhelmus à Brakel, *The Law, Christian Graces, and the Lord's Prayer*, vol. 3 of *The Christian's Reasonable Service*, ed. Joel R. Beeke, trans. Bartel Elshout (Grand Rapids, MI: Reformation Heritage Books, 2015), 103–4; italics in the original.
9. Jim Berg, *Essential Virtues: Marks of the Christ-Centered Life* (Greenville, SC: JourneyForth, 2008), 173.
10. Berg, *Essential Virtues*, 173.
11. H. D. McDonald, "Courage," in *New Bible Dictionary*, 3rd ed., ed. D. R. W. Wood et al. (Downers Grove, IL: InterVarsity, 1996), 234.
12. À Brakel, *The Law, Christian Graces, and the Lord's Prayer*, 334.
13. Jerry Bridges, *The Practice of Godliness* (Colorado Springs: NavPress, 1983), 164; bold added; italics in the original.
14. Excerpt from the work by Robert C. Roberts entitled "Temperance" from the anthology book Virtues and Their Vices (by editors Kevin Timpe and Craig A. Boyd © 2014. ISBN: 9780199645541). Reproduced with permission of Oxford Publishing Limited through PLSclear.

## Chapter 7: Virtues, Part 2

1. Jerry Bridges, *The Practice of Godliness* (Colorado Springs: NavPress, 1983), 91.
2. Bridges, *The Practice of Godliness*, 91.
3. Bridges, *The Practice of Godliness*, 220.
4. Taken from page 208 of *Known by God: A Biblical Theology of Personal Identity* by Brian S. Rosner. Italics in the original. Copyright © 2017 by Brian S. Rosner. Used by permission of Zondervan. www.zondervan.com.
5. Chromatius, "Tractate on Matthew 17.4.1–2" in *Matthew 1–13*, ed. Manlio Simonetti, vol. New Testament 1a of Ancient Christian Commentary on Scripture (Downers Grove, IL: IVP Academic, 2001), 82.
6. John MacArthur, *The Quest for Character* (Nashville, TN: Thomas Nelson, 2006), 25.
7. MacArthur, *The Quest for Character*, 72.
8. Jim Berg, *Essential Virtues: Marks of the Christ-Centered Life* (Greenville, SC: JourneyForth, 2008), 181. Berg seems to be building on William Barclay's description of *agapē* love in *New Testament Words* (Philadelphia: Westminster Press, 1964), 28.
9. Jonathan T. Pennington, "A Biblical Theology of Human Flourishing," Institute for Faith, Work, and Economics, March 4, 2015, https://tifwe.org/wp-content/uploads/2015/03/A-Biblical-Theology-of-Human-Flourishing-Pennington.pdf.
10. Bernadette Deron, "This Is How 15 Other Countries Around the World Celebrate Thanksgiving," All That's Interesting, updated November 9, 2021, https://allthatsinteresting.com/thanksgiving-in-other-countries.
11. Bridges, *The Practice of Godliness*, 127.
12. Bridges, *The Practice of Godliness*, 145.
13. Pennington, "A Biblical Theology of Human Flourishing."
14. Pennington, "A Biblical Theology of Human Flourishing."
15. John Webster, "The Fruit of the Spirit 4. Peace," Reformation21, August 26, 2015, Section IV, https://www.reformation21.org/articles/the-fruit-of-the-spirit-4-peace.php.
16. MacArthur, *The Quest for Character*, 86.
17. MacArthur, *The Quest for Character*, 40; italics in the original.
18. Taken from *Christian Ethics: An Introduction to Biblical Moral Reasoning* by Wayne Grudem, © 2018, p. 311. Used by permission of Crossway, a publishing ministry of Good News Publishers, Wheaton, IL 60187, www.crossway.org.
19. Adapted from Grudem, *Christian Ethics*, 311–12.
20. John Calvin, *Commentaries on the Four Last Books of Moses Arranged in the Form of a Harmony*, trans. Charles William Bingham (Bellingham, WA: Faithlife, 2010), 1:34–35.

## Chapter 8: A Method for Handling Ethical Issues

1. Taken from page 43 of *Invitation to Christian Ethics: Moral Reasoning and Contemporary Issues* © Copyright 2020 by Ken Magnuson, Invitation to Theological Studies Series. Published by Kregel Publications,

Grand Rapids, MI. Used by permission of the publisher. All rights reserved.

2. "The Shorter Catechism" in *Westminster Confession of Faith*, rev. ed. (Glasgow: Free Presbyterian Publications, 1994), 287.
3. Magnuson, *Invitation to Christian Ethics*, 45.
4. The questions that follow and their later expansion owe most to Magnuson's ethical method as articulated in *Invitation to Christian Ethics*, 43–54. However, our method and questions have also been influenced by other writers, including pages 33–34, 49–51 of *The Doctrine of the Christian Life* by John M. Frame. Copyright 2008, P&R Publishing, Phillipsburg, NJ; and from *Christian Ethics: An Introduction to Biblical Moral Reasoning* by Wayne Grudem, © 2018, pages 107, 149–60. Used by permission of Crossway, a publishing ministry of Good News Publishers, Wheaton, IL 60187, www.crossway.org.

## Chapter 9: The Ethics of Life and Death

1. 18 U.S.C. 1111(a), http://uscode.house.gov/view.xhtml?req=granuleid:USC-prelim-title18-section1111&num=0&edition=prelim; bold added.
2. See 18 U.S.C. 1111(a).
3. 18 U.S.C. 1112(a), http://uscode.house.gov/view.xhtml?req=granuleid:USC-prelim-title18-section1112&num=0&edition=prelim; bold added.
4. See 18 U.S.C. 1112(a).
5. "Self-Defense Law: Overview," FindLaw, last updated September 10, 2022, https://www.findlaw.com/criminal/criminal-law-basics/self-defense-overview.html.
6. "Self-Defense Law: Overview," FindLaw.
7. Taken from page 685 of *The Doctrine of the Christian Life* by John M. Frame. Copyright 2008, P&R Publishing, Phillipsburg, NJ.
8. Douglas K. Stuart, *Exodus*, New American Commentary (Nashville, TN: B&H, 2006), 503.
9. See Frame, *The Doctrine of the Christian Life*, 325.
10. Centers for Disease Control and Prevention, "Leading Causes of Death Report, 2019," WISQARS Injury Data, https://wisqars.cdc.gov/fatal-leading.
11. Taken from *Christian Ethics: An Introduction to Biblical Moral Reasoning* by Wayne Grudem, © 2018, p. 587. Used by permission of Crossway, a publishing ministry of Good News Publishers, Wheaton, IL 60187, www.crossway.org.
12. Andrew Dugan, "In U.S., Support Up for Doctor-Assisted Suicide," Gallup News, May 27, 2015, https://news.gallup.com/poll/183425/support-doctor-assisted-suicide.aspx.
13. Julie Lowe, "Teens and Suicide: Recognizing the Signs and Sharing Hope," *Journal of Biblical Counseling* 35:1 (2021): 13.
14. Grudem, *Christian Ethics*, 566.
15. Melissa Webb, "Healing in Even the Darkest Places," *Answers Magazine*, January 1, 2019, https://answersingenesis.org/sanctity-of-life/healing-darkest-places/.
16. Taken from page 342 of *Invitation to Christian Ethics: Moral Reasoning and Contemporary Issues* © Copyright 2020 by Ken Magnuson, Invitation to Theological Studies Series. Published by Kregel Publications, Grand Rapids, MI. Used by permission of the publisher. All rights reserved. Magnuson cites Lawrence B. Finer et al., "Reasons U.S. Women Have Abortions: Quantitative and Qualitative Perspectives," *Perspectives on Sexual and Reproductive Health* 37, no. 3 (September 2005): 113 (Table 2), https://www.guttmacher.org/sites/default/files/article_files/3711005.pdf. Higher percentages of women (though still below fifteen percent) did cite health concerns for themselves as contributing factors, according to this table.
17. Magnuson, *Invitation to Christian Ethics*, 342.
18. Magnuson, *Invitation to Christian Ethics*, 339, who cites Doe v. Bolton, 410 U. S. 179, 192 (1973) and Francis J. Beckwith, *Defending Life: A Moral and Legal Case against Abortion Choice* (Cambridge: Cambridge University Press, 2007), 339.
19. Magnuson, *Invitation to Christian Ethics*, 340–41.
20. See Magnuson, *Invitation to Christian Ethics*, 339–40; Ariana Eunjung Cha and Rachel Roubein, "Fetal Viability Is at the Center of Mississippi Abortion Case. Here's Why." *Washington Post*, December 1, 2021, https://www.washingtonpost.com/health/2021/12/01/what-is-viability/.
21. Roe v. Wade, 410 U.S. 113 (1973) at 163.
22. See "Dobbs v. Jackson: A New Opportunity to Protect Life," The Heritage Foundation, December 2, 2021, https://www.heritage.org/citizens-guide-fight-america/2021-action-items/dobbs-v-jackson-new-opportunity-protect-life; Leah Savas, "Abortion Battle Lines," World, January 29, 2022, https://wng.org/articles/abortion-battle-lines-1641864614.
23. Dobbs v. Jackson, No. 19–1392, 597 S. Ct. slip opinion (2022).
24. See Avery Foley, "When Does Life Begin?," *Answers Magazine*, December 1, 2021, https://answersingenesis.org/sanctity-of-life/abortion/when-does-life-begin/; David Menton, "Plan B: Over-the-Counter Abortion?," *Answers Magazine*, July 21, 2008, https://answersingenesis.org/sanctity-of-life/abortion/plan-b/.
25. Sarah Terzo, "Abortion Activists Admit: 'I Knew It Was a Baby,'" LifeNews.com, January 22, 2013, https://www.lifenews.com/2013/01/22/abortion-activists-admit-i-knew-it-was-a-baby/.
26. See "Ectopic Pregnancy," Mayo Clinic, accessed May 17, 2022, https://www.mayoclinic.org/diseases-conditions/ectopic-pregnancy/symptoms-causes/syc-20372088, and "Ectopic Pregnancy," Cleveland Clinic, last reviewed January 18, 2023, https://my.clevelandclinic.org/health/diseases/9687-ectopic-pregnancy.
27. See Abolghasem Pourreza and Aziz Batebi, "Psychological Consequences of Abortion among the Post Abortion Care Seeking Women in Tehran" *Iran Journal of Psychiatry* 6, no. 1 (2011): 31–36, https://www.ncbi.nlm.nih.gov/pmc/articles/PMC3395931/.

## Chapter 10: Ethical Government

1. See summaries of and responses to these positions in pages 406–19 of *Invitation to Christian Ethics: Moral Reasoning and Contemporary Issues* © Copyright 2020 by Ken Magnuson, Invitation to Theological Studies Series. Published by Kregel Publications, Grand Rapids, MI. Used by permission of the publisher. All rights reserved.
2. Magnuson, *Invitation to Christian Ethics*, 395–96.
3. Magnuson, *Invitation to Christian Ethics*, 395–404, 412–20.
4. "Percentage of Americans Who View the Death Penalty as Morally Acceptable Remains Near Record Low," Death Penalty Information Center, June 16, 2022, https://deathpenaltyinfo.org/news/percentage-of-americans-who-view-the-death-penalty-as-morally-acceptable-remains-near-record-low, citing Megan Brenan, "Americans Say Birth Control, Divorce Most 'Morally Acceptable,'" Gallup News, June 9, 2022, https://news.gallup.com/poll/393515/americans-say-birth-control-divorce-morally-acceptable.aspx.
5. See "Atom Spy Case/Rosenbergs," Federal Bureau of Investigation, https://www.fbi.gov/history/famous-cases/atom-spy-caserosenbergs.
6. "Death Penalty for Offenses Other Than Murder," Death Penalty Information Center, https://deathpenaltyinfo.org/facts-and-research/crimes-punishable-by-death/death-penalty-for-offenses-other-than-murder.
7. Magnuson, *Invitation to Christian Ethics*, 404.
8. "Life Imprisonment in Norway," Wikipedia, accessed May 21, 2022, https://en.wikipedia.org/wiki/Life_imprisonment_in_Norway.
9. See discussion in Magnuson, *Invitation to Christian Ethics*, 409–10.
10. Maurice Possley, "Donald Eugene Gates," The National Registry of Exonerations, last updated November 20, 2015, https://www.law.umich.edu/special/exoneration/Pages/casedetail.aspx?caseid=3233.
11. Magnuson, *Invitation to Christian Ethics*, 404.
12. Taken from page 703 of *The Doctrine of the Christian Life* by John M. Frame. Copyright 2008, P&R Publishing, Phillipsburg, NJ.
13. Taken from page 704 of *The Doctrine of the Christian Life* by John M. Frame. Copyright 2008, P&R Publishing, Phillipsburg, NJ.
14. Oliver O'Donovan, *The Just War Revisited* (Cambridge: Cambridge University Press, 2003), 11; Charles Hodge, *Systematic Theology* (Peabody, MA: Hendrickson Academic, 1999), 3:367.
15. Hodge, *Systematic Theology*, 3:367.
16. O'Donovan, *The Just War Revisited*, 11.
17. Plymouth Brethren Christian Church, "Brethren Served in Both World Wars," What We Believe–Other, https://www.plymouthbrethrenchristianchurch.org/beliefs/other/; Mennonite Church USA, "Article 22. Peace, Justice, and Nonresistance," Confession of Faith in a Mennonite Perspective, https://www.mennoniteusa.org/who-are-mennonites/what-we-believe/confession-of-faith/peace-justice-and-nonresistance/.
18. Michael Walzer, *Arguing about War* (New Haven, CT: Yale University Press, 2004), 22.
19. O'Donovan, *The Just War Revisited*, 5.
20. The following box is taken from page 2555 of *The ESV® Study Bible*

(The Holy Bible, English Standard Version®), Copyright © 2008 by Crossway, a publishing ministry of Good News Publishers. Used by permission. All rights reserved. Some formatting has been altered; deleted material is indicated by ellipses; added material is in brackets.

21. Andrew Fiala, "Pacifism," under 2.1 Absolute vs. Contingent Pacifism, *The Stanford Encyclopedia of Philosophy* (Fall 2021 Edition), ed. Edward N. Zalta, https://plato.stanford.edu/archives/fall2021/entries/pacifism/.
22. Taken from *Christian Ethics: An Introduction to Biblical Moral Reasoning* by Wayne Grudem, © 2018, p. 514. Used by permission of Crossway, a publishing ministry of Good News Publishers, Wheaton, IL 60187, www.crossway.org.
23. Malcolm Shaw, "Geneva Conventions," *Encyclopedia Britannica* online, last modified October 20, 2022, https://www.britannica.com/event/Geneva-Conventions.
24. Walzer, *Arguing about War*, 20–21.
25. "Major Cold War Events," *Encyclopedia Britannica* online Student Center, accessed March 3, 2022, https://www.britannica.com/study/major-cold-war-events.
26. See O'Donovan, *The Just War Revisited*, 9, and Paul Ramsey, *The Just War: Force and Political Responsibility* (New York: Charles Scribner's Sons, 1968), 142.
27. Mark R. Amstutz, *Just Immigration: American Policy in Christian Perspective* (Grand Rapids: Eerdmans, 2017), in the introduction to Chapter 4, https://search.ebscohost.com/login.aspx?direct=true&AuthType=sso&db=e000xna&AN=1703973&site=ehost-live.
28. Amstutz, *Just Immigration*, in the introduction to Chapter 4.
29. Amstutz, *Just Immigration*, in the introduction to Chapter 4.
30. Amstutz, *Just Immigration*, in Chapter 1, under "Christian Ethics and Immigration."
31. Gretchen Frazee, "Four Myths about How Immigrants Affect the U.S. Economy," PBS News Hour, Making Sen$e, November 2, 2018, https://www.pbs.org/newshour/economy/making-sense/4-myths-about-how-immigrants-affect-the-u-s-economy; "How Does Immigration Affect the U.S. Economy?," The Science Behind It, National Academy of Sciences, accessed May 3, 2022, https://thesciencebehindit.org/how-does-immigration-affect-the-u-s-economy/.
32. Michael T. Light, Jongying He, and Jason P. Robey, "Comparing Crime Rates between Undocumented Immigrants, Legal Immigrants, and Native-Born US Citizens in Texas," *Proceedings of the National Academy of Sciences* 117, no. 51 (December 7, 2020), doi:10.1073/pnas.2014704117.
33. See Amstutz, *Just Immigration*, in Chapter 3, under "Shortcomings of the Current System," who mentions a similar policy as a recommendation of the Jordan Commission on Immigration Reform (among others) and cites William A. Kandel, "US Family-Based Immigration Policy," Congressional Research Service (November 19, 2014), 2.
34. "Rights and Responsibilities of a Green Card Holder (Permanent Resident)," U.S. Citizenship and Immigration Services, last updated July 15, 2015, https://www.uscis.gov/green-card/after-we-grant-your-green-card/rights-and-responsibilities-of-a-green-card-holder-permanent-resident.
35. Average number from 2010–19 from 2019 Yearbook of Immigration Statistics, Table 1, U.S. Department of Homeland Security, https://www.dhs.gov/immigration-statistics/yearbook/2019/table1.
36. 2020 Yearbook of Immigration Statistics, Table 6, U.S. Department of Homeland Security, https://www.dhs.gov/immigration-statistics/yearbook/2020/table6.
37. 2020 Yearbook of Immigration Statistics, Table 20, U.S. Department of Homeland Security, https://www.dhs.gov/sites/default/files/2022-07/2022_0308_plcy_yearbook_immigration_statistics_fy2020_v2.pdf.
38. "Naturalization Statistics," U.S. Citizenship and Immigration Services, last updated September 21, 2022, https://www.uscis.gov/citizenship-resource-center/naturalization-statistics.
39. "Naturalization Statistics," fiscal year 2020, U.S. Citizenship and Immigration Services, accessed March 16, 2022, https://www.uscis.gov/citizenship-resource-center/naturalization-statistics.
40. Bryan Baker, "Estimates of the Unauthorized Immigrant Population Residing in the United States: January 2015–January 2018," Population Estimates (DHS Office of Immigration Statistics, January 2021), Figure 1, https://www.dhs.gov/sites/default/files/publications/immigration-statistics/Pop_Estimate/UnauthImmigrant/unauthorized_immigrant_population_estimates_2015_-_2018.pdf.
41. Ryan Baugh, "Refugees and Asylees: 2019," Annual Flow Report (DHS Office of Immigration Statistics, September 2020), 1, https://www.dhs.gov/
42. Justin Gest, quoted in Quoctrung Bui and Caitlin Dickerson, "What Can the U.S. Learn from How Other Countries Handle Immigration?," *New York Times* online, February 16, 2018, https://www.nytimes.com/interactive/2018/02/16/upshot/comparing-immigration-policies-across-countries.html.
43. Lily Kuo, "In China, They're Closing Churches, Jailing Pastors - and Even Rewriting Scripture," *The Guardian* online, January 13, 2019, https://www.theguardian.com/world/2019/jan/13/china-christians-religious-persecution-translation-bible.
44. "Russian Revolution," History.com, last updated January 11, 2023, https://www.history.com/topics/european-history/russian-revolution#; "Nov 7, 1917 CE: October Revolution," *National Geographic* online education resource, accessed April 27, 2022, https://www.nationalgeographic.org/thisday/nov7/october-revolution/.
45. Mario F. Morelli, "Civil Disobedience," in *Civil Disobedience, Social Justice, Nationalism & Populism, Violent Demonstrations and Race Relations*, ed. Editors of Salem Press (Hackensack, NJ: Salem Press, 2017). https://online-salempress-com.eu1.proxy.openathens.net/articleDetails.do?articleName=GHCT17_0002.
46. Taken from page 618 of *The Doctrine of the Christian Life* by John M. Frame. Copyright 2008, P&R Publishing, Phillipsburg, NJ.
47. John Calvin, *Institutes of the Christian Religion* 4.20.31, vol. 1, ed. John T. McNeill, trans. Ford Lewis Battles, The Library of Christian Classics, vol. 20 (Philadelphia: Westminster Press, 1960), 1519.
48. Bradford Littlejohn, "Christian Citizenship and the Rule of Law," The Gospel Coalition (Canadian edition), December 9, 2020, https://ca.thegospelcoalition.org/article/christian-citizenship-and-the-rule-of-law/.
49. Littlejohn, "Christian Citizenship and the Rule of Law."

## Chapter 11: Ethical Society

1. Colin Kidd, *The Forging of Races: Race and Scripture in the Protestant Atlantic World, 1600–2000*, (Cambridge University Press, 2006), 9.
2. Herman Bavinck, *Reformed Dogmatics: God and Creation*, vol. 2, ed. John Bolt, trans. John Vriend (Grand Rapids, MI: Baker Academic, 2004), 523.
3. *Oxford English Dictionary* online, s.v. "racism", last modified March 2022, https://www.oed.com/view/Entry/157097?redirectedFrom=racism#eid.
4. Noted in George Yancey, *Beyond Racial Gridlock: Embracing Mutual Responsibility* (Downers Grove, IL: IVP Books, 2006), 67.
5. Yancey, *Beyond Racial Gridlock*, 67.
6. Dictionary.com, s.v. "reparations", accessed July 21, 2022, https://www.dictionary.com/browse/reparations.
7. Taken from *Christian Ethics: An Introduction to Biblical Moral Reasoning* by Wayne Grudem, © 2018, p. 642. Used by permission of Crossway, a publishing ministry of Good News Publishers, Wheaton, IL 60187, www.crossway.org. Grudem quotes the same Scripture passage that follows and adds the same emphasis, but in a different English translation.
8. Declaration of Independence (1776), https://www.archives.gov/founding-docs/declaration-transcript.
9. Taken from *Love in Hard Places* by D. A. Carson, © 2002, p. 97. Used by permission of Crossway Books, a publishing ministry of Good News Publishers, Wheaton, Illinois 60187, www.crossway.com.
10. Grudem, *Christian Ethics*, 685–88.
11. Randy Jaeggli, *Christians and Alcohol: A Scriptural Case for Abstinence* (Greenville, SC: Bob Jones University Press, 2014), 11–36.
12. For more information, see Kevin J. Vanhoozer, "Should Followers of Christ Use Recreational Marijuana?," The Gospel Coalition, January 16, 2020, https://www.thegospelcoalition.org/article/followers-christ-use-recreational-marijuana/.
13. See John Rosengren, "How Casinos Enable Gambling Addicts," *The Atlantic*, December 2016, https://www.theatlantic.com/magazine/archive/2016/12/losing-it-all/505814/?utm_source=nl-atlantic-daily-112816.
14. *Collins COBUILD Advanced Learner's Dictionary* online, s.v. "recreational drug," accessed April 4, 2023, https://www.collinsdictionary.com/us/dictionary/english/recreational-drug.

15. Grudem, *Christian Ethics*, 1039.
16. Grudem, *Christian Ethics*, 676–77.
17. Grudem, *Christian Ethics*, 691–92.
18. Rosengren, "How Casinos Enable Gambling Addicts."
19. Grudem, *Christian Ethics*, 1040–41.
20. Mark E. Shaw, "What Does God Say to those Who Struggle with Addiction?," The Gospel Coalition Podcast, July 29, 2020, 8:02, https://www.thegospelcoalition.org/podcasts/q-a-podcast/what-does-god-say-to-those-who-struggle-with-addiction/.
21. Vocabulary.com, s.v. "profanity," accessed July 28, 2022, https://www.vocabulary.com/dictionary/profanity.
22. Vocabulary.com, s.v. "vulgarity," accessed July 28, 2022, https://www.vocabulary.com/dictionary/vulgarity.
23. Kevin DeYoung, "The One Indispensable Rule for Using Social Media," *DeYoung, Restless, and Reformed* (blog), The Gospel Coalition, June 13, 2012, https://www.thegospelcoalition.org/blogs/kevin-deyoung/the-one-indispensable-rule-for-using-social-media/.
24. *Cambridge Dictionary* online, s.v. "bribery," accessed July 29, 2022, https://dictionary.cambridge.org/us/dictionary/english/bribery.
25. *Cambridge Dictionary* online, s.v. "extortion," accessed July 29, 2022, https://dictionary.cambridge.org/us/dictionary/english/extortion.
26. Jeffrey Moriarty, "Business Ethics," under 6.1 "Hiring and Firing," Stanford Encyclopedia of Philosophy (Fall 2021 Edition), ed. Edward N. Zalta, https://plato.stanford.edu/archives/fall2021/entries/ethics-business/.
27. Summarized from Moriarty, "Business Ethics," under 6.1 "Hiring and Firing."
28. Grudem, *Christian Ethics*, 1060.
29. Grudem, *Christian Ethics*, 1062.
30. The preceding six principles have been adapted from Grudem, *Christian Ethics*, 1059–63.
31. See Grudem, *Christian Ethics*, 1066–72.
32. *Cambridge Dictionary* online, s.v. "exploitation," accessed July 30, 2022, https://dictionary.cambridge.org/us/dictionary/english/exploitation.
33. William G. Messenger, review of (and in this case, summarizing a theme of) *Why Business Matters to God (And What Still Needs to Be Fixed)*, by Jeff Van Duzer, *Themelios* 36, no. 2 (August 2011), https://www.thegospelcoalition.org/themelios/review/why-business-matters-to-god-and-what-still-needs-to-be-fixed/.

## Chapter 12: Ethical Science

1. "Stem Cells: What They Are and What They Do," Mayo Clinic, accessed April 13, 2022, https://www.mayoclinic.org/tests-procedures/bone-marrow-transplant/in-depth/stem-cells/art-20048117.
2. Leonardo M. R. Ferreira, "Stem Cells: A Brief History and Outlook," Science in the News (Harvard University Graduate School of Arts and Sciences), January 2, 2014, https://sitn.hms.harvard.edu/flash/2014/stem-cells-a-brief-history-and-outlook-2/.
3. Andy Coghlan, "Stem Cell Timeline: The History of a Medical Sensation," NewScientist, January 30, 2014, https://www.newscientist.com/article/dn24970-stem-cell-timeline-the-history-of-a-medical-sensation/.
4. Joe Carter, "The FAQs: Chinese Scientists Create First Monkey-Human Embryos," The Gospel Coalition, April 19, 2021, https://www.thegospelcoalition.org/article/create-monkey-human-embryos/; bold added.
5. Carter, "The FAQs: Chinese Scientists Create First Monkey-Human Embryos."
6. Joe Carter, "9 Things You Should Know about Human Cloning," The Gospel Coalition, May 17, 2013, https://www.thegospelcoalition.org/article/9-things-you-should-know-about-human-cloning/.
7. Carter, "9 Things You Should Know about Human Cloning."
8. "Cloning Fact Sheet," National Human Genome Research Institute, last updated August 15, 2020, https://www.genome.gov/about-genomics/fact-sheets/Cloning-Fact-Sheet.
9. Carter's term (although he is focused more on cloning for research) in "9 Things You Should Know about Human Cloning."
10. See Carter, "9 Things You Should Know about Human Cloning"; "Cloning Fact Sheet," National Human Genome Research Institute.
11. "Cloning Fact Sheet," National Human Genome Research Institute.
12. Joe Carter, "The FAQs: What Christians Should Know about CRISPR Genetic Scissors," The Gospel Coalition, October 14, 2022, https://www.thegospelcoalition.org/article/the-faqs-what-christians-should-know-about-crispr-genetic-scissors/.
13. Gabriella Beer, "Science Surgery: 'What's the Difference between the Words Genome, Gene and Chromosome?,'" Cancer Research UK News, May 29, 2018, https://news.cancerresearchuk.org/2018/05/29/science-surgery-whats-the-difference-between-the-words-genome-gene-and-chromosome/.
14. Carter, "The FAQs: What Christians Should Know about CRISPR Genetic Scissors."
15. "How Does Genome Editing Work?," National Human Genome Research Institute, last updated August 3, 2017, https://www.genome.gov/about-genomics/policy-issues/Genome-Editing/How-genome-editing-works.
16. This evaluation generally follows and partially summarizes that of Carter, "The FAQs: What Christians Should Know about CRISPR Genetic Scissors."
17. Francis J. Beckwith, "The Human Being, a Person of Substance," in *Persons, Moral Worth, and Embryos: A Critical Analysis of Pro-Choice Arguments*, ed. Stephen Napier (New York: Springer, 2011), 67–68.
18. "Placental Tissue with CryoMaxx Processing," Americord, accessed April 8, 2022, https://www.americordblood.com/placental-tissue/.
19. Ferreira, "Stem Cells: A Brief History and Outlook."
20. Ferreira, "Stem Cells: A Brief History and Outlook."
21. Gilbert Meilaender, *Bioethics: A Primer for Christians*, 3rd ed. (Grand Rapids, MI: Eerdmans, 2013), 42.
22. Carter, "The FAQs: What Christians Should Know about CRISPR Genetic Scissors."
23. Anjana Ahuja, "'God Is Not in Charge, We Are'; Interview," *Times* [London, England], July 24, 2003, 6, https://link.gale.com/apps/doc/A105815467/STND?u=bju_main&sid=bookmark-STND&xid=d1445762.
24. Angel Corona, "Disease Eradication: What Does It Take to Wipe out a Disease?" American Society for Microbiology, March 6, 2020, https://asm.org/Articles/2020/March/Disease-Eradication-What-Does-It-Take-to-Wipe-out.
25. Corona, "Disease Eradication."
26. "History of Living Donation," United Network for Organ Sharing, Transplant Living, accessed April 19, 2022, https://transplantliving.org/living-donation/history/.
27. "Donate Organs While Alive," Health Resources & Services Administration, organdonor.gov, last reviewed April 2021, https://www.organdonor.gov/learn/process/living-donation.
28. "The Organ Transplant Process," Health Resources & Services Administration, organdonor.gov, last reviewed April 2021, https://www.organdonor.gov/learn/process/transplant-process.
29. "Organ Donation Statistics," Health Resources & Services Administration, organdonor.gov, accessed April 19, 2022, https://www.organdonor.gov/learn/organ-donation-statistics.
30. "What Does the Bible Say about Blood Transfusions?," JW.org, Bible Questions Answered, accessed April 20, 2022, https://www.jw.org/en/bible-teachings/questions/bible-about-blood-transfusion/.
31. Bodie Hodge and Roger Patterson, eds., *World Religions and Cults*, vol. 1 (Green Forest, AR: Master Books, 2015), 208.
32. Hodge and Patterson, *World Religions and Cults*, 207.
33. Meilaender, *Bioethics*, 104.
34. "Organ Donation Statistics," Health Resources & Services Administration.
35. Meilaender, *Bioethics*, 90.
36. "Man Given Genetically Modified Pig Heart Dies," BBC News, March 9, 2022, https://www.bbc.com/news/health-60681493.
37. Carter, "The FAQs: Chinese Scientists Create First Monkey-Human Embryos."
38. United Nations Meetings Coverage and Press Releases, March 28, 2019, https://www.un.org/press/en/2019/ga12131.doc.htm.
39. See video, "Here's What to Expect from Our Planet in the Next 100 Years If We Take No Action on Climate Change," World Economic Forum, July 2, 2021, https://www.weforum.org/videos/20257-2021-what-to-expect-from-our-planet-in-the-next-100-years-if-we-take-no-action-on-climate-change-uplinkmp4-a6c42fe4ce.
40. Taken from page 504 of *Invitation to Christian Ethics: Moral Reasoning and Contemporary Issues* © Copyright 2020 by Ken Magnuson, Invitation to Theological Studies Series. Published by Kregel Publications, Grand Rapids, MI. Used by permission of the publisher. All rights reserved.

41. "Our Partners," The Partnership Project, accessed April 3, 2023, https://partnershipproject.org/partners/.
42. "Who We Are," The Partnership Project, accessed April 3, 2023, https://partnershipproject.org/who-we-are/#our-story.
43. "What PETA REALLY Stands For," People for Ethical Treatment of Animals, accessed May 4, 2022, https://www.peta.org/features/what-peta-really-stands-for/.
44. Why Animal Rights?," People for Ethical Treatment of Animals, accessed May 4, 2022, https://www.peta.org/about-peta/why-peta/why-animal-rights/.
45. Magnuson, *Invitation to Christian Ethics*, 504.
46. Abraham Kuyper, *On Business & Economics*, ed. Peter S. Heslam, Collected Works in Public Theology (Bellingham, WA: Lexham, 2021), 78–79.
47. Jo Ann Stover, *If Everybody Did* (Greenville, SC: BJU Press, 1989).

## Chapter 13: Sexual Ethics

1. Taken from page 202 of *Invitation to Christian Ethics: Moral Reasoning and Contemporary Issues* © Copyright 2020 by Ken Magnuson, Invitation to Theological Studies Series. Published by Kregel Publications, Grand Rapids, MI. Used by permission of the publisher. All rights reserved.
2. See *Christian Ethics: An Introduction to Biblical Moral Reasoning* by Wayne Grudem, © 2018, p. 802. Used by permission of Crossway, a publishing ministry of Good News Publishers, Wheaton, IL 60187, www.crossway.org. Grudem cites Judith Wallerstein and Sandra Blakeslee, *Second Chances: Men, Women, and Children a Decade after Divorce* (New York: Ticknor and Fields, 1989), 41.
3. W. Bradford Wilcox, "The Evolution of Divorce," *National Affairs* 1, Fall 2009: 81–94, https://www.nationalaffairs.com/publications/detail/the-evolution-of-divorce.
4. Taken from page 747 of *The Doctrine of the Christian Life* by John M. Frame. Copyright 2008, P&R Publishing, Phillipsburg, NJ.
5. Frame, *The Doctrine of the Christian Life*, 766–67.
6. Taken from page 14 of *Transforming Homosexuality: What the Bible Says about Sexual Orientation and Change* by Denny Burk and Heath Lambert. Copyright 2015, P&R Publishing, Phillipsburg, NJ.
7. Grudem, *Christian Ethics*, 843–44.
8. See *The Rise and Triumph of the Modern Self: Cultural Amnesia, Expressive Individualism, and the Road to Sexual Revolution* by Carl Trueman © 2020, p. 176. Used by permission of Crossway, a publishing ministry of Good News Publishers, Wheaton, IL 60187, www.crossway.org.
9. See Trueman, *The Rise and Triumph of the Modern Self*, 176.
10. Grudem, *Christian Ethics*, 874.
11. Rick Phillips, "Should We Equate Homosexual and Heterosexual Sin?," Reformation21, June 4, 2015, https://www.reformation21.org/blogs/should-we-equate-homosexual-an.php.
12. Godefridus Udemans, *The Practice of Faith, Hope, Love* (Reformation Heritage, 2012), Kindle edition, loc. 7235.
13. Jonathan V. Last, *What to Expect When No One's Expecting: America's Coming Demographic Disaster* (New York: Encounter Books, 2014).
14. "Current Contraceptive Status Among Women Aged 15–49: United States, 2015–2017," CDC National Center for Health Statistics, Data Brief 327 (December 2018), Figure 2, https://www.cdc.gov/nchs/data/databriefs/db327-H.pdf.
15. Grudem, *Christian Ethics*, 752.
16. Rachel Nall, "Everything You Need to Know about Artificial Insemination," last updated December 22, 2017, https://www.healthline.com/health/artificial-insemination#process.
17. Rebecca Buffum Taylor, "Using a Surrogate Mother: What You Need to Know," last updated November 04, 2021, https://www.webmd.com/infertility-and-reproduction/guide/using-surrogate-mother; "Surrogacy," Yale Medicine, Fact Sheets, accessed March 31, 2023, https://www.yalemedicine.org/conditions/gestational-surrogacy.
18. "Carrier Screening FAQs," The American College of Obstetricians and Gynecologists, last updated December 2020, https://www.acog.org/womens-health/faqs/carrier-screening.

## Glossary

1. Taken from *Christian Ethics: An Introduction to Biblical Moral Reasoning* by Wayne Grudem, © 2018, p. 566. Used by permission of Crossway, a publishing ministry of Good News Publishers, Wheaton, IL 60187, www.crossway.org.
2. David Mathis, "We Will See His Face: What Is the Beatific Vision?" Desiring God, March 11, 2021, https://www.desiringgod.org/articles/we-will-see-his-face.
3. *Cambridge Dictionary* online, s.v. "bribery," accessed July 29, 2022, https://dictionary.cambridge.org/us/dictionary/english/bribery.
4. Joe Carter, "9 Things You Should Know about Human Cloning," The Gospel Coalition, May 17, 2013, https://www.thegospelcoalition.org/article/9-things-you-should-know-about-human-cloning/.
5. Jim Berg, *Essential Virtues: Marks of the Christ-Centered Life* (Greenville, SC: JourneyForth, 2008), 164.
6. Wilhelmus à Brakel, *The Law, Christian Graces, and the Lord's Prayer*, vol. 3 of *The Christian's Reasonable Service*, ed. Joel R. Beeke, trans. Bartel Elshout (Grand Rapids, MI: Reformation Heritage Books, 2015), 103–4; italics in the original.
7. Grudem, *Christian Ethics*, 587.
8. *Cambridge Dictionary* online, s.v. "exploitation," accessed July 30, 2022, https://dictionary.cambridge.org/us/dictionary/english/exploitation.
9. *Cambridge Dictionary* online, s.v. "extortion," accessed July 29, 2022, https://dictionary.cambridge.org/us/dictionary/english/extortion.
10. John Calvin, *Institutes of the Christian Religion* 3.2.7, vol. 1, ed. John T. McNeill, trans. Ford Lewis Battles, The Library of Christian Classics, vol. 20 (Philadelphia: Westminster Press, 1960), 551.
11. Joe Carter, "The FAQs: What Christians Should Know about CRISPR Genetic Scissors," The Gospel Coalition, October 14, 2022, https://www.thegospelcoalition.org/article/the-faqs-what-christians-should-know-about-crispr-genetic-scissors/.
12. Carter, "The FAQs: What Christians Should Know about CRISPR Genetic Scissors."
13. James T. Dennison, Jr., comp., "Calvin's Catechism (1537)," in vol. 1, *Reformed Confessions of the 16th and 17th Centuries in English Translation* (Grand Rapids, MI: Reformation Heritage Books, 2008), 378.
14. Jerry Bridges, *The Practice of Godliness* (Colorado Springs: NavPress, 1983), 91.
15. Taken from page 34 of *The Defense of the Faith*, 4th ed., by Cornelius Van Til, ed. K. Scott Oliphint. Copyright 2008, P&R Publishing, Phillipsburg, NJ.
16. Michael Walzer, *Arguing about War* (New Haven, CT: Yale University Press, 2004), 22.
17. Oliver O'Donovan, *The Just War Revisited* (Cambridge: Cambridge University Press, 2003), 5.
18. Augustine, *On Christian Teaching* 3.10.16, in William Harmless, ed., *In His Own Words* (Washington, DC: CUA Press, 2010), 170.
19. Grudem, *Christian Ethics*, 311.
20. 18 U.S.C. 1112(a), http://uscode.house.gov/view.xhtml?req=granuleid:USC-prelim-title18-section1112&num=0&edition=prelim.
21. See 18 U.S.C. 1112(a).
22. See 18 U.S.C. 1112(a).
23. 18 U.S.C. 1111(a), http://uscode.house.gov/view.xhtml?req=granuleid:USC-prelim-title18-section1111&num=0&edition=prelim.
24. See 18 U.S.C. 1111(a).
25. See 18 U.S.C. 1111(a).
26. *Oxford English Dictionary* online, s.v. "racism", last modified March 2022, https://www.oed.com/view/Entry/157097?redirectedFrom=racism#eid.
27. Collins COBUILD Advanced Learner's Dictionary online, s.v. "recreational drug," accessed April 4, 2023, https://www.collinsdictionary.com/us/dictionary/english/recreational-drug.
28. Bridges, *The Practice of Godliness*, 164.
29. "Self-Defense Law: Overview," FindLaw, updated September 10, 2022, https://www.findlaw.com/criminal/criminal-law-basics/self-defense-overview.html.
30. Joe Carter, "The FAQs: Chinese Scientists Create First Monkey-Human Embryos," The Gospel Coalition, April 19, 2021, https://www.thegospelcoalition.org/article/create-monkey-human-embryos/.
31. Carter, "The FAQs: Chinese Scientists Create First Monkey-Human Embryos."
32. See Augustine, *City of God* 15.22, trans. Marcus Dods, with an introduction by Thomas Merton (New York: Modern Library, 1993), 511.

# glossary

## A

**abortion** "Any action that intentionally causes the death and removal from the womb of an unborn child."[1]

**abstinence** With respect to alcohol use, the position that emphasizes both the necessity of avoiding drunkenness and the wisdom of abstaining from that which gets one drunk.

**addiction** Dependence on getting pleasure from a substance or behavior regardless of the negative consequences.

**adultery** Marital unfaithfulness; lust for someone or sexual activity that violates the marriage covenant of one or both people involved.

**anger** Intense displeasure arising from strong disagreement with a situation.

**animal rights** The idea that animals are entitled to the same rights and privileges that humans are entitled to—no exploitation and no abuse; generally includes the notion that any killing or prolonged caging of animals to benefit humans is unethical.

**artificial insemination from a donor** Collecting semen from a man other than a woman's husband and injecting it into her cervix or uterus.

**artificial insemination from a husband** Collecting a husband's semen and injecting it into his wife's cervix or uterus.

**asceticism** The severe denial of the normal physical needs of the body, usually for the purpose of gaining spiritual merit.

**assisted reproductive technology (ART)** All types of medical technology used to promote reproduction in order to overcome infertility.

**authenticity** Being true to oneself, being transparent, and following one's heart—most often leading to transparent sinfulness.

**beatific vision** "The sight that makes happy,"[2] specifically the direct sight of God Himself, which believers will experience in their glorified state.

**bestiality** Sexual behavior with animals.

**birth control** A general term that refers to preventing pregnancy; contraception through the use of artificial or natural methods.

**bisexual** According to LGBTQ+ advocates, someone with sexual desires for or who engages in sexual behavior with both men and women.

**bribery** "An attempt to make someone do something for you by giving the person money, presents, or something else that he or she wants."[3]

**capital punishment** A government's use of execution as a criminal penalty.

**categorical imperative** A maxim (or principle) that a person is convinced would guide all people to do the right thing if it were a universal law. This maxim is always true regardless of circumstances and is an obligation for all people at all times, according to Kant's formulation.

**Christian disobedience to authority** A refusal to obey a legitimate authority's laws or commands that contradict the commands of God.

**Christian ethics** The branch of theology that studies how man ought to live in light of Scriptural teaching, creational norms, and moral reasoning.

**cloning** A form of reproduction that does not use a sperm and an egg but takes genetic material from a single person to manufacture a new, almost identical, but separate, individual.[4]

**cohabitation** Living together before or apart from marriage.

**commercialism** The abuse of profit-making that dehumanizes people by reducing them to cogs in an economic machine, by appealing to their covetousness.

**communitarianism (on immigration)** A framework that when applied to immigration defends the prerogative of each nation to govern its borders with moral appropriateness, keeping in mind the challenges immigrants and refugees face that host nations can help overcome.

**compassion** An external manifestation of loving-kindness that sympathetically and indiscriminately meets a need.

**compatibility** The popular idea that, in order for a marriage to work, couples must have a lot in common.

**consequentialist ethics** Ethical choices are governed by the results or ends they will achieve. The proper end is that which achieves the greatest amount of good. The good is often happiness, as defined by the individual or by society.

**conservation** The effort to preserve or improve certain

natural resources so that they remain available for use in the future.

**corruption** Any harm done to God's good design and moral will for His creation.

**cosmopolitanism** A framework that when applied to immigration focuses on the needs and well-being of the individual regardless of a person's immigration status.

**courage** Spiritual strength to unashamedly do the right thing at the right time even at risk of one's own harm.[5]

**covenantal identity** Who a person is—based not on individual characteristics but based on his or her relationship to a representative head whom God established, either Adam or Christ.

**cowardice** Running away from danger; refusing to stand up to defend what is true and right when threatened.

**creational norms** Standards for how life in God's creation works, discerned by observing the design of the created order in light of Scripture's teaching.

**cruelty** The willful causation of distress or discomfort in others.

**cunning** Involves shrewdness as well as deception. Like prudence, cunning employs a thorough analysis of the situation, but it does so in order to obtain something through immoral means or to an unethical end.

## D

**deontological ethics** Ethical choices are governed by objective, absolute, universal rules or principles and a selfless commitment to duty.

**despair** Hopelessness; describes giving up and being pessimistic about the outcome of a situation.

**diligence** *"The exertion of the spiritual and physical powers of a believer whereby he willingly, joyously, and earnestly executes that task which God assigns him, doing so because it is the will of God."*[6]

**disloyalty** Disregard (without a legitimate ethical reason) for any commitment to remain faithful and loyal to something or someone.

## E

**environmentalism** A movement that seeks the protection of the environment from human destruction and the improvement of the conditions of the environment through social and political action.

**ethical egoism** A consequentialist approach in which pure, individual self-interest directed toward fulfillment of personal happiness is the governing goal.

**ethics** The branch of philosophy that studies how man ought to live.

**eugenics** The quest to bolster human genetics by preventing people with traits deemed undesirable from reproducing, while encouraging people with traits deemed desirable to procreate; has often been associated with the idea that some races are superior to others.

**euthanasia** "The act of intentionally ending the life of a person who is elderly, terminally ill, or suffering from some incurable injury or disease."[7]

**existentialist ethics** Ethical choices are determined by the freely choosing individual. In the absence of absolute truth or meaning, the individual creates his own meaning and essence by the choices he makes and must take full responsibility for the outcome of these choices.

**exploitation** "The use of something in order to get an advantage from it."[8]

**external coherence** The test of whether an ethical system aligns with real life.

**extortion** "The act of getting something, especially money, by force or threats."[9]

**faith** "A firm and certain knowledge of God's benevolence toward us, founded upon the truth of the freely given promise in Christ, both revealed to our minds and sealed upon our hearts through the Holy Spirit."[10]

**faithfulness** Steadfast loyalty to that which is morally acceptable and good, despite difficulty and conflict.

**falsehood** As a vice, describes the endorsement of untruths to harm someone else or for personal gain.

**fornication** Sexual immorality.

**gene editing** "A form of genome engineering in which DNA is inserted, replaced, or removed from the genetic material of a cell using artificially engineered enzymes, or 'molecular scissors.'"[11]

**gentleness** Tender care for others even when they are hard to deal with.

**germline** An individual's sex cells (ovum or sperm) or "the lineage of [sex] cells spanning generations of individuals."[12]

**goodness** Generously seeking others' happiness and well-being, as determined by God's righteous standards.

**gratitude** An attitude of thanksgiving to God for His provision and governance of all things.

**harshness** Unpleasantness, roughness, or meanness directed toward someone.

**homosexual** According to LGBTQ+ advocates, someone with sexual desires for a person of the same sex and/or who engages in sexual behavior with a person of the same sex.

**honesty** A devotion to truthfulness where one affirms and acts in accord with what is true and righteous.

**hope** "The expectation of the things that faith has believed to be truly promised by God."[13]

**humility** A lowly view of one's own importance, resulting from "a high view of God's person"[14] and a profound sense of one's own weakness and sinfulness.

**image of God in man** The essence of being human; a bestowed status whereby the whole person is made to be "like God in everything in which a creature can be like God."[15]

**immigrant** Someone who relocates to a country other than his or her own.

**immodesty** Dress, or undress, that draws sexual attention.

**incest** Sexual relations among family members aside from between a husband and wife.

**indifference** Apathy toward others and utter lack of concern for the ethical good of a situation.

**inequality** The treatment of certain groups as less worthy of respect and dignity than other groups.

**ingratitude** Taking things for granted, overlooking what is clearly worthy of thanks, and being unthankful for all the good one has.

**internal consistency** The test of whether an ethical system contradicts or undermines itself.

**in vitro fertilization (IVF)** Joining together a wife's egg and a husband's sperm to form an embryo in a laboratory.

**joy** A confident delight in God's sovereign work in all of life's circumstances.

**just war doctrine** A perspective on war that recognizes war as a moral matter[16] and also recognizes that war can be a legitimate way for governments to ensure justice[17]; sets ethical parameters on when war is ethically viable and how to conduct oneself in war.

**kindness** An internal sentiment, cultivated by the Holy Spirit, that motivates believers to indiscriminately do good to others.

**kingdom of God** The reign of the risen and enthroned Lord Jesus Christ; includes Christ bringing the saints to fulfill the Creation Mandate as well, so that they rule the creation as God intended.

**legalism** Trying to earn justification with God through works, or trying to earn a higher standing with God by the performance of works or rituals.

**LGBTQ+** An abbreviation that stands for lesbian, gay, bisexual, transgender, queer (or questioning), and several other terms that are used to denote various types of gender identity confusion.

**love** "Any movement of the soul to enjoy God for God's own sake, and to enjoy one's self and one's neighbor for God's sake."[18]

**lying** Verbally declaring something that one knows to be false.[19]

**manslaughter** "The unlawful killing of a human being without malice."[20]

**manslaughter (involuntary)** Manslaughter that results from carelessness or occurs in conjunction with the commission of a minor crime.[21]

**manslaughter (voluntary)** Manslaughter that takes place impulsively in response to a heated exchange or serious provocation.[22]

**marital purity** Forsaking all forbidden sexual activity and partaking in the sexual activity God designed for a man and woman within the bounds of marriage.

**masturbation** Sexual self-stimulation.

**meekness** A humble and calm disposition in situations that can lead to pride or anger.

**militarism** A perspective that sees war as the means to fulfilling the desires of a country or its leaders.

**moralism** Trying to be a good, upstanding person through one's own good works; focused on social acceptability.

**murder** "The unlawful killing of a human being with malice aforethought."[23]

**murder (first-degree)** Premeditated murder or murder committed alongside another serious crime.[24]

**murder (second-degree)** Any murder that does not fit the definition of first-degree murder.[25]

**naturalistic fallacy** This fallacy assumes that what is natural is good. In other words, it assumes that if a behavior is found in nature, it must be morally acceptable.

**no-fault divorce** Divorce law that allows for divorce without the need for either party to demonstrate that the other has violated the marriage covenant.

**organ donation** Voluntarily giving one's organs or tissues to replace someone else's defective or damaged organs or tissues.

**organ transplantation** The replacement of a defective or damaged organ or tissue in one person with a healthy organ or tissue taken from another person.

**pacificism** A perspective on war that, in its most extreme form, opposes all forms of violent action, even those which would avoid great harm or promote a great good.

**patience** A believer's faith-filled and hopeful endurance under long-lasting difficult circumstances.

**peace** A harmonious wholeness produced when God's design of the world, including human relationships, is rightly ordered; as a virtue, describes the mindset and character of a believer, even during difficult and unpleasant circumstances.

**polygamy** Having multiple spouses at one time.

**pornography** Pictures, videos, or graphic descriptions intended to stimulate sexual desire.

**pride** An inflated estimation of oneself which attempts to rob God of His rightful place as sovereign Lord of all.

**prostitution** Providing sex acts for pay or in return for some benefit.

**prudence** The ability to choose the best course of action, having considered all the constraints of the situation, to obtain the most righteous and beneficial outcome.

## R

**race** The single race of humans (all descended from Adam and distinct from animals) or a distinct cultural, ethnic, social, or people group within the human race.

**racism** "Prejudice, antagonism, or discrimination by an individual, institution, or society, against a person or people on the basis of their nationality or (now usually) their membership of a particular racial or ethnic group, typically one that is a minority or marginalized. Also: beliefs that members of a particular racial or ethnic group possess innate characteristics or qualities, or that some racial or ethnic groups are superior to others; an ideology based on such beliefs."[26]

**rashness** Acting in the moment with no regard for whether one's actions are the best way, or even a good way, to reach a desired end.

**realism (on immigration)** A framework that when applied to immigration recognizes that each government will act according to its best interests in relation to its own people. Borders and immigration laws feature positively in this framework.

**realism (on war)** A utilitarian and pragmatic perspective on war that views wars as necessary evils, where any moral considerations either don't exist or are very flexible.

**rebellion** The rejection of a current government's authority and the assertion of an opposing agenda through violence.

**recklessness** Throwing all caution to the wind and acting or reacting impulsively.

**recreational drugs** Drugs "that some people take occasionally for enjoyment, especially when they are spending time socially with other people."[27]

**righteousness** The conformity of an individual's life to God's standards of moral perfection.

**self-control** "The exercise of inner strength under the direction of sound judgment that enables us to do, think, and say the things that are pleasing to God."[28]

**self-defense** "The right to prevent suffering force or violence through the use of a sufficient level of counteracting force or violence."[29]

**self-indulgence** Having no inhibitions, a total letting go of oneself to do as one pleases.

**sexual abuse** Any criminal activity that forces any kind of sexual perversion on another person; includes rape and pedophilia.

**situation ethics** A consequentialist ethical approach. A form of ethical relativism that holds that a person should always act in the way that is most loving in each situation. Love is not tied to any moral absolutes, and what love requires may be different in different situations for different people.

**sloth** Laziness; a lack of motivation to do necessary and productive work.

**stem cells** Cells that "have not yet obtained a special structure and function."[30]

**stem cells (embryonic)** A type of stem cell found in embryos in their first few days of development that can develop into any type of cell in the body.[31]

**strife** Adversarial contention that leads an individual to verbally disagree with, ideologically break away from, or physically engage the conflicting party.

**suicide** The intentional and voluntary taking of one's own life.

**surrogacy** Using the womb of a third party (a surrogate mother) for the gestation of a baby.

**temperance** Self-control and the avoidance of excessive behavior.

**transgender** According to LGBTQ+ advocates, someone who thinks of him- or herself as having a gender different from his or her sex.

**ungodliness** Anything that is contrary to God's nature or opposed to God's ways.

**utilitarianism** The most common consequentialist approach to ethics. Believes that the utility (usefulness) of an action to bring about an intended helpful end determines what is right or best. The end justifies the means, and the proper end (or goal) is to do the greatest good for the greatest number of people, usually understood as that which brings the most happiness and the least pain.

**utopian** Relating to an ideal society of perfect peace, justice, and prosperity; often intended as a description of an unrealistic hope.

**vice** A character trait or consistent behavior that is recognizably wicked or immoral; a deviation from God's upright standard. May be the exact opposite of a virtue or may be the twisting of a virtue into a counterfeit.

**virtue** Rightly ordered love,[32] which manifests itself in a person's character and behavior.

**virtue ethics** An approach to ethics that focuses on discerning what virtues lead to a flourishing life and on developing those virtues so they become habitual.

**volunteerist perspective** The belief that God's law is simply whatever He wills it to be and that right and wrong could have been opposite what they are, merely at God's whim.

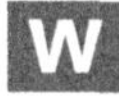

**wisdom** The art of living well by observing creational norms through the lenses of Scripture, by listening to the counsel of the wise, and by being conscious that all of life is lived before the face of God.

**workaholism** Excessive engagement in work that leaves no room for and gives no attention to the other good and necessary parts of life that aren't work.

**worry** Emotional instability where someone rehearses all the what-ifs about a given situation and fails to trust God and His Word.

# scripture memory

## 1. Creational Foundations for Ethics

**ROMANS 1:18–20**

For the wrath of God is revealed from heaven against all ungodliness and unrighteousness of men, who hold the truth in unrighteousness; Because that which may be known of God is manifest in them; for God hath shewed it unto them. For the invisible things of him from the creation of the world are clearly seen, being understood by the things that are made, even his eternal power and Godhead; so that they are without excuse.

## 2. The Fall's Effects on Ethics

**ROMANS 3:10–12**

As it is written, There is none righteous, no, not one: There is none that understandeth, there is none that seeketh after God. They are all gone out of the way, they are together become unprofitable; there is none that doeth good, no, not one.

## 3. The Role of Redemption in Ethics

**COLOSSIANS 3:1–3, 12**

If ye then be risen with Christ, seek those things which are above, where Christ sitteth on the right hand of God. Set your affection on things above, not on things on the earth. For ye are dead, and your life is hid with Christ in God. . . . Put on therefore, as the elect of God, holy and beloved, bowels of mercies, kindness, humbleness of mind, meekness, longsuffering.

## 4. Becoming Like Christ

**2 PETER 1:3, 5–7**

According as his divine power hath given unto us all things that pertain unto life and godliness, through the knowledge of him that hath called us to glory and virtue: . . . And beside this, giving all diligence, add to your faith virtue; and to virtue knowledge; And to knowledge temperance; and to temperance patience; and to patience godliness; And to godliness brotherly kindness; and to brotherly kindness charity.

## 5. Three Central Virtues

**1 CORINTHIANS 13:13**

And now abideth faith, hope, charity, these three; but the greatest of these is charity.

## 6. Virtues, Part 1

**PHILIPPIANS 4:8**

Finally, brethren, whatsoever things are true, whatsoever things are honest, whatsoever things are just, whatsoever things are pure, whatsoever things are lovely, whatsoever things are of good report; if there be any virtue, and if there be any praise, think on these things.

## 7. Virtues, Part 2

**GALATIANS 5:22–23**

But the fruit of the Spirit is love, joy, peace, longsuffering, gentleness, goodness, faith, Meekness, temperance: against such there is no law.

## 8. A Method for Handling Ethical Issues

**PSALM 119:97, 101–4**

O how love I thy law! it is my meditation all the day. . . . I have refrained my feet from every evil way, that I might keep thy word. I have not departed from thy judgments: for thou hast taught me. How sweet are thy words unto my taste! yea, sweeter than honey to my mouth! Through thy precepts I get understanding: therefore I hate every false way.

## 9. The Ethics of Life and Death

**EXODUS 20:13**

Thou shalt not kill.

**MATTHEW 5:21–22**

Ye have heard that it was said by them of old time, Thou shalt not kill; and whosoever shall kill shall be in danger of the judgment: But I say unto you, That whosoever is angry with his brother without a cause shall be in danger of the judgment: and whosoever shall say to his brother, Raca, shall be in danger of the council: but whosoever shall say, Thou fool, shall be in danger of hell fire.

## 10. Ethical Government

**ROMANS 13:1, 4**

Let every soul be subject unto the higher powers. For there is no power but of God: the powers that be are ordained of God. . . . For he is the minister of God to thee for good. But if thou do that which is evil, be afraid; for he beareth not the sword in vain: for he is the minister of God, a revenger to execute wrath upon him that doeth evil.

## 11. Ethical Society

**MATTHEW 7:12**

Therefore all things whatsoever ye would that men should do to you, do ye even so to them: for this is the law and the prophets.

## 12. Ethical Science

**GENESIS 1:28–30**

And God blessed them, and God said unto them, Be fruitful, and multiply, and replenish the earth, and subdue it: and have dominion over the fish of the sea, and over the fowl of the air, and over every living thing that moveth upon the earth. And God said, Behold, I have given you every herb bearing seed, which is upon the face of all the earth, and every tree, in the which is the fruit of a tree yielding seed; to you it shall be for meat. And to every beast of the earth, and to every fowl of the air, and to every thing that creepeth upon the earth, wherein there is life, I have given every green herb for meat: and it was so.

## 13. Sexual Ethics

**1 THESSALONIANS 4:3–5**

For this is the will of God, even your sanctification, that ye should abstain from fornication: That every one of you should know how to possess his vessel in sanctification and honour; Not in the lust of concupiscence, even as the Gentiles which know not God.

# instructional aids

# 4.2 Counterfeits and Integrity Chart

In the chart below, define the counterfeits of virtue. Then describe the aim, source, means, and end result of each counterfeit. And finally, do the same for the biblical solution, integrity.

For help, see pages 70–72 in your textbook.

| | LEGALISM | MORALISM | AUTHENTICITY | INTEGRITY |
|---|---|---|---|---|
| **Definition** | | | | |
| **Aim** | | | | |
| **Source** | | | | |
| **Means** | | | | |
| **End Result** | | | | |

# 6.1 Virtue and Vice Chart

| VIRTUES | VICES |
|---|---|
| faith | unbelief |
| hope | despair |
| love | lust, hate |
| righteousness | ungodliness |
| goodness | corruption |
| prudence | rashness, cunning |
| diligence | sloth, laziness |
| faithfulness | disloyalty |
| courage | recklessness, cowardice |
| self-control | self-indulgence, addiction |
| temperance | addiction, asceticism |
| patience | strife |
| humility | pride |
| meekness | anger |
| gentleness | harshness |
| kindness | cruelty |
| compassion | indifference |
| gratitude | ingratitude |
| joy | despair |
| peace | worry |
| honesty | dishonesty, falsehood |

# 6.2 Virtues and Vices in the Bible

## VIRTUES

**1 CORINTHIANS 13:13**
And now abideth faith, hope, charity, these three; but the greatest of these is charity.

**GALATIANS 5:5–6**
For we through the Spirit wait for the hope of righteousness by faith. For in Jesus Christ neither circumcision availeth anything, nor uncircumcision; but faith which worketh by love.

**GALATIANS 5:22–23**
But the fruit of the Spirit is love, joy, peace, longsuffering, gentleness, goodness, faith, meekness, temperance: against such there is no law.

**PHILIPPIANS 4:5–8**
Let your moderation be known unto all men. The Lord is at hand. Be careful for nothing; but in every thing by prayer and supplication with thanksgiving let your requests be made known unto God. And the peace of God, which passeth all understanding, shall keep your hearts and minds through Christ Jesus. Finally, brethren, whatsoever things are true, whatsoever things are honest, whatsoever things are just, whatsoever things are pure, whatsoever things are lovely, whatsoever things are of good report; if there be any virtue, and if there be any praise, think on these things.

**COLOSSIANS 1:4–5**
Since we heard of your faith in Christ Jesus, and of the love which ye have to all the saints, for the hope which is laid up for you in heaven, whereof ye heard before in the word of the truth of the gospel.

**COLOSSIANS 3:12**
Put on therefore, as the elect of God, holy and beloved, bowels of mercies, kindness, humbleness of mind, meekness, longsuffering.

**1 THESSALONIANS 1:3**
Remembering without ceasing your work of faith, and labour of love, and patience of hope in our Lord Jesus Christ, in the sight of God and our Father.

**JAMES 3:17–18**
But the wisdom that is from above is first pure, then peaceable, gentle, and easy to be intreated, full of mercy and good fruits, without partiality, and without hypocrisy. And the fruit of righteousness is sown in peace of them that make peace.

**2 PETER 1:5–7**
And beside this, giving all diligence, add to your faith virtue; and to virtue knowledge; and to knowledge temperance; and to temperance patience; and to patience godliness; and to godliness brotherly kindness; and to brotherly kindness charity.

# 6.2 Virtues and Vices in the Bible

## VICES

### MATTHEW 15:19
For out of the heart proceed evil thoughts, murders, adulteries, fornications, thefts, false witness, blasphemies.

### MARK 7:21–22
For from within, out of the heart of men, proceed evil thoughts, adulteries, fornications, murders, thefts, covetousness, wickedness, deceit, lasciviousness, an evil eye, blasphemy, pride, foolishness.

### ROMANS 1:29–31
Being filled with all unrighteousness, fornication, wickedness, covetousness, maliciousness; full of envy, murder, debate, deceit, malignity; whisperers, backbiters, haters of God, despiteful, proud, boasters, inventors of evil things, disobedient to parents, without understanding, covenantbreakers, without natural affection, implacable, unmerciful.

### ROMANS 13:13
Let us walk honestly, as in the day; not in rioting and drunkenness, not in chambering and wantonness, not in strife and envying.

### 1 CORINTHIANS 5:10–11
Yet not altogether with the fornicators of this world, or with the covetous, or extortioners, or with idolaters; for then must ye needs go out of the world. But now I have written unto you not to keep company, if any man that is called a brother be a fornicator, or covetous, or an idolater, or a railer, or a drunkard, or an extortioner; with such an one no not to eat.

### 1 CORINTHIANS 6:9–10
Know ye not that the unrighteous shall not inherit the kingdom of God? Be not deceived: neither fornicators, nor idolaters, nor adulterers, nor effeminate, nor abusers of themselves with mankind, nor thieves, nor covetous, nor drunkards, nor revilers, nor extortioners, shall inherit the kingdom of God.

### 2 CORINTHIANS 12:20–21
For I fear, lest, when I come, I shall not find you such as I would, and that I shall be found unto you such as ye would not: lest there be debates, envyings, wraths, strifes, backbitings, whisperings, swellings, tumults: and lest, when I come again, my God will humble me among you, and that I shall bewail many which have sinned already, and have not repented of the uncleanness and fornication and lasciviousness which they have committed.

### GALATIANS 5:19–21
Now the works of the flesh are manifest, which are these; Adultery, fornication, uncleanness, lasciviousness, idolatry, witchcraft, hatred, variance, emulations, wrath, strife, seditions, heresies, envyings, murders, drunkenness, revellings, and such like: of the which I tell you before, as I have also told you in time past, that they which do such things shall not inherit the kingdom of God.

### EPHESIANS 4:31
Let all bitterness, and wrath, and anger, and clamour, and evil speaking, be put away from you, with all malice.

### EPHESIANS 5:3–5
But fornication, and all uncleanness, or covetousness, let it not be once named among you, as becometh saints; neither filthiness, nor foolish talking, nor jesting, which are not convenient: but rather giving of thanks. For this ye know, that no whoremonger, nor unclean person, nor covetous man, who is an idolater, hath any inheritance in the kingdom of Christ and of God.

### COLOSSIANS 3:5, 8
Mortify therefore your members which are upon the earth; fornication, uncleanness, inordinate affection, evil concupiscence, and covetousness, which is idolatry: . . . but now ye also put off all these; anger, wrath, malice, blasphemy, filthy communication out of your mouth.

### 1 TIMOTHY 1:9–10
Knowing this, that the law is not made for a righteous man, but for the lawless and disobedient, for the ungodly and for sinners, for unholy and profane, for murderers of fathers and murderers of mothers, for manslayers, for whoremongers, for them that defile themselves with mankind, for menstealers, for liars, for perjured persons, and if there be any other thing that is contrary to sound doctrine.

### 2 TIMOTHY 3:2–4
For men shall be lovers of their own selves, covetous, boasters, proud, blasphemers, disobedient to parents, unthankful, unholy, without natural affection, trucebreakers, false accusers, incontinent, fierce, despisers of those that are good, traitors, heady, highminded, lovers of pleasures more than lovers of God.

### TITUS 3:3
For we ourselves also were sometimes foolish, disobedient, deceived, serving divers lusts and pleasures, living in malice and envy, hateful, and hating one another.

### 1 PETER 2:1
Wherefore laying aside all malice, and all guile, and hypocrisies, and envies, and all evil speakings.

### 1 PETER 4:3, 15
For the time past of our life may suffice us to have wrought the will of the Gentiles, when we walked in lasciviousness, lusts, excess of wine, revellings, banquetings, and abominable idolatries: . . . but let none of you suffer as a murderer, or as a thief, or as an evildoer, or as a busybody in other men's matters.

### REVELATION 9:21
Neither repented they of their murders, nor of their sorceries, nor of their fornication, nor of their thefts.

### REVELATION 21:8
But the fearful, and unbelieving, and the abominable, and murderers, and whoremongers, and sorcerers, and idolaters, and all liars, shall have their part in the lake which burneth with fire and brimstone: which is the second death.

### REVELATION 22:15
For without are dogs, and sorcerers, and whoremongers, and murderers, and idolaters, and whosoever loveth and maketh a lie.

# 4.2 Counterfeits and Integrity Chart

**In the chart below, define the counterfeits of virtue. Then describe the aim, source, means, and end result of each counterfeit. And finally, do the same for the biblical solution, integrity.**

**For help, see pages 70–72 in your textbook.**

| | LEGALISM | MORALISM | AUTHENTICITY | INTEGRITY |
|---|---|---|---|---|
| **Definition** | trying to earn a right standing with God through works or a higher spirituality through external ritualism | trying to be seen as a good person in the eyes of others through good deeds and outwardly pious practices | being your true (sinful) self; being transparent and being naturally who you want to be without any inhibitions | being who God wants you to be |
| **Aim** | earning a right standing with God | earning a right standing in society | freedom to be oneself | Christlikeness to the glory of God |
| **Source** | self | society | one's own heart, desires, and dreams | Christ, by the regenerating work of the Holy Spirit provided in the New Covenant |
| **Means** | practicing religious rituals (externalism) | doing good works and outwardly pious actions in the community | removing all inhibitions to be and do as one wants | yielding to the Spirit's work by practicing the spiritual disciplines |
| **End Result** | pride, hypocrisy, guilt, and hopelessness | self-righteousness, self-serving hypocrisy | embrace of what's most vile; transparent sinfulness | virtues |

# student edition scripture index

## LEVITICUS



## NUMBERS



## DEUTERONOMY



## JOSHUA



## JUDGES



## RUTH



## 1 SAMUEL



## 2 SAMUEL

## 1 KINGS



## 2 KINGS



## 2 CHRONICLES



## EZRA



## NEHEMIAH



## ESTHER



## JOB



## PSALMS



## PROVERBS

## ECCLESIASTES



## SONG OF SOLOMON



## ISAIAH

## MARK



## LUKE



## JOHN



## ACTS



## ROMANS

## 1 CORINTHIANS

## 2 CORINTHIANS



## GALATIANS



## EPHESIANS

## JAMES



## 1 PETER



## 2 PETER



## 1 JOHN



## JUDE



## REVELATION

# student edition topical index

Page numbers followed by "i" indicate an image on that page.

## A



## B



## C

## D



## E



## F

## S



## T



## U



## V

## W

# student edition photo credits

**Key:** (t) top; (c) center; (b) bottom; (l) left; (r) right

## Cover

Pyrosky/E+ via Getty Images

## Throughout

(crinkle paper) Phecsone/Shutterstock.com; (crinkle paper) Ton Photographer 4289/Shutterstock.com

## Introduction

**4** skynesher/E+ via Getty Images; **5** brizmaker/iStockphoto via Getty Images; **6l** bigacis/Shutterstock.com; **6r** liquidtenerife/iStockphoto via Getty Images; **7** Maryna Patzen/iStockphoto via Getty Images

## Chapter 1

**13** Hulton Archive/Staff via Getty Images; **14, 25** vadik4444 /Shutterstock.com

## Chapter 2

**34** Grafissimo/Digital Vision Vectors via Getty Images; **43** Ho Ngoc Binh/Moment RF via Getty Images

## Chapter 3

**46** IanDagnall Computing/Alamy Stock Photo; **51** Guillem Lopez/ Alamy Stock Photo; **52** Victor Korchenko/Alamy Stock Photo; **54** Krakenimages.com/Shutterstock.com; **55** kate_sept2004/E+ via Getty Images; **57** TommL/E+ via Getty Images; **58** biletskiyevgeniy.com /Shutterstock.com

## Chapter 4

**63** Alberto Gagliardi/iStockphoto via Getty Images; **66** Historical/Corbis Historical via Getty Images; **68–69** Atid Kiattisaksiri/E+ via Getty Images; **70** Chronicle/Alamy Stock Photo

## Chapter 5

**75** Matveev Aleksandr/Shutterstock.com; **78** Valdis Skudre/Shutterstock .com; **85** CHAINFOTO24/Shutterstock.com

## Chapter 6

**94** Draga Saparevska/RooM RF via Getty Images; **95, 110** Floortje/ iStockphoto via Getty Images; **97** Khosrork/iStockphoto via Getty Images; **101** RTRO/Alamy Stock Photo; **103** Prostock-studio /Shutterstock.com

## Chapter 7

**113** mashabuba/E+ via Getty Images; **120l** kieferpix/iStockphoto via Getty Images; **120c** Prixel Creative/Shutterstock.com; **120r–21b** jacoblund/iStockphoto via Getty Images; **121t** SDI Productions/E+ via Getty Images; **128** iShootPhotosLLC/E+ via Getty Images; **130** Rapid Eye Media CC/iStockphoto via Getty Images

## Chapter 8

**137** Monkey Business Images/Shutterstock.com; **142** cirano83/iStockphoto via Getty Images; **144** Olivier Blondeau/E+ via Getty Images

## Chapter 9

**152** The Washington Post/Contributor via Getty Images; **154** Ghislain & Marie David de Lossy/The Image Bank via Getty Images; **158** Motortion/Shutterstock.com; **164** Ground Picture/Shutterstock.com

## Chapter 10

**167** imagedepotpro/E+ viaGetty Images; **170** BERIT ROALD/AFP via Getty Images; **173** 3D_generator/iStock/Getty Images Plus via Getty Images; **176** Carl Court/Getty Images News via Getty Images; **181** Michele and Tom Grimm/Alamy Stock Photo

## Chapter 11

**194** kali9/E+ via Getty Images; **196t** Science History Images/Alamy Stock Photo; **196bl** Niday Picture Library/Alamy Stock Photo; **196br** Tibbut Archive/Alamy Stock Photo; **202** mrs/Moment via Getty Images; **203** Igor Sandra/Alamy Stock Photo; **206l** michaeljung/Shutterstock .com; **206r** TheVisualsYouNeed/Shutterstock.com; **207** Felix Junker/ EyeEm via Getty Images; **211** tsyhun/Shutterstock.com; **213** fizkes/ Shutterstock.com

## Chapter 12

**217, 235** luismmolina/iStock/Getty Images Plus via Getty Images; **218** PA Images via Getty Images; **221** Yvonne Hemsey/Hulton Archive via Getty Images; **222** Carlos Fernandez/Moment via Getty Images; **223** PA Images/Alamy; **224** Akarawut/Shutterstock.com; **228–29** Christoph Prokop/Alamy Stock Photo; **230** Mitch Kezar/Design Pics via Getty Images; **231t** mustafagi/E+ via Getty Images; 231b Africa Studio/Shutterstock.com; **232** georgeclerk/E+ via Getty Images; **233t** Science History Images/Alamy Stock Photo; **233b** ~UserGI15633185 /iStock/Getty Images Plus via Getty Images; **234** Peter Summers/Getty Images News via Getty Images

## Chapter 13

**237, 261** Olga Moreira/Shutterstock.com; **242** ©Kevin Dodge LLC /Tetra images RF via Getty Images; **247** Alessandro Biascioli/iStockphoto via Getty Images; **250** DNY59/iStockphoto via Getty Images; **255** Srdjanns74/iStockphoto via Getty Images; **256** AS photo family /Shutterstock.com; **258** Eddie Gerald/Alamy Stock Photo; **259** monkeybusinessimages/iStockphoto via Getty Images

## Back Matter

**264** kieferpix/iStockphoto via Getty Images **278-9** Prixel Creative /Shutterstock.com

# explaining the gospel

One of the greatest desires of Christian teachers is to see their students repent and believe in Christ. Relying on the Holy Spirit, you should take advantage of the opportunities that arise for presenting the gospel. You may find the following outline helpful, especially when dealing individually with a young person.

### 1. THE LORD GOD IS KING OVER ALL HIS CREATION (REV. 4:11).

- God created everything that is (Gen. 1–2).
- God created the world with laws about how His world is to work and the way people are to live.

### 2. ALL HAVE SINNED—INCLUDING ME (ROM. 3:23).

- Since Adam first sinned, all people are born rebels against the rule of God (Rom. 5:12).
- God has made me in His own image so that I might declare His glory by being like Him (Gen. 1:26–27).
- But I am a sinner. I disobey God's Word. The Bible teaches that I am to love God more than anything or anyone (Mark 12:30). It also teaches that I should love other people at all times (Mark 12:31). But I don't enjoy doing what God wants me to do, I don't delight in obeying my parents, and I don't like being kind to other people.
- God will punish me for my rebellion and sin (Rom. 6:23). God hates sin, and there is nothing I can do to get rid of my sin. I can try to change my behavior, but I can never change my heart.

### 3. JESUS DIED AND ROSE AGAIN FOR ME (ROM. 5:8).

- God loves me even though I am a sinner.
- He sent His Son, Jesus Christ, to live a perfect life and to die on the cross, suffering the punishment for my sin.
- Three days later, God raised Jesus from the dead and made Him the ruler of His eternal kingdom. Jesus is alive today. This is the gospel of Jesus Christ: He died on the cross and was raised up to be God's appointed King (1 Cor. 15:1–4).
- God desires to restore me to bear His image fully by making me like His Son, the perfect image-bearer of God (Rom. 8:29).
- God gives a new heart—new loves and desires—to every one of His children (Ezek. 36:26–27).

### 4. I NEED TO PUT MY TRUST IN JESUS (ROM. 10:9–10).

- I must repent (turn away) from my sin and let Jesus control my life. I must also believe what God has done through Jesus (Mark 1:15).
- If I repent and believe in what Jesus has done, I am putting my trust in Jesus.
- Everyone who is trusting in Jesus is forgiven of sin.
- Everyone who is trusting in Jesus submits to having Him as his or her King.
- Everyone who has been saved by God will continue trusting and obeying Jesus for the rest of his or her life (Heb. 3:14).

When talking individually with a young person, ask questions to discern sincerity or any misunderstanding. What is sin? Are you a sinner? What is the gospel? What does it mean to repent? Read the verses from your Bible. If a student shows genuine sorrow for sin and a sufficiently accurate understanding of the basics of the gospel, encourage him or her to call on the Lord as you listen. Perhaps he or she will pray something like the following:

> God, I know that You hate sin. But I also know that You love me. I believe that Jesus died for me and rose from the dead for me. I now turn away from my sin, and I am trusting in Jesus to forgive me and to be my King forever. I want to follow Him wherever He leads me.

Show the student the Bible's command that believers unite together in regular fellowship (Heb. 10:24–25), and encourage him or her to get involved right away in a gospel-preaching church. Tell the student that whenever he or she sins, God will grant forgiveness as he or she confesses those sins to God (1 John 1:9).